PRAISE FOR
GEORGE MICHAEL: A LIFE

"This is one of my favorite biographies ever."
—Jon Bream, *Minneapolis Star-Tribune*

"*George Michael: A Life* enlightens and answers. And with it,
James Gavin has done the legacy of George Michael and in fact the
business of proper biographical writing an immeasurable service."
—Christian Josi, *Washington Times*

"Revealing (and often shocking) . . . This biography is moving,
eye-opening, and essential, even for readers with just a casual
interest in pop culture." **—Jim Piechota, *Bay Area Reporter***

"Scintillating . . . eloquent and meticulous."
—Jamie Brickhouse, *Interview*

"Gavin's acclaimed new bio is a detailed, meticulously researched,
definitive look at the life of the late superstar singer."
—ExtraTV.com

"Poignant . . . definitive."
—John Murph, *Tidal*

"There has been no shortage of revisionism and analysis of George since,
but *George Michael: A Life* is by far the most authoritative to date.
A must-read for GM fans." **—*Classic Pop* (UK)**

"A meticulously researched, fascinating deep dive into a man
whose music shattered hearts." **—Patrick Kelleher, *Pink News* (UK)**

"A comprehensive . . . detailed, evenhanded biography . . .
Gavin handles Michael's problematic years as equitably as
the storybook ones . . . his first-rate reporting makes this
biography sing. Gavin's real stories of triumphs and tragedies
poignantly explain one of pop's most enigmatic stars."
—*Kirkus Reviews*

"Gavin's fluent, gripping account of Michael's roller-coaster
music career will draw readers in. An emotionally fulfilling read."
—*Library Journal*

"Truly definitive . . . emotionally satisfying and meticulous."
—**Kevin Howell**, *Shelf Awareness*

"James Gavin has delivered a stunning, empathic, and peerlessly
knowledgeable biography of George Michael. Gavin's attention to his
subject's artistry, his honest treatment of Michael's struggles, his sharp-
eyed understanding of the last days of record-company dominance, and
his comprehension of the shifting tides of gay acceptance in our culture are
sublime. The author of biographies of Chet Baker, Lena Horne, and Peggy
Lee has, with this book, firmed up his place as one of our very best writers
about music and life." —**Sheila Weller, author of *Girls Like Us: Carole
King, Joni Mitchell, Carly Simon—and the Journey of a Generation***

"James Gavin is a biographer of the highest order, with a gorgeous
sense of narrative and insight galore. His *George Michael: A Life*
is a backstage, all-access pass into a glittery world filled with dark
corners and trap doors. It's a thrilling, albeit cautionary tale of success,
excess, and a remarkable performer who met his destiny head-on."
—**Bob Spitz, *New York Times* bestselling author of**
The Beatles: The Biography* and *Led Zeppelin: The Biography

GEORGE MICHAEL

A LIFE

———

JAMES GAVIN

ABRAMS PRESS, NEW YORK

Library of Congress Control Number: 2022930494

Paperback ISBN: 978-1-4197-6835-4
eISBN: 978-1-64700-673-0

Printed and bound in the United States
10 9 8 7 6 5 4 3 2 1

ABRAMS The Art of Books
195 Broadway, New York, NY 10007
abramsbooks.com

To my friend David Munk

For believing in this project and in me

PROLOGUE

IN EARLY 2016, AFTER thirty-three years of near-ubiquity in the U.K. press, George Michael, age fifty-three, vanished from public sight. For years, one of British pop's favored sons had sent out as many as a dozen tweets a day from his various homes in London and from dressing rooms, limousines, and posh vacation spots. But on February 11, he posted his last tweet for months to come. "Hi lovelies!" it read. "Enjoy this playlist on Valentine's Day."

The Spotify link he shared didn't send listeners to "Faith," "I Want Your Sex," or any of his other dance hits about romantic and physical obsession, which were favorite subjects of his. Instead, he called the playlist "Heartbreak by George Michael." The songs ranged from "Last Christmas," the vengeful tearjerker he had written at twenty as half of England's premiere boy band, Wham!; to "Jesus to a Child," an elegy for the love of his life, Anselmo Feleppa, who had died of AIDS years before Michael was out of the closet; to the Billie Holiday lament "You've Changed," featured in his last touring show, Symphonica, in 2012–2013.

The tweet was a smoke signal from a man in despair, yet almost no one perceived it as that—not even in the wake of a series of public scandals and accidents, one of which had left him in a bloody heap on a London expressway. Memories lingered of Michael in his late-eighties heyday: a butch, stubbly, leather-jacketed pinup boy who had become one of the hottest pop stars in the world. It had always been his gift to raise people's spirits, to make them feel less alone; just the mention of his name made people smile. Even when Michael was at his darkest, Danny Cummings, his longtime percussionist, felt a healing power in his voice. "It had a frequency in it that was very sweet to the ear—angelic," he said.

To Lynda Hayes, who had delivered an uncredited but famous rap chorus on the Wham! hit "Young Guns (Go for It!)," Michael had "an everyman voice—innocent, natural-sounding, with no frills. He just sounded like himself singing, and it was beautiful. Who couldn't relate to that?" Performing in stadiums, Michael could transmit those sensations to thousands of people; his shows invariably ended with fans on their feet, dancing. He had done it on the tour for *Faith*, the 1988 album that had made him a superstar. And he did it again in Symphonica.

After the tour had finished, though, guitarist Ben Butler, who had played all sixty-plus performances, lost contact with Michael. "I sensed that things were not well in his world," said Butler. "He seemed to have gone completely off the radar."

The most recent published pictures of him came from Switzerland, where he had checked in for treatment at one of the priciest rehab facilities in the world. Photographers had snapped him on a street holding hands with his handsome Lebanese boyfriend, Fadi Fawaz. In his other hand was a cigarette. His goatee had turned gray; he looked bloated and weary.

Since the beginning, Michael had been adamantly private. "No one will ever know any more about George Michael than they probably do about the next man on the street," declared Andrew Ridgeley, his partner in Wham!. But for some time, an artist known for his ironclad grip on every facet of his career had been spinning frighteningly out of whack. He could not face the day undrugged, whether by chemicals or anonymous sex. His once-burning ambition to make music had waned. In 2012, his worn-out body had nearly succumbed to pneumonia.

Brits regarded the troubled star with sadness, Americans with pity. Few people, even most of his friends, looked much deeper. "When you thought of George Michael," wrote Dan Aquilante in the *New York Post*, "you thought of this carefully crafted image, amply displayed in his groundbreaking videos." The one for "Faith" showed him in his iconic pose, that of a leather-jacketed, shimmying, butt-shaking, post-*West Side Story* biker dude with stubble and an earring. For a star who had been terrified of opening the closet door, that revealing gay look implied a clutching at the truth, yet it flew over the heads of his mostly female audience. To them, said Johnny Douglas, one of his recording engineers, Michael was "the most beautiful human being on earth." At the same time, Douglas added, "he was the white male soul singer that I think every British lad aspired to be."

In interview after interview, however, he spoke of his longing to be embraced as a serious artist. His Top 10 single, "Freedom! '90" found him pleading to be seen for who he really was. "Sometimes the clothes do not make the man," he warned. But fame and its trappings had consumed him since childhood; he defined himself not as a singer-songwriter but as a "pop star," which to Michael was a synonym for king. "He pops the two *p*'s when he says it, and his eyes gleam, giving the term a noble air," wrote the music journalist Rob Tannenbaum.

Yet he sang about freedom with his eyes hidden behind dark glasses. Writer Richard Smith saw numerous Michaels on display, none of them quite convincing. "He always appears to be creating some new fantasy self," said Smith, "and as soon as that betrays him he tries to kill it off, but then creates a new one to take its place." In the *Guardian*, Jim White wrote of Michael as a grand contradiction: "a songwriter of real depth compromised by an addiction to the superficial, the glamorous, the unreal." David Geffen, whose mid-nineties record label, DreamWorks SKG, released the singer's most candid album, *Older*, sensed a man in deep discomfort with all he had fought to attain. "He never seemed to be able to live in the career he'd created for himself," said Geffen. Earlier, he had witnessed Michael's quixotic battle to cut himself loose from the record label, Sony, that had made his superstardom possible. The outcome had not been happy.

Michael yearned to hide, yet stood on gigantic stages in front of thousands. The front door to his home in the fashionable London neighborhood of Highgate was clearly visible from a low gate a few feet in front of it; anyone could see his comings and goings or wait there for an autograph. He nearly always obliged with a smile, for Michael was a gentleman. "It was impossible not to like him," said David Bartolomi, one of the countless photographers who took his picture. Yet most of the time, Michael couldn't bear to look at his own face.

A companion of his since Wham! called the singer a "sad, angry little boy." Friends such as Chris Cameron, his longtime keyboardist and musical director, were very worried about him. Cameron overheard a tense exchange between Michael and his manager, Andy Stephens, over Michael's self-destruction. The singer lashed out: *"Stop trying to save me from myself!"*

CHAPTER ONE

ALMOST EVERYTHING TO DO with George Michael, from his gut ambition to his sometimes crippling insecurities, in some way pointed back to his father. Jack Panos was the model of a self-made 1960s man's man. Born Kyriacos Panayiotou in 1935, he had grown up with seven siblings in Patriki, a dirt-road village in Cyprus, an island in the Eastern Mediterranean. In later years he would boast of the life he had transcended: that of a shoeless child who survived on bread and olives and used a hole in the ground for a toilet.

Poverty had given him a fierce resolve to better himself. He and a friend, Dimitrios Georgiou, set their minds on the restaurant business, and in 1953 they emigrated to London, a popular destination for Greek Cypriots. They started as busboys, then became waiters. Kyriacos knew that if he were to keep climbing, his given name had to go.

His next step was to find a wife. At a dance, he caught the eye of Lesley Angold Harrison, a British girl from a working-class family. Reared in convent school, Lesley was a lady, fastidiously neat, quiet but firm, and gracefully spoken, with an almost Victorian reserve. She had all the makings of a proper mate, and Jack proposed.

Early in their marriage, they and another immigrant friend of Jack's shared a flat in Finchley, a suburb of North London. He and Lesley could only afford to live above a laundromat, especially as the kids started coming. In 1959, Lesley gave birth to daughter Yioda; two years later came Melanie. Jack was impatient for a son to carry on his name, though, and on June 25, 1963, in East Finchley, Lesley delivered a hazel-eyed, screaming baby boy.

Despite having anglicized his own name, Jack christened the child Georgios Kyriacos Panayiotou, which no Brit could pronounce. But he wanted to establish that Georgios was his father's son and a proud bearer of Jack's Greek heritage. Once the boy was old enough, Jack would send him off, grumbling, on Saturdays to Greek school.

Where Jack had come from, tradition meant everything. Sons were more important than daughters, and if Yioda and Melanie sensed his attitude, so be it. Georgios certainly did. "I grew up with this terrible feeling of guilt," he said later. "I was always the one that was gonna get the easy ride."

In fact, the pressures of being Jack's son were stifling. Dimitrios's boy, Andros Georgiou, who for much of Michael's life was closer to him than almost anyone—they were often referred to as cousins, although they weren't—cringed at Jack's iron fist: "He was a mean bastard, using fear, not respect, to rule and keep control of his household." During a family vacation in Cyprus, Andros and Georgios stole sweets from a shop, and the owner caught them. Jack punished his son the old-fashioned way. "You could hear the belt swinging down on his arse and legs," said Andros. "His screams echoed around the building."

Luckily for Georgios, Jack spent most of his time working. Now an assistant restaurant manager, he could afford to move his family, in 1969, to a semidetached house in Burnt Oak, a suburb of Edgware. He and two Greek headwaiters pooled their money and leased a dilapidated property on the main road; they turned it into the Angus Pride, a steakhouse that also offered Greek specialties.

The restaurant took off, making Jack—who had far more charisma than his partners—a local celebrity. As soon as customers stepped inside, there he was—a broad-shouldered hulk with a shock of thick, graying hair and a hearty hello spoken in a thick Greek accent. Soon he grew tired of sharing his success; Jack dreamed of earning enough money to buy his partners out.

He was a shining immigrant success story, but Simon Napier-Bell, the co-manager of Wham!, sensed "a great coffin of angst somewhere in that family." Lesley had dutifully helped her husband ascend, but he worked her so hard, said George, that she wound up angry and exhausted. Even though Lesley had a home to run and three children, her "extremely unreasonable husband," as their son later called him, expected her to hold a day job while the kids were at school. She went to work in a fish-and-chip shop and hated it. The smells permeated her hair, skin, and clothes; she could never fully wash them out. Jack then demanded that she spend evenings working at the restaurant. With almost no spare time, she kept the house in impeccable shape;

her son wondered how on earth she did it. She seldom complained, but he sensed her unhappiness. "Depression runs in my family," he said as an adult.

He had inherited it, but Jack didn't seem to notice. Interviewed years later about his son, the older man had little to say. "He was a quiet boy," Jack recalled. Georgios had a mop of mousy brown, curly hair; eyebrows that met in the middle and looked like a long, furry caterpillar; and such impaired vision that he wore Coke-bottle glasses. He hated his appearance, and Jack, intentionally or not, made things worse. "I was never praised, never held," said Michael. Though once a peacock, Jack tolerated none of that from his children. "Conceit of any kind was considered an absolute sin," explained Michael. Jack took further steps to keep his son humble. "A few things were said which would probably take your breath away if you heard them from a parent to a child," Michael explained. "I never got over them. It's as simple as that."

Feeling lonely and flawed, Georgios retreated into his own world. He rose at dawn, then walked in his pajamas to an overgrown field behind the house and dug up worms, caterpillars, and ladybugs, which he stored in matchboxes and jars. At the end of the road was a lilac tree that attracted butterflies; he stared at them and tried to catch them. Playing on the radio then was the Stevie Wonder hit "My Cherie Amour"; the boy sang bits of it outdoors in his boy soprano. A neighbor reported to Lesley that her son had a lovely voice.

He thought little of it until the age of eight, when an accident at Roe Green Junior School in nearby Kingsbury made his whole world swerve around. Barreling down a hallway on the way to lunch, he tripped at the top of a flight of stairs and tumbled to the bottom, where he banged his head on the metal pipes of a radiator. The impact knocked him cold, and he awoke in a pool of blood; it had covered his glasses and splashed into his eyes, and he could barely see. Only one student—a girl with a crush on him—came to his aid and called for help. A teacher ran over and removed his glasses, then walked the young man to the nurse. He felt humiliated.

Yet the injury brought an almost magical epiphany; somehow it jogged his brain and opened a new channel. Within six months, his infatuation with creepy-crawlies was gone. Now, he said, "all I wanted to know about was music."

He and his closest playmate, David Mortimer—their mothers were best friends—crafted a song together and recorded it on the Mortimer family's tape recorder, with Georgios singing; presciently, they called it "The Music Maker of the World." That tape machine became their favorite toy. David strummed a guitar; Georgios banged on a biscuit tin in lieu of a drum. He began learning songs off the radio and mimicking the lead vocals. In one of his solos, he imitated Olivia Newton-John singing her top-ten hit "Banks of the Ohio," a traditional murder ballad in which a woman impetuously plunges a knife into her lover's chest: "My God, what have I done? I've killed the only man I love!"

He couldn't stand the Greek music his father played, but there wasn't much else in the house. In the garage, however, he found discarded treasures—mementos of his mother's carefree dancing days. The boy laid his hands on her abandoned windup gramophone and some battered 45s. They included the Tom Jones blockbuster "Delilah" and two chart-toppers by the Supremes, "Baby Love" and "Stop! In the Name of Love." One disc was chipped, making part of it unplayable; another of the records kept skipping. Undaunted, he spun them again and again, transfixed by the voices. Jones, a Welsh sex god, sang "blue-eyed soul"—the term coined for R&B sung by white artists. Jones's hypermasculine, semi-operatic belting, with frills borrowed from Elvis Presley, Little Richard, and Jackie Wilson, suffused George's consciousness; it had qualities he would one day emulate. From the Supremes, the reigning girl-group of Motown, Michael got his first taste of the catchy hooks and beats that made a pop song unforgettable.

Around the same time he began tuning into BBC Radio 1, which, as the seventies progressed, played an ever-growing bounty of the decade's sounds: disco, punk, reggae, psychedelica, Top 40. Georgios wanted desperately to buy records, but Jack forbade it. Longing to get closer to music, he took up the violin. For a few weeks he struggled to play it, then announced he was quitting. His parents insisted he stick with it, and he studied the instrument halfheartedly for years. When his father dragged him out at family gatherings to flounder his way through some formal composition, the boy was mortified.

But it was Jack's money that paid for a series of gifts that made his dream take wing. Georgios had begged for a cassette recorder, and for his birthday he got one. He began taping songs off the radio, holding the mic close to the speaker. After learning them by heart, he sang them into his recorder, then proudly played the recordings for his pals.

Some of the tunes he singled out from the early-seventies airwaves gave glimpses into the mind of a child who felt like a weirdo. They included "Chirpy Chirpy Cheep Cheep," a number-one U.K. hit for Middle of the Road, a Scottish bubblegum band. Using kids' language, the song told an unsettling tale of a boy who winds up deserted: "Last night I heard my mama singing a song / Woke up this morning and my mama was gone." Michael Jackson's "Ben" was the title tune of a horror film about a geeky outcast and his pet rat: "With a friend to call my own / I'll never be alone." Having adopted all those slithery insects from his backyard, Georgios could relate. His favorite song was "Little Willy." Recorded by the Sweet, a quartet of androgynous hippie rockers, it portrayed a London lad who defies his disapproving parents to become the strutting, dancing "king around town": "Willy wears the crown . . . you can't push Willy 'round."

When he saw the Sweet perform the song on his favorite TV show, he was mesmerized. Like fifteen million other Brits, Georgios tuned in every Thursday night to the country's favorite musical variety show. At 7:35, the boy watched an explosion of multicolored flames followed by a flock of dancing teenyboppers. Then came the announcement that made his pulse race: "Yes, it's number one, it's *Top of the Pops!*" For the next thirty minutes, Georgios's eyes and ears were glued to a parade of mostly British acts, from the Beatles, the Who, and the Rolling Stones to the latest one-hit wonders. *Top of the Pops* filled his head with daydreams about how it must feel to stand on that pedestal, adored and applauded by all. Georgios studied the performers, pondering what had gotten them there. He stared at the long-haired youths strumming electric guitars, at the skintight spandex and bare midriffs, the beards and platinum hair, and analyzed every phrase, looking for clues.

In 1974, David Cassidy, star of the American TV show *The Partridge Family* and a chart-topping, international pinup idol, had begun his first U.K. tour. Girls from eight to eighteen were his fans, but Cassidy's soft, pretty features, his shoulder-length hair, and his lanky torso—photographed shirtless, even down to his pubes, by countless magazines—had also stirred desire in a legion of budding gays. Eleven-year-old Georgios didn't quite perceive it at the time, but he, too, had a crush on Cassidy.

His bedazzlement was sealed as he watched a TV appearance of Cassidy kicking a football on top of the twenty-four-story London Television

Centre. The camera panned the streets below, where screaming girls stared heavenward, wishing they could somehow get to him. But when an adolescent girl died amid the crush of fans at one of his British shows, Cassidy began having second thoughts. "I feel burnt up inside," he told the *Daily Mail*. "I'm twenty-four, a big star . . . in a position that millions dream of, but the truth is I just can't enjoy it."

His conflict mirrored what would happen to George Michael at almost the same age. But for now, the boy looked at Cassidy and saw a man who had seduced the world. "I didn't want to be rich; I just wanted to be filthily famous," said Michael in 1998. That alone, he decided, would make up for the pains of his daily life: "It was feeling not listened to; it was lots of feelings of low self-worth, all the kind of screwed-up things that go together to make someone who becomes well-known. . . . It's the things that are missing that make you a star, it's not the things that you have."

He shared his dream with his father, who angrily told him it was pie-in-the-sky nonsense that would go nowhere. According to Andros, his friend's dad had a deeper concern than that: "Jack hated pop music because he thought all pop stars were gay." Back in Cyprus, he had grown up amid Greek Orthodox Christianity, a religion that is both strikingly liberal and punishingly conservative. Priests marrying and divorcing is permitted, but homosexuality is seen as an abomination. Michael Mavros, a doctor, grew up in Cyprus in the 1980s. "People absolutely didn't like gays there," he said. "But at the same time, there is a lot of homosexuality. People would try to hide it."

Like many men of his generation, Jack used homophobic slurs; he referred to certain men, including a waiter at his restaurant, as poofs. Clearly he had worries about Georgios, who was far from the virile heir he wanted. Instead of being proud of him for excelling in English language and literature, Jack, recalled Andros, was "always trying to toughen his son up." He even bought two pairs of boxing gloves and pitted the boys against each other. As Andros clobbered Georgios, Jack bellowed, "Don't just sit there, boy! Hit him back! Are you a coward?" His taunts made Georgios so angry that he began pummeling Andros with both fists.

According to Danny Cummings, Jack had meant no harm: "For the old generation, fathers wrangling with their sons, putting them down, was nothing unusual. That's just how Jack was." But his belittlement was chipping away at the boy's confidence. Georgios joined the school choir then lost heart, deciding he wasn't good enough. He switched to playing timpani in the school orchestra, but the instrument left him cold. Jack softened enough to buy him a small drum set; with that, too, Georgios felt average at best. He consoled himself by bingeing on ice cream at his father's restaurant—then his weight rose, which made him even more self-conscious. When he entered the nearby Kingsbury High School at eleven—the age at which secondary schooling in Britain starts—his self-esteem had sunk to a new low. "I was fat and ugly and I had glasses," he recalled. He grew his bangs long in an effort to hide his bushy unibrow, but he was still certain his looks made people cringe.

Homely as he felt, a strong sex drive was welling up in him. He had begun masturbating before puberty; in 2004, he told Adam Mattera, who edited the British gay magazine *Attitude,* of having had "clichéd straight fantasies like nuns with their tits out." Later, the boy got down to serious petting with a classmate whom he dated briefly. At a party he got "in between her legs," he said. She removed his glasses and told him sweetly, "Haven't you got beautiful eyes!" Crushed by what he took as sarcasm, he bolted for the door. At twelve, he lost his virginity to a girl. So "horrifically embarrassing" was the experience, he said, that it frightened him off sex for years.

• • •

After about six years as a restaurateur, Jack had saved enough money to move various family members from Cyprus to the United Kingdom, and in the summer of 1975, he placed a down payment on the four-bedroom home of his dreams. It was in Radlett, Hertfordshire, northwest of London. Radlett was one of the most posh towns in Britain; to live there was a badge of achievement for a former peasant boy from the Mediterranean. Jack could afford it because the house was a wreck; he renovated for a year, during which he lived with his brood in a flat above the restaurant. After they had settled into Radlett, he managed to buy out his business partners, leaving him as the sole owner of the Angus Pride. Jack had finally made it.

Next door was a pub called the Railway Hotel. One day Georgios heard a soul-blues band rehearsing inside. He sat on the steps, riveted. The musicians—drummer Peter Van Hooke, whose father owned the pub;

guitarist and pianist Chaz Jankel; singer Ric Parnell; and the leader, saxo-phonist John Altman—had bright futures ahead of them. Years later, Altman would arrange a track, "Kissing a Fool," on George Michael's *Faith*. "You inspired me," Michael told him.

But in the seventies, Altman had heard Jack lamenting his boy's ambitions. "He would say to people, 'Can you have a word with my son and tell him not to bother with this music?'"

Little did Jack know that by moving his family to Hertfordshire, he had placed his son on a one-way track to where he longed to go. Having finished one year of high school at Kingsbury, Georgios switched to the Bushey Meads School in Bushey, about three miles from Radlett. He started class on September 9, 1975. Shyly, he found an empty desk in his assigned classroom; he tried to blend in but imagined ridicule in his schoolmates' eyes. He wore the Bushey uniform, a forest-green blazer and striped tie; above his collar was a rash of pimples, glasses that covered half his face, and hair so dense and curly he could barely run a comb through it. Georgios was mortified when the teacher mangled his name as she introduced him to the class. He spoke as little as possible, but when he did, out came his mother's refined middle-class diction; given his gawky appearance, it sounded almost comical. Perhaps sensing his discomfort, the teacher asked for a volunteer to look after him. For reasons that mystified everyone, the star of Bushey Meads, twelve-year-old Andrew Ridgeley, raised his hand.

Unlike his primly garbed classmates, Ridgeley was a standout—the lad whom all the girls wanted, the one with a hint of danger. Slender, with pouty lips, delicate bone structure, and a dark, tousled shag hairdo, he was as pretty as the swooners who fronted boy bands on *Top of the Pops*. His eyebrows arched above a coolly superior gaze. As a child, he had starred in a school production of *Joseph and the Amazing Technicolor Dreamcoat*; though he looked fetching in the lead character's coat of many colors, the vocal demands of the Andrew Lloyd Webber score were far beyond him. Ridgeley had studied piano as a child, but it bored him, and he gave it up. Still, he had ambitions, however vague, for a career in music.

Now the pubescent youth had cast himself as one of the New Romantics, a movement of fashion-obsessed London clubgoers who milled about in elaborate costumes based on the Romantic age. The trend was inspired largely by the glam rock pageantry of David Bowie. Ridgeley's template, though, was apparently Adam Ant, the New Wave idol who dressed like the Beau Brummel dandies and swashbuckling pirates of the nineteenth century. Michael never forgot the vision of Ridgeley in tight trousers of "cherry silk" and "cerise satin," with his hair, like Ant's, tied in little braids. Occasionally he wore eye makeup. Some wondered if Ridgeley was gay—Georgios did, too—but he wasn't; he was just supremely self-possessed.

Georgios was both captivated and jealous. Ridgeley had all the swagger he lacked; he seemed so free, while Georgios, a nerd with a violin case, was timid. Ridgeley's touch of androgyny might well have attracted a boy with nascent gay urges; never had the notion of physical appeal occurred to him until he met Ridgeley, who "just oozed confidence out of every pore," he observed. The package was intimidating. His teacher, Michael recalled, "ordered me to sit next to this horrible little boy, who then took charge of me." They were the oddest couple at Bushey Meads, but Ridgeley liked the idea of being a mentor, and Georgios had a lot to learn.

They had a few things in common. Ridgeley's father, Albert, was also an immigrant (from Egypt), though more intellectual and cultivated than Jack. He too had climbed his way to prosperity, and worked as an executive for Canon. Andrew and Georgios both revered pop music; the former was teaching himself guitar. They bonded over their love of Elton John, the clown-like British wonder. Both young men had memorized *Goodbye Yellow Brick Road*, John's conceptual double-album, full of lush cinematic metaphor and allusions to such Hollywood goddesses as Judy Garland and Marilyn Monroe.

Georgios invited him home. Andros, who was there with his father, Dimitrios, recalled Ridgeley's outfit: a kilt, a ponytail, and eyeliner. Jack was appalled; Lesley didn't like him, either. Later, at dinner, talk between Dimitrios and Jack turned casually homophobic. Their sons boldly challenged them by arguing that many ancient Greek males had been known to have sex with other men; the older men swore it was a lie.

Andrew seemed unruffled. He began visiting the Panos house regularly, and vice versa. Jack made no secret of his disdain. Finally, however, he knew he had no choice but to give in. "They were so close," he explained, "that at the end of the day I thought, well, I have to trust my son's judgment on his friends."

With Ridgeley as his role model and Svengali, the boy began to blossom. The unwieldy name of Georgios Panayiotou made eyes roll, so Ridgeley gave him a nickname. His new friend's family called him Yorg; Ridgeley told his classmates, with amusement, that Georgios's family called him Yog. Ridgeley's mispronunciation caught on, and Yog proceeded with his transformation. He had his hair trimmed and got contact lenses. As a student, Andrew goofed off; Yog, too, began doing the minimum to avoid flunking out. His focus shifted instead to partying, drinking, and to the pursuit of pop stardom. Andrew brought his guitar to the Panos house; the teenagers amateurishly recorded songs and fantasized about fame. They went together to parties; girls flocked only to Andrew, which left Yog miserable. "Everyone called me a sissy," he said, as Andrew did his best to comfort him.

Yog struggled to keep up with his pal, especially in bars, where Andrew could outdrink almost anyone. At one party, Yog wore a pair of green trousers that he had bought to try to impress a certain girl. She snubbed him, and in response he got blind drunk. On the way home, Ridgeley had to prop him up, but Yog fell on the grass and burst into tears. "No one said I've got new trousers!" he moaned. "Now I've got them dirty. I'm *sooooo* ugly! No girl will ever like me!" He would later claim he had "lots of girlfriends" but "never fell in love." Yog had no such feelings for Ridgeley, but they acted like a couple, conversing in shorthand, swapping inside jokes, and finishing each other's thoughts. Ridgeley's middle-school girlfriend, Shirlie Holliman, knew that even she could not compete: "They had such a strong relationship that no girl—not even if Andrew was head over heels in love—could have stopped it at that time."

•••

He now had three close mates to listen to music with: Andrew, Andros, and David. While he "lived for the radio," as he put it, Yog used most of his pocket money to buy albums, which he and his pals debated and sang along with. They devoured ABBA, the Sex Pistols, and Donna Summer, and they wore out the two-LP soundtrack, mostly by the Bee Gees, of *Saturday Night Fever*, the 1977 box-office sensation that had thrust disco to its worldwide zenith. As "Stayin' Alive," "Jive Talkin'," and "Night Fever" pounded from their stereos, the boys tried to copy the elastic dance moves of the film's star, John Travolta, who played a working-class Brooklyn teen who rules his local disco.

Unconsciously, Yog found himself drawn to pop music's gay stars. Although nearly all of them were professionally in the closet, several were flaunting a splashy gay sensibility. The teenager treasured his imported copies of albums by Sylvester, the American soul singer whose gender-bending, sequined outness and high-flying falsetto had made him known as the Queen of Disco. Yog's enrapturement with his key influence, Elton John, kept growing. John's albums were treasure-chests of hummable tunes, wrapped in production values that tattooed almost every song on the brain. Writing about "Bennie and the Jets," a glam rock satire by John and his lyricist, Bernie Taupin, Robert Christgau marveled in the *Village Voice*: "The whole damn song is one enormous hook." John's blue-eyed-soul baritone, peppered with Motown mannerisms, had enough of an ache to hint at inner turmoil.

Born to an upscale and rather stuffy British family, John was a short, doughy, balding nerd who had remade himself into a one-man circus. Seated at his piano bench, he wore rose-tinted glasses as big as headlights and sparkly suits in clashing, psychedelic colors; he added plumes, feathers, and headdresses. In that naive age, John could pass as a goofy straight guy and fool much of the public, but he was "living a lie," he confessed later, and it tortured him. Though still in the dark about his own sexuality, Yog felt an immediate kinship—"because I could *feel* he was gay."

The same thing happened when he and Andros went to Earls Court Exhibition Centre, a London arena, to see Queen. In 1975, the British band had topped the U.K. charts for nine weeks with "Bohemian Rhapsody," a six-minute suite whose camp overkill spoofed the hammiest excesses of opera, stadium rock, and confessional singer-songwriter balladry. The lead singer, Freddie Mercury, galvanized Yog. Mercury had a tenor with near-operatic range and heft; his over-the-top theatrical grandeur filled the biggest arenas. His sequined leotards plunged to the waist, making his furry chest the center of attention. He slicked back his dark hair and grew a Latin-lover-style mustache—a look reminiscent of Ramon Novarro, the secretly gay post-Valentino film idol. Though in interviews Mercury only hinted coyly at his homosexuality, his band's name and his persona told gay fans all they needed to know. When he sang "We Are the Champions," they felt he meant it for them.

"He had such a profound effect on me," said George Michael. "I was such a total worshipper of his music. I kind of drank in everything he did." He memorized every song on Queen's albums, then stood in his bedroom and performed them to the mirror, copying Mercury's breathy way of ending phrases and his sweeping arm gestures.

Outside the sanctuary of his bedroom, he stayed polite and contained. But he noticed that gay men were showing an interest in him. When one of them made a pass he panicked and didn't give in, but he was also excited, and his fantasies began shifting toward men. Around the age of sixteen he started cruising for sex, of course in top secret.

By now his mother had spotted telltale signs in her sensitive son, and they troubled her. Following her husband's lead, she had made him feel, in unspoken ways, that he "wasn't manly enough," he said, "or boy enough." It wasn't homophobia but fear that drove her to share with him the skeleton in her family closet. Lesley's older brother, Colin Harrison, had been secretly gay, she believed; that along with paranoid schizophrenia had literally tortured him to death. Colin made a suicide attempt in 1963, after which he was sent to a mental hospital. A few days after his release, he committed suicide. He was thirty-eight.

Apparently Lesley withheld some of the details from her son, who for some reason believed that his uncle had put his head in the oven and that his mother had found the corpse. To compound the drama, he claimed that his mother's father, George James Harrison, had done the same thing within days of Colin, and that Lesley had discovered his body, too.

Her father had indeed killed himself, but in 1960, years before his son's death. The *Daily Mail* would later report that Colin had been released from the psychiatric ward for a few days in January 1964 to visit his mother, Daisy. During that time, Colin was found dead in bed, having overdosed on his schizophrenia medication. Reportedly he had left a suicide note. "This man was very, gravely, mentally ill," said the coroner.

Lesley shuddered to think that her son, too, might turn out to be gay. For now, she let her husband remain "supposedly protectively homophobic," as George Michael put it. The waiter he called a "poof" lived upstairs from the restaurant; Yog was forbidden from going up there—"in case I caught something. In case I caught gay."

Lesley's stories of Colin haunted him forever. As a young man, he feared he had inherited the gene for schizophrenia. And while Elton John and Freddie Mercury had shown him an exuberant, triumphant vision of gay life, the truth seemed much darker. "Deep down, part of me thinks the wrath of God is the reality," he told the *Guardian*'s Simon Hattenstone in 2005. "I don't believe that for a moment, but when I was younger it was hard not to feel that way as a gay man."

Not long after Lesley had spoken of his uncle's and grandfather's suicides, he poured his dread into his first significant composition, "Stephen," which he and David Mortimer had written it in their mid-teens. With the latter playing guitar, Yog made a demo. Nothing he recorded for years would approach the helplessness and fear in that performance. "Stephen" tells of a man who is wracked by the death of a girl he loves. He hears her calling him; he can't bear the thought of losing the memory of her touch. "There's only one way to see her again . . . Stephen, Stephen, you can join her now."

By now he had developed a real voice—a muscular, in-tune, high baritone with a velvety texture. As he sang, he reached up into a falsetto that sounded like a cry of pain. That desolate ballad, with its suicidal overtones, was too raw and bleak for a teenager with his eye set on *Top of the Pops*, so he shelved it.

He yearned to hear his own name called out by the program's announcer, but how would he get there? On Fridays, he and Ridgeley took their first awkward steps toward the stage by playing hooky and busking in London tube stations. In their tiny repertoire was a cover of the Queen showstopper, "'39," about a team of astronauts on a space journey. Multitudes passed by them, but few people noticed.

• • •

In 1979, when he was sixteen, Yog began wearing a close-trimmed beard, a slim-fitting white jacket, a skinny black tie, straight-leg white trousers, and white loafers. This was the look of the "rude boy," and it was all the rage in late-seventies England. Rude boy was Jamaican street slang for rebellious youths who liked ska, the reggae-like beat that scores of young British bands were playing. They tossed in strains of punk, New Wave, rock, Motown—and out came a mishmash called 2 Tone. That summer, the sound was adopted by five middle-class suburban British teens, who formed a band with a posh name: the Executive. Michael sang lead. David played guitar, as did Andrew Ridgeley, whose brother Paul was the drummer. A third guitarist, Andrew Leaver, seemed at least as cute and cool as his namesake; he had tousled hair, a boyish grin, and a record collection stocked with the latest New Wave sounds: David Bowie, Roxy Music, the B-52's.

For the moment, Jack and Lesley were uncharacteristically lenient, and allowed the boys to rehearse in their home. Leaver's father loaned them his keyboard. Yet the boys were neophytes, and as various members vied for the upper hand, arguments erupted and egos flared. Andros recalled Mortimer "having a tantrum" when Yog hijacked his guitar amp and hooked it up to his own vocal mic. "It was so obvious he just wanted to be the singer," said Andros of David. Georgios showed much more promise, but his father's putdowns persisted. "I always told him he couldn't sing," confessed Jack, and the chiding worked. "As a young performer he never believed in himself as a singer," recalled David. But Yog soldiered on, determined to prove Jack wrong.

He had absorbed his father's control-freak instincts. For him, this band was no lark; he took it more seriously than any of his mates and vowed to whip it into shape. They began working through a hodgepodge of tunes, including another of his first originals, "Rude Boy," and a ska version of the Andy Williams hit, "Can't Get Used to Losing You," which their favorite ska band, the Beat, had been performing around town. The oddest choice was the Beethoven piano piece "Für Elise," with incongruous Jamaican rhythms pasted on. Michael demanded that he and his bandmates rehearse the songs again and again; he scrutinized what he heard, trying to figure out ways to make it better.

But Jack still wasn't impressed, and he grumbled to Lesley, who felt no choice but to take her husband's side. As they left the house one night to go work in the restaurant, she forbade the boy from having another rehearsal. At last he stood up to her. Raising his voice, he warned her: If she didn't back off, he would quit school and do as he chose anyhow. It was the last time she threatened him.

The Executive booked an early November debut at a Methodist church hall in Bushey. Rehearsing in the Leaver dining room, they left the French doors open, and neighbors and friends gathered on the lawn to listen. "There was a real buzz, and it felt like something great was on the horizon," said Leaver's brother, Scott. Yog's ambitions shifted into overdrive. For him, this was the first step on the road to stardom. Changing his impossible birth name, just as his father had done, was the next. George Panos seemed an option, but he didn't want to be regarded as Jack's son. Elton John and Rod Stewart, he recalled, both had two first names. He decided to borrow a surname from a Greek schoolmate, Deno Michael, and call himself George Michael. Following suit, David Mortimer became David Austin.

Leaver's mother pitched in by driving the equipment to the venue. When an item punctured the backseat cushion, George, recalled Scott, said cockily, "Don't worry, Mrs. Leaver—we'll buy you a new one when we're rich and famous!"

That church performance revealed five bumbling lads whose attempts at Jamaican music seemed as ill-fitting as their Rude Boy costumes. To Michael's ears, the instrumental and vocal blend sounded awful.

After a subsequent performance, the group met James Sullivan, an exchange student from Brooklyn College who was backpacking through Europe to study languages. Punk was his passion, and he made his first of several stops in London to seek it out. Sullivan was eye-catching; he had dark curly hair, a mustache, and earrings, along with a disability that made his head tremble. He was also openly gay, and had courageously come out to his Irish Catholic family. To his amazement, his father was tolerant. But his mother had voiced an ultimatum: "You either obey the rules and regulations of the church or get out." He chose the latter.

A British boyfriend, Eddie, told him about the Executive, and he went to hear them. Sullivan was impressed, particularly with Michael. All the members were "very curious," recalled Sullivan, about this "young gay guy from New York City." In the course of several meetings, they asked him all about Manhattan and its music scene. Sullivan was struck by Ridgeley's friendliness; not only did he show obvious concern for his shyer buddy George, he gave Sullivan tips on bed-and-breakfasts to stay in as he traveled through Britain.

Michael was attracted to Sullivan, but didn't let on. Still, he was full of questions: When had Sullivan come out? How had his family reacted? "He said to me, 'You're Catholic, you're openly gay, and you have no problem with it?' I said, 'I didn't say I have no problem with it.'" Sullivan described his life in Brooklyn: "You're raised in a home where everything is religion. And then you're told that what you were born as is sinful."

As a teen, Sullivan had bought an issue of *Mandate*, a gay adult magazine, at a newsstand; a snitch leaked word to his father, who confronted him. "He thought it was just a phase," explained Sullivan. "I said, 'Dad, I'm gay.'" Wracked with shame, Sullivan considered entering the priesthood, but when the written application required that he list his sexual history he stormed off, disgusted. He sought counsel from a priest, who sent him for conversion therapy, which Sullivan refused. "I started to drink and take tranquilizers," he said.

Michael listened, riveted, and confided his resentment of Jack. "I think he was curious about my relationship with my father because he accepted me in many ways," said Sullivan. "I think George's father was a homophobic bastard who caused George a lot of pain. He found happiness in music and in Ridgeley's acceptance of him. But I think George was miserable his whole life. He was confused and scared—scared of rumors, scared of a lot of things."

Sullivan saw Leaver as a troublemaker. "There was a mean streak about him," he observed. "He was constantly getting stoned, and he would talk to me a lot." After Sullivan returned from his first deep conversation with Michael, Leaver snarled, "You must be queer if he's asking you all these questions." Sullivan was irate: "I said, 'Who the fuck is this asshole?'"

But Leaver seemed to like taunting him. He mentioned gossip at Kingsbury High School about a masturbation session that Michael had allegedly had with another male student. When Michael disappeared from the group, Leaver cracked that he was probably messing around with boys. "How the fuck do you know that?" asked Sullivan.

He felt sure that Leaver was doing exactly what he had accused Michael of.

"I remember one time we were in some gay club," said Sullivan. "I was with Eddie, and Andrew Leaver said, 'You fucking queer.' I took a bottle and broke it and held it to his throat. I said, 'Me, a fucking queer? You motherfucking slutty bastard, to call me a fucking queer—who the fuck do you think you are? If you ever, *ever* say anything like that to me again, I swear to God I will slit your throat open!'"

Leaver had left the Executive by 1980, when the group booked studio time and made a demo of the small handful of tunes in their repertoire. The results were traffic jams of psychedelic guitar, bashing drums, and a mild ska rhythm. Michael was the tentative main singer; at times he affected a Caribbean accent. Still, he felt proud of his work. In the car with his father, he played the cassette, hoping it would change Jack's mind. It didn't. Jack again berated his son. "Dad was horrified," said Melanie. "He didn't think Yog had any talent." Michael exploded: He was *not* going to quit, no matter what happened.

The young man ran off cassette copies of the demo, and he and Ridgeley began researching record companies. Thereafter, they sat in a string of waiting rooms and more than once bluffed their way into some staffer's office; the meetings were invariably brief, and the demos wound up in the trash.

Word came that the Vibrators, a rising British punk band, had been booked to play London's Harrow College, which Ridgeley attended. Austin promised to arrange for the Executive to open the show. It seemed too good to be true, and a week before the gig, Michael and Ridgeley decided to phone the school to confirm. The person on the other end had never heard of the Executive. As furious as the two teenagers were at Austin, it didn't really matter: 2 Tone was on the wane, and they had to admit that nobody wanted this "useless band," as Michael called it. As the other members stopped coming to rehearsals, the group finally broke up.

It pained Michael to think that his father had been right, but he wouldn't give up. Against his better judgment, he begged Jack to buy him a pricey four-track recording machine for his eighteenth birthday. Instead, Jack presented his son with a long, heavy box. Michael tore it open and found two antique muskets. Jack explained the gift: When George had finally failed for good at being a musician, he could sell the guns, which were sure to increase in value.

In time, Michael sensed that his father, at least in part, wanted to cushion him from getting his feelings hurt. But Jack, he felt, could border on sadistic, and Michael burned to prove him wrong. "The fact that I had my father as an adversary was such a powerful tool to work with," he recalled. "I subconsciously fought him to the degree that it drove me to be one of the most successful musicians in the world. . . . It's a good coincidence, in a way, to have both musician ability and a lack of self-belief, a kind of damage, that drives you on like an insane person."

•••

Michael graduated from high school with no desire to go to college. He knew what he wanted to do, so what was the point? Jack had strongarmed him into waiting tables, washing dishes, and bartending in the restaurant; Michael hated every minute of it. But one night he heard a song playing there and began rewriting it in his head; that moment gave him his first inkling that he had the talent to compose. Suddenly, he recalled, "I had a feeling that I had a huge advantage over other people in the industry and a lot of other people in my own life." That included Ridgeley, who, having also graduated, was living "on the dole," cashing benefit checks for the unemployed. "He was a lazy bastard who just didn't want to go out to work," complained Michael. Determined to earn his own money, he took a series of mundane jobs: on a construction site, in a carwash, in a department store, as a ticket-tearer in a movie house.

In 1980, he tried his hand at deejaying. A restaurant in Bushey, the Bel Air, frequented by older couples, hired him to play music for post-dinner dancing. Michael was situated behind a pillar. Around the time dishes were cleared, a disembodied voice cut through the chatter. "Good evening, ladies and gentlemen," announced Michael awkwardly. "Welcome to the Bel Air restaurant. We hope you will partake of a little dancing . . ." Confusion fell over the room as diners looked to the left and the right, trying to figure out who was speaking. Michael spun such square selections as "Chicken Dance," a 1950s accordion tune, and Julio Iglesias ballads; they were the likeliest choices to lure couples onto the small dance floor. Every few tunes, he snuck in a mild disco record. "It was so embarrassing, so tacky," he said.

But his brief stint at the Bel Air taught him about pacing; he learned how to shift moods and tempos in order to keep an audience engaged. On nights off, he and Ridgeley tried their hand at writing songs. Michael's best mate had moved into a seedy flat in a cool neighborhood, Peckham, with Shirlie Holliman. Despite his study of violin, Michael couldn't notate music, but dreaming up tunes and lyrics came easily to him. Around that time, an idea entered his brain. It grew out of an episode with a young woman he had dated; she had spied him with another girl, and it broke her heart. His small twinge of guilt vanished as the indiscretion burgeoned into a song. In his head he worked out a rangy, sinuous, melodramatic tune, teeming with tragedy and sex. He jotted down some words on the bus to the Bel Air: "I'm never gonna dance again / Guilty feet have got no rhythm."

A seductive four-bar passage occurred to him as he approached the restaurant. He began devising words to fit, then decided it would sound better played instrumentally, maybe on saxophone. He sang what he had to Ridgeley, who provided chords, and they made a demo on a rented tape deck. On his last night at the Bel Air, Michael played "Guilty Feet," as he called it—"and the floor filled. I remember thinking, 'That's a good sign.'" The song, he decided, was a No. 1 hit.

Hipper dance floors called to both boys, and he and Ridgeley spent Friday nights on the town. Holliman had a car, and she chauffeured the young men to every cutting-edge spot in London: the Mud Club, the Wag Club, the Dirtbox, the Camden Palace. Michael's favorite was Le Beat Route, a Soho disco that exploded with every color and sexual preference in the rainbow. The trendiest styles were on display: piercings, poodle haircuts, purple lipstick, pale skin with garish eye-makeup.

Even in that company, one of Le Beat Route's key habitués, Boy George, born George O'Dowd, stood out. The New Wave singer and his band, Culture Club, were about to break with their first hit, "Do You Really Want to Hurt Me." But it was his campy geisha look—Kabuki makeup, plaited hair that hung from a straw hat, junk-store print frocks, shaved eyebrows, and a menacing glance—that grabbed most of the attention.

Michael, who had grown to just under six feet, wore what he hoped was a slick outfit: a black open-necked shirt topped by a bright orange jacket. He exuded suburban uncool. His cheeks were pimply and still round; he had a frizzy, untended beard and no mustache, and his unibrow hooded his sheepish eyes. One night a videographer inadvertently caught a snippet of George Michael in the crowd. He looks self-conscious and awkward as he tries to fit in. His eyes dart uncomfortably as they scan the couples around him, all of them looking as though they were born to dance.

He himself was anything but carefree, as James Sullivan knew. In 1981, the American student and the fledgling singer had their last encounter.

Michael had come out to him halfway, as bisexual. "I knew that he wasn't bisexual, but gay," said Sullivan. Michael seemed frightened: What would his parents think if they found out? Becoming famous meant everything to him, and "he was terrified that being gay would ruin his chances," observed Sullivan.

•••

That spring and summer, the first articles appeared about a mysterious "rare cancer" that had afflicted forty-one gay men in the United States. Purple blotches had burst through on their skin, and their lymph glands had swollen painfully. Researchers called the disease GRID (Gay-Related Immune Deficiency). The news brought the first chilling sense that gay life, which had only emerged from the underground a few years before, was about to become more perilous and stigmatized than ever. Photographer Robert Mapplethorpe—a victim, in 1989, of what would soon be renamed AIDS—summed up this grim new age to a friend. "You know," he said, "faggots are dying."

Michael heard the reports. Although he had done little sexually—and did not want to believe he was exclusively gay—he was still shaken; the physical contact he craved had taken on a new level of danger. He grilled Sullivan for information. "What happens?" asked Michael.

"You get it, you die."

Around that time, Sullivan's boyfriend told him that he had slept with Andrew Leaver. "When I found out what happened," recalled the American, "I said, 'I'm going back to the States. I'm not gonna get this fucking disease.'" On December 23, 1982, Leaver died—from cancer, his family said. He was nineteen.

Recently Michael had attended a benefit for Patrick Cowley, a disco composer who had helped create electronic dance music. Cowley had been diagnosed with AIDS. He had led the backup band for Sylvester, who would die of the disease in 1988. At the event, Michael heard further frightened talk about the virus. Up to then he had not used condoms; now he started. Everything about his sexual future seemed fraught with alarm, even as he set out to remake himself as the sex symbol every girl desired.

CHAPTER TWO

AFTER THE EXECUTIVE HAD fizzled, its members wondered if they would ever make a living from music. Austin became a public-pool attendant; Michael kept his job in a movie house; Ridgeley remained "on the dole," which was the national pastime. A recession had swept England, leaving about three million Brits unemployed. The young were enraged; their hard-earned college diplomas seemed worthless. Riots had broken out, aimed largely at the conservative government of prime minister Margaret Thatcher.

Jack warned his son that he had six months to land a record deal or get a real job; otherwise, he would throw him out. Taunted by his father and prodded by Ridgeley, he felt his determination growing. Michael had no doubt he was better than Duran Duran, Spandau Ballet, and Culture Club. He wasn't interested in being arty or underground. Michael had his mind on pop, a language everyone could understand. James Spencer, a teenage American pianist who would soon start a New Wave band, Common Hours, met Michael on a trip to England. "He told me he had thought a lot about what sounds were in, what image was going to help them make it," Spencer said. "In London, dance music and soul were hot."

Punk was wheezing its last; so were the New Romantics. But he and Ridgeley numbered themselves among a booming subculture of "soul boys," a British movement of young working-class males who worshipped soul music—the funkier the better—as an escape from suburban blandness. Rap was its latest incarnation. While hip-hop had barely reached the United Kingdom, Michael loved two singles from the States: the Sugarhill Gang's "Rapper's Delight" and Blondie's No. 1 hit, "Rapture," in which Debbie Harry, a blonde from Miami, did the first rapping that most Americans had ever heard.

Joined by Shirlie, who could dance, and Andrew, who was surprisingly stiff, Michael continued to haunt the discos. He had made strides since his first clumsy forays into Le Beat Route; now he was having his own *Saturday Night Fever* moments. "George used to make up all these dance routines which we'd do in nightclubs," noted Shirlie to Louise Jury in the *Independent*. "We were either great or so bad that everybody cleared the floor." Out of those dances, Wham! emerged.

One night on the floor, Ridgeley, in the heat of the moment, let loose with a rap-like chant: "Wham! Bam! I am the man!" He was referencing one of the first records he had ever bought, "Wig-Wam Bam" by the Sweet. The phrase "wham bam" had also appeared in another song he and Michael knew, David Bowie's "Suffragette City."

As strobe lights flashed, Michael had an epiphany. "That's a great name for a band!" he shouted. "Wham" meant hitting the bull's-eye so fast that people reeled. Ridgeley loved exclamation points, which added a cocky level of excitement to any name. Henceforth, he and Ridgeley would be known as Wham!.Within weeks, Michael had written "Wham Rap! (Enjoy What You Do?)." Later he explained: "It's very much based on Andrew's lifestyle—the idea of living off the state when your mother's a teacher and your father works at Canon, and you've got a perfectly healthy life at home and they're not making you put anything towards the housekeeping and you just go off and get your money every week."

•••

In February 1982, Michael and Ridgeley stood around another rented four-track tape deck in the latter's home. With the aid of Paul Ridgeley on backup vocals and a cheap synthesizer, they made a primitive demo of "Wham Rap! (Enjoy What You Do?)." At a time when activists were proclaiming every Brit's right to work, Michael cheered on the jobless and prodded the card-punchers. "Don't need this crap!" he snarled. "Do you enjoy what you do? If not—just stop!" Though he'd heard just a few rappers, Michael had the nimbleness and wit to mimic them; he chanted "get, get on down" with the beatboxing rhythm of hip-hop. The sheepish nerd of Bushey Meads was now channeling his bad influence, Andrew Ridgeley. He implored Britain's youth to raise a middle finger to the rules: "Listen, Mr. Average—you're a jerk!" The theme wasn't original; in 1977 the Sex Pistols had spat out a similar message in "Seventeen": "I don't work, I just speed . . . I'm so lazy." But now it had a fresh relevance.

The two other recordings on the demo went in different directions, which gave the group a cloudy persona. In "Guilty Feet," Michael's smoldering lament for the girl he'd wronged, an amateur sax player whom they had met in a pub played a schmaltzy solo. "Club Tropicana," also written by Michael, reached for the lushness of upscale Studio 54 disco while exalting the carefree beach life.

But Michael felt sure that their demo—an amateurish edit of chunks from their three songs—contained gold. Running off cassette copies, he and Ridgeley resumed the grind of sending their music to record companies or dropping it off in person. Once more they bluffed their way into the offices of a couple of A&R (Artists and Repertoire) executives, who scouted and developed talent. Again, nobody was interested. One producer tossed the cassette back across his desk and told Michael he had a nice voice. "Now go home and write some hit songs," he said.

In about a month, they seemed to have exhausted their options. Michael fumed: "I don't know why record companies hire people twice the age of the kids who are buying the records!"

There had been talk of David Austin joining Wham!, but the band seemed doomed, as he declared bluntly. Austin announced he was off to Thailand to play with a friend's group. One possibility remained. Near the Ridgeley home in Bushey lived a drinking buddy of Andrew's, Mark Dean, who had just founded a tiny label, Innervision. Then in his early twenties, Dean was a working-class street kid with dark and wavy hair, chipmunk cheeks, and small, surly eyes. In his previous job at Phonogram, the parent company of several British labels, Dean had helped launch two prominent New Wave bands, Soft Cell and ABC. That gained him a reputation as a talent-spotter. Dean talked CBS Records into funding a startup label that he and his Indian partner, Shamsi Ahmed, would run. The budget was minuscule, but at least it included manufacturing and distribution. Since CBS had a controlling interest in Innervision, the larger company had very little to lose and—if Dean unearthed a winner—a lot to gain.

But dealing with him could be maddening. David Chidekel, a New York-based music lawyer, represented Dean later in the decade. "I would say Mark was a brilliant, narcissistic sociopath," he said. "He would be generous and funny, a really cool guy to hang out with, then he could be the most cruel and inhumane person I'd ever met. He had a hair-trigger temper. He could verbally rip artists apart. I would take him off to the side and say, 'Are you out of your mind, man?' He'd be like, 'Aw, he was nothing without me, he was washing cars, look at him now.' I'd say, 'Yeah, but that's no reason to treat him like dirt.' "

Though painted as Wham!'s last resort, Dean claimed that Ridgeley had been hounding him to hear the demo even before he'd left Phonogram. Dean brushed him off, assuming Wham! was another deadbeat garage band. At the Innervision office, little more than a cubicle above a clothing store, a coworker insisted that Dean give the tape a listen. To his surprise, he loved it: "It was just George singing songs with scratchy guitar, but it was still great."

When he offered to sign Wham!, they were ecstatic. But the contract, dated March 5, 1982, and similar to almost every deal offered to unknowns, seemed harsh. Innervision could demand up to ten albums, based on how well the previous one had sold. The band would receive an 8 percent royalty rate per unit in the United Kingdom, 6 percent elsewhere; for twelve-inch singles—a growingly popular format among disco fans—they would earn 0. Before Michael and Ridgeley saw a pound, all expenses would be deducted.

Even with such puny terms, Innervision was taking a chance. No one else wanted Wham!. Paul Russell, a lawyer and music executive whom CBS U.K. appointed that year as managing director, acknowledged that Dean was working on a shoestring. CBS had paid him an advance—essentially a loan— of £225,000; out of that he had to cover all production costs. "He did his best for Wham! within the confines of the CBS-Innervision contract," said Russell. "Mark was not a shady character. My sense was that his overriding and perhaps naive interest was in signing artists, not becoming a music mogul."

As a formality, Michael and Ridgeley showed the contract to a lawyer, Robert Allan, whom a customer of Michael's father had recommended. Allan had serious reservations about the terms and wrote to Dean's lawyer, Paul Rodwell. Dean agreed to add £500 advances for Michael and Ridgeley. As for the rest, Dean's attitude was clear: Take it or leave it.

Fearful of losing the deal, Michael advised Allan to back off; the prospect of confronting his parents and telling them he'd gotten a deal was too sweet to risk losing. He marched into the cinema where he worked and brashly gave notice, "as though I'd just become a diamond dealer." On March 24,

Dean brought the contract to a studio in North London where Wham! was rehearsing. Michael recalled "almost kissing the ground" when Dean walked in. The label owner made it clear that if Wham! didn't accept his offer, he might move on to another band.

That day, just four weeks into their search for a deal, Wham! joined Innervision. Michael recalled the joy of pocketing his modest advance; he'd never had so much money. "Remember that when they were signed they were nobody," said the record-industry mogul David Geffen, with whom Michael would one day work. "They weren't in a position to negotiate. All artists that start from the bottom have crummy contracts. They're lucky to have them and they're thrilled when they get them. As was George."

The celebration continued when Michael went home and told his incredulous parents the news. He sealed it with an act of defiance. Jack had been appalled by Ridgeley's pierced ears, and had recently barked at his son, "You ever come home with two earrings, you'll be out that door!" On March 25, Michael had both ears pierced. He walked into the house and came face to face with his father. "Not a word was said," Michael recalled.

• • •

Before the songs could be released, they had to be published. Dean played the Wham! demo for Dick Leahy, a former record executive who had teamed with Bryan Morrison, an ex-manager of pop artists, to form a publishing company. Like Dean, Leahy heard possibilities; he certainly didn't know another suburban, teenage, British rapper. In their first meeting, Leahy saw the most strongheaded, focused teenager he had ever met. "George had a plan from day one," he said. "Wham! was his vehicle."

Although Leahy—a forty-four-year-old Brit with a sixties-style mop of dark hair streaked with blond highlights—had worked with David Bowie and Donna Summer, something else made Michael hire him: While running the London office of Bell Records, a 1970s label that had specialized in bubblegum pop, Leahy had helped nurture David Cassidy's British stardom. Whatever Cassidy had, Michael wanted, and Leahy became Michael's trusted advisor until the singer died. "George would play him music, and he trusted Dick's taste," said Rob Kahane, Michael's future agent and manager. "I thought Dick was very much a yes-man; he was always siding with George. I had to battle him a lot of times."

Now that they had a little seed money, they could record a proper take of "Wham Rap!," which would be their first single. A session was booked at Halligan Band Centre, a London studio. Prior to Wham!'s arrival, producer Bob Carter and engineer Chris Porter worked on the demo. Michael's fake American accent made Porter cringe; the synthesized rhythm track sounded amateurish and cheap. Suddenly, he remembered, Michael and Ridgeley "came bouncing into the room, dressed in tennis shorts" and looking fresh out of a tanning salon. Ridgeley wore movie-star shades and his familiar air of detached cool, while Michael still had the earmarks of the nerd he'd always been: baby fat, tight curls, acne. "I looked at the two of them," said Porter, "and I thought: Never. We might as well all go home. But it became apparent that George had a good handle on what he wanted to get out of this song and how he was going to achieve it."

Though he had almost no technical vocabulary, he gently told Porter just what he wanted. Ridgeley did little. "Early on there was a bit of guitar work," said the engineer. "But I'd be misleading people if I said that Andrew had a voice or much musical ability. What he had was a great personality. George in that first session was very, very shy, a bit gauche. But Andrew could be fun, easy to talk to, and he gave George the confidence to do these things." Michael was in the process of building a musical family, and Porter would remain his engineer for the next thirteen years. With a bassist and drummer present, "Wham Rap!" was complete.

Soon Wham! would have to start performing live—something that both Michael and Ridgeley had seldom done, and never too well. For window-dressing as well as moral support, they enlisted Shirlie Holliman to be their backup singer. She could barely carry a tune, but as a blonde, choppy-haired ex-punker who now leaned toward the girl-next-door look of Doris Day, she would add visual spice. Because she would seem lonely standing up there by herself, Michael and Ridgeley planned to pair her with a sexy sixteen-year-old blonde, Amanda Washbourn.

Michael quickly began having second thoughts. If Wham! wanted to be taken seriously as a rap and soul band, it would need street credibility, and it wouldn't get it by employing two white blondes. Washbourn was unceremoniously dumped. Dean and Ahmed recommended a replacement: Dee C. Lee (born Diane Catherine Sealey), a young soul singer from London who recorded demos for EMI Publishing. The job required a vocal correctness that did little to show off her sultry R&B style; it also hid her high-cheekboned beauty, which presaged that of Sade.

Lee met with all four young men at Innervision. This was ostensibly an audition, but no one asked her to sing; the Wham! team wanted to see how she looked. Amid some conversation, they played her the demo. Lee loved it. More than her voice, Michael wanted her look. She left Innervision with the job.

Soon she was at Michael's home, rehearsing with the group. The Innervision signing had warmed Jack and Lesley to their son's ambitions, and Lee wondered how the family setting she saw could have inspired "Wham Rap!," which evoked switchblades and delinquency. "I thought, is this guy really gonna become a pop star?" she recalled. "Musicians are like wildcats and weirdos. These people seemed far too nice and normal."

But as Michael spoke of his dreams for Wham! and his goal of celebrating soul music, Lee's hopes rose. She barely knew how he sang; she had mainly heard him rap. Nonetheless, she got the feeling that Wham! was on an express train to the top.

On June 16, 1982, Innervision released "Wham Rap!" Deejays and critics ignored it; nobody had heard of Wham! Watching his company's one hope fizzling, Dean told Michael and Ridgeley that they had to go out and perform. CBS stepped in. Dave Novik, a new member of the A&R department, had heard the record and put in a good word. "I was blown away by what they had done," he said. A member of the publicity department, Lorraine Trent, contacted Norman Scott, a popular deejay on the London club circuit, and asked if he would present Wham! somewhere. Scott spun at Bolts, a gay Monday night meetup at Lazer's, a North London disco. Since Wham! consisted of two young, cute boys and a pair of flashy girl singers, the act had obvious gay appeal. Luckily Scott, who himself was gay, loved "Wham Rap!" and booked them for an upcoming Monday. He began playing the record nightly to start a buzz.

On a chilly Monday in September, Michael, Ridgeley, Holliman, and Lee, along with a gang of their friends, climbed the steep flight of steps to

Lazer's. It was a seedy place that stank of beer, and on this night, only about twenty men milled around. Michael and Ridgeley maximized the opportunity by changing into gym shorts. When the moment seemed right, Scott faded out the dance record he was playing and introduced a rising pop sensation known as Wham!. He cued up "Wham Rap!" and the young foursome awkwardly took their places at the front of the club. Michael lip-synched; Ridgeley held a guitar and shimmied to the beat; Holliman and Lee enacted some rudimentary moves. All eyes stayed on Michael, including those of Richard Tay, the China-born future owner of a record label, Sepia. "We were all young and camp," said Tay, "but George outcamped us by a million times. Lots of makeup, and when he danced I thought he was boneless. He moved like a snake and looked at ease and confident, and clearly in charge. Andrew could not dance and was always one beat behind, and looked clumsy and uncomfortable."

The girls made up for it. "The little dance routine and the way we mimed to the record just seemed to go down so well," said Lee. "I'd always been in bands but I'd never gotten adoration like that before." Michael, however, emerged as the star. "I think everyone at Bolts that night was quite aware that George Michael was gay," said Stephen, another customer. When admirers asked about his plans, Michael stated nonchalantly that he was going to be a pop star.

Scott invited them back. This time he pulled a surprise. He cued up the B-side of "Wham Rap!," which was an instrumental version of the song. Instantly realizing what had happened, Michael began rapping live. Rather than being upset, he seemed thrilled. He liked Bolts as much as the customers liked him. As a conflicted gay nineteen-year-old, he found the club tantalizing and showed up every week, absorbing the latest sounds. "If you listen to what Wham! was doing and the music getting played in the gay discos, there's a connection," said James Spencer.

Ridgeley seemed completely at ease around gays, but he did not yet realize he was working with one; by all appearances, his friend was straight. Aside from that, androgyny was in, and there on the London club scene, even the most finely tuned gaydar could err. "The boys and girls looked the same," explained Lee. "I knew a lot of straight guys who were a bit effeminate."

Still, Michael was hanging out in a gay club, which held risks. Wham!'s performances at Bolts helped launch the persistent rumor that he and Ridgeley were boyfriends. Years later, Michael laughed the rumblings off: "I cannot think of anything less likely than Andrew and I sleeping together," he said. But he didn't hesitate to milk the gay interest. Soon he and Ridgeley would affect the look of brooding, sexy young bikers in tight jeans and leather jackets. As he admitted later to writer Adrian Deevoy: "It was all definitely very ambiguous. We had a very strong gay following."

Even so, Michael took precautions. He began showing up at Bolts with a young Portuguese woman, Pat Fernandes, on his arm. Fernandes was a club kid who loved hanging out with gays, notably Boy George, who had used her as his assistant. Because she had a car, she was at the ready to drive friends around. "She was a pretty little thing," said Dee C. Lee. "She was always good fun in the clubs."

Fernandes became the first in a series of young women who served as Michael's "beards," or faux-girlfriends. They danced with him, served as his dates at events, and would soon provide grist to columnists who were eager to know who Michael was sleeping with. Michael called Fernandes a "really sweet girl," but things turned messy when she fell madly in love with him. Still, she came in handy. Since she was dark-skinned, Michael inserted her in videos and shows as an ersatz backup singer to up Wham!'s soul quotient.

• • •

Image was crucial as the band stood poised on the brink of one of the biggest revolutions ever to hit pop. At the New York offices of Epic Records, a subsidiary of Columbia, Debbie Samuelson was the young woman who helped set up a division to handle a burgeoning promotional tool. "There were these things called music videos, which nobody knew what to do with," she said. Still painfully cheesy, they showed acts lip-synching to their latest singles. The concept harked back to the 1930s, when coin-operated machines played "soundies," three-minute performance films of current tunes. In the fifties, a new version, Snader Telescriptions, provided filler on early TV; the sixties brought in Scopitones, sixteen-millimeter musical shorts shown in their own special jukeboxes. "Then when MTV came," said Samuelson, "the world changed." The year was 1981. She began hiring directors and supervising shoots. "It was exciting," she said. "It was new. It was renegade. We were making these little minifilms that added an extra dimension, and there were no rules as to what could or could not be done."

Many old-guard artists fumed as they saw their songs taking second place to the way they looked. "I hate fucking videos—they're fucking loathsome!" spewed Elton John. "I make music, I don't make fucking films!" Art Garfunkel, sharing a BBC TV panel later on with Michael and Ridgeley, remarked dryly: "Isn't that what videos are, the look? Who needs music?"

But Michael understood from the beginning that an eye-catching video could cinch a song's success faster than a single; MTV could make artists famous almost overnight. By 1982, his generation expected to see a song, not just hear it. "The video was an essential part of both the marketing and the experience," said Michael Pagnotta, one of Michael's future press agents. "Does anybody not think of the 'Thriller' video when they hear that song? Does anyone not remember Madonna in the gondola when they hear 'Like a Virgin'?"

Supplied by Innervision with a tiny budget, Michael, Ridgeley, and director Chris Gabrin shot the video for "Wham Rap!" It shows Ridgeley in a suburban living room, lazily leafing through a magazine as his parents demand he get a job. Out struts his brother George, leather-clad, primped, and defiant as he hits the street. He breezes past street cleaners, office staff, and other members of the dreary working class. The video cuts to him and Ridgeley in an all-white room, dancing their hearts out on top of white blocks. Emblazoned on the wall behind them is the password to excitement, WHAM!. Holliman and Lee flank them, shimmying in black pantsuits. The camera pulls in for a closeup of Michael shaking his behind in leather pants; he also wears a spiked leather jacket over his bare chest—styling straight out of Bolts. But the scene is heterosexualized by Holliman and Lee, the latter of whom poses as Michael's interracial love interest. By the end, this parents' nightmare has turned into an *American Bandstand*-like shindig, as the group's friends and even the sour mom and dad dance with Wham!.

Lee marveled at how effortlessly in control Michael seemed. "I wasn't that used to being in front of the camera," she said. "George helped me. 'Walk like this, a bit slower, tilt your head down!' I remember thinking, is this really gonna be my life? Doing things I love, hanging out with people that are hilarious, funny, and getting to wear lovely clothes—and sing? Oh, yeah. This was it, baby."

Only the singing part failed to materialize. Lee wasn't heard on the next Wham! single, "Young Guns (Go for It!)," another teen-rebel rap song, written by Michael. It finds him running into an old "soul boy" pal, now with his fiancée, and taunting him for wanting to settle down: "See me, single and free / No tears, no fears, what I want to be." In the end, the betrothed "sucker" takes his buddy's side. Michael knew that some people were bound to be offended—and the more controversy Wham! stirred up, the better.

With Blondie's "Rapture" in mind, Michael wanted a female rapper to play the part of the scorned girlfriend. Shamsi Ahmed found the ideal voice. Lynda Hayes was an American jingle and session singer who had recently moved to London; she could channel almost any style, including rap. On August 18, 1982, Hayes arrived at the studio to find a group of horn players and other musicians, producer Steve Brown, and Wham! getting ready. Michael was still writing Hayes's lines. He could not come up with a couplet for the moment when the betrothed "young gun" snaps at his fiancée for rebuking his friend. Hayes rattled off a solution: "Shut up, chick, that's a friend of mine / Watch your mouth, baby, you're out of line." Michael loved it. He sang very little on "Young Guns"—all the rest was rap—but Hayes saw a star in the making.

"George was so cool!" she said. "It went beyond his voice—it was his aura. He was a hardworking little son of a gun. At such a young age, to be that tuned-in to who you are and what you wanna hear—that made all the difference. Steve Brown may have produced the record, but George was driving that train." She did all the backing vocals and harmonies, and when a modulation took Michael a few notes above his range, she sang them for him.

Soon thereafter, Wham! called Hayes into Innervision for a meeting. They had been talking her up to Dean, they said, and he wanted to sign her. They played her the "Guilty Feet" demo and proposed it as her first single, to be produced by Michael. "I would *love* to do that song," she told them. A week later they handed her a contract. The terms appalled her. She could make that much in a day of jingle work, she told them. Hayes declined.

When "Young Guns" was shipped in October, the sleeve did not mention Hayes, but not even the name Wham! seemed to matter. The group's appearances in non-gay clubs weren't going so well, and despite the best radio promotion Innervision could provide, the single stalled at No. 48. Everyone began losing faith in Wham!, Mark Dean included. Michael, recalled Ridgeley, turned "almost suicidal." In attendance at one of Wham!'s club dates was a staff member of *Saturday Superstore*, a BBC TV variety series for kids. With three hours of airtime to fill every Saturday morning, the bookers were in constant need of talent that was suitable for children. Luckily, the *Saturday Superstore* booker knew nothing of Wham!'s performances at Bolts. Michael and Ridgeley were ecstatic when an invitation came to perform "Young Guns" for the show's vast prepubescent audience.

Wham! orchestrated that appearance as though their lives depended on it. On the set were a pair of American sports cars; flanked by those, the young men staged the song as though it were a scene from *Grease*. Shirlie Holliman, playing the fiancée, wore prim, secretarial white and lip-synched to Lynda Hayes's sassy rapping. Ridgeley, as the bad boy turned dullard, wore a drab short-sleeve shirt. Michael, in jeans and a leather vest in lieu of a shirt—a spicy outfit for a kids' show—led the pack, breaking into his *Saturday Night Fever* moves, some of them enacted with Lee. Clearly, only one young gun had star quality. "It would have been fabulous to have some of that stardust sprinkled upon me," recalled Ridgeley. The studio audience clapped so loudly that suddenly Wham! felt hopeful again.

But *Saturday Superstore* wasn't turning anyone into a star, and the show bumped "Young Guns" only to No. 42. Then came another break. A producer from *Top of the Pops* had seen Wham! on *Saturday Superstore*. An act had dropped out at the last minute, and the show needed a sub. Wham! would do.

It all happened so fast that Michael and Ridgeley barely had time to feel nervous. On November 17, 1982, the night before the eight A.M. rehearsal, the two nineteen-year-olds slept at a cheap hotel on a London side street, courtesy of Innervision. Michael's bed was child-size. "I was sitting with my feet over the end of it thinking, this isn't how it's supposed to be. If you're on *Top of the Pops* that means you're famous." The next morning, he and Ridgeley reported to work. Michael glanced around, stunned at "how crummy the studio was."

Lynda Hayes wouldn't have minded. She had missed Wham!'s *Saturday Superstore* appearance, but word reached her about *Top of the Pops*, where everyone lip-synched. Hayes knew that Shirlie would be miming to her voice.

Why couldn't they let Hayes do it? "I was on the phone to Steve Brown, saying, 'Please, please don't do this to me.' He said, 'If you make a fuss about this, you will never work in this town again.' I needed to work in this town. I didn't have any money; I was just good at what I did." She backed off.

Hayes was at home, scrubbing the floor, when *Pops* came on. Out bounced Wham! to repeat their "Young Guns" performance as a crowd of youths danced behind them. The ugly duckling of Bushey Meads was now a sexy and slightly menacing swan. Michael had lost weight even since *Saturday Superstore* and looked in fighting shape, down to his flat, shaved stomach. Makeup covered his blemishes. His hair was straightened and cut into a feathered bouffant. Michael had morphed into an Andrew Ridgeley fantasy—and Shirlie had become Lynda Hayes.

On her hands and knees with a soapy brush, Hayes burst into tears. "The idea of wanting to sign me may have been a little consolation prize, because they knew at that time that someone else would be miming to me."

Initially, however, not even Wham! seemed to have gotten much out of the *Pops*. Michael rode the bus home with Ridgeley. The next day he walked down the street, and no one showed a hint of recognition. The lack of response suggested how different he looked offstage, without makeup and in street clothes—for at that moment, "Young Guns" was climbing steadily into the Top 40. It peaked at No. 3. Only eight months after they had signed their small-time record deal, Wham! had made it. Michael told friends he had expected it to happen all along.

• • •

Wham! still lacked a manager, and Dean reached out to a powerful one, Ron Weisner, in Los Angeles. Weisner's clients included Madonna and Michael Jackson; he had also worked with an eye-popping array of Brits, notably Steve Winwood, Frankie Goes to Hollywood, Bananarama, and ABC. Weisner flew to London to meet with Dean. He was interested, and proved it by getting Wham! some of its earliest U.S. airplay; he also booked the group on *American Bandstand* and *Solid Gold*, two U.S. television shows that had jettisoned many a family-friendly single up the charts. For the first time, Wham! flew to Los Angeles. The young men arrived for the *Solid Gold* taping in their rumpled airplane clothes, which annoyed the producers. Things went downhill from there. The show's gimmick was its troupe of six Spandex-and-lamé-clad Solid Gold Dancers, who enacted kitschy choreography. As much as Michael dreamed of conquering America, he was appalled at what they planned to do during "Young Guns." He announced that Wham! would not perform with those hacks; the group, he said, already had its own lousy dancers. The segment was taped, then killed.

American Bandstand, on the air since 1952, had long ago passed its prime. But Michael didn't dare blow this appearance, too. On March 5, 1983, host Dick Clark introduced Wham!'s two hotshot Brits to the States. "They are hot!" he said. "They are just knocking everybody on their head over there." But the spot was somewhat wasted, for "Young Guns" hadn't been released in the States. Ultimately, Michael decided he didn't want to pay Weisner and his partner, Freddy DeMann, the percentage they wanted.

Back in London, Wham! had caught the eye of Gordon Summers, a drummer and low-level manager known by his nickname, Jazz. A weathered, chain-smoking thirty-eight, Summers had blotchy skin and a balding head with a fringe of scraggly hair. He spoke frantically; his favorite adjective was "fucking." Summers had bummed around the business for years, playing with jazz bands, rock groups, and folk singers and representing a few obscure clients. On a visit to a record company, he heard someone playing a single. At first he thought he was hearing the Sugarhill Gang, who hailed from New Jersey, but the song mentioned the DHSS (Department of Health and Social Security), which stamped checks for Brits on the dole. He asked who this was. Wham!, he heard.

"Wham!" he said. "What a fucking great name."

He learned that Wham! recorded for Mark Dean, whom he knew slightly. Summers paid him a visit. Dean told him what he had hoped to hear: that Wham! had no manager. He played the demo of "Guilty Feet." As if by magic, in walked the young duo. Though straight, Summers found them "luminous," and gushed over them like a teenage girl. They all but ignored him.

Summers knew he had no clout. But Simon Napier-Bell, a far more prominent British manager, had loads of it. Then forty-three, Napier-Bell had helped detonate the Yardbirds, the band that had launched three star guitarists—Eric Clapton, Jimmy Page, and Jeff Beck; he had also handled

Marc Bolan, a glam rock giant. With Vicki Wickham, the former manager and lover of Dusty Springfield, Napier-Bell had written the words to Springfield's only No. 1 British hit, "You Don't Have to Say You Love Me." He was something of a star in his own right; openly gay and flamboyantly well-to-do, he had a highbrow tongue, a flashy wardrobe, and the cleverness to charm almost anyone.

He agreed to see Summers. "I crossed his white, shag pile carpet and passed under a huge chandelier," said Summers in his memoir, *Big Life*. "His living room was dominated by two cocaine-white leather sofas." Effusing about Wham!, Summers proposed a joint management venture. Napier-Bell had seen the duo on *Top of the Pops*. Aside from their fetching looks, Wham! had captured him with their rapport, what would one day be dubbed a "bromance"—a deep though nonsexual intimacy between two apparently straight men. Napier-Bell didn't suspect that either of them was gay, even when Michael tossed an arm around Ridgeley. It was a fascinating pop image. He wanted in.

Through Bryan Morrison, Summers arranged a meeting with Wham!. At the appointed time, the two older men waited, and waited. Wham! stood them up. It wasn't mere arrogance; Michael had already developed an allergic reaction to the businessmen of music. He was starting to feel had by Mark Dean, who kept him and Ridgeley on forty-pound allowances per week even after a top-five hit. But Summers was furious and let Morrison know it.

Two days later, Ridgeley lay stretched out on Napier-Bell's sofa, looking indifferent. Michael, however, sat warily on a chair and displayed a toughness he had never quite shown before. "He could shoot mistrust from his eyes like fire from a flamethrower," said the manager. Although Marc Bolan was a favorite of his, Michael made sure not to seem too impressed. He grilled the two older men as to what they had done in the past and what they could do for Wham!. Michael made his intentions clear: "Our ambition is to become the biggest band in the world. And I think it's within our reach."

Napier-Bell and Summers, he announced, could have world management rights, except for America. Bluffing, he claimed that Wham! already had Michael Jackson's manager. But in a moment of truth, he confessed that both he and Ridgeley were broke. Summers read the Innervision contract, which he deemed one of the most "awful, unfair fucking record deals that

ever got signed." If Wham! were to go with Summers and Napier-Bell, the
two would have to renegotiate it. Furthermore, declared Michael, after a
thirty-day trial, Wham! could leave whenever they chose. No contract was
signed. Nomis Management, as Napier-Bell called his office, took on Wham!.

On the same day that the trade papers had announced the news, he
learned that their defensive new client had a secret. "At least four friends
called me up and said, 'George is gay.' I said, 'No, he's not.' They said, 'I've been
in a toilet with him.' 'I've seen him in that club.'" Napier-Bell had gotten his
first taste of the trials that lay ahead. "There was nothing uncomplex about
George. He would be incredibly cautious about anybody knowing he was
gay, and ridiculously incautious. But I worked on the basis of, what George
doesn't tell me I don't know. He knew I'm gay—that's certainly one of the
reasons he wanted me to manage him—but he didn't want to talk overtly
about himself, and I respected that. If he'd have asked me about coming out,
I'd have said, don't, because Wham! was a fake Hollywood image devised by
him. And he had to stay heterosexual."

Michael achieved that in the "Young Guns" video, which was shot in one
of their favorite haunts, the Wag Club. Though again shot on a shoestring,
the video, directed by Tim Pope, has an expensive look and enough tongue-
in-cheek to leaven its juvenile premise. The camera follows Michael and Dee
C. Lee down winding stairs and onto a packed dance floor. Michael sees an
old friend and his prim betrothed and starts rapping his discouragement.
The lights flash and the beat pounds, turning Michael once more into a British Travolta. Shirlie and Dee C. break into a catfight, and the boys escape
together into the London tube.

The video, observed James Spencer, was "macho enough not to look
effeminate. Women like men with tight jeans and a nice package. It worked
for everyone. That's why George went that way with his early marketing."
But video aroused Michael's every insecurity about his looks. The camera
scrutinized him closely, and when he saw the playbacks he cringed; no
amount of styling could banish the George he was used to seeing in the
bathroom mirror. All he cared about, he said, was "not having to look at
what I don't like about my face." He hated its right side—but on the left he
had this "mangy ear." He shunned backlighting because he thought it made
his hair look thin.

But the Wham! image was clicking. A slightly updated version of "Wham Rap!" was released in January 1983, and it shot to No. 8. "Bad Boys," the next single, repeated the formula. Michael recast the young-rebel theme as a slap at his parents: "When you tried to tell me what to do / I just shut my mouth and smiled at you."

This time, Wham! leaned closer to Hollywood than the backstreets of London. In the video, a little boy can't stand his punishing parents and the monotony of family life, depicted in quaint sepia. He flees the house, along the way punching a dorky, bespectacled boy, much like Michael was before Wham!. One striking sequence shows the boy's feet in closeup as he runs away; they metamorphose into the feet of the grown-up George, now a menacing James Dean-like greaser with studs on his leather and a chain on his jeans. He climbs into a car with Andrew and a girl and they speed off to dangers unknown.

To Napier-Bell, Wham! consisted of "a real Andrew and a fake Andrew." But on camera, Michael had become the bad boy, Ridgeley the nondescript second fiddle. The song itself embarrassed Michael, who knew he had written a pale knockoff of "Young Guns." But it took Wham! to No. 2. Innervision took a chance and released it in the States. It only reached No. 60, but that was a start. Michael decided that Wham! was done with rap. The time had come to start singing.

CHAPTER THREE

THOUGH UNCOMMONLY SHREWD, MICHAEL was, in many ways, still a kid. Like Ridgeley, he lived with his parents. He loved Mars bars, slathered mayonnaise on much of what he ate, and annoyed Ridgeley by chewing with his mouth open. They spoke in boyish shorthand, finishing each other's sentences and bursting simultaneously into laughter at childish jokes. Asked by a reporter about the cover photo of their upcoming debut album, Michael said: "There's these two boys in it; they're really pretty ugly, you know?" He and Ridgeley giggled.

At home, said percussionist Danny Cummings, who would soon join the band, Michael was now "the center of everybody's world. They were all satellites." Chris Heath, a young reporter for *Smash Hits*, a monthly bible for British pop fans, interviewed him at home. "He seemed close with his family, although clearly his family was a complicated issue. I remember how he reverted to being a young son rather than a pop star, meekly asking his mother things."

On the job, though, he was as controlling as his father. "You couldn't tell George what to do," said Jazz Summers. When he and Ridgeley disagreed, the latter gave in. Michael complained that his partner was a lazy stoner who contributed little. Sometimes they stopped speaking. But Michael didn't want too much of Ridgeley's input. While he could carry a tune, his singing, like his guitar-playing, wasn't really needed. Ridgeley had inspired Wham!; that was enough. Sometimes he skipped record dates and slept through other opportunities, such as a photo shoot for *My Guy*, a teen magazine that comprised comic-strip picture stories about young adults and their problems. Michael was asked to play girl-crazy Tony; Ridgeley his best friend Des. But according to editor Frank Hopkinson, he "couldn't get out of bed," so David Austin stepped in.

Ridgeley soon realized that if Wham! were to reach the top, he had better leave Michael in charge. All Ridgeley had to do was look good, be a sometime consultant (especially on matters of style), and enjoy the ride. He certainly knew that the Wham! brand hinged on smart-ass cockiness. It was he who dreamed up the name for their first album, *Fantastic*. But in the studio, Michael took command.

His choices "weren't negotiable, really," said Paul Gomersall, who would soon join his team of engineers. "If you made a slight change to something overnight, he'd come back and say, 'What's happened there?' George had great ears." But Michael's technical know-how remained weak; he could fish out notes on a bass or a keyboard and invent simple chord changes, but it took hours. Other bands learned their craft by "woodshedding"—long sessions of experimentation at home or on casual gigs—but Wham! had skipped that. "George was a child of the computer age, and I think that tempered his perception of music a lot," said Henry Hey, the musical director for his final tour. "For George, a song might start with a drumbeat on a sequencer and then some keyboard parts. He would spend a lot of time manicuring a track and *then* go perform it live."

Colleagues began recommending heavyweight players to make Wham! sound funkier. The group acquired its first maestro in Tommy Eyre, the organist on Joe Cocker's chart-topping cover of the Beatles' "With a Little Help from My Friends." Drummer Trevor Murrell knew all about the Motown beat. But the backup band's star became Deon Estus, a Detroit-born bassist who had worked with Marvin Gaye. A handsome, mahogany-skinned hulk with massive shoulders and dreadlocks, Estus was full of charisma, and his burning rhythm made Wham! swing. Michael looked to him in awe. "We were like brothers," Estus said.

He, in turn, loved Michael's sweet soul sound, which recalled Smokey Robinson and Al Green. Michael shunned melisma, the multisyllabic out-pouring that had sprung out of gospel and invaded soul; he preferred not to decorate. "He didn't oversing," said Estus, "but the way he delivered was beautiful." Michael insisted the backing, too, be as basic as possible. "It was to make the voice and the vocal arrangements shine," said Chris Porter. "No fluffy high hats, not too much cymbals, bass. He would say, 'You're playing too much! Keep it simple!'"

By now he and Andrew could no longer pose as backstreet thugs; they were stars. "I've stopped trying to pretend that I've got anything important to say or anything that needs an angry young man to say it," Michael explained. "We're putting back into pop the idea that records should be there for three-and-a-half minutes and buzzing around your head for a while and not much else."

In the tracks that fleshed out *Fantastic*, the mature sound of Wham! took hold. "A Ray of Sunshine" had a beat out of Studio 54 and a tapestry of George Michael backup vocals, processed to sound like basso he-men, chirpy children, and the neutered falsettos of the Bee Gees. In a cover of "Love Machine," the Miracles' 1975 disco hit, he gave pinpoint imitations of its vocals, from the guttural growls to the sweet falsetto of singer Billy Griffin. Michael's head was a packed jukebox of sixties and seventies pop; he seemed to know every hot riff, vocal quirk, and Motown rhythm that made people want to move. He had spent most of his life dissecting these sounds, analyzing their inner workings. He could draw them up in an instant, reshuffling them in ways that sounded fresh.

"There's not much that I write that doesn't stem from some other influence," he confessed. "I have no shame about that at all. . . . There is something about those clichéd chord patterns that I love." Michael was learning the science of pop—how to push pleasure buttons in listeners' minds that would make them buy the record.

But one of his new songs, "Nothing Looks the Same in the Light," shunned those devices; instead it looked ahead to an adult George Michael. The song is a morning-after reverie sung to a figure sleeping in the sheets. "Only a fool like me would take to heart / The things you said you meant last night," sings Michael in a soft, breathy, reverberant cry. Six minutes long, the track foreshadowed the hypnotic, drawn-out grooves of Sade. "I remember hearing that and thinking, 'Oh, this is new and interesting, sort of jazzy,'" said James Spencer. "And two years later everybody was doing it. George was on the cutting edge of that. He was very proud of that track."

But Michael knew it wasn't chart material. For that, he had souped up another song from the original Wham! demo, "Club Tropicana," about an imaginary summer oasis in which "castaways and lovers meet." Its inspiration was Club 18–30, a British company that booked frisky young singles on resort vacations.

Michael revamped it to sound like lush European disco. The track opened with sound effects—footsteps in the night, party noises, crashing waves—that conjured up a boozy, balmy oasis. Horns and a Latin-jazz keyboard solo made the rhythm sail along. As Michael sang of a "place where membership's a smiling face," he sounded cool and sexy—just the type of guy one would hope to meet on the dance floor. Michael had borrowed the groove as well as the idea of using sound effects from a recent No. 1 hit, the Gap Band's "Burn Rubber on Me (Why You Wanna Hurt Me)." The travelogue theme had been used in Duran Duran's "Rio," then on the American charts. But Michael saw it as his ticket to the Reagan-era U.S. market, in which dreams of affluence reigned and Club Med vacations were booming. And with British youth still reeling from unemployment, what better fantasy could there be than "Club Tropicana"?

Heard at the end of the track, in a few multitracked repetitions of the word "cool," was Dee C. Lee. Otherwise, Wham! fans had barely heard her voice. For Shirlie Holliman, the group was a lark; she went along with whatever its leaders wanted. But Lee fought to sing. When Michael and Ridgeley tried to dress her in skimpy outfits, she rebelled: "You don't pay me enough! I'm not a freakin' porn model, I'm a singer!" She refused to lip-synch onstage anymore or to appear in videos for songs she hadn't sung on. "I used to forget that George was quite sensitive and occasionally very insecure," recalled Lee. "I could be quite full-on and freak him out."

But he couldn't be swayed. "No," he said. "We're gonna do it this way." No voice would be allowed to compete with his.

In the spring of 1983, with no Wham! jobs on her calendar, Lee went on tour with another Innervision band, Animal Nightlife. In the midst of it, she got a last-minute call from London: Wham! needed her for the video of "Club Tropicana," to be shot on the Spanish island of Ibiza. In order to use her, they would have to squeeze the shoot into a two-day gap in her schedule. The Wham! team was furious.

Nonetheless, she soon found herself in a hedonist's paradise of crystal-blue beaches, sex, and drugs. Ibiza's tone was set by Tony Pike, the mustachioed and frequently naked owner of the Pikes Hotel, the island's notorious boutique resort. It lured such boldface names as Freddie Mercury, Julio

Iglesias, Frank Zappa, and Grace Jones, the Amazonian singer, model, and club icon whom the married Pike recalled as "the best fuck I've ever had in my life." Showing a reporter the hotel in 2018, the year before he died, Pike boasted: "Along this fucking bar it'd be all lines of cocaine."

Wham! had made stunning strides in just over a year, yet Michael was impatient to catapult the band higher. The "Club Tropicana" video was designed to give Wham! the decadent glamour of *La Dolce Vita*. After a movie-style credit crawl comes a touch of mystery: Lee and Holliman arrive by jeep in the dead of night, heels clicking as they walk through the dark. Suddenly day breaks and there is Pike in a straw hat, welcoming them to a candy-colored pool party at his hotel. The star is Michael in sunglasses and a white Speedo, his body shaved, tanned, and slimmed-down, his smile gleaming white. He and Ridgeley float on inflatables, splash in the water, and ogle girls in bikinis—particularly Lee and Holliman, with whom they flirt from afar. At the end, the two women don their work clothes—they're stewardesses—and fly off, leaving two crestfallen beach boys behind.

Duncan Gibbins was ostensibly the director, but Michael ran the show tensely and with dead seriousness; when Lee and Holliman giggled during one of their shots, he scolded them as though they were naughty schoolgirls. His hair remained his biggest concern; the splashing and humidity were turning it frizzy. Compulsively, he checked his looks in the monitor; each time he frowned, hating what he saw.

But female Wham! fans beheld a pair of teenybopper dreams—the Frankie Avalon and Fabian of British pop. In the *Sunday Times*, Mick Brown called Wham! "an exorcism of all the things that were negative about pop music in the seventies and eighties." Punk rock may have dwindled, but its hostile imagery was hard to erase. Barb Jungr, a British cabaret singer, had started out as half of the Stroke, a duo that she formed with her husband, Dan Bowling. "I had silver boots with stack heels and this blue working-man's boiler suit, and in my hair I had a big panel of bright red," she said. "Dan wore a T-shirt that said FUCK YOUR MOTHER. And we were bone-thin from all the drugs."

A subsequent wave of star bands, including Frankie Goes to Hollywood, the Smiths, and Eurythmics, replaced the anarchy of punk with cynical and wounded art-pop; Eurythmics' 1983 hit, "Sweet Dreams (Are Made of

This)," urged a generation to "hold your head up" in a world of opportunists and users.

But there was nothing arty or embittered about Wham!. Michael and Ridgeley were two cute lads on top of the world, exulting in privilege and in each other. They spoke in the language of pop—a genre, said Chris Heath, "that communicates very directly and emotionally to a large audience. It's a skill that is not respected as much as it should be. It can seem superficial."

With the recession in England starting to fade, Wham! spoke loudly to what the *Daily Telegraph* called "the Thatcherite youth," whose goal was capitalism. They were "conformists rather than rebels . . . highly pragmatic realists who know exactly what they want and where they are going.'" Michael and Ridgeley provided the soundtrack. "They danced and looked cute; they didn't look like they were gonna come 'round and destroy your furniture," said Jungr. "They were magnets for nice young people who wanted to get married and have a garden and still have fun."

• • •

In 2009, the *Independent's* Simon Price would marvel at how hardly anyone had caught "the slightest whiff of gayness" in the "Club Tropicana" video, which showed "our heroes gazing at each other's tanned torsos in mutual admiration, larking about in the pool. . . . Only in the unique context of the eighties, in which far more blatant gender-bending abounded, could such high levels of camp have gone undetected."

It all seemed like a calculated tease; Michael knew that gays had helped ignite Wham!'s ascent. The girls who loved them seemed none the wiser. James Spencer recalled watching the video with his sister, who had a crush on Michael. "I said, 'Oh my God, this is so gay.' She said, 'He's not gay! You just want him to be gay because you like him!'"

Homosexuals were all over the Top 10, yet just a few bands dropped their cover. Soft Cell made its *Top of the Pops* debut in 1981 with its first hit, "Tainted Love"; though warned to "tone it down," the lead singer, Marc Almond, performed with studded leather wrist bands and eyeliner. Frankie Goes to Hollywood's video "Relax," banned by MTV and the BBC, was set in a gay S&M club. The video for Bronski Beat's "Smalltown Boy" depicted cruising at a public pool and a gay-bashing. Onstage with Culture Club, Boy George was known to shout: "Any queers in the audience?"

But for nearly everyone else at or near the top ranks, the cost of coming out seemed too high. The Pet Shop Boys and the Village People played coy with the media; Elton John admitted only to bisexuality. "I'm not gay," declared Michael Jackson. "I just don't know why people say these things about me." In a faux-naive "defense" of Jackson, the *Sun* cited "his neatly permed hair, teased into careful curls across his forehead" and "his almost feminine cat-like movements." They were far less delicate about John, whose diva histrionics made the press love to bait him. In 1984, when he married Renate Blauel, his recording engineer, the *Sun's* front page screamed: "Good On Yer, Poofter!"

Wham!'s formula for fame depended on selling sex to girls, which for Michael made telling the truth about his sexuality seem impossible. So discreet was he that not even his inner circle knew his secret, but Dee C. Lee had her suspicions. One day she asked him outright: "Are you gay?" "Nah," he said. She took his word for it. The two of them even whipped up a rumor that they were dating, just to arouse publicity.

In fact, Michael had not dated a girl in some time. So far he had come out only to his sister Melanie, for whom Michael was a hero. She took the news lovingly and vowed to keep it hidden. But the anything-goes spirit of Ibiza encouraged him to crack open the closet door another inch. In his memoirs, the sexually fluid Tony Pike claimed that on the night before the video shoot, a flirtation with Michael led to a session of "tender and passionate" lovemaking.

Perhaps it made Michael yearn for more honesty. While still in Ibiza, he came out to Shirlie. At first she didn't believe him. Then she urged him to inform Andrew. In his memoir *Wham! George Michael & Me*, Ridgeley recalled Michael summoning him to his hotel room. Shirlie sat on the sofa for moral support; Michael was in bed. "I didn't know whether to tell you this," he said, "but I'm going to: I'm gay."

Ridgeley didn't flinch. "Oh, okay," he said. "Well, that's a bit of a surprise!" With that, he recalled, "the three of us went to breakfast as if nothing had happened." Michael recounted the incident somewhat differently. Shirlie, he claimed, had offered to break the news to his partner, but Michael told her to let him handle it. Ridgeley walked into his room—"and of course she told him straight away!"

Everyone agreed that Michael should *not* tell Lesley, and definitely not Jack. The three youths shared a vow of silence. Wham! had come this far; nothing so dangerous as Michael's sexuality could stand in its way.

• • •

In her few months with Wham!, Dee C. Lee had watched the band's image turn into manicured unreality. On TV, she said, Michael would have his "cool-looking friends pose as band members. None of them could play." He loved the foxy African-god look of Deon Estus; otherwise, said Lee, "the sort of people whose sound he wanted didn't look like he wanted the band to look."

He loved Lee's voice, but he wasn't letting her use it, and she knew her reputation would suffer if she stayed. She gave Wham! her notice, then joined the Style Council, a New Wave band whose leader, Paul Weller, became her boyfriend. In 1985, Lee made a solo leap to No. 3 with "See the Day," a song she had written and recorded for CBS.

She had promised Michael she would find a replacement. Helen DeMacque, better known as Pepsi, was a young singer with a slim resume; no one at a Wham! show would ever hear how she sounded, but she looked something like Lee, and provided the same striking contrast to the blonde and sunny Holliman. Michael treated the two women like a gay boy's Barbie dolls, dressing them in what Sheryl Garratt of the *Sunday Times* called "the worst the decade had to offer . . . at a time when white stilettos and shoulder pads were seriously cool." On one occasion they had to wear rubber dresses, which felt sticky and suffocating under the lights. They designed their own synchronized moves; so long as they stayed in motion, that was enough. "We were always doing it wrong," said Holliman. "We were pretty useless, really."

But the duo became a friendly part of the Wham! image, and they basked in their leaders' stardom. Fans cornered them with phone numbers and even underwear for the boys—a laugh, given what both of them knew about Michael.

At the moment, Michael was feeling more annoyed than lascivious. For all their success, he and Ridgeley were still broke. Michael fought with Mark

Dean over everything. In his memoir, Jazz Summers remembered pleading with Dean to sweeten the band's terms. "Fuck you, Jazz," he said. "I've got a signed contract." Summers warned that they would sue; CBS, he added, would "shit on you." Dean wouldn't budge.

A petulant Michael hid the finished master for *Fantastic* in his mother's bedroom. The move irritated everyone, notably Paul Russell, who had recently joined CBS as managing director, from which he graduated to president and CEO. Russell, recalled Michael, was so incensed that he called him a thug. Dick Leahy talked Michael into surrendering the tapes. "If you are going to have a legal fight," he advised, "then fight with a number-one album."

In July 1983, Innervision released *Fantastic*. The cover showed Michael and Ridgeley back-to-back in the guise that had made them famous: carefully coiffed pretty-boys posing as leather-clad street toughs and peering at the camera with defiance. It wasn't the look of "Club Tropicana." But buoyed by the video and a return appearance on *Top of the Pops*, the single hit No. 4 in Britain and popped onto a few other European charts.

In the States, the reception was dismal. Columbia Records had given *Fantastic* a half-hearted release; the *Vancouver Sun*'s Ian Gill dismissed it as "effete, ephemeral" blue-eyed soul. "Perhaps the boys should have called themselves Spam!—canned, perishable when opened, and not as good as the real thing." The album stalled at No. 83; the single of "Club Tropicana" saw no American issue.

Michael blamed Dean. He and Ridgeley craved world stardom; Innervision was too puny to provide it. When Dean bypassed Wham!'s consent to release "Club Fantastic Megamix," a hodgepodge single of bits from the album, Michael was enraged. He demanded control over *everything*. Sweeter terms would no longer do; in order for Wham! to truly explode, it would have to sign directly with CBS. Mark Dean had to be edged out. Unfortunately, Wham! was bound to him in an ironclad deal—and only a shrewd and ruthless attorney could break it. Wham! found one in Tony Russell, who represented Dick Leahy. Stout, with owlish glasses, Tony would later be termed "a skilled and tough negotiator of recording agreements" by the British courts. Summers described him more bluntly: "Tony Russell might literally eat a man if that man stood in the way of legal victory. He had ball-breaker hands, viper eyes."

A war lay ahead; the bill might end up costing Wham! thousands of pounds. Napier-Bell scrambled to find work for them. He arranged for Wham! to film a Japanese commercial for Maxell cassettes; soon the two young men were dangling by wires in a studio, pretending to fly above Tokyo.

The fee didn't go far. Wham!, who had never done a full show, would have to go out on the road for the first time. Napier-Bell and Summers appealed to Harvey Goldsmith, England's premiere rock impresario. Having booked tours by Bob Dylan, Eric Clapton, and Bruce Springsteen, Goldsmith viewed Wham! as the pinkest of bubblegum; and when Napier-Bell demanded a £110,000 advance, he laughed. "This band has never sold a ticket," he said. Napier-Bell didn't mention that Wham! had a repertoire of only nine original songs, plus a couple of covers. But he pleaded, cajoled, and switched on his brightest charm, and the promoter succumbed.

Wham!'s Club Fantastic Tour would make thirty-three stops in October and November, mostly in venues that held two to three thousand. Napier-Bell talked Fila, a sportswear brand, into sponsoring the band by promising that Wham! would wear its products onstage. He and Summers wined and dined tabloid writers into hyping the tour. Wham! needed the boost: Instead of economizing, Michael blew up costs by enlisting eight musicians, five backup singers, and a crew of seven.

During rehearsals, a crucial addition to Wham! came aboard. Danny Cummings had recently left the group of John Martyn, a venerated blues-rock guitarist and singer. At twenty-six, Cummings was considered a master of Latin, African, and R&B percussion. Now he was auditioning for a band whose average listener was fifteen years old. Wham! planned to use "A Ray of Sunshine" as its false closer; the percussionist would have to pound out a storm on the bongos and make the girls scream for the band to come back on. Michael heard Cummings play and nodded his approval. The relation-ship lasted nearly thirty years.

"Wham! was pop music," Cummings said. "I thought I was vastly supe-rior. I didn't realize then that I was looking at someone who would teach me so much about how music is made." But as more and more of those around him all but genuflected in Michael's presence, Cummings—a hard drinker with a dry, sarcastic sense of humor—needled him shamelessly, and vice versa. "Danny was the only guy I ever knew who was able to take the piss out of George Michael and get away with it," said Phil Palmer, Michael's future guitarist.

September 1983 brought the first proof of what Michael could be without Andrew Ridgeley. Both Michael and Wham!'s managers felt that "Guilty Feet," by now dramatically retitled "Careless Whisper," had No. 1 potential. Napier-Bell had reached for the stars by hiring Jerry Wexler, the former Atlantic Records producer, who had masterminded classic discs by the label's stars—Aretha Franklin, Ray Charles, Dusty Springfield, Led Zeppelin, the Rolling Stones. Ridgeley wasn't needed. Wexler booked the mecca he had helped finance, Muscle Shoals Sound Studios in Sheffield, Alabama. There, thanks to the Swampers, the studio's founders and house musicians, R&B and southern soul formed a seductive brew—just the kind needed for a song of heated betrayal.

Michael was known as a smug young man, but in this fabled home of hits, located on a rural street in America's Deep South, he had to hide his jitters. Wexler treated him gently, but as Michael stood in the booth, ready to sing, the producer hit the intercom button to remind him that he was standing in the same spot where Ray and Aretha had created masterpieces. Wexler wanted to pump him up, but Michael was petrified.

Worse still, he did not like the tenor saxophonist that Wexler had flown in from Los Angeles. Michael wanted grand, flaming passion, the soundtrack of two lovers rolling around in the sheets; this musician sounded like a studio whiz-kid—clean and precise but with no sex, no swagger. There was another problem: The solo lay more comfortably in the higher range of an alto, and the saxophonist had to strain to make the upper notes. For two hours, Michael struggled to "correct" the flustered musician's efforts: "It has to twitch upwards a little . . . not there, but here. . . . Not too much!"

Wexler promptly imported a substitute from New York. The new player made Michael no happier, but reluctantly he bowed to the judgment of the great Wexler. Back in London, he played his cassette dub of the track for a few trusted friends, hoping it was better than he thought. All were underwhelmed. To Chris Porter, it sounded "like Europop—soft-edged and a bit old-fashioned."

For now, Michael put it aside. On October 9, less than a month away, Wham! would perform its first actual show, at the Capitol Theatre in the

Scottish city of Aberdeen; there, they would have to prove they really were "fantastic." That night, while radio host Gary Crowley warmed up the crowd with a deejay set, Michael sat in his dressing room, trying to look like the sun god in his videos. He was suitably bronzed courtesy of London's pricey Uvasun tanning salon; Melanie stood behind him with a hot comb in her hand, struggling to tame her brother's curls. "Smoke poured off the hair as she tried to get it straight," said Cummings. Michael flinched as she plucked the hairs from the center of his unibrow. From there, he and Ridgeley donned Fila white sneakers, gym shorts, and sweatshirts. Ridgeley's outfit was red, Michael's lemon-yellow.

After a thunderous musical fanfare, they bounded onto the Capitol stage to an ear-piercing torrent of screams. Two thousand adolescent fans, nearly a full house, saw what was essentially a kids' show. As Wham! hopped around, a slideshow of family photos reminded viewers that for Michael and Ridgeley, childhood was a recent memory; now the stage was their playground. "A Wham! show was so energetic, and piercingly loud," said the American gossip columnist Billy Masters. "This was not a concert with peaks and valleys and a nice slow song that everyone sat down and took in. You were on your feet the whole time. It was a party."

During "Come On!," a track from *Fantastic*, the young men pretended to play badminton, a sport Ridgeley loved. In a stunt that would mark Wham! forever, they reached inside their shorts and pulled out shuttlecocks, which they tossed at the audience; girls screamed and flung their hands in the air, trying to catch a souvenir from inside Wham!'s pants. Midway through the tour, Max Bell of the *Times* reviewed Wham! at Hammersmith Odeon, the London venue that had hosted everyone from the Beatles to Ella Fitzgerald. Michael, he wrote, was "alternately lascivious and embarrassing and always hilarious." His "slimmer foil," Andrew Ridgeley, "simpers shyly at Michael's side, clutching a decorative guitar with minimum effect."

But Wham! fans packed each venue, and the band and its entourage formed a merry caravan as they rode by bus from town to town. In order to cut costs, the group had few nights off. Throughout each show, Michael shouted above the din. Tommy Eyre warned him to ease up or he might lose his voice. Sure enough, on the second of Wham!'s three nights at Hammersmith, Michael's top notes began to crack. By the last, it hurt him to even speak. A throat doctor warned Michael that if he didn't take two weeks off he might seriously damage his voice. Despondently, he and Ridgeley went home as Goldsmith's office scrambled to reschedule eleven dates—a tedious and costly chore.

•••

At least Tony Russell had been earning his high fees. On October 7, 1983, the lawyer had sent Innervision a bone-chilling letter. It declared Wham!'s contract unenforceable, citing misrepresentation (dubious claims made to encourage a deal), undue influence (coercion to sign), and restraint of trade (an unfair advantage held by one side over the other). Consequently, he insisted, Wham! owned its masters. The far-fetched charges were meant to scare. Next, Russell phoned the tiny label's lawyer. Playing nice, he said he hoped the company would avoid litigation by letting Wham! sign directly with CBS; in return, Innervision would get a modest cut.

Dean did not back down. On October 18, he filed an injunction against Wham!, blocking them from signing elsewhere and claiming breach of contract. For now, he won. Tony stepped up his attack. He phoned Paul Russell and implied strongly that if CBS took Dean's side, Wham! would go elsewhere. Tony needn't have worried. Mark Dean, said Paul, "was a lovely guy, and we didn't want to piss on him; but equally, we knew we couldn't risk losing Wham!."

As the pressure grew, Dean buckled. He took a buyout deal, severed ties with CBS, and handed over his two discoveries. Russell negotiated a deal with Epic, a division of CBS. Wham! signed it in March 1984. They would get somewhat larger budgets, advances, and royalties, along with full artistic control; CBS would own all masters and copyrights, and after the next album it would hold options for five more. These included solo Michael and Ridgeley releases, should Wham! split up. "In the record business," observed Napier-Bell, "you get out of one bad contract, you get into another that is slightly less bad."

Dean would go down in pop history as the epitome of a small-time record-label shark. But to Napier-Bell, the real villains lay elsewhere. "CBS behaved in the ruthless corporate way that big business behaves. They completely threw Mark under the bus. They didn't fund his legal case with Wham!; they didn't fund his company sufficiently to give Wham! a better contract because they didn't want Innervision to have them. I wasn't sympathetic because it wasn't my job. I was employed by George to get him out of that contract." Even Michael mustered a grain of compassion. Speaking to Simon Garfield, author of *Expensive Habits: The Dark Side of the Music Industry*, he noted how Dean had "really counted on CBS coming to help him, which they didn't."

Paul Russell acknowledged that Dean could never have given Wham! the kind of contract Tony Russell had negotiated with CBS—"for the simple reason that it was better than the deal Innervision was getting from CBS! All the know-nothings who subscribe to the popular rip-off mythology are totally full of shit. In my view, Simon Napier-Bell, Jazz Summers, and Wham! 'deliberately and knowingly,' as the lawyers say, threw Mark Dean under the bus."

Dean felt had by all of them. "He was definitely bitter; he talked about it a lot," said David Chidekel. "But it didn't hold him back." Innervision folded in 1985, and Dean moved on to an A&R position at MCA. Shamsi Ahmed didn't fare so well. Bipolarity and alcoholism plagued him for years; driving on Christmas Eve, he hit and killed a teenage boy and spent years in jail. In 2010, the forgotten half of Innervision jumped from a ten-story building.

In years to come, Michael spoke gratefully of having signed Innervision's deal—"because otherwise I wouldn't be here." But it led him to mistrust all record companies, the entities on which his hopes rested. Until now, he said, the Wham! experience had been "just magical"—a magic-carpet ride "with your best mate, playing out your fantasies." But he sensed that Wham!'s honeymoon was over. "Everyone feels the same when they're entering the business; they're just desperate," he told the BBC's Chris Evans. "And desperation makes you think that you love everything that you're doing."

• • •

Critics had begun to wonder exactly what Andrew Ridgeley did in Wham! besides holding a guitar. Michael was quick to defend him: "If he was not important to the group, I would be solo by now. He is responsible for many of our ideas, presentation, and style." Ridgeley "always seemed to be at the cutting edge of what was going on in clubs, music, fashions," said Paul Spong, a trumpeter who would soon join the band. But Michael didn't share his visual flair. "George never had style, even when he had a stylist," said Bret Witke, the future co-owner of one of Michael's favorite Hollywood clubs, Boys & Girls. Now it didn't matter; Michael had become an object of widespread lust. "I was thrilled to be suddenly looked upon as a physically attractive human being," he said. Yet the more it grew, the more he felt like a fraud.

Only his talent made him feel secure. "I was supremely confident I was writing pop classics," he said. Songwriting would never come so easy to him as it did in the early days of Wham!. In February 1984, he and Ridgeley sat in the Panos living room; *Match of the Day*, a football show, was on TV. Michael got a flash of inspiration. He ran upstairs to his bedroom and sat at his little keyboard, recorder at the ready, and began poking out a tune. It had a nursery-rhyme simplicity, and sounded a bit like Peaches & Herb's "Reunited," a hit from his high-school days. The words had a childlike sweetness turned sour: "Last Christmas I gave you my heart, but the very next day you gave it away." A year from now, he warned, he would save it for "someone special." Michael played it for Ridgeley. This, he announced, would be Wham!'s No. 1 Christmas hit.

He put it away; another song seemed far more pressing. Late one night after a drunken spree on the town, Ridgeley came home and left his mother, a grade-school teacher, a note in the kitchen, asking her to wake him before she left for work. According to Summers, Wham! was flying that day to Rome; Michael was coming to take him to the airport. He arrived and saw the note. Ridgeley had written, in error, "Wake me up up." He turned it into a joke, adding, "before you go go." Michael grinned at its silliness. He sensed a song in there.

Sixties girl groups and the sock hop dancers on *American Bandstand* flooded his mind as he scratched out the words. They formed a sugar rush of love aimed at a girlfriend who had acted mean. "You make the sun shine brighter than Doris Day," he told her, while suggesting they "cuddle up" in bed to make things better. He tossed in keywords—"jitterbug," "yeah-yeah," "ha-ha"—that added percussive bursts. Then he whipped up a refrain so catchy that it astonished even him. It popped into his head as he sat in a public bathroom. "It kept coming back to me every time I went to the toilet!" he said. "Every time I was straining away!"

This, he decided, was the song that would break Wham! through to the entire world. He, Ridgeley, and a retinue of musicians convened at SARM West, the London studio where Queen—as Michael well knew—had recorded "We Are the Champions." Chris Porter and his assistant, Paul Gomersall, would engineer, but as usual, Michael took charge. First he oversaw the recording of a rhythm track, the basis of any Wham! concoction. When the drummer was late, he programmed the LinnDrum machine. A small horn section would play an instrumental break. Danny Cummings had recommended Paul Spong, who had played trumpet with bandleader Shorty Rogers, a kingpin of cool West Coast jazz. "I was intrigued by George's lack of schooling but complete understanding of what he wanted," said Spong. Unable to write out parts for his musicians, he sang them instead. Sometimes they didn't quite fit what a horn could play. When Spong suggested an alternative, Michael said, "Yeah . . . that's not what I want, though." Spong took his line up an octave, "because he didn't know the trumpet could play that high."

In a day and a half, "Wake Me Up Before You Go-Go" was done—a frothy punch bowl of jitterbug rhythm with a shuffle beat lifted from "Heat Wave," a 1963 hit by Martha and the Vandellas. Tommy Eyre's Hammond and Deon Estus's bass made it swing. Michael's vocal—breathy and boyish all the way up to a recurring falsetto high note—was electronically processed to sound much like Lesley Gore's on her tearjerking hit of 1963, "It's My Party."

Michael was giddy with the song's potential. The month before, while promoting her first album, Madonna had appeared on *American Bandstand.* Dick Clark asked about her dreams. Famously, she responded: "To rule the world." At SARM West, Michael told Porter he wanted the same.

For the video, he envisioned clouds of pink, a sea of toothy smiles, and everyone dancing as Wham! performed. Michael and his director, Duncan Gibbins, rented out Brixton Academy, a venue in South London. There he would unveil yet another new look. He had let his hair balloon into a blownout, layered shag with blond tinting—the trademark style of Lady Diana. It was a deliberate feminizing of his image. "That's what young girls want at a certain age," he explained. "Nothing that looks vaguely hairy or threatening."

Snowy white would dominate the video's first section. Michael and Ridgeley donned T-shirts emblazoned with the words CHOOSE LIFE. They were the work of Katharine E. Hamnett, a British retail clothing designer whose two-tone apparel, stark as a tabloid headline, bore activist slogans. This one was intended as an antiwar message, but other causes had adopted it, including drug prevention and safe sex. No matter; it marked Wham! as a band who cared. The musicians' shirts read GO-GO—one more way of branding the song onto viewers' minds. Everyone wore neck-to-toe white and stood on white platforms; the spotlights would make them glow like angels.

Wham! had advertised for an all-girl audience, dressed in white or pink. A packed house was expected. But the filming took place on a school night, and it rained. Peeking outside before the shoot, Michael spotted less than a hundred sodden girls with umbrellas. Once inside, they were creatively arranged to suggest a full house.

The record played, and a row of musicians, singers, and friends, including Pat Fernandes, began to lip-synch. Ridgeley strummed a guitar, then faded from the attention as the star took the foreground. Michael glided as though on air; he pranced through the crowd as they waved their arms. After countless takes, the lighting changed to Day-Glo, and the group switched to candy-colored Fila gymwear. Shirlie wore a mishmash of yellow, orange, and pink, a look she found "horrendous." But somehow it worked. "It was such happy music, toothpaste happiness," she said. Day-Glo turned to ultraviolet, showing off Michael's tan, pearly teeth, and blond highlights.

Jazz Summers was nauseated. "I thought it was tacky, and I said so," he recalled. "But my management partner, Simon Napier-Bell, was more camp than a row of tents. He thought it was lovely." To pound the video's true purpose home, it closed with a pink-lettered command:

GO-GO
buy it
Thank you

It was almost dawn when the shoot ended. As the musicians packed up to leave, Michael and Ridgeley sat on the rim of the stage and signed an autograph for every fan who wanted one.

"Wake Me Up Before You Go-Go" was released in the United Kingdom on May 14, 1984, and launched on *Top of the Pops*. In the chilly realm of eighties electronic pop, the song seemed to come out of nowhere. "If you took away what made it modern for 1984—that cheesy synth—it could have been 'Sunshine, Lollipops and Rainbows,'" said Kenny Mellman, an American pianist and cabaret performer. Even Doris Day was surprised. "I love that record!" she exclaimed. "It doesn't matter that my name is in it. I think it's so good!" Then the video hit—and Wham! scored its first No. 1, just as Michael had planned.

CHAPTER FOUR

THE ENHANCED BUDGET OF the Epic deal had enabled Wham! to hire a publicist. Connie Filippello was a friend of Napier-Bell's; at the time, she promoted a hair salon. Buxom, blonde, and Australian-Italian, with a thick but indeterminate accent, she was a living cartoon. "We never quite knew where Connie was from, whether she might even be a guy," said a tabloid music columnist. "We only ever saw Connie in dark restaurants, so nobody got a really good look at her."

Her true language was hyperbole, and she knew how to butter up anyone, including the Wham! boys. "Dahlinks, hullo—my two wonderful sex gods," she exclaimed. That was the image she aggressively helped whip up, with an emphasis on Michael's purported heterosexuality. Many assumed she was following orders, but Napier-Bell insisted that neither he nor Michael had given any. She and the singer, he said, "never, *ever* talked about George being gay."

Certainly she was clever enough to know what would make the Wham! fantasy fly; had Michael objected, he would have spoken up. "George might have been somewhat oblivious to the fact that Connie was dropping stories on us every day," a columnist recalled. "For the most part they were perpetuating the myth he wanted to put out there. 'Dahlink, dahlink, George and Shirlie, they're so in love!' We would print this garbage. People had an insatiable appetite for everything to do with George." Numerous tidbits were attributed to unnamed "friends" of Michael's. "That would have been Connie! 'Dahlink, just say a close friend told you!'"

• • •

Michael had proceeded halfheartedly with the "Careless Whisper" video, to be filmed to a track he didn't like. For this release, Michael would get his first solo billing. Plans were made for him, Duncan Gibbins, and a crew to convene in Barbados in February 1984. Gibbins had hoped to sidestep the song's schmaltz by staging the video as "a fairly hard-edged *Miami Vice*-type story." But Michael wanted a scorching tale of infidelity, highlighted by sun and sea. Arriving on the island first, he found the weather cloudy. On the day Gibbins was set to fly, Michael phoned and demanded a change of plans: They would all gather in Miami instead.

After a rush to rebook flights and hotels, Gibbins and his team arrived in the Florida heat and hurried to rent a sailboat and a helicopter for aerial shots. With this video, Michael's goal was to brand himself as a straight stud with a heart. As the saxophone wails, he and a blonde make torrid love in a cabana. His mousy girlfriend, with whom he was vacationing, flings the door open in shock then storms off. Later he sits in a towel, wracked with guilt; then he stands on a balcony and belts his song into the Florida night. In a cameo appearance, Ridgeley hands Michael a note. It's a kiss-off from his one-night fling, who drives off, smiling sarcastically.

When he saw the shots, he cringed at his hair. "It's dreadful," he told Napier-Bell. "Too long. Too posey. Too poofy." He flew in Melanie to restyle it, and demanded the footage be redone.

Once edited, the video looked like a five-minute version of a Lifetime TV melodrama, and Michael was having second thoughts. He'd grown to hate the Wexler track, and wanted it redone. That meant that his lip movements in the video wouldn't match the vocal. All the film would have to go. This was his first solo showcase; his whole post-Wham! future depended on it. He harbored no illusion that he was creating high art. "I totally threw away my musical credibility for a year and a half in order to make sure my music got into so many people's homes," he told writer Rob Tannenbaum. Pete Townshend of the Who, the high-concept British superstar band, mocked Wham! as sellouts. At the time of "Wham Rap!," he noted, "they were considered to be quite subversive . . . street kids who weren't going to be part of the system. And now what are they? They're actually completely integrated into the machine."

But the hits had to keep coming at any cost. It was time for Wham!'s second album, which would be called *Make It Big*—and the pressure was on to do just that. The budget had taken a leap; the band would be that much bigger. Almost everything rested on Michael's shoulders: He would write, sing, and produce the songs.

His bravado crumbled; for the first time, Michael encountered writer's block. By the summer, he had almost no new songs. He found a costly solution. Michael had heard about Miraval, a recording studio with living quarters in Correns, a rustic village near the French Riviera. Pink Floyd, Sade, and the Cure had settled there for weeks of album-making amid a rolling countryside. In July 1984, CBS flew Wham!, various musicians and pals, Chris Porter, and Paul Gomersall to France. For the first week, Michael and company ate breakfast under the sun, took pleasure trips to Saint-Tropez, and basked by the pool. Michael blasted Motown from a boom box, hoping it would seep into his writing. He looked in annoyance at Ridgeley, who treated the trip as a holiday and had no apparent intent to work. But there wasn't much for him to do; at this point, Michael wasn't too interested in his partner's input.

After goofing off for a week, Michael announced: "All right. Let's go." Leaning on Spong, Estus, and his other band members, who played inspiring licks in the studio, he felt his creativity stirring. The results sounded clearly derivative of the music he had been playing by the pool. "Credit Card Baby" had a slinky horn arrangement and a high-flying vocal that sounded like Smokey Robinson and the Miracles; "Freedom" could have been a Supremes B-side. But the hooks were exciting and the beats as danceable as anything on *American Bandstand*.

Beyond those two songs, Michael was stuck. Estus suggested they cover "If You Were There," an obscure dance track from an Isley Brothers album of 1973. The Wham! arrangement copied the original, but it enabled Michael to prove, more than ever before, what a natural gift he had for singing. He could set a swinging soul groove and soar upward with ease; he exuded a summery, boyish zest. Michael's voice, wrote Stephen Holden in the *New York Times*, "has a vestigial teen-idol sob that complements his furry-eyebrowed, pug-nosed good looks."

During the sessions, stardust fell upon Miraval in the form of Elton John, who arrived by helicopter to record a commercial. Michael remained in awe of John, and it wasn't one-sided. Apart from beholding a beautiful young man, John saw formidable talent, and he took on the role of fatherly cheerleader. "He's going to be a major, major songwriter," announced John. "He has one of the best voices I've ever heard. Technically it's way ahead of mine."

Michael began to view John as a gay surrogate father; they even took trips together, hanging out in glamorous, jet-setting locales. But both men were obsessed with being No. 1, which made for a complicated friendship. "From my observation," said David Geffen, for whose label, Geffen, John recorded, "Elton wanted to be friends with all the biggest stars. He admired them until they surpassed him, making him only human. George had replaced Elton at that moment in time. And Elton's so competitive that if you play pool with him, you turn around, he'd move the ball."

Michael would never approach his hero's productivity; John wrote songs almost faster than he could record them. But after months of work on *Make It Big*, Michael was still one song short. In August, he went to Paris with Porter and Gomersall to mix the tracks he had. One night at dinner, he exclaimed, "I've got an idea!" Back he went to the studio, where he began playing with the LinnDrum machine and poking out a bass line on synth. The engineers tried to help him flesh out the fragments, but by two A.M. they had nothing decent. Michael told them to meet him there at ten the next morning.

By the time he returned to the studio he had written a whole song in his head, including backup vocals. "Everything She Wants" gave the strongest evidence to date of the songwriter inside him—the one that Wham!'s image had not served. Michael sang of a working man in an unhappy marriage, with a baby on the way. "If my best isn't good enough," he asked, "then how can it be good enough for two?" After a drawn-out, suspenseful intro, the song unfolded in several parts, shifting form throughout—a trademark of Michael's best future work. Yet it kept coming back to one of the nastiest, most insinuating hooks Michael would ever write. His voice lashed, it pleaded, it wailed; he convincingly portrayed a broken, desperate man. Those "embittered lyrics," observed Simon Price later on in the *Independent*, "express a lifetime's experience from a mere twenty-one-year-old."

"Everything She Wants" was finished at SARM. Working with a keyboard player, Andy Richards, Michael took the song into the realm of modern R&B. The synth-playing had a tough, robotic whir; it underlined the lyrics with a snarl. One phrase stood out. Singing the words "won't you tell me why," Michael descended, step by step, into a bass register no one had known that he had.

For the last of the album's eight tracks, he had to redo "Careless Whisper." The Wexler version had come out in Japan, but Michael didn't want it heard anywhere else. He reworked the arrangement with Estus and Tommy Eyre, then asked Porter to meet him at SARM on a Monday morning. Word was sent out for saxophonists to come and audition. "We wanted someone who could play it with a great tone, who could do it with soul and character, without taking breaths to interrupt the flow," said Porter.

That was a tall order. Nonetheless, saxophonists showed up throughout the day and tried, using the new backing track and a lead sheet. Every time, said Porter, "George and I looked at each other and said, 'He didn't quite get it, did he?' George would say, 'He's not doing it. Get rid of him.'"

Shortly before midnight, in walked Steve Gregory, who had played on the Rolling Stones' "Honky Tonk Women" and other classic rock and blues records. That day he had spent hours in the studio, then done a gig, and he was exhausted. Already waiting his turn was Ray Warleigh, a ubiquitous session player for the likes of Stevie Wonder and Dusty Springfield. Michael had stepped out, and Porter didn't know when he'd be back. Sick of waiting, Warleigh left.

Gregory asked Porter if they could get going. Gregory's sax was a 1950s model that lacked the tenor's highest note, an F sharp; that happened to be the highest note in Michael's solo. He asked Porter to slow the track by a semitone; that way he could play an F instead of an F sharp. Gregory recorded the solo intact, then had Porter raise the pitch back up.

During the playback, Michael walked in. He listened, then announced, like Professor Henry Higgins to Eliza Doolittle: "I think we've got it!" Gregory humbly noted that he had cracked on one note. "No, I like that," said Michael. "That's real."

What Gregory had recorded in less than an hour would become one of the most memorable sax solos in pop history. Its writhing, sinewy sound would be copied in countless movie sex scenes, shot with fluttering curtains and satin sheets. Michael confessed to not liking the song; he felt it was a string of clichés. He might not have disagreed with Andrew D'Angelo, a New York jazz saxophonist, who said of the solo: "Technically it's not that profound. So lame, so cheesy. But it's so fucking bad, it's good." Allen Mezquida, an alto player from Los Angeles, appreciated its mysterious sound; was that an alto or a tenor in the high register? "The fact that the track was re-tuned might account for why I could never quite place what the notes were," he said. "These unknowns gave it an ethereal quality that took it beyond a simple pop saxophone solo—like a magic trick that defies explanation."

Now Michael could redo the video. With Gibbins directing, he performed "Careless Whisper" without an audience in London's Lyceum Theatre. Intercut with film salvaged from the Miami shoot, this new performance footage made the video look less sappy. On July 24, 1984, Epic released the single under the name George Michael. He premiered the song on *Top of the Pops*—just him on a bare stage in a white shirt and jeans.

He invited Gregory to reprise his solo on TV, but never used him again. "I was a bit pissed off about that," the musician said. The following year, Gregory played on "One Year of Love," a track from the Queen album *A Kind of Magic*. "You played the saxophone on 'Careless Whisper,'" said Freddie Mercury. Yes, answered Gregory. Observed Mercury: "Best bit of the record."

One night after a Wham! rehearsal, Paul Spong sat with Danny Cummings in a Greek restaurant. A Greek recording spun in the background; on it, the two musicians heard a familiar tune, played on balalaika. It sounded nearly identical to the "Careless Whisper" sax line. "We sat there and said, '*That*'s where George got that hook from!'" recalled Spong.

• • •

"Careless Whisper" hit No. 1 in Britain, and Jazz Summers and Simon Napier-Bell flew to Manhattan to try and convince Columbia to give Wham! a proper U.S. launch. Indifference awaited him. "Wham! was a joke, even though it had huge hits," said Ellyn Solis, director of publicity at the label's Epic subsidiary. "But those songs stuck in your head." Napier-Bell's suave English charm proved no match for Walter Yetnikoff, Columbia's foul-mouthed, bludgeoning president. "He was every cliché, every extreme, crazy, irresponsible characterization of a record company executive," recalled a department head. When Napier-Bell, in an early discussion, branded one of Yetnikoff's ideas tasteless, the executive shot back: "Don't be such a fag. Good taste never got anyone anywhere."

No one was calling Wham! elegant, but in a meeting with another group of executives, including Al Teller, who ran Epic, the band's managers faced rolled eyes and bored glances. Napier-Bell and Summers hyped Wham! as the hottest British band since the Beatles; they screened the "Careless Whisper" video. The Americans thought it was schlock. Even if they hadn't, there were no bragging rights in releasing records by a band that someone else had discovered, and they would have to split the earnings with the parent label. When Napier-Bell moved into his hard sell, Teller let loose a torrent of expletives.

Howard Thompson, an A&R manager at Columbia, felt differently. Thompson, who was English, had previously held the same position at CBS U.K., where he signed Adam and the Ants, Motörhead, and the Psychedelic Furs. Wham!, he said, "seemed to be doing something that hadn't been done before. They were, in my mind, a super-commercial club act that had employed R&B and hip-hop quite successfully. Don't forget, in 1983, rap was very underground in America. I think that's why it took a while for anybody in the American company to take them seriously."

Thompson managed to slate the U.S. issue of "Wake Me Up." To work up a buzz, he went to clubs and handed advance copies to deejays, who played them on the spot. "People would dance like crazy," he said. To prepare for the August release, Debbie Samuelson flew in Wham! to do promotion. MTV put the video in rotation; meanwhile, Samuelson booked Wham! on *New York Hot Tracks*, a syndicated series of such importance that Madonna and David Bowie had hosted episodes. On his first visit to Columbia's offices, Michael wandered from department to department, introducing himself to people who could be helpful and charming everyone. "George struck me as being genuine, modest, and respectful," said Samuelson.

To much of the press, however, Michael and Ridgeley seemed like two puffed-up boys, drunk with success. Part of that was intentional; they enjoyed riling people up, and it fit their image of tongue-in-cheek entitlement. The Andrew known to friends was impishly funny and bemused by the charmed life he'd fallen into, but for the public he affected a blasé superiority. In an interview, he called Mick Jagger "beyond a joke," adding: "He's an old man. Well . . . he seems it. He just seems stupid on stage now." Responded Jagger: "Ask Andrew Ridgeley if he's written any good songs lately."

But nothing could stop him from playing enfant terrible. "Andrew wanted to be seen," said Paul Spong. "A group of us would go to a nightclub in London. We'd stand in the VIP area. He'd see the press, who had followed us there, and he'd go, 'Okay, let's make the papers in the morning, shall we?' Then he'd walk out and do something. Next day, all over the front page was Andrew falling over, grabbing a photographer's camera, whatever."

Ridgeley's exploits got him dubbed "Randy Andy" by the *Sun*. In a cover story, the tabloid listed his perhaps apocryphal shenanigans at a student party: "TRIED to take down a girl's trousers. OFFERED autographs in exchange for 'gropes.' STAGGERED about twanging girls' suspenders. FONDLED a man in drag, mistaking him for a girl."

Connie Filippello issued a denial—"this story is total fabrication"—yet when Ridgeley had a nose job, she didn't hesitate to send out a report that he had gotten into a fight in a bar and been hit by an ice-bucket. Journalists demanded to know who had thrown it. David Austin was named as the imaginary culprit, which prompted Wham! fans to call for his arrest. In another publicity grab, Michael joined Ridgeley in donning drag at a party after a show.

Michael's hubris wasn't just for fun; he aimed to pump up his image as a larger-than-life pop titan. "I'm twenty-one years old and I'm not saying this to brag, but I've achieved more as a performer, writer, and producer than anyone else ever has by the same age," he noted. "We take getting into the top five for granted. We're the biggest duo since Simon & Garfunkel." In one of his first major U.S. interviews, he kept Dennis Hunt of the *Los Angeles Times* waiting at lunchtime in front of the Polo Lounge, the posh restaurant in the Beverly Hills Hotel. When he finally arrived, he greeted Hunt by saying, "Well, let's get this over with." He did not come off well in the piece. "His arrogant, aloof, condescending attitude grates on you instantly," wrote Hunt.

George Martin, the Beatles' record producer, foresaw trouble. "His songwriting talent is phenomenal—on a par with McCartney's," remarked Martin in the *Daily Mail*. "But I'm scared for him. He's had his success too soon. He hasn't really had to slog for it. . . . Success has gone to his head, and that superstar attitude can prove very dangerous in the long run. I hope that he calms down—or he risks losing everything. . . . Arrogance is usually born of fear."

•••

Much of Michael's panic involved the risk of being seen for who he thought he really was: Georgios Kyriacos Panayiotou, the fat, pimply, gay outcast of Bushey Meads. He lived in growing dread of the tabloids, which could sniff out stars' dirty secrets like bloodhounds. Centered mostly on Fleet Street in London, the tabloids held up a revealing mirror to the country's class system. Hinging on the exploits of the rich and famous, they provided reassurance to those who weren't that the elite were as screwed-up as anyone.

Several of these publications, including the *Daily Mail*, the *Daily Mirror*, and the *Daily Telegraph*, offered more than a little journalistic credibility. At the opposite end were the *Sun* and *News of the World*, rival tabloids that were owned by Rupert Murdoch, the libertarian media mogul. The papers served up endless titillation; the *Sun*'s ranged from bare-breasted "Page 3" girls to prurient cover stories: Michael Jackson sleeping in a coffin-like glass chamber, Saddam Hussein in his underwear, the Deputy Speaker of the House of Lords snorting coke off a table.

To obtain material, some tabloid reporters would bribe, threaten, harass, and stalk. Fact-checking was loose; the papers could afford lawsuits. Where scandal didn't exist, they created it by hounding celebrities until tempers flared or the invariable misstep was witnessed. Stars complained endlessly, but the smarter ones used the tabloids to their advantage. To Caroline Graham, a longtime reporter for the *Sun*, the Princess of Wales "was the best manipulator of the press of all time. She would call the *Sun*'s offices. She was on the front page more than anyone else because she sold newspapers. She was gold dust." Elton John and Boy George used the tabloids to shamelessly dish their rivals. "The music business hasn't got any personalities apart from me," said the latter in the *Sun*. He called Bananarama "unimportant and talentless," the Wham! boys "pretty, but they've not got a lot to say."

Wham! and Boy George's band, Culture Club, had begun nearly simultaneously, and rivalry existed on both sides. Both groups were led by soul boys named George; they ran neck-and-neck in the Top 10. Michael, said Boy George, was "always so snotty," and the press, he felt, had bought into it: "I hated the way he was portrayed as a serious songwriter while I was treated like a pop joker." But Boy George had handed them considerable rope. Shooting heroin and wreaking havoc, he seemed a portrait in gay misery as well as bitchery. He had publicly branded Michael as "camp" and made a string of public digs at the singer's bogus heterosexuality; worse was still to come.

The press was all ears. By now homosexuals were in the news almost daily as the so-called "gay plague" gave the tabloids a bonanza of lurid material. At every newsstand Michael passed, front pages screamed at him about this disease that had turned gays into lepers, to be shunned, quarantined, and condemned. "AIDS Blood Donor Who Infected 41 People Dies," announced the *Sun*. "AIDS Panic at British Airways" detailed the terror of seven thousand employees when the virus killed three male flight attendants. The headlines kept coming: "AIDS Is the Wrath of God, Says Vicar." "Don't Sleep Around, Gays Told."

Paranoia and homophobia raged. There was talk of banning gay actors from the London stage. Some funeral workers refused to embalm AIDS casualties; certain doctors and nurses refused to treat patients. "The health of the nation is more important than homosexuals," declared a health workers-union representative.

Since Wham! was peddling sex, albeit an antiseptic brand, to girls, curiosity arose about Michael's bed habits. For some time, he had worried that if his secret got out, it would wreck his career. He still feared his father, and knew that the suicide of his gay uncle haunted his mother. Now AIDS, an incurable and shameful disease, was everywhere. If he confessed he was gay, it would petrify her and likely enrage Jack.

Rumors had circulated about his sexuality for at least a year. The *Sun* reported that Michael had been seen snorting the "gay sex drug," poppers (amyl nitrate inhalers), at a club, Taboo. Hints were dropped even in the *Times*, which noted his "high-pitched giggle" and less-than-manly appearance, "graceful and pampered-looking and just this side of feminine."

Michael was sure that the press, notably the *Sun*, stood poised to out him. He considered banning interviews altogether, but he felt too strong a compulsion to speak his truth; that way, he believed, he could control the narrative. He learned the art of evasion. When *New Musical Express* broached the gay rumors, Michael gave a carefully premeditated statement: "I don't think anyone should have to answer a 'gay or straight' question. Mind you, I actually like the ambiguity. That sort of thing has helped Bowie and Jagger."

Seldom would an interviewer make him squirm more than the breathless peroxide blonde Paula Yates, Britain's premiere rock 'n' roll party chick of the eighties and nineties. Married to Bob Geldof, the mastermind of Live Aid and other charity rock extravaganzas, Yates—who died of a heroin overdose in 2000—spent much of the eighties as a presenter on a hit music TV show, *The Tube*. She became famous for coaxing celebrities into bed for flirty "pillow talk" interviews. Playing with fire, Michael joined Yates under a maroon satin sheet, TV lights blazing down on them and crew members milling everywhere.

The two stars made strange bedfellows. Yates caressed her bare arms and batted her eyes at Michael, whose sexuality could not have been unknown to her. Yet she egged him on with one personal question after another. He stammered through his answers while pretending to flirt back.

Do you find girls a great inspiration? I mean, are lots of your songs written about girls?
Of course. [Michael smiled tensely.]

What sort of people do you fantasize about?
Um . . . I never fantasized about people in the public eye, like film stars or pop stars or anything, but, uh [nervously picking at his hair] . . . but people I knew, and I had my eye on or whatever, but never film stars or anything like that.

And what kind of things were they doing?
[He presses his face into the pillow and smiles.] What do you want from me? I don't know . . . Well, the normal things, all the normal things you'd like to do but most of the time don't get around to.

Are they really naughty?
Ask me for a demonstration later!

All the tabloid "scoops," some accompanied by dubious George Michael quotes, helped enhance his smokescreen. The *Daily Mail* quoted him on his life before Wham!: "I gorged myself on girls, taking everything I could get." Now all that had changed, he said. "There's nothing I'd like to do more," declared Michael, "than marry and have kids."

• • •

Michael was still barely more than a kid himself. He proved it in November 1984, when he recorded his lullaby of juvenile scorn, "Last Christmas," at London's Advision Studios. Paul Gomersall had arrived early and hung yuletide decorations, "so that when George walked in it was Christmas." Working with a LinnDrum machine and a Juno-60 synthesizer, Michael played all the parts himself, including simulated sleigh bells. The rhythm, like the trot of a horse-drawn carriage in the snow, was copied off a recent hit that he loved, Kool & the Gang's "Joanna." Years later, Michael looked back on that record with amusement. "I can't believe how young I sound," he said. "It sounds like a little girl singing."

In November 1984, Wham! and a gaggle of friends—among them Shirlie, Pepsi, Andros, Spandau Ballet's Martin Kemp, and Jon Fowler, who would one day team with Michael's future manager, Andy Stephens—were in a Swiss ski resort, taping a video that looked like a Hallmark Christmas special. The youngsters frolic in the snow, ride the lift, decorate the tree, then gather at the dinner table, where Michael becomes moony-eyed while looking at Ridgeley and his girlfriend. Apparently she is Michael's ex—and although a new sweetheart is on his arm, he can't help but flash back to fun times with the other girl, who had broken his heart. Will Ridgeley's get broken, too?

For Christmas, Michael wanted nothing more than a No. 1 hit. So did Bob Geldof, a gaunt, long-haired Irish rocker. Geldof was the lead singer of the Boomtown Rats, a formerly chart-topping band. Now Geldof's "career was in the sewers," said his friend James Ure, better known as Midge Ure, leader of the New Wave group Ultravox. Watching a BBC report on famine-wracked Ethiopia, Geldof saw a way to rescue both the poor and himself. With Ure, he wrote a yuletide tune about the crisis, then cajoled every rock star he could into recording it with the Rats. "Do They Know It's Christmas?" launched a new craze in pop: the all-star fundraiser, which gave rockers golden opportunities to appear conscientious and giving. Ure wasn't fooled. "Their standard response is, 'Who else is doing it?' It's not about the charity; it's about their profile."

Michael was no exception. "One day," said Simon Napier-Bell, "he came to Jazz and me and said, 'I think it's time I did a charity thing. I need to connect myself to charity.' We said, 'What sort of thing?'"

"Oh, I don't know—you're my manager."

Summers suggested that Wham! join a benefit at London's Royal Festival Hall to aid the National Union of Mineworkers. Margaret Thatcher had authorized the closing of a vast number of British mines, and the workers had gone on strike.

"Miners on strike, they're good," said Michael. "Okay, I'll do that one."

He termed himself a socialist, and even joined the Young Communist League of Great Britain under his birth name. It was mostly for show, however; a socialist stance was de rigueur then in British rock. Michael exposed his true feelings to Mick Brown in the *Sunday Times*. "A lot of stubborn and not terribly bright left-wing groups"—some of whom were fighting to dethrone Margaret Thatcher in the next election—were "pissing in the wind," he felt. As for Arthur Scargill, the Marxist president of the miners' union, Michael, like many others, disapproved of his handling of the strike, and publicly termed him a "wanker."

But the singer was quick to sign on for Geldof's record; even though it posed a threat to "Last Christmas," he did not want to be left out. Furthermore, Geldof had screamed expletives at any artist who balked: "*I'll tell the world that you've fucking turned it down!*" On November 25, 1984, a string of musicians straggled reluctantly into SARM, eyes hidden behind dark glasses and guitar cases in hand. Geldof gave them the collective name of Band Aid. They included Bono, Sting, Boy George, Paul Young, Spandau Ballet, Bananarama, Duran Duran, and Wham!, minus Andrew Ridgeley, who overslept.

According to the *Daily Mirror*'s Robin Eggar, who attended the all-day session, wine and cocaine helped keep the stars engaged, especially as each of them sang an assigned line of Geldof's trite lyrics. ("At Christmastime, we let in light and we banish shade.") Michael, said Andros, "was one of the only stars that could hold a tune that day." A making-of video omits a confrontation between him and Paul Weller, the left-wing leader of the

Style Council. Michael's comment about Scargill had made his blood boil. In front of other artists, Weller snapped at Michael: "Don't be a wanker all your life. Have a day off."

On the way home, Michael was in a foul mood, but not because of Weller. The Band Aid single was certain to hit No. 1, thereby blocking "Last Christmas" from the same slot. Indeed, "Do They Know It's Christmas?" topped the charts in fourteen countries, including the United Kingdom, and stayed there until after the holidays. "Last Christmas" spent five weeks at No. 2. For Michael, that constituted failure. "No one remembers number two," he liked to say.

His irritation mounted as he heard members of Geldof's chorale congratulate themselves for their philanthropy. He spouted off to the *Los Angeles Times*. "That didn't cost anything more than a day of their time. There was an incredible amount of wealth in the studio. People were singing, 'Feed the world' . . . and I thought, 'Did you actually do anything else about it?' . . . I couldn't reconcile singing a lyric like that with just giving a bit of my time. So I did something about it."

Wham! donated its royalties for "Last Christmas" to the famine victims. Neither he nor Ridgeley realized that Michael had written a holiday evergreen, one that would earn a bounty every December—for charity, not for them. The cover versions would surpass five hundred. In 2010, a Bulgarian poll named it the most annoying holiday song of all time. Michael recalled his gift to the poor with rolled eyes, but there was a small consolation prize. Barry Manilow's publisher had filed suit against Michael, charging plagiarism of Manilow's 1978 hit, "Can't Smile Without You." The chord sequence was undeniably similar, but the case was withdrawn. It would not have looked good to deprive starving Ethiopians of money for food.

• • •

In December 1984, Wham! set out on The Big Tour. It would start on home turf—the Whitley Bay Ice Rink, on England's northeast coast—then take them throughout Britain, Asia, Australia, and the United States. The thought of months of shows filled Michael with fear. The loss of his voice in the Club Fantastic Tour haunted him; he took to wrapping a cashmere scarf around his mouth when he walked on the street. Even worse, a decaying vertebra was causing him chronic pain.

Still, he smiled gamely during what one critic called "a floor show that could rival anything out of Las Vegas." In its first moments, a huge black curtain, emblazoned with MAKE IT BIG in white letters, cascaded to the floor, revealing the Wham! troupe. The shrieks of female fans were deafening; Paul Spong compared them to a rush of "wind noise going past your ear—*WHEEEESH!*" Wham! manipulated the crowd shamelessly. Michael shook his behind and twirled like a top, his white jacket flailing out to expose his almost bare chest. Ridgeley patted the backsides of Pepsi and Shirlie, who dressed as chorus girls, cheerleaders, and cowgirls. For "Freedom," the group did a Supremes impersonation. Pepsi and Shirlie gesticulated in magenta sequined gowns with elbow-length black gloves; Michael became Diana Ross.

All the running and jumping inflamed Michael's spine. After eight shows he was in agony, and he had to postpone five U.S. dates. He was determined not to miss a sold-out four-night engagement, including Christmas Eve, at London's Wembley Arena, the 12,500-seat adjunct to Wembley Stadium. Word came that Princess Diana was attending the opening; Michael *had* to appear. Though hurting, he delivered a high-octane show. He donned white tights; Ridgeley shook jingle bells. Later they dressed as Santa Clauses and led a "Last Christmas" singalong amid fake snow. "George Michael's cliché-ridden bumps and grinds appear to have been borrowed from a Tom Jones television special," wrote Mick Brown.

But Diana seemed enchanted. Mark Ellen, the editor of *Smash Hits*, recalled seeing the princess—who was two years older than Michael and Ridgeley—"reduced to a blushingly hysterical schoolgirl, head-in-hands as he pirouetted beneath her stand." Afterward she was brought backstage, where she acted like a shy but starstruck teenager.

The fans in Japan were less restrained; after a radio appearance, a swarm of them almost trampled Michael and Ridgeley. In late January, the band made its Australian debut with a three-night stand at the Entertainment Centre in Melbourne. "It was difficult not to be infected by the excitement of about seven thousand twelve- and thirteen-year-olds," wrote Rebecca Batties in the *Age*.

But belting, anxiety, or both did Michael in; he felt his voice going during the first show and canceled the second. Pressures mounted. At a press conference in Sydney, a sea of girls outside screamed, WE WANT WHAM!. "It's all become a bit terrifying," confided Michael to a reporter. "I don't know how much longer I can stand losing my privacy, which I have always valued so much."

A North America tour, his lifelong dream, awaited him. On February 4, 1985, Wham! would make its U.S. debut at a legendary venue, the Hollywood Palladium; five more American shows would follow. Michael had cause for confidence. Columbia had issued "Careless Whisper" in the States—the label read "Wham! Featuring George Michael"—and it was slowly rising up *Billboard*'s Hot 100 chart.

As the Wham! ensemble arrived at Los Angeles International Airport (LAX), a crowd of fans waited to cheer them on. Later, in a vehicle headed down Sunset Boulevard in West Hollywood, they passed Tower Records. Above it, a billboard proclaimed: WELCOME WHAM!. As the curtain rose on the Palladium stage, Wham! beheld a sellout crowd of over four thousand fans. The group moved on to full houses in Oakland and Dallas. From there, Michael and Ridgeley returned briefly to London to attend the BRIT Awards, England's equivalent of the Grammys; Wham! had been nominated as Best British Group. On February 11, the two young men sat in the ballroom of the Grosvenor House Hotel as their fellow nominees were read off: Bronski Beat, Frankie Goes to Hollywood, U2, and Queen. The winner: Wham!. Onstage, Michael and Ridgeley, dressed in matching white, seemed genuinely shell-shocked and almost speechless.

Back they went in triumph to the States, where they sold out Philadelphia's Tower Theater and the Beacon Theatre in New York. On February 16, they reached the Orpheum Theatre in Boston. That day, Wham! learned that "Careless Whisper," which had topped the charts in ten countries, had just made No. 1 in the States.

• • •

Michael's displays of ego had continued to sour him to the press. Two weeks earlier he had informed the *Boston Globe*: "I think we're going to sell America to the Americans with much more professionalism than they do it." The *Globe*'s Steve Morse wrote a predictably harsh review of the Orpheum show. "You really have to invent an entirely new category of wimpiness to describe Wham!," he observed. Michael and Ridgeley, said Morse, had performed "like cardboard cutouts from a Fruit Loops commercial." Pejoratives shot from his typewriter like bullets: "powderpuff pop," "bubblegum Motown," "cheesy," "contrived." He saved a barb for the "preening" Ridgeley, "running his fingers through his hair and staring up at the balcony like an Olympian god."

Sitting alone in the back of the Orpheum was Billy Masters, sixteen and as dazzled by Wham! as Morse was repelled. In a few years, the painfully shy young man would make his name as the author of a syndicated gay gossip column. A nearby woman at the Orpheum soundboard saw Masters with eyes agog and started a conversation. After the show, she thrilled him by taking him backstage and introducing him to Michael. He was startled to find that the colossus he had just seen onstage "was not much more than a boy. His eyes had a worldliness that was older than his body. He was magnetic in many ways."

Suddenly, a swarm of fans barreled toward them. Michael grabbed Masters's arm and they vanished inside a passageway that led to the Parker House Hotel. The Wham! crew was occupying several rooms on the same floor. Michael rushed Masters to his suite, where an after-party was in progress. "I realized that George was high," said Masters.

Michael began kissing him. The teenager was shocked; he had thought for sure that the pinup idol the girls had just screamed for was straight. Michael led him into a private room. Then, said Masters, "things began to progress. I had never been with a guy, and I started shaking." Michael asked what was wrong, and Masters broke into heaving sobs. Embarrassed, he confessed this was his first gay experience. "You could have been with anyone but you got me!" blubbered Masters. Michael, he recalled, "was so comforting and sweet. He said, 'We can just hang out.' It seemed to amuse him. It showed him I wasn't there to score with George Michael."

Masters stayed overnight. They lay in bed, kissing and cuddling; Michaels asked the teenager everything about himself, including his study of classical piano. "The impression I got," said Masters, "was that all this was something he was craving but didn't get to do very often." The next morning, Michael hired a car to send him home.

Their date had been terribly romantic, but they never repeated it; Michael could not yet risk a gay relationship, especially when Wham!'s success had reached dizzying heights. In both the United Kingdom and the United States, *Make It Big* had made No. 1. In it were four No. 1 hits: "Wake Me Up Before You Go-Go," "Freedom," "Everything She Wants," and "Careless Whisper." On March 13, Michael was back at the Grosvenor House Hotel. The Ivor Novello Awards, named after a fabled British theater composer and given annually to songwriters, honored "Careless Whisper" as Most Performed Work, and Michael as Songwriter of the Year. No one so young had ever won the award—and its presenter was Elton John. Michael's hero proclaimed him "the greatest songwriter of his generation—in the league of Paul McCartney." The tribute shattered his cocky façade. Choking back tears, Michael said, "This award is the most important thing that has ever happened to me."

The next month, he embarked on an adventure that would make Wham! known all over the world. An outrageous publicity scheme, over a year in the making, had borne fruit: Wham! would soon become the first Western pop group to perform in Communist China. It was Summers's idea, but Napier-Bell had made it happen. He knew China well, for he had a penchant for Asian men. "Messing about in Asia," he confessed, was "what I'd always enjoyed best."

Chinese authorities viewed Western pop as the soundtrack of degeneracy; it was more or less banned, along with almost every other worldly pleasure. Andrew Jacobs, the longtime China correspondent for the *New York Times*, made his first visit there within months of Wham!'s. "Everyone looked the same," he said. "They were all wearing army green or navy blue and nerdy glasses. Any kind of attention to your looks was considered decadent. People were horribly repressed and had no freedom; everything was monitored. You never touched a girl before you were married. Anything Western was considered evil. Just having a book in your house from the West could get you tortured and killed."

Now the government was loosening its reins, though very slightly. Teenagers had access to records by bands like the Beatles and ABBA, and they held timid dance parties. Some girls began wearing makeup and heels. A flicker of capitalism arose via posters and television ads for electronic equipment. A potentially huge new market for Wham! seemed within reach. With that in mind, Napier-Bell had begun flying to China to romance government officials. No one there, of course, had heard of Wham!, but he pointed out that everyone else had, and that a tour by the band would make China more attractive to the West, thus encouraging foreign investment.

In January, Chinese officials had agreed to fly to Tokyo to see Wham! perform. Michael and Ridgeley gave their most wholesome show possible, reducing the amplification and the butt-wiggling. It worked. After hacking through a sea of red tape, Wham! was approved for two stadium concerts.

This would be anything but lucrative. Wham! would have to pay all expenses; proceeds would be divided between Beijing's All-China Youth Federation and Guangzhou's Ministry of Culture, which had made the invitation. It was essential that the group behave. The "Careless Whisper" video, if shown, had to be shorn of all tumbling in the sheets. Wham!, announced Willy Newlands in Sydney's *Sun-Herald*, were about to become "the prized symbols of the new revolution."

CHAPTER FIVE

CHINA MEANT LITTLE TO Michael or Ridgeley, and although they didn't relish the thought of playing for no money, they saw the PR value. En route there in late March, Wham! gave two shows in Hong Kong to help subsidize the tour. Then, on April 4, 1985, the partners and their ever-growing entourage—musicians, crew, managers, parents, friends, Melanie, invited press, Connie Filippello—landed in Beijing. In his book about the China visit, *I'm Coming to Take You to Lunch*, Napier-Bell called the city a place of "grim, never-ending drabness." As the group trudged through the airport, children in Mao caps stared at the two long-haired Brits as though they were Martians; men in suits nodded and smiled at them nervously. A Chinese journalist asked Michael if he were Andrew Ridgeley.

Culture shock erupted on both sides. Once they had reached town, said Danny Cummings, "all you could hear were bicycle bells and the sounds of people clearing their throats, spitting endlessly." The first show was on April 7; until then, two boys who had yanked shuttlecocks out of their shorts onstage had to act as foreign dignitaries. Swarms of international press snapped their photos as they kicked a soccer ball around on a field and took a walk along the Great Wall. China's centuries-old fortification was a tourist magnet, but the Wall puzzled Ridgeley. "I can't imagine why they built it," he said. "I can't see who would want to invade this place."

As guests of honor at a government banquet, they stared at tables filled with Chinese delicacies, such as hundred-year-old eggs. "It was so alien to all of us," said Paul Spong. "None of us could eat any of the food. Nothing tasted like it looked." Michael and Ridgeley walked around shaking hands and looking like guests at the wrong party. At a podium, Michael read a statement. Wham!'s visit, he hoped, would provide "a cultural introduction between young China and young people in the rest of the world." He was nervous, but for Deon Estus, this was the lark of a lifetime. "I had a ball in

China," he said. "People would come up to me and touch my face because I was black. It was a trip."

This experience was costing Wham! well upward of a million pounds. Napier-Bell had persuaded CBS to foot the bill if a concert video could be made. Aiming for greatness, Summers obtained a yes from director Lindsay Anderson, a kingpin of 1960s British New Wave cinema. Anderson's *if. . . . ,* a 1968 film about antisocial teens at a British boys' boarding school, had been called "a landmark of British countercultural cinema."

He was now sixty-two, and had no interest in Wham!'s music. Instead, he sensed a profound story about the crumbling of a historic cultural barrier. Michael, though, envisioned a fun promotional film with travelogue footage and the prettiest photography possible, especially of him. Secretly, Anderson saw the two young stars as entitled and arrogant, and his regal cordiality vanished when he tripped on the Great Wall and hurt his leg. Thereafter, he barked at people from a wheelchair.

Over a thousand young Chinese lined up at the Workers' Gymnasium on Friday to buy admission to Sunday's show; many waited all night. In their pockets were the required letters of permission from their employers. Each ticket came with a cassette of *Make It Big* to give them an idea of the alien sounds they were about to hear.

On the evening of April 7, the Workers' Gymnasium, which held thirteen thousand, began to fill up. The show had sold out. Young Chinese gingerly took their seats amid walls of red and gold, inscribed with quotes by Chairman Mao. Tension hung in the air; nobody knew how to behave at a pop concert, and soldiers and police stood everywhere, poised to maintain order. "If we react too violently, then we will never have another concert," said Ai Li, a student. Trevor, an English break dancer, opened. Breaching protocol, Napier-Bell had advised him to weave through the audience and work people up. Some rose and tried to imitate him. After he finished, a stern announcement in Chinese filled the arena: "Stay in your seats. Don't dance!" Everything else about the show was meant to turn the country's obedient youth into a raucous Wham! audience. Blue and purple strobe lights scissored over the crowd's heads. Out came the musicians, then Shirlie and Pepsi bounced into view wearing purple polka-dot miniskirts. Then came the band. "We walked onstage to silence," said Spong. Michael saw a line of photographers and momentarily froze. But they seemed far more interested in the reactions of the audience; that was the real show.

Wham! launched gamely into "Wake Me Up Before You Go-Go." When the song ended, all they heard was rustling and a few murmurs. "This was mortifying for them," said Craig Peikin, an actor friend of Michael's who had flown in from Los Angeles for the occasion. "You could see the looks on their faces. But that was the custom in China—nobody applauds until the end of the show. George and Andrew left the stage for a minute while they were told this. George told me it was probably the toughest night of his life."

He and Ridgeley soldiered on. With each song, they watched fearful and confused faces melt into smiles. Michael asked the audience to clap along. They tried, but couldn't maintain the time; they didn't know Western rhythms. Nor could most of them understand the words, but it scarcely mattered. In the stadium's upper tiers, people started dancing. From the stage, Danny Cummings witnessed one of the night's most famous moments: "One guy stood up and started chanting about freedom and liberty, and was arrested and dragged away by men in uniform."

Newly emboldened, Michael turned around and twitched his behind. Everyone gasped. He sang "Love Machine," with its groans of "push it, push it, baby." At intermission, Wham! committed its biggest sin by showing the unedited "Careless Whisper," which in Communist China was akin to pornography.

But his ploys were working. One dancing fan called Wham!'s show "much better than Chinese music—it really gets your insides moving." Yibi Hu, an animator who would create one of Michael's last videos, was just a year old when Wham! came to China, but he grew up hearing about that historic visit. "If all your life you grew up in this Communist regime and only heard patriotic songs, then suddenly someone broke in with a really confident swagger to sing about love, you got a feeling that maybe music could be different. When Wham! hit China, it was like a bomb."

The next day, Michael and Ridgeley stayed behind in Beijing to do a TV interview; everyone else proceeded to Guangzhou (also known as Canton), Wham!'s next stop. About fifteen minutes into the flight, the weirdest incident of the trip occurred. The band included a young Portuguese trumpeter who boarded in a state of altered consciousness and turned the flight into the ride from hell. By one report, he barged into the cockpit, startling the pilot so much that the plane fell into a nosedive. Crew ushered him to his seat and tried to calm him, but according to Dave Moulder, Wham!'s bodyguard, the musician began "screaming and foaming at the mouth. No one was sure what was going on and we were very frightened. He was hallucinating and seemed to be in a trance. He thought he was possessed by the devil and dying."

The trumpeter pulled out a fake Swiss Army knife that he had bought in Hong Kong and began jabbing at his stomach. "Had he used a real knife he would have died," said Spong. Luckily he only nicked himself, but the pilot turned back and made an emergency landing in Beijing. The trumpeter was taken to the hospital and the flight resumed. Once settled at their hotel in Canton, the traumatized band members slept together in one room, some of them sprawled out on the floor. "It was quite bonding," said Spong. "Nobody would leave anybody."

The show there went more smoothly, and the response was almost unanimously positive. Cheng Fangyuan, a young singing star, seemed deeply moved. "We knew nothing about Western culture," she said. "This gave us our glimpse." But according to Andros Georgiou, Michael and Ridgeley had hated the experience. Michael stepped into London's Gatwick Airport on April 13, 1985; Ridgeley, who had stayed over to visit Hong Kong, flew in the next day. Reporters rushed over to query the young men about China. "I am not in a huge hurry to get back there," said Ridgeley dryly. "I like the people, but there were a few problems." His partner was more blunt: "I'd never go there again."

The changes they wrought were not immediate. Later in 1985, Chinese officials nixed efforts by the Australian rock band Men at Work and even by the most wholesome of American singer-songwriters, John Denver, to perform there. "There's a general feeling that the Wham! show had over-stimulated the youth," said Carrillo Gantner, Australia's cultural affairs officer. Nevertheless, rock exploded throughout the country the next year thanks to singer-songwriter Cui Jian, whose "Nothing to My Name" became an anthem for alienated Chinese youth. He performed the song in 1989 at one of a series of bloody student uprisings at Tiananmen Square in Beijing. For years, Cui Jian's songs—along with most other forms of protest—were squelched. But Wham! had shown a repressed generation how freedom could taste.

That was Lindsay Anderson's ambition, too. To attain it, he had issued countless demands, and his filming of this cultural milestone had cost a fortune. Soon, Summers, Napier-Bell, Harvey Goldsmith, and the film's producer, Martin Lewis, screened the eighty-five-minute cut. "He'd made the film so achingly boring we could scarcely sit through it," said Napier-Bell. Predictably, Anderson had put the story's sociological bent ahead of the music, and long expository scenes interrupted the fun. Summers panicked—what would happen when Michael saw the film? He rushed to draft a list of edits for Anderson. Sure enough, Michael hated the initial cut, primarily because of how he looked. He decided to take over the project in conjunction with a young British director of music videos, Andy Morahan.

A desperate Anderson tried pleading his case in a letter to Michael. "Jazz and Simon both seem to be terrified of you," he remarked. No answer came. Costs took another leap when Michael decided that the China performances had to be reenacted. A shoot was booked at Shepperton Studios, one of London's best-known soundstages. Since returning home, Ridgeley had cut his hair; for the filming, he had to wear a painfully obvious wig. When Anderson saw Michael and Morahan's re-edit—which still bore Anderson's name—he was appalled. Sitting at his typewriter, he fired off letter after angry letter. He blamed Summers ("a fearful idiot") and Napier-Bell ("with his endless appetite for destructive intrigue") for kowtowing to Michael, their meal ticket: "a spoiled, conceited dumbbell . . . whose every command his minions must dash to execute."

In the end, *Foreign Skies: Wham! in China* caused hardly a ripple. John Peel of the *Observer* called it "pretty dull fare . . . a gaudy home-movie which proved little beyond the awfulness of being followed everywhere by cameramen."

• • •

For all its problems, the China tour brought Wham! a prestige it had never known. In June, Michael and Ridgeley were invited to a cocktail party at the Guards Polo Club in Windsor; there, at her request, they met Queen Elizabeth II. She chatted politely with them about China, and knew their hits.

But Wham! still bore the stain of bubblegum. "I can write very good pop songs," insisted Michael. "I'm a capable musician. So is Andrew. But some people don't think we're much." Respect, he realized, would only come to him on his own.

That spring brought an opportunity that stunned him. Michael was invited to sing on *Motown Returns to the Apollo*, an NBC-TV special that celebrated the fiftieth anniversary of the fabled Harlem venue. The Motown hook was a stretch, for only a few of the guests (Smokey Robinson, Stevie Wonder, Martha Reeves, Diana Ross, Mary Wells) had recorded for the label. The others included four renowned British soul boys: Rod Stewart, Joe Cocker, Boy George, and George Michael. In a coup that would bring him dream validation, Michael would duet with Robinson on "Careless Whisper" and also sing one of his favorite songs, "Love's in Need of Love Today" from Wonder's *Songs in the Key of Life*, with the composer himself. At a run-through before the May 4 taping, he was greeted warmly by everyone but Boy George, who resented his presence, for he, too, would be singing with Wonder. To Michael's disappointment, his idol stood him up at rehearsal; shortly before showtime, he managed to grab a few minutes with Wonder and Robinson.

At the concert's seven-minute mark, host Bill Cosby gave Michael a rote introduction. The singer walked nervously onstage, his blond shag hairdo brushing his shoulders, to perform "Careless Whisper." Midway through, Robinson strode out to join Michael.

The Motown god's high-flying, buttery tones and warbly vibrato sounded much as they had on the singles that Michael had worn out as a kid. But the song made no sense as a duet, and Robinson's cool suaveness stood in Michael's way as he tried to build to an emotional peak. In the last chorus, Michael bit into his song with renewed gusto as though trying to save it. The crowd cheered him more loudly than they did Robinson. At the end, Michael gave the star an obligatory hug. Boy George was "relieved," he said later, to hear Robinson "murdering" his rival's hit: "He sounded like a throttled duck."

Michael had far worse jitters before he sang with Wonder. "The Stevie thing," he told writer Rob Tannenbaum, "was either going to make me scared shitless and I was going to sing like crap, or it would bring something out in me—and it did." That something was deference. Joined on stage by only

Wonder at a keyboard, Michael glowed with awe. He had long ago learned "Love's in Need of Love Today" off the record, and when he opened his mouth his identity vanished, replaced by an almost perfect Wonder imitation.

The duets amounted to a double consecration. But they couldn't quite ease the sting of a seeming snub from Bob Geldof. "Do They Know It's Christmas?" had reached No. 1 in fourteen countries, making Geldof seem like the savior of Ethiopia. In the summer of 1985, he teamed with Harvey Goldsmith and the American rock promoter Bill Graham to present Live Aid, the grandest rock benefit in history. Once more, Ethiopian famine was the cause. Live Aid would be telecast from Wembley Stadium and the John F. Kennedy Stadium in Philadelphia on July 13, 1985. The event would run for sixteen hours.

Geldof had reached for the stars and gotten them: Bob Dylan, David Bowie, Paul McCartney, the Who, Queen, Madonna, the Rolling Stones, Led Zeppelin, Phil Collins, Elton John. Simon Napier-Bell skipped the whole affair, vacationing in Thailand instead. "There's something obscene about people starving in Ethiopia, and everybody going off in helicopters to drink champagne and sniff cocaine all day," he explained.

He wouldn't be missing his clients there; although Spandau Ballet and Duran Duran had been invited, Wham! had not. Elton John saved the day by having them perform one song with him. John knew the value of allying himself with a rising, sexy young star like George Michael, especially now, when John's career needed a boost. Earlier that year, he had engaged Michael for *Ice on Fire*, his first new album in nine years. Michael was inaudible amid the backup vocals on "Nikita," the album's big single, but they shared equal space on "Wrap Her Up," written with Bernie Taupin. The video shows John as a boogying paparazzo, hot on the trail of a parade of female gay icons, shown in old newsreel clips. The two men meet on a stage, where Michael, in a brown fringe jacket and shades, breaks into kitschy disco moves while incanting diva names with John: Marilyn Monroe, Marlene Dietrich, Joan Collins, Grace Jones, Tallulah Bankhead.

John's coming-out was three years away, but when he finally did, said Gill Pringle, the *Daily Mirror*'s pop-music columnist, "it was a bit of a joke, because everyone knew." Far less of the public perceived the truth about Michael, though, and at Live Aid he watched his two foremost gay role models display their highly differing approaches to performing. Like everyone else, Michael was dazzled as Freddie Mercury delivered the benefit's most showstopping segment. Mercury had not come out of the closet either, yet he proclaimed his gayness to the world whether they grasped it or not. His look—tight faded jeans with a bulging fly, a scooping white tank top, a mustache, a studded leather bicep band—defined the clone style, and his manner took it to epic heights. Standing with his legs in a V in front of seventy-two thousand viewers (nearly two billion more were watching on TV), Mercury seemed drunk with power; his moves were oversize and theatrical. Never had "We Are the Champions" held such a pronounced gay subtext.

Shortly before nine P.M., Elton John entered in a pink polka-dotted, gold-trimmed black jacket with a feathered cap and sat at a white Liberace-style grand piano. After obliging with a few of his hits, he played the intro to another one, "Don't Let the Sun Go Down on Me," and announced, "Mr. George Michael!" The young man walked out, wearing the Mercury-inspired butch look that foretold his next phase: a beard, sunglasses, snug jeans, a white tee, a leather jacket, and an earring. Ridgeley trailed behind him. Hastily John added, "And Mr. Andrew Ridgeley!" Michael's partner disappeared into the line of backup singers and sang into a dead mic.

Having sung along with John's power anthem countless times in the bedroom of his family home, Michael got to emote it for an estimated 40 percent of the global population as the composer played. To have sung his Wham! hits would not have meant nearly so much. Live Aid gave the first indication of the breadth of Michael's presence, which effortlessly filled one of the world's largest stadiums.

In attendance was England's most distinguished rock-star groupie, Princess Diana. According to the *Daily Mirror*, Diana allowed that she found Michael "very gorgeous." Michael issued a public response: "Thank you, ma'am—you're pretty smashing yourself." Thus began the awkward twelve-year friendship between a smitten aristocrat and a closeted sex idol.

•••

Clearly there was more money to be made off Michael than ever. For months, Summers had been laboring to arrange a late-summer U.S. tour for Wham!.

Now that Michael had gotten a taste of touring, the prospect of doing it again made him recoil. Nonetheless, Summers began conferring with Rob Kahane, a young agent at Triad Artists Inc., a Los Angeles talent agency. Kahane was eager to acquire Wham! as a client, and he rushed to help Summers with a far-fetched scheme: an America stadium tour.

Almost everyone, including Dick Leahy, argued against it. Wham! was not a superstar act in the States; despite its hits, it had only played a few modest-sized U.S. venues. Yet Kahane and a colleague, John Marx, cobbled together about twenty dates. The two men flew to London and met Michael in a recording studio, where they laid out their plans.

Their hearts sank as he announced that he would only play six shows. What Ridgeley wanted didn't seem to matter. Though disappointed, the agents booked an abbreviated though still-risky tour: five arenas in the States and one in Toronto. Now everyone involved had to figure out ways to fill them. They decided to hire radio promoters and to paper local record shops with Wham! material. Summers lined up a selection of three opening acts—Katrina and the Waves, the Pointer Sisters, and Chaka Khan—who were stars in their own right.

After all that, Michael phoned Summers. He had changed his mind: He did not want to tour at all. Dumbfounded, the manager begged him to explain why, but he got no clear response. Only years later would Michael talk about how phony he felt in front of audiences as he pretended to be what he wasn't.

Summers could only panic as he saw his potential windfall evaporate. He insisted that Kahane fly to London to help him save the tour—by lying, begging, whatever it took. By the time Kahane arrived, Summers had dreamed up a solution. It was too late to cancel, they told Michael; lots of tickets had sold, and the Miami Stadium was already full.

It wasn't. But the news appealed to Michael's ego, and he told Summers he had changed his mind. The manager set out to fool the American press as he had fooled Michael. He pumped out hype about sellout shows; columnists printed it without checking. The ploy worked: Whamamerica!—also known as the Make It Big Tour '85—came close to packing six stadiums.

In all of them, Wham!-mania, as the British media called it, was in full flight. Barricades in front of the stage kept surging girls at bay. They knew every word of every song. Wham!'s wardrobe induced swoons: Michael wore fringed yellow hip-hugger pants and a matching jacket over no shirt; Ridgeley looked prince-like in his high-collared, red-orange coat. They strutted into the crowd on runways and teased fans with safely naughty talk. "Are you horny?" asked Michael; a din of excited squeals came back at him.

At Hollywood Park, Wham! played to fifty thousand; Sidney Poitier, Dionne Warwick, and Stevie Nicks sat in the VIP section. Michael's cliché patter betrayed his youth. "Good evening, Los Angelees! We want to give you our best all evening!" James Spencer attended. "It was a crazy fucking hot day, like a hundred and six degrees, and they had to hose off the audience," he recalled. "I nearly got heat stroke. At one point George did a costume change and forgot to zip up his pants, so he did part of the show with his fly open."

Critics called the music "decent-enough Bazooka-formulated pop" . . . "more derivative of Broadway or Las Vegas than an arena rock 'n' roll show." One writer, Iain Blair, made Michael seem like a laughing stock: "Will he be strangled by his own hair before they can fly his sister to the rescue again? Will it get even wilder, and challenge Tina Turner's wig to a duel? Could it provide valuable shelter for the world's homeless? Stay tuned."

• • •

Michael was not opening his heart to many people, but he poured it out in Los Angeles to his friend Craig Peikin, a nineteen-year-old, openly gay actor whom he had met on a previous visit to California. Peikin's family owned a "one-stop," a business that distributed albums to small record shops; in the last year, the company had moved a landslide number of Wham! discs. Michael felt at home in Los Angeles, where celebrities were abundant and less fiercely pursued. He especially liked West Hollywood, the predominantly gay town-within-a-town.

Over dinner, Michael leveled with Peikin. He had grown to hate Wham!'s featherweight image; he knew the band's shelf life would expire soon, and he couldn't wait to make a solo album. Michael believed that a lot of people were out to take advantage of him, particularly his management. "It's going to be a long time before I trust people in a total sense ever again," he admitted. Michael had not explicitly come out to Peikin, but when the subject turned to AIDS, he remarked: "Yeah, I'm trying to be careful." Peikin asked, "Careful with a girl or careful with a boy?"

"What do you think?" answered Michael.

He had over a week off before September 15, when Whamamerica! would close at Veterans Stadium in Philadelphia. Michael made his way to nearby Rehoboth Beach, Delaware, a summer resort town that was popular among gays. At the Blue Moon, a restaurant that offered live music, a young singer and part-time model named Carolyn Montgomery sometimes performed. One night, someone pointed out Michael at the bar. Montgomery marched up to him and offered to buy him a drink. "I don't care what you are, gay, straight—you're adorable!" she said. He loved it.

As they talked, however, she detected a young man in turmoil. "He said he was bisexual, but he was gayer than a goose," she said. Michael kept drinking—"and he got very handsy and very needy. I was attracted to him, but I knew the difference between a gay man who was trying to straighten himself out and somebody who was really attracted to me. I was like, 'Oh, sweetie, you might be able to go through the motions, but who wants to do that?'"

Two female acquaintances of Montgomery's invited her and Michael home. One of the women broke out a mound of cocaine. Until that summer, Michael had hardly dabbled in drugs; alcohol was his main escape. But recently in London, Michael had discovered Ecstasy, the nightlife drug that had swept the gay party circuit. Just one of those flat, round tablets, which looked like candies, made inhibitions melt, releasing in their wake a rush of happy, sexy feelings. But Michael had also begun experimenting with coke, and at the gathering, said Montgomery, "he did a tremendous amount," which turned him even more desperate. When she announced she had to leave, Michael begged her to join him at brunch the next day. She said yes, but couldn't bring herself to go. "He was so closeted and scared and sad," she said. "The need to be loved and desired was huge."

Throughout his weeks in the States, nearly two hundred thousand people showered him with adoration. Michael returned to London in triumph, yet he felt a strange disapproval, as though people were looking through him and spotting things he didn't want them to see. He confided in a reporter: "An hour ago I wanted to get a paper, and I sat here for thirty minutes trying to decide whether to or not, because I can't stand the way people look at me . . .

as if I shouldn't be walking down the street. Musically, things get better and better; personally, things get worse and worse."

Michael was still attempting to sleep with occasional women, but he had to get drunk first, and the efforts invariably led to embarrassment. What's more, in the age of AIDS, he felt compelled to divulge the fact that he had slept with men. For the next several years, recalled Michael, "I had an absolute rubbish level of sex."

On his arm at many a public event was his purported girlfriend, Pat Fernandes. Since the Bolts days, she had proven useful in keeping the tabloids sated. In the *Sun*, Lesley-Ann Jones noted how "dusky Pat Fernandes" was keeping Michael "occupied until dawn." But Fernandes was in love with him and wanted more, as humiliating as that pursuit was. Years later, in the gay magazine *Attitude*, Michael told Adam Mattera of having once taken Fernandes to a gathering at a club. "I announced to this whole fucking party, pissed out of my head, that I wanted to have sex and invited the whole room, basically!" He dumped the young woman and went to a downstairs lounge with an American man and a British woman. Fernandes was apparently heartbroken, but she wouldn't give up.

Michael hated confrontations, but finally, in 1985, he told her that this affair would never happen and that they were done. In response, she threatened to write a book—not to out him, but to claim they had been lovers. It never happened; instead she fed items to the tabloids about their alleged affair. Michael's publicity machine stepped in, recasting Fernandes as the woman who had broken his heart. Boy George told a reporter that the headline should have read, "How Pat Broke My Hoover."

Michael found a replacement for Fernandes. Kathy Jeung was a Chinese-American, Los Angeles-based club kid and deejay turned makeup artist. She and Michael had met on a photo shoot and bonded. Henceforth, Jeung became his tour guide in the after-dark fast lane. She quickly realized he was gay, but that didn't stop her from falling for him. For the next few years they remained inseparable, sharing everything from "silly drugs," said Michael, to their innermost secrets. "Kathy looked after him," said her best friend Bret Witke. "And he was very protective of her. He really loved her—the way he could." Word about their "affair" reached the *Mirror*, which reported that Michael had "found happiness . . . with his beautiful girlfriend Kathy Jeung."

But one flame wasn't enough; sex gods were supposed to have revolving doors on their bedrooms. In the fall of 1985, columnists feasted on Michael's purported fling with Brooke Shields, the winsome brunette beauty who had costarred in *The Blue Lagoon* as a mermaid-like adolescent who winds up shipwrecked on an island with an equally pretty blond boy. When *Tonight Show* host Johnny Carson asked Shields to name her dream companion on a desert island, she didn't hesitate: It was George Michael. Shields's mother, who managed her, finagled a meeting.

Michael escorted the twenty-year-old actress to a party for Grace Jones; soon word was released of their "passionate affair." It followed Shields's rumored entanglements with Michael Jackson and John Travolta. "Brooke Shields was the person you wheeled out any time you had a guy who was being called gay," said Simon Napier-Bell. "A young, pretty-looking fag-hag. So George went off with her for a week, and now he was straight after all." *Rolling Stone* was skeptical: "We hear the highlight of their dates has been . . . shopping."

But Shields seemed oblivious to the truth. After a handful of public appearances together, Michael told her goodbye. "I think he believed he was getting in too deep," she explained. Someone asked about the rumors that Michael was gay. "I know he's not," she asserted. "You get a feeling about a man—and I can definitely tell you, he's *all* man." Unfortunately, noted Shields, she had tried phoning him—"but he seems to have changed his number." In 2011, she laughed about the episode. "He was such a gentleman! He didn't even kiss me goodnight! I was like, oh my God, he's so Prince Charming, he respects me!"

Michael was facing actual heartbreak in the person of Brad Branson, a friend of Kathy Jeung. Dark-haired, stubbly, and handsome, Branson worked as a nightclub cashier, but liked taking pictures; he would eventually become the protégé of the fashion and celebrity photographer Paul Jasmin. Though gay, he was still as sexually ambivalent as Michael. The singer fell for him to the point of obsession, but although they had a couple of make-out sessions and even slept in the same bed, Branson let it go no further.

Early in 1986, Michael played him a new ballad, "A Different Corner." He had written it about the two of them, he said. He clicked on the cassette, and Branson heard a breathy, pleading voice, set in a bed of synthesizer and trimmed with an electronically produced Spanish guitar solo. "Little by little you've brought me to my knees / Don't you care?" sang Michael.

Branson's heart wasn't in it, as he told Michael. They stayed in each other's lives for years, but as he said years later, "I just never really wanted to be a rock star's wife." To find love while pursuing his dreams, Michael feared, was going to prove nearly impossible.

CHAPTER SIX

AT LAST MICHAEL HAD left his parents' home and rented a mews in the well-to-do London district of Kensington. Soon he would buy a £1.3 million mansion in Oak Hill Park, Hampstead, not far from his parents' house. He acquired a Mercedes coupe and treated himself to a £1.8 million villa in Saint-Tropez on the French Riviera. Elton John had a villa there, which he called the Pink Palace, and keeping up with him mattered to Michael. "It's not a bad thing if your competition's Elton John," said Danny Cummings. "You're doing pretty well." He christened the house Chez Knobby, based on a nickname friends had given him; it was an abbreviation of "knobhead," the British equivalent of "dickhead."

Currently airing on MTV was a video for Wham!'s latest No. 1 hit, "I'm Your Man." Michael had written most of it in five minutes on an airplane during the Whamamerica! tour. The song was his most contagious spin yet on Supremes-style dance music and the pleading-for-love theme that he adored. One of his catchiest hooks was sung to the line, "If you're gonna do it, do it right!"; it meant nothing, but that didn't matter—people remembered it. Michael's voice panted, purred, growled, and leapt into a silky falsetto, backed by an intricately arranged choir of his own vocals.

The video took Wham! into comedy, for which both young men had a flair. Shot in black and white, it shows Michael and Ridgeley out on the freezing street in front of the Marquee, a London club, as they beg passersby to see their show. Inside the stage door, Michael grouses on the phone to Napier-Bell about having to work this tacky dump. "Simon, don't cry," he says. A white-jacketed ticket-taker, played by Cummings, tries to move more tickets. Having seen Scarface, the film about a Cuban drug lord, Cummings decided to adopt a Spanish accent, which came out sounding like Speedy Gonzales.

Onstage in the packed Marquee, Shirlie and Pepsi are absent; the star is Michael, who had adopted a new visual sophistication. Spanking a tambourine and gliding across the stage as though floating on air, he wore designer black, a streamlined haircut, and fashionable stubble. This was Michael's first of many collaborations with videographer Mike Southon, formerly of the BBC; in his hands, Michael looked like a *GQ* model.

Otherwise, the Wham! image had become a joke, and he confided to Rob Kahane that he planned to end the group. "You've been on the tour," he said. "You know Andrew doesn't even play the guitar."

Michael shared his news with a crushed Napier-Bell; the manager was looking ahead to a worldwide stadium tour and massive earnings. But Michael couldn't wait. "He had let the pressure build until he couldn't stand it," said Napier-Bell. "It was, 'I cannot go on another day.'" Jazz Summers had secured a Pepsi commercial for Wham! at a staggering fee, but Michael turned it down; he knew the ad would make it even harder for him to dissociate himself from Wham!. "He desperately wanted to be seen as a serious artist," said Paul Spong. "For some reason George wasn't happy writing fantastic feel-good songs."

The formal announcement would come later. For now, he set out to reeducate the press. The "bloke prancing about in the pretty blond hair with the shorts and the teeth," he explained, was just "a role I was playing." He had a lot more to say as a songwriter than that pose had ever allowed. Michael was instantly ridiculed for his ambitions. "This Thatcherite dream—born Finchley, a self-made millionaire at twenty-two—wants to be taken seriously," wrote Phil Shaw in the *Guardian*. The more he was mocked, the less patience he had with all things Wham!.

Word came in late December that the group had been nominated twice in the American Music Awards, an annual gala to be televised live from Los Angeles on January 27, 1986. Michael didn't care at all about winning Favorite Pop/Rock Video by a Group (for "Freedom"); but "Careless Whisper" was up for Favorite Pop/Rock Song, and that award would boost his solo future. Even so, attending would require him to cut short his vacation in Australia. He demanded that Napier-Bell sleuth out his chances of scoring the second award. Industry insiders did the voting, and an organizer leaked word to Napier-Bell: Yes, "Careless Whisper" was ahead.

Michael attended without Ridgeley, who had slept late and missed his flight. Seated in the Shrine Auditorium, he saw Prince, one of his current fascinations, announce the winner for Favorite Pop/Rock Song: "The Power of Love" by Huey Lewis and the News. Michael flashed a frozen smile and applauded, while fuming inside. Other winners were giving speeches by satellite; he could have done that, too. He cursed himself for having agreed to announce a special award for Bob Geldof. Michael took the podium in a bulky black suit with his chest exposed. As girls screamed, he read half-heartedly from a teleprompter. Late in the show he returned, for "Freedom" had won the video award. Michael could barely manage a smile. Standing without Ridgeley at the podium, he kept it brief: "I'm not gonna lie to you; he missed his plane."

Afterward, he tore into Napier-Bell. "You were meant to get me Favorite Single. You didn't do your job properly, man. You fucked up."

• • •

Nomis Management *was* Wham!; none of its other clients could compare. With his cash cow soon to expire, Napier-Bell decided it was time to unload the company. In late 1985, Summers arranged a dinner with Harvey Goldsmith. Britain's dean of rock promoters had sold his production company to Kunick Leisure, a sprawling conglomerate, but Goldsmith remained in charge, and he offered to buy Nomis. The deal was irresistible: £1.2 million up front, and as much as £5 million in the future if certain projections panned out. Napier-Bell withheld the news that Wham! was splitting. Luckily, Goldsmith didn't ask to see Nomis's contract with the group; Wham! had never signed one.

In a follow-up meeting, Summers and Napier-Bell learned that Kunick was funded partly by Sol Kerzner, South Africa's premiere hotelier. Kerzner owned Sun City, the country's grandest and gaudiest resort and casino. It contained a six-thousand-seat arena where Frank Sinatra, Cher, Liza Minnelli, Queen, Shirley Bassey, and Elton John had performed. Kerzner had lured them there with staggering fees—enough to stifle concerns about entertaining in an apartheid nation. Sun City was not discriminatory in its staffing or guest policies, but the prices ensured a clientele of mostly well-to-do tourists from nearby Johannesburg. Activists denounced the resort as an emblem of apartheid; on a 1985 benefit protest album, *Sun City*, Bono, Peter Gabriel, Ringo Starr, and other rockers proclaimed, "I ain't gonna play Sun City."

For Nomis to talk business with Kunick was risky; during the negotiations, Michael, too, denounced apartheid in the *Guardian*. But the offer was too tempting to pass up—especially because Wham!'s breakup would soon go public. In January 1986, Kunick announced the acquisition. According to Summers, Michael gave his blessing. The sale didn't matter to him; Wham! would soon be history.

Over the next few days, Rob Kahane lunched with Michael in Los Angeles. Kahane showed him a show-business daily. A headline declared bluntly that Sun City had bought Wham!. Michael was livid. On his behalf, Kahane grilled Summers by phone; he pleaded innocent, then immediately confronted Goldsmith, who did the same. Summers kept calling Michael to try and explain. He wouldn't answer.

Ridgeley had seen the end coming for some time; however reluctantly, he began the process of saying goodbye to Wham!. He and Shirlie had long since parted, and in January 1986, Ridgeley and his new trophy girlfriend, Donya Fiorentino, an eighteen-year-old model and the ex of actor Don Johnson, flew to Monte Carlo. He knew that a solo musical career would be next to impossible, but he had dreamed up a glamorous alternative: Formula 1 race car driving. "Motor racing is my passion now," he told the *Daily Express*. "There will be no more late nights or drinking, because my life is at stake." Soon he had gotten a French auto manufacturer, Renault, to sponsor him.

Ridgeley had an ulterior motive. A growing wave of Britain's top earners were seeking part-time exile to avoid the country's stifling taxes. The government stood to drain 60 percent of Ridgeley's income. One more award was no consolation prize, but on February 10, he and Michael sat in the Grosvenor House Hotel ballroom to be honored by the British Phonographic Industry (BPI). Wham! had been singled out for having brought British culture to China; Elton John was lauded for having successfully performed in Russia. Michael and Ridgeley looked bored as Norman Tebbit, chairman of the conservative party, gave a lavishly laudatory speech, trimmed with pallid jokes. Tebbit called Wham! to the stage along with Napier-Bell and Summers, who were seated elsewhere. Ignoring them, Michael read a bland statement; Ridgeley, with a tinge of sarcasm, added: "It's gratifying to feel that the British music industry takes us seriously."

That month, Michael summoned the managers to lunch. The time had come, he said, to tell the world of Wham!'s demise. Afterward, said Napier-Bell, Michael pulled him aside to share a word about the South African fiasco. "He said, 'I wish you'd been able to do it more privately. I don't really care at all. It's just that I've got a career. I can't live with this.'"

Nomis rushed to release a carefully worded statement. Michael, it announced, would leave the company in three months. Ridgeley would stay, first establishing himself as a race car driver, then making his film debut. Napier-Bell hoped the news would cloud over the Sun City mess.

The next morning, the *Daily Mirror*'s front page screamed: "WHAM STARS SPLIT!" Michael had released his own statement. This was a "personal decision," he explained, without elaboration; he had not even consulted Ridgeley, who was "out of contact," he said, in France. A "close friend" of Michael's gave more details: "George is fiercely anti-apartheid and couldn't bear to have any involvement with South Africa."

Napier-Bell and Summers insisted to the press that "this didn't mean the end of Wham!" But the acquisition deal exploded in their faces. Their company, said Napier-Bell, was "finished. Done. Gone. We lost everything."

At least he still had half of Wham!. "By the end of the year," he told a reporter, "Andrew Ridgeley will be the superstar name on everyone's lips, not George Michael." That wasn't to be. By late February, Ridgeley had crashed five times in seven races, gaining him the nickname Smasher. Renault withdrew its sponsorship. "Andrew is a great disappointment to us," said his team manager, Robert Fernley.

A British reporter tracked down Ridgeley in France. He wasn't ready to quit racing just yet, he said. As for Michael's announcement of February 21, he "discussed the decision in unprintable terms."

Michael opted to speak for them both. Wham!, he told the *Daily Mail*, had been an exercise in "ignoring my own intelligence." The "bright young thing image," he said, had been Andrew's idea, not his; now it reflected "an optimism I no longer have. . . . I can't pretend I'm a young man with no problems anymore." Nor, he declared, could Ridgeley. "The fact that he didn't contribute anything must have been a terrible blow to his ego. Wham!'s been bad for him in the last couple of years. He's relieved that it's all over."

There would be a huge farewell show, he decided—only one. To preclude any thoughts of extension, it would be called The Final. Michael wanted a spectacular goodbye. Wembley Stadium was booked for June 28, 1986.

Once more, Ridgeley had not been consulted. Wistfully, he told the *Daily Mail* that he saw Wham!'s abrupt demise as a betrayal of their fans. "I thought we should have toured," he said. Danny Cummings sensed that Ridgeley was heartbroken—"But every aspect of that thing had run its course. George had a vision of what the next stage had to be. It couldn't include Andrew."

Word of the farewell brought the expected tearful sentiment, along with a sense of what low regard some other bands had held for Wham!. Joe Strummer, former lead singer of the Clash, told the *Guardian*: "Ten years from now, when Thatcher's gone, we'll look back at this decade of nightmare, and their songs will be a part of the soundtrack to it."

Wham! gave CBS one more album, in two forms. *Music from the Edge of Heaven*, comprising new songs and recent singles, would come out in Japan and the United States. Most of those tracks, plus older hits, would fill a European double-LP, *The Final*. Michael wanted to show off the tougher, edgier persona he was concocting. Wham!'s last single, "The Edge of Heaven," with Elton John on piano, would be "really filthy," he promised. It even contained hints of S&M: "I would chain you up if I thought you'd swear." In "Wham Rap '86" he updated their first hit with a nastier, more snarling delivery and updated hip-hop electronics. A new dance track, "Battlestations," gave a decidedly non-teenage look at love: "We spend more time in battle than we ever do in bed." An extended remix of "Last Christmas" trounced the song's confectionary sweetness with harder percussion and a wailing vocal. Ridgeley was non-existent even in the artwork. The jacket of *Music from the Edge of Heaven* had no photo; instead, it showed a midnight-blue sky with WHAM! written across the top.

The video for "The Edge of Heaven," directed by Andy Morahan, reused the "Wake Me Up" formula, minus the bubblegum. It would be filmed in black and white in a recording studio in front of three hundred female students from the Epsom School of Art & Design. Each was paid thirty pounds to wave her arms and shout on cue. Anne Barrowclough of the *Daily Mail* joined them.

She saw that Wham!'s boyish rapport had vanished. Michael and Ridgeley, she wrote, "presented an icily polite front," addressing the musicians yet keeping their distance from each other. "As filming began, George tried to choreograph his ex-partner. . . . Andrew stared out over the crowd, ignoring the orders." As the shoot dragged on for hours, Barrowclough heard bored students making fun of Michael's brown, fringed jacket and suede leggings. "How could he have so much money and so little taste?" asked one young woman.

The final cut betrayed no hostility. Instead, it summed up four action-packed years that had sped to a close. The Wham! story flashed by via quick, momentary cuts to their previous videos. Now, however, Ridgeley had been reduced to an extra. GOODBYE rolled back and forth across the bottom of the screen, followed by THANK YOU.

• • •

Even before the Wembley farewell, Michael would be making his solo recording debut with the Queen of Soul, Aretha Franklin, an extraordinary coup. Franklin was riding high with a platinum album, *Who's Zoomin' Who?*, and a Grammy-winning hit single, "Freeway of Love." Potential songs for Franklin poured in to Clive Davis, president of her label, Arista. One of them was a dance tune, "I Knew You Were Waiting (for Me)," co-authored by Simon Climie, who had written the Pat Benatar top-ten hit "Invincible." His partner, Dennis Morgan, came from Nashville.

Davis already had his eye on a George Michael duet, but not with Franklin; instead, he proposed Arista's skyrocketing golden girl, Whitney Houston. But Michael found Houston's singing mechanical and cold. Shooting for the stars, he suggested Franklin instead, and got her. Michael knew she liked him; when "Wake Me Up" was on the charts, she had communicated a request for him to write and produce a single for her. Out of intimidation, Michael declined. Now she was willing, even eager, to sing with him. Franklin was revamping herself as a modern dance diva, and he had the audience she wanted. Michael, in turn, wanted further soul cred, and nothing could provide it like a duet with Franklin. To produce, Davis chose Narada Michael Walden, the hotshot who had masterminded *Who's Zoomin' Who?*

It took the notoriously difficult and moody Franklin months to commit to a session. Finally, time was slated for May. Accompanied by Rob Kahane, Michael flew to Detroit, near her home, for two days of recording. Michael phoned Andros from the studio, which stood in a neighborhood that had made him shudder. "He reckoned at first they were trying to scare him off; then, after a while, hanging out with the crowd, he said he felt like the 'acceptable honky.'" But Kahane got a sense of how Franklin's crowd actually perceived him. The agent had brought a video camera, and at the studio, he asked members of Franklin's entourage to comment on Michael. "They'd say, 'Who?' No one knew who he was."

For Michael, this session was an anointing; for Franklin, it was a gig. "She wasn't cold to me; she just seemed unimpressed by everything," he told Rob Tannenbaum in *Musician*. Franklin placed an order for baby back ribs, and she perked up when they arrived, wrapped in newspaper. She laid the heap on Michael's lap. "She'd put a whole rib in her mouth across the room and take all the meat off the bone," said Kahane; then she would toss the remains across the room and into a bucket, always hitting the bull's-eye. When Michael rose, everyone could see a line of grease across his crotch.

Franklin entered the booth to sing a solo part. "She's belting out the song," said Kahane. "Just killing it. She stopped and said, 'Narada, you know I can do much better than that!'" Michael turned to Kahane. "I wanna go," he said. "There's no way I'm gonna be able to sing like that." The agent had to talk him into staying. Franklin wanted to sing with him at the same mic; as the tape rolled, he stood opposite her, "just freaking out," he said, because she was "treating me like an equal." He wasn't impressed by the accompaniment, which sounded like routine eighties pop: twinkly synthesizer and a backbeat that pounded out a medium dance groove. But it didn't hold Franklin back. She plunged into the gravelly depths then swooped raspily to heaven. Her partner delivered breathy pillow talk, punctuated by growls and wails.

Michael's team waited for months for Franklin to become available to shoot the video; without it, the single could not be released. Finally, Michael, Andy Morahan, Mike Southon, and the rest of their group flew back to Detroit. A production meeting was held the night before the shoot. Everyone waited until well past the appointed time for Franklin to appear. At last she barreled in, accompanied by "the Reverend": her brother and manager, Cecil

Franklin, the replacement pastor for their late father, Reverend C.L. Franklin, at the New Bethel Baptist Church in Detroit. Her brother announced: "Hey, man, we've gotta make this quick—I've gotta go see the man about some blow!'" Shock flashed on Michael's face. Cecil—who died three years later of a heart attack—asked a few questions, then left. His sister stayed, and the meeting proceeded. About an hour later, Cecil returned "in a very different mood," said Southon. "He sat down and immediately fell asleep. That was our introduction to the world of Aretha Franklin."

At the shoot, she and Michael recaptured their spark. As the video opens, two hulks escort Michael down a dark passageway, en route to the Queen. Michael stands before a video screen that shows Franklin singing. He sings back to it. Cut to Franklin performing in front of a video image of Michael. Will they come together, the viewer wonders, or did they film separately? But unite they do, for a few joyous moments that show the mercurial diva clearly loving her company.

"I Knew You Were Waiting (for Me)" went into the can for a 1987 release. For now, Michael's former chapter needed closing. He and Ridgeley had planned a multi-act spectacle that would go on for hours. Michael scheduled weeks of rehearsals. According to the *Mirror*, Ridgeley was in France. Columnist John Blake quoted an unnamed friend of the duo's: "I don't suppose it matters whether he's there or not." Seventy-two thousand seats sold out in twelve hours. To appease four thousand of the shutouts, Wham! held a pop-up performance at Brixton Academy, where they had been rehearsing. The proceeds went to one of Michael's pet charities, Help a London Child, which gave cash assistance to needy youth. On the day of the Brixton show, "The Edge of Heaven" made No. 1. Onstage, Michael announced he would turn twenty-three at midnight. His fans sang "Happy Birthday," followed by an explosive cheer.

Two days later, the Wham! brigade made its way to Wembley. Blazing sunshine had pushed the temperature above a hundred degrees. Backstage, Wham!'s surprise guest, Elton John, had set up a mini-village, complete with a blowup swimming pool and barbecue. John had gifted Michael with a Reliant Robin, a small three-wheel car. "We just drove it around backstage all day," said Andros.

Outside, stewards hosed down the audience. Vendors stood behind stacks of Wham! souvenir programs, Wham! T-shirts, Wham! LPs, and

Wham! posters. To warm up the crowd, Gary Glitter, a bouffant-haired, Elvis-like glam rock star of the early seventies, reprised his old hits, followed by Nick Heyward, a New Romantic singer-songwriter.

After him, two giant video screens showed *Foreign Skies: Wham! in China.* As night fell, impatience for the real Wham! mounted. Behind a giant black curtain that read THE FINAL, the musicians got in place. "We were all a bit sad and wishing it would go on forever," said Danny Cummings. "I remember seeing Andrew looking rather glum. You weren't encouraged to ask penetrating questions."

The synth intro to "Everything She Wants" began, and so did the screaming. With a "ONE-TWO-THREE-FOUR!" from Michael, the curtain dropped. He strutted out, not with Andrew but with a pair of male dancers. After they had milked the applause for two minutes, out came Ridgeley, followed by Shirlie and Pepsi. If the girls, with their wedding-cake wigs and miniskirts, still looked like fugitives from a sixties girl group, the boys of Wham! had grown up. Ridgeley, in a long black cape, seemed like a combination of Dracula and Superman; Michael had donned his black-leather gear. He and Ridgeley strutted along catwalks that reached far into the crowd and basked in the shrieks.

But The Final was essentially a solo concert; Ridgeley moved his lips, but there was still no sign that his guitar was plugged in. On this night, wrote Antony Thorncroft in the *Financial Times*, Michael "finally managed to shake off Mr. Ridgeley, an old school chum who, for four years, has attached himself to Michael." The partners pushed every nostalgic button in their listeners' short memories. "All right, we're gonna go a *long* way back now," said Michael as they uncrated "Wham Rap!"—"composed in our friend Mr. Ridgeley's front room." With Shirlie and Pepsi dressed as cowgirls, they recreated their old *Saturday Superstore* choreography for "Young Guns." Michael led a sentimental singalong of "Last Christmas." Later, everyone left the stage except Michael and two musicians. The lights dimmed, and he sang "A Different Corner" quietly. A sea of lighters glowed in front of him.

Crew members wheeled out a white concert grand. "Would you please welcome . . . Mr. ELTON JOHN!" shouted Michael. His hero waddled out as Ronald McDonald, dressed in a red floppy wig, a red rubber nose, yellow overalls, and a red-and-white striped shirt. John Peel of the *Observer* called it "a doomed attempt to upstage the ebullient Michael"; but when John accompanied him on "Candle in the Wind," Michael had to hold back tears. After "Freedom," Wham! walked off, only to charge back out for five encores. Simon Le Bon, the lead singer of Duran Duran, joined Michael and John to sing "I'm Your Man." Finally, Michael and Ridgeley embraced "like two old comrades who know a war is finally over," wrote the *Mirror*. As fans filed out, fireworks lit the sky over Wembley.

For Jim White of the *Guardian*, Michael had given "the best pop performance I have ever seen. . . . He knew how to tease, how to flirt, how to exploit his moment shamelessly. There was no doubt in the minds of anyone who saw him that day: This was a star." Right after Wham! had first wowed twenty gay men at Bolts, Michael's ambitions had grown to the size of Wembley. In the *Times*, Julie Burchill called him "exactly the stuff that stars have always been made of: the oddball adolescent outsider with a lust for revenge and a desire to submerge the old, unloved self in a new giant-sized being."

After the show, he and Ridgeley, their friends, everyone connected with the performance, and the press convened at London's Hippodrome. That night the club looked like an enormous playpen; huge beach balls hung above the dance floor, and there were enough inflatable animals to stock a kiddie parade.

A month later, Ridgeley and Donya Fiorentino would visit Michael in Saint-Tropez; thereafter they maintained an amiable but mostly distant relationship. According to reports, Wham! had netted each of the partners about £12 million; Michael had earned an additional five from songwriting. Royalties from the four Wham! songs that bore Ridgeley's name, notably "Careless Whisper," would extend his windfall. But according to Simon Napier-Bell, Michael revised the royalty split on the song in his favor. "I couldn't understand that, because the credit would still say George and Andrew, and George didn't need the money. There was some underlying ego thing in George, maybe to prove that the song was more his than Andrew's."

• • •

Success had further complicated Michael's relationship with his father. The young man had disproven every word of Jack's discouragement; he had also threatened his ego by surpassing him. But for Jack, the situation had advantages. In 1986, he opened a new restaurant, Mr Jack's, in Edgware. Wham! fans knew who his son was, and droves of them turned up. Jack capitalized on their interest by playing Wham! records and naming a taramasalata (a vegetable and fish-roe dip) after his son. "My son is not a great salad lover," Jack told the *Mirror*. "He prefers the fattening things with sauces."

Jack acquired a racehorse, and, soon, an entire stud farm, paid for by George. With that, the power dynamics between them shifted radically. Speaking with the BBC's Chris Evans, Michael recalled how, even after Wham! had scored three hits, Jack "was telling me to save my money because it wasn't gonna last. Now my father says, thank you very much for my stud farm!"

For years, Lesley had dutifully echoed Jack's disapproval of their son's dreams; she now regretted it deeply and expressed her remorse for years. Michael forgave her. His sexuality remained unspoken—but "his mother always knew," said Deon Estus. Though sensing his conflict, she never pressured him to come out; instead, she lavished him with loving care, and he returned it. Whenever he made a new single or demo, he rushed to play it for her. He hoped to make her proud, and he did. "She was as sweet as could be, and just wanted him to be happy," said Rob Kahane.

In 1986, while visiting Los Angeles, Michael had his first of many conversations with Judy Wieder, a young music journalist. Wieder would later become editor of the *Advocate*, the national LGBT newsmagazine. But when she first met Michael, both were in the closet. "I suspect he knew I was gay," she said. "I didn't know he was gay, although many did." In future talks, they revealed themselves. "He was up against so many things," she recalled. "He didn't like the feeling of being dishonest with his audience. He was really lonely, and he'd been trying to explore being straight to be sure that he couldn't make life easier for himself. When you reach the end of that exploration you start to look for what's more appropriate for you, and hope that nobody makes it public."

CHAPTER SEVEN

BY NOVEMBER 1986, CBS WAS eager for Michael's first album under his own name. He informed Tony Russell that he wanted superstar contractual terms. Russell warned him that he wasn't yet a superstar, but Michael could not be dissuaded. An American solo breakthrough—the faster and bigger the better—was key to his plans; Columbia's U.S. division was the true seat of the company's power. For some time, Rob Kahane had been managing him on the sly; Kahane was itching to become his full-time manager, but he was contractually tied to Triad as an agent. At the end of the year, Kahane broke free. He partnered with a lawyer, Michael Lippman, to found Lippman Kahane Entertainment. On January 1, 1987, the company acquired Michael.

The singer was hell-bent on erasing his boy-band image, and his collaboration with Aretha Franklin helped. Released that month, "I Knew You Were Waiting (for Me)" became a top-ten hit in sixteen countries; in seven of them, including North America and the United Kingdom, it hit No. 1. The song gave Franklin her first No. 1 hit in the twenty years since "Respect." Freddie Mercury had no congratulations. "I'm mad that George Michael did a duet with her," he said. "I could have done it better!" Michael had since teamed with the rising R&B singer Jody Watley, formerly of the group Shalamar, on "Learn to Say No," which gave him an added dash of soul validation. Now he had to show people who *he* was, un-partnered—even if it meant devising a character as fictitious as the one he had played in Wham!.

Before starting his album, he did one of his best mates a favor. David Austin had become a client of Simon Napier-Bell, who had talked EMI into releasing an album with Austin—one that would bear the hot-button name of George Michael as producer. In 1984, Michael had loaned some of his prestige to his best mate by cowriting a single with him and providing backup vocals. The record, "Turn to Gold," rose only to No. 68, but now Michael had a song for Austin that showed more promise. "I Want Your Sex" was a page torn from Michael's growingly chaotic personal life. He had written it about Tony Garcia, a swarthy, curly-haired, handsome French playboy and occasional record producer with whom he had spent glamorous times in Saint-Tropez and elsewhere.

Although it was a largely unrequited crush, Michael took it seriously. He had fallen in love "for the very first time," he acknowledged later, and it banished any lingering doubt about his sexuality: "I knew I was gay, gay, gay." Garcia lived across the road from him in Saint-Tropez—the main reason Michael was spending so much time there. In Polaroids taken of them at Chez Nano, a local celebrity hotspot, Michael sits shoulder-to-shoulder with Garcia, gazing at him in bedazzlement. Nano habitués assumed that Garcia was Michael's boyfriend. In fact, he was the shiny toy that Michael "couldn't get to fuck . . . even though I knew he was fucking crazy about me."

That may have been wishful thinking, for Garcia knew his charms and how to wield them. Garcia acquired a home in Hampstead, Michael's London neighborhood, which only served to torture the singer more. He was "tired of waiting for this French guy," he said, and wrote "I Want Your Sex" out of frustration. Though intended for one unattainable man, it preached a broader message: "Sex is natural, sex is good / Not everybody does it / But everybody should." Controversy was assured.

Working on "I Want Your Sex" with Austin at SARM West, he sensed possibilities, as Napier-Bell soon learned. "David called me up in tears at three in the morning and said, 'George has just told me he's gonna take the song away from me—he wants to do it himself!' I said, 'Well, he can't. I'm your manager, and I shall tell George, and we have legal writing in the contract.' David said, 'No, no, no. I'm gonna let him have it.'"

"I Want Your Sex," he decided, would be his first post-Wham! solo single and the seed of the new album. Michael wanted no outside producer; he knew the sound he wanted, and it wasn't anything like Wham!. His head was exploding with musical influences; channeling them into catchy hooks was his second nature. And he knew the allure of his voice. But on this album, George Michael would grow up.

In February, he flew to Denmark. Michael had booked about two months at a high-tech hit factory, Puk Recording Studios, a residential oasis for pop stars such as Elton John and Depeche Mode, who had limitless budgets and no pressing deadlines. Puk stood on acres of rural land about an hour's drive from Denmark's second largest city, Aarhus. By necessity, Puk enabled its clients to live there; it offered four three-bedroom homes, a spa, a pool, a gym, and a restaurant.

Michael had brought most of his trusted musical family. By now it included Chris Porter, Paul Gomersall, Deon Estus, Paul Spong, and a new-comer, Chris Cameron, a funky and versatile keyboard player. He would serve as Michael's musical director on and off until 2012. But according to Peter Iversen, Puk's head engineer, this was a "one-man show," and the singer was "completely in charge. . . . He was a workaholic, and involved in everything." Michael knew his entire future depended on this album, and he worked on it with burning concentration each day, starting in the late morning and often continuing until past midnight.

No one perceived that he was feeling "massively unhappy and lonely," as he confessed later, due presumably to Tony Garcia. Obviously, Michael knew how to keep secrets. "He always had his headphones on, listening to music," said another new member of his team, trumpeter Steve Sidwell, whose relationship with the singer would span twenty-five years. Michael was hell-bent on stirring up controversy, and it would start with "I Want Your Sex." Spong knew him well enough not to mince words. "George," he said, "you can't call a song that. It's gonna be banned."

Michael said simply: "Yeah?"

"He knew what he was doing," said Spong. "He was a master at things like that." Michael had not forgotten that the song that had bumped "Wake Me Up Before You Go-Go" out of No. 1, Frankie Goes to Hollywood's "Relax," had zoomed to the top on the wings of a BBC ban—apparently from its suggestive repetitions of "come" and "shoot it."

More recently, Michael had snickered at a campaign by Tipper Gore, the wife of U.S. senator and future vice president Al Gore, to sanitize the music industry. As her husband took a traditional stance—including a rejection of homosexuality as "wrong"—Tipper joined with three other so-called "Washington wives" to found the Parents Music Resource Center, a watchdog organization that sought to shield children from obscenities in pop lyrics. Among the PMRC's "Filthy Fifteen" were "Darling Nikki," a Prince song about his one-night stand with a "sex fiend . . . masturbating with a magazine"; Sheena Easton's "Sugar Walls"; AC/DC's "Let Me Put My Love into You"; and Madonna's comparatively tame "Dress You Up."

Gore and her partners succeeded in having a warning stamp placed on all potentially offensive releases. But the effort backfired; it won the "taboo" songs huge publicity and made them almost irresistible to the young. Michael knew that his timing could not have been better.

He had worked out his approach to "I Want Your Sex" at the David Austin session, and he replicated it at Puk. Nothing was on paper. "George," asked Spong, "tell me how you've written this song. There's so much going on in it."

"It's in my head," said Michael.

"What's in your head?"

"The finished record is *in my head*. I can hear it. I can see it. All I'm doing is deconstructing what I see in my head."

The music was hardly deep, nor was it original. The archetype for that track and for much of Michael's emerging persona, was Prince, the gaunt, enigmatic, gender-bending, hyper-eroticized funk-rock star. "He manages to capture the compulsions of sex in his amazing unholy screams over a relentless beat," wrote Baz Bamigboye in the *Daily Mail*. Prince sang, composed, played multiple instruments, and produced his own records, giving him an autonomy that Michael sought to copy, just as he mimicked Prince's stubble and, later on, his aversion to publicity.

For "I Want Your Sex," Michael had borrowed the lo-fi sound of a recent Prince single, "Kiss," that used synthesizer and the clatter of a drum machine to heat up its blatantly sexual message: "I just need your body, baby / From dusk till dawn." Cameron played elementary keyboard lines while Estus added funky bass; a programmed drum loop kept a raunchy beat going. In recording, Michael preferred a drum machine to a drummer. "It was convenience, I think," said Danny Cummings, who added real-life percussion. "He liked the perfect tempo; he liked the controllable sound which you could go in and alter afterward."

The vocals were trickier, and they took many hours to record. Michael wanted to turn himself into a sex machine. By the time he'd finished, his heavily processed singing—true to the song's title—was stripped of sweetness and romance-free. It was robotic and menacing, full of growls, groans, and guttural outbursts of "OW!" and "HOO-wah!." His vocal sounded like a parody of porno-film sex, addressed to a "girl"—but no one at the sessions recalled any tongue-in-cheek in Michael's attitude. He had worked hard to analyze Prince's signature tapestry of background vocals, whose richness stemmed from a microscopic delay between vocal tracks. Michael kept Chris Porter working at it for hours: "I want it close—no, closer. No, not that close."

Prince's influence did not end there. On "Kiss," Michael's new idol had sped up his vocal to give it a female sound. He christened his electronic alterego Camille and cast her in numerous songs as a sexed-up but androgynous ghost. For "I Want Your Sex," Michael created his own Camille to sing with; they sounded like two frantic, twitchy figures on a dance floor.

Looking ahead to the twelve-inch extended-play version, he had spun the song into three parts: "Rhythm One: Lust," "Rhythm Two: Brass in Love," and "Rhythm Three: A Last Request." In the last one, the tempo eased so that Michael could purr some pillow talk about "sexy baby's . . . sexy body."

He moved on to the rest of the album. For this crucial solo debut, Michael showed up with no finished compositions besides "I Want Your Sex"—just ideas. Nurtured by his musicians and by painstaking experimentation in the studio, the songs took shape. To Michael, as Stephen Holden wrote in the *New York Times*, "songwriting, arranging, and producing are all indivisible parts of a process in which rhythmic groove, melody, texture, and message are developed more or less simultaneously." It was like assembling a jigsaw puzzle, and it could not be rushed. "I always imagined him in the laboratory with a white coat—his vocals, the production, the harmonies, they were so perfectly executed," said Boy George.

The first step in each song, said Cummings, was to create "a semicomplete musical backdrop that he could manipulate"; its purpose was "to trigger something in him so he could do what he did best, which was melody and lyrics." Sometimes Michael sang or played a phrase for his musicians, who vamped on it; often they did the same for him. He freely quoted other artists' songs; "Monkey" grew out of a riff he liked from "Relax." The process was not unlike sampling, in which hip-hop artists lift a small portion from an existing song, reprogram it, and rap over it.

In each case, Michael knew exactly what he liked, even if he couldn't always explain it. "Because of his shyness," explained Chris Cameron, "he was not great at communicating what he wanted. Over time we got to read him, to second-guess." He wanted nothing fancy. The album anticipated a future genre known alternately as bedroom pop and DIY (Do It Yourself): sparse, bare-bones music based on synthesizer and drum machine. Michael liked that style. Before he'd begun singing to them, most of the backgrounds sounded so bland, it was hard to imagine how magic could be spun out of them.

As he listened, however, ideas for lyrics rushed into his head. Seldom at this stage did he aim for the profound; he preferred something rhythmic and blunt. "George couldn't write lyrics unless he was moving," said Rob Kahane. "He needed to be in his car, a plane, or a train. He'd write part of the song, he'd go for a two-hour drive or more, and then come back and write a few more lyrics to the thing." In the recording booth, said Porter, "he would come in and start singing, whether or not the lyric was finished. We worked on it sometimes phrase by phrase, sometimes syllable by syllable."

At his first session with Michael, Chris Cameron sat at the keyboard, improvising. "I started playing some old Atlantic soul things that come from the church," he said. Michael stopped to listen. "Oh! I like that. Do that again."

Subsequently, at around two A.M., Porter and Gomersall sat in the control room, with Michael in the booth. The studio was darkened, as Michael preferred it to be when he sang. His only human accompaniment came from Estus and Cameron; a drum machine was programmed to play a slow, gospel-like backbeat. From out of the booth, "this thing came at us," said Gomersall. It was "One More Try," the album's big ballad, about that moment, he said, "when you've really had your guts ripped out by someone"—in this case, Tony Garcia. The two engineers heard a chilling wail in the night, flung to the heavens: "I'm looking out for angels / Just trying to find some peace." On a recurring phrase, "touch YOU," Michael soared up an octave, landing on the highest note he'd ever recorded. "It was one of those shivers-down-the-spine moments that you don't normally get with recording," said Gomersall. The lyric, about feeling lost and alone and crying out to a higher power for peace, spoke to the album's eventual title, *Faith*. Asked why he chose it, Michael said, "just because I think I've a renewed optimism that I lost during the last couple of years of Wham!."

At Puk, he kept bursting with ideas. Another song came together in about a week of painstaking trial and error. "Father Figure" used hypnotic

Middle- and Far-Eastern motifs, religious undertones, and veiled homo-eroticism to flesh out a tale of forbidden seduction. Michael cast himself as a priest-like seducer of someone younger, someone who might be "warm and naked at my side." The invitation had a strong hint of taboo: "I will be your father figure / Put your tiny hand in mine . . ."

Tension built from the opening bars, with a funereal synthesized organ and the metronomic cymbal sounds ticking away, everything bathed in churchlike echo. A keyboard suggested the undulating tone of a pungi, a snake-charmer's instrument. Michael played everything except the exotic, Japanese-sounding acoustic guitar, plucked by Hugh Burns. Singing over a hypnotically revolving pulse, Michael gave a vocal tour de force unimaginable in his Wham! days. He panted, pleaded, whispered, sighed, and finally burst into a thunderous shout to cajole his "sacred" love object into submitting.

Over the coming weeks, a growingly confident Michael bounced from style to style. "Hard Day" began with the hollow wail of what sounded like a Japanese bamboo flute; then it broke into slamming hip-hop. "DON'T BRING ME DOWN!" yowled Michael at a lover who was bugging him; in those four notes he jumped octaves twice. "Monkey" used stone-cold house music to frame a message of concern for Kathy. He explained later that she had taken "some drugs that I didn't know she took" with her pals; Michael was referring to Bret Witke and his boyfriend Chris Daggett. "We were the bad influence in her life, he thought," said Witke. The song warned: "Oh, I hate your friends / But I don't know how and I don't know when to open your eyes."

In "Hand to Mouth," the nouveau riche Michael took a slap at British life under Thatcher, whom he saw as coldly oblivious to the poor. The song, he said, had sprung from "the way our country is leaning towards American values in terms of welfare. . . . It's just a comment on how vicious it is. It leaves such a huge number of people who can't fend for themselves with no choice." Over a Latin beat, Michael told of "Jimmy-Got-Nothing"—a starving boy who goes on a killing spree—and a prostitute who dies, leaving a baby on a stoop. He cast himself as the third pauper: "With empty hands I pray / And I tell myself one day / They just might see me."

Rock didn't interest him much, but "Look at Your Hands," written with David Austin, was "the nearest thing to a rock 'n' roll song he ever did," said Danny Cummings, "and I played on it. He didn't like it." Michael may have included it as a favor to Austin—perhaps as a consolation prize for having taken "I Want Your Sex" away from him.

Back at SARM, Michael threw cocktail jazz into his album's grab bag of genres. Three years earlier, Alison Moyet, the blue-eyed-soul singer-songwriter, had revived the Billie Holiday trademark "That Ole Devil Called Love," which portrayed romance as a Pandora's box of danger and seduction. Moyet had belted it in her bluesy contralto while a big band echoed the mellow ballroom sound of the original. Michael loved Moyet's record, a No. 2 single in Britain; he wanted his own retro-jazz hit.

He showed up at SARM with a few fragments in his head. As Cameron played what he called "that beaten-up old piano in there," Michael sang a line: "You are far, when I could have been your star." He and Cameron threw lines and ideas back and forth until a song took shape. It evolved into "Kissing a Fool."

He sought out the man who had arranged Moyet's track: John Altman, the jazz saxophonist and bandleader who had worked with everyone from Jimi Hendrix to Chet Baker. As a teenager, Michael had sat on the steps of a pub in Edgware, listening to Altman's band rehearse and wishing he were in it. Now Altman was arranging for him. He gave "Kissing a Fool" an intimate, floating-on-air dance-floor sound. Michael sang in a breathy croon—not his usual style at all. For over twelve hours, Michael labored over his vocal; Altman didn't know why, for "each take sounded as good as the previous one."

Michael cranked up the reverb; it wrapped his voice in clouds of vapor. He also employed other processing that thickened and textured his already velvety sound. "Personally, I think a lot of it was insecurity," said Paul Spong, "and he was the last person who needed to feel insecure. Every time he opened his mouth it was correct."

In general, though, Michael's instincts astounded those around him. Michael had an idea for a rockabilly song in the style of early Elvis or Bo Diddley. One day at Puk he asked Hugh Burns if he'd brought his acoustic guitar. Burns didn't have one. Michael fished around the studio; all he found was "this horrible aluminum-body guitar," as Porter called it—not much better than a toy. Michael began strumming it with a rockabilly beat.

Out of that came "Faith," in which he chanted about shedding a cruel lover and holding out for the real thing.

Michael had Burns overdub himself into a whole band of Bo Diddleys; a simulated tambourine took the song to church. Dancing above the rhythm was a chorus of grunting, breathy George Michaels, all of them echoing the beat he had played on that junk guitar.

"Faith" he decided, would be the album's crucial opening track, the first one deejays and critics would hear. He set it up with a grand display of mock-saintliness. At SARM, Cameron sat at a Yamaha DX7, the first digital synthesizer, which could emulate all sorts of instruments. Switching some controls, he set down his hands on the keys; out came the sound of a thundering cathedral organ. "I remember George chuckling," he said. What fun it would be, Michael thought, to have that sacred pomp fade into a non-churchy message: "I guess it would be nice if I could touch your body . . ."

• • •

On April 3, 1987, near the end of recording *Faith*, Michael stepped onto a stage for the first time since Wham!. Pasteur Institute, the French biomedical research center that had isolated HIV in 1983, had declared an International AIDS Day. Wembley Arena hosted a gala concert, the Stand by Me AIDS Day Benefit.

Michael was asked to perform. Given what he had to hide, he might well have declined, as did many celebrities who feared any connection with the most stigmatized disease in history. Yet he was among the first to say yes. "George Michael, by setting such a wonderful example, has really made a lot of difference," said a spokesman for the event. Boy George and Frankie Goes to Hollywood's Holly Johnson agreed to appear for the first time without the bands that had made them famous. Then Elton John signed on—and the concert could boast the four biggest gay stars in British pop. Of them, only Michael remained professionally in the closet.

He stepped onstage in an Andrew Ridgeley-style black waistcoat. Since the show was subtitled The Party, he hauled out a frothy dance hit from 1965, "1-2-3," by Len Barry, a Motown-loving soul boy. Standing alone at last, he was scared, and let Deon Estus play and sing for almost half the song. From there Michael acknowledged the evening's cause with "Love's in Need of Love Today" ("Hate's goin' 'round, breakin' many hearts / Stop it, please.")

Then came the moment that explained his choice of outfit. Michael began singing "Everything She Wants." Suddenly he announced: "Ladies and gentlemen, Mr. Andrew Ridgeley!" Out came his ex-partner in one of Michael's preferred looks, a white T-shirt and faded jeans. The audience, said the *Daily Mail*, was "ecstatic"—and for a few minutes, Michael seemed complete again.

His other duet, with Boy George, was closer to oil and water. Perhaps to be a good sport, Michael joined his nemesis on the Culture Club hit, "That's the Way (I'm Only Trying to Help You)." "I was standing with them backstage as they were working it out," said Chris Heath. "It was weird, because they had such an awkward rapport." They ended the performance with an embrace, but the duet was conspicuously absent from the home-video release of the show. Later they reunited to record Boy George's "Freedom," written after the Wham! song of the same name had become a hit. "He wasn't happy with it," said Boy George ruefully, "so it was never ever released."

• • •

"I Want Your Sex" would come out on June 1, and the advance publicity rolled forth with symphonic precision. Word went out to columnists, who dutifully published it; the title alone made good copy. Michael Lippman and Rob Kahane had scored a coup by getting "I Want Your Sex" onto the soundtrack of what was sure to be one of the summer's hottest films, *Beverly Hills Cop II*. But one unwelcome question was sure to arise: Whose sex did Michael want? On the back of the sleeve, he had printed a message intended for Tony Garcia: "This record is dedicated to my hopeless conquest." Anyone who read it would be curious. Michael had to build a smokescreen.

The video, shot in the weeks before the single's release, sought to make it clear that he wanted the sex of only Kathy Jeung, who would costar. To assist, he called back Andy Morahan and his videographer, Mike Southon. Visually, Michael tried to evoke the sexual pas de deux in Prince's "Kiss" video, where the singer and a model cavorted seminaked on a mostly bare set. But where "Kiss" seemed semicomedic—Prince wore lipstick and a bare-midriff top and seemed to be playing Camille, while a guitar-playing woman in lipstick-lesbian garb rolled her eyes at his sashaying—"I Want Your Sex" is dead serious and verges on glamorous but campy soft-core porn. A couple writhes beneath a huge blue satin sheet on a bed; Jeung's fingers, with blood-red nails, slip out. Wearing lingerie and a short platinum wig, she makes smoldering glances at the camera. Michael ties a scarlet blindfold around her eyes and lip-synchs into her ear: "Don't you think it's time you had sex with me?"

The camera pulls in on Michael as he and Jeung, both nude, sit on a crumpled white satin sheet. More fleeting nudity is sprinkled throughout the video, but a Spanish model handled some of Jeung's racier shots—and as Michael would later reveal, the naked man wasn't him, but a buff substitute. "I'm afraid that my body is nowhere near as good as that," he confessed.

Michael wanted to push things as far into R-rated territory as he could. "George knew the furor this was gonna cause," said Southon. "MTV in that period was like network American television in terms of what you could or couldn't show or imply. It was an incredibly conservative channel."

The singer had anticipated one possible danger. With the AIDS threat at its peak, he knew he had to add a conscientious touch. He did so as suggestively as possible: On camera, he writes EXPLORE on Jeung's thigh and MONOGAMY across her back in red lipstick. This was Michael's idea, as Morahan stressed in Craig Marks and Rob Tannenbaum's book *I Want My MTV*. "Personally, I find the blindfold and lipstick to be embarrassing—it was a bit obvious, even at the time—but George was exploring the boundaries of what he could get away with." Still, John Diaz, who produced some of Morahan's other music videos, gave the director strong credit: "Andy Morahan made a man out of George Michael. George never exuded any, um, manhood prior to working with Andy." The director, said Diaz, "toughened him up, make him a ladies' man." As always, Michael took a firm and meticulous hand in the editing.

By the end, he had contrived a new George Michael—one that he hoped the world would believe.

• • •

On May 20, 1987, *Beverly Hills Cop II* opened throughout America. Midway through the film, as two detectives (played by Eddie Murphy and John Ashton) infiltrate a strip club full of naked women, George Michael is heard panting "I Want Your Sex." Despite mixed reviews, the film was a hit, and its all-star soundtrack album bolted to No. 1. Columbia released "I Want Your Sex" as a single on June 1. Michael, wrote Cliff Radel of *Gannett*, was a "nervy little twerp," his record "just another neo-disco concoction." Other reviewers smirked at the title: Who would say, "I want *your* sex"?

Trevor Dann, the head of BBC Radio 1, the music channel, deemed "I Want Your Sex" a cheap grab for attention. Many at the network, he said, considered it a piece of fluff. "I remember that producers who were under pressure to ban the song would say, 'It's not worth fighting for; it's not very good.'" But that didn't stop the BBC from taking the moral high ground. "At a time when we are trying to help fight AIDS," declared a spokesman, Michael's single "tries to encourage sex."

Within days, the BBC had blocked "I Want Your Sex" from airplay before nine P.M. Many American stations banned it outright. Local newspapers published letters by appalled listeners. Michael's song, wrote one protester, was the sort of thing that led to "child sexual molestation, spouse abuse, child abuse, child pornography, teenage pregnancy, abortion, and suicide among our youth." Christian churches petitioned to yank the song off the radio. "We feel it encourages sexual behavior in our youth," argued one representative. The scandalized editors of Kentucky's *Paducah Sun* printed some of the words; an angry reader responded: "Of course they are offensive to any God-fearing Christian—do you read your Bible? . . . I pray God will forgive the *Sun* for contributing to the immorality in our nation today."

Even Barry White, whose testicular bass had filled the seventies airwaves with soulful hymns to making love, called the song "blatant" and "vulgar." Added White: "I would never say to a lady 'I want your sex.' I always tried to use class and be a gentleman."

Michael admitted: "I'll be perfectly honest. I was expecting the BBC to ban it." Somewhat disingenuously, given his avowed goal to ruffle feathers, he balked at the outrage "I Want Your Sex" had caused in the States. "I thought Americans were more liberal than we were," he said. "Considering all the sexual innuendo on radio and television, the whole fuss over this one song strikes me as rather hypocritical."

Such quibbles paled against a separate complaint. Sex was now synonymous with sickness and death, and many denounced Michael for crassly exploiting a global tragedy. Cliff Richard, the British Elvis of the 1950s and later a born-again though closeted Christian, scorned Michael's single. "I find that an irresponsible title," he declared. "With all the TV publicity trying to get people to be serious about AIDS, suddenly there was this."

Michael had worked out a response. Before the record had gone on sale he told a reporter: " 'I Want Your Sex' is about attaching lust to love, not just to strangers." Safe-sex campaigns, he said, had ignored the safest sex there was: monogamy. "Kids aren't going to *stop* having sex," he told Chris Heath. "There's a backlash against AIDS being the *end* of sex, and if my single is part of that then that's a good thing. There hasn't been enough emphasis on the strength and safety of monogamous relationships. . . . Sex is not the public enemy. Promiscuity is."

The problem was that nothing in the lyrics made that message clear. The line that came closest—"Sex is best when it's one-on-one"—proved too murky to make an impact. In the first half of 1987, other songs on the subject had driven the point home. Motown singer Carrie McDowell had scored an unlikely dance hit: "Uh Uh, No No Casual Sex." Abstinence was the theme of Janet Jackson's demure "Let's Wait Awhile," which reached No. 2. Rapper Kool Moe Dee did not mince words. In "Go See the Doctor," he declared: "I don't wanna do the sick sick dance / So I'm keeping my prick inside my pants." Now here was George Michael, urging the youthful masses to hit the sheets.

Unwilling to miss out on a rising hit, a San Francisco radio station edited in the word "safe" before "sex." Atlanta's WZGC-FM replaced "sex" with "love," snipped from elsewhere on the record. According to J.D. Considine of the *Baltimore Sun*, Columbia acquired a copy of the station's edit and offered it to interested stations.

Michael was furious. "In no way, shape, or form would George endorse any edit like that," announced Rob Kahane in the *Los Angeles Times*. MTV incensed them further by holding up the premiere of the video, whose EXPLORE MONOGAMY shot might have bolstered Michael's defense. Nudity, not safe-sex concerns, had tripped up MTV's censors. The network "suggested" cuts; Michael conceded only to some. Two re-edits were rejected. According to the *Los Angeles Times*, an addition was made "per the channel's orders." At the start of the video, Michael could now be seen speaking in shadowy close-up. "In the past there were arguments for and against casual sex," he intones. "Then it was a question of morality. These days, it *can* be a question of life or death. It's as simple as that. And this song is *not*"—he shakes his head—"about casual sex." At the end, the words EXPLORE MONOGAMY appear on a blank screen.

To have to do all this galled him. He tried insisting that he had "started writing the song before the public scare about AIDS," which was far from true. Years later he told Richard Smith and Steve Pafford of London's *Gay Times*: "I didn't have the courage of my convictions, did I? I needed to put something in to pacify the AIDS hysteria." Michael released all three parts of "I Want Your Sex" on a twelve-inch "Monogamy Mix," as he called it. To "accommodate" his "actual current long-term relationship" with Kathy, said Michael, he had added the quizzical phrases, "now that we're friends" and "we've waited so long."

On June 18, at eight P.M., the video made its much-hyped MTV premiere. (The channel had banned it from broadcast before seven.) Chris Willman of the *Los Angeles Times* didn't buy its "contrived gyrations," nor its opening disclaimer. "The message that comes across as he blindfolds his one-and-only is more like: 'Explore Monogamy If You Have a Beautiful Model for a Girlfriend Who Will Wear Different Wigs So You Can At Least Pretend You're Sleeping with Half the Western World.'" To Michael, Willman added, AIDS was "just another selling hook."

Soon, however, none of the complaints seemed to matter. "I Want Your Sex," boasted Michael Lippman, had "snowballed beyond our wildest dreams. The more radio stations refused to play it, the more people talked about it." No. 1 eluded it—"I Want Your Sex" reached No. 3 in the United Kingdom and No. 2 in the United States—but the disc eventually went platinum. "No doubt a few of those American sales came from Tipper Gore's efforts," noted Michael.

•••

With *Faith* on its way, Michael still felt he had some explaining to do. He booked an appearance on *The Last Resort with Jonathan Ross*, the United Kingdom's new late-night talk show hit. Its collegiate-looking host, then twenty-seven, faced an impeccably tailored and poised George Michael, with a snow-white smile. But as he sought to justify "I Want Your Sex" while sidestepping the minefield of his sexuality, Michael got tangled in a mass of half-truths and evasions. He couldn't tell Ross about Tony Garcia; instead, he reiterated that it was "fairly obvious" he had written the song "from the point of view of someone who's in a relationship with one person." Somewhat confusingly, he noted: "I'm not planning on getting married."

Conversation drifted to the tabloid press, who, he said, seemed "hell-bent on ruining me." Ross asked Michael if personal questions bothered him. "I get annoyed when people go past a certain point," he said calmly.

The host crossed it. Had Michael had an AIDS test? Looking downward, he admitted he hadn't. Stammering, he said he didn't need to; he had not been promiscuous since his "unselective" days "a long way back." Ross pressed on. "Did you used to use a condom when you were unselective? Do you use one now?" Michael laughed nervously. Yes, he claimed; he did. It would not be the last time someone asked him those questions.

Jeff Davis, a columnist for the *Press & Sun-Bulletin* in Binghamton, New York, wanted to know what all the fuss over Michael's video was about. He arranged a viewing with three local high-school boys, all sixteen. "That places them near the bull's-eye of MTV's target audience," Davis wrote, although they were hardly typical George Michael fans. They sat before the TV and watched him "singing, gyrating, and generally emoting over a fairly standard dance rhythm track," wrote Davis, whose eyes went elsewhere. "She is an extremely good-looking woman," he observed. Replied one of the boys: "You mean George Michael?"

"From what we had read," concluded Davis, "'I Want Your Sex' is supposed to impress upon us the virtues of 'safe sex' and monogamy. But the panel was not convinced. 'I wasn't impressed,' said Larry, reaching for the remote control. 'Neither was I,' said Dan, heading for the door. 'I was disappointed, actually,' Larry added."

In the end, so was Michael. "Musically," he said of his second-place hit, "it was a rather limp attempt to do a Prince." But success, he held, had placed him fully in charge of his life. "I'm very free," he told Jonathan Ross. "I have the freedom to go where I like and do what I like." For a closeted man, however, he had set himself a dangerous trap: He wanted to titillate with sex *and* keep his secrets untouched.

CHAPTER EIGHT

THE GEORGE MICHAEL KNOWN to his friends was funny, talkative, and loyal. He had keen perception and relentless drive. But his fears were growing. "When George left Wham! and did 'I Want Your Sex,' I think that's when everything changed," said Bret Witke, whom Michael had apparently forgiven for his perceived bad influence on Kathy Jeung. "He was on his own. He was getting bigger and bigger. The videos got better; everything got stepped up. He was afraid of all of it. The gay thing was hard for him, really hard. He didn't want anybody to know. Kathy was his beard."

The "I Want Your Sex" video had made her famous; she was often mobbed when they went out in public. True to plan, Michael had bolstered the myth of their affair. Jeung knew her role, and the two of them kept up appearances. Kahane still believed Michael was straight, and asked no questions. "I didn't want to know," Kahane said, "because I did not want to lie." A few pals who hung out in Michael's hotel suites after shows saw him and Jeung disappear behind the bedroom door when it was time to sleep. "But they had adjoining rooms," said Phil Lobel, who would soon handle Michael's tour publicity, a job that consisted mainly of turning requests down.

Jeung was doing her best to ignore the truth; Michael encouraged her by claiming he was bisexual. The affair was "basically fucked-up," said Michael to Adam Mattera. "But I was E'd off my tits half the time," he said—a reference to Ecstasy.

He could at least give her gifts in compensation. For her birthday, he offered her the car of her choice. "She was like, 'Do I get the BMW or something else?'" recalled Witke. "I was like, 'Get the BMW!' She got a Toyota because she didn't want him to spend that much money." The car was bright red, like the lipstick and blindfold in the video, and the license plate read IWANTYOURSEX.

Keeping his secret involved carefully screening his social circle. In Los Angeles, his companions were typically Jeung, Witke, and Chris Daggett. "He didn't want any other people around," said Witke. "We would go to restaurants and book pretty much the whole restaurant just to have dinner. His social skills were fine but he was afraid of crowds. We had some great laughs, but never for any length of time. He was kind of charming and sweet, but not too much came out of him. He would listen. He was so fearful of anybody finding out about anything. I think his whole life was based on that fear, and I think he never reconciled it. There was also a lot of anger in him. He would see us, and we were doing what we wanted to do, and in his mind he couldn't."

In time, Michael opened up to Witke. He would sometimes show up in the middle of the night at his apartment "just to hang out. He did *not* like to be alone."

Michael often went with Jeung to Boys & Girls, the small but trendy dance club that Witke and Daggett had started in Hollywood. But Michael did not mix. "He would be hidden in a corner with Kathy or in the kitchen," said Witke. One striking exception occurred at a Christmas party at the club. The two partners had decorated Boys & Girls with dolls that evoked the baby Jesus. Daggett took a Polaroid of Kathy and George holding one of them like proud new parents. The photo showed Michael looking genuinely happy; the love they had for each other was undeniable. "He was like a little kid playing," said Witke.

Career-wise, he had boundless bravado. Certain that his album would reach No. 1, Michael instructed Tony Russell to have CBS sweeten the terms of his 1984 contract. The company had no obligation to do so, but it was important to keep its moneymakers happy. Rob Kahane had nurtured a friendship with Walter Yetnikoff, president of CBS Records; now he could take his requests straight to the top. Yetnikoff was glad to help. "He thought George was gonna be the biggest star on the label," said Kahane. "He used to say, 'He's gonna be bigger than Springsteen, he's gonna be as big or bigger than Michael Jackson.'"

When Kahane mentioned wanting to hire an American lawyer for the renegotiation, Yetnikoff all but insisted he use one of two that he preferred. Michael chose Allen Grubman, whom Beth Landman and Alex Williams of *New York* magazine termed "the industry's sole superpower attorney" as well as "a man of almost cartoonish crudeness." If the ethics of Yetnikoff's referral seemed dubious, this was nothing new. "Grubman has often played both sides of the fence, representing a Sony artist like Springsteen while simultaneously representing Sony," wrote Landman and Williams. "Miraculously, both sides will come out happy (except Billy Joel, who had a nasty legal dispute with Grubman over just such an issue)."

Thus began a months-long battle whose many participants, in the end, would profit dearly. In the middle of it was Michael, the new golden goose. British stardom didn't concern him; he already had that. His overwhelming goal, he declared, was "to become as big in America as I am in the rest of the world. . . . I want to know that *everyone* knows my stuff." He burned to make himself "a star of the proportion of Madonna, Bruce Springsteen, and Prince. And I believe that's just about to happen."

Michael had wanted no interference from his label in the creation of *Faith*, and they didn't exert any. But Paul Russell advised that it was in Michael's best interest for the New York executives to hear more of the album than "I Want Your Sex." Joined by Dick Leahy, Michael dropped in on Columbia's president, Al Teller, and played him some tracks. The move worked: Teller raved that the album was sure to be a smash. Now Michael was much more likely to cash in at the negotiating table.

As he completed *Faith*, both sides began the discussions. In Wham!'s 1984 contract—the reference point for the new one—the duo had signed on to make one album, with options for another five. (CBS held the right to exercise or decline those options.) Tony Russell and Allen Grubman agreed: In order to pry superstar money from the company, they had to promise more product. Russell proposed offering four albums, with options for four more. He asked a £6 million advance for the first album (*Faith*) and £2 million for each one thereafter; he also demanded a 22 percent royalty per unit sold in the United Kingdom and the United States—nearly double the norm, and higher than even the 20 percent Michael Jackson was receiving. Russell later explained that he had calculated these numbers based on the assumption that *Faith* would sell at least ten million copies.

CBS found the proposal absurd, but Russell wouldn't budge. It was decided to delay the renegotiation until after the release of *Faith*, when the company would have a clearer sense of Michael's worth.

The singer's confidence got everyone excited; he knew he could use it to get what he wanted from people. Columbia staffers grew used to seeing him walk through the corridors, smiling. "George always showed up in a suit, impeccably dressed," said marketing director Jane Berk. "They'd roll out the red carpet. Walter Yetnikoff would want to see him. George was very businesslike and extremely polite. He had some really good ideas."

Plans were made to fly him by private jet (or sometimes the Concorde) to key cities to do advance promotion. On July 6, 1987, he attended an international CBS sales convention in Vancouver, Canada. Tracks from *Faith* were played. "We were all completely blown away," said Dave Novik, who had left British CBS to become head of A&R at CBS Australia. "From the moment it started it was clear that it was a very good song record, but a great production record, developed in a new style. It sounded different than everything else: his ability to create very percussive music with the acoustic guitar, the way he was using the keyboard sounds, the style of the drums or programming. In other records of the era there was much more emphasis on a big-sounding, thick, snapping snare-drum sound, whereas *Faith* sounded much more subtle in that sense. It was a perfectly crafted record. He had produced it himself, working with engineers. He had every aspect of it down creatively. Everybody realized that George had major talent."

Marketing teams excitedly realized that *Faith* would fit all over the radio dial. "I'm gonna milk this album for everything," Michael said. He planned to have most of the tracks released as singles—"because I couldn't bear for them just to be album tracks."

He knew that most if not all of them would hit No. 1. But this album was his ultimate soul/R&B statement, and he wanted to be welcomed onto the same pedestal as Smokey and Stevie. After all, he reasoned, he had recorded rap before almost anyone. Wonder had sung with him; so had Aretha. Michael had played the Apollo. But he wasn't just looking for respect. In 1976, Elton John's "Bennie and the Jets" had made No. 15 on the *Billboard* Hot Soul Singles chart. "I Need Your Lovin'," by Motown artist Teena Marie—known as the Ivory Queen of Soul—had made No. 9 on the same chart, which by then had been retitled Hot Black Singles. Madonna and Hall & Oates had also made its Top 10. Style, not skin color, determined inclusion—a fact that so far had escaped much resistance.

Michael was no stranger to that chart. "Everything She Wants" had gone to No. 12 there, "Careless Whisper" to No. 8, the Franklin duet to

No. 1. Now he wanted to surpass Elton John's old achievement and top not only Hot Black Singles but Top Black Albums. The names of those charts rankled him. *Faith*, he felt, was as soulful as anything on them. He flew to New York and enlisted the help of Columbia's radio and promotion people. "I've been accused of being just an impersonator for so long," he said. His new sound, he felt, needed a radical change of image. What he came up with was one of the most dramatic visual self-recreations in pop history, a rejection of almost everything his critics thought him to be.

●●●

On a trip to Los Angeles, Michael began work on the video for "Faith," which he had picked as the album's first single. It would show him dancing alongside a jukebox against a plain white background. A stylist brought in some sample wardrobe items. He liked none of them. In his mind was the black leather bomber jacket he'd worn on *Top of the Pops* just before Wham!'s breakup. Emblazoned on its back were the words ROCKER'S REVENGE in Gothic type (a reference to Rockers, a 1950s British motorcycle gang) and BSA (Birmingham Small Arms), a brand of motorcycle. Michael set out to build on that look. He and Andy Morahan drove down Melrose Avenue, where they passed an array of clothing shops that stressed punk, biker, and vintage. At Leathers and Treasures, Michael picked up metal tips and heel plates to dress up cowboy boots. From King's Western Wear in the town of Van Nuys, Michael chose silver belt-buckles and weathered-looking, button-fly Levi's jeans. His purchases also included aviator sunglasses and a dangling crucifix earring, which Madonna had worn. At a pawnshop, he bought an old acoustic guitar.

He had toyed with this Elvis-style look in Wham!'s early days; Mick Brown of the *Sunday Times* called it "a middle-class, north London boy's idea of the iconography of macho cool." Added Bret Witke: "It was a straight-guy image in his mind." Instinctively, he knew it was right for *Faith*, even if it embarrassed him slightly. For the "Faith" video, he wound up hanging strands of pearls from the left shoulder of the jacket. "I somehow wanted to make people understand that I wasn't stupid enough to think I was butch," said Michael years later.

They understood the opposite, thanks in part to the stiletto-heeled model posed against the other side of the jukebox. Below camera range, Michael stands on a turntable. As it revolves slowly, the camera pulls in for a tight closeup of his behind. That image defined him for years to come.

So did the album cover, which shows Michael shirtless in his shiny black, silver-zippered jacket. His nose points toward his armpit and a tuft of chest hair; his eye becomes a black cavern. But the focus of the picture is his fist, which clutches his collar as the crucifix earring dangles above it.

For Michael, "that strange picture where I look like I'm smelling my armpit" gave the perfect touch of sacrilege to an album called *Faith*. Michael had chosen an image that was full of encoded signaling—classic macho on the surface, but homoerotic for anyone in the know. "He was probably consciously or unconsciously testing what would people accept," said his journalist friend Judy Wieder. "He was sending up balloons, as we used to say back then." Jane Berk was puzzled. "I said, 'What does it mean? Don't people want a gorgeous pic of George?' But I think George liked the mystery of it all."

The videos, then in production, further heterosexualized his image. In "Father Figure," which was shot in downtown Los Angeles, Michael played a taxi driver who picks up a forlorn, distracted model. Having gazed at her in longing, Michael broods at the wheel, exhaling clouds of cigarette smoke. He takes her home to his tiny room, where they wind up in bed following prolonged kissing and shedding of clothes.

The part of the model went to a real-life one: twenty-one-year-old Tania Coleridge. In an interview with Marc Tyler Nobleman, she recalled Michael as "a very intelligent, witty dude," but a man who was struggling with a lie. "He was clearly gay to me," said Coleridge. "I remember it being quite tricky for him but we got through it. . . . I had to say, 'George, just kiss me properly so we can get out of here!'"

Michael had still managed to fool nearly everyone. "If you said to somebody, George Michael is gay, they'd say, you're out of your mind," recalled Witke. In time, many would conclude that his record company had pressured him to stay closeted; Michael himself admitted that wasn't true. "It never came up in any conversation that I had about George or Wham!" said Columbia A&R manager Howard Thompson.

Before the release of *Faith*, an interviewer asked Michael about the rising tide of rumors over his sexuality. His answer came closer to the truth than anything he had thus revealed. "If I turn around tomorrow and say, 'Oh, I'm gay,' and everyone that has been saying it for the last five years had been right all along, there's no doubt it would have a huge effect on my career."

Elton John had felt the same way, but in 1988 he would end his four-year marriage to a woman; four years later he came out as gay and never looked back. A year younger than Michael and far less fearful was Andy Bell, half of the New Wave duo Erasure, a British Top 40 fixture starting in 1986. A blond, flamboyant gay-boy-next-door, he made his announcement just as Erasure was scoring its breakthrough hit, "Sometimes." He discussed his sexuality briefly in an interview with the British magazine *Melody Maker*: "I don't want to go out of my way to talk about it but I'm not going to pretend I'm not." In what seemed like a dig at Michael, he declared: "I won't portray a heterosexual in videos."

But Michael didn't wish to be labeled a gay pop star; he wanted to seduce everyone. "I'm sure that George thought, if I'm not pegged as either gay or straight then everybody's interested in me," said Michael Pagnotta, his nineties press agent. "Those young girls that are the pop record buyers, they're the radio listeners. When you're singing a love song they want to think it's about them."

Almost every week, the tabloids continued to regale readers with tales about Michael's heterosexual affairs—"none true, obviously," said Rob Kahane. Even with Jeung still in the picture, those items paired Michael with a staggering array of gorgeous women, including French socialite Helen Tennant and models Gail Lawson and Kay Beckenham. According to John Blake of the *Daily Mail*, Michael was currently "on the town" with his "beautiful, new girlfriend, June Montanna, who sings with the band Brilliant." Michael, wrote another columnist, had been spied at his favorite London nightclub, Browns, "with a French girl by his side by the name of Babette." (That was Tony Garcia's sister, who looked after Michael's home in Saint-Tropez.) The *Daily Mail's* Garry Jenkins noted the "reported" romance between Michael and Fawn Hall, the former secretary to U.S. Lieutenant Colonel Oliver North and an accessory to one of the biggest political scandals of the eighties, the Iran-Contra affair. She and Michael had done little more than talk at a party.

In public, sometimes the truth was clear. Michael loved dancing in nightclubs, especially under the influence of Ecstasy, which eased inhibitions and made the user feel very affectionate—a perfect disco drug. But he could not be seen getting intimate in public with the wrong people. In a 1998 essay in the *Guardian*, columnist Jim White recalled spotting the singer in a club. With him, White wrote, was a woman who "appeared to have been mail-ordered from a perfection catalogue." They danced next to White and his companion, a man. "George moved in the most fluid way I've ever seen," White said. "But it was blindingly obvious as they gyrated around, never getting close, that there was no chemistry whatsoever between him and his partner. Indeed, he could barely keep his eyes off my mate. A couple of days later, there were the inevitable pictures in the papers of George snapped with a mystery girlfriend. These were shots he had presumably engineered, in order to maintain a veneer of heterosexuality which was assumed to be vital in preserving his fan base. Seeing those snaps, I couldn't help feeling sorry for the bloke, trapped by his role, obliged to hire a fake girlfriend just to enjoy a night's dancing and so uncertain of his appeal, he thought he'd lose everything if the fans found out the truth."

Slowly, Michael was coming out to a few more people in his innermost circle—ones he trusted not to breathe a word. Michael had delayed telling Andros; such was his talent for hiding things that his lifelong friend had not guessed, despite two years of swirling rumors. But one day Michael took him to lunch. The singer seemed uncomfortable; wine flowed until both men were drunk. Finally, Michael made his admission.

"I was stunned," recalled Andros. "Why hadn't he told me before?" Michael, he said, "poured his heart out. . . . He had tears in his eyes."

But in interviews, he maintained his pose. Asked if he planned to marry, he answered that he hadn't "met that person" who would make him want to settle down. Yet he continued to utilize Kathy Jeung. "One More Try," he explained, was "about my attitude coming out of my last relationship"—he let the press assume he meant Pat Fernandes—"and into this new one, when I was pretty unwilling to be open to anything." Fear of AIDS, he said, had caused him to narrow his sex life just to her. "These days it can be a matter of life and death," he noted.

•••

For Michael, so was the success of *Faith*. With this album, said Danny Cummings, "he had arrived at a new chapter. He showed diversity, he showed maturity. It was the making of him as a solo artist, exactly what he had hoped for."

On November 2, 1987, *Faith* was released. In a market rife with the blare of heavy metal, the brutish anti-melodicism of rap, and the overripe production and romantic platitudes of such power-ballad divas as Whitney Houston, *Faith* fit no category. In the *New York Times*, Stephen Holden handed him a crown and scepter. "At twenty-four, Michael is the most talented heir to the tradition of pop craft that embraces Paul McCartney, Elton John and the Bee Gees. He has the golden touch. . . . If asked to nominate the one contemporary pop star most likely to be as successful ten years from now as today, I'd cast my vote for George Michael." Paul Grein of *Rolling Stone* called *Faith* "a startling state-of-the-art dance album."

But many of the reviews, including some of the raves, reconfirmed the sense that Michael was no original. *Rolling Stone* writer Mark Coleman wrote about *Faith* in code words that signaled a borrower at work. He called Michael "one of pop music's leading artisans, a painstaking craftsman who combines a graceful knack for vocal hooks with an uncanny ability to ransack the past for musical ideas and still sound fresh. . . . It would be easy to dub George Michael the Elton John of the eighties."

Tom Moon of the *Philadelphia Inquirer* was more blunt. He called *Faith* "a collection of cocky 'I can do that!' derivations. . . . Forced to use one phrase to describe *Faith*, it probably would be 'influenced by Prince.'" To the *Daily Mail*'s Marcus Berkmann, *Faith* was "less of a coherent album than a '32 flavours' sampler for what he can do." Berkmann smirked at the cover, "which shows George edging his nose under his leather jacket and inhaling deeply from his no-doubt fragrant right armpit."

Saxophonist Dave Bitelli, who would play with Michael in years ahead, had his own qualms. "George was in awe of R&B," he said. "You can see that in clips of him with Stevie Wonder. He does well. Yet he never allowed that freedom or danger into his own work. Everything was nailed down. His music remained pop, and pop music does not take you to the same transcendent state that you achieve with African-based music." Michael read the reviews, fixating on the less flattering lines and taking them all personally. He fumed when the *Independent*'s Dave Hill called him "a pastiche songwriter" and when Robert Hilburn, in a long and largely complimentary *Los Angeles Times* profile, declared that his music had "an anonymous quality."

Michael responded by breaking a cardinal pact between artists and their critics: He spoke out bitterly. *Faith*, he declared, was a "work of genius" and "close to perfection," adding: "Critics are nobodies with absolutely no right to use their position to put forward their own personal prejudices. . . . I spent over a year working like hell to get a brilliant album out, and then some unknown critic spends less than ten minutes racing through the tracks." Speaking with Adrian Deevoy, Michael sounded less angry than hurt. "I resent the fact that people think my songwriting is contrived and calculated," he said. "Sure, you draw on influences but that's more often than not a subconscious process. Everybody does it."

He wanted the glory, the sales, *and* the respect. Prince had them; so did Elton and Paul. But his confidence stayed firm: "I really think that anyone who doesn't like anything on my new album has no right to say they like pop music."

Michael had chosen the order and approximate release dates of the singles; the title song was first. Released on October 12, it began lurching up the Hot 100: 54, 37, 27, 19. But was it strong enough to hoist a whole album to the top? He and his people pored over the rankings in each new issue of *Billboard*. On November 21, after an agonizing three-week wait, *Faith* blipped onto the album chart at No. 41. Up above, it faced a seemingly impenetrable wall: the blockbuster soundtrack of *Dirty Dancing*, whose theme, "(I've Had) The Time of My Life," sung by Jennifer Warnes and Bill Medley, was bulleting to No. 1. *Dirty Dancing* vied with Michael Jackson's *Bad* for the top rung.

Faith's second single, "Hard Day," came out on October 30. It reached the top five on *Billboard*'s Hot Dance Club Songs chart, which didn't help the album much. But on December 12, the "Faith" single made No. 1 in the Hot 100 and stayed there for four weeks. It nudged the album to No. 3, but *Dirty Dancing* and *Bad* blocked it from climbing higher. Christmas passed, then the New Year. In between, "Father Figure" was released as a single. On January 9, *Faith* bumped *Bad* out of No. 2. The next *Billboard* held glorious news: *Faith* had displaced *Dirty Dancing* at No. 1.

In months to come, *Faith* resumed its fight with *Dirty Dancing* for the crowning slot. Ultimately it spent a total of twelve weeks at No. 1—nowhere near as many as *Thriller* (37) or *Dirty Dancing* (18), but more than *Bad* (6). The album stayed in the Top 10 through November 1988. Surprisingly, it had spent only one week at No. 1 in England, but it reached that zenith or the Top 10 in fourteen additional countries. "One More Try" followed "Father Figure" as a No. 1 U.S. hit. *Billboard* named *Faith* the No. 1 pop album of 1988 and its title song the year's biggest single. In a Gallup Youth Survey, Michael was named No. 1 Teen Favorite, ahead of Jackson and Prince. "He was so proud of being ahead of those guys, trust me," said Kahane.

An even unlikelier dream came true: "One More Try" made No. 1 on Hot Black Singles; it displaced "Wishing Well" by Terence Trent D'Arby, a hot young soul singer. "Father Figure" followed, hitting No. 6. Most shockingly, *Faith* climbed to No. 1 on the Top Black Albums chart. A Bee Gees LP, *Spirits Having Flown,* had done that too, but they were a group; as a solo artist, Michael had set a precedent. He proclaimed it "the highlight of my career. For above everything else, it means that the music is stronger than prejudice." What followed made him prouder still: In 1990, due in part to *Faith*, Hot Black Singles was renamed Hot R&B Singles and Top Black Albums became Top R&B Albums, just as he had hoped.

Robert Rosenthal, the press agent for two African-American music organizations, defended the changes, which to him reflected a new age of crossover tastes "You have to be realistic," he said. "The music business, and radio stations in particular, accommodate what is desired by the people."

Hardly any of the chart's mainstays responded for publication. One who did was Freddie Jackson, a Harlem-raised soul balladeer. Then in his early thirties, Jackson had scored a string of No. 1 Hot Black Singles and a No. 1 Top Black Album, *Rock Me Tonight*. Jackson seemingly had little to complain about, yet he aired a ferocious resentment of Michael. "Who does he think he is?" fumed Jackson to Dennis Hunt in the *Los Angeles Times*. White singers, he declared, could have their own kind of soul, but it couldn't be compared to the kind Jackson had, which was "not acquired in some singing school or from copying what you hear on records. I *live* soul. That George Michael hasn't been through any of that. . . . We've gotta stop him."

• • •

Nothing could. Once *Faith* was out and on the rise, renegotiation of Michael's contract had resumed. On December 1, 1987, Michael's representatives—Tony Russell, Allen Grubman, and Grubman's junior colleague Bob Flax—met with Paul Russell and Thomas Tyrrell, CBS's Vice President of Business Affairs, at the company's New York offices.

With Michael set to become a superstar earner, Tony revived his previous demands for rates above even what the titans were getting. Paul recalled him as "unbelievably aggressive and unpleasant," to the point of pounding the desk and acting as though he were about to storm out. Tyrell recalled the lawyer voicing an unsubtle threat to declare Michael's 1984 agreement unenforceable: "You don't even have a contract with George Michael so you ought to consider that when you're negotiating your offer points."

Not much was resolved. After the meeting, Russell placed a top-secret call to Flax to voice an issue he hadn't mentioned. In 1988, the lawyer explained, Michael would be on a mammoth world tour for *Faith*. Britain's top earners were now subject to a whopping 60 percent tax rate. In order to spare him a bill that could reach eight figures, Michael's accountants had advised him to spend most of the year away from England as a tax exile. Andrew Ridgeley, Cat Stevens, Rod Stewart, Shirley Bassey, Roger Moore, Tom Jones, and many other stars had done it. Russell told Flax he wanted as much record money as possible paid to Michael in 1988 via CBS U.S., thus avoiding British taxes. All this had to be noted in his contract. In anticipation of his tax-exile status, Kathy Jeung began shopping for a house that Michael could buy in Los Angeles.

December 17 found him in New York to attend a follow-up meeting at CBS. It dragged on for nearly twelve hours. CBS offered to commit to three albums (including *Faith*) with options for five more. The company refused to cave on Russell's royalty demands, but it offered to retroactively pay a whopping $5 million advance for *Faith*, followed by $3 million for the subsequent album and $2–4 million for the next two, based on how well the previous album had sold. Michael would not earn more for compact discs, even though they sold at double the list price. This was standard practice then, thanks to Walter Yetnikoff. Knowing that many people still viewed the format as a fad, Yetnikoff had gotten artists to accept something close to old vinyl royalty rates for CDs. The medium, of course, skyrocketed, erasing vinyl from the marketplace.

Even so, the proposed terms of Michael's deal were extraordinarily sweet. CBS even agreed to Russell's tax scheme. Throughout 1988, the company would wind up paying £11.5 million in advances for *Faith*, premature ones for the next album, and current and projected royalties. The rest of the contract was boilerplate. The label would own all masters; Michael held creative control, but the company had no obligation to release what he submitted.

The singer was disappointed. He felt betrayed by Grubman, who, he claimed, had promised him better. The fact that, with his first solo album, he had secured terms that were known only to the biggest pop stars in the world, yet still he felt unsatisfied, suggests how far above reality he had floated. What troubled him most was the fact that the contract tied him to CBS for (potentially) eight albums spread out over twelve years—perhaps longer, if he couldn't turn them out every eighteen months, as Columbia wanted.

But he knew it would not be in his best interests to alienate Yetnikoff, and he backed down. On January 4, 1988, Michael signed. By then, *Faith* had sold over four million copies. He did not yet know that the ground was shaking underneath the company to which he had sold the prime time of his career.

Laurence Tisch, the billionaire president and CEO of CBS Inc., had so little faith in its record division that he wanted to unload it. Yetnikoff knew just the man to help. Mickey Schulhof, once a CBS executive, had become Vice Chairman of Sony Corporation of America, the world's leading electronics and hardware firm. Yetnikoff phoned him with a proposal: Did Sony want to buy the CBS Music Group?

It did. Schulhof negotiated the sale. Later in January, Sony acquired the division for $2 billion. It went on to buy Columbia Pictures and a major

Hollywood production company, Guber-Peters Entertainment. Sony was now the world's largest entertainment group—and the music industry had made its first leap into corporatization.

Inadvertently, Michael had helped. To pump up the value of the CBS Music Group, Yetnikoff had rushed out as many anticipated goldmine discs as possible: Michael Jackson's *Bad*, Bruce Springsteen's *Tunnel of Love*, and the biggest smash of them all, *Faith*. Michael's association with Sony would help make him one of the richest men in England and a worldwide superstar. No one could have foreseen how terribly unhappy that contract would make him.

CHAPTER NINE

ON FEBRUARY 19, 1988, the Faith Tour would start in Japan—eight shows in nine days—then proceed to New Zealand, Australia, and dozens of European countries. Michael would take July off, then resume in the United States and Canada. Approximately one hundred and thirty shows were booked.

As Lippman Kahane Entertainment piled on dates, many on consecutive nights, Michael panicked. Wham!'s The Big Tour had shown him that he and his voice could not stand the pressure, but his managers pushed back. "They were making money—lots of money," said Deon Estus. In the end, Michael agreed to every show. "All the really huge artists in the world now have done one huge tour," he reasoned. "I know I have to do it at least this once." He hoped that the thrill of performing to masses of adoring fans would override the fear.

As in his Wham! phase, the vast majority of them were women in their teens and twenties. Though *Faith* was seen as an abundantly heterosexual statement, the album was also striking gay chords. Ben Rimalower, a theater director and monologist from New York, was an elementary-school student in Encino, California, when Michael's music was playing "constantly, everywhere," he said. " 'Father Figure' would come on and I felt like everybody could see my boner. I felt like it shined a light on how gay I was. It made me embarrassed. George Michael was the hot guy that every girl was in love with, but I somehow knew he was gay. It was weird to me that nobody acknowledged it when he'd gotten to be this objectified sex symbol, with his butt in those jeans as he stood with his back to the camera. Even though things were more conservative with Ronald Reagan as president, they were also becoming more graphic and explicit. George Michael was branded as SEX. We were supposed to take him the way we would take Elvis or Burt Reynolds or Tom Cruise."

•••

The layers of protection around him grew. On the road, he needed his personal teddy bears: a rotating circle of up to twenty pals (notably Kathy, Andros, and David Austin) to keep him company. On days off between concerts, they would accompany him on side trips to luxury vacation spots. "I had to be at every single show or he wouldn't go on," said Kahane. "I said, 'Why is that?' He said, 'Because you're making fifteen percent. And I don't want to deal with any of the other fucking people out here. That's your job.' I'd have to fly from Rome for my kid's birthday and then fly back the same day to Milan."

Michael knew what he wanted to sing and wear; he had strong ideas about stagecraft and lighting. At last he would employ the talents of real backup singers. As for choreography, he hired the trendiest name in music videos, Paula Abdul, one of Kahane's clients, whose funky-cheerleader moves were all over MTV.

Whatever his fears about the punishing agenda that would consume his life for six months, Michael knew he would deliver a stellar performance. He skipped the first few rehearsals, leaving the musicians to work out the accompaniments. They began embroidering upon the album sound. Once he arrived and heard what they were doing, every bit of improv was cut. He claimed it was to keep his fans happy—"They want to hear what is essentially on the records with some live ambiance," he told Adrian Deevoy—but those arrangements were his security blanket; he did not want any tampering. Throughout the tour, certain songs sounded so similar to the album versions that some critics thought he was lip-synching. Reverb made him more confident in how he sounded, and he wanted it layered on thick. When Chris Cameron heard the raw vocal in his headphones, he thought: "You're a great singer, man—what do you need all that stuff for? Just sing."

Michael could move, too, of course, but Paula Abdul was there to lift his dancing out of the *Saturday Night Fever* era and make it look fresh. Abdul gave him lateral hops, fist punches, and hip shakes to punctuate the rhythm; she taught him to use the depth of the stage by jumping forward and backward to the beat. Michael asked her to design a "monkey" move for the song of the same name, in which he planned to shout, "DO THE MONKEY!" and teach the audience a new dance. She had him raise his arms and shake them back and forth like King Kong. Michael aced it all.

He thought Deon Estus deserved to be a star, and he asked the bassist to open the shows. Michael had already lent his clout to *Spell*, Estus's forthcoming debut album as a singer-songwriter, to be released on Mika Records, Kahane and Lippman's homegrown label. Michael cowrote, produced, and added backup vocals to *Spell*'s big single, "Heaven Help Me." The single made *Billboard*'s Top 10, but Estus had a tough road ahead: Michael's audiences were so eager to see him that they could barely sit through a warm-up act.

In mid-February, the star and his hefty entourage landed in Tokyo. The first stop was Budokan, the nearly fifteen-thousand-seat arena that Wham! had played. Michael had flown in his sister and hair stylist, as well as his parents; he wanted his mother to be proud of him, and indeed, Lesley was bursting with pride. Jack stared incredulously as fans filled that massive space. Even after the Wham! farewell at Wembley, Michael's popularity seemed incomprehensible to him. "All these people are here for my son?" he asked Kahane.

That night, Jack watched Georgios become a megastar. As the lights dimmed, the word FAITH stretched across the back wall in huge blue letters. Laser beams crisscrossed above the audience; the organ sounds that began *Faith* boomed out. The *Daily Mail* called that opening "the most portentous since *2001: A Space Odyssey*."

Michael and the band waited inside a huge white cage. In the shadows, he began "I Want Your Sex." Light flooded the stage, the cage was lifted, and there, engulfed in clouds of dry ice, was the star, wearing tight, torn, faded jeans, a white tank-top under a black leather jacket, and his crucifix earring. Chanting his sex anthem, he bumped and grinded along the vast length of the stage, running up and down ramps on either side as Latin jungle percussion pounded. Everything was sexualized. Projections of strip-show neon signs and the words LUST and SEX flashed on the back wall. Michael turned around and peeled off his jacket, revealing a silver-studded eagle on the back of his shirt. He broke into his famous fanny-shake, followed by a Michael Jackson-like clutch of the groin.

From there the bombast eased off. Michael didn't need flashy moves to rivet an arena of fans; when he stopped posing and preening, he became what he was: young, sweet, and a bit bashful. He roamed through almost all of *Faith* and the milestones that had preceded it—"Careless Whisper,"

"Everything She Wants," "I Knew You Were Waiting (for Me)"—plus covers of a few pop-soul hits. The show was at times surprisingly intimate; on several songs, notably "A Different Corner" and "Love's in Need of Love Today," he stood nearly motionless and sang softly, with a maturity that belied his outfit and his puffed, frosted hair. For all his insistence on duplicating his album's sound, Michael had no trouble equaling or even surpassing his recorded vocals. The octave leaps in "One More Try" shot skyward like reverse lightning. From time to time, he had a musician descend from the risers and join him up front. "He chases Deon Estus around the stage with the same gleam in his eye he reserved for Andrew Ridgeley when the two lads looked as if they were enjoying it all," wrote a critic.

Michael closed with a little more trashy audience-pleasing. For his recreation of Labelle's funk-dance hit "Lady Marmalade," about a hooker who works the streets of New Orleans, a backup singer strutted lasciviously while Michael made pumping motions behind her. After a reprise of "I Want Your Sex," the cage lowered over him and the band, organ tones thundered, and the show ended.

The relative restraint of the Japanese audiences did not prepare him for the hysteria that lay ahead. Wherever he played, thousands sang along, often without prompting. At times he found himself pleading with them to quiet down. "We couldn't hear counts of songs," said Chris Cameron. Every one of his calculated devices pushed the desired buttons. Yet as he stood in front of more fans than the eye could see, he felt empty. "He'd thought this was gonna make his life complete," said Bret Witke. "It made him more unhappy. He couldn't figure it out." Years later, Michael confirmed it: "I was even more miserable than when I'd split up Wham!—and the reason I split up Wham! was because I was miserable."

He knew that people were shrieking for someone he wasn't. His worshippers, he decided, were not there for his voice or words; they had fallen for the image, and it was a lie: a gay man packaged as a modern-day Elvis. "His most ardent fans are still gape-mouthed and miniskirted teenage girls," wrote Jon Bowermaster in the *Chicago Tribune*. "They 'ooh!' and 'aah!' his every thrust and pout." Michael still agonized over his looks; his Ray-Ban shades, he said, "meant that I could hide. . . . there was only so much scrutiny that could be paid to my face."

David Geffen saw in Michael a tendency he'd found in many an artist. "Self-loathing is not unusual," he said. "Everyone is saying how great you are, how hot you are, but if you're not feeling good about yourself it doesn't matter."

There were no visible issues; Michael performed impeccably every night. Benji LeFevre, the British concert engineer who mixed Michael's vocals on the Faith Tour, used the word "same" to describe the shows. "He was absolutely right," said Chris Cameron. "No room for anything other than what had been programmed or played beforehand; every night exactly the same—a micro-managed environment." In many ways, Michael was doling out standard arena fare: the laser light show, the sprints from side to side, the singalongs. To the *Guardian*'s Adam Sweeting, it all seemed rote: "Where Whitney Houston has a gift from the Almighty, George Michael has a job. He does it with energy and thoroughness, but with none of the sly magic of a Prince or the Hollywood dazzle of a Michael Jackson."

• • •

With over a hundred shows ahead, Michael dreaded the year to come. "You have to stay with it," he said, "when all you want to do is go home and forget about it—forget about what you do for a living." He loved to sing, and at times the music thrilled him. But rumors circulated that he was snorting coke—a drug he loathed—in order to keep his energy up. "Believe me, I was not rock 'n' rolling on tour," he told the BBC's Kirsty Young. "I was taking care of my vocal cords and was in bed by eleven-thirty at night, every night." And still he was "desperately lonely," he said: "The adulation from this huge, huge record put that loneliness into such stark contrast." He missed Andrew Ridgeley. "There is twice as much pressure on me without him," admitted Michael.

He was finding it hard to know who his real friends were. "The more people you employ," he said, "the more people you have in your life who can't be honest with you, and that's what I find most distressing about touring. People are terrified of me. I don't know why. I very rarely fire people. . . . I like to know that if I make a joke and the room laughs that it was funny."

Fearing what reporters might ask, he avoided them whenever possible and measured his words carefully; once in a while he let something revealing slip. When Deevoy referred to the *Faith* cover's "fairy biker" look, Michael laughed. "Fairy biker! That's really good. Yeah, that's probably what it is, really. . . . This look is natural to me." But when Deevoy pressed him further, he defaulted to his standard response. "I'm so used to speculation. Lies bother me. Whether or not people say I'm gay doesn't bother me."

The more he dodged the matter, the more the curiosity grew. When Chris Heath broached the subject, Michael snapped: "What's the point in denying it? If people want to believe it they will. *I* have no doubts about my sexuality. Anyway, if I had thought about sleeping with men and I was going to do it I wouldn't sit here and say it to *Smash Hits*. Sexuality is a totally private thing and it should always stay that way." Yet he couldn't resist titillating reporters with hints. "I often think it would be hard to decide which I'd give up first—walking on stage in front of tens of thousands of people who have been waiting for me, or sex," he said.

The first bullet to pierce his façade came in March of 1988, when the Australian version of *60 Minutes*, the U.S. magazine-style TV series, profiled him in a highly controversial face-off. The interviewer, Jeff McMullen, had helped make *60 Minutes* the country's number-one Sunday night show; apart from having the strapping blond handsomeness of an ex-surfer, he was known for casting a penetrating eye at a wide range of topics, from rock-star culture to the plight of indigenous populations. Although straight, he worked on numerous AIDS-related stories, one of them about a much-bullied teenager with AIDS, Ryan White, whom Elton John had befriended.

McMullen prepared for the Michael piece by reading everything he could find on the singer and listening to the music, including "I Want Your Sex." Its monogamy spin did not convince him. "I thought the marketing was alarmingly insensitive in the midst of a global epidemic," he said. "It was a defiant taunt, in my view; it rejected the counseling of the international gay community that said this was a time for prudent personal behavior. And that was not confined to gay men." Michael's artistry didn't interest him, but the "mask and the secrecy" did. "The challenge was, how do I get closer to the truth? How do I expose the lie?"

On the appointed day, McMullen and his crew set up in a hotel suite in Sydney. Michael had donned his superstar armor for the occasion. Entourage in tow, "he swept in like a prince," said the host. "It was kind of like, I'm here—spotlight, please." Michael insisted that the camera angles be changed to favor his left side. "There were a couple of people that were fiddling with everything that went on," McMullen recalled. "They were more hands-on in controlling the manufactured image than people were on any film set I've ever worked on. There was an obsessive concern with what he was projecting. It made me understand what was going on here. This was the image; it wasn't the real man."

As the camera rolled, Michael found himself staring into one of the most skeptical faces he'd ever encountered. The fact that it was also one of the most attractive magnified the tension. Fixing the star with a barbed smile, McMullen posed his first question: "George, are you gay?"

Everyone in the room gasped.

Michael flinched, then grinned tensely. "Am I gay? That's a pretty direct first question." He pulled out one of his standard responses: "Um . . . I've never said no, I've never said yes." Seldom had he lied outright, but this time he did: "No, I'm not. But the main thing I like to express is I don't think it's anybody's business."

He tried to defuse his anger with humor. Boy George, he said, had told him in their first meeting: "You're so straight, you must be gay." But in the end, he added testily, none of that mattered: "I don't think it benefits anyone listening to my music to know whether or not I was in bed with a dog or a man or a woman last night." McMullen then quizzed him about "I Want Your Sex." He read several lines, calling them "tasteless and trite." Michael defended the song. "I don't think it's trite," he asserted. "It's definitely an outstanding pop lyric. It's going to be there in five, ten years' time."

Time came for the film cartridge to be changed. Michael leapt out of his chair and paced around, infuriated. "*Why did you ask that question?*" he snapped.

"Because it's for you to consider," said McMullen. "You can say it's none of my business and leave it there and I will find other ways to talk to you."

Michael could have walked out, but he didn't. The interview resumed, and McMullen only got tougher. He asked Michael about a series of tabloid rumors. Did he, in fact, use cocaine? Had he brandished a large bottle of poppers in a club? Keeping his cool, Michael denied everything. Their talk ended, and no second blowup followed. Clearly troubled, Michael "just kind of wrapped it up briskly," said McMullen.

The segment, entitled "Gorgeous George," set off a firestorm. It was aired both in Australia and on England's Sky TV network, which shared the same owner as the *Sun*: Rupert Murdoch, the Australian-American news magnate. Many viewers denounced the piece as sensationalistic, moralistic, perhaps even homophobic; some believed it was a Murdoch conspiracy. McMullen's first question was seen as scandalous. "Friends that I deeply respect thought I should never have gone there," he said. "But once you've gone into the marketing of sexuality as a product, it's fair territory to explore."

American *60 Minutes* passed on running the piece. It was sold to the Los Angeles station KTTV to use in *The Reporters*, a short-lived, tabloid-style magazine show produced by the Fox Broadcasting Co., which Murdoch also owned. To stoke advance publicity, KTTV sent out dozens of transcripts to print and television outlets. Michael's interview brought *The Reporters* its highest-rated installment of the year. The *Los Angeles Times* took his side. In an article by Patrick Goldstein, "The 'George, Are You Gay?' Scandal," Rob Kahane called Australia's *60 Minutes* a "video scandal-sheet" and the interview a "set-up," probably tailored to goad Michael into walking out on the interview, thus goosing press potential even further. To Goldstein, Michael had "emerged with dignity intact, projecting self-confidence, good-natured wit, and a refreshing lack of pretense."

Years later, though, McMullen recalled him as a tortured soul. "I had a sense of the internal anguish involved in living that grand a lie. It's an extraordinary thing to do if in your heart you are drawn toward an honest life." His George Michael piece, he felt, "was about more than secrecy. It was about the manufacturing of lies. These big liars, posing, profiting from the lie. I think it was a necessary conversation for the time. I do believe homophobia only exists because people are denying the truth of things."

The dreaded question—"George, are you gay?"—would arise with growing frequency. In April 1988, the *Sun* ran a feature, "The Poofs of Pop," in which Piers Morgan and Peter Willis surveyed gay singing stars, drawing upon both rumor and fact. Morgan and Willis didn't write about Michael, but they included a photo of him with Boy George. By now Michael was used to printed gossip that his constant mates, Andros and David, were his boyfriends.

He claimed he didn't care, yet deflection and denial had become his second nature. Speaking to Adrian Deevoy, he declared his old "feminine-looking" hair and earrings "disgustingly embarrassing." Sometimes he hid altogether. After *60 Minutes*, Michael cancelled his final Sydney show and four other Australian dates. Connie Filippello released conflicting excuses. "George went to a party on Saturday night and when he woke on Sunday morning found he couldn't speak," she told the *Daily Mirror*. "He was seen by a doctor in Sydney and told he has a severe throat infection and must not sing under any circumstances. He is not even allowed to speak. . . . He is confined to bed and ordered to rest." Nine days later came a more glamorous report: "He sprained his back while playing tennis with his keep-fit trainer. The doctor told him that under no circumstances could he perform."

The tour's massive European leg awaited, and the hype machine started up again. Michael's people continued to issue stories about the glamour of it all. In a *Daily Express* column, "Riding George's Dream Machine," Louise Court touted a thirty-foot tour bus equipped with "a satellite dish, tinted bulletproof windows, fax machines, bunk beds, tables and plush leather seating, a waiter serving endless food and drink, CD and video players, washing and toilet facilities." A sexy trainer from New Zealand had been hired to work on Michael every night to keep his back in check. Gianni Versace would give the star a break from hotel life by loaning him his Italian villa.

Michael would relaunch the tour with four shows at Ahoy Stadium in Rotterdam; a huge press conference would precede the first. It was a necessity he feared, for he knew the British tabloid press would be there, and he felt sure they were out to get him. Held in an event room above the stadium, the event drew an estimated two hundred European journalists, photographers, and TV cameramen. An executive from CBS moderated. "Sensible questions, please," he warned. Attendees had to sit through a slickly edited half-hour George Michael promotional video, MUSIC MONEY LOVE FAITH—"a neat device to parry any thorny topics that might crop up during the conference," noted Adrian Deevoy. In the carefully laundered interview within it, Michael declared: "I have to have total control over everything in my life."

Now he was about to be thrown to the wolves. The video ended, but where was George? Minutes passed and irritation filled the air. The host stammered out excuses: "Er . . . in fairness to the guy, his plane was an hour late landing this morning." Finally, the relieved moderator announced, "Ladies and gentlemen, Mr. George Michael!"

He entered unsmilingly in dark glasses and sat at a table up front. Flashbulbs popped and photographers asked him to remove his glasses. He declined, making a tense joke: "If you saw my eyes you'd know I was lying through my teeth." All he wanted was to get this over with. "What I'm not here to do is to make a series of denials about my private life," he announced. A series of mostly drab inquiries came and went. The moderator called for one last question. The *Daily Mirror*'s Gill Pringle—who like a number of her colleagues had run even the most outlandish tidbits about Michael's alleged liaisons with girls—cut in.

"Have you had an AIDS test, George?"

Michael froze. No, he said quietly, he had not. The conference was over.

He went on to deliver four smash shows at Ahoy. Over the next six months, however, he would cancel half of his remaining sixty European concerts. "I was very close to what I would call a breakdown," he recalled.

Elton John blamed Kahane and Lippman. "The people that set this tour up made it too long for someone so inexperienced at touring, which can be very stressful indeed," he told the *Daily Mirror*. "They have taken all the love out of it for him." Speaking privately to Michael, though, he let him know which of them was better equipped for the road: Michael was about to miss more performances in one tour than John had in his whole career.

The reported throat problems were true; so much full-throttle singing with an untrained voice had gotten him into trouble. In late April, an exploratory operation uncovered a cyst on one of his vocal cords. Surgery was scheduled for June 29, at a clinic in London. In the meantime, Michael was ordered to rest in silence for at least two weeks.

The fact that he was canceling certain dates and honoring others, while always sounding fine, cast doubt on his claims of vocal problems. "People thought that was just part of my being temperamental," he said. On June 10, Michael began a six-show run at Earls Court, a London arena with a capacity of nineteen thousand. This was home turf, and the shows had sold out; he had to do them. Onstage, he never faltered. But the same star who dirty-danced his way through "I Want Your Sex" and "Lady Marmalade" turned self-righteous with anger when he hissed: "This country's position on South Africa is a fucking disgrace!" He then sang Stevie Wonder's "Village Ghetto Land," which told of blood in the streets and families eating dog food.

On the afternoon of his second Earls Court show, Michael went to Wembley to join the Nelson Mandela 70th Birthday Tribute, subtitled Freedomfest. South Africa's most famous anti-apartheid revolutionary had been imprisoned since 1964, for having helped plot a violent but thwarted overthrow of the government. The concert, a worldwide telecast, was presented as a call for his release. (Two years later Mandela went free, and he became the country's first democratically elected president.)

The producers had warned against political ranting. What they got instead was a six-hour marathon of pop stars singing their hits, no matter how ill-suited to the occasion. Only a handful seemed appropriate, notably Peter Gabriel's "Biko," in memory of a murdered South African activist. Otherwise, standup comics joked awkwardly while Hollywood stars recited earnest testimonials. Peter Watrous of the *New York Times* called Freedomfest "a sorry mixture of good intentions and show business."

The songs Michael sang showed his persona at its most muddled. He repeated "Village Ghetto Land"; turned Gladys Knight & the Pips' "If I Were Your Woman" into "If You Were My Woman"; and finally, in his most incongruous "tribute" to Mandela, replicated Marvin Gaye's "Sexual Healing" with karaoke precision.

The Earls Court shows thrilled his British fans. All that week, however, he pored over his reviews, looking for affirmation. The critics were not kind. Marcus Berkmann of the *Daily Mail* called him "narcissistic," "self-absorbed," and "a bit porky." In the *Financial Times*, Antony Thorncroft sneered at Michael's "mechanically suggestive gestures" and "bland sentiments"; the star, he wrote, was "dressed like an Ibiza gigolo."

One afternoon during the run, Mick Brown of the *Times* waited for Michael to turn up at a hotel for a two P.M. interview. He didn't show. Brown phoned the publicist, who made no false excuses: So upset was Michael over the reviews that he did not want to speak with the *Times*. The writer pleaded with the publicist; the publicist begged Michael to come. Finally, Brown saw the star heading his way. Michael claimed a hangover, yet looked immaculate. In the discussion that followed, Brown became a combination psychiatrist, soft shoulder, and whipping board. "I feel terrible," said Michael. His master plan, almost flawlessly executed, had veered out of his grasp. He blamed the pans on "jealousy and envy"; the critics, he snarled, could "all fuck off." A young man who had sold out arenas worldwide felt happiest, he said, while alone in his car; only when he was out of view was he at peace. "For that to constitute freedom," observed Brown, seemed "rather sad."

• • •

On June 25, 1988—his twenty-fifth birthday—Michael played his last show before the operation. At the Genting Arena in Birmingham, he gave the crowd a thrill and himself a reminder of sweeter days: Andrew Ridgeley joined him on "I'm Your Man."

The vocal-cord surgery, a simple procedure, worked. Michael spent the next month in Saint-Tropez, recuperating and working with a vocal coach. He went back to work in August for the North American and Canadian legs of the tour—three solid months of shows. This time, Michael canceled nothing. From August 14–16, he played New York's Madison Square Garden, which held twenty thousand; all three performances sold out. In March, Michael Jackson had done a single night there; two years prior, in her debut Virgin Tour, Madonna had done two. Michael's plan had come true: For the moment, at least, he was bigger than both of them.

On August 29, Michael sang at the Palace, a sixteen-thousand-seat arena in Auburn Hills, Michigan. Shoring up his courage, Michael had phoned Aretha Franklin with an invitation. Midway through the concert, he paused before singing "I Knew You Were Waiting (for Me)." "Normally at this point of the show," he said, "my spiel goes, 'The lady is not with us tonight.'" With a tremble in his voice, he announced: "Ladies and gentlemen, Miss Aretha Franklin!" There in her own kingdom (Detroit was just a few towns away), the Queen of Soul walked out to give Michael one last consecration.

Afterward, Michael told the elated crowd: "No bullshit, this was the best night of the tour." Franklin raved to a reporter: "It was wonderful, fabulous, just great. He's very, very talented. I would say that he's definitely a perfectionist."

Bouquets kept coming his way. In October, near the close of the tour, Michael played a three-night stand at the Forum, an arena in Inglewood, California. Despite his Wham!-era snub of the *Los Angeles Times'* Dennis Hunt, the critic was won over: "Michael exuberantly performed what may be the best body of dance music this side of Michael Jackson." Michael, Hunt added, "often seems like the reincarnation of Marvin Gaye."

By the time he'd gone home, the *Faith* album and the tour had grossed an estimated £50 million. *Billboard* would name him the biggest pop star of the year. Michael had surpassed his most lavish boyhood dreams.

In the course of the tour, he had finally parted from Kathy Jeung, which brought bittersweet feelings tinged with relief. But a heavier burden weighed on him, for now, he said, "I absolutely knew that I was gay." He yearned for a relationship, yet knew he could never have a healthy one unless he came out of the closet, and he wasn't ready to do so. Left with his own thoughts about the meaning of success, Michael told the *Sunday Correspondent*: "I can honestly say most of 1988 was a complete nightmare for me."

CHAPTER TEN

MICHAEL HAD EARNED PLENTY of barbs, but the praise outweighed them. Bryan Appleyard of the *Times* marveled at how astutely the star grasped the world of music and his role in it. "When he talks of the rap phase, the pop phase and so on, he links them with extraordinary perfection to autobiography, cultural history, and market pressures." The veteran jazz singer Carmen McRae, a tough critic, had told the *Detroit Free Press*: "There's good artists out there right now, too—George Michael, Sting, Chaka Khan." Andy Williams, the hit-making crooner and 1960s variety-show host, spoke philosophically about handing his mantle to those who had followed. "I had my day; now it's George Michael's day," he said. That's just the way the music business is. You're only hot for a while."

Rob Kahane knew Michael as both a client and a houseguest, for the singer began hiding out at Kahane's home in Encino, California. Michael, he said, was "the most artistic person I've ever been around. A reader. Loved to learn more about life and things outside music. He was very giving. I saw the way he treated his friends, the way he treated my family. He was a control freak, but in the best ways, because the results were amazing."

The British press looked in awe at his financial success. In 1983, Michael had been broke and living with his parents; in 1988, he ranked as one of the highest-paid entertainers in the world. He admitted to Adrian Deevoy that he'd forgotten how it felt to be broke. When friends on hard times came to him for help, he asked them what it was like. "Everyone owes me money. And they all say, 'You're the last person to come and ask for it back.' So, I'll probably be owed it for a long time."

Kahane advised him that he needed to unload some of his cash for tax purposes, and in early 1989, he made one of his most spectacular purchases: a $3 million home in the foothills of Santa Barbara, the coastal city in Southern California. The hexagonal house, designed in the style of Frank Lloyd

Wright, boasted a pool, tennis court, sauna, and breathtaking views of the Pacific Ocean and the Santa Ynez mountain range. It was the residence of a rich man, but Michael was surprisingly unostentatious. "His homes, while exquisitely furnished, were not overly opulent," said Danny Cummings.

The way he himself looked was much more important to him, and he agonized over it. "Like that other former ugly duckling, Michael Jackson, his desire to control his public image borders on the pathological," wrote Richard Smith. He demanded approval of press pictures, and sometimes refused to be photographed for interviews, for he tended to hate the results. Whenever possible he bought back entire photo shoots. His frequent rejection of film shot of him for his videos was part of his growing myth.

He took that effort a step further in January when he taped a commercial for Diet Coke. Pepsi and Coca-Cola had begun paying pop stars mammoth sums to promote their soft drinks, both through tour sponsorships and commercials. The seven-figure payoffs were hard to decline. Pepsi had nabbed Madonna, Michael Jackson, David Bowie, and Tina Turner; Whitney Houston, Paula Abdul, and Julio Iglesias had all hawked Coke. Songwriters began lampooning the trend in such songs as "Soda Pop" (John Fogerty) and "How Much Did You Get for Your Soul?" (Chrissie Hynde).

Though plagued by money troubles at the time, Billy Joel refused an offer from Diet Coke. "Whatever celebrity I have was given to me by people," he explained. "To trade in on it would be a betrayal of that." The company turned to George Michael. Wham! had done a Diet Coke commercial in 1984 for a modest sum; now Michael would cost a reported $3 million.

Coke didn't skimp on the director, either: The choice was Stephen Frears, known for one of the most acclaimed films of 1988, *Dangerous Liaisons*, starring Glenn Close and John Malkovich. With Michael's firm input, Frears storyboarded a commercial that, at the extravagant length of ninety seconds, would cost as much to produce as some feature films. The location: Madison Square Garden.

Michael was flown to Manhattan by Concorde. The commercial allied him with an iconic image of machismo: the bullfighter. Shots of a sexy matador dressing in ceremonial, embroidered gold were intercut with glimpses of Michael in a dressing room, preparing to conquer an audience. His face is not shown; the camera zooms in only on his visual trademarks from the

Faith cover. As the matador takes his dignified walk to the bullring, Michael is shown from behind, strutting in rock-star glory down a runway toward the Garden stage. Only then does his famous face appear. Vamping on the "You deserve a Diet Coke break," Michael had adapted a bit of "Hard Day." He yowls: "Won't you gimme a break, somebody gimme a break, now!" Then he flings a fist upward in victory for the screaming masses.

In the *Chicago Tribune*, Barbara Lippert wondered: "Is he suggesting that singing for the millions of young fans who've made him rich and famous has the life-and-death struggle, the blood, the violence, the gore of slaying a bull? And if that's the case, why increase the martyrdom by doing a Diet Coke commercial?"

But the guise of a conquering hero suited that year's American Music Awards, where the commercial would premiere on January 30. The awards spoke for the public; twenty thousand record buyers had voted. This time, Michael would vie for Favorite Pop/Rock Male Artist, Favorite Soul/R&B Male Artist, Favorite Soul/R&B album, and Favorite Pop/Rock Album.

He arrived at the Shrine Auditorium with a streamlined haircut and a black jacket over a white shirt, with just one button undone—his most mature look, meant to show the world that he was a lot more grown-up than the industry thought. Early in the show, the winner was announced for Soul/R&B Album: *Faith*. Michael had won over Gladys Knight and a new R&B hotshot, Keith Sweat. At the podium, Michael kept tapping his fist against his heart in disbelief. Through a din of female screams, he stammered out: "I just don't know what to say. . . . I can't believe it."

A while later, he was back onstage. This time he had beaten out Michael Jackson and Steve Winwood as Favorite Pop/Rock Male Artist. Given *Faith*'s staggering success, he wasn't surprised, and he had a humble statement prepared. When he had broken up Wham!, he explained, "I knew I had a tough job ahead of me, and I thought that maybe people weren't gonna give me much of a chance. So, I'd just like to thank everybody in radio, the record company, everybody, the public especially, just for giving me that chance and letting me prove myself."

The *Dirty Dancing* soundtrack beat out *Faith* for Favorite Pop/Rock Album—no surprise; it had doubled the sales of *Faith*. But gasps were heard amid the screams as Michael was announced as Favorite Soul/R&B Male

Artist over Jackson and rapper Bobby Brown. Michael strode up and smiled in triumph as he reeled off more thank-yous.

Resentment still lingered over Michael's No. 1 hits on the *Billboard* soul charts; now the outrage came to a boil. Gladys Knight avoided comment on the category in which Michael had beaten her, but she spoke out angrily about his other two awards: Why had an "outsider" like Michael been allowed to muscle his way into "that area"?

Dionne Warwick, not a nominee, had a sharp rejoinder to Michael's win as Favorite Soul/R&B Male Artist. "It's a puzzle how that was even considered. Where were the likes of Luther Vandross, Freddie Jackson? I don't appreciate it. I don't like it."

Don Cornelius, the creator of *Soul Train*, seemed just as perplexed, but when queried by *TV Guide*, he answered diplomatically. "This being a quote-unquote, free country, people are entitled to call George Michael a soul artist and, in effect, change the meaning of the word 'soul,' " he said.

The AMAs, of course, were not industry-chosen; they reflected public opinion. Michael felt compelled to respond. "I didn't ask to be given those awards," he said. "I'm not gonna pretend that I wasn't happy to get them." But he understood how some would find his efforts at soul laundered and inauthentic. "It goes way back to Elvis, obviously," he said. Michael swore he wasn't trying to "steal" African-American heritage—"all I think that's happening is I'm trying to make good music." Michael had burned for a lot more than that, of course, and he had stopped at almost nothing to get it, which had left him wide-open for parody. That February, *Saturday Night Live* roasted him. Dana Carvey, posing as Michael, sat down with an interviewer, played by Dennis Miller.

"Before we talk with him," says Miller, "let's take a look at why he's so popular." He cuts to a montage of close-ups of the star's wiggling behind. Then Carvey, sprawled on a floral armchair, has his say. "I just want to apologize to my fans for my appearance in that Diet Coke spot," he declared in a North London accent. "They shot this extravagant commercial featuring me, and I ask you, where was my butt? . . . I wanted to bloody kill the editor! It went, boot shot, beard shot, belt, bullfighter, hair, crowd, face, hands, bull, boot, hair. And I told them *specifically* it was supposed to be, butt shot, shot of the hand, back to the butt, hand, butt, hand, butt, hand, butt, belt, butt, beard, butt. . . . *It's a formula, but it bloody works!* . . . It's the best butt in video today. I mean, look at it!" Carvey leaps up, turns around, and shakes his behind back and forth. "It's perfectly round, Dennis. *Look at my butt!* Bow down before it, Dennis! LOOK AT IT!"

Miller turns to the camera and says, deadpan: "What an ass."

According to Rob Kahane, Michael thought the bit was funny—"because he never thought of himself as George Michael. That's the way he put it to me—'That's not me. That's just who I pretend to be.'" But where his career was concerned, he had little humor. The most important validation arrived on February 22, when Michael made a flashbulb-popping entrance at the Shrine for the Grammy Awards. David Browne noted in the New York *Daily News* that Michael and his label were "reportedly miffed" that *Faith* had earned only two nominations. For Best Pop Vocal Performance, Male, "Father Figure" would compete against songs by Sting, Phil Collins, Steve Winwood, and Bobby McFerrin. Album of the Year pitted Michael against McFerrin, Winwood, Sting, and Tracy Chapman, whose hugely successful debut disc had tackled a range of social causes. Although "Father Figure" lost to McFerrin's "Don't Worry, Be Happy," *Faith* won Album of the Year.

Its win was a "surprise," wrote Robert Hilburn in the *Los Angeles Times*. "The album was widely praised for its pop craft, but it lacked the originality and boldness—to most critics—associated with the Chapman LP, which is filled with themes of welfare mothers and victimized children." Richard De Atley of AP was likewise startled that "an album of lightweight pop tunes such as 'I Want Your Sex'" had beaten Chapman for the night's most hallowed award.

Michael took the criticism to heart; in response, he showed the public his worst. On April 5, he returned to the Grosvenor House Hotel to collect two more Ivor Novello Awards—one for the song "Faith," the other for Songwriter of the Year. There at his table were Michael's entire family along with Andros Georgiou and Andrew Ridgeley; seated elsewhere in the ballroom were Sting and fellow winners Paul McCartney and Cliff Richard.

Called to the stage, Michael staggered up in jeans and a cowboy hat, a half-full bottle of red wine in one hand. "I am completely pissed," he slurred, as uneasy titters and murmurs spread throughout the room. "I wish I had got this earlier in the afternoon. I was more sober then." Called back to accept his second honor, he was even drunker. "Over the last year," the singer muttered, "everything has turned out the way I wanted it, and more . . . I think I'll have another drink."

• • •

For Michael, the fun of music-making had dimmed, replaced by pressure. *Faith* had sold approximately fifteen million copies. How could he ever equal it?

Sony hoped his new album would repeat the winning formula of *Faith*, but Michael had other plans. He told Stephen Holden in the *New York Times*: "I think it will be obvious from my next record that *Faith* was a transitional album. There was a lot of aggression on *Faith*, which has been worked out. . . . The next record will probably be softer, more relaxed and acoustic and probably not as aggressively commercial."

He had recently discovered guitarist-singer João Gilberto, Brazil's feather-voiced bossa nova pioneer. He loved Gilberto's soft, caressing sound, and hoped to capture it on the new album. Acoustic guitar, Michael decided, would be the record's foundation. While he was scaling down, he was also pumping up. Though songwriting was getting harder for him—"I'm not prolific, I'm just not," he told Kahane—he envisioned a double album that dealt with social issues as well as personal ones. He wanted an adult audience, not an army of screaming girls.

Starting in the spring of 1989, Michael's home-away-from-home became the downstairs Studio 2 at SARM. He gathered a handful of trusted musicians, including Danny Cummings, Chris Cameron, and Deon Estus, along with a new addition, guitarist Phil Palmer, a top-call session player since the seventies. Michael would lean on them heavily for the next several months.

He was developing other crutches, too. Until now, Michael's anesthetics of choice had been alcohol and Ecstasy. But by the time of these sessions, said Palmer, Michael was relying on pot, which he would famously smoke for the rest of his life. It helped unlock his creativity, he said. During the making of this album, recalled Palmer, "he was often spaced-out. But it seemed he could function best under those conditions and nobody really questioned it."

Michael showed up in the studio with nothing but ideas, and sometimes not even with those. "I would get a call to go in for an afternoon and strum around a few ideas," said Palmer. He would ask Cameron and Estus to do the same. Using a drum machine, Michael experimented with rhythms. "Then he'd say, 'Okay, let me work with that for a few days,' " Palmer said. With the help of Porter, Michael would edit and shuffle pieces around on a computer; all the while, melodic and lyric ideas would occur to him. Once he had enough words, Michael would create a guide vocal. "He would do odd things," said Cameron, "like pasting ten-bar vocal phrases over eight-bar passages." Then he would call back his musicians for further rounds. "It was a vague process," said Palmer. "He never actually completed one song in one go."

By the time he brought in Cummings, the rhythmic patterns were programmed rigidly on computer; it was his job to play his bongos and congas over them—"to bring animation, some percussive life to the thing," he said. Michael couldn't always explain what he wanted; his musicians had to figure it out. Whatever they played, it could *not* be "distracting," the word Michael used constantly. He looked for support, nothing more. It frustrated Palmer to see his every standout contribution buried, but Michael's foremost concern was his singing. "He wanted to find his vocal comfort zone in every song," said the guitarist. "He would spend days figuring out little sensitive bits of vocal. If he didn't find it then he would reject the song."

More often than not he succeeded, and the tracks slowly blossomed. So it was with "Freedom! '90," the song that would define the album. Michael had burned to write a song in which he told people he wasn't who they thought he was. But he had only vague fragments in his head in the winter of 1990 when he started working on it at SARM. That February saw the release of "Loaded," a Top 20 dance single by the Scottish indie band Primal Scream. Seven minutes long, it incorporated a shuffling Afro-Cuban beat, a gospel-like piano part, choral invocations ("We wanna be free to do what we wanna do!"), and an orchestral energy that built and built.

With "Loaded" as his blueprint, Michael got to work with his band. He demonstrated the piano line he wanted Cameron to play by singing it for him. When Cummings arrived for the day, he found that Michael had already computer-programmed the percussion part. It sounded stiff; Cummings piled on congas, bongos, hi-hat, and tambourine to give the track swagger.

Weeks went by in what Porter called a "torturous" process of experimenting, saving, rejecting, cutting, pasting, and piecing together. As the music evolved, it reminded the musicians more of the Aretha Franklin hit "Think," another of Michael's favorites, than of "Loaded." Yet it also revealed a new sophistication in Michael's lyric writing. Never had he crafted anything so explicitly autobiographical. Singing in a gravelly, confrontational voice, he opened with a promise—"I won't let you down"—then told the story of his life and of his shifting personas, from grade-school nerd to teenybopper heartthrob to MTV idol, and of how his soul was nearly destroyed along the way. He had to show people the truth whatever the cost, and grab some happiness. The moral: "Sometimes the clothes do not make the man."

Like "Loaded," the song changed forms as many times as Michael had, while building suspense. To Will Automagic, half of the New York deejay duo the Carry Nation, the buildup and eventual release were orgasmic: "It's like he's having sex with you and teasing you—like building up to come, you know?" The explosion happens midway through when a choir of overdubbed George Michaels chants out "FREEDOM!" with an ecclesiastical fervor.

Michael and his band had created a mid-tempo yet eminently danceable disco tune. Nothing sounds electronic—he seemed to sense that in a song about finding the human being under the armor, only flesh-and-blood playing would ring true. The lyrics were downbeat; the music made them triumphant. Using specific details from his life, Michael had written a universal anthem about breaking free.

That theme followed him throughout the making of the album. In "Waiting for That Day," Michael is haunted by the wounds of rejection and past mistakes as he begs a lover to take him back. The grief, he admits, will probably never leave: "Something in me needs this pain." Records he loved kept passing through his thoughts; Michael referenced them unapologetically. The wistful folk-rock setting recalled Van Morrison's "Into the Mystic"; Michael added a hook that sounded like a slowed-down version of the "Do-do-do . . ." motif of Lou Reed's "Walk on the Wild Side." Likewise, he used a famous sample of the drum break that Clyde Stubblefield had played on James Brown's single "Funky Drummer," but cut the speed. Michael closed by incanting a line by the Rolling Stones: "You can't always get what you want."

Michael's influences kept popping out. He planned one track, he said, "to show how much I love Lennon, another to show how much I love McCartney." The seeds of "Praying for Time" occurred to him on his way to a gas station. Like John Lennon's "Mind Games," the song was an anthem for world enlightenment; an emphatic backbeat, surging keyboards, and oceans of reverb signified a big statement. "These are the days of the open hand," he sang—an era stained by the desperation of the poor and the selfishness and hypocrisy of the rich. "Charity is a coat you wear twice a year," he wrote, and God was nowhere to be found. Michael was as emotive as Freddie Mercury in full cry; he whispered, he yowled, he let out a stadium-sized cry of frustration.

Adam Sweeting of the *Guardian* would describe "Heal the Pain" as "the Paul McCartney ballad the Fab One never wrote." The song, with its dreamy bed of acoustic guitar and tapestry of vocals, recalled McCartney's band Wings; the words were an offer of love to someone whose heart had been broken: "How can I help you / Please let me try to."

One of the album's most seductive tracks drew upon Michael's memories of his unrequited French love, Tony Garcia. In "Cowboys and Angels," Michael wrote about the masochism of clinging to an obsession: "It's the ones who resist that we most want to kiss." But he found a way to bring the song an almost celestial lightness: It floated along in graceful six-eight time on a swirl of synthesized strings. Michael's singing sounds breathless and numb; an icy cloud of reverb surrounds it. The album's only cover, "They Won't Go When I Go," revisited a song written by Stevie Wonder and his sister-in-law, Yvonne Lowrene Wright, after a 1973 auto accident that had left Wonder comatose. His recording, on the album *Fulfillingness' First Finale*, evokes a funeral march in Harlem. Wonder plays a Chopin-influenced piano part and sings of ascending to a place where "the greed of man will be / Far away from me / And my soul will be free." Behind him, what sounds like a choir of female voices—actually all by Wonder—sings mournfully. As the end draws near, his voice erupts into a state of gospel-like ecstasy.

Michael undertook to copy that recording, and came close to capturing its mixture of anger, sanctity, and elation. But, as a few critics noted, he took the song nowhere new. Faced with a masterpiece, he could only genuflect before it, not reimagine it.

In his own song, "Mother's Pride," he equaled Wonder's depth. Michael took an age-old subject in popular song, the tragedy of war, and looked at it through the lens of a woman who had lost her husband to battle and knows their son is doomed to the same fate. Over a course of weeks, the lyric came together; the imagery is so stark and precise that the boy's short life seems to fly past the listener's eyes. Michael writes of an innocent child who grows into "a soldier waving at the shore"; soon he will lie on the battlefield, a frozen vision of one more fallen soldier. "He'll hold a gun till kingdom come," sings Michael as Cameron makes a synthesizer rise into the grandeur of film music. The song made Cummings flash back to the Michael he had met in Wham!. "Can you believe the same person who wrote 'Club Tropicana' wrote 'Mother's Pride'? He was developing and growing constantly, always full of surprises, and the music got gradually more and more melancholic."

The recording of these songs took much more out of him than *Faith* had. "All you have to do is listen to the lyrics to understand what he was going through," said Rob Kahane. "It's kind of a tortured-soul record."

But at the MTV Video Music Awards, which honored him on September 6, 1989, manufactured images were extolled, and Michael wasn't ready to part with his. He, Madonna, Prince, and Michael Jackson were the network's reigning creations; each had masterfully concocted a public character and sold it to the world. There at the Universal Amphitheatre in Los Angeles, Madonna presented Michael with the Video Vanguard Award. She stepped to the podium flanked by two young women; all three held cigarettes aloft in their right hands. In between puffs, Madonna "saluted" Michael with the ostensibly tongue-in-cheek arrogance that had helped make her famous. "Though I'd rather be getting an award than giving one away," she said, "it is my distinct pleasure to present the Video Vanguard Award to an artist that has made outstanding contributions to the world of music video." Taking another puff, she added: "Like me."

After reading further comments off a teleprompter, she introduced "the diva himself, George Michael." Though "stunned and pissed," said Andros, at the bitchy dig, Michael sailed out, beaming a dazzling smile, and gave Madonna the obligatory bear hug. With his perfectly gelled and tinted hair, fashionable stubble, and a black-and-gold bolero jacket, he looked every inch the jet-setting, multi-millionaire pop star.

This was the image that had helped make Michael a superstar, but its phoniness had become hard for him to bear. What would happen, he wondered, if he took it off his new album entirely and let the songs speak for themselves? Many years later, he explained his thinking to Kirsty Young: "If I take away the image, if I take away this face, I'll see whether they still love me." Whether or not Sony would support him in that choice remained to be seen.

•••

Amid the creation of his new album, Michael went to three Spanish cities to make up shows he had canceled the previous year. The thought of reliving the Faith Tour felt excruciating, but they were government-sponsored, sold-out stadium shows, and he had a contract. Besides that, Kahane had insisted that all the money be paid up front and deposited into a British escrow account.

To sweeten a bitter prospect, Michael insisted that a bevy of friends be flown with him to Ibiza for an all-expenses-paid vacation. The first show, in Madrid, went well, but hell broke out just before the flight to Málaga, Andalusia. The singer had his sister Melanie call Kahane, who was in the same hotel, to say that Michael would not be doing the show. "His eyes were burning, he put the wrong contacts in, or some bullshit," recalled the manager. "I went over, and he was crying and carrying on—'I'm not doing it, I'm not doing it!' I said, 'Well, if you don't do it you're gonna end up in a Spanish prison along with your family and friends. You've taken their money. You have to at least show up and go to a doctor at the concert in order to cancel it.'"

Kahane warned the promoter that Michael was unwell and might not perform. The news aroused suspicions that he might try to flee the country and pocket his fee. As Michael and his entourage reached the airport, a military jet waited to take them to Málaga. From there, a jeep with armed personnel drove them to the stadium. Michael cried all the way.

The audience waited an hour: no George Michael. They grew loudly angry. A doctor administered to Michael's eyes with soothing drops. Michael pouted to Kahane: "If I go onstage, I'm just gonna sit in a chair. I'm not gonna move." Fine, Kahane told him. "Then you'll become Stevie Wonder for the night. I don't care. Just get onstage." Finally, Michael stepped out before forty-four thousand fans. He sat for the first song. Then he rose to his feet—"and it ended up being one of the best gigs on the whole tour!" said Cameron. "It was possibly the only time I remember George throwing caution to the wind. He was definitely not on autopilot that night." Two nights later he performed in Barcelona, where the show reverted to its old quality: "same."

CHAPTER ELEVEN

AFTER THE DEATH OF Wham!, Michael had taken the cockiness he'd learned from Andrew Ridgeley and built it into an epic persona. But Ridgeley's dream of becoming a star drag-racer had literally ended in smoke as he wrecked car after car. Ridgeley had bought a home in Los Angeles to bring him closer to a film career, but that dream, too, had crashed and burned. "He was pretty despondent about the way the press treated him," said Michael. "And it's not just the press. The public treated him with a great degree of disdain. He was seriously pissed off." Finally, Michael's ex-partner made the safer choice of opening a restaurant with friends in a town outside London.

Sony retained an option on a Ridgeley solo record. Announcements of it had appeared as early as 1987; Michael had pledged to write songs for it, but the comeback was a risk that Ridgeley didn't rush to take. Finally, three years after the breakup of Wham!, he began work on the album, to be called *Son of Albert*. With Michael's encouragement, Kahane and Lippman took him on as a client. The former trumpeted Ridgeley's potential to the *Los Angeles Times*: "This album will show that he's more than just a sideman . . . that he is a very talented writer, producer, and performer."

If Michael had ditched his bubblegum façade, maybe Ridgeley could do the same. Having fallen for Def Leppard and Van Halen, he hoped to create "very macho, very raunchy rock. . . . My music is rooted in sexual energy, though intellectual energy is important, too." Ridgeley seemingly didn't want too many of Michael's thumbprints on the project; he wrote with other collaborators, including his coproducer Gary Bromham, who played bashing drums and blaring electric guitar. Amid the metal, Ridgeley's voice was heard at last: a high, braying, boy-band sound that aimed to lash and snarl.

He was no leader, and his old partner—who sang backup on one track, "Red Dress"—saw him floundering. Michael revealed later that he had urged Ridgeley in vain to redo certain vocals. The video for "Shake" cast him, none too convincingly, as a rocking sex machine surrounded by writhing, seminaked women.

With *Son of Albert* due out in May 1990, Chris Heath interviewed a "super-suspicious" Ridgeley for *Smash Hits*. "My personal view," recalled Heath, "is that he wasn't that committed to being a solo artist and felt awkward about it." Chrissy Iley, a blonde-bombshell celebrity profiler for the *Daily Mail*, found Ridgeley a lot more receptive. Iley noted the "breezy insouciance" and "confidence overspill" of old as Ridgeley downed five cocktails, mooned over the opposite sex ("Dark women appeal to me"), and boasted of his style sense: "I don't go shopping because I have a shoemaker, a shirtmaker, and a tailor who makes everything to my specific instructions. I have personal motifs—laurel leaves for strength, a rose for love, and angel's wings for purity." With so little irony in his words, it was hard to believe him when he stressed that the lyrics on his new album were "meant to be funny. They're a satire on male sexuality."

The humor was lost on *Entertainment Weekly*'s Greg Sandow, one of the few critics to review *Son of Albert*. He called it "fake-raunchy rock 'n' roll" unsuited to Ridgeley's "eager, tiny voice." Sandow's rating: C+. Ridgeley would never release another album. Nearly thirty years later, when *Son of Albert* appeared in a new edition, Ridgeley said in the booklet: "I am surprised the album is being reissued, baffled in fact—particularly in view of how poorly it performed first time 'round!"

In the original credits, he had thanked his former partner "for never doubting me." Even after *Son of Albert* had come and gone, Michael defended him. "I'd never have believed that this stigma would have held that strong. . . . He knows it's not a great voice, but he fucking *tries*. . . . I don't know what he's going to do now."

• • •

Michael was in the throes of a much more elaborate self-recreation.

His album was due out in September 1990. Michael had chosen the title *Listen Without Prejudice*—a plea to listeners to wipe his old image from their minds and embrace the new George. To the main title he added "Vol. 1," in anticipation of a sequel. The front of the album wouldn't show his name, the title, or his face; Michael assumed he was so famous that none of them were needed. Instead, he and Simon Halfon, his favorite cover designer, found an image they loved in a photography book Halfon had given him for his birthday. The new album would display a square-sized portion of a photo, *Coney Island at Noon Saturday, July 5, 1942*, taken by Weegee, the photographer known for his stark black-and-white street photography. His picture showed a sea of swimsuit-attired bathers huddled together and staring at the camera; Weegee had danced and screamed to make them look his way. The photo, with so many near-naked men standing shoulder to shoulder, had a homoeroticism that Michael liked.

To mark what the *Sunday Times* called his "transformation to serious respectability," there could be no higher anointing than his hour on *The South Bank Show*, the long-running U.K. documentary series hosted by an aristocrat of British TV, Melvyn Bragg. The show had begun as a lofty celebration of high-art figures and venerated popular artists: Sir Laurence Olivier, Sir Alec Guinness, Francis Bacon, Oscar Peterson. More recently it had swerved toward such ratings-friendlier subjects as the Pet Shop Boys.

Even so, Kevin Jackson of the *Independent* found Michael—"a bright crafter of dance-floor numbers"—to be an "odd candidate for Melvynization." Jackson was puzzled to hear the host "speak of George's origins in Bushey in the same tones he might apply to Beethoven's in Bonn."

Chris Heath reported that the star had exercised "considerable editorial control" over the show, which detailed how he had shed all traces of frivolity and was now, above all else, a songwriter. Michael was shown working intently in the studio, reinforcing "I Want Your Sex" as a pro-monogamy statement, defending his soul singing against charges of cultural appropriation, and offsetting his old arrogance with a newfound show of humility. "I don't believe that I am important as a pop star," he said. "I believe I can leave songs that will mean something to other generations."

That month also brought the publication of *Bare*, Michael's "official" life story. Though marketed as a memoir, the book was more of a biography, written by Tony Parsons, a scuffling music writer whom Michael liked. Parsons had proposed the book to Michael, who consented because he "had become sick of the Niagara of lies, innuendo, and trivia that a tabloid deity has to endure," explained Parsons.

On February 23, 1989, the day after Michael's Album of the Year Grammy win, the scribe began interviewing him for *Bare*. With the star's okay, he also quoted several of Michael's intimates, although his family was off-limits. Michael chose the title, with its two-pronged thrust of titillation and candor. But *Bare* was "superficial stuff," said Rob Kahane. "It was more of a PR move."

He and Parsons wove a portrait of a contented young genius who had left drugs, sex, and other glamorous excesses behind. Michael discussed romance in gender-nonspecific terms, while letting Andros effuse at how his studly friend used to sleep with "everything that moved, from air hostesses to unbelievable amounts of girls . . . I'm talking about three or four girls a night." As for the present, Michael left things vague: "I've settled into a life on my own so well that I find it really difficult to imagine living with somebody."

A few revealing statements slipped through, including a poignant admission of how hard it was to find love when most people couldn't see past his stardom: "It wouldn't matter if I met someone tomorrow and fell hopelessly in love with them, and they with me. I would still always be George Michael to them." The real Michael, of course, could not bare his soul to the public; he had a major secret to hide. The tabloids kept hunting down old pals and associates, tempting them with payoffs and hoping, said Michael, "that someone's going to be much more down than they were the last time they called."

Most of his true friends stayed fiercely protective. When Shirlie and Pepsi did a show in Providence, Rhode Island, on a solo tour, Billy Masters went backstage to chat. The women were charming—until Masters mentioned that he had spent time with Michael in Boston during Wham!'s first U.S. tour. "They immediately shut down with me," he said.

Michael knew he could also rely on Tony Russell to protect his interests. In February 1990, months before the anticipated blockbuster release of *Listen Without Prejudice Vol. 1*, Russell resumed his testy contract renegotiations, notably for a boost in Michael's royalties to American superstar rates. For now, he and the singer withheld a major piece of news: As part of his rebranding, Michael planned to "kind of disappear." He would halt interviews indefinitely and appear in no new videos—an explosive gamble at a time when they were crucial to a pop star's success. "Very little in this album is right for video," he explained to Adrian Deevoy. "When you are trying to express things with metaphors and much more subtlety, that's when you are doing yourself a disservice by making a video. . . . I just want people to use their imaginations." Kahane saw him scrambling to banish his fake façade: "He was just never comfortable in his own skin. I lived with him so I saw the pain he was going through in terms of living as something that he wasn't."

But there was more to it than that. Maybe if he withdrew from the spotlight he could at last find love and a stable personal life. He expected a "sharp drop in sales," but would accept the tradeoff.

•••

On September 4, Sony president Norio Ohga had stunned the industry by firing Walter Yetnikoff, Kahane's closest ally. Sales were dwindling, and rumors had spread that Michael Jackson and Bruce Springsteen, with whom Yetnikoff had clashed, might leave. As the new president of CBS Records Group, Ohga chose Don (Donnie) Ienner, who had recently joined CBS after having managed Arista. At thirty-six, Ienner was as volatile as Yetnikoff, with his eye ruthlessly set on boosting the sagging family of labels to number one.

Dave Novik, who worked with him, recalled Ienner as "very brash, very arrogant. He wanted to be right all the time, and he didn't want anybody else to take credit." As Ienner told Chuck Philips of the *Los Angeles Times*: "Our job is to take the artist's vision into the street and to get as many people to hear it as we possibly can. And when that process gets messed up, I get angry. I get loud. I get excited. That's who I am."

A member of the company's art department had been warned that when he entered Ienner's office to show him a design, he should stand at least six feet away—"because there was a very good chance he'd throw his stapler at you during the presentation. People were genuinely terrified of being around him."

That June, Michael played his new tracks for Paul Russell; the next month he did the same for Donnie Ienner and Tommy Mottola, Sony Music's Chairman/CEO, when they visited London. Michael would later claim he had explained his intentions fully to all executives. But according to Mottola, Michael merely said he didn't want to appear in the album's first video.

With time running out to seal his client's demands, Tony Russell stepped up the pressure. Sylvia Coleman, Sony U.K.'s Director of Corporate Business

Affairs and a lawyer herself, was Paul Russell's contract advisor. One day, Tony Russell called. If she and Paul did not agree to everything he wanted, he would tell Michael how difficult they were being—thus poisoning the star against his record company. In subsequent calls, he turned even nastier. "I was extremely concerned," she recalled, "because I felt that throughout the negotiations the U.K. company had acted with the utmost good faith, and we had genuinely endeavored to see that George Michael received full superstar status."

In late July, the renegotiation agreement was signed. Michael had gotten everything he wanted. Only then, as marketing meetings for the album began, did Michael reveal the extent of his plans to "disappear." He had decided to grant interviews to only three newspapers: the *New York Times*, the *Los Angeles Times*, and *USA Today*. As for videos, he would not appear in any. "If my life goes the way I want," he said, "I would like never to step in front of a camera again."

Paul Russell and Andy Stephens, Epic U.K.'s Head of International Marketing, begged him to reconsider. He wouldn't budge. "It was very hard for me to deal with," said Rob Kahane, "because I had helped create that character and it was incredibly successful. He and I had huge fights over it. Yelling, screaming, throwing shit. My wife was always on his side, like, 'You have to respect what he wants.' I was like, 'Yeah, I just worked my ass off all these years to build this thing and now he wants to tear it down.' Can you imagine going back to the label and saying, 'But you're not gonna have George there to promote it'? They went nuts. I don't blame them." As Jerry Blair, a Columbia executive in charge of radio promotion, pointed out: "If you bought a piece of property and spent millions to make it more valuable, would you just sit there and go, 'Hey, no problem,' and write it off?"

Nonetheless, Mottola issued a peacemaking statement. There would be "a lot of disappointed fans," he said, "but when they get to understand his point of view and hear the record, I don't think there will be any problem." Paul Russell, too, played the gentleman. "I told George Michael that I respected his position, so long as he was fully aware that we would have more difficulty marketing the album, which he was. I said we would still be fully behind the album and would do everything we could to ensure that it received maximum promotion."

At a Columbia convention, held in a ballroom, Mottola gave the sales and marketing team and other staff a preview of the hotly anticipated follow-up to *Faith*. Jay Landers, one of the company's Vice Presidents of A&R, was present. "Nothing on the album sounded like *Faith*," he said—and as the somber "Praying for Time" floated out of loudspeakers, "people sat there incredulous. This is what they were gonna have to sell. George had taken this darker turn, and the music didn't feel as celebratory and fun." Only "Freedom! '90" seemed to show hit potential, and Sony chose it as the first single. Michael insisted on "Praying for Time." MTV would need a video. Once more, Prince became his blueprint. Michael's hero had declined to appear in two of his own videos; in one, "Sign O' the Times," the lyric unfolded onscreen in multicolored graphics. Something similar would have to do in "Praying for Time."

All the while, Michael kept giving publicity about his desire to avoid publicity. His "escape" seemed like a series of therapy sessions as he struggled to explain himself to reporter after reporter. No more, he insisted, was he "driven by an insatiable desire for everyone to love me. . . . I now believe that I'm worth loving and I don't need the world to tell me anymore." He cited Bob Dylan as an example of what he never wanted to happen to him. "I can't see the mystique anymore," he told Bryan Appleyard. Dylan, he said, "writes great lyrics still, but as a person he seems such a casualty. And that documentary made about him in the sixties—*Don't Look Back*—what an arsehole! He wouldn't get away with that now."

On September 9, 1990, the *Los Angeles Times* gave him pages of talking space. "I'm not stupid enough to think that I can deal with another ten or fifteen years of major exposure," he told Robert Hilburn, the newspaper's pop critic. "I think that is the ultimate tragedy of fame . . . people who are simply out of control, who are lost. I've seen so many of them, and I don't want to be another cliché." But what did he want? Michael, wrote Gary Graff in the *Detroit Free Press*, "doesn't seem to know. . . . Never has someone who's been so successful complained about it so much. . . . He's a pop star wailing 'This is what I'm not!' without defining what he is."

On the day the *Los Angeles Times* article ran, the ultimate legend of classic pop felt moved to send a response. To him, Michael was a spoiled brat. A first-person letter from Frank Sinatra to Michael was sent by his office to various newspapers, then syndicated widely. Although Michael doubted that Frank had written it himself, its hardboiled, wisecracking, all-knowing air was pure Sinatra.

"Come on, George," the letter said. "Loosen up. Swing, man. Dust off those gossamer wings and fly yourself to the moon of your choice and be grateful to carry the baggage we've all had to carry since those lean nights of sleeping on buses and helping the driver unload the instruments. And no more of that talk about 'the tragedy of fame.' The tragedy of fame is when no one shows up and you're singing to the cleaning lady in some empty joint that hasn't seen a paying customer since St. Swithin's Day."

Michael was furious at having been publicly shamed by a legend; why couldn't Sinatra have simply sent the letter to him? The memory of that letter stung; its advice went unheeded. Following Sinatra's death, Michael released a comment: "I think that Sinatra was the finest singer of his time and probably ours too, but I did not respect him because of his connections, and his actions towards others were well documented. And respect is earned by what you do, not just what you do with the gifts that God has given you."

To Marcus Dunk of the *Daily Express*, the letter had "merely voiced what a lot of people felt about George Michael." Even some of his friends were losing patience. "George coveted fame like nobody I know outside of Madonna," said one of them. "It used to piss me off no end when he went on about the pitfalls of fame. George enjoyed his fame. His problem was that, as a control freak of the highest magnitude, he wanted to control it and he couldn't."

Through it all, Michael's self-confidence hadn't wavered. While he claimed he was content to trade sales for artistic integrity, he still had his eye on No. 1. As soon as *Listen Without Prejudice* was released, said Rob Kahane, "he was as competitive as he was back in the *Faith* days."

For critics to heed the plea in the title proved almost impossible. Michael had deluged them with advance press about the weightiness of this artistic statement, but they had not forgotten the butt-wiggling, the Diet Coke commercial, and the "hot pursuit of fame and notoriety at almost any price," as Robert Sandall wrote in the *Sunday Times*.

A TV commercial, directed by the singer, also clashed with his rebranding. It features an interracial couple—a Michael-like stud in jeans and a leather jacket and a female model in designer sportswear. While listening to his album on Sony Walkmans, they strip. Michael had wanted to show them nude from the rear, but that would have cost him his American airings; he had to settle for showing the models seated with their backs to the camera, the tops of their behinds blurred.

In the first week of September, reviews of *Listen Without Prejudice Vol. 1* began appearing. Its star, said Tom Moon in the *Philadelphia Inquirer*, had "gone from the silly controversy-baiting of 'I Want Your Sex' to the sanctimonious hot air of 'Praying for Time' . . . Michael sounds vain or spoiled far more often than he sounds concerned or engaged." In the *Daily Telegraph*, Chris Heath showed no patience for the star's loud rejection of stardom: "Singing pop songs opening up about your unhappy feelings about being a pop icon is like giving press conferences to explain why you're a recluse." Deborah Wilker of the *South Florida Sun Sentinel* was even more skeptical. "In reinventing himself (a ritual so common now among pop idols that it's boring already), in looking inward to find something a bit more meaningful than he has put forth in the past, Michael has forgotten how to write the bright melodies and catchy phrases that have always made him so appealing."

Others saw the record as a breakthrough. "That the eloquent music featured here comes from a sex symbol who could easily have continued traveling more profitable paths makes the album all the more exciting," wrote Bruce Britt in the *Los Angeles Daily News*. The *Daily Mail's* Marcus Berkmann almost managed to listen without prejudice: "George may have an ego the size of Bulgaria and a touchingly Garboesque desire to be left alone (as long as we continue to buy his records), but he remains our most adventurous and talented pop all-rounder, a consummate craftsman who, with this album, has finally fulfilled the promise that he has shown in snatches for so many years." Michael even received a modest benediction from *Rolling Stone*: "For the most part," wrote James Hunter in his three-and-a-half-star review, "the album succeeds in its effort to establish Michael's seriousness and deliver him from caricature."

David Munk, an artist manager turned music blogger, saw it as the first truly honest statement Michael had made. "We don't get much insight into what Elton endured because he wasn't a lyricist. Because George wrote his own lyrics he gave us clues. That's why I think his work has such a poignant quality in *Listen Without Prejudice*, when a lot of his pain was sublimated into the music. It has such tenderness."

For the pop-jazz singer-songwriter Spencer Day, who was then in junior high, the album held deep meaning. Born Mormon, Day moved from rural Arizona to San Francisco, then to Manhattan; in his early thirties he came out as gay. *Listen Without Prejudice* had given him clues to himself. "Long before I understood what queer culture meant or how that applied to me," he said, "I got the bittersweet, unrequited nature of 'Cowboys and Angels.' 'Freedom! '90' has a sense of triumphing over a narrative that's been written for you that you don't agree with. When I heard it I thought, this sounds like New York City! Sophisticated and urbane. It was a world I didn't know at all, and that record made me feel I could belong there."

• • •

For most record buyers, reviews mattered far less than MTV and VH1. Even though he wasn't seen in it, the video for "Praying for Time" had helped boost the song to No. 1 in the United States and Canada, though only to No. 6 in England. But when he chose another somber track, "Waiting for That Day," as the second U.S. single, Sony stood up to him and insisted on "Freedom! '90."

Michael grumbled, but made the best of it. He recalled a recent cover of British *Vogue*, for which German photographer Peter Lindbergh had gathered five of the hottest supermodels of the day—Naomi Campbell, Cindy Crawford, Linda Evangelista, Tatjana Patitz, and Christy Turlington—for a black-and-white photo that showed them dressed down and looking fresh and not overly styled. The look seemed to match the spirit of Michael's new image.

He became "fixated," said Crawford, on the notion of persuading all five models to star in a video for "Freedom! '90." Michael was in awe of these aloof, self-assured beauties who had transformed themselves into boldface-name celebrities and money magnets. They peddled Maybelline and Diet Sprite; they appeared on *Vanity Fair* covers, MTV, and late-night talk shows, all the while delighting in getting others to pay them sky-high sums. Evangelista had made a comment that would famously define supermodel avarice. "We have this expression, Christy and I: We don't wake up for less than ten thousand dollars a day." Profiling Evangelista in the *Daily Express*, Louise Gannon observed: "Look deep into her green eyes and you will see dollar signs."

Michael felt sure that they would jump at the chance to appear in one of his videos. Their hard-nosed detachment about it shocked him. "He thought it would make us into a big deal, that it would be good for us," said Evangelista. "I was like, 'Please, we're here. We've already arrived!' "

The bargaining began. "Convincing them, then flying all the models in, negotiating with these people—that was the biggest stress of my life," said Kahane. It was finally decided that all five would receive $15,000 per day. With that settled, Michael kept thinking big. Five male models were added to the roster, along with a rising It Boy of music videos, director David Fincher, who at twenty-eight had already worked with Madonna on "Express Yourself," "Oh Father," and "Vogue." *Alien 3*, his feature-film debut, was in preproduction; and the studio, 20th Century Fox, was not pleased to learn that Fincher would be moonlighting on a time-consuming and high-profile video. A Fox representative attended the "Freedom! '90" shoot to log how many hours he spent on it. "Apparently it was a contractual thing," said Mike Southon, the video's cinematographer. "So, Fincher was under pressure."

Extravagances continued to pile up. The models would be flown via Concorde to London, which helped the budget to balloon to a reported $1 million. Desperate for a "real" video, Sony okayed the costs.

The shoot took place in a sprawling building in the neighborhood of Merton; a set was built that simulated a deserted mansion. Per the star's wishes, the video would signal the destruction of the *Faith* image and the reduction of George Michael to what really counted: his music.

Fincher's testiness made the beginning of the shoot tense. "David was getting quite difficult," said Southon. "People were scared of him. He would say, 'No, that's no good' to a prop, so they'd come back with ten different versions of it." Southon managed to calm him down, and the atmosphere on the set lifted. "It was fun but it wasn't silly," said Southon. "George was drinking champagne and chatting people up and feeling very nice that this shoot was happening and that all the girls were happy."

In the video, each supermodel lip-synchs a portion of his song, with its frustration at the shallowness of image and stardom. The camera worships every styled inch of the cover girls and boys, finding not a hint of irony. Evangelista, whose platinum-bleached coif looked far from "undone," is shown in a mohair sweater, leggings, and a headband, pouting and "curled up kitten-like in a corner," as one writer described her. Crawford sits naked in a bathtub, glycerin rubbed on her to make her look wet. Campbell writhes in a black bra and miniskirt and biker boots. Turlington struts, runway-style, in a sixty-foot-long white sheet. A male model seductively peels an orange; another one aimlessly throws paper airplanes. A third, in boxer shorts, swings upside-down from a chin-up bar. Like the women, they all look blasé and inscrutable.

Amid all the enticing surfaces, three symbols of the former George Michael are immolated. A leather jacket is ritualistically burned; a Wurlitzer jukebox and a guitar are blown to bits. The shots came at the end of the final night of shooting. The set was cleared except for essential personnel. Southon and his cameramen were positioned far back; all of them wore safety gear, including goggles. A special-effects man set off the explosions, which filled the studio with smoke.

Fincher's edits pulsed to the rhythm. In a throwback to the "Faith" video, which opens with a phonograph stylus touching an LP, "Freedom! '90" shows the cuing-up of a CD: *Listen Without Prejudice*. The video would become MTV legend, as well as a defining moment in Michael's career. "It was a genius idea, you've gotta admit," he told Adam Mattera. But the supermodels and the vivid imagery overwhelm Michael's lyrics; if the song had aspired to tear down his façade and reveal the human inside, the video did the opposite. Michael is a ghost in a bubble of high-gloss fantasy, glamorous but vapid. His voice stays in the background, singing "sometimes the clothes do not make the man." Objects that had held deep meaning for him wind up destroyed.

However confusing its theme, "Freedom! '90" was Michael's most sophisticated video to date. "Little did I know that to this day, when someone meets me for the first time, they bring up that video," said Evangelista to *Allure's* Patrick Rogers. "So, yeah, George was right." It helped make the pop video a fashion statement—an ever-costlier platform for designers, makeup artists, and directors—though less of a musical one. "Freedom '90" proved that as a medium for messages, the video was superficial at best, with too many elements vying for attention. MTV style involved cuts every one to three seconds; this made it nearly impossible for deeper meanings to sink in.

Sales-wise, the single disappointed Michael; it made No. 8 in the United States and only No. 28 in Britain. *Listen Without Prejudice* topped the U.K.

album chart, while making the Top 10 in thirteen other countries. In the States, the album peaked at No. 2 on October 20, 1990. Rapper MC Hammer's *Please Hammer Don't Hurt 'Em* blocked it from the top slot.

By December, *Listen Without Prejudice* had dropped to No. 10. Ultimately the album would sell 7.5 million copies worldwide—a phenomenal success by almost any measure, except the dizzying "superstar" zenith that he and his team had insisted he deserved. Michael was wounded. For all his insistence that numbers no longer mattered to him, he deemed the album a failure. Michael had opened his heart, allowed a glimpse inside his life, shared his world view. He wanted everyone to get it. "Selling those records meant all those people desire what you want to say, how you want to sing it," he admitted. He wasn't just hurt; he was angry. "He figured that he was important enough to be successful under any circumstances," said Phil Palmer. "It didn't really matter what the product was; it had to be successful because it was George Michael. And if it wasn't then it was someone else's fault."

He couldn't understand that follow-ups to blockbuster albums seldom sell so well. "The white-hotness always wears off, *always*," said Jerry Blair. Yet stratospheric sales tended to make artists believe that the public would follow them anywhere. Michael Jackson's 1982 album *Thriller* had set a world record: thirty-two million copies sold. Jackson announced his ambition to sell a hundred million the next time. Five years later he released the edgier *Bad*. Within a year, it had sold only eighteen million copies. Madonna's *Like a Prayer* equaled the sales of *Faith*; her next album, *Erotica*—a shift from confessional pop to sexually themed dance music—did half as well. Bruce Springsteen explored the problems of America's heartland in *Born in the U.S.A.*, whose sales topped thirty million. Then came *Human Touch* and *Lucky Town*, two albums of smaller, more personal songs. They sold about a million copies each.

In Michael's case, there was another problem: His music had already begun to lag behind the times. "Music had gotten faster in clubs," explained Reed McGowan, a New York deejay. "The style was more electronic. Trance and techno were big. 'Freedom! '90' was not easily programmed into a set. I liked *Listen Without Prejudice* but as a deejay I thought, what am I gonna do with this?"

Mickey Schulhof spoke of the issue philosophically. "Every artist at that level is entitled to the freedom to experiment. The record company doesn't want to lose money, but what could it lose? That its top line might be a little bit lower than its budget? What the record company had at stake was just a financial forecast. What George had at stake was whether he would continue tapping into an audience that would appreciate what he had to say creatively."

But in a year when Sony's sales were dipping, high hopes had been attached to Michael, a cash machine for all involved. Rob Kahane had a lot riding on the album. He and Michael Lippman had parted ways; now Kahane was the singer's sole manager. He had recently made an extravagant request of Sony: a $1 million advance, to be drawn against his commission from Michael's royalties. He needed it urgently; the reasons were left vague. After Michael had consented, Paul Russell reluctantly gave his approval. On October 30, Sony sent Kahane half the sum; the rest came a few months later. Before it arrived, Sylvia Coleman picked up the phone; it was Kahane. Later, on a witness stand, she recalled his greeting: "*Where's my fucking money?*"

"It was not a pleasant experience, dealing with Rob Kahane," she said. "He was a difficult individual. I was terribly English about it and thought he should have at least said, 'Hello, Sylvia, how are you?'"

Both he and his superstar client were losing faith in Sony. In Jay Landers's view, the company "did *not* do wrong by George. They worked their asses off. It was twenty-four-seven George Michael. They did everything they could. It was just a difficult record to sell, and artists rarely understand that. It's hard sometimes for them to look inward and say, maybe the record I made was not as accessible as the one that preceded it."

But with Kahane sowing discontent, Michael decided that the company had buried *Listen Without Prejudice* out of spite, and he took none of the blame. "I heard they said the album's shit, he's not promoting it, and let's let it go. . . . I thought if I told them the truth and I was transparent with them that it would pay dividends and they would be patient with me. But they just shat on me!"

CHAPTER TWELVE

IN HIS SECOND SOLO tour, to launch on January 15, 1991, Michael took revenge. Cover to Cover amounted to a public disowning of *Listen Without Prejudice*. Of the new batch of originals that he regarded so proudly, he planned to perform only "Freedom! '90." From *Faith*, he chose only "Father Figure." Wham!, which he had tried hard to leave behind him, got greater play than either of those albums. The rest of the show was his teenage playlist: songs by the Temptations, Elton John, David Bowie, and others. Critics wondered: With all his pleading for respect as a songwriter, why a tour devoted to covers? "Like most of the things he's done as part of his current anti-stardom campaign," wrote Chris Heath, "it's all a little contradictory."

No one at Sony knew how angry he was, but for now he was done explaining. "He was determined to be so fucking pigheaded to the point where he was acting stupid," wrote Andros in his memoirs. "What he wanted to do was piss off all the right people at his record company." Michael hired a young publicist, Michael Pagnotta, who loved *Listen Without Prejudice* and had aggressively pursued Kahane for the job. Pagnotta had promoted the Rolling Stones, the Moody Blues, and the Beach Boys, but it was another of his credits that cinched the deal: He worked for Prince. Since 1983—the year before his album *Purple Rain* made him a superstar—Michael's youngest role model had shunned the press. "I make records, I make movies," he explained tersely. "I don't do interviews." That elusiveness, as Michael knew, was key to Prince's mystique.

With that in mind, Michael instructed Pagnotta to turn down all media requests and release only prepared statements. "No, I'm sorry—he's not doing any interviews now," said Pagnotta on the phone to countless journalists. It proved frustrating. "I thought, Jesus Christ, can't we just do one? Can't you just let me find one of my people and put you in a room with him so we can get the story out in the right way and push back against all this other bullshit?

Instead, it was like a sniper campaign of finding places to get George's point of view out without directly quoting him."

Having suffered through the Faith Tour, Michael kept this one shorter. For two months, he played a handful of European cities plus Japan and Brazil; not until October, after crucial promotion time had passed, would he hit the United States and Canada. "The pressure was off," said Danny Cummings. "It was a bit of a nonevent because it wasn't a creative thing for George; it was an indulgence."

Still, the show was no throwaway. It had the earmarks of a souped-up arena production: the fog machines, the multilevel set, the klieg lights cutting through the dark, the row of backup singers emoting and swaying in unison. For "Father Figure" and "Freedom! '90," he employed what was becoming a pop star cliché: a heavenly backup choir of robed gospel singers.

Michael unveiled Cover to Cover at the National Exhibition Centre (NEC) Birmingham, an arena of nearly sixteen thousand seats in central England. As the lights dimmed, the audience heard not a George Michael song, but the opening vamp of the Temptations' "Papa Was a Rolling Stone." The curtain rose, and there, wrote Jasper Rees in the Times, was "a spotlit Michael in Gorgeous George mode, incorporating eleventh-hour shadow, starlite-brite smile, and Maoist suit unzipped to expose a long sliver of pectoral." Emblazoned on his back was the logo of one of Birmingham's most famous creations, the BSA Motorcycle. Having burned his biker jacket in the "Freedom! '90" video, Michael seemed determined to baffle. Why, with his own new single to promote, did he open with "Killer," the British house-music deejay Adamski's No. 1 hit? True to the show's name, cover followed cover: McFadden & Whitehead's disco smash "Ain't No Stoppin' Us Now"; the Doobie Brothers' "What a Fool Believes"; Elton John's "Tonight."

To some critics, this was high-end karaoke. "Obsessive George has carefully studied every vocal pirouette and arranger's curlicue, and reproduced them diligently," wrote the Guardian's Adam Sweeting. "'Desperado' followed the Eagles' blueprint to the letter, the vital difference being that George can't approach the cracked world-weariness of Don Henley. . . . He cannot sing 'Superstition' or 'Living for the City' better than Stevie Wonder. . . . What George Michael does best is George Michael music." At the start of "Freedom!

'90," wrote Spencer Bright in the *Daily Mail*, "there was an audible sigh of relief from the audience." Tossing out the hit arrangement, he sang with just Danny Jacobs's acoustic guitar and Deon Estus's bass.

But few other singer-songwriters could have handled the vocal challenges of that set, which Bright called a "musical voyage of self-discovery." Touching on every genre that had made him want to sing, Michael sounded unmistakably like himself. In "Calling You" a chilling cry in the night from the movie *Bagdad Cafe*, Michael's high notes shook with fear. The Adamski song found him bearing down on the key lines: "It's the loneliness / That's the killer." A theme emerged of unrest, searching. Michael had sung along quietly in his bedroom to Culture Club's "Victims"; now, in arenas, he barely raised the volume as he told of feeling "like a child on a dark night / Wishing there was some kind of heaven." When he switched to a stadium-sized belt, his tone remained sweet. Yet even while revealing himself to thousands, he barred picture-taking, including that of photographers from publications that were covering the show. Security seized cameras at the door. "You were about to enter the presence of a superstar far too famous to be snapped," scoffed the *Independent*'s James Rampton.

The ban seemed like one more effort to make "the George Michael character," as Kahane called it, disappear. But a lot of his fans might not have accepted what was underneath. Pagnotta recalled a phone-in radio show in which a caller wondered why this obviously gay star drove girls crazy. "All these women came to his defense, saying, 'He's not! I'm gonna marry him, I love him!' I think we all saw it as a useful illusion." Michael's sexuality "had nothing to do with his performance," explained Pagnotta, "so why discuss it?"

The deception left Michael sad, yet afraid to break free. Love, he felt, might never be his. "I felt I couldn't come out and live a full gay life and still have my devotion to what I did," he said.

Matthew Parris, a political columnist and former member of British parliament, had come out as gay in 1984, and he felt for Michael. "If you tell everyone, they call you indiscreet," wrote Parris years later. "If you keep it to yourself, they call you secretive. George Michael couldn't win." Even if no record company executive had forced the matter, the industry, wrote Parris, "pressurizes young musicians to lie at a time when they need the record label more than the label needs them. Then they get stuck with the lie. By the time they gain the independence and clout to speak out, they're carrying too much history, too much deception, to dare. Think of what would have been made of an 'I am gay' announcement by George Michael halfway through his career—after Wham! split, for instance. Maybe Michael hoped he could avoid all that by saying nothing and getting on with his private life in private. Can you blame him for trying?"

That year and the next, Michael witnessed a messy public debacle involving Jason Donovan, an Australian-born theater singer and teenybopper pop star. Donovan, whom Michael knew, had made the United Kingdom's biggest-selling album of 1989, *Ten Good Reasons*, out of which had come four No. 1 singles. With his "lemon-bleached hair," as the *Guardian* called it, and considerable gay following, he was widely rumored to be gay himself, despite a romance with the pop star Kylie Minogue. Now he was suing *The Face*, a British pop-culture magazine, over his appearance in an article on celebrity outing. It reproduced a poster that had shown up in London's Soho district; there was Donovan in a T-shirt that had been altered to read, QUEER AS FUCK.

The author, Ben Summerskill, had alleged nothing. Nevertheless, Donovan's team sued *The Face*. "This sort of libel tends to spread," declared the singer's lawyer. "Poison spreads as people talk." His remarks incensed Out-Rage!, a gay activist group that was Britain's answer to the New York-based ACT UP. "We're very concerned by the homophobia that has surrounded this action," said OutRage! cofounder Peter Tatchell. "We do not accept that it is a slur to say that someone is gay."

Donovan won, but only after he had defended his sexuality on the witness stand. "People look up to me as an influence," he said. "Young kids certainly do." Michael could only imagine what messes awaited him if he came out or, worse, if he were outed.

•••

In January, he set off for Brazil, a place he envisioned as a full-time, anything-goes bacchanal. He didn't know that in that heavily Catholic country, homophobia reigned, and even the gayest stars stayed adamantly in the closet. Though he had never sung in Brazil, Michael was famous there. One of the most successful telenovelas in Brazilian history, *Vale Tudo* (Worth Everything), had featured a soundtrack of international hits, including "Father Figure." The song caught on in Brazil. So did "Freedom! '90," thanks to the video, a favorite there on MTV.

All this enabled him to receive a $1.5 million for two shows at Rock in Rio, the most extravagant music festival Brazil had ever known. For nine nights in January 1991, it would occupy the country's biggest sports arena, Maracanã Stadium. The promoter, Roberto Medina, had famously brought Frank Sinatra to Maracanã in 1980 for a triumphant Brazilian debut. Now, drawing from the hottest names on MTV Brazil, Medina once more aimed for the stars: Guns N' Roses, Prince, New Kids on the Block, Billy Idol, Judas Priest, Megadeth, INXS, Deee-Lite, George Michael.

It was all very risky. An earlier edition of Rock in Rio had lost money. Undeterred, Medina agreed to pay astronomical fees. In a time of bad economy, he had over a million tickets to sell. Medina lined up Coca-Cola as a sponsor, and worldwide TV rights would further defray costs. But there was another worry: Rio crime syndicates had been kidnapping powerful Brazilians and demanding seven-figure ransoms; one of the victims was Medina, whose wealthy family could afford to buy his release. Some of the stars he booked for Rock in Rio canceled out of fear.

But not Michael; instead, he made more demands. He wanted a posse of friends flown to Rio and put up at Medina's expense; after the shows, the whole gang would enjoy an all-expenses-paid trip to Búzios, a fashionable resort peninsula east of Rio. Medina said yes, but the planning "was stressful as shit," said Kahane. "George always wanted crazy stuff." Further requirements included four palm trees in his dressing room, which had to be painted in baby blue and white. And according to Luiz Felipe Carneiro, author of the book *Rock in Rio*, Michael, for unspecified reasons, insisted on twenty plates of kosher food, which had to be blessed by a rabbi. Only half of one plate would be eaten.

In late January, Michael arrived in Rio, protected by four armed guards. All artists and their crews would be staying at the Royal Rio Palace, the luxury Copacabana hotel where Sinatra had stayed. But Michael complained about noise bleeding in from the street, and Medina moved him to the even pricier Copacabana Palace. He booked Michael into the suite once occupied by Princess Diana.

On January 25, hours before the first show, Michael summoned Kahane to his hotel suite. Kahane feared the worst: "I thought, fuck, he's gonna cancel." The singer greeted him with his hair shorn into a short, spiky-banged Caesar cut. He was "wearing fucking pink," said Kahane, as well as a gold hoop earring. "I said, 'Excuse me. I'm in shock. Why'd you do that?' He said, 'I *knew* you'd hate it. I just wanted you to come over. Because *I* love it.' I said, 'Well, why don't you just tell everybody in the world you're gay?' That's how we used to talk to each other."

Perhaps Michael felt free enough in Rio to lower his guard, but he changed his mind and switched to a charcoal jacket, a black T-shirt, and sunglasses. The earring stayed, as did the hairdo. Michael Snyder of the *San Francisco Chronicle* later wrote: "He looked like Eddie Munster guest-starring on *Miami Vice.*"

The star made his entrance after midnight. It was raining, and the audience was soggy and sparser than hoped. As Michael began singing other bands' signature songs, fans were confused. The covers may have been famous in America and England, but many were unknown in Brazil. In the crowd was twelve-year-old Luiz Felipe Carneiro, the rock-crazed son of a lawyer who worked for Medina. "I think that everyone at Maracanã was hoping for a show of his greatest hits," said Carneiro. The audience still cheered continuously, but delirium broke out only for the finale, "Freedom! '90."

Onstage, the musicians were struggling. "The stadium was a huge echo chamber, so you couldn't really hear what you were doing," said Danny Cummings. "The delay of the sound coming back to you made it impossible to play properly in time. So, the gig itself, to my mind, was a mess." Chris Cameron was no happier: "I'm a football fan, so I'm thinking, Maracanã, Brazil, great. It was *hell*. The sound wasn't good at all. And it stank of piss."

Two days later, at one A.M., Michael closed the festival with his second performance. A surprise moment turned out to be a nonevent. In the last twenty minutes, Michael brought out Andrew Ridgeley, who lent his presence to "Careless Whisper" and "I'm Your Man." The crowd seemed indifferent. "I don't think the public remembered Wham!," said Carneiro. "No one wanted to know." Still, he said, "it was a very classy show. The band was wonderful; George Michael was singing very well. It wasn't very popular, but I consider it the best show of that edition of the festival."

At least one audience member at the first performance had overwhelmingly agreed. Perched on a stool and peering at Michael through binoculars was Anselmo Feleppa, an assistant stylist and sometime clothing designer, age thirty-four. His boyish looks—shiny brown hair, a snow-white smile, puppy-dog eyes—projected great sweetness, but Feleppa was aggressive about what he wanted. And what he wanted on that hot and drizzly summer night was George Michael.

Feleppa had not gone to see Michael; he was there for the whole spectacle. His companion was Rosa Fernandes, a casting agent for commercials and film. They lingered in the rain through act after act. When Michael finally appeared, Feleppa was entranced. He told Fernandes in Portuguese: "He's beautiful. I'm going to get to know him. He's mine!"

"Are you crazy?" she asked. "We can't get to where he is!"

Undeterred, he spent the next day investigating. Learning that Michael was staying at the Copacabana Palace, Feleppa asked Fernandes to have breakfast with him at the hotel on the morning after Michael's second show. Shortly after they had arrived, they looked across the lobby and saw the star heading for the exit, surrounded by security. "Anselmo went crazy," said Fernandes. Not until later did he learn that Michael had spotted him, too. "I saw him with this beautiful girl," recalled the singer, "and I looked at him and I looked at her and I thought, lucky bitch."

Feleppa bolted outside. He bribed a taxi driver into telling him where the star was headed: to Búzios. Wasting no time, Feleppa called in sick to work. From there he phoned a close friend who owned a house in Búzios. Lucia Guanabara was the jet-setting wife of a banker and a common name in Brazilian society columns; she and Feleppa had met in Petrópolis, where her family lived part-time. If anyone could help him find Michael in Búzios, it was she. "I have to go!" he told her.

They went. Once there, they learned that Michael was throwing a party in a club for himself and his "merry throng," as Danny Cummings put it. The revelers included Cummings, Ridgeley, his girlfriend Keren Woodward from the group Bananarama, Brad Branson, and Jon Fowler, who kept things irreverent. Fowler was far from in awe of Michael; he ribbed the star mercilessly, even calling him light in the loafers, and Michael gleefully tore back into him.

With Guanabara on his arm, Feleppa gained access. "We split in the party," she said, "and that is where they finally met." In heavily accented English, Feleppa told Michael that he had seen the concert. Said the singer later: "He'd followed me for two hundred miles—that would send me running for the hills, normally." Instead, he was captivated. In his mind, Feleppa became "this angel." Michael was sure he'd seen him standing ringside at Maracanã: "He wasn't jumping up and down; he wasn't clapping his hands; he wasn't going wild. He was absolutely static, just looking at me . . . and he was really cute." The chances of Michael having spotted a face, poised in rainy darkness, in that enormous crowd, as blinding spotlights hit the stage from all angles, was extremely slim—and Feleppa wasn't that close, hence his binoculars.

But Michael had made up his mind. Feleppa's reappearance at the Copacabana Palace, he felt, had meant that they were fated to meet. Before the party, Michael claimed, he had been eating breakfast at the hotel when Feleppa "walked up the hill towards me from the swimming pool, and I thought, my god, I'm right. I'm right! I'm gonna know this man."

Feleppa was just as enchanted. To him, said Fernandes, all this "was a dream, like *Alice in Wonderland*. He was looking at someone with a passion, someone almost intangible, someone he couldn't get; he was watching a guy through binoculars and saying, 'He is mine.'"

After the party, Michael took Feleppa to his suite. Suddenly Michael's world had turned bright. Their Brazilian idyll was brief; Michael only stayed a couple of days, then flew to Los Angeles. He told Rob Kahane to get Feleppa there as swiftly as possible.

CHAPTER THIRTEEN

MICHAEL SANG OF FREEDOM while living in a cage he'd built himself; Feleppa seemed truly free—of secrecy, of shame, of self-loathing. He was all that Michael yearned to be. Feleppa "was such an incredibly positive person," the singer marveled. "Everybody loved Anselmo," said Lucia Guanabara. "He was funny, smart, handsome, with a lot of heart." From him, Michael learned his first lessons about living without fear. "Life is not going to hurt you if you just open up to it a little bit more," he told himself.

Feleppa had shored up that courage in a place where coming out was almost unheard of. He was born in August 1956 in Petrópolis, reachable by car from Rio de Janeiro in just over an hour. The cooler climate made it a popular place for Rio's well-to-do to keep summer homes. For all its relaxed charm, Petrópolis was a town of Catholic family values and rigid sex roles. Men buzzed around on motorcycles. "Petrópolis was only for guys who had that machismo," said Marcelo Lago, a visual artist and one of Feleppa's best friends there. "Society there was very old-fashioned."

Feleppa's father, Amodeo, was "extremely macho," said Sylvynho, a photographer who had known Feleppa in his teens. "The brother, Alexandre, was the same way." As much as his family adored him, they disapproved of homosexuality—and although nothing was discussed, Feleppa was clearly different. "He was very beautiful—an angelic beauty," said Lago of the young Anselmo. "Delicate. He didn't have a beard." When Lago stayed two nights at the house and slept in Feleppa's room, word got out, and Lago's friends made cruel fun of both of them. At other times, Feleppa watched angrily as local bullies ganged up on cross-dressers and stripped them naked in the street.

By his twenties, however, he found that a lot of people wanted to get close to him. "He dressed so well, people paid attention to him," said Lago. "He was very elegant. People thought he was very handsome." Sylvynho recalled him as a hub of excitement: "He gave wonderful parties in his house. He was a happy guy with many friends. Everyone wanted to be there. He used to cook very well. We realized that he had a tendency that was different from ours, but he didn't make it explicit."

He seemed destined for the big city. His first trip to Rio was an epiphany; returning home, he felt the crash. "He was very sad," recalled Lago. "I said, 'Dude, get away from Petrópolis. It's not the place for you. You need a place where you can reinvent yourself. Here you will never be able to be who you want to be.' He understood perfectly. He was super-emotional over this. He felt relieved."

Instead of moving to Rio, Feleppa chose Paris, where he supported himself by cutting hair. He stayed for three life-changing years, during which he learned French and spread his wings as a sexually active, party-loving gay man. He also reunited with Lucia Guanabara, who was then living in Paris. "From that time," she said, "he was my best friend, like a brother." When his parents flew there to visit him, Feleppa scrambled to hide all traces of his homosexuality. "He would change the whole decoration of the house," said Sylvynho, "and make it much more conservative."

By the late eighties, Feleppa had moved to New York. He found work as a designer of men's bomber jackets; he also grew close to Prince Egon von Fürstenberg, the handsome, bisexual German fashion and interior designer and socialite, who employed him as an illustrator. Through an American boyfriend he met Patricia Agressot, a hair and makeup artist with whom he lived for a time. "We were always laughing," she said. "He was very funny and extremely generous. Every time we went out he would never let me buy anything."

He finally settled in Rio, where he worked for a stylist. Feleppa began moving in a well-heeled, fashionable crowd who went to gay dance parties and did recreational drugs. "Anselmo was like most of the gay guys here," said Rosa Fernandes. "If there was a party anyplace, he'd go." But he wanted something deeper.

The meeting with Michael struck both men as a miracle. But before they could be together in Los Angeles, the singer had to tour Europe; after that was a seven-month break between the European and North American legs of the tour. In that time, he was expected to work on *Listen Without Prejudice Vol. 2*. But his mind was on Feleppa.

"This was the first love of my entire life," he told the BBC's Kirsty Young years later. "I was happier than I've ever been. Fame, money, everything else just kind of paled by comparison to finally, at twenty-seven years old, be waking up in bed with someone who loves you." He and his new boyfriend stayed in Kahane's house, where they had privacy. But soon Michael swept Feleppa off to his house in the Santa Barbara foothills. In the master bedroom, they lay opposite a fireplace; outside the wraparound windows were stunning views of mountains and sea. He was in awe. On his first visit, he called Guanabara. Exclaimed Feleppa in Portuguese: "I'm here in the living room. He's playing the piano just for me! I can't believe it!"

Michael showered his love with gifts: a Cartier watch, designer clothes, a Mercedes. Together they listened to bossa nova, especially that of Antônio Carlos Jobim. Michael had heard some of those songs before, but never with a boyfriend who could sing them and translate the words. Over time, they looked like a perfectly matched pair, as Feleppa adopted Michael's stubble and black attire.

Lots of people were attracted to Michael's new partner, who had a big sexual appetite and a wandering eye. But Feleppa was so in love that, for the most part, he lost interest in partying and playing the field. Gradually, Michael introduced him to his inner circle. An overjoyed Michael introduced him to Chris Porter in a recording studio. "This is my partner, Anselmo," he said. "They were quite discreet, though," observed the engineer. "No kissing and cuddling on the couch." It wasn't long before Feleppa realized that this great love affair would be kept mostly in the shadows. He would never meet Michael's parents, although he wanted to; the singer breathed not a word about him to either of them. In retrospect, Michael realized that Lesley had deduced why her son was spending so much time in Los Angeles. She never phoned the house; another man might answer, and she didn't want her son to have to explain who it was.

Feleppa confided his frustration to friends. "Everything was so secretive, and he didn't like that," said Agressot. Fernandes recalled the relationship as "kind of blocked; you couldn't really see it. George didn't want to show it in public because he was a public figure. Anselmo was very upset with that. He would stay in the house, or they would go out to dinner as friends."

The Brazilian certainly wasn't on his arm at that year's BRIT Awards, in which *Listen Without Prejudice* was nominated for Best Album by a British Artist. Producer Jonathan King had booked Michael to close the show. Word arrived the day before that Michael was seriously ill and had to cancel. King scrambled to find a replacement. The next day he learned that Michael would indeed show up—not to perform, but to accept. He had doubted his record would win over Elton John's *Sleeping with the Past*, but somehow he had learned otherwise. Thus followed an exchange with King that Michael would not have wanted Feleppa to see.

"George turned up fit as a fiddle," recalled King. "Two minutes before he was about to be announced, I said, 'George, you've turned into a cunt. Your talent is slipping away; your ego is taking over. Do you realize how many people got you booked and planned your performance, and you just felt you didn't want to do it so you canceled at the last moment. You're not concerned with anyone else.' George said, 'Nobody's ever spoken to me like this—how dare you?' I said, 'Because I'm speaking the truth. The very fact that nobody ever said anything like this is exactly why you all turn into these ghastly monsters!' "

Award in hand, Michael began his thank-yous. "Actually, I've got a piece of paper in my pocket," he said. "It's not like I thought I was going to win or anything." He injected a note of sarcasm: "I'd also like to say hi to everybody at Epic Records, even the people on the top floor," which contained the executive offices. "Not really—joke, joke."

• • •

Michael had promised to deliver *Listen Without Prejudice Vol. 2* in June. But as of late March, he had completed just a handful of tracks. He planned a dance album, free of the loftiness that had gotten him branded as "pompous" and "self-absorbed."

But the new songs did not reveal the contented soul he claimed to be. Instead of romance, he served up bleakness set to drum programming and aggressive house-music beats. The most promising track was "Crazyman Dance," a portrait of a man whose fallen big-city dreams send him to the brink of a nervous breakdown. "It just dawned on me what a huge number of homeless and really loony people there are in New York, everywhere you look," he said. "It made me feel how many people must come to New York and they arrive normal and what happens to them—who come there thinking they're gonna make something out of themselves and are gradually driven into the ground." The song opens with a baby's crying. Then, with cold electronics pounding, Michael yowls out in panic and rage: "Yesterday's newspapers / I wrap them around my body . . . For all the pushing and shoving / I've still got nothing."

On "Happy," Michael switches to a sinister growl and bitterly takes down the kind of sycophants who cling to stars: "You don't dig men / But you'll fuck 'em if they're rich." "Do You Really Want to Know?" found him rethinking his most famous declaration—"Sex is natural, sex is good"—as he pondered promiscuity in the age of AIDS. "What you don't know," he sang, "can kill you, baby." He stayed in the closet by casting himself as half of a straight couple whose pasts had given them plenty to worry about: "If you knew every woman and I knew every man / We never would have made it past holding hands."

Sony didn't know it yet, but those tracks, which were intended for the next album, would wind up elsewhere. Michael loved *Red Hot + Blue*, the first in a decades-long series of starry benefit albums produced by the Red Hot Organization, whose CDs, TV specials, and events earned millions for HIV and AIDS causes. Annie Lennox, Tom Waits, U2, and other luminaries had signed on for *Red Hot + Blue*, a tribute to a gay songwriting master, Cole Porter. But John Carlin, the charity's cofounder, had been turned down by numerous artists who feared association with an AIDS-related project. One was Luther Vandross, the closeted soul superstar whose plush bedroom voice had won him a largely female following. "Luther doesn't want people to think that he's gay," explained his manager.

Carlin was stunned when Andy Stephens phoned him from Epic to say that George Michael wished to contribute something to the forthcoming *Red Hot + Dance*, which Sony would distribute. Apart from wanting to help in the fight against AIDS, Michael longed to take another step toward honesty, if a veiled one. Most of all, by giving away the music for *Listen Without Prejudice Vol. 2*, he began the process of dismantling the most important professional relationship of his career.

• • •

In October, when he returned to the final stretch of his tour, Michael took his lover on the road with him, but there was still no public hand-holding; Feleppa would blend into the entourage. By now he had been talked into singing two more songs from Listen Without Prejudice, "Mother's Pride" and "Waiting for That Day." Reviewing him at the Forum in Southern California, Richard Cromelin of the Los Angeles Times sensed a major change in Michael: Now, the critic wrote, "emotional expression, not glitz, is his real stock in trade."

He even began hinting at his sexuality, perhaps to test the response. Michael, reported Cromelin, made "a ringing endorsement of the current demonstrations against Governor Pete Wilson's gay job-rights bill veto." To the San Francisco Chronicle's Barry Walters, who saw Michael at the Oakland Coliseum, the star's gayness was no longer a secret. "Dropping the leather-and-501s clone look was smart (now that straights have appropriated it), but he's got to come up with something better than dress slacks that make him look like a waiter."

But whenever strangers were around him and Feleppa, Michael maintained a smokescreen. Often Guanabara came along as a third wheel. She attended the shows with Feleppa; then, during the closing "Freedom! '90," they were whisked past the crowds and ushered through backstage corridors. Minutes after Michael had left the stage, they followed him into a limo and sped off to some private destination.

In the United States, as in Brazil, Cover to Cover proved somewhat of a letdown to fans; his concert at Dallas's eighteen-thousand-seat Reunion Arena drew only half capacity. The tour would be best remembered for the moment in which Michael interrupted "Don't Let the Sun Go Down on Me" to announce: "Ladies and gentlemen, Mr. Elton John!" The resulting duet was recorded, and Michael begged Sony to release it as a single. He planned to donate his profits to Rainbow House, a charity for critically ill children. The company resisted; it was still trying to sell singles from Listen Without Prejudice.

Michael got his way, although Sony did not issue the single until November. In its hunger for a video, Sony agreed to bankroll one for the duet. As cameras rolled, Michael and John recreated their Wembley summit at Chicago's Rosemont Horizon, a stop on the Cover to Cover tour; and before an invited audience at an airplane hangar in Burbank, California.

At Live Aid, John had generously accompanied him on the same song; six years later, Michael was a superstar, and the performance on the video amounts to a standoff. Wearing a black baseball cap, a zippered black jacket, and his trademark deadpan aloofness, John felt no need to impress anyone; he was the writer. Each man ascends a small riser on opposite ends of the stage. As John sings, Michael beams at him and grooves eye-catchingly to the music. With that, the designer-clad sex machine and the unabashed nerd meet center-stage.

John's diction—"losin' av'ruh-*thang*"— verges on a parody of soul, but Michael had absorbed the genre's feeling while avoiding the clichés. As he thrusts his arms into the air and emotes his heart out for a screaming audience, John shoots a glance his way, frowns, then enacts a couple of strained shimmies. At the end, the men bow to each other and embrace, but Michael had won.

Competitiveness aside, the video was one of the great gay summits in nineties pop. Michael had triumphed over Sony—the single hit No. 1 in fifteen regions—and over John, for the duet far outsold the original. Why, reasoned Michael, should he risk that kind of popularity by telling the world he was gay? Because it was honest, John argued. "Elton wanted George to be out of the closet," said Kahane. "George thought it was too soon, and it wasn't anybody's business."

•••

For years, Michael had used Rob Kahane's Encino home as a secret hideaway, but Kahane had finally put an end to that. "I had to say to him, 'George, my daughter is asking questions because you're sleeping in the room with Anselmo and she doesn't get it.' There was an ashtray full of these smiley-faced things. I thought they were mints. My kid was reaching up and I moved it away. I found out they were Ecstasy." Michael would later complain to friends that Kahane had been charging him for the lodging.

Before he moved out, that house had become the setting of an incident that Kahane would cite as the tipping point in Michael's rejection of Sony.

The manager was in his living room when the phone rang. It was Donnie Ienner. With Michael nearby, Kahane put the call on speakerphone. Ienner's side of the conversation was overheard by his colleague Dave Novik. "Donnie was extremely aggressive, as was his style," said Novik. "He was telling Rob that George should get off his ass and do another video, or be in the video." Ienner, claimed Kahane, referred to Michael as "that faggot client of yours."

Word of Ienner's smear spread throughout Sony; by the mid-nineties, references to it had begun appearing in print. In his 1996 book *Off the Charts*, Bruce Haring writes that Michael "overheard a slur about his personal life from a senior Sony executive." Ienner repeatedly swore that the incident had never happened, and the singer himself neither mentioned it, at least in public. At the time he couldn't; he was in the closet. From then on, however, both he and Kahane were on the warpath. Michael later said: "I think that Ienner felt that if he showed me . . . in extreme what could happen without video in the States, that I would be scared into changing my mind for the next album."

But the causes were not confined to any phone call. A judge would later conclude that "Mr. Michael's attitudes to and opinions of Sony, and his suspicions of Sony's motives, owe far more to Mr. Kahane's input than Mr. Michael can have realized." Years later, Kahane allowed: "He wasn't unhappy until I was unhappy."

From that point on, it was hard to know where to draw the line between Kahane's rancor and Michael's paranoia. In October, Ienner and Tommy Mottola flew to Toronto to see Cover to Cover. Afterward, Kahane told him the executives had left early. Michael was furious, and took it as a snub. Later on, Mottola insisted that he and Ienner had tried to greet Michael before the show and had been told he wouldn't see them—and that they had, in fact, stayed to the end then come backstage, only to be told that Michael was having a massage.

Whatever Kahane's or Michael's issues with Sony, both men had squeezed exorbitant sums from the company. But those had not been enough. On November 27, 1991, Kahane faxed Tony Russell to report personal financial fears. He would be in "deep trouble," he wrote, without "some type of new plan to expedite funds for Kahane Entertainment." Sony was highly unlikely to loan him any more money; he implored Russell to arrange a personal loan from Michael.

A few days later he faxed Russell again to report that Michael had promised a new album, *Extended Plaything*, which would follow *Listen Without Prejudice Vol. 2.* "Please pass this information on to Sony and also start the wheels in motion for my $400,000 advance," wrote Kahane. The "album" was, in fact, a four-track EP that Michael had contemplated, but would never complete. "If further advances could not be obtained from Sony," decided the judge, "then it was in Mr. Kahane's interest, as Mr. Kahane well realized, that Mr. Michael should break with Sony and enter into a fresh recording agreement—providing for higher advances—with another record company."

Michael still wasn't determined to sue, but that attitude changed as Kahane fumed that Sony had cut off promotional funding for *Listen Without Prejudice*. All the while, his team kept requesting money. At Kahane's urging, Michael commanded Tony Russell to ask for yet another increase in his royalty rate. The lawyer scheduled a meeting with Paul Russell, Sylvia Coleman, and Andy Stephens. Yes, Tony learned, Sony would raise the percentage—*if* Michael would produce and appear in three videos.

That demand, recalled Paul Russell, was "the straw that broke the camel's back." Apparently no one at Sony had understood a word he'd said about his need to reclaim his life. He asked Tony Russell: What would it take to get him out of his contract? It wasn't a prospect any of them relished. The litigation would be ugly and perhaps unwinnable, but Michael insisted they find a way: He wanted out.

•••

AIDS remained his and Feleppa's greatest fear, and they had reason to be scared. Michael confessed to Andros that he and Feleppa had not always used condoms. Both men had resisted getting tested for HIV. But in the late fall of 1991, Feleppa told Michael he felt sick. He was about to fly to Brazil to spend the holidays with his family; he would get tested there. Michael feared the worst. In a 2004 documentary, *George Michael: A Different Story*, the singer recalled "looking at the sky and saying, 'Don't you dare do this to me.' I went home to my family for Christmas and sat at the table not knowing whether my partner, who the people around the table did not know about—this man I was in love with—was terminally ill, and not knowing whether I was terminally ill. It was possibly the loneliest time in my life."

In Brazil, Feleppa got the news: He had AIDS.

For a time, he avoided telling his partner. "He didn't want to worry George," said Lucia Guanabara. But he had no choice. Back in California, Feleppa let Michael know the truth. They cried together. Feleppa, he said later, was "the first love of my entire life, the person I cared for most in the world"—and he had received a death sentence at thirty-five.

The Brazilian begged him to tell no one. But in his desperation, Michael had found a therapist, to whom he revealed the whole story. In London, he met with Andros. Bursting into tears, he shared the news. His friend panicked. "Have you got AIDS?" he asked. No, said Michael. In fact, he didn't know—he still hadn't been tested.

Michael's secrecy climbed to a crushing new level. He forbade Andros from breathing a word about Feleppa, whose family knew nothing about his secret life with George Michael. But the star had other concerns: He envisioned career-destroying tabloid headlines about how George Michael's gay lover had AIDS. Michael decided to stay as much as possible in Los Angeles. Reporters, he said, "knew I was gay" but "left me alone out there." In California, Feleppa would have access to the best doctors. Michael did not accompany him—the risk of being seen was too high—but Kahane could help arrange things; and Michael had the funds to pay for any possible treatment that might keep Feleppa alive.

CHAPTER FOURTEEN

KNOWING THAT HIS DAYS with the love of his life were probably numbered, Michael tried to maximize their time together. Feleppa missed Rio, so Michael bought them an apartment in Lagoa, one of the city's most fashionable neighborhoods; it bordered Ipanema and offered stunning views of a blue-green lagoon. The couple never lived there, however; and as with other glamorous homes he'd bought on a whim, Michael wound up loaning it to vacationing friends.

On November 24, 1991, news broke that sent a cold stab of fear through Michael. Freddie Mercury, whom he had met only twice but continued to worship, had issued a statement: He had AIDS. At forty-five, Mercury was bedridden and going blind. The following night, he died of bronchial pneumonia. He had lived secretly with HIV for four-and-a-half years. His press release contained a line to which Michael could relate: "My privacy has always been very special to me and I am famous for my lack of interviews." But as he had grown gaunt and reclusive, the tabloids hounded him into confessing he had AIDS. It was an end that Michael could easily envision for himself.

Now Mercury, who had sung "We Are the Champions" like a gay Apollo and empowered millions, would be extolled like a savior at Wembley Stadium on Easter Monday, April 20, 1992. The Freddie Mercury Tribute Concert for AIDS Awareness would launch the Mercury Phoenix Trust, an HIV/AIDS charity; the concert would be telecast worldwide. In it, Michael, at Queen's request, would sing two of Mercury's songs.

The lineup ranged from pop-rock royalty (Michael, Elton John, David Bowie, Roger Daltrey, Annie Lennox) to heavy metal (Metallica, Def Leppard, Guns N' Roses) to Liza Minnelli, whose "warbling and thoroughly out-of-place voice in the encore of 'We Are the Champions,'" wrote Jim Farber in the New York *Daily News*, "was just the wildly camp touch Mercury would have loved." An impassioned plea for safe sex came from Elizabeth Taylor, president of the American Foundation for AIDS Research (amfAR) and the first screen legend to lend her support to the cause.

The show teemed with contradictions that mirrored the stigmatized nature of the virus. This four-and-a-half-hour appeal for compassion and acceptance honored a pop star who had led a band called Queen, yet never come out to the public. Nearly everyone onstage, wrote David Keeps in the *New York Times*, "sidestepped the matter of his sexuality." The presence of Guns N' Roses gave many viewers pause. It was led by the at-times openly homophobic Axl Rose, who in one of his most notorious songs, "One in a Million," sang of "immigrants and faggots" who "spread some fucking disease." Yet Rose listed Mercury, Elton John, and George Michael among his idols. Above the stage was a white eagle, a symbol of the freedom Mercury had never quite had.

Then there was Michael, whose clandestine boyfriend had AIDS. Michael cared deeply about supporting the cause, but his frequent assertion on the subject—"I don't care if people think I'm gay; it's beating this disease that matters"—belied the fact that he cared a lot. No one knew he was singing to Feleppa, who was in the audience. Michael insisted upon five days of rehearsal with the band. "I was just not gonna get this wrong," he recalled.

While waiting to make his entrance, Michael stood in the wings between Rose and Elton John. He wore an orange jacket over a black T-shirt and a red AIDS ribbon. Finally, he emerged to the roar of seventeen thousand fans.

His fifteen-minute segment opened with the folklike "'39," a Queen song that he had once sung as a metro busker. With Lisa Stansfield, a young British soul singer whom he admired, he sang "These Are the Days of Our Lives," the No. 1 hit that Queen had recorded when Mercury was dying. He closed with "Somebody to Love," Freddie's combustive prayer to the Lord to ease his loneliness: "I start to pray 'til the tears run down from my eyes, Lord . . . can anybody find me somebody to love?" Asked about that choice, Michael told the *Daily Mirror*: "Everybody is looking for one person to love, ultimately. Nobody really sets out to change partners on a regular basis. It's a dangerous thing to do these days."

Michael had memorized Mercury's roller-coaster glides, his gospel-like cries and quavers. Now he could become his idol—a "childhood fantasy," he said later. "It was probably the proudest moment of my career."

In stadium-filling voice, Michael came closer than anyone to channeling Mercury's thunder. He incanted "somebody" over and over while, in the distance, a white-robed gospel choir kept echoing the word. "I want to hear every single person, hear every single pair of hands," he said; instantly he beheld a sea of hands clapping in the air. He pointed the mic at the crowd and demanded they sing along. He held the final "to" for several moments. "That's probably the bravest note I ever hit," he said later.

The performance was cloaked in autobiography. "Try to imagine that you fought with your own sexuality to the point that you've lost half your twenties," he told the *Independent*'s Johann Hari. When "real love" had finally found him, along came a fatal disease to destroy everything. Fate had never seemed crueler. "I couldn't go through it with my family," he said, "because I didn't know how to share it with them; they didn't know I was gay. I couldn't tell my closest friends, because Anselmo didn't want me to. So, I'm standing on stage, paying tribute to one of my childhood idols who died of that disease . . . the isolation was just crazy."

Michael's between-songs comments about AIDS were much quoted. That night and for years to come, he strained to avoid sounding as though he were speaking as a gay man; he tilted his public concern in the direction of heterosexuals and bisexuals. "People here are probably taking some small comfort in the fact that though Freddie died of AIDS, he was publicly bisexual. It's a very, very dangerous comfort." He quoted a forecast that by 2000, HIV would infect at least forty million people. "If any of you out there really think that all of those are going to be gay people or drug addicts, then you're pretty much lining up to be one of those numbers. So please, for god's sake and for Freddie's sake and your own sakes, please be careful, all right?"

After the concert, After theMichael threw his attention into compiling *Five Live*, an EP to benefit the Phoenix Mercury Trust; perhaps it would somehow accelerate treatment that might save his lover's life. He chose "Somebody to Love"; the Stansfield duet, "These Are the Days of Our Lives"; and three songs from Cover to Cover: "Killer," "Papa Was a Rolling Stone," and "Calling You." He added a surprise, performed not by him but by Freddie. Michael remembered a minute-long Queen song, "Dear Friends," written by bandmember Brian May. Accompanied only by May on piano, Mercury had sung as plaintively as a choirboy. The song was a hymn of hope, sung after a loved-one's death to the ones who were left behind: "Go to sleep and dream again. . . . From all this gloom life can start anew." Michael dedicated the disk to Mercury: "who probably saved me from life as a waiter." *Five Live* hit No. 1 in England. In the United States, it stopped at No. 46.

•••

Still, AIDS was giving him a cause beyond himself. *Red Hot + Dance* was in production, and Michael, said John Carlin, "wanted to be the star of the album"—even to the point of having his own people design the cover. Michael had decided to donate three of his *Listen Without Prejudice Vol. 2* tracks to the disc, the rest of which consisted of remixes and previously issued songs, notably by Madonna. Michael handed over "Happy," "Do You Really Want to Know," and "Too Funky," an urban-funk dance track with a laid-back groove. It sounded like an Ecstasy-fueled come-on: "I'd love to see you naked, baby." The song, he explained, was "the biggest pile of bollocks I've written in ages. But I like it."

He chose "Too Funky" for a video that would appear in the *Red Hot + Dance* TV special. Since Sony was financing the project—although it would recoup expenses before proceeds went to charity—Michael did not hold back on spending the company's money. To that end, he invited back the five supermodels from the "Freedom! '90" video. Michael made it clear that all participants would donate their services for AIDS.

He was stung when only Linda Evangelista said yes. Substitutes for the rest would have to be found. In the meantime, Michael lined up a glamorous first-time director: Thierry Mugler, the fiery French fashion designer whose runway shows were circuses of outrageous spectacle—just the kind Michael wanted to depict in "Too Funky." Mugler, wrote a *Vice* blogger, was "obsessed with doing things on an extreme, massive scale." Drawing on bondage, video-game action figures, sci-fi superheroes, and golden-age Hollywood, he turned his models into everything from insects to dominatrixes. Even his simpler clothes were skintight, broad-shouldered, and flesh-exposing. "It's all about getting a great fuck, darling," he explained.

Mugler was exhaustively capricious and demanding, but his confidence attracted Michael. If anyone in fashion owned the word freedom, it was he. Observed Danilo, the video's hairstylist: "I think Thierry and his views on sexuality and sensuality were things that very much titillated George."

In advance of the shoot, Mike Southon, on board as cinematographer, flew to Paris to meet the designer in his atelier. Southon walked up a sweeping white staircase and was ushered into Mugler's office. He waited an hour before the designer appeared; then they had a five-minute meeting. Southon asked about his concept for the video. "Well, it's a fashion show," said Mugler. "I just want to have a high shot of the catwalk and the models will walk up and down. But I want to do some stuff with a boy lip-synching to George's lyrics."

Southon thought, "That ain't gonna happen!"

Mugler sketched out the storyboards. He had devised a spoof of "fashion heaven and fashion hell"—a portrait of the backstage mayhem that went on during a seemingly flawless show. Everyone, of course, would wear his designs. He brought aboard the eighteen-year-old supermodel Tyra Banks and veteran Hollywood sexpot Julie Newmar, who would play a seamstress with hidden ambitions. Dipping into the New York drag scene, Mugler cast one of its icons, the performance artist and singer Joey Arias, to portray a bossy couturier based on Edith Head, the fabled movie costumer.

Evangelista would frolic with cover girl Shana Zadrick on a bed and another rising supermodel, seventeen-year-old Beverly Peele, in a shower. That was fine with Michael, who had visions of another seminaked cause célèbre. He assured Mugler that he would leave the direction in his hands. Both men agreed that Michael would not appear on camera.

Three shooting days were scheduled at Boulogne Studios in Paris. By nine A.M. on the first morning, crew members swarmed on a giant sound-stage; tables filled up with extravagant French catering and bottles of wine, served by waiters. Mugler walked Michael around, introducing him to everyone, including Arias. "Oh, it's a pleasure!" Michael said. "Do I call you Mistress Arias? Or Madame Arias?" With mock hauteur, Arias answered, "Just call me Mistress." The singer loved it.

He had allowed a few journalists onto the set, including Chris Heath, who covered the shoot for the *Daily Telegraph*. But Michael would still not be interviewed.

Heath did slip in a question: What did this song have to do with fashion? "Nothing," answered Michael. "Are you *joking*?"

Giddy with excitement, he boarded an overhead camera platform, which ascended and glided over everyone's heads. "If you have enough money you can do anything you want!" he told Heath. But Mugler stayed flamboyantly in charge. Arias recalled "hundreds of people running around, talking in French, no English. I think George was intimidated." Indeed, Michael sat down with the designer and grilled him over what he had in mind. When Mugler got to the part about having a pretty lad moving his lips to Michael's voice, the singer froze. "*Nobody* lip-synchs me," he said. It was fine when supermodels did it, "but he wasn't gonna have some young, attractive boy pretending to sing his lyrics," said Southon, who was there at the meeting. Michael went on to explain that this was a pop video; he wanted movement, energy, rhythm, not plot development and characterization. "They were not seeing eye to eye," recalled Southon. Sensing he was being discarded from his own video, Michael made an announcement: He wanted to appear in it after all. Mugler informed him that it was too late to change the storyboards. "I knew he took it badly," said the designer.

In an attempt to assert control, Michael approached Arias, who was styled à la Head with a dark pageboy, tinted glasses, a plain but stylish black suit, and a cigarette holder. "Okay, Mistress Arias," said Michael. "I want you to go to that guy and grab his cock and then kiss him."

"I looked at George," recalled Arias, "and said, 'I'm a lesbian. There's no way I'm gonna grab a man's crotch.' I could see Mugler was kind of smiling. George said, 'Well, you do have a point there.'"

Julie Newmar, the only TV pro among them, took the reins. In her big scene, behind-the-scenes chaos sent her into a comic meltdown. Per Mugler's direction, Arias grabbed her arm and shook her. "No," said Newmar, "I want you to really slap the hell out of me." Arias gave her a hard whack on the behind. From there, Newmar darted onto the runway and tossed off her white robe, revealing a black latex catsuit. At fifty-nine, Newmar fell onto her back, flung her legs in the air, and improvised a split that wowed everyone.

But tension grew as Mugler obsessively pursued his vision, oblivious to timeline and budget. "It was all about detail—the way the nails looked, the way the lashes sat," said Arias. "Mugler would always check everything to perfection." Two days passed and the designer still hadn't shot the runway footage Michael wanted. "That's what keeps the rhythm of the song going!" the singer declared. Mugler, he felt, was also too busy shooting the drag queens instead of the Evangelista-Peele shower scene. "*What are you doing wasting all this film shooting closeups of the extras?*" he yelled. That night, he ran into Mugler at the hotel. "Thierry was crying," recalled Michael, "saying that I was about to ruin his artistic vision."

By the third day, the shoot had devolved into what Newmar called "hysteria, lots of smoking, and raw nerves." She told Arias: "I don't really drink, but man, I could do with a whisky and Coke!" Mugler asked for two more shooting days, which would have sent the video soaring even higher over budget. Michael exploded.

On an empty stage, everyone met to discuss the warfare. "There were the ones who sided with Thierry," said Southon, "and there were the ones who sided with George. It was very French Revolution." Michael screamed at Mugler: "*I'm* the one who's made the millions of dollars, *I'm* the recording artist—*you're* a fashion designer!" He told the designer he was fired. Mugler recalled "a deathly silence on the set," followed by the imperious voice of Newmar rebuking Michael—"We're all here for Mugler and not for you!"—and vows from the supermodels to leave if the designer did. "George stalked out and locked himself in his dressing room," said Mugler, "after his bodyguards had tried in vain to throw me out."

Exasperated crew members finally spoke up. Recalled Danilo, "We the collective said: 'You know what? This is all about AIDS. It's not about anything but that. We need to move ahead.'" According to Arias, Evangelista played peacemaker and got them to talk more calmly, and the shoot got finished.

Mugler was still in charge of editing, or so he thought. He produced an unexpectedly hilarious and savage spoof of the fashion world in which he lived—a candy-colored explosion of gay camp and bitch-fighting that evoked Bette Davis and Joan Crawford in *Whatever Happened to Baby Jane?*, Gloria Swanson in *Sunset Boulevard*, and every absurd excess of the nineties runway. The drag queens are indistinguishable from the female models; shirtless male ones pose, preen, and do go-go boy moves. Evangelista's giant blonde wig looks like a lacquered space helmet. Even Mugler's trademark latex and leather bondage-wear is played for laughs. Backstage, Arias tussles with Newmar; temperamental models snarl at being endlessly primped. Once on the runway, they strut to the voice of George Michael as though this were a Fire Island drag show. A fawning crowd applauds.

At the end, Mugler gives a homoerotic spin to the famous image from the "I Want Your Sex" video. A muscle god is shown from behind, arms outstretched, with a serious message penned on his back: WE MUST PRO-TECT OURSELVES.

This was no sexually ambiguous George Michael video; it was blazingly out of the closet, and certainly too gay for MTV. The singer scrapped nearly the entire edit and designed one of his own. Out went almost all the camp humor, homoeroticism, and backstage satire. Michael opened the video with the voice of film actress Anne Bancroft in *The Graduate*, intoning the famous lines: "I am not trying to seduce you. . . . Would you like me to seduce you?" With that, "Too Funky" turned into conventional MTV fare. The drag-queen footage was mostly axed to provide extra screen time for the supermodels to strut to the beat. After all of Michael's campaigning for safe sex, WE MUST PROTECT OURSELVES was cut.

There was a bigger surprise. Throughout the video was Michael, who had cast himself as a cameraman in a baseball cap. It was his way of telling the world who had really directed. Having initially demanded an onscreen credit, Mugler now insisted his name not appear. Michael twisted the knife. The video ends with a reference that only insiders would have understood:

Directed by

?

Then comes a closeup of Michael, one eye peering through the view-finder, the other glaring out sarcastically. "He completely butchered the video," said Mugler, "and we ended up with something insipid because his only goal was the promotion of his album."

• • •

In the summer of 1992, *Red Hot + Dance* and the "Too Funky" single were released. With no new solo album in sight, these projects had to prove that a world full of fans still loved him. *Red Hot + Dance* made the Top 10 in several countries, but in the United States it sold a modest 240,000 copies. In Michael's mind, the project had flopped; never mind that little on it, aside from his tracks, was new. The video—which had cost more than the whole remainder of the project—proved a nonevent. For all the cost and talent involved, it seemed like a poor man's "Freedom! '90," and it vanished quickly.

Carlin had no issue with Columbia's handling of the album, but Michael was quick to agree with Rob Kahane, who called the marketing a "complete joke." The singer didn't help matters when he made an appearance at the CD's New York launch party. "George immediately sat in the deepest, darkest corner of the event space with his back to everyone," said Carlin. "When Don Ienner came in, George would not get up and shake his hand."

Michael had made up his mind: He had to leave Sony. His lawyers had contrived the only possible way out: They would need to prove that his contract was unenforceable due to restraint of trade. Sylvia Coleman defined that gray term as "basically a concept whereby the courts will intervene if they feel that it was a heavyweight against a lightweight, with an unfair advantage that one party had over the other."

Michael and his camp knew that *Listen Without Prejudice Vol. 2* would never happen, but for now they held back that information. The problem was an advance check that Stephen Brackman, one of Michael's accountants, had requested and received earlier that year on the star's behalf. It had gone uncashed; to do so would have confirmed Michael's acceptance of a deal that his lawyers planned to contest.

On August 3, 1992, Tony Russell faxed Brackman a letter to accompany the check. Since work on the new album had barely begun, he noted, it was only fitting that the advance be returned.

Paul Russell smelled trouble, and phoned Michael's lawyer for an explanation. "I told him that I didn't want the money back," remembered Paul in court. "He said, 'You've got to have it back. It has to do with George's tax.' I then said, 'Tony, are you telling me that there's no hidden agenda here?' He said, 'I am telling you there's no hidden agenda.' I said, 'So I can take this money back and I don't have to worry about anything?' And he said, 'You do not have to worry.'"

The following month, Michael had Dick Leahy fax Norio Ohga and Mickey Schulhof. His client wanted to arrange, "as a matter of the utmost urgency, a meeting to discuss matters of extreme importance."

Ohga, they learned, was out of the country. Michael sent him a curt fax. Their relationship was "irreconcilable," he wrote; he could no longer record for the company Sony had become. "The purpose of meeting with you is to prevent a very public fight, which quite frankly I would have thought would be very damaging to Sony. . . . Without your intervention this fight will go ahead immediately. The decision is yours."

Michael's suggestion that Sony was a cold money machine run by philistines rankled Schulhof. "Norio Ohga was a former opera singer," he explained. "The fact that Sony nurtured and grew the record company significantly after the acquisition and signed contracts with quite a few talents, many of whom grew their careers only after they had joined Sony, speaks, I think, to the fact that we were very sensitive to the artistic process. To me the statement is what a publicist writes trying to rattle everyone's cage leading into litigation."

In Ohga's absence, Schulhof sent a peacemaking fax. He proposed that Michael's unhappiness with Sony might in some way stem from his management. Soon a rebuttal appeared on Schulhof's desk. "Mr. Schulhof, you do not know me," wrote Michael. "But if you did, you would realize that these thoughts are mine, and that I do not come to important decisions lightly. As far as I am concerned, the question now is not whether I leave Sony, but *how* I leave Sony. There are distinct options—a private resolution or a public fight. . . . If this meeting does not take place before the end of next week by the latest, one of those options will no longer apply."

Michael was crossing swords with the man who had masterminded the most complicated and costly acquisition in record-company history. "Threats don't go down very well with me, ever," said Schulhof. "Nor with Sony, ever. But trying to figure out if the relationship can be repaired is always worth the effort."

At last, Ohga returned to New York. On Monday morning, October 26, 1992, Michael, accompanied by Kahane and Leahy, rode the elevator to the forty-third floor of Sony's New York headquarters. Minutes later, they were seated with Schulhof, Ohga, and Paul Russell. Michael took control. In frigid tones, he reiterated what they already knew: He wanted out. The settlement amount was negotiable. But make no mistake—he would never record another song for them.

Perhaps in an effort to inject friendliness into the tense gathering, Schulhof asked for autographs for his children. Michael complied, but inside he was seething. "He didn't feel Schulhof was getting the message," said Leahy.

That afternoon, Michael flew home to Los Angeles. On Tuesday came Sony's response: They had no intention of letting him go.

Tony Russell began preparing a lawsuit to file in Britain's High Court. With that, as Mike Ellison later wrote in the *Guardian*, he "set in motion what industry insiders regard as the most significant legal case ever to hit the music business." Its thirty pages charged Sony with restraint of trade and many more injustices. The company, Russell noted, retained ownership of Michael's recordings even though all costs had been charged to him. Sony had earned several times as much per unit sold as Michael had. Despite this, Sony could decline to release anything he gave them.

Every point that Russell now pronounced unfair had appeared in the contract that he had vetted and that his client had signed. All were standard to big-label recording deals. Convincing the court that Michael had been had would not be easy.

The lawsuit sent shockwaves throughout Sony. Why was Michael doing this? For those who had heard about it, the Ienner phone incident would have been reason enough, but the explanation proved more complex. "I think there was plenty of blame to go around," said Schulhof. "The relationship had deteriorated. What does a relationship mean? It boils down to one word: trust. The artist has to trust that the record company is doing the best it can in terms of marketing and getting the right exposure and building up the sales. And the record company has to trust the artist not to go into left field and become a hermit. In that relationship, the trust broke down."

Sony, of course, did not know the secret that Michael would recall as his driving force: "Had Anselmo not been diagnosed with HIV, I don't think I would have had the anger to take Sony to court for treating me badly. I was too happy." Now, he said, he was "terrified, and angry—*angry*—about my beautiful boy being taken from me."

The only solution he saw was to exorcise a career that had left him mostly unhappy. "I think he was battling his own demons," said Kahane. "It spiraled out of control."

CHAPTER FIFTEEN

FOR MICHAEL TO MAINTAIN any semblance of privacy in London was nearly impossible, but in California he felt free.

Michael had lived there intermittently since the late-eighties, including in his home in Santa Barbara; finally, he acquired his dream house in Los Angeles's most fashionable zip code, 90210. Standing in the hilliest part of Beverly Hills, 1149 Calle Vista Drive became his main headquarters for the next dozen years. "He bought the property, knocked the house down that was there, and put a new house up," said his neighbor, Don Goldstone. The living room had a towering ceiling; glass walls looked out onto a balcony, gardens, a deck, and a pool. Properties in that neighborhood were typically gated, sequestered down long driveways, and hidden by hedges. But Michael's entrance was on the street. Tony Parsons saw the contradictions: "He is a very private man yet he lives in a glass house. He desperately wants his own space yet there is also something in him that compels him to bare his soul to the world."

With him lived Feleppa, safe from inquiring glances. When Michael was there, all seemed romantic. The singer filled the house with orchids, his favorite flowers. Feleppa sent his friend Rosa Fernandes a postcard. "He was so emotional," she recalled. "He said the house was so beautiful."

Then Michael would leave, and Feleppa stayed there alone—"like the lady who waits for the husband to come home," Fernandes said. "He didn't want to see anyone, but he would call his friends in Brazil and say how much he missed them." His illness and the strain of secrecy kept him aching with fear. Friends noticed he had lost weight and that his usually broad smile seemed forced. Rob Kahane had a newborn baby, and his wife handed the child to Feleppa. "He was reticent to hold the baby, to put it near his face," said Kahane. "I started to think, something's wrong."

Feleppa decided he had to go home and see his family. Though visibly unwell, he revealed nothing about his health. They pleaded with him to move back to Brazil, but Michael begged him to stay in California, even though his presence was a constant reminder of the grief that lay ahead. "I was absolutely terrified," Michael said. "I didn't know when I would ever be happy enough to write another song. It was such a dark period of my life."

In lieu of making music, he poured his attention into the case against Sony. He claimed a lofty motive: "I thought, maybe in this period where my destiny is not to make great music because I cannot even think of a note. . . . Here is my chance to do something truly special and altruistic and change the path of artists' lives." But not even Dick Leahy saw magnanimity in Michael's actions. "He's not trying to change the world," said the publisher. "He just hates his bosses and wants a divorce."

The case had some encouraging precedents. In 1988, Holly Johnson, leader of Frankie Goes to Hollywood, had sued the group's label, ZTT, for restraint of trade and won; a judge ruled their nine-year contract unfairly restrictive. Another English band, the Stone Roses, had released a celebrated debut album in 1989; afterward it sued its small label, Silvertone, to escape a contract that Dorian Lynskey of the *Guardian* called "so comically unreasonable that it listed among the territories covered 'the world and its solar system.'" The judge ruled restraint of trade. But a three-and-a-half year absence from recording had dealt the Stone Roses a nearly fatal blow.

Michael faced the same danger, but with so much rage to fuel him he would not be intimidated, even by the likes of Sony. The corporation released a statement. "We are saddened and surprised by the action George has taken. Our contract with George is valid and legally binding. There is a serious moral as well as legal commitment attached to any contract, and we will not only honour it but vigorously defend it."

Since he couldn't record, he groped for outside projects. Andros had helped him score a hefty advance from Warner Music for *The Trojan Souls*, a proposed album of Michael songs to be sung by superstars (including Aretha Franklin, Elton John, David Bowie, and Whitney Houston). Contractually, Michael wasn't allowed to sing on it; instead, he would produce. *The Trojan Souls* dragged on for years until it fizzled. To Chris Cameron, the concept had been shaky from the start. "George wasn't that great at producing other people," he said, "maybe because he always heard himself singing the song."

Whitney Houston had helped inspire another possibility. In 1992, the pop star made her acting debut in *The Bodyguard*, the second-biggest box-office smash of the year. If she could do it, why not George? Months later, the *Sun*'s Piers Morgan announced the launch of Rob Kahane's "Disney-backed company Generation Films." Morgan quoted Kahane: "Our plan is to unleash George in films in a really big way." Michael's supposed movie ambitions added up to nothing more than fantasy. Offers came in "a million times," said Kahane. "George didn't want to do it."

•••

By now Kahane had learned that Feleppa had AIDS. When the Brazilian told him he was about to fly home for a blood transfusion, Kahane urged him to have it done under superior conditions in an L.A. hospital. Feleppa refused. "He preferred to stay close to his family," said Fernandes. "He knew he was going to die." Yet he fought on, as much for Michael's sake as for his own.

Feleppa's family still didn't know he had AIDS, nor did his friend Patricia Agressot. She hadn't seen him in some time, and wasn't aware of how visibly he had deteriorated. In what turned out to be their last phone conversation, Feleppa mentioned he'd been under the weather, but offered no details. After that, Agressot kept calling him in Los Angeles. No one answered. Finally, a woman picked up. Once Agressot had introduced herself, the woman told her that Feleppa was back in Brazil. "He's not doing well," she said.

"My heart hit the floor," recalled Agressot. She had many gay friends, and she knew what those words probably meant.

In February 1993, with his beloved Carnaval in full swing, Feleppa was in Rio, gaunt and fading. His old friend from Petrópolis, Sylvynho, saw him. "He was really, really sad," said the photographer. "Everyone was happy and excited, and he was sitting down. He said he was sick with HIV. He loved life and he realized he was going to lose it. The truth is that he came here to die."

No longer could he withhold the news from his family. His mother accepted it with staunch compassion, and she stayed with him in the Lagoa apartment while he went to doctors, accompanied by Lucia Guanabara.

The next month, Guanabara phoned Michael in Los Angeles. Andros answered. Feleppa, she told him, was in the hospital in Rio and very sick.

"Yog wanted to go to him immediately but we decided to wait a few days," recalled Andros. A while later Feleppa called, sounding frail. "We still thought it would pass," said Andros, "and he'd be well enough to come home to L.A." Why Michael didn't rush to the side of his gravely ill partner was open to speculation. But had he gone, the possibility existed that his secret might have leaked out, especially if he were visiting Feleppa in the hospital.

The choice would haunt Michael for the rest of his life. A few days later, Feleppa underwent his latest blood transfusion. It triggered a brain hemorrhage. At thirty-six, Feleppa was dead.

If fell to Guanabara to call Michael. Once more, Andros answered. In tears, she told him the news. "YOG!" he yelled. Michael ran in. "He got halfway across the lounge when he saw my face. He collapsed." Andros put Michael on the phone. "He couldn't believe it," she recalled. "He started crying."

Feleppa was buried in Petrópolis. Michael did not attend the funeral. "There was no time," explained Guanabara. A few days later, the singer flew to Rio with Andros and his wife. "He came incognito," Guanabara recalled. "Nobody knew he was there." They all went to Petrópolis. By now the family had become aware of Michael and the relationship. Guanabara introduced Feleppa's mother, Alice, to her son's boyfriend for the first time. The group visited Feleppa's grave. Michael marveled at the steadfastness of Alice's faith, even amid the agony of having lost a son.

Conspicuously absent was Feleppa's father, Amodeo. Five years later, after Michael's sexuality and his affair with Feleppa had become common knowledge, a reporter from the *Sun* got Amodeo on the phone. "We cannot talk of this terrible thing," he said. "I can't deny George and my son had a relationship. But this subject is far too painful for us." Around the same time, the *Daily Mirror* questioned Feleppa's brother, Alexandre. "Maybe George sent flowers to his funeral," he said. "If he did, they weren't under his name."

In his agony, Michael looked for people to blame. Feleppa, he believed, had fled to Brazil out of fear that the press would expose everything and mortify his family. The singer's hatred of the tabloids hit a new high. The singer felt certain that in Brazil, Feleppa had received shoddy care—and that "with the right help I think he could have stayed alive."

Years later, Michael would look back wistfully at what he'd gained. Anselmo, he said, "was the most beautiful, kindhearted, angelic person I've ever met, which is sometimes hard for my partners since his death, because you can't rival a ghost." With Feleppa in mind, he returned to Rio in 1995 and hang-glided off Sugar Loaf Mountain.

For now, though, he was wracked with guilt and exploding inside. "If you'd been in the closet for that long," said Chris Porter, "and denied yourself the kind of relationship that you really want, then you find someone whom you think ticks all the boxes, and then that person dies—it was a huge blow. And sent him spinning off on a course that no one would have predicted or wanted."

One happy surprise came out of it. He sensed that this would be the right time to come out to his parents. Michael sat down to write a letter, and four emotional pages poured out of him, including the story of Anselmo. Michael directed it to his mother, not his father. "It was the easiest thing I've ever written," he recalled. Lesley called her son with love in her voice. She told him it was the most beautiful letter she had ever read. But she was afraid: What if he had AIDS, too? Michael assured her he did not.

His revelations had not shocked her. "But his dad lost it," said Deon Estus. "It hit him like a ton of bricks. It was a hard day for him."

•••

Most of 1993 passed with no new work from a star who had been omnipresent for a decade. "If his goal on *Listen Without Prejudice* was to remove himself from the George Michael image," recalled Rob Kahane, "this part of the journey was to completely destroy that image." Michael, wrote the *Daily Express* of the lawsuit, "threatens he will never sing another note if he loses."

But neither the press nor the public had great sympathy for "Bachelor Michael," as the *Express* called him. The star was railing against the unfairness of a contract that had helped make him 238th on the *Times*' list of England's five-hundred richest people. According to the paper, he was worth £80 million. "I've got more money than I know what to do with," he had told Adrian Deevoy in 1990. He confessed to the *Times* that he had willingly sold his soul to the record business: "I would have done whatever they told me in order for them to make me a pop star."

The only way to win would be to frame the trial as a David and Goliath battle for artistic freedom and fairer terms industry-wide. Michael was certainly taking an unprecedented stand. "Hardly anyone can afford to do what he's doing," said Ed Bicknell, manager of the rock band Dire Straits and an advocate for contractual reform. Bicknell called Michael "either insane or very brave." He added: "At least 98 percent of artists would show sympathy with George's complaints." So did Mark Lepage, rock critic of the *Montreal Gazette*. "The record industry is still run like a slave shop," he wrote. "Rock is the last plantation, a place where people with talent and star visibility routinely get suckered into onerous decade-long contracts wherein the power balance is completely tilted toward the 'employer.'"

The trial, which began on October 18, 1993, and occupied seventy-four days in court, would depict the record industry as a place of greed, lies, backstabbing, and massive conflicts of interest. If Michael won, he would upend the whole business, undoubtedly triggering a flood of similar lawsuits. If he lost, wrote the *Daily Mail*'s Spencer Bright, it "could signal the end of one of the most successful pop careers of all time." The outgoing message he recorded on his home answering machine, to the tune of "Careless Whisper," suggested as much: "No, I'm never gonna sing again / Bastards! Bastards! Bastards! Bastards!"

In any event, the case was a guaranteed ordeal for Michael. Unwelcome rumors sprang up. Some people held that he was creatively on the skids and using the lawsuit to hide it. The "more prurient rumormongers," wrote Melinda Wittstock of the *Times*, "hint darkly at Sony's unease with Michael's refusal to deny claims of bisexuality." She warned: "Instead of adoration from twenty thousand squealing teenage fans, he will face the stony stares of the legal establishment."

On the first day at around ten A.M., a black Mercedes parked on the Strand, the main throughfare in the London neighborhood of Westminster. As fans cheered, out stepped Michael in front of the white, castle-like Royal Courts of Justice. He wore a black Armani suit over a black T-shirt, silver-tipped black boots, combed-back and blown-dry hair, and designer stubble. "Only his face looked different," wrote the *Independent*. "He was wearing a pair of horn-rimmed glasses—to add an air of gravitas, perhaps." Surrounding him was a cluster of handlers, most of whom had dressed with the same studied cool, accessorized by tough-guy scowls.

Photographers mobbed him and his entourage as they approached the front door of the High Court. Michael waved to fans and shot them a winner's smile, but Michael Pagnotta saw through it: "Based upon the chitchat we had on the way over and in the hallway, he was very nervous." A reporter approached Dick Leahy for a comment. "George thinks he's going to win," said the publisher. "So do I."

The procession took them to the library-like sanctity of Courtroom 39, with its shiny hardwood walls, red curtains, and seating that looked like church pews. Only a few fans had gathered in the courtroom's public gallery; others were having trouble finding the courtroom because Michael was listed on a card outside as Georgios Panayiotou. The singer's parents had come to lend moral support. Barristers in long black coats and powdered horsehair wigs gave the proceedings an archaic formality. Moments before starting time, His Lordship, Justice Jonathan Parker, took his place at the elevated desk up front. Waves of horizontal blond curls framed his face, making him look as though he were entombed in an Egyptian sarcophagus.

Once inside, Michael passed dozens of large white files, the creation of which had cost him seven figures. His discomfort showed. "This was not the stage he is used to," wrote the *Independent*'s Nigel Cope. Onlookers tried to avoid gawking as he took his seat in the front row.

But not even he could top the formidable entrance of the lawyer known as "the Bruiser": Sony's lead counsel, Gordon Pollock, Michael's foe for the seventy-four court days to come. Pollock, who commanded top cases, hobbled in: tall, hulking, with electric blue eyes, fair brown hair, and a shepherd's crook—"like Moses used," said Kahane, a key witness. That was Pollock's cane; he had injured his back, which had delayed the trial for a week. Throughout the trial he brandished that stick with an actor's flair, banging it on the floor for emphasis, intimidating opponents with it. He even quoted *Rubáiyát of Omar Khayyám*, intoning a quatrain about a man who had dreamed of mending the mess caused by his own bungling ways:

> *Ah Love! could thou and I with Fate conspire*
> *To grasp this sorry Scheme of Things entire,*

Would we not shatter it to bits—and then
Re-mould it nearer to the Heart's Desire!

The *Telegraph* called him "a man seemingly unchallenged by modesty"; he didn't hesitate to belittle or to flaunt his superiority. Most of the time, it worked: Years later, he would guide the surviving Beatles to victory in a trademark lawsuit against Apple, the computer manufacturer, whose name the rock group had long ago copyrighted.

But except for him and other participants in Michael's case, nobody quite understood what "restraint of trade" meant. It was up to Mark Cran, head of Michael's legal team, to explain it. Cran sought to make Sony seem like an oppressive corporate monster that had taken advantage of a great artist, forcing terms upon him that would stifle him almost indefinitely.

Cran's opening statement revealed how shaky a charge it was. A nondescript man in a business suit and rectangular glasses, he could not hope to downplay Michael's wealth. This case, he stressed, was not about loss of money, nor "the wish of somebody to benefit from being free of a contract which he has freely entered into. . . . It is about an agreement which binds George Michael for the whole of his professional career in terms which are capable of being worked to his substantial disadvantage. . . . Without recording, he seriously underachieves or fades entirely from the scene." With that, Cran revealed the first flaw in his argument. No one had told his client he couldn't record. Sony was desperate for new George Michael product; he had declined to give it to them.

Cran went on to list the perceived injustices of the relationship. From 1988 through 1992, Michael's worldwide recording income totaled £7.35 million, compared to the £52.45 million that Sony had made off him. The discrepancy seemed outrageous—except for the fact that Sony was a massive corporation in which hundreds of people in two countries worked to create and sell that music. Sony, continued Cran, had "almost no obligation" to "exploit" his records, which meant it could promote them or not as it saw fit. But how could he prove that Sony had fallen down on that job—especially when Michael had refused to help?

Other grievances, common to record deals, were easier to grasp. Recording costs were deducted from the artists' profits; then why, Cran argued, did companies permanently own master tapes they hadn't paid for? If they could opt out of recording less-profitable artists, why didn't the artists, too, have the right to leave? Major-label contracts, including Sony's, also included this eyebrow-raising fine print: Up to 25 percent of royalties were skimmed off to cover the costs of packaging, "breakages," and promotional copies. But Michael's contracts had spelled those points out. Moreover, there seemed to be no evidence that Sony had hindered Michael's earning abilities.

It was up to the singer to reveal otherwise. On October 28, after eight days of rote information-gathering, he was called to the witness stand for the first time. There he sat for five hours of grueling examination, as Gordon Pollock set out to prove that Michael's "broken promises" and demands "for more and more money" were the true injustices. Pollock's disdainful frown and pinched, aristocratic tones, edged in sarcasm, left no doubt as to what he thought of spoiled pop idols and their defenders. Sylvia Coleman, who testified on Sony's behalf, watched the attorney in fascination. "I have a vivid recollection of him sitting reading a novel whilst Cran was talking. I also remember that, when Cran was cross-examining me and taking me down a path which wasn't working for him, Pollock actually guffawed with laughter. Running circles 'round Cran was a blood sport to him, I think."

Early on, Michael had promised: "This court case will be embarrassing to Don Ienner." No mention, of course, was made of Ienner's phone call with Kahane, but Pollock sensed something between the lines.

> POLLOCK: Would you agree with me that the motives on your side for this litigation, the motives which are driving you in this litigation, have very little to do with the legal reasons which appear in the pleadings?
>
> MICHAEL: Yes.
>
> POLLOCK: And that your reason for this litigation is simply that you do not get on with Sony anymore?
>
> MICHAEL: My reason for wanting to part with Sony is because I don't believe that one part of the world which is very important to me [the United States] has any belief in me or any motivation to exploit my work.

Michael went on to state his "strong impression" that *Listen Without Prejudice Vol. 1* "had been killed in order to teach me a lesson." Pollock grimaced. "You are saying that the company deliberately decided to stultify sales of this album in America to teach you a lesson, despite the loss of money it would involve for themselves."

"Yes," insisted Michael. "In this country I am one of the few very large-selling artists for Sony, but in America CBS is a hugely successful label with multi-million-selling artists and the failure of my album there would hardly make a dent in their profits." Michael couldn't resist adding that a newer star at the label, Mariah Carey, had gotten much more attention than him. "It may be irrelevant," he noted, but Carey "was having a relationship with Mr. Mottola at the time and is now his wife."

Pollock showed no sympathy. With every question, he defined Michael as nobody's victim, but a cunning young man who had manipulated the system and squeezed everything he wanted out of it. Pollock drew out the star's most vulnerable admissions. "Although I had worked specifically to achieve the status of an American superstar," Michael said, "I found the results slightly overwhelming and felt I was losing control. More frightening to me than anything else was the feeling that I had become distant from people around me, even my closest friends."

But no pained revelation softened Pollock. He turned back the clock to the Wham! days, when Michael, he'd learned, had held back the duo's first album from CBS until the contract was revamped to his liking. "So, this is the first example of you breaking your promise to get what you want?" he asked.

"Yes," said Michael.

Pollock turned personal. "You have got more money than you know what to do with—true?"

Michael smiled. "I think you might be a bit shocked, actually."

"Give us some idea of what you're worth," prodded Pollock.

"Do I really have to?" asked Michael with a grin.

Pollock suggested he write it down. An usher darted over with pen and paper. Michael jotted something and folded the slip in two. The usher handed it to Parker, who read it and smiled. It was handed next to Cran, who did the same thing. Finally, Pollock got it. Peering at the figure, he remarked drily: "This is intended, I take it, to be a decimal point."

Laughter rolled throughout the courtroom. But Pollock wasn't through. Michael owned eleven companies, all managed by Tony Russell, who had holdings in them. Did the figure include those? It did not. Michael added a second amount.

Pollock broached the issue of Michael's change of persona, which Sony had allegedly opposed. The lawyer set out to show that nobody but Michael had ever controlled it; in fact, he had contrived an "image of blatant sexuality" to become a star. Unintentionally, the lawyer pushed the trial into comedy as he sniffed that Michael had made "a particular virtue of the pelvic waggle." He even compared the "I Want Your Sex" video to "soft-core porn."

Michael protested that the risqué footage wasn't him. "I used a body double," he explained. "He was considerably larger than me and had no hair on his chest." His fans burst into laughter.

In the course of four appearances on the stand, Michael piled up grievances. He blamed Allen Grubman for having added two more albums to his contract; he mentioned his anger that Sony had allowed an album by another of its artists, Luciano Pavarotti, to bump *Listen Without Prejudice* from No. 1. He cited Sony's reluctance to release his duet with Elton John and the company's supposed burial of *Red Hot + Dance*. He cited the promotion—against his will, he said—of "Mother's Pride" as a Gulf War protest song, even though it had an antiwar theme. And he brought up the story that Ienner and Mottola had skipped out on one of his concerts. "I was very offended by this," Michael told the court. "Relations were already strained and I felt this was a fairly deliberate move on their part."

His complaints were working against him. Though he praised Michael's believability and candor, Parker found him unreasonably "touchy"; the judge also flagged a statement the star recalled making to Ienner and Mottola—"that if I made albums over a period of twenty years, each of which sold five million copies, we would all be happy." Michael, in other words, had viewed his relationship with Sony in the long term, not as a straitjacket.

And had CBS denied him anything?

No, admitted Michael. "CBS had not tried to interfere artistically. My career had progressed as I and my record company had wanted it to progress."

Pollock incurred the judge's wrath only once, when he read a pan of a

Wham! show. His Lordship cut him off. "Anyone can get a lousy review," he said, "even leading counsel." Michael's fans applauded.

With each attack, Michael seemed to be gaining in sympathy. "It was difficult not to like him," wrote Michael Skapinker in the *Financial Times*. "He was confident and personable, and Mr. Justice Jonathan Parker was clearly not immune to his charms."

Rob Kahane made five trips to the witness stand, more than even Michael, and gave the most controversial testimony of the trial. Much of it had Parker and Pollock listening in stunned disbelief. The suit hinged upon Michael's alleged vulnerability at the hands of Sony; contrary to that, Kahane revealed a "detail freak," intent upon controlling everything. "Ever since I've managed George, he's called the shots. At many times he was interfacing with the label at the same time I was. . . . When George has a record active, I might speak to him on the phone a dozen times a day. It's a blow-by-blow account he gets."

The judge sensed a strong vested interest at play. Kahane admitted to Pollock that he had "desperately needed" funds in the form of fat advances for his client, from which Kahane could draw commissions. A fax was produced in which Kahane had promised Sony a George Michael album, *Extended Plaything*, that did not and would not happen. Asked about the letter, Kahane said he couldn't remember. "I am satisfied that Mr. Kahane's memory was a great deal better than he was prepared to admit," said Parker later. Kahane could not hide his hatred of Ienner and Mottola; this, the judge decided, had led him to sour Michael on Sony and urge him to look elsewhere.

Kahane's remarks about Mottola had reporters grabbing their pens and notebooks. He described the CEO as "a scary guy. . . . I mean, we've all seen *The Godfather*. I was afraid of his reputation . . . a lot of friends of his had vowels. You know, their last name ended in a vowel." After several such digressions, Pollock slammed his shepherd's crook on the floor and barked: "*Answer the question, Mr. Kahane!*"

A few days later, Mottola took the witness's seat. He was "outraged, shocked, and offended," he said, at Kahane's mafia accusations. As for Sony's purported ill-promotion of *Listen Without Prejudice*, he told the court that he had not heard of Michael's plan to withdraw from the cover and the publicity until a month before the first single was set to land.

The evidence continued to stack in Sony's favor. In seven days of exhaustive testimony, Paul Russell convincingly portrayed the company as having gone to extraordinary lengths to give Michael "whatever made him happy." Tony Russell, however, came off as a bully who would stop at almost nothing to get his way. Sylvia Coleman told of his extreme unpleasantness during the 1990 renegotiations. The lawyer, she said, unleashed an anger "which I had never encountered in my entire working life." Russell, recalled Coleman, was "extremely abusive and divisive" as he threatened to sour Michael on CBS by trashing its executives' behavior.

Tony took the stand. Pollock zeroed in on the weakest link in Michael's case: his attorney's seeming attempt to hide the planned lawsuit as he and the star went on reaping maximum benefits from Sony. The red herring, as Pollock knew, was Russell's return of a months-old, million-dollar advance check which, had they kept it, would have affirmed the contract they intended to dispute. Russell's accompanying letter—a claim that he was sending back the check as a good-faith gesture, for Michael had not delivered his album— was torpedoed by Pollock. That letter, he sneered, was intended to mislead; Russell knew perfectly well what Michael had in mind.

Russell stammered a disjointed response, alleging that his client had not yet decided what he wanted to do. Russell denied that he "could ever stop him doing one thing or another. I can advise him; I cannot stop him."

CHAPTER SIXTEEN

MICHAEL FELT SURE THAT Justice Parker agreed with Sony and Pollock; all he wanted now was for the whole ordeal to end. "I was expecting to lose the court case as of about two or three days after I got in there," he said later. He awoke each day in a rage, and tried to let off steam by running on his treadmill for an hour. The press shed no tears for a multi-millionaire pop star. His arrivals at the courthouse struck Imogen Edwards-Jones of the *Sunday Times* as farce: "A wave, a smile, an autograph, then he and his entourage would strut up the steps in the sort of perfect arrow-head formation that would have made Michael Jackson's choreographer ever so proud."

That November, not only Michael but Elton John and Boy George were in court, eliciting snickers from the tabloids. John was suing the *Daily Mirror* for libel over a story that he was bingeing and purging to keep his weight down. He wound up receiving a quarter of a million pounds. "Stars get awarded more for their hurt feelings than parents get if their child is killed by a drunk driver," wrote Tony Parsons in the *Daily Telegraph*. Boy George was fighting a paternity suit. "I have never penetrated a woman in my life!" he said. "My boyfriend and my mother think it's hilarious."

Michael's trial held far greater weight, because he had more to lose. Throughout the trial, he received matchless consolation in the form of calls and occasional meals with the Princess of Wales. If anyone understood the loneliness and cold scrutiny known to those who lived in that unimaginable stratosphere, it was Diana. She and Michael were close in age and had become famous at approximately the same time. Michael called her "my darling," and even gave her a gold watch. They confided in each other, knowing their secrets would go no further.

Gill Pringle, the *Mirror*'s former pop columnist, had observed the relationship from afar: "I think they shared a sense of being such hugely public figures that it was hard to know whom you could trust. It was hard for them to make real friends, to be their authentic selves without being watched.

Obviously both of them enjoyed their gilded cages but felt trapped by them. The fact that she had his home number and was calling and chatting with him—that's not a relationship you normally see with the royal family, where somebody's secretary would call up the other person's secretary and make a very formal meeting."

Still, he kept Diana at a careful distance, and called her rarely. Michael didn't want it to seem as though he were badgering one of the most pursued women alive, even though he suspected she was "lonely and would love to hear a friendly voice." He had another reason to step back: He sensed she had a crush on him. That suspicion was borne out later in the *Daily Telegraph* by writer Cassandra Jardine, who reported that Diana had "tittered about her fancy for the singer George Michael."

Between them, of course, such things went unspoken. And as 1993 ended, they shared a project that lifted Michael out of himself and refocus him on the truly unfortunate. On December 1 at Wembley Stadium, Diana commemorated World AIDS Day with her first annual Concert of Hope, headlined by Michael and televised worldwide. It would benefit two organizations, National AIDS Trust and Crusaid. For Michael's British fans, this was the first chance to see him onstage in over two years. Largely because of Anselmo, he stayed driven to help fight AIDS; that aside, the show gave him positive PR when he needed it most.

Diana had asked him to organize the show. David Bowie came aboard to host and deliver a dignified opening speech, but he didn't sing. For that, Michael chose two supporting acts, and gave them as much stage time as he claimed for himself. k.d. lang was a Grammy-winning country-pop favorite; Mick Hucknall led Simply Red, a blue-eyed soul band that had topped the British and American charts.

Known for his long ginger dreadlocks, Hucknall walked out in a black cape over a colorful vest and made everyone rock along with his mellow R&B groove-funk. The Canadian-born lang, then thirty-two, had a golden tone and an acquired twang; she wielded both with a confidence that surpassed even Michael's. lang steeped her love songs in irony; she viewed romance and heartbreak through a superior wink. At Wembley, she stood before the princess in black boots and a white dress that looked like a cross between a Druid's robe and a bedsheet. She worked the stage with big, sweeping gestures, rapture on her face as she luxuriated in making creamy-toned, arching phrases that swelled and soared.

Offstage she had another distinction: The year before, she had come out as a lesbian and suffered little fallout. Michael had noticed. But lang seemed almost oblivious to who he was. Later she told a reporter: "I did a show for Princess Diana and George Michael was on the bill. He came up to me and said, 'You're so comfortable onstage.'" Somehow lang concluded "that he hadn't really played live before, which took me by surprise because he was really huge at the time." Her conclusion: "With the technology we have today, anybody can make an album. But not everyone can cut it live."

Michael, though, not only lived up to his highest standard but showed a poise and maturity that truly befit the occasion. For his segment, which closed the show, he wore an exquisitely tailored dark blue-green, three-piece plaid suit; he was tanned and groomed impeccably, his hair combed back and his stubble now a close-trimmed beard. To Danny Cummings, who played for him that night, Michael "looked absolutely wonderful, a picture of health and vitality." As twinkly, electronic space-age music filled the night air, lights rose on Michael, posed on a round platform in the middle of Wembley as though he were rising from a 45 rpm single. He stayed there for "Father Figure" then leapt off for "Killer"; clapping his raised hands, he strolled amid the band and backup singers and danced his slinkiest moves, reveling in his own charisma. He dedicated "Love's in Need of Love Today" to everyone in the audience who had lost someone to AIDS. It was "unbelievable," he announced, that "we're not conceivably much closer to finding any end to this awful situation."

Michael made sure to thank "the lady who made this evening possible." As a spotlight sought her out, Diana, wearing a white suit with a red AIDS pin, looked down, hands folded in her lap, then waved demurely.

The special showed the world the George Michael everyone wanted to see: a winner at what he was born to do. Michael had made certain it would. Janet Street-Porter, who worked at the BBC, recalled what happened after the concert. "George demanded to see the film and completely re-edited it so that he came first rather than last in the running order, and then he re-cut all the bits of himself on stage, adding extra shots, because he thought his bum looked big! 'Never work with children, animals, or George Michael' became an industry mantra after that."

• • •

Afterward, he returned to professional limbo. His courtroom testimony was done; the trial proceeded without him. It dragged on into the dead of winter, with secondary witnesses and industry experts providing reams of extra evidence. Finally, on February 21, 1994, the attorneys gave their closing statements. Sony, reiterated Cran, had imprisoned Michael in a contract that had taken outrageous advantage of him. Pollock reminded the court that the plaintiff had grown immensely rich and powerful due to the company he was suing. Restraint of trade, he reminded the court, meant that one party was injured. "The person complaining has been wholly successful in achieving the exploitation of his talent, which it was the purpose of the contract to achieve," he declared.

With that, the two camps went home. Ahead of them was an agonizing four-month wait as Justice Parker pored over thousands of pages of testimony and background. In that time, Michael remained silent and largely reclusive. Songwriting proved impossible. He had begun to wonder if he could ever do it again.

Four months passed with no music-making, save for one small project. Béco Dranoff, a Brazilian event producer and promoter from the Red Hot team, reached out to Michael to sing on the next album in the series, *Red Hot + Rio*. Having loved bossa nova and a man from Brazil, Michael said yes. He picked Antônio Carlos Jobim and Newton Mendonça's "Desafinado," which had entranced him as sung in the breathy, nasal murmur of João Gilberto. He wanted João's wispy-voiced ex-wife, Astrud Gilberto, who had made "The Girl from Ipanema" famous, to be flown in from her home in Philadelphia to join him. Both would sing in Portuguese.

The doe-eyed, raven-haired singer met him at Master Rock Studios in London. They did not record together; Michael was too self-conscious about singing in her language, which of course he didn't know, to have her there listening. Instead, he played her a rough demo of his effort. She corrected some of his pronunciation and he promised to fix it, although he never did. Gilberto taped her part quickly and left. Only then did Michael record his half. The process was tedious: engineer Paul Gomersall played a phrase at a time of the João Gilberto original, then Michael would mimic it. The backing was synthesized smooth jazz, bathed in reverb. Saxophonist Andy Hamilton replicated the feathery playing of Stan Getz, Astrud's partner on "The Girl from Ipanema." In the end, Michael sounded like João with a British accent. "Desafinado" was only a brief distraction in a torturous stretch of waiting. Finally, on June 21, 1994, Michael returned to Courtroom 39 to hear the decision. Photographers had climbed atop ladders, eyes glued to the road; finally, a Mercedes arrived. Michael emerged, shrouded by a phalanx of keepers and bodyguards holding walkie-talkies. Rob Kahane, Andros Georgiou, David Austin, Dick Leahy, and his parents were there, too. No one smiled.

The singer and his entourage made their way inside the High Court and through the glass door of a packed courtroom. The many fans who had been shut out waited in the hallway; throughout the proceedings they peered through the door as though trying to read lips. Michael sat solemnly alongside Mark Cran as Justice Parker entered and assumed his throne.

What followed took less than twenty minutes. In a calm and measured voice, Parker refuted every one of Michael's charges. The singer's contention that Sony had tried to "kill off" *Listen Without Prejudice* for spite had "no foundation in fact," said the judge, who pointed out the extreme unlikelihood that any business would want to sabotage a major investment. "If the public are not buying an album," he added, "a record company cannot go on indefinitely spending more and more on marketing. And the fact is that, whatever its intrinsic merit, *Listen Without Prejudice* did not prove nearly as popular with the public as *Faith* had been." Nor did the judge scorn Sony for its allegedly weak marketing of *Red Hot + Dance*: "It would have been understandable had Sony been disappointed at having three George Michael tracks included in a charity album rather than in the new George Michael album, the delivery of which Sony had been led to believe was imminent."

The company, stated Parker, had not, in fact, opposed Michael's new direction. "On the contrary, Paul Russell told Mr. Michael that he respected his position"—and that Sony would do its best regardless. Michael, the judge added, had expected to lose sales: "He cannot blame Sony for the fact that he was right."

Parker singled out Sylvia Coleman as a "most impressive witness in every respect," and voiced similar praise for Mottola and Paul Russell. The Michael camp fared less well. Parker gave a scathing assessment of Kahane, branding him "a thoroughly unreliable and untrustworthy witness whose evidence must be approached with the greatest caution." Kahane, declared the judge, had prodded Michael into believing "that Sony was acting in bad faith and spitefully towards him by feeding him with exaggerated and misleading reports concerning Sony's incompetence and the degree of support which Sony was giving to *Listen Without Prejudice*."

But Parker's most damning conclusions pointed to the advance check that the star's camp had requested in February 1992. It was clear, said Parker, that Russell—whose "negotiating tactics" he deemed "angry and thoroughly intemperate"—had tried to find some way of returning the check "without raising Sony's suspicions that Mr. Michael was about to announce his intention of breaking with Sony." From that point on, concluded the *Daily Express*, Michael's "legal battle to free himself from Sony was doomed."

All the terms that the lawyer and Michael were challenging had gotten Russell's approval; each renegotiation, said Parker, "proceeded on the basis that Mr. Michael's current contractual obligations were valid and enforceable."

The judge had to agree with Cran that the standard terms of a major-label deal were harsh, and that shorter deals as well as a ten-year limit on the ownership of masters "would lead to a freer marketplace." That said, he felt that Michael had negotiated from a position of strength, not weakness—thus invalidating the restraint-of-trade charge. "I am satisfied that the terms of the agreement are reasonable and fair," said Parker. "I conclude that this complaint has no substance whatsoever. . . . Mr. Michael's claims are dismissed."

The singer shook his head and stared out blankly. As everyone rose to leave, Michael accepted comforting hugs from his parents and uncomfortable downward glances from his team. He huddled with them briefly. How could the judge have saluted his frankness and honesty then taken Sony's side? In the hallway, reporters surrounded him, clamoring for a quote. He seemed dumbstruck. "What can I say?" said Michael. "It's very upsetting."

On the way out, Kahane told Giles Smith of the *Independent*: "I am stunned. I've had my integrity and my reputation questioned. It felt almost like a personal attack."

Michael's handlers had arranged for him to flee through an alternate gate. Bodyguards whisked him into a gray Jaguar, a different car than the one in which he had arrived. A few minutes later, Michael entered the nearby Hotel

Howard for a press conference. As reporters and paparazzi streamed through the lobby, the hotel manager scrambled to find a bigger event room. An announcement came down from Michael: Shutterbugs had to leave. "When they refused," said Joe Joseph in the *Times*, "the mood turned ugly. Wilier photographers hid cameras down trousers and inside shirts until they had more bulges than the Elephant Man."

Michael entered to no applause. Seething with anger and humiliation, he read a hastily prepared statement. "I am shocked and extremely disappointed at the judgment," he said. "Effectively, you sign a piece of paper at the beginning of your career and you are expected to live with that decision, good or bad, for the rest of your professional life. . . . Even though I both created and paid for my work, I will never own it or have any rights over it."

He tried to summon his dignity. "I am convinced that the English legal system will not support Mr. Justice Parker's decision, or uphold what is effectively professional slavery. The initial view is that we have very strong grounds for appeal."

He stormed out. No questions.

The next day, Parker and the lawyers convened in court—this time without Michael—to tally the cost of the trial and how much of it Michael would have to cover. The total came to £3 million. It took Parker less than a minute to decide: Michael would pay it all.

The outcome, in Michael's view, had been a disaster. High on the list of people he blamed was Kahane. Obviously their eight-year relationship was through, although the Sony debacle wasn't the only cause. In 1993, Kahane and a partner had founded their own label, Trauma; Hollywood Records, a Disney-backed company, would distribute. Their signings included Bush, an up-and-coming band. "George was very resentful of me, I thought, for starting the label," said Kahane. He announced he would leave Michael on November 1, 1994, "due to the pressing demands" of launching Trauma. Added Kahane: "We look forward to maintaining our long friendship."

That, of course, was PR-speak. "I remember after the trial, George said, 'You know, when you first started the record label I thought maybe that's the time we should part ways, but I needed you for the trial.'

" 'You needed me? Oh, you *used* me for the trial. That's not too cool.' It was mutual—I was done." Michael, he believed, had "ended up sinking his own ship." Michael Pagnotta could not disagree: "Usually guys get a little bitter when their mantle is taken. In George's case he kind of relinquished it."

Opinions on the judgment flooded in. Pete Waterman, who had produced twenty-two No. 1 U.K. hits, called it a "great day" for the industry, one that proved that "the contracts we have are worth the paper they are written on." Karl Wallinger, leader of the British band World Party, asked: "Who feels sorry for George Michael? He doesn't need to worry about the daily drudgery of life. If he was really concerned about artistic freedom in the true bohemian sense he wouldn't be on Sony Records in the first place; he'd be sitting in a field singing to the birds."

Jonathan King wrote a *Daily Mail* editorial about the judgment. "When Mr. Michael had the choice of getting a small deal (and artistic freedom) for a little money or a big one (to make him a megastar) for big money but very binding clauses, he chose the latter. . . . Sony, and its little people, spent time, effort and expense on his behalf. So it's not right for anyone to ask for vast investment, promise a long-term return and then moan that it's not fair."

But for Sony, it was a tainted victory. "There are just no winners in a battle like this," said Sylvia Coleman. "Sony won the court case but they lost the artist. You think what could have been." The *Independent* may not have heard the Ienner speakerphone story, but still it saw the case as a cautionary tale: "A skillful record company . . . should remember that a talented artist is a rare commodity that needs careful handling—whatever the contracts say." Sony issued an optimistic statement. "We have great respect for George Michael and his artistry, and look forward to continuing our relationship with him."

Following the trial, Michael granted only one interview, in a place where he could speak unedited: on the BBC in a talk with Sir David Frost, England and America's genial interviewer of political, show business, and literary royalty. Michael could not hide his fury. "It's a ridiculous situation to sign a contract when you are eighteen years old and be held to it for your entire professional career," he said. "Why would any court uphold that situation? The judge seems to have found in my case that I reaffirmed this contract at all the given points of my renegotiations. But did I really have any choice?"

Frost reminded him gently that he had entered into those highly lucrative deals "voluntarily and with expert advice . . . and that's why you're left with the consequences." The singer bristled. Any artist who signs a record deal at eighteen is "desperate" and in a "very vulnerable position," he maintained. As he once more listed his complaints—that "Sony in the U.S. was refusing to release the singles that I wanted in the succession that I wanted"; that "once the album was effectively dead in the U.S., even though it was still selling around the world, they just said, well, we don't want to release any more singles"—Frost stared. Michael knew he wasn't winning.

"I'm not looking for public sympathy," he insisted. "I just don't believe that if you are wealthy that you're not supposed to fight for your principles."

Frost extracted one revelation from Michael; it came closest to the heart of what had caused him such unhappiness. "Being paid less than other artists has always been a problem for me in terms of pride," he confessed.

He had one last hope of saving face. On August 8, 1994, Michael's attorneys filed their appeal. Per Michael's pleading, they asked for rush consideration. Charles Gray, the lawyer in charge, told the judge that as things stood, Michael would not get to record until at least 2003, when his Sony contract ran out. "Millions and millions of people all over the world listen to this man's music," implored Gray. "There is deprivation over a huge field."

The judge was unmoved. Michael's deal with Sony stood intact; he could record for them anytime he wanted—and his stardom in no way entitled him to leap to the front of the queue. His appeal would not be heard until February 1996.

• • •

A few people in the industry cheered Michael's effort. He and Cran had made the more punishing bullet points of record deals public knowledge. In his willingness to risk all, the singer had empowered some of his peers to fight back. "He showed you can go up against the system," said Pagnotta, "and after he did it, others have, too." In 1993, Don Henley, formerly of the Eagles, sought release from Geffen Records due to a long list of charges, including poor marketing and the company's acquisition by Matsushita Electrical Industrial Co. In a statement almost identical to Michael's, Henley complained that the company was "no longer the one I signed with. . . . I feel like a commodity, like soybeans or pork bellies."

Michael had also inspired one of his idols. Throughout the Sony lawsuit and its long buildup, Prince, too, was in the process of an awkward rebranding, the prelude to a nasty war with his label, Warner Bros. Whereas Michael had withheld his face from an album cover, Prince had gone further. The star had changed his name to an unpronounceable symbol—it looked like a bugle fused with a downward-pointing arrow—and made this the title and cover image of a 1992 album. Rechristening himself The Artist Formerly Known as Prince, he blamed Warner for his diminished sales, and began appearing in public with SLAVE written on his face. During that time, said Pagnotta, "Prince was actually in contact with George Michael."

Both Prince and Henley reconciled with their labels. But the thought of doing that repelled Michael. If the appeal failed, he vowed to sit out his contract. In the end, his suit had no effect on the way such agreements were written. But Jonathan King saw "enormous ramifications" ahead. "Those giant corporations who sadly now own most record companies are going to get very nervous about sinking millions into so risky a business. . . . Many chairmen will now cut their music-division budgets to the bone. New, fresh young talent will not get the hefty launch or expensive nurture it deserves."

No one, at that moment, could foresee the rise of the internet, which in time would cause the whole power structure of the music industry to implode. "A lot of record companies in those days were run by an arrogant set of people who thought that they would always hold the power," said Anthea Benton, one of Michael's future video directors. "We've seen since then that artists can create in their own bedroom and market themselves very well. I think what George did was incredibly courageous and altruistic—although I feel it was an almost impossible thing to win."

Looking back on that period, Pagnotta pondered one of the key questions to come out of the lawsuit: "Did all the talk about money and lawyers replace what should have been songs on the radio?"

Sony could have held Michael to his deal, but the company wanted no more litigation with him; it would have been pointless. Artists were not factory workers; quality work could not be forced out of them. That left him with only one option: to buy back his freedom.

"I was fat and ugly and I had glasses," recalled George Michael of his childhood self. Never would he like what he saw in the mirror.

In 1982, a nineteen-year-old Michael visits Innervision, the British start-up label that launched Wham!

During its Club Fantastic debut tour, Wham! makes a smash appearance on the British TV music show *The Tube*. Upstairs, L to R: Janey Hallett, Gee Bello, Janet Mooney, cameraman, David Baptiste, Paul Spong, Colin Graham. Stage, L to R: Tommy Eyre, Deon Estus, Michael, Robert Ahwai, Andrew Ridgeley, Danny Cummings. November 18, 1983.

At Studio Miraval in the South of France, Wham! records its 1984 album, *Make It Big*. It made No. 1 in ten countries. L to R: Engineer Chris Porter, Michael, and best mate David Austin.

Photo by Paul Gomersall

"George is the greatest songwriter of his generation," said Elton John, who gave him the Songwriter of the Year honor at the Ivor Novello Awards. Hero worship and jealousy marked their long friendship. Wham!'s co-manager Jazz Summers hovers above them. Grosvenor House Hotel, London, March 13, 1985.

Columbia Records

Wham! rocks communist China in April 1985. Their breakthrough tour there made them "the prized symbols of the new revolution," but after visiting the Great Wall, Andrew Ridgeley said: "I can't see who would want to invade this place."

Goddard New Era/Alamy

Above: China's youth had seen nothing so brazen as Wham!
"People were horribly repressed and had no freedom. . . . Anything
Western was considered evil," said journalist Andrew Jacobs.

Photo by Paul Gomersall

Below: Wham! at the Workers' Gymnasium in Beijing, April 7, 1985.
On riser, L to R: Tommy Eyre, Deon Estus, Trevor Murrell, Danny Cummings.
In front, L to R: Janet Mooney, Pepsi DeMacque, Michael, Shirlie Holliman,
Ridgeley, Raoul D'Oliveira.

AP Photo/Neal Ulevich

Michael's sister, hairdresser Melanie Panayiotou, worshipped him unreservedly and helped groom him into a teen girl's heartthrob.

MediaPunchInc/Alamy

Michael awaits his turn onstage at Harlem's Apollo Theater, where he would duet with Stevie Wonder and Smokey Robinson—a double benediction—in the TV special *Motown Returns to the Apollo*. May 4, 1985.

Photo by Walter McBride; MediaPunchInc/Alamy

At London's Marquee, Wham! tapes one of its last videos, "I'm Your Man," in 1986. Onstage, L to R: Deon Estus, Michael, Ridgeley, Trevor Murrell, Andy Hamilton, Danny Cummings.

Goddard Archive 2/Alamy

At Michael's choosing—not Ridgeley's—Wham! says goodbye with a single show at Wembley Stadium, not a tour. "I remember seeing Andrew looking rather glum," said Danny Cummings.

Photo by Roger Bamber; Alamy

Michael parties in London with Pat Fernandes, one in his string of faux girlfriends in the 1980s.

Landmark Media/MediaPunchInc/Alamy

High times in Saint-Tropez, where Michael kept a home starting in the late eighties. Top: Michael in 1987 at Chez Nano, the town's hottest nightspot, with Tony Garcia, the unattainable inspiration for his song "I Want Your Sex." Middle: The singer celebrates the birthday of his friend Cordy Thomas, society columnist. Bottom: An evening at Chez Nano with Garcia (far left); German film composer Peter Thomas, Cordy's husband (sipping espresso); and owner Jean Tantot Dit Nano (far right), among others.

All photos courtesy of Philip Thomas; peterthomas.tv

Michael at London's Gatwick Airport with purported girlfriend Kathy Jeung, March 1987. That year, Jeung rolled naked in the sheets with him in his scandalous video for "I Want Your Sex."

Photo by David Parker/Alamy

Sometime record producer Andros Georgiou was one of Michael's shadows from childhood until 1998, when he spoke too freely to a tabloid about his close mate's indiscretions.

Photo by Mark Blumire/© Alpha Press/Alamy

Michael and Chris Porter during the making of *Faith*. Puk Recording Studios, Kærby, Denmark, 1987.

Photo by Paul Gomersall

Michael at Tokyo's Budokan for the opening night of his Faith Tour, which made him a superstar and an icon of biker-dude butchness. February 19, 1988.

Photo by George Chin; IconicPix/WENN.com/Alamy

The love of George Michael's life, Anselmo Feleppa, with best friend Lucia Guanabara. Less than two years into the relationship, Feleppa died of AIDS.

Courtesy of Lucia Guanabara

At the starry Freddie Mercury Tribute Concert for AIDS Awareness, Michael (above left) sang "Somebody to Love" in secret dedication to Anselmo, who had AIDS.

Photo by Kevin Mazur/Hollywood Records

Liza Minnelli (below) added a "wildly camp touch," wrote critic Jim Farber, to the finale. L to R: Queen's Brian May, Michael, Minnelli, Black Sabbath's Tony Iommi, and Def Leppard's Joe Elliott. April 20, 1992, Wembley Stadium.

Group photo: PA Images/Alamy

Michael's parents, Kyriacos (Jack) Panayiotou and Lesley Angold Harrison, help celebrate his thirtieth birthday at Newmarket Racecourse, Suffolk, England. Lesley offered unconditional love; Jack's intimidation scarred him for life. June 25, 1993.

Michael arrives at London's High Court to begin his fight to extricate himself from Sony Music. "They just shat on me!" he insisted. David Austin is on the right. October 18, 1993.

Invited by his friend Diana, Princess of Wales, Michael headlines the Concert of Hope for World AIDS Day at Wembley Arena on December 1, 1993. Costars k.d. lang and Mick Hucknall help him greet the princess.

Photo by Martin Keene; PA Images/Alamy

The Concert of Hope. Michael, said Danny Cummings, "looked absolutely wonderful, a picture of health and vitality."

AP Photo/Gill Allen

On April 7, 1998, Michael entered the men's toilet of Will Rogers Memorial Park in Beverly Hills; minutes later he was arrested for lewd behavior. The scandal made world headlines.

Photo by Peter Jordan/Alamy

Friday, November 21, 1998: Michael fulfills a day of community service at one of his favorite charities, Project Angel Food, in Hollywood. On Monday, the enraged singer called a press conference after a judge had forced him to serve elsewhere.

Photos courtesy of Richard Ayoub

Three members of *Older*'s dream team:
studio assistant turned engineer Niall Flynn,
programmer Steve McNichol, and engineer
Paul Gomersall. SARM West, London, 1995.

Courtesy of Paul Gomersall

At the Stonewall Equality
Show at London's Royal Albert
Hall, Michael dedicated "I
Remember You," a ballad
from his overlooked album of
standards, *Songs from the Last
Century*, to Anselmo. Corky Hale
accompanied him celestially on
harp. November 28, 1999.

Courtesy of Corky Hale

Elton John, George Michael, and Geri Halliwell as portrayed
on *2DTV*, the British satirical cartoon series, in 2001.

Courtesy of Tim Searle

The official *Patience* publicity photo by James Dimmock, 2004. Michael had spent five troubled years making the album. In Britain it hit No. 1; in the States it flopped.

Epic Records

An unretouched shot of Michael in Basel, Switzerland, promoting *Patience* on *Wetten, dass . . . ?*, the German TV variety show. Michael had long sought to control or buy back as many images of himself as possible.

dpa picture alliance archive/Alamy

With boyfriend Kenny Goss, Michael attends the tenth anniversary party for the British gay magazine *Attitude*, to which he had told some of his deepest gay secrets. Atlantic Bar & Grill, London, May 4, 2004.

Photo by Myung Yung Kim; PA Images/Alamy

Michael leaves Brent Magistrates Court in London after a judge had pronounced him guilty of driving under the influence of drugs. His bodyguards, David White and Ronnie Franklin, flank him; behind him stands his sometime manager, Michael Lippman. June 8, 2007.

Photo by Andrew Parsons; PA Images/Alamy

The day after his sentencing, Michael was at Wembley Stadium with 25 Live, his immensely lucrative greatest-hits show. His blazing outness had not deterred his female fans.

Photo by George Chin; Iconic Pix/WENN.com/Alamy

In Michael's last tour, Symphonica, he showed Europe a regal but somber crooner, singing of disappointment and lost hope. Mediolanum Forum of Assago, Milan, November 11, 2011.

Photo by Fabio Diena; Alamy

Having barely survived pneumonia, a weak but grateful Michael greets the press outside his Highgate home. December 23, 2011.

Photo by Hoo-Me; Storms Media Group/Alamy

On August 12, 2012, in front of 750 million TV viewers, Michael made a misbegotten appearance at the Olympics in London.

Sport in Pictures/Alamy

Michael accompanies his boyfriend, Fadi Fawaz, as they leave the singer's Highgate home. Fawaz was the last person to see him alive. March 14, 2012.

Photo by Hoo-Me; Storms Media Group/Alamy

Mourners gather outside Michael's Highgate home. December 27, 2016.

WENN Rights Ltd/Alamy

CHAPTER SEVENTEEN

MICHAEL'S DEFEAT WOULD HAUNT him for years; never would he fully recover. It had turned him from one of pop's mightiest winners into its most public loser.

Creatively he was almost paralyzed, and he feared he might never write another song. He had begun taking Prozac, the antidepressant that calms panic attacks, but that wasn't enough; he stayed high on pot from the time his feet hit the bedroom floor each morning until he went to sleep. Jonathan King detailed Michael's state of mind in the *Daily Mail*: "George has, in some ways, become the Howard Hughes of pop music. Sitting in a darkened room brooding. Or suitably attired in trademark shades and designer stubble, walking his dog in lonely misery."

There were now two George Michaels, and to keep them separate was exhausting, even for him. "Talk to his friends and colleagues and what emerges most strongly is the contrast between the frowning, self-absorbed icon and the personable, unpretentious private man," wrote the *Observer*. His public image was in dire need of repair, and the pipe dream of a successful appeal wasn't helping.

David Geffen found the whole business absurd. The film and record-industry magnate, whose labels had released some of the defining albums of the seventies and eighties, had met Michael years before through Elton John. Geffen's insight into pop artists' careers and choices was like a well-aimed machete, and he cringed at seeing Michael wage his quixotic battle. "I kept telling him he needed to get back and make a record, and fuck this lawsuit. Whether he was right or wrong didn't really matter. It was a huge, huge error. Nobody can stay away from their audience that long and expect to come back and be what they were. You need to have product in front of your audience or they will replace you."

This wasn't just friendly advice. Geffen was about to launch a new record label that would turn out to be his last, and he wanted Michael as its flagship star. No one doubted he knew what he was doing. He had sold his last company, Geffen Records, to MCA for a reported $710 million thanks to its fruitful back catalogue: Donna Summer, John Lennon, Elton John, Guns N' Roses, Peter Gabriel, Nirvana. Prior to that, Geffen and his partner Elliot Roberts had created Asylum Records, home of Joni Mitchell, Bob Dylan, Linda Ronstadt, and Tom Waits. Geffen held a firm belief that artists should be left free to express themselves; enduring product meant as much to him as the fast buck. Often the two coalesced. Asylum's *The Eagles: Their Greatest Hits (1971–1975)* became the biggest-selling album in U.S. pop history; another one, *Hotel California*, trailed behind at number three.

Geffen's energy could prove almost unbearable in large doses. He was ferociously persuasive and obsessed with winning; asked how he managed to swim in the sea of sharks that comprise the music and film businesses, he grinned and said: "I'll take on any shark!" He pumped people for ideas and information and felt he could run their lives better than they could. Geffen mingled with the biggest power brokers in America—presidents, superstars, fellow moguls, and others whose ambitions matched his.

In 1994, he teamed with the most successful filmmaker in Hollywood, Steven Spielberg, and the ousted chairman of Walt Disney Studios, Jeffrey Katzenburg, to form a multimedia entertainment conglomerate, DreamWorks SKG. It would include a record label. To Geffen, George Michael remained a white-hot property, and he was poised to go to any lengths to acquire him. "I was a big fan of his," he explained. "I liked him. He was gay and I'm gay. What can I tell you?" Due to its victory, however, Sony still owned him. Once again, some of the most powerful men in the business prepared to do battle over George Michael.

In August of 1994, Geffen phoned Mickey Schulhof and suggested that this chaos could be resolved to everyone's satisfaction. There was little chance, he noted, of getting inspired product from an artist who hated his employers. Over the course of several discussions, Geffen convinced Schulhof and the president of Sony International, Mel Ilberman, to let Michael go. By the following month, Michael had gotten the news: Sony would be willing to sell his contract.

The process would be neither easy nor cheap. The company still saw him as an exorbitantly precious gem, maintained at staggering cost and about to slip through their fingers. Nonetheless, Geffen had won the first round. Now he had to vie with other labels who wanted Michael and who might offer a sweeter deal. Tony Russell and Dick Leahy had narrowed the list to Warner Music Group, Arista, Virgin, and DreamWorks. The requirements were stiff: Not only would Michael's new label have to fork over a huge buyout, it would get him for just one or two albums—more if Michael, not the company, chose. Despite his recent depression and writer's block, Michael had never doubted his worth, nor his control. "He had a huge sense of himself," said Geffen.

At Warner's Manhattan headquarters, the Michael party sat with CEO Robert Morgado; Rob Dickins, chairman of the company's U.K. division; and other executives. Morgado was a nouveau record-company head who typified everything Michael detested about the business. His background lay in New York State politics, not music; he was all about money and acquisitions, and he had helped force out several beloved Warner executives, which made him a hated figure at the label. At the Michael meeting, colleagues cringed as he kept referring to the star as George Michaels. Months later, Morgado himself would get the sack.

Arista, too, fell short. For Geffen, that left only one rival: Virgin, a division of EMI and the home of stars ranging in age from the Rolling Stones to Janet Jackson. Michael was keen on Ken Berry, the handsome president of the parent company. Berry's statement of intentions could have been written with Michael in mind: "It's always been our policy not to pressurize or dictate to our artists. But we are very aggressive about supporting them in the market." Berry and his wife, Nancy, were as bohemian as two residents of Los Angeles's swanky Bel Air section could be; the *Wall Street Journal* described their home as "a late-night crash pad for itinerant rock stars and music producers."

Virgin wanted world rights, which would have shut out the still-embryonic DreamWorks. But Geffen was thrown a bone: He could have North American and Canadian rights—far less lucrative markets for Michael—while Virgin got everywhere else. The labels would have to divide the buyout costs, plus a $12 million advance for two albums, and pay Michael a sky-high 21 percent royalty. Both Geffen and Berry tried offering more money for a longer-term deal; Tony Russell wouldn't budge. To accept these terms, said Geffen, "was a huge mistake on my part. I wanted George so badly that I agreed to it."

In January 1995, Sony got to exact revenge on Michael. The company demanded $50 million for the buyout plus a royalty on future sales. Sony announced its intention to release a Greatest Hits collection at the end of the year, just when Michael's camp had hoped to issue a new album; the compilation would likely outshine a new album. Russell rolled up his sleeves. Over the course of several grueling months of negotiation, the buyout cost was dropped to $40 million; Sony threw in a prize by agreeing to pay its own legal costs for the trial, even though the judge had pinned them on Michael. The company also agreed to delay its Greatest Hits album if Michael would give them three new bonus tracks that he would produce and own. Michael agreed to do promotion.

On July 11, he signed a dual contract with Virgin and DreamWorks. Amid almost a year of testy haggling over money and terms, someone did a basic piece of math. Michael's next album would have to sell over ten million copies—a quarter-million more than *Listen Without Prejudice Vol. 1*—for his two new labels to turn a profit. But it was best not to dwell on that. Press releases were whipped up, trumpeting the news that George Michael's comeback CD and single were on the way. Observed Simon Garfield in the *Independent*: "Nobody is even entertaining the thought that these will not be hits of considerable magnitude."

•••

Michael had gotten the deal he'd wanted; now he had to prove he'd been worth the cost. Dick Leahy magnified the pressures in a comment he gave to the *Sunday Times*: After the pummeling that Michael's reputation had suffered, nothing but "the biggest album in the world" would make him happy.

Five years had passed since his last one, and the market had changed. In the month of the double-signing, Michael opened the *Guardian* to read a sobering quote from Simon Napier-Bell: "I haven't met anyone in the business who cares about George Michael anymore." The British press was smitten with two scruffy, brooding young stars, Damon Albarn (lead singer of the band Blur) and Jarvis Cocker (head of another group that critics loved, Pulp). England's favorite boy band was Take That, Britpop's answer to an American sensation, New Kids on the Block. Take That rode a wave that Wham! had once topped as it scored six No. 1 singles and headlined at Wembley. In 1995, Take That invaded the U.S. market with "Back for Good," a top-ten hit. The arm-in-arm youths went even further than Wham! in teasing with ambiguous sexuality: the *Observer* smirked at their "camping about in leather, studs, boots, and codpieces."

The group's lead singer and songwriter, Gary Barlow, held forth with mooning eyes, Michael-like bushy eyebrows, and fussily spiked bangs; his light, pretty voice matched the pained sensitivity of his looks. Barlow was highly vocal about his dream to become the "new George Michael," as though the old one were dead and gone. "Of course," he enthused, "it's a great compliment when people compare me to George. . . . I used to idolize George when I was growing up. I wanted to be everything he was. So, in my early years, I did fancy men. Or a man. He is bloody good-looking, isn't he?"

The remarks made Michael cringe. Take That's breakout star, however, wasn't Barlow but Robbie Williams, a cute, funny, playful bloke, adorable to girls and anything but self-serious; onstage and in videos he camped it up and didn't care if people thought he was gay. Williams, too, adored Michael, and even released a cover of "Freedom! '90." Their relationship was cordial, but Michael could never forget that Williams was the It Boy who had usurped his British crown; in TV interviews he kept noting it with a strained smirk.

Michael could have accepted the ephemeral nature of pop and let go of his sales obsessions; in Europe, at least, his fans remained as fervent as ever. But unless he were No. 1, nothing else seemed to matter. Across the dinner table, Geffen faced a deeply depressed man for whom little, in his mind, had worked out. "I'm not sure George could have been made happy. In fact, I don't know that he was ever happy. I never saw it. Everybody had disappointed him—professional people, friends. He talked about how hard it was because people were trying to borrow money from him. Columbia Records was to blame, his managers were to blame. He did not take any responsibility. He was attached to being a victim. He couldn't be told what to do. He didn't listen."

Things got worse when the singer occasionally went off Prozac, which caused his mood to seesaw. "I never knew who I was gonna have a meeting with," said Geffen. "He could be a doll, really nice, warm, friendly, or he could be aggressive."

At least now he had a cause: to eulogize Anselmo in music, to make his spirit live, while exploring the nature of bereavement. "If you have loved," he said, "then the love you felt never goes away. It is with you forever." That is what drove him through the excruciating recording that lay ahead. The new album, he decided, would spell out what loss had taught him; it would tell the world about the man who had made him grow up—without divulging too many details about their relationship. Ageist pop charts be damned: He would call it *Older*. Michael aimed to prove he'd grown into a more sophisticated artistry. In his mind were the Jobim songs Anselmo had played for him. He wanted the album to sound sensual, melancholy, like Rio felt.

This formula wasn't likely to catapult him back to the top, but for now, Michael had a graver problem: He could barely compose a line. Pot, he said, dulled his grief and made him feel like composing. Yet he had struggled to sketch out songs in Los Angeles and come up with almost nothing usable.

In the fall of 1994, he returned to London and put a hold on SARM's Studio 2. Michael kept it booked for months, Monday through Friday, at an approximate cost of £1,500 a day. He placed Chris Porter on constant call; Andros was there to lend moral support and prep the joints. (The booklet would credit him as "roller.")

To simply sit down and write songs was now beyond Michael; he would have to cobble them together through trial and error in the studio. Though he brought in trusted musicians, notably Chris Cameron and trumpeter Steve Sidwell, Michael would play most of the keyboards himself, as well as bass guitar, while operating new computerized recording and synth equipment that he didn't fully understand.

Thus began an agonizing and lonely process that mirrored his broken internal state. Lights dimmed, Michael sat at a keyboard, a spliff burning; the acrid smell filled the air. However much the pot may have eased his fear, it also slowed him down and made it hard for him to stay focused. With almost nothing on paper, he wracked his brain for ideas and recorded "total stream-of-consciousness rubbish," as he called it later. He repeated lines and phrases every which way, groping for the notes that sat the most flatteringly in his voice, then discarding nearly everything. Often he finished a chorus only to say, "No, that's not right"; he would scrap it and start all over again.

Outside in the reception area, his colleagues waited and waited. Porter would arrive in the late morning; Michael was never there. Occasionally he failed to show up; more often he wandered in at some point in the afternoon. "I just need to be alone for a minute," he would tell Porter. "I've got to work out some ideas." Sometimes hours passed before he summoned the engineer briefly to record a few fragments of music. Michael kept a programmer, Steve McNichol, on hand to help him with computer issues; he would call upon Chris Cameron for help in coming up with chords or shaping a phrase, a rhythm, a vamp. "We'd do four bars," said Cameron, "then I was told to go sit outside."

Daytime television or PlayStation videogames kept the musicians amused to a point. Rather than waste so much time, Cameron sketched out other projects. Sometimes Michael saw him busy with someone else's arrangements and became angry: These were *his* sessions. But Michael tended to quit within a couple of hours and go to dinner. "Not only was I doing an awful lot of nothing," said Porter, "I was also starting to be excluded from any involvement in any actual work. He wanted to keep it all to himself."

After months, they had three songs. "Star People," a midtempo dance track, returned to a theme that haunted him: the emptiness of celebrity and the dysfunction that drove the famous to seek the love of millions. "Where would you be without all that attention / You'd die / I'd die." That track excited no one; "Freedom! '90" had covered the same theme more enticingly. "The Strangest Thing" showed more promise. It featured a guitar line, played by Michael on keyboard, that sounded like a bouzouki, the Greek string instrument that he had heard on his father's records. Its hard, metallic twang lent a chill to a song about a lost man stumbling through the night, searching for warmth: "There's a liar in my head / There's a thief upon my bed . . . I am frightened for my soul."

Inspiration was sparse until November, when the muse of Anselmo descended. Michael sat in solitude at the keyboard, noodling synthesized instrumental sounds, including a soft guitar line. He flipped on his vocal recorder and sang a phrase: "You smiled at me like Jesus to a child."

"Oh my God," thought Michael. "That's him and me."

As other lines followed, he was exhilarated to find he could still write, and that he had cracked open his heart like never before.

In "Jesus to a Child," Michael found redemption for the young man's death: "The lover that you kissed will comfort you when there's no hope in sight." While he remained nonreligious, themes of Christianity brought him comfort, while serving as dramatic devices. The melody lay high in his range; it made him sound like the child in the song—one who looked up to his savior with vulnerability and submission. Soft cries ended many of his phrases. Michael framed the song in caressing sounds, notably acoustic guitar, that drew from bossa nova. He poured on his trademark reverb; it enhanced the churchlike atmosphere.

The bulk of the song was finished in a day and a half, "which is really unusual for me," he said. He couldn't wait to share it with the world. Michael premiered "Jesus to a Child" at the inaugural MTV Europe Music Awards, telecast from Berlin on November 24. The ceremony would take place in front of the Brandenburg Gate, the white-pillared, neoclassical row of arches that symbolized the hard-earned unity of a long-divided country. But the show's intentions were murky. While purporting to honor music that typified international social change, it seemed more like an excuse to throw together miscellaneous pop idols (including host Tom Jones and Take That) with supermodels, fashion designers, and other celebrities, who handed out awards for vague displays of activism.

At present there was no reason to celebrate Michael, yet he received fifteen minutes of airtime. His opener, "Freedom! '90," might have passed for a tie-in with the fall of the Berlin Wall five years earlier. But the segment was pure pop exhibitionism, performed so frenetically that he seemed desperate to prove he still had it. A parade of female models, notably Naomi Campbell, rose one by one like Venuses through a hole in the ground, wrapped in white sheets and preening haughtily; Michael leapt out from behind them in a black leather suit and sang about the hollowness of the pop-star façade while mining it to the hilt. He reenacted his old disco moves with a vengeance, jumping on and off risers, clapping feverishly, and traversing runways.

Michael sported a puzzling new look. Sheryl Garratt, in the *Sunday Times*, led a chorus of ribbing: "George Michael, as even his most ardent fans will admit, has not had so much a bad hair day as a bad hair life. Now we have this severe crop with a fringe, a clipped centurion look that no doubt worked fine on the imperial faces of Ancient Rome, but which makes a good-looking Greek lad from north London appear unfairly round-faced and chubby." Replacing his famed stubble was a Mephistophelian goatee met by long sideburns.

Later he returned, now stationary in front of an orchestra, and lip-synched to his track of "Jesus to a Child." The song created a spell; its imminent release would have made sense. But *Older* was far from complete, and both Chris Cameron and Chris Porter had lost patience with his process and moved on. *Older* would be the last project in Porter's dozen-year association with Michael. Paul Gomersall, his longtime assistant, took over. On Gomersall's first day, Michael met Niall Flynn, a young apprentice engineer at SARM, raised in Limerick, Ireland. Flynn would work with Michael for the rest of his life.

Months of studio time continued to drag on. But "Jesus to a Child" *had* helped Michael to break through his block, and songs gradually came together. "George pretty much mixed everything himself," said Flynn. "You did your homework and made sure there were no issues, but he was a self-contained unit in a lot of ways. He knew how to make a record sound like a record."

Marijuana, of course, had much to do with *Older*'s sound; it helped make the songs sound like dreams, blurred around the edges, not quite literal. Striking instrumental details break through the mist; the singing is breathy and anguished. "To Be Forgiven" is the cry of a drowning man—"I'm going down, won't you help me / Save me from myself"—set to a celestial strain from Debussy's symphonic poem, *Prélude à l'après-midi d'un faune*. In the album's title song he floats in a stoned haze, trapped in unhappiness: "Change is a stranger / Who never seems to show." The muted trumpet of Steve Sidwell cuts through the dark, like a cold reality Michael can't escape. He had asked Sidwell to double-track his solo, as though a ghost were shadowing a ghost. Michael labored for months on the saddest song, "You Have Been Loved," a portrait of Anselmo's funeral and the strength of his mother, who clung to her faith even after a senseless loss: "Now we meet to take him flowers / And only God knows why."

In "It Doesn't Really Matter," a bed of pingy electrobeats and casual percussion lighten a song that seems directed at his father: "I changed my name / To be rid of the things that I want from you. . . . Why tell me you don't understand when you do?"

Almost everything he'd recorded was somber and bleak; the success of *Older* would depend on punchier hit singles. The path to those pointed upstairs, where Johnny Douglas, a fledgling record producer in his mid-twenties, was grooming the debut album of Lisa Moorish, a Jamaican-British singer-songwriter. He had her covering Wham!'s "I'm Your Man." Douglas idolized Michael, and in the "very hick northern England town" where he'd grown up, he said, "I wanted to be him." He had sung the star's songs and even copied his eighties bouffant hairdo. The Michael image had helped lure Douglas to London, where for a time he slept on a park bench. He quickly realized he couldn't sing as well as his idol, though, and he switched to producing and songwriting. So far, none of his efforts had charted high enough to be noticed.

But now Michael was a flight below him, and Douglas was determined to make his presence known. He tracked down a stack of old Wham! CHOOSE LIFE T-shirts and asked everyone in the studio to wear one. Word leaked to Studio 2, and as hoped, Michael walked in. Douglas played him some of Moorish's tracks, and Michael liked what he heard. In Douglas he encountered a lifeline to present-day pop, with which he had lost touch; Douglas, he sensed, could give *Older* a shot of energy and youth. Michael thrilled him and Moorish by volunteering to sing backup on "I'm Your Man."

But first he invited Douglas downstairs, where he proudly played him "Jesus to a Child," along with various other songs in rough or fragmentary states. Douglas singled out "Fastlove," a medium-tempo dance track about using quick sex as a drug to bring "some peace of mind," "some affirmation." When he sang, "I ain't Mr. Right . . . but if you're looking for fast love," any gay man would have understood. And while Douglas was straight, he got the message.

The Latin percussion and sluggish pace on the demo weren't working. Michael asked Douglas to record a library of samples, drum loops, bass lines, anything that might trigger his imagination. As they worked together, Michael's gloom lifted. He showed up every day, increasingly certain he was creating something special. The producer aimed to revive what he called the "dirty sexy fucker" in Michael, who was drowning in seriousness. Dipping into G-funk (gangsta funk), a slow-groove form of hip-hop, he gave "Fastlove" one of the style's earmarks: a high-pitched, synthesized whistle that spun out a countermelody. Douglas devised a hook: "Gotta get up to get down," which he sang throughout the track in what he called "this silly American accent."

Just when the producer thought "Fastlove" had been put to rest, Michael recalled "Forget Me Nots," a mellow R&B dance hit by singer Patrice Rushen. It had a hypnotic groove and a throbbing bass line that he fused onto "Fastlove."

A week later the track was done, and Michael returned to Douglas's tapes. He found an eight-bar drum-and-keyboard loop in a style known as trip-hop: a psychedelic fusion of hip-hop and electronics. The loop recalled the soundtrack of *Twin Peaks*, the early-nineties cult TV series about murder and supernatural intrigue in a suburb of Washington state. Angelo Badalamenti's music, created on a Fender Rhodes synthesizer, had proven as vivid as any character: It was slow, sinister, and full of eerie silences, implying footsteps in the night and danger lurking around the corner.

Michael locked himself away with Douglas's recording. Out of it grew a far bolder gay statement than "Fastlove." In "Spinning the Wheel," as Michael called it, he tells a chilling story of anonymous sex and infidelity in the age of AIDS. As the clock inches toward dawn, a man waits for his lover to come home. As he does, he ponders his mate's obsession with a sexual form of Russian roulette and his own willingness to put up with it: "How can you love me when you are playing with my life?" It's all about the thrill of danger, he decides, and it's just a matter of time before he, too, will pay the cost: "One of these days you're gonna bring some home to me."

The song seemed far more mature and candid than the made-for-scandal "I Want Your Sex." It mirrored his vulnerability as a gay man who yearned for love and commitment, while foretelling the promiscuity that would soon consume him. The track wedded fear, excitement, and a hint of black humor. One of Michael's most evocative touches comes at the end, when one hears the flicking of a lighter and the crackle of a cigarette being lit. That action and the pale flash of light it brought were how gay men signaled their presence in dark cruising areas. Michael had simply recorded himself lighting a spliff in the studio.

After ten months of work, *Older* was done. In its course, Douglas had watched Michael come back to life. "I didn't see George suffering in any way," he said. "I saw an invigorated pop star who knew he had something great. I think my enthusiasm and energy helped pushed him over the line."

•••

Eager to bolster this new beginning, Michael had hired the gentlemanly but direct Andy Stephens, the longtime Epic executive, to manage him. Stephens asked why Michael had chosen him when he could have had almost any pop manager in the world. "Because I think you will tell me what you believe, not what you think I want to hear," said Michael. "Most importantly, you've always been honest with me, and I trust you."

Michael knew that his British audience would devour whatever he gave them; it was America that he had to reclaim. Geffen had left him alone throughout the making of *Older*—"I didn't have any input and I didn't want any"—but whatever hopes he may have had for another *Faith* were dashed when he heard the finished album. From the opening measures of track one, "Jesus to a Child," to the *Twin Peaks*-inspired coda, "Free," *Older* was a mournful affair. It closed with Michael gasping: "Feels good to . . . be . . . free." From Sony? From his pain over Anselmo? From the closet? Once more, the notion of "freedom" in Michael's life was tinged with irony.

Geffen had to level with him. "George wanted to be a big star in America. And that album wasn't gonna do it. I don't think it took a genius to figure that out."

His lukewarm response infuriated Michael. Geffen had already inflamed the singer at a dinner with him and Andros at the mogul's Malibu home. Geffen, claimed Andros, had inexplicably offended Michael by offering him the "use of his black book of gay men in Hollywood that were safe to use"—most likely escorts who could be counted on for discretion. "From that moment," said Andros, "Yog decided he didn't like Geffen anymore and soon pissed him off by blanking his phone calls."

As for *Older*, though, Michael refused to get discouraged. "Fastlove" and "Spinning the Wheel" would be the first two singles, and to direct the videos he engaged a British couple, Vaughan (Arnell) & Anthea (Benton), whose videos for Terence Trent D'Arby, Dead or Alive, and other artists of the day had a feel and a rhythm he liked: moody, sensual, full of evocative imagery, and devoid of MTV-style rapid-fire editing. Like countless women and gay men, Michael had felt a tingle from the duo's Levi commercial of 1993. Shot in their preferred black and white, it borrowed the visual style of Ansel Adams, who famously photographed the American West, by showing a shirtless hunk in skintight jeans, bathing in a creek while two minister's daughters peek in shamed excitement from behind a tree.

That sense of high-gloss, fashion-influenced eroticism, heterosexual on the surface but with a discreet homoerotic flicker, was Michael's safe space; it had dominated his videos and public persona for years. To break past it, as he had in "Spinning the Wheel" and "Fastlove," would not be easy. Benton sensed his conflict. "He said, 'Look, this is why this album is different for me. I am a different human being. At last, I feel free. And I want to try to make things that will represent what I'm feeling.'" Yet he left no doubt that the specifics were off limits. "It was always a dichotomy for George," said Benton, "because he wanted to retain his privacy while being strong enough to say, 'This is me, this is who I really am.'"

While respecting their views, he took control. The couple found him positive and enthused, full of ideas, and highly organized—the opposite of the despairing Michael in the early stages of *Older*. "He was really funny, really engaging," Arnell recalled. "On the shoot he'd come down and meet everybody. He could light up the room with loads of stories, make everybody feel relaxed." Shades of the pre-*Faith* Michael shone through as he spoke about how to manipulate the press: "He was always looking for a really good angle, what could be a front cover of a certain paper, just to get the hype going."

As ever, he knew how he wanted to be photographed. "He'd watch his reflection in the filter screen in front of the camera," said Arnell, "and he could tell exactly when he was at the right angle." At the editing deck he sat at their sides, politely but firmly directing the choices.

What resulted were two impressionistic, visually seductive fashion statements, populated with models who gazed out with a studied, weary-of-it-all ennui while Michael cast his eyes downward in pained introspection. "Spinning the Wheel" finds him in dark glasses and a designer suit as he grooves with his band in a 1930s Harlem-style nightclub. In a nod to the "I Want Your Sex" video, a woman's body becomes a billboard; LUST and TRUST are written on a model's bare back. Aside from the presence of beautiful men, the video ignores the song's gay theme.

The same is true of "Fastlove." Michael sits in a large swivel chair, barefooted, cross-legged, and dressed in black; in his hand is a remote control that makes his fantasy figures turn up on a screen. Beautiful female models caress themselves; a man sensuously unbuttons his shirt. Some of the models, and Michael, too, dance under a cascade of water. His bitterness toward Sony makes an appearance when the camera pauses on a pair of headphones; the brand reads FONY.

"Jesus to a Child" also got a video, and for this one Michael employed director Howard Greenhalgh, who had done several for the Pet Shop Boys and Elton John. The video was rife with symbolism. A kitchen chair floats in the air behind a mound of dust; entranced figures are shown in churchlike rooms, bathed in an orange glow. The "child" is a nude blonde woman. A naked man lies on the wet ground; a woman in a Venetian ball mask saunters through a hallway. Michael is shown singing in deep, prayerful reflection.

While still refusing to utter the words, "I'm gay," he hoped *Older* would serve as his coming-out statement. In the *Daily Telegraph*, Tony Parsons gave him a seeming push by rhapsodizing over the "hairy love god" and his "hairy back." Michael adopted his gayest look to date: a handlebar mustache, lambchop sideburns, a goatee, and closely buzzed hair. He later explained to interviewer Phil Marriott: "I was trying in every way to say, look, I'm not trying to hide something here—I just don't want to talk to the press."

In the back of the booklet, Michael expressed the following: "This album is dedicated to Antônio Carlos Jobim, who changed the way I listen to music, and to Anselmo Feleppa, who changed the way that I look at my life. May they rest in peace."

The black-and-white cover image, chosen by Michael, clashed with the music's pained openheartedness. The right side of his face—the one he didn't like—is blacked out; the other peers out defiantly under an arched eyebrow. Michael, wrote Stephen Holden in the *New York Times*, had "the look of a jaded Mephistopheles." To Richard Smith of *Gay Times*, that image was "the perfect metaphor for George Michael. He's one of the world's best-known faces but he leaves half of that famous face hidden in the shadows."

Over a year after he'd premiered it on the MTV Europe Music Awards, "Jesus to a Child" was slated as the flagship release on DreamWorks SKG. It was Michael's first single since 1993, when his live mashup of "Killer" and "Papa Was a Rollin' Stone" had reached a disappointing No. 69 in the United States.

"Jesus" would be available to radio on December 14, 1995, yet not for sale until January 8. This "increasingly fashionable marketing ploy," wrote David Sinclair in the *Times*, was "designed to manipulate the public into providing a massive first-week sale and thereby produce an instant No. 1 hit." Sinclair didn't help; he gave the single one star, calling it "a long, meandering ballad . . . swathed in layers of introspection and self-pity." Jim White, a columnist for London's *Independent*, was no more encouraging. "Five years is a long time to be away," he warned. "Members of the Live Aid generation of which he was the greatest talent are now cast as laughable has-beens, and for the first time in his professional life George Michael is way out of kilter with the prevailing fashion. Compared to Noel Gallagher, Damon Albarn, or Jarvis Cocker, the big players of the mid-nineties, George is too slick, too well-coiffured, too concerned with his looks. His style is all cappuccino, glossy magazines, and well-tailored suits; theirs is all lager, fanzines, and sports labels. He's a gent; they're lads."

But tremendous loyalty and affection for Michael remained in the United Kingdom, and on January 14, "Jesus" hit No. 1 there. A week later it was knocked off its perch by the techno dance band Babylon Zoo's "Spaceman," the theme of a Levi's commercial. While "Jesus" lingered on the British charts for months, it fared worse in the States. On February 24, it peaked at number seven, then began a swift tumble. At seven funereal minutes, the single was shunned on U.S. radio. Outranking Michael were the divas of the day (Mariah Carey, Celine Dion), the stars of hip-hop (Coolio, LL Cool J, Mary J. Blige), and Alanis Morisette, queen of a new wave of confessional female singer-songwriters whose savage revelation and self-scrutiny had captured their generation.

At least "Jesus" had made the Top 10. But *Older* would not come out until May—another long and ill-advised wait that allowed momentum from the single to sag.

No matter what, people expected excitement from him. To that end, the singer loaded about thirty friends, including Douglas, onto a private jet from London to Paris for an *Older* launch party. The Michael for whom money was no object, and who played the pop star like few others could, had returned, at least for a moment. He put up his friends at the Ritz, where Princess Diana liked to stay. Deciding while there that he wanted to go to the Versace boutique off the Champs-Élysées, Michael gathered some pals in a car. Paparazzi chased them on motorbikes, snapping pictures. The group arrived at Versace, which had been closed to the public in Michael's honor. Michael added his signature to those of Madonna, Elton John, and other boldface names in the store guest book.

The launch event was a relatively dry affair, attended by press and record-company executives. Michael and his friends proceeded to the after-party in the Ritz basement. He took over the deejay booth and put on "Fastlove," then proceeded to the dance floor, where he recreated his moves from the video. Everyone around him basked in the intoxicating orbit of a superstar whose presence alone could give off sparks.

•••

In mid-May, *Older* was released. Nicholas Barber of the *Independent* spoke for the majority of reviewers: "For this we've waited five-and-a-half years? As Paul McCartney once said, 'Plastic soul.' As John Lennon once said, 'Muzak to my ears.'" Tom Moon of the *Philadelphia Inquirer* deemed the album a "crashing bore," adding, "Say goodbye to the carefree, hit-making George Michael. *Older* is so old, it's hard to find a pulse under the swirling strings and wandering Quiet Storm saxophones."

The pans kept coming. "George Michael returns with a whimper on *Older*," wrote Edna Gundersen of the Gannett news service. "Hardly triumphant, Michael comes across as a tormented martyr in these lugubrious lyrics and anemic melodies." The grievances he aired in "Freedom! '90" had been cloaked in fun sounds you could dance to. Now Michael, according to Jim White, was like "a comedian who yearns to play Hamlet." He even chided "the comedy narcissism of the cover."

There were a few voices of approval. "This is a brave, downbeat album, true to its dominant themes of pain, loss, and fitful regeneration," wrote Andrew Smith in the *Times*. The *New York Post*'s Dan Aquilante found *Older* "mature, assured, and even elegant." In *Newsweek*, Karen Schoemer called it "gorgeous and romantic, ambitious and revelatory, featherweight and exquisitely listenable."

But who was this Anselmo Feleppa to whom Michael had dedicated *Older*? A few writers inquired about his relationship to Michael. As ever, Connie Filippello answered evasively: "Anselmo was a friend of George and his family. He was a lovely person." Pressed further, she doubled down. "George is a very private man," she reminded them, "and has not given any explanation." Michael would later insist that the lyrics and the dedication were all the truth-telling the public needed: "For anyone who had a clue about any kind of symbolism, I was coming out."

The gay themes of "Spinning the Wheel" and "Fastlove" were overlooked by nearly every writer; somehow the production and the grooves had overridden the content. Only the *Daily Mirror* noted the "overtly homosexual sentiments expressed in the lyrics," while expressing no doubt that Michael and Feleppa had been lovers. "Pop songs are the legacy of the two men's relationship—songs accompanied by videos of George with beautiful women."

By almost anyone's standards but his own, however, *Older* was a success. It hit No. 1 in thirteen countries and the Top 5 in others; within its first month, two and a half million copies had sold. "Fastlove" had topped the charts in four countries, including England, where the song gave him his last No. 1 hit. In the United States, it climbed to No. 8.

But Michael had wanted this uncommercial effort to hoist him back up into the *Faith* stratosphere, especially in the United States. Touring would have helped, but the thought of that repelled him. Soon the phrase "eighties pop star" would start creeping into his press.

Douglas created various dance remixes of *Older* tracks. But if Reed McGowan, the New York deejay, had found little on *Listen Without Prejudice* that would get a crowd dancing, *Older* was almost useless to him. Tempos in clubs had continued to quicken; Michael, like an old clock, was slowing down. "Madonna was in clubs, listening," said McGowan. "George Michael didn't want anyone else giving him advice. When you're dealing with depression and drugs, when your whole life has been turned upside down, how are you going to understand the industry?"

Michael praised Virgin for its promotion of *Older*, ignoring the fact that in Europe, his releases almost sold themselves. But he blamed Geffen for the low U.S. sales, which had wounded him deeply; Michael had bared his heart, and America hadn't cared. "George ended up being as miserable with me as he was with Columbia," said the mogul.

He canceled Michael's contractual agreement for a second DreamWorks album and set him free. The gamble had lost Geffen's company millions. "We never complained to George," he said. "We put it out and did the best we could with it." Other DreamWorks releases by artists Geffen believed in, such as the gay singer-songwriter Rufus Wainwright, fared worse. Shifting tastes in pop had likewise left Geffen behind, and he bowed out of the record business gracefully. "Nobody can remain contemporary forever," he admitted.

It was a lesson Michael wouldn't accept. Years later, the two men ran into each other socially. "I was happy to see him," said Geffen. "He wasn't quite so happy to see me. He started to talk about the sales of *Older*. Ancient history. I said, 'Are we really gonna talk about *Older* now? It sold what it sold. Has your last record sold more?' Which it hadn't. He was furious that I said that."

It took a long time for *Older* to gain wider respect. Johnny Douglas began receiving notes from gay Michael fans who had connected with the album's subtexts. "A lot of gay men say it helped them come out, or that they had wanted to commit suicide, and *Older* got them through those times." Douglas did, however, mourn the excision of a couple of dance tunes that were "absolutely fucking brilliant" and that might have provided a blast of energy. "One of the tracks was about his drug dealer who's seeking him out at two in the morning. His management and everybody were like, 'Ugh! You can't say you do drugs,' 'cause nobody even knew he smoked."

Until the end of his life, Michael viewed *Older* as his best work. But for now, it hurt him to think about it. "My next album is not going to be a down album," he announced. "I want to make some great pop music before I get too old. And for it not to be about the pain in my life." The record had taken too much out of him: "I don't ever want to be that inspired again."

CHAPTER EIGHTEEN

WITH NO TOURING PLANNED and little incentive to struggle through the writing of more songs, Michael was at loose ends. Though not yet thirty-five, by pop standards he was aging out; his next step seemed unclear. Now he was searching for something quieter to give his life meaning. He had begun giving discreetly yet lavishly to charities.

With Anselmo in mind, he had been sending large donations to the Los Angeles-based Project Angel Food, a meals-on-wheels program for those afflicted with HIV. "He donated a gazillion dollars to AIDS," said Rob Kahane, "and he helped build the wing of a hospital in England." Another of his favorite causes was the Thalassaemia Society, which addressed a blood disease that afflicted Greek Cypriots. Michael secretly donated the royalties from "Jesus to a Child" to ChildLine, a telephone and email support service for troubled children. ChildLine's founder, British TV host Esther Rantzen, sensed "personal interest" on Michael's part. "It may have been tough for him when he was younger," she said.

Watching *Deal or No Deal*, a game show, Michael saw a man talking about his wife's need for costly fertility treatments. He sent them an anonymous £15,000 grant. One day he observed a woman crying in a café; he said hello, and she confessed she was mired in debt. He sent her £25,000. Michael tipped a bartender £5,000 when he learned she was struggling to repay a loan for her nursing studies. Periodically he loaded up his Range Rover with soup and sandwiches made in his home and drove to Cardboard City, a food dispensary in the poor London neighborhood of Holborn. He doled out meals by hand, chatting freely. "The funniest thing about it all is that no one seems to recognize him," said a fellow volunteer. "He comes down in jeans and a baseball cap and mucks in with the rest of us. George is a genuinely nice bloke. The youngsters often tell him he looks like George Michael and he laughs and says people tell him that all the time. When anyone asks what he does for a living, he tells them he's self-employed."

Michael hadn't performed a full show in about three years, and he longed to reconnect with what his life was all about. In October 1996, he returned to pure music-making in a BBC radio concert, "An Audience with George Michael"; he also taped an installment of *MTV Unplugged*, the series of handsomely produced specials that showcased established stars in acoustic settings. In both shows he stressed *Older*, whose songs he hoped to keep alive.

MTV Unplugged was an adult oasis on a network whose target demographic topped out at thirty-four. Michael taped it at a studio in East London for an invited crowd of fewer than two hundred. He sat for the whole show, with seventeen musicians and singers arranged artfully around him in a circle; like him, they wore black. At both the *Unplugged* and BBC shows he could look into nearly every listener's face, which he found scarier than singing into a dark sea of fifteen thousand. Now, though, he felt no pressure to deliver to the back of an arena, moving all the while. Michael just sang, and with his voice free of the usual reverb, it had rarely sounded so supple and free.

He lingered over some of his saddest songs: "You Have Been Loved," "Older," and "Praying for Time." The one cover he sang, "I Can't Make You Love Me," written by two Nashville songwriters, Mike Reid and Allen Shamblin, came from Bonnie Raitt's biggest-selling album, *Luck of the Draw*. Raitt sang of a bedtime scene between her and the man who had drifted away from her: "I'll close my eyes / Then I won't see / The love you don't feel / When you're holding me."

In the five years since, "I Can't Make You Love Me" had been covered widely; even Prince had recorded it—the likely reason that Michael was now singing it, too. But Michael's version mimicked no one's. He sang as though he were recalling his first heartache; his voice sounded years younger. His version climbed to No. 3 in the United Kingdom.

After that, there would be no more chart-toppers for Michael. But the playing field of pop recording was shifting rapidly. The public was losing patience with the zooming list price of new CDs, which in the States had reached $18.99. In 1999, two computer developers, Shawn Fanning and Sean Parker, neither of them yet twenty, developed Napster, an internet file-sharing service through which tracks could be bootlegged and downloaded for free. A court injunction halted Napster in 2001, but now millions had discovered the pleasures of downloading songs at little or no cost.

Well before his failed lawsuit against Sony, Michael had tired of corporations. "Let's start our own label—fuck 'em," he told Andros, who for years
had dabbled in record producing, frequently with Michael's help. Once more
Michael's template was Prince, who had founded his own label, NPG (New
Power Generation). But Andros took that ambition further; he saw a future in
which artists could produce and sell their music directly on the internet. He
got Michael excited over the possibilities. The singer told the *Times:* "I can't
help but believe that music will become one of the first things that the public
will buy online." If that happened, he predicted, record stores would crumble.

Thus was born Ægean Records, paid for by Michael and run by Georgiou.
As an experiment, he posted Michael's recording of "Ain't No Stoppin' Us
Now" on the label's website for a $0.99 download. Sales were strong.

He and Georgiou sketched out a plan to offer the sort of artist-friendly
deals Michael had fought for. Once production costs were recouped, performers would receive 50 percent of the profits; anyone who felt unhappy
could leave.

It was a gallant plan, but Michael left most of the work to Andros. He
was feeling neither ambitious nor social, except with regard to sex. Michael
had begun frequenting Beverly Hot Springs, a day spa in the Koreatown
neighborhood of Los Angeles. Though ostensibly straight, it had a substantial gay clientele; it was also known for attracting celebrities and those who
wanted to meet them. It was there, in June 1996, that Michael met Kenny
Goss, his next boyfriend.

Goss, who had recently moved to Los Angeles from his native Texas,
was hardly Michael's type; he was smooth, cornfed, and all-American, not
hairy and swarthy. He spoke with a hint of a twang and had a gleaming
smile with "very expensive teeth," as a friend of Michael's called them.
Goss, who was two years older than Michael, had worked for the National
Cheerleaders Association, selling uniforms and teaching cheerleading
technique. "He acted like a star," said a colleague, "even when he was selling cheerleading clothes."

In Los Angeles, he set up a business as a gym-equipment salesman, but
he had grander ambitions, which he attained once he had caught Michael's
eye. "It wasn't the big love-at-first-sight thing that he'd had with Anselmo,"
said Lesley-Ann Jones, a columnist who knew Michael. But Goss was an

antidote to Michael's loneliness; he seemed like a nice, solid boyfriend at a time when Michael had lost hope of finding one. He yearned to show Goss off, but he was still programmed to be secretive. Johnny Douglas recalled walking into the lounge of a recording studio and seeing Michael on the sofa with his arm around Goss; spotting Douglas, Michael yanked his arm away.

Even so, Goss gave Michael a shoulder in the hard times ahead. Monogamy, however, was not in the deal, on either side. "He knows who I am," explained Michael. In June 1997, Goss moved in with him.

"I think he was good for George," said Douglas. "I think he helped keep him on the straight and narrow a lot of the time." Others were leery. In his memoirs, Andros recalled Goss telling him he had never heard of Michael until the day he had arrived in Los Angeles; the friend who picked Goss up, Andros said, played "Fastlove" in the car. "It would have been impossible for a man of Kenny's age, being the party animal that he was, not to have danced to or heard one of his songs." One of Michael's band members felt a continual chill from the star's new boyfriend. "He was terribly self-important, I felt. If you said, 'Hi, Kenny,' he wouldn't stop and talk. Just 'How ya doing?' and he kept walking." Phil Palmer recounted an afternoon when Michael, with Goss at his side, arrived at a venue and was shown to his lavishly stocked dressing room. Goss, said Palmer, "demanded that he have his own dressing room. And that's what he got on subsequent occasions."

But Goss made Michael feel lovable again. The thought of her son being alone had worried Lesley, and Michael decided to tell her "this fantastic news." She had evolved into his best friend; from her he got "a completely unwavering feeling that nothing I can do can stop this person from loving me, supporting me, and believing in me."

She couldn't do enough to show her son how much she loved him; Lesley even made regular visits to his homes to clean and do laundry. Shortly before the holidays of 1996, he phoned her and effused about Goss. After telling him how happy that made her, she divulged some news she'd been keeping secret: She had recently had surgery for skin cancer. Michael panicked, but Lesley assured him that she was fine. "Lesley was a very proud woman," said Andros, "putting on a smiling face for everybody all the time." In truth, her condition was serious, and she was on strong painkillers. But she didn't want to burden her son or spoil anyone's holidays.

After the New Year, however, there was no hiding the fact that Lesley was gravely ill. She spent much of the next few weeks in the cancer ward of Charing Cross Hospital in Hammersmith. So traumatized was Michael that he didn't have the heart to visit. But by February 24, 1997, word had come that Lesley's hours were numbered.

That night, Michael was due at Earls Court, the twenty-thousand-seat venue in London's West End, for the BRIT Awards. *Older* had earned him a nomination for Best Male Solo Artist. His opponents were poised to outshine him from every angle. Sting's album *Mercury Falling* had gone platinum in both the United Kingdom and the United States; *Greatest Hits* by Simply Red (Mick Hucknall) had sold platinum six times over. Twenty-three-year-old Mark Morrison was England's hottest R&B singer of the day; Tricky, twenty-nine, had helped create trip-hop, the music Michael had dipped into in *Older*. Elton John would present the award.

Unlikely as a win seemed, Michael had hoped to make his mother proud of him one last time. He had hoped against hope that he might make it to Earls Court; instead, he and his family were gathered by her bedside. John, who knew the situation, stood at the podium and solemnly read off the nominees.

He popped open the sealed card containing the winner's name. Looking pained, he announced it to a roar of approval: George Michael. "Unfortunately, George cannot be here tonight," said John. He read a message that Michael had prepared in case he won. "To everybody here, and everybody watching at home, I would like to apologize for not attending tonight's award show. . . . My love to my family and friends and to everybody that has helped to make music my life for the last fifteen years. Thank you, thank you, thank you. George Michael." Clutching the award, John added: "I'd like to add to that how proud I am of him, and to send my love to his family as well, and to George; he's a dear friend."

At the hospital, their excruciating vigil wore on. "We slept on the hospital floor that night," said Andros. The next morning, Lesley died. She was fifty-nine.

• • •

The memory of Anselmo haunted Michael daily; now he had lost the mother who loved him as no one else in his life ever would. "He never recovered from either of those things, I think," said Phil Palmer. "The songs reflected it for the next twenty years."

In the car on the way home, he and Andros played a demo by Ægean's first signing: Toby Bourke, an Irish singer-songwriter, two years Michael's junior. Bourke had a rugged, weathered voice and a slightly surly delivery, laced with hurt. The song, "Waltz Away Dreaming," reminded Michael of his mother's passing: "She had a history, joy and pain, and she chose to leave. . . . Now you fly like an eagle above while I waltz away." As it played, Michael vowed to plunge back into work, just as Lesley would have wanted, and turn tragedy into beauty. He would produce "Waltz Away Dreaming" as a duet between him and Bourke. All this proved an unimaginable dream-come-true for Bourke, a pub performer who had been hungry for a break. Michael asked him to write a new chorus that would address the loss of Lesley.

Three days later they were together at SARM. Grief and pot had nearly immobilized Michael; that day and at the sessions that followed, Bourke was shocked by what he saw. "George would turn up stoned out of his mind. He would smoke skunk joints in the studio when we were meant to be working. He was easily getting through twenty joints a day. I remember how smelly and pungent it was when he was smoking them. But nobody was allowed to complain."

In the midst of all this, Michael was helping plan his mother's funeral service, which was held as secretly as possible in a small church. Michael was numb; he remembered not crying, which enabled him to give a soft-spoken, dignified eulogy. "Sometimes," he said, "God can't wait for his angels and takes them early."

Harrowing as it had been to produce, "Waltz Away Dreaming" turned into a track that all concerned could be proud of. It had the homeyness of Celtic folk; the two singers seemed as sympathetically matched as brothers. Bourke sounded like the toughened elder; Michael, as high as he was, sang with a boyish innocence. He delivered the song's closing words: "She's waiting."

Prior to the single's release, Capital Radio held a fundraising weekend for Help a London Child. Michael and Georgiou offered the song as a premium for donors. When he heard that donations had reached £904,000 he phoned in and donated another £96,000 in Lesley's memory. "I didn't think I'd have a good day like this for a long time," he said, "but I had a fantastic time just listening to the radio."

The publicity cinched the success of "Waltz Away Dreaming," which rose to No. 10 in England. Michael even paid for the production of a video that matched the track in its poignancy. It showed Bourke playing guitar and singing the song in a dim room of a family house, filled with candles and letters. An old man, seemingly widowed, wanders off as the room morphs into an enchanted forest. Michael is there in a black top coat, walking and singing amid flowering trees and nymphs. One was played by his friend Kate Beckinsale, a beautiful young British film actress. Michael and Bourke, also dressed in the color of mourning, meet and finish the song together.

If the video implied sympathy toward his father, Michael felt little; on the contrary, he blamed him for Lesley's fate. Even Andros, who hated Jack, could not agree. But as the winter ended, Michael was doing his best to put on a public face. On March 26, 1997, he made his first live appearance since Lesley's death; at the Capital FM Radio Awards in London, he collected honors for Best Male Vocalist and Best Album. Two weeks later, Michael was in Los Angeles to make a "surprise" appearance at the fourth annual VH1 Honors. There he would sing with Stevie Wonder, for the first time since their 1985 duet at the Apollo.

The show was devoted, as *Variety* put it, to "rock 'n' roll's golden oldies": James Taylor, Lou Reed, Steve Winwood, Emmylou Harris, Chaka Khan, and Wonder, all of whom, like Michael, had mellowed into cherished elder statesmen.

At the April 10 taping at the Universal Amphitheatre, Wonder was at the piano and in the midst of the song when Michael strode out, looking every inch the ultra-assured pop star in his trademark black Armani and shades. Their song was "Living for the City," Wonder's 1973 portrait of poverty and prejudice in a Mississippi ghetto. When Michael sang, out came a copy of Wonder, just as it had at the Apollo. For all Michael's eminence, awe could still make his identity crumble.

Then he took the podium and read a statement geared to the night's cause: the VH1 Save the Music Foundation, which seeks to bring music education into schools. Unlike the evening's safely worded, stiffly delivered testimonials, Michael's was a personal statement of dismay over hip-hop, which had helped push the show's veteran participants aside. "For the first time in human history," he announced, "music became the mouthpiece for anger, fear, and racial division, driving young people apart and even more tragically offering no solutions, no hope. . . . Surely we know that music's greatest values are joy, elation, and that old favorite, pure escapism. Of course, there have always been protest songs, songs of political frustration; we just did one. But they've never overshadowed the heart of popular music in this way before. I'm sure I'm not the only musician in this room that believes it's time for our business to wake up and admit that it has a responsibility to the children of the future."

Out of the spotlight, Michael remained almost inconsolable over his losses. He was distracted, often in a foul mood, and, for all his charitable gestures, increasingly self-obsessed. "It seemed his dad's arrogance was taking over," said Andros. Yet Michael was humbled by a surprise invitation from Ron Weisner, the manager who had almost signed Wham!. Weisner was overseeing a duets album by Ray Charles, who was nearing seventy and in declining health. Weisner wanted Michael aboard; the stunned singer consented immediately. He flew to California to meet with Charles in his Culver City offices. The two of them chose a tortured lament for lost love, "Blame It on the Sun," by Stevie Wonder and his then-wife Syreeta Wright. Michael and Charles recorded together, although the soul titan didn't like how he sounded and redid his vocals later. "Ray became a fan of George," said Weisner. The duet, released after Charles's death in 2004, took on a father-and-son vibe; Charles sang like a ravaged, embittered old man, while Michael, in his sweetest voice, could have been a teenager wracked with heartbreak.

In Charles's intimidating presence, Michael had been the ultimate professional. But Michael had more or less abandoned Toby Bourke, whose dreams of an album on Ægean were fading. For weeks and weeks Bourke heard not a word from Michael, whose dependence on antidepressants and pot were troubling. He engaged Paul McKenna, a famous British TV hypnotist and self-help guru, to try and break him of his smoking habit. It didn't work.

The singer had lost all interest in Ægean, which under Andros's direction had floundered. But Michael wasn't helping. "We could do nothing without getting the okay from George," said Andros, "but he was too hammered to give us that okay." Niall Flynn had quit SARM to work there; in dismay he watched Andros and his cronies "throw around pie-in-the-sky ideas with nothing but bravado to back them up."

A handful of artists besides Bourke were signed, to little or no avail. Michael had found Trigger, a British-based trio with an ethereal chillwave vibe. Ægean launched the band with a single, "Chameleon (Shed Your Skin)"; Michael's heavily processed backup vocal was in the blend. But like Bourke, Trigger had to go elsewhere to get an album released. In one of their numerous yelling matches, Michael told Andros to shut the label down. From then on, the singer would release some of his own music under the Ægean imprint, but no more would he record outside artists.

• • •

For the moment, Andros remained one of Michael's "shadows," as Danny Cummings had termed the group of acolytes who followed him everywhere. A few of its members, such as Shirlie Holliman and her husband, Spandau Ballet's Martin Kemp, to whom Michael had introduced her, seemed sincerely caring. Others, said Phil Palmer, did not. "George was a gravy train. He surrounded himself with people who seemed to do absolutely nothing except smoke joints with him or get drunk with him. They were kind of employed to bolster his ego and to support his lifestyle. What should have happened, and what never did, is that his proper friends should have been more protective of him, I think."

Of late, Michael's best gal pal was Geri Halliwell, the former Ginger Spice of the Spice Girls, the five-member British girl-power band. At its mid-nineties peak, the group had eclipsed Michael in popularity. Now, on her own, she had a solo singing career to build—a challenge, for Halliwell could barely hold a tune. Based on her interviews, the *Times* wrote a satirical first-person diary that depicted her as a vacant namedropper with a monstrous ego. "One minute I'm a pop star, and a UN Goodwill Ambassador, the next I'm a children's author. That's me all over. I'm an enigma. Like Madonna. But nicer. Although she's great."

She revealed a dream to a reporter. "When I was a little girl," she said, "I thought I was going to marry George Michael." While it couldn't come true, she had achieved the next best thing. "Geri Halliwell has been inseparable from the millionaire singer," wrote the *Daily Mirror*. They were seen shopping together in Beverly Hills, hand in hand, prompting the *Mirror* to call them "the oddest couple in town." She and Kenny Goss had quickly forged their own friendship; it brought Goss close to another star and took Halliwell closer to Michael.

Michael's friendship with Princess Diana had been more sporadic, limited mostly to occasional lunches—some with Elton John at Kensington Palace—and the odd phone call. She had touched him with a consoling call after the death of his mother. But Michael sensed a lonely woman. If his stardom and wealth had made it hard for him to form honest relationships, for Diana it was almost impossible. A doctor of hers, Michael Skipwith, described the princess in terms to which Michael could relate: "All she wanted was to be treated like other people, and for those she trusted not to talk about her."

A brief recorded memento exists of her friendship with Michael. In July 1996, as Diana underwent a painful and humiliating divorce from Prince Charles, Michael's phone had rung late at night. As he sat in the living room with Andros, a familiar voice began leaving a message. Michael ran to the phone and picked up. The tape kept rolling; it wound up in the possession of Andros, who eventually sold it for publication.

"How are you, my darling?" Michael asks the princess. She refers delicately to her divorce from Charles, which was then in progress. "It's been pretty grim but we're near the end of it," she says. "A very loving, compassionate family, this one I'm leaving." With a demure laugh, she thanks him for having called to wish her a happy birthday.

> G: You know I missed it.
> D: That's quite all right. . . . You're so sweet. Well, thank you ever
>   so much. We saw you in Elton's film last night . . . Oh, what
>   was it called?
> G: That's right, he did that documentary; he actually invited me
>   'round to see it. With his boyfriend. I must admit I was kind
>   of horrified.
> D: [*Laughs*] George, is life treating you kindly?
> G: Fantastically at the moment, actually. . . . The album's doing
>   pretty well everywhere. Actually, it's doing great everywhere

but America, and I'm not worried; I'm not really that bothered
by the Americans, actually. I'm madly in love, so I'm doing very
well at the moment.

D: Oh, lucky you!

G: Lucky me, yeah! . . . I'd love to see you.

D: Well, George, at the moment, can I wait 'til this is all quieted
down?

G: Absolutely.

On August 31, 1997, Michael and the rest of the world heard the shocking news. Just past the stroke of midnight, a chauffeur-driven car had sped
through a tunnel in Paris; it held the former Princess of Wales; her bodyguard,
Trevor Rees-Jones; and her new boyfriend, Emad "Dodi" Fayed. A battalion
of paparazzi had trailed them in cars and on scooters. The driver, Henri Paul,
lost control of the car, which crashed; an autopsy revealed that he had been
driving under the influence of alcohol and prescription drugs. Only Diana's
bodyguard survived. Among her last murmured words as photographers
with cameras surrounded the totaled car: "Leave me alone."

Instantly a feeding frenzy began, with "intimates" selling stories to
tabloids: hairdressers, a medium, a masseur. The situation, over time, would
play itself out again with Michael. For him, the circumstances of Diana's life
and death hit unnervingly close to home.

On Saturday, September 6, 1997, two billion TV viewers watched the
funeral. Untold thousands of mourners crowded the grounds of Westminster
Abbey; giant video screens monitored the proceedings as though the funeral
were a concert at Wembley.

But the press was more focused on the dream explosion of boldface
names: Diana Ross, Sting, Luciano Pavarotti, Steven Spielberg, Tom Hanks,
Tom Cruise, Nicole Kidman. Overhead photos show Michael and Elton John
arriving together, trudging forward amid the sea of VIPs in black. Among
the celebrity quotes about Diana, Michael's was among the most heartfelt
and perceptive: "I think she was there to remind people of their humanity."

The funeral uncorked his deepest grief over Lesley. "I bawled my eyes
out," he said later. "It was almost like I was reliving my mum's funeral." Elton
John had hastily rewritten "Candle in the Wind," his sentimental 1973 hit

about Marilyn Monroe, the first line, "Goodbye, Norma Jean," to make it "Goodbye, England's rose." He wasted little time in recording the song as a benefit for some of Diana's pet charities.

John, like Michael, was obsessed with hitting No. 1, and "Candle in the Wind '97" could not have been better poised to get there. Plans were underway for the release of yet another single from *Older*, "You Have Been Loved." Its hoped-for ascent to the top would undoubtedly be blocked. "I think he asked Elton to delay the release of his record, and Elton wouldn't do it," recalled Danny Cummings. Sure enough, on September 20, "Candle in the Wind '97" peaked at No. 1, while "You Have Been Loved" stayed in second place.

•••

The whole Diana episode was a reminder of the brittleness of the fame he'd achieved and that still obsessed him. At its heart was his assumed heterosexuality. Michael argued repeatedly that he had shared the truth with everyone that mattered to him, but that was a small group, and did not even include his band members. Toby Bourke recalled Michael's "deep-seated paranoia": "He was terrified his big secret was going to come out."

It was already such a rampant rumor that it threatened to overshadow his music. But the more reporters asked, the more stubbornly he withheld. "If there's one question I know is gonna come up it's that," he told an interviewer. "You can almost see people sitting there waiting for a moment to throw the question in—where's it gonna be received best?" Asked by Richard Smith what he would do if he were outed, Michael lost his cool. "I can sue them but they'll still have ruined my career. . . . Once something's printed the damage is done. Who fucking believed Michael Jackson when he said he wasn't gay? . . . Because I don't make my sex life public, there's a section of Fleet Street who are desperate to know who I'm fucking. They're certainly not going to find out."

James Collard, the editor of *Attitude*, perceived the price the singer was paying. "George Michael often looks like a man not physically at ease with himself," he wrote. "For all the expensive clothes, the friends in the fashion industry, and the accoutrements of rock stardom, there is something about him which will always be slightly reminiscent of a bouncer: that rather self-conscious machismo, that hint of spiky, 'what-you-looking-at?' defiance. . . . There is something ironic about the star of the 'I Want Your Sex' video keeping his private life private. He can't have it both ways, surely?" To the *Daily Telegraph*'s Tom Leonard, Michael seemed "desperate to be candid, but at the last minute [he] can't be."

He wasn't alone. The late nineties remained a risky time for celebrities to come out. Managers, agents, and others on the payroll discouraged it, warning that it would spell career death. Many stars longed to do so, but were afraid. They faced mounting pressure from gay activists to come clean; those who refused were scorned as traitors to the cause or were outed in print.

The bulk of their audiences probably didn't want to know. Ellyn Solis, Sony's head of publicity in the nineties, recalled seeing Barry Manilow in Las Vegas. The singer and songwriter of earnest AM-radio love songs had earned his first No. 1 hit, "Mandy," in 1975; but his sexuality stayed an open secret until 2017, when he finally came out at seventy-three. To have done so earlier, he insisted, "would have killed my career" and perhaps alienated his mostly female fan base. "I thought I would be disappointing them if they knew I was gay," he explained. To some degree, he may have been right. Solis talked with one of them in Las Vegas. "I said, 'Don't you think Barry probably has a boyfriend?' This woman was mortified that I would say such a thing."

By 1997, TV star Ellen DeGeneres could no longer ignore an insistent chorus of demands that she come clean about her sexuality, which had passed the stage of rumor. The droll comedienne with the blonde crewcut had a lot at stake: She had fought her way up from years of doing standup to star in a long-running sitcom, *Ellen*. She wanted out of the closet, but she was scared: "Would I still be famous, would they still love me if they knew I was gay?"

Rather than utter the words that people wanted to hear, she dropped hints, which only served to frustrate the gay media. Finally, she orchestrated a double-barreled coming out. After months of arguments between her and ABC, it was decided that her character would come out to a therapist, played by Oprah Winfrey, on April 30. With that established, *Time* put DeGeneres's face on its cover, accompanied by the headline, "Yep, I'm Gay." The placement proved what explosive news this was in 1997.

The episode scored *Ellen* its biggest audience ever—forty-two million viewers. Now out with a vengeance, DeGeneres shifted her show's focus to LGBT themes. Then the fallout came: JC Penney and Chrysler pulled their ads; televangelist and Moral Majority cofounder Jerry Falwell christened the star Ellen DeGenerate. The Media Research Center, a powerful conservative watchdog group, took out a full-page ad in *Variety* declaring that ABC was "promoting homosexuality."

Buckling to pressure, the network placed viewer-discretion warnings at the start of her episodes. DeGeneres was stung by Elton John's remark that she should ease up on the gayness and go back to being funny. When she put her arm around girlfriend Anne Heche at a White House Correspondents' Association dinner, the *New York Times* noted her "ostentatious display of affection with her lover."

In 1998, *Ellen* was canceled. It took years for the star's career to bounce back. Months after the show's demise, she saw *Will & Grace*—a sitcom about a female interior decorator and her funny, nonthreatening gay pal—premiere on NBC and zoom its way to a ten-season run.

Michael had been in the closet for far longer than DeGeneres; the more pressure he felt to come out and the more open his secret became, the more he resisted. Yet in interviews, it was often he who broached the subject—defensively, evasively, yet with a burning desire to somehow come clean. In the discussion that opened "An Audience with George Michael," his live BBC concert, the singer said to host Chris Evans: "Everyone presumes I don't do interviews 'cause I've got loads of things I don't want to talk about, which is not the truth at all."

"People are obsessed with your sexuality, aren't they?" asked Evans.

Michael spent minutes analyzing the issue. All this badgering, he insisted, grew out of homophobia. Most straights, he explained, were so insecure about their sexuality that they rushed to "out" those whom they perceived as gay. "And *that's* why you get a huge debate over somebody like me," he declared. "Because you've got all these guys, for instance, maybe their girlfriend likes me or whatever. And they're like, he's a fairy! It's obvious to me! Now if they were proved to be wrong, that would be unsettling for them. If they were proved to be right, that would be comforting."

But as always in interviews, Michael withheld. "All the people that I know and care about are perfectly clued in. Everybody knows who I am. So, for the sake of people that I never speak to, I really don't feel any desire to define myself."

As ever, Boy George was there to point out the irony of Michael's words. "George says he has nothing to hide and that he has never considered his mysterious sexuality to be wrong," he told the *Daily Express*. "If that's the case, then why can't he get it past his lips? Is it really that awful?" To Peter Tatchell, the London-based campaigner for LGBT rights, Michael and other closeted gay stars were not helping the cause. For years, he said, he had tried "discreetly" to encourage the singer to come clean. Michael's refusal to do so had left Tatchell "hugely disappointed."

CHAPTER NINETEEN

MICHAEL HAD STAYED FRIENDLY with journalist Judy Wieder, who had become editor-in-chief of the *Advocate*, the foremost American LGBT news magazine. In her memoir, *Random Events Tend to Cluster*, Wieder recalls her respectful but persistent efforts to talk gay and lesbian celebrities into opening up in print. There were more defeats than wins, but overall, women were easier to persuade; Wieder persuaded Rosie O'Donnell, Janis Ian, and other stars to speak out.

Her friend Melissa Etheridge, the platinum-selling, leather-voiced rocker, had done so in 1993, inspired by k.d. lang, who had leveled with an *Advocate* reporter, Brendan Lemon, in 1992. Like lang, Etheridge had evaded the issue for years; she now felt freed. "I really enjoy being totally honest," she explained. "I enjoy sitting down in an interview and not thinking, 'Oh, I *hope* they don't ask me that.' Or I'd do live radio shows and think, '*Please* don't have that dyke call in!'" Laughing, she added: "I mean, please don't have that *lesbian* call in! But now it's like, 'Go ahead! Ask me!'" A year later, Neil Tennant of the Pet Shop Boys shed the open secret of his gayness in the British magazine *Attitude*.

But Michael seemed a dead end, even with Wieder. She appealed to him through Andy Stephens, and even flew to the manager's London office to plead her case. But Michael had never broached the subject of coming out with Stephens, who would have been powerless, in any case, to sway him. "Andy would just kind of shoo me away," Wieder said.

Few in England seemed to notice that Michael was seemingly outed by his *Bare* coauthor, Tony Parsons, in a November 1997 *Daily Mirror* cover story. Parsons referred to Anselmo Feleppa, "the good-looking Brazilian," as "the great love of his life." After quoting Michael's rhapsodic memories of Feleppa, Parsons noted: "There has always been a certain mystery about George's sexuality." But unless Michael said the magic words, "I'm gay," the truth would not register.

Periodically he flew to Los Angeles, where he spent weeks at a time at his Beverly Hills home. "He was a very, very private guy," said his neighbor Don Goldstone. "You would see glimpses of him every once in a while going in and out of his house, with males." If Goldstone could have peeked inside, he would most likely have spotted the star in his living room watching TV through a curtain of marijuana smoke; or he might have spied Michael lying by the kidney-shaped pool with Kenny Goss.

When Goss wasn't around, and sometimes when he was—their relationship was open—Michael would often emerge from his bedroom in a uniform of sweatpants or shorts, a T-shirt, a hoodie, a baseball cap, sneakers, and sunglasses. From there, one of pop's most recognizable stars stepped into his Mercedes and drove to various community toilets, mainly in parks. His new fix for depression was a national pastime in the United Kingdom; it was called "cottaging," anonymous gay sex in public places. The deed took its name from the design of many outdoor British lavatories, which looked like Victorian country cottages.

Michael had joined in a furtive hunt, fueled by the thrill of risk but also, for many years, by the lawlessness of homosexual activity, which had been forced into the shadows. Not until 1967 was it decriminalized in England. After three more decades, the targeting of cottagers by British sting operations softened; most cops had learned to look the other way.

A cottager quoted by the *Independent* in 2011 explained the appeal: "People want the thrill of it, the anonymous sex, the sex on tap. It isn't a gay thing; it's a man thing. If there were a place where heterosexual men could get sex so easily, they'd go. Men are biologically formed that way. They spill their seed."

But the psychology of cottaging was often more complicated, involving lives lived in secrecy and shame or wounds that reached back to childhood. Sometimes it bespoke a need to constantly affirm one's desirability. Bradley Jones, a New York psychologist whose patients included many sexually addicted gay men, called the compulsion "an ersatz attempt at repair. In other words, I'm going to repair myself by doing this over and over again. I never quite get what I want from it, but I'll keep doing it because somewhere along the line I'm going to get something that will make me feel better."

Michael, of course, had grown up gay under the disapproving eye of a homophobic Greek orthodox father. From the beginning, he had confined his gay sex life to the shadows. Hiding it had long been his reflex; he even concealed his cottaging from his therapist.

His cruising picked up speed in Los Angeles. There, Michael felt free enough to drop into Rage, a gay bar in the heart of West Hollywood, the city's verdant gay ghetto. "He comes in here about ten P.M., sits with a group of his friends, and is perfectly charming," recalled the manager, Charlie Geary. Los Angeles was a bonanza of beautiful men, and quite a few turned up at Will Rogers Memorial Park. Just a mile from Michael's home, it stood on Sunset Boulevard near the border of Beverly Hills and West Hollywood. Across the street was the Beverly Hills Hotel, a green and cotton candy-pink blast of old Hollywood.

Will Rogers boasted stately palm trees, a pond filled with fish and turtles, a fountain, and an impeccably groomed geranium bed and rose garden. In the air were the scent of freshly mowed grass and the squeals of children. The park was an idyllic spot for weddings and photoshoots, as well as afternoon sunbathing. One saw a lot of shirtless men, along with a fair amount of traffic in and out of the yellow stucco toilet block. It contained one urinal, one cubicle, a sink, and a water fountain with a glitzy gold tap. But there was room enough to engage in sexual activity when no one was around, and many did; Will Rogers earned a listing in at least one internet cruising directory.

Complaints were coming into the Beverly Hills Police Department; according to Lieutenant Edward T. Kreins, it incensed parents "that they couldn't take their young children into the park bathrooms because men were having sex in there." The charge was somewhat disputed by J. T. Anderson, a retired schoolteacher who lived in West Hollywood. "As a person who has frequented restrooms in my life," he said, "I can't remember one time when people continued to have sex when someone walked in." That wasn't the case, he said, in Griffith Park, which occupies over four thousand woodsy acres in the neighborhood of Los Feliz. "I have come upon straight couples fucking away and not stopping when you walk by," said Anderson.

But gay public sex, not straight, had triggered sting operations—also known as "potty patrol"—all over Southern California. John Duran, a

West Hollywood-based attorney who eventually became the town's mayor, specialized in defending the accused from what he deemed widespread entrapment. "It was common practice then," he explained, "for various police agencies to take young, strapping, sexually attractive cops and place them in tight-fitting clothing, often with handkerchiefs in their back-left or back-right pocket"—a popular cruising symbol. "They would stand, sit in, or lean against the walls of public restrooms in known cruising spots, where they would pretend to be gay or feign interest in sexual activity with those whom they perceived to be gay. If there were any sort of response that made it seem like these men were taking the bait, an arrest would be made for solicitation."

In 1997, there were over twenty arrests in Beverly Hills, two at Will Rogers. Anderson had his own brush with entrapment in the men's room of Roxbury Park, also in Beverly Hills. Anderson walked in, followed by an attractive man who stood a few urinals away and made eye contact, hand on his crotch. "He kept nodding, like, come over here. He didn't say anything. No one speaks." Something didn't feel right, and when Anderson stepped outside he was arrested. Duran got the case thrown out of court. "When I read the police report it was two pages of exaggerations and lies," said Anderson. "It said there were children around, that the restroom was crowded—none of that was true."

Even so, this was a dangerous hobby. But that didn't deter Michael, and word got out. Back in August 1997, Steve Payne, a British celebrity photographer, was on the lookout. One day around five P.M., he got lucky. Michael had just parked his Mercedes alongside Will Rogers. Onto the grass he walked, wearing a T-shirt and shorts. His black baseball cap was pulled low, but he wore no glasses, and his trademark goatee left no doubt that this was George Michael. He pulled off his shirt and sat under a tree, knees spread apart. A gray-haired man with glasses walked by and cruised him. Michael rose and entered the men's room. The other man followed. About five minutes later, both men emerged.

Michael got in his car and drove off; discreetly Payne drove behind him. The singer stopped at another Beverly Hills park and went inside the toilet. Payne would later claim that Michael drove back and forth between the parks at least ten times. The photographer trailed him for over two hours, taking pictures all the while, until the star drove home, where Goss awaited him. Payne managed to snap photos of the couple by the pool; one showed Goss kissing Michael.

In the months to come, there were further George Michael sightings at Will Rogers. If his partners recognized him, and "if they were nice," he said, he invited them home. The following March, Janet Charlton, gossip columnist for the *Star*, an American tabloid, published a blind item. "This megastar has a multimillion-dollar home in Beverly Hills but he chooses to sunbathe shirtless in a public L.A. park, which happens to be frequented by gays cruising for anonymous sex. Our celebrity was seen ducking into the men's room with three different total strangers he picked up during the course of one sunny afternoon. What he doesn't know is that he was photographed with his boy toys. The photos are circulating around Hollywood but so far no one's had the nerve to print them!"

It was hard to imagine that no one told Michael about the blind item, but he persisted. On a gray, rainy day near the end of March, J. T. Anderson drove by an empty Will Rogers and decided to check it out, knowing it was unlikely that undercover police would be there. He parked nearby and waited. In a few minutes, a black Mercedes Benz parked in front of him. Out came a tall man in sunglasses, a T-shirt, blue-and-white Adidas sweatpants, a baseball cap, and a sweat-jacket, the hood pulled over his head. He entered the restroom; Anderson followed. He sat inside the stall with the door open. Within seconds, the man, who was hairy, swarthy, and silent, had approached the door and lowered his sweatpants. "I gave him a blowjob," said Anderson. "No reciprocation." Only later, via photographs and published descriptions, would he recognize his partner as Michael.

Word of the closeted star's cruising—as well as his relationship with Goss, with whom he had exchanged rings—had been hot gossip for some time on the gay grapevine. More than ever, Boy George could not contain his annoyance. In an interview, the singer declared: "I have been waiting a long time for him to admit he had a boyfriend and once again, it hasn't happened. George Michael should stand up for what he believes in."

Boy George found an enraged opponent in Tony Parsons, who launched a knockdown mud fight. In the *Mirror*, Parsons heaped invective upon the "limp-wristed gay caricature"—a "vain, spiteful little creep" and "sad old queen" (Boy George was thirty-six) who was "getting his XXL frilly knickers in a dreadful twist." Michael, claimed Parsons, had revealed enough via his loving remarks about Anselmo—"so what exactly is Boy George's problem?" Michael, he insisted, was a "real man" who, in his youth, had "had more girls than Boy George has had hot dinners."

Those comments were published on April 6, 1998. No one knew how prescient Boy George's remarks would become, and how soon.

• • •

That same day, an interesting opportunity arose for George Michael. A&R Vice President Jay Landers had been hoping to lure him back to Columbia to team with Barbra Streisand, for whom Landers served as executive producer. Streisand's largest-selling album to date was *Guilty*, released in 1980. Its coproducer, Barry Gibb of the Bee Gees, had written or cowritten all the songs, played guitar, and dueted with her on two tracks. That No. 1 LP, with its three top-ten singles, had brought Streisand the biggest pop credibility of her career.

Landers hoped to replicate that feat by pairing Streisand with another younger star who could custom design a vehicle for her. When he proposed Michael, she seemed barely familiar with one of her own label's former superstars. He played *Older* for her, and she loved it, particularly "Jesus to a Child."

Landers managed to arrange a three-way conference call. To his astonishment, Michael reverted to the adoring fan-boy he had been in 1976, when he was galvanized by "With One More Look at You," the hyperemotional love song that Streisand had sung to her dead rock-star husband in a remake of *A Star Is Born*. That performance, Michael said, had lifted him from the depths of adolescent depression. He told her he longed to write for her and maybe find a few covers she might like. Could they meet the following week and run over some ideas? Of course, she said. Landers was ecstatic. "I hung up from that call thinking: I'm a genius!"

The next day, a Tuesday, Michael had lunch with Goss in Beverly Hills; he downed several glasses of wine and a Prozac. Sometime after four P.M., he pulled up across the street from Will Rogers. He saw a young male wearing a T-shirt and jeans and apparently cruising. The man would later be described as a "six-foot, two-inch hunk" with a "perfect set of white teeth." Michael had no way of knowing that this was Marcelo Rodriguez, a member of the Beverly Hills Police Department's plainclothes "Crime Suppression Unit." Rodriguez and two colleagues, Shan Davis and Sgt. Sammy Lee, were there to keep an eye out for "loiterers." One offender had already been arrested that afternoon.

Michael and Rodriguez would each claim that the other had entered the restroom first and waited. Whatever the order of events, they found themselves together and alone. Michael stood at the urinal, pretending to use it. Rodriguez entered the adjacent stall and did the same, leaving the door open—a common ploy for cruising. According to the policeman, Michael stepped closer, yanked down his sweatpants, and started masturbating. The singer admitted that he did so, too, but only when his companion started to masturbate first. Rodriguez noticed what looked like a round Band-Aid on Michael's right buttocks. It was a nicotine patch; Michael was making one of his many attempts to quit smoking. All the while, he kept glancing at the door. There was no physical contact.

Rodriguez claimed he walked out while Michael was still masturbating; Michael insisted that both of them finished the act. In either case, the officer left first and quickly informed Davis, who was in the vicinity, that he had caught a man behaving indecently. At 4:48 P.M., Michael walked out and was apprehended. As Davis explained the nature of his offense, Michael blurted out: "This is ridiculous! This is entrapment!"

Asked for ID, Michael said he had none. Davis drove the handcuffed star and Sgt. Lee to the police station. There Michael was photographed, holding a numbered card, for a mugshot. In the *Telegraph*, an unnamed source—who could only have been a department employee—reported that Michael was "visibly shaking when he came in. But he was well-spoken and very cooperative with the officers. He answered every question clearly. He looked totally shocked but was trying to hold it together."

Name? "Georgios Kyriacos Panayiotou," said Michael, helping with the spelling. "Profession?" "Singer." Did he call himself anything else? Yes: George Michael.

Rodriguez had probably not recognized him; in his written account he referred to the subject as George Michaels. But others at the station knew.

Bail was set at five hundred dollars. Reluctantly, Michael phoned Goss to tell him he'd gotten into trouble. "I left Kenny a message and said, 'Darling,

I'm in big trouble. You're going to have to get me from the police station.'
He called me back and said, 'What did you do, darling?' I said, 'Use your
imagination.' And he said, 'DUI?' I said, 'Fuck—if only. Think again.' He
said, 'Oh, no.' I said, 'Please just come down and get me.'" Goss drove to the
Beverly Hills Police Department with the bail.

At 8:05 P.M., Michael was released. The arraignment would take place the
next month at Beverly Hills Municipal Court. He faced up to six months in jail.

Around four A.M., Caroline Graham, a British, L.A.-based entertainment reporter for the *Sun*, awoke to a ringing phone. An informant of hers
at the BHPD had news. She leapt out of bed and raced to the office, where
she announced: "I've just had this crazy tip that George Michael has been
arrested!"

Graham raced to his home. She saw a light on in one room and his Range
Rover in the driveway, a baseball cap on the back seat. Dawn was breaking
as she and a *Sun* photographer proceeded to Will Rogers. They found it
empty. But that didn't last, for Lt. Kreins had wasted no time in sending out
a press release about the arrest; the police report was also made available. On
Wednesday morning, Kreins led a press conference in front of the BHPD.
As a crowd of newspeople waited, cameras poised, Kreins—bald and gray-
haired, with a mustache and a business suit—made his entrance through the
front doors and read a statement into a cluster of mics.

A member of his Crime Suppression Unit, he explained, had entered
the Will Rogers restroom and found "the singer known as George Michaels
[*sic*] . . . engaged in a lewd act." The officer, Kreins stated, "did not recognize
that he was a pop star"; the timing was "sheer coincidence."

The arrest provided a bombshell teaser for American TV breaks. But
for the British press, it was the scandal of the year. A battalion of *Sun* staffers
were sent out to dig up whatever they could find. Calls to Andy Stephens
went unanswered; Connie Filippello offered no comment. Photographers
and journalists swarmed Michael's front door in Beverly Hills, ringing the
bell to no response. Helicopters hovered overhead.

In England, reporters sped to the home of Andrew Ridgeley, a secluded
farmhouse in Cornwall, a coastal county in the country's southwest region.
They confronted him with questions about his ex-partner's arrest. Ridgeley
"looked shocked," wrote the *Daily Mail*, and "declined to comment."

Meanwhile, in the small town of Coleman, Texas, the phone rang at the home of Kenny Goss's parents, Earl and Ozell. According to the *Mail*, the startled couple seemed unaware of their son's relationship with a male superstar; Earl had apparently never even heard of George Michael. "I'm sorry," he said, "but I cannot comment any more about this at the moment." Reportedly he told the *National Enquirer* a bit more: "I've got to talk to Kenny and sort this out. Kenny needs to come back home to Texas."

Michael's now former publicist, Michael Pagnotta, was on a plane that had just landed; he checked his phone and found it flooded with text messages. "I guess I was the only U.S. contact still on record for George," he said. "I read them and thanked God that it wasn't my responsibility. I was surprised that he'd been so careless and self-sabotaging, because that wasn't like him, but maybe it was."

On April 9, the newspaper coverage began. The *Sun*'s cover brandished a headline that made tabloid history: ZIP ME UP BEFORE YOU GO GO. Staffers milked the scandal over "Gay George" for numerous stories. In her lead article, Graham reported the facts more or less straightforwardly; other *Sun* coverage showed no mercy. "Heavy smoker George Michael wears a nicotine patch on his bum because he wants to quit FAGS," wrote entertainment editor Dominic Mohan. "Sorry, George," he added. "You really have been nicked and you'll go down, for want of a better phrase, in history as the Hugh Grant of pop"—a reference to the British film actor who had been busted for receiving oral sex from Divine Brown, a prostitute, in his BMW, parked off Sunset. Continued Mohan: "The whole of Britain had heard the careless whispers that George was a careless woofter. If, in 1982, George had been more frank and open about his sexuality, I don't think any of this would have happened."

A swarm of Fleet Street reporters had ganged up on Boy George's London doorstep, hoping for a quote from Michael's saltiest critic. He wrote an uncharacteristically humane letter for the next day's *Express*. "Some might see this as a reason to gloat right now," he wrote, "not least of all George's close friend, journalist Tony Parsons, who wrote a damning piece about me only this Monday in the *Mirror*. . . . I wonder how Mr. Parsons is feeling today? George Michael's current predicament is further reason why all public figures must be upfront about their sexuality. I personally think that sex in public places is no big deal and that the Los Angeles Police Department [*sic*], which arrested George, should be concentrating on real crime. . . . I wish him much strength at this time because when push comes to shove, we are sisters under the skin."

Michael's arrest "rocked gay California," said Billy Masters. "You went out, people spoke of nothing else. Suddenly everybody had a story. 'I've been to that bathroom!' We heard that David Geffen was getting involved, the gay mafia. One of our own was being targeted and attacked, and we had to stand up and defend ourselves. The older people who had fought for any rights saw this as a very dangerous situation that could start some sort of a major antigay movement. On the other hand, there were people who said, 'If he hadn't been in that bathroom this wouldn't have happened,' which was also true."

But in the hours after his arrest, where was Michael?

Masters's source was correct: Immediately after his release, he had fled to Malibu to hide out at the home of Geffen. Ill feelings about *Older* were put aside; a traumatized Michael needed the advice of a man who seemed vulnerable to nothing.

Upon hearing the news, Geffen had limited patience. "I said to him, 'That's why God invented hookers! They'll come to your house and if you don't get exactly what you want you just give them some money and they'll go away!' But that was not the turn-on." For now, said Geffen, "we tried to figure out how to deal with all this in the best possible way." Michael needed to reemerge and convince the world that he was fine; he had to tell his story in the most sympathetic way possible, and fast. Geffen suggested an interview with Maria Shriver, contributing anchor for *Dateline* and the wife of Arnold Schwarzenegger. Within forty-eight hours it had been slated.

Michael returned to Beverly Hills in time to greet Andy Stephens and Tony Russell, who had flown in to do damage control. Michael gave Andros the unpleasant job of canceling his appearance at the Capital FM Radio Awards, which was yet again honoring Michael. Just as the singer had feared, his arrest was the talk of the party, with reporters pouncing on celebrities for comments. "Live and let live is what I say," declared Robbie Williams.

The U.S. press wasn't so forgiving. *Newsweek* called the nineties a decade in which "Americans became obsessed with fame and disgrace." With the bar ever dropping as to how much could be exposed in the media, sex scandals, reported in lurid, voyeuristic detail, were bigger business than ever. A gleeful dehumanizing of wayward and sometimes troubled stars took place; their life-damaging mishaps were reduced to tabloid fodder. At the same time, they became a platform for high moralizing.

In 1994, Michael Jackson had made his first reported out-of-court settlement on a child molestation charge; from then on, disgrace and ridicule overwhelmed his artistry. In 1997, police questioned (but did not arrest) comic actor Eddie Murphy for having picked up a transgender prostitute in West Hollywood. Months later came the sex scandal to flatten them all, when President Bill Clinton's long-running indiscretions with White House intern Monica Lewinsky exploded in the press. In England, it was open season on Parliament, dozens of whose members found their secret sex lives splattered on the front pages of the *Sun*, the *Daily Mirror*, and *News of the World*.

Most of the transgressions were heterosexual, however. George Michael's downfall involved the outing, by his own hand, of a closeted sex idol who had marketed himself as straight. The incident was seamy, especially given his image as an Armani-clad, loudly "private" superstar with the money to buy almost anything. Now the British masses were getting an education that they hadn't bargained for on renegade gay sex. As Hugh Grant told Emily Yoshida in *Vanity Fair*: "My parents, I can remember, if the subject of homosexuality came up, they had that kind of 1950s, 1960s attitude. It was sort of, 'Well, it happens, darling. And it's a little bit disgusting. We don't talk about it very much.'"

Michael had phoned Andros in London to explain himself. "I made a mistake," he said. "I went for lunch, had a few glasses of wine, got horny, and started looking for some action."

"*In a fucking toilet?*" sputtered Andros.

He was appalled by the doting reactions from Michael's inner circle. "You should have heard them. 'Never mind, George, these things happen.' And you would see the fear on their faces, scared to rock the boat and lose their huge salaries, their gifts and bonuses." Though horrified, Jack, according to Andros, acted unfazed: "'Don't worry about it, son. I understand . . . And oh, by the way, I've just seen a new horse. It's only half a million, George, can I buy it?'"

The British press responded a lot more heatedly, as everyone from gay activists to right-wing commentators began editorializing over gay public sex. The *Daily Mail's* Lynda Lee-Potter, a defender of traditional family values, wrote about "preying homosexuals . . . selfish exhibitionists who care only about satisfying their own unpleasant urges. . . . Unfortunately, if they're allowed to carry on like this, their behavior becomes contagious."

On her side was the *Sun's* Richard Littlejohn, Britain's highest-paid columnist. "What he gets up to with another consenting adult in private is none of our business," Littlejohn wrote. "When he chooses to do it in public he deserves to be humiliated. Imagine if a child had walked into that toilet just as George decided to get his rocks off. . . . Instead of addressing the problem with tear gas and batons, the police turn a blind eye. The local health authority actually encourages it by hanging free condoms and lubricants on trees." Added Littlejohn: "I suspect that no one is more ashamed than George Michael himself."

In the United States, the coverage was even more damning; there, Michael was portrayed not only as a laughingstock, but as a has-been who had "crashed and burned," as the *New York Post* wrote. DOWN AND OUTED IN BEVERLY HILLS, read the tabloid's front page. "Michael once gave a world full of females a touch of the vapors when he wailed 'I Want Your Sex.' By George, he was telling a little fib. Now, nobody gives a damn if he is gay—but a public john, for crying out loud! You are rich, you are famous, and you throw it all away in a Beverly Hills outhouse?"

Perhaps most hurtfully to Michael, Elton John appeared on VH1, snickering over his friend's misstep. "In a *toilet*?" he said, rolling his eyes. Simon Napier-Bell felt the same. "Gay people won't accept that this has nothing to do with being gay or straight," he said. "If you were caught in the toilet doing this with a woman, I would feel that's tacky."

Amid the righteous indignation were a few sympathetic voices. One of them was the *Daily Express* sports columnist Martin Samuel. Michael, he noted, "has lost overnight his two most important possessions—image and dignity. . . . There is no way the punishment fits the crime." Samuel scorned the Beverly Hills police for not having simply released Michael with a warning. "They say they did not recognize one of the world's most famous faces until it was too late. Believe that and you'll believe George and Anselmo Feleppa were golf partners."

The *Sun* gave a forum to Matthew Parris, the out-gay columnist who had served in Parliament. He had once been assaulted while cruising Clapham Common, a London park frequented by gays. "What flaming hypocrisy all this fake astonishment and pumped-up commentary is," Parris wrote. "The offense of which he is accused is a minor misdemeanor. Thousands like it come before our courts every year. . . . Nobody dies. Nobody is assaulted. Nobody is robbed. Nobody is hurt. Nobody bleeds. Nobody suffers. Except the poor fellow caught." Most of the pontification, he felt, was self-serving: "Every Tom, Dick, or Harry who's ever met George Michael becomes a lifelong pal, pens a column, gives a quote, offers sympathy in his 'sad ordeal' and 'darkest hour,' pledges continued friendship—then carefully covers their own back by expressing shock that George could do this dreadful thing."

The conservative-leaning *Sunday Times* defended Michael in the voice of its rock critic, Lesley White. In England, she wrote, "we pride ourselves on loving the campest drag acts, transvestite comedians, committed campaigners, effete aesthetes, but an otherwise harmless entertainer caught at a tricky moment suddenly incurs an outrage that belongs to fifty years ago."

But as long as there was money to be made, the scandal would roll on. The *Independent* reported that *News of the World* had paid five figures for the 1997 Steve Payne park pictures. Allegedly the tabloid had first purchased them the year before then lost them; now that the dreamed-of tie-in had occurred, the pictures had to be repurchased at a higher price. Eventually Michael found some humor in the images: "I *never* take my shirt off in public, ever. Even when I'm slim I never take my shirt off in public. And the day the picture was taken I was a little overweight. One tabloid headline actually said, FAT AND GAY. . . . It was like, 'Here are two things you'd hate to be. And he's both!'"

* * *

For now, however, Michael wasn't laughing. His advisors had convinced him he had to face the world and seem nonchalant. On April 9, two days after his arrest, Michael made what the *Daily Mail* would call a "carefully staged" appearance at Spago, the exclusive Beverly Hills restaurant where Elton John had just held his hot-ticket Oscar party, a benefit for his AIDS foundation. Spago was a few minutes' drive from Michael's house; for him to dine there would seem natural. Word was leaked to the press. Spago was fairly new; this would bring the restaurant a feast of publicity, while enabling Michael to appear cool and unruffled.

Dressed in designer black-on-black, the singer, with Tony Russell and Andy Stephens in tow, approached the restaurant as though strolling down a red carpet. As he passed flowering bushes in planters and stepped onto Spago's earth-toned marble floor, flashbulbs popped and reporters thrust microphones in his face, pelting him with questions. He offered platitudes: "It's good to get out." "I feel great." "I'm fine." "It's been a bit of a rough time, but I'm okay."

Seated at his table, he faced a continual parade of fans asking for autographs and journalists seeking comments. His patience cracked just once. "Guys, do us a favor and leave us alone," he said. Disingenuously, he added: "I have come here to have a meal, that's all." He ordered a rich man's feast—filet mignon tartare with quail's eggs, saffron fettucine with Maine lobster—and exchanged carefully worded pleasantries with celebrities who dropped by to say hello; they in turn were pumped by journalists. Actor Tony Curtis obliged with some good cheer: "He said he couldn't be better. I told George to keep smiling, and he replied, 'Don't worry, I will.'" Pop star Lionel Richie claimed that he and Michael had "talked about everything but the arrest." The star was in "good spirits," Richie added, "considering everything that he has been through recently."

The press lingered for the length of his meal. When Michael wanted to use the men's room, word was sent to the management, and the space was emptied for him. As he left through the main entrance, the media trailed him with their last questions. Michael disappeared into a black limo with smoked glass and slumped into his seat.

Michael Sitrick, one of the many L.A. publicists who specialized in celebrity damage control, was not alone in feeling that Michael should have merely issued a statement through a publicist, "implying that the Beverly Hills police should have better things to do," and grabbed the opportunity to stress that this was a new beginning for him as an out-gay male, thus casting him in a positive light.

But Michael had other ideas. He was furious at the press for having—he felt—viciously outed him; he was enraged at the police and sick of keeping silent. "If I'm going to be remembered in America as the guy that got caught playing with himself in the toilet," he said, "then I want people to know my take on it."

The *Dateline* segment with Maria Shriver would not air until Sunday; and it would be edited, raising the possibility of an unkind spin. When CNN expressed interest and agreed to air a taped, unedited interview on Friday, April 10, in the United States and on Saturday in the United Kingdom, *Dateline* lost out to CNN.

Jim Moret, the reporter assigned to Michael, had calmly anchored one of CNN's ratings bonanzas, O. J. Simpson's 1995 murder trial. As cohost of *Showbiz Today*, which had covered all manner of scandals, including the pedophilia charges against Michael Jackson, Moret exuded impartiality.

On Friday, Michael showed up at CNN's Hollywood studios alone— something no star did, even on a routine press junket. The composure he had feigned at Spago was gone. Visibly agitated, he sat with Moret in the green room for nearly an hour and vented his fears over how he would be portrayed. The host assured him he was not under attack; Michael would tell his story with minimal interference. Moret didn't even have prepared questions.

They took their place before the cameras, underneath news-show lighting that recalled an operating room. "He was stammering and fumbling and nervous," recalled Moret. "He couldn't focus; he couldn't answer. He was so uncomfortable it was making *me* uncomfortable. I thought, this is going to be a disaster, and I wasn't interested in the spectacle of it." Stopping the cameras, he took Michael back into the green room and tried to calm him. "I really felt for the guy," Moret said. "He seemed to be a genuinely nice, decent, gentle soul. He was contrite, he was humble. He was extremely polite. When he finally smiled, he had a great smile and a sense of humor."

Back on the set, Michael appeared calmer. "This is as good a time as any," he announced, to come clean. The worldwide TV audience would get a close-up look at the least likely cottager they could have imagined: one of the richest and most famous men in England, privileged beyond imagination yet drawn to a forbidding sexual netherworld of public toilets and parks.

Moret didn't ask him to recount the events inside the men's room; Michael spent most of his air time trying to justify the years he had spent in the closet before being forced out of it in the least flattering way possible. The effort was, at times, rambling, vague, and defensive as Michael insisted, fidgeting all the while, that he had never really hidden anything. "My sexuality was *not* cut and dried," he said. "I spent the first half of my career being accused of being gay when in fact I hadn't had anything like a gay relationship. . . . So, I spent my years growing up being told what my sexuality was, really, which was kind of confusing." In truth, Michael had already come out to himself and his closest friends; and until the nineties, few journalists had tried to out him. But he was so mad at the press, he told Moret, that he had vowed never to give them what they wanted.

"So, in unambiguous terms, what is it that you want to say?" asked Moret.

"Uh, I want to say that I have no problem with people knowing that I'm in a relationship with a man right now." His last relationship with a woman (Kathy Jeung) had ended almost ten years earlier, he said. He went on to assure his female fans that "there was no bullshit" (the word was bleeped) in his songwriting: "The songs I wrote when I was with women were really about women and the songs that I have written since have been fairly obviously about men."

He made one point more emphatically than any other. "I don't feel any shame," he said. "I feel stupid, and I feel reckless, and weak, for having allowed my sexuality to be exposed this way, but I do not feel any shame whatsoever and neither do I think I should."

Six minutes later, Moret and Michael returned to the green room. "He looked like he could breathe again," said the host. Still, there wasn't much to celebrate. "I found George Michael to be a sad man. But he still had dignity. I can't even imagine being able to function at that point. I would have been in bed with the covers over my head, probably under the influence of God-knows-what, just trying to stay calm so I didn't shoot myself."

Those around him contributed as best they could to his image repair. During Capital Radio's latest on-air fundraiser for Help a London Child, his sister Melanie phoned in on Michael's behalf to tell them he was donating £50,000. "He's a very nice man, you know," she said.

For all his worries over how the incident might alienate fans, Chris Heath saw hardly any fallout, at least in England. "He was treated like a national treasure. Even if parts of the British public are still homophobic, they've got that sort of blinkered homophobia where it doesn't count for people who are beloved."

The *Sun* polled its female staff for their reactions. Said newsdesk secretary Tara McCole: "Everyone has known for years that George was hiding a big secret, but he seemed more bothered about his sexuality than anyone else. At least now he will have to be honest with his fans. That is all we ever wanted." Remarked Sam Watson, a secretary in the sports department: "Any man who spends hours grooming his chin must be suspect. But he is a fantastic-looking bloke, and a real loss to us girls."

Even Michael was surprised at how "nice" his London public had been; some of them, he said, even seemed to like him more. "It's almost like they didn't think I was human before. You can't get much more human than getting caught with your trousers down."

• • •

The fact remained that Michael had been accused of a crime. How he would defend himself had not been decided. In mid-April, John Duran received a phone call from the office of an attorney who was representing Michael. Duran was asked for advice. Told the circumstances of the arrest, he smelled entrapment; he had heard similar stories from hundreds of clients. "Gay men don't just walk into public restrooms and get sexual," he said. "There has to be some sort of dance that occurs. Sustained eye contact. Lingering about for too long. Something that indicates, I'm on your team. Otherwise, nothing is going to happen. No gay man who wants to avoid a violent confrontation is going to go in the middle of a restroom with somebody he's never seen before, pull his dick out, and start masturbating. The fact that George Michael said, 'This is entrapment,' tells me that the officer did something, said something in order to give George the idea that he was another gay man interested in having sex."

Entrapment had existed at least since the 1950s. It was considered a homophobic ploy; certainly there were no reports of female undercover officers who tried to seduce straight men into acting out sexually in public. For Duran, this constituted "denial of equal protection under the law." Furthermore, many of the lewd-conduct cases he encountered didn't fit all four requirements of California law: a) the touching of one's genitals or the female breasts or those of another person, b) the specific intent of sexual arousal, c) a location open to public view, and d) the clear presence of someone who would be offended.

Frequently, said Duran, "the defendant wouldn't have any reason to believe that the person who had just grabbed his own crotch, smiled at him, winked at him, would be offended by anything that was done sexually in response. Without the presence of somebody whom the defendant knew would be offended, there's no violation of the law. I thought that the George Michael case would be a great opportunity to continue to test the boundaries of what was fair and just. I would have fought it. I would have taken it to a jury, and shown the inequities of what the police were doing."

But he quickly learned that Michael and his team wanted the problem whisked away as swiftly as possible; they had no interest in making the singer a poster boy for gay-rights legislation. That left nothing to do but wait for the judge to announce the punishment on May 14. Whenever he left his house Michael sensed scorn in the eyes of almost everyone who looked at him, but still he ventured out. On April 17, he attended the twenty-eighth birthday of Tamara Beckwith, a young British socialite and reality TV performer. Approximately two hundred guests had gathered in Beverly Hills; Michael, reported the *Daily Express*, "sat in the garden by himself, slumped in a chair with a baseball cap over his forehead."

The Barbra Streisand project had gotten lost in the chaos. With nothing else to work on, he spent most of his waking hours getting high and reflecting. For years to come, the scandal would fascinate journalists; Michael answered their questions eagerly, using the process as therapy. In a 2007 discussion with the BBC's Kirsty Young, Michael revealed much pained self-analysis.

"I always knew it was gonna happen sometime," he admitted. "I was absolutely tempting fate. I think I was sick of the secret. . . . It wasn't really something that needed holding onto anymore, but I just couldn't do it in the regular way. I think I had to do it and fool myself that it had been dragged out of me."

CHAPTER TWENTY

MICHAEL DIDN'T HAVE TO turn up to hear the decision at Beverly Hills Municipal Court. His attorney, Ira Reiner, pleaded no contest. Judge Charles Rubin pronounced the singer guilty of lewd conduct, fined him $910, and sentenced him to two years' probation. During that time, the singer would be barred from Will Rogers. He would have to undergo at least five hours of therapy, serve eighty-one hours of community service, and pay seventy dollars into a "victims' restitution fund." Rubin informed Reiner: "Let Mr. Michael know if he commits a similar offense in the future it will be the county jail for sure."

Slim as the terms were, Michael was sure he'd been made an example of. "I got double the normal probation," he said. "If you pay the fine, you normally don't do community service. I got both." His cry of entrapment hadn't helped. A statement was released by the Beverly Hills Police Department: "If Mr. Michael felt it was entrapment, why did he agree to a conviction?" The *Los Angeles Times* warned gays to watch their step: "Officials have stepped up undercover police patrols and have placed rangers in various parks during special hours to discourage such sexual adventurism." At Will Rogers—now known to some as Willie Rogers—concealing bushes were chopped down and the men's toilet reconfigured. Jay Leno, host of *The Tonight Show,* gave a mock news flash: "Singer George Michael, out and about on the town again. . . . Last night I saw him at one of his favorite restaurants, The Palm."

There had to be a way for him to save face and engender compassion, to join in on the joke while reclaiming his power. On July 21, 1998, Andros organized an internet talkback between Michael and his fans. Seated at his computer, Michael enjoyed the chance to address his public directly. The chat found him at his wittiest and most endearing; he extended it well beyond the promised hour.

Your last album was called 'Older'—what will you be calling the next one?

It's a long way off, as the greatest hits will be released this year but the working title is 'Fatter with a little more grey hair' :-)

Have you been offended by jokes or satires or did you take it all in good humour?

Ok . . . the truth is that I've been seriously offended by the lack of decent jokes on the subject . . . Actually, I heard a good one last week. George Michael is worried about going through customs next time he visits the States. Why? They might do him for handling swollen goods. And they are mighty swollen, I can tell you.

George, why don't you record a song in Greek—I always liked Vasilis Papaconstantino!!

Who? Sounds like a cross between a lubricant and a musical instrument! Sorry, Vasilis! I don't think I will be performing in Greek anytime soon. I've tried, but it always sounds like someone trying not to throw up.

Humor got him through the embarrassment, at least publicly. A new song and video, he decided, would be the best way to acknowledge the elephant in the room, while getting his side of the story across. Sony's two-disc compilation, *Ladies and Gentlemen: The Best of George Michael*, was in the works; the new track could be added. Maybe it would hit No. 1.

He sent Johnny Douglas a cassette containing a sketch of the song. Startled by how quickly Michael could create music when he wanted to, Douglas pulled it into shape and added synthesized strings. For extra spice, he inserted bits he'd recorded from news reports about the arrest.

Michael swapped in real strings, recorded his vocal, and "Outside" was born: a risqué but tongue-in-cheek celebration of public sex, steeped in the sounds of 1970s disco. "I think I'm done with the sofa; I think I'm done with the hall," sings Michael in a comically butch voice. "I'd service the community . . . but I already have, you see."

To direct the video, he called back Vaughan Arnell, now parted from Anthea Benton. Michael had numerous agendas besides fun. He strove to portray the cops as hypocritical buffoons and the American justice system as a farce. Michael planned to slip in some added revenge: He would "out" Officer Rodriguez.

His premise was to depict a shagfest in a public toilet—one that transforms into a disco as the hijinks heat up and attracts cops (one of them played by Michael) who participate. Michael had hoped to return to the scene of the crime, but that would have been illegal; "Outside" was shot mostly in the beachside town of Venice, California.

The singer rode in the van with Arnell as they scouted locations—not just a public bathroom but outdoor spots where couples would explode in lust. The sex, Michael decided, would be unsimulated, which would entail finding hidden places to film as well as real porn actors. Two triple-X starlets, Rebecca Lord and Brittany Andrews, signed on. The 1950s B-movie actress Jeanne Carmen (featured in a 1957 cult potboiler, *Untamed Youth*) agreed to play a blonde dominatrix who leads a boy around on a chain.

"Outside" starts by simulating a grainy-looking, straight Swedish adult film of the seventies. As a sleazy saxophone plays, a man in a restroom is enticed by a blonde Venus. Opening titles and credits appear in ersatz Swedish, made up by Michael and Arnell. One of the stars is billed as Marchelo Üffenvanken (meant to sound like "often wankin'"). As soon as their lips meet, a badge fills the screen and the blonde morphs into a wrinkled old crone. HOLLYWOOD flashes in red, white, and blue.

A police helicopter whirs above and the man is dragged out, bullied, then pushed into the back of a van. Suddenly Michael appears with the smirk he'd worn on the cover of *Older*, and the men's room becomes a glittering, strobe-lit disco. Michael is shown in a policeman's uniform, clutching a phallic nightstick. Heterosexual couples grope and kiss in the toilet; Michael dances furiously with two female cops.

From there, the video depicts Los Angeles as a Sodom where cruising and public sex are everywhere. The homoeroticism, however, is fleeting: Two bodybuilders cruise at a gym; a male couple make out in a truck. Then the cops start busting people. Thinking they're out of view, two policemen—including the Rodriguez stand-in—start kissing. Cut to Michael making a wink-wink smile. The closing image was his idea. Shot from a helicopter, a red neon rooftop sign comes into view:

JESUS

SAVES

Then comes an onscreen caption: "all of us. all." That statement of hopelessness suggests that the freewheeling fun has been a lie.

Like his other videos, "Outside" was predominantly straight. The point, he explained, was that any heterosexual man would have done what he did if tempted by a sexy woman, and the police wouldn't have cared. But in a dance-pop video with hundreds of cuts and diverting if distant flashes of soft-core porn, that theme got lost. "Outside" suggested a man with one foot still in the closet.

On October 19, 1998, Sony released "Outside" as the advance lead single from Michael's compilation. *Billboard*'s review filled the singer with hope. After so many songs that were "heavy in lyric and short on hook," here, at last, was "a vocal filled with simple joy. . . . This celebratory track could be the one to return George Michael to the hearts of the masses."

But his tune didn't even make the Hot 100, although it reached No. 3 on the dance charts. In the United Kingdom, "Outside" rose to No. 2; the top slot was held stubbornly by "Believe," a massive comeback record for Cher, who was seventeen years Michael's senior. It became the gay disco anthem he had wanted with "Outside." Apart from its cutting-edge house-music style, "Believe" boasted a technology that would soon dominate commercial pop. Cher's vocal had been processed through Auto-Tune, the pitch-correcting software that made even the worst singers sound perfect. When used to the maximum, it turned a voice into a robotic hum—an electronic sound that caught on.

Michael's commercial instincts were faltering. Richard Wallace branded the video "laughable" in the *Daily Mirror*. "Ooh, very shocking," he wrote. "Yippee, you're out and you want to shout about it but enough already. . . . Nobody's really all that interested. George, take a tip from your old friend

Elton John. He's gay, he's proud of it, and works tirelessly for charities—all with the minimum of personal fanfare. Now get back to what you do best and write us all a hatful of great songs."

Tony Parsons turned his disdain for Michael's recent behavior into more *Daily Mirror* copy. "Come on, George. You don't honestly believe that grown men—gay, straight, or somewhere in between—really have the right to have sex in a public park, do you? . . . In both real life and your video, aren't you presenting a negative image of gay men? . . . And aren't you just trying to put a brave face on the most crushing and humiliating experience of your life, George?"

Andros was equally weary of Michael's post-outing publicity campaign. In his memoirs, he told of having been contacted by *Hello!*, the British gossip magazine, for an interview. He consented—and in the fall of 1998, *Hello!* readers learned what Andros really thought of his close pal's shenanigans. "I was the only person who went ballistic at him over his arrest," Andros declared. "I was so furious with him that he didn't know how to handle it. I can do that with him. . . . George and I are one-hundred-percent brothers."

Andy Stephens would tell a different version of the incident. Connie Filippello, he said, had heard that Andros had, in fact, approached *Hello!*, offering not only comments but precious candid photos of Lesley. Working at high speed with Filippello, Stephens managed to get the writer to call and tell him, on tape, about Andros's offer. When Michael heard the recording, he was enraged. He couldn't stop the piece from running, but from then on he refused to speak with Andros; instead he sent a barrage of livid emails, accusing his lifelong friend of betrayal. After that, he cut off contact.

With each new attack, Michael became more determined to speak his truth. On November 9, the release day for *Ladies and Gentlemen: The Best of George Michael*, the star stepped onto the set of America's second most important nighttime talk series (after the *Tonight Show*), *Late Night with David Letterman*. The snarky comedian seemed unimpressed. "It's not your first time on the show, is it?" Letterman asked.

Michael momentarily flinched. "Excuse me—you should know, shouldn't you? *Yes*, it is!" Then he laughed. Letterman fast-forwarded to the arrest. The singer wound up disarming and finally charming him. Grinning devilishly, Michael explained: "I've been told backstage that I can't say the 'm' word. So,

God knows, if you're not allowed to say it, no wonder I got arrested doing it!" The audience burst into laughter. Letterman pressed him for details. Waving a hand with a gold band on his ring finger, his guest revealed: "I'm no stranger to outdoor nookie." Applause erupted; he rose and bowed.

Michael worked in some digs at the puritanism of America and at the arresting officer: "The police report said he was simulating urination. . . . If you try to simulate urination doing that with your hand you'll get wee all over the shop." He had seldom been funnier, yet he failed to sing, which would have affirmed what really mattered about George Michael.

• • •

The star still had community service to fulfill. On Friday, November 21, Michael, with Goss there for moral support, drove to Project Angel Food's headquarters on Sunset Boulevard in Hollywood. Nobody had decided what type of work he would do. The front-desk staff called on head dessert-maker Derbeh Vance. "They said, do you guys have a job for him?" recalled Vance. He handed white aprons to the singer and Goss and assigned them the job of making thirty-four pans of white cake. They took the work seriously, and seemed to be enjoying it.

On Monday they returned, only to learn that Judge Charles Rubin had opted to move him elsewhere. The star would have to complete his time by phoning schools and children's centers, urging youngsters to work for charity. He later heard that there were suspicions that, because of his philanthropic history with PAF, the organization might reward him by cutting his hours. A vow to the contrary by executive director Ken Hurd did not sway the court. Michael was also told that Rubin knew of his "Outside" video and of his highly public charges of entrapment against the BHPD. The judge refused to comment.

Michael hastily arranged a press conference outside Project Angel Food. A swarm of media gathered on the street as Michael stood before them, wearing his apron. Though outraged, he calmly read his statement. "I am fully aware that in all likelihood I have prompted Judge Rubin's sudden change of heart by my own actions. Obviously I will accept the court's decision. I have no choice. But I feel that I must at least ask Judge Rubin this question:

Why should Project Angel Food now suffer the loss of funds that my time here would raise? . . . I felt that my misfortune could at least bring some attention and funds to an amazing organization. Judge Rubin, I remain at your mercy, but whatever you think of me, please, please do not let this unusual opportunity for good go to waste." But the judge would not relent.

On December 5, Michael gave his first U.K. interview since the arrest. *Parkinson* starred Britain's most beloved TV interviewer, Michael Parkinson. The singer made a royal entrance, descending a staircase to a huge, sustained ovation. Within seconds he had scored his first laugh. In his childhood, he explained, his mother would let him stay up late only if he were watching Parkinson. "She probably wouldn't have been quite as thrilled," he added, "that I had to take my willie out to get on here."

The laughter ended as he shifted to an angry attack against the BHPD. "As far as I was concerned, it was completely an encounter between two adults and it was completely private. . . . You don't see it as a massive risk if there is no one else around, and there's someone waving their genitals at you; you don't think that they're an officer of the law. . . . I fell for the trick. It was a stupid moment and obviously I've suffered for it. Believe me, I'd rather have run up and down Oxford Street saying 'I'm gay, I'm gay,' than have it happen the way it did."

The appearance drew over eight million viewers. To the *Independent*, the interview stood as "a watershed in making the most out-there gay male behavior seem understandable to the public at large." The singer was applauded by Michael Cashman, one of the United Kingdom's most prominent LGBT activists and politicians. Cashman was also an actor whose defining moment—the first gay kiss on a British soap opera, *EastEnders*—had made an impact on Michael.

"Whether he knows it or not," wrote Cashman, "he has advanced the rights of lesbians and gay men. In time, people across the world will be saying, 'Who cares?' And in a strange way, the events in that park have let us understand the human being and the pressures he has had to live with. . . . Finally, George Michael can now be himself, he can openly celebrate his sexuality, who he is and who he loves."

But as the most trying year of his life concluded, the singer was at his bitterest. *Ladies and Gentleman: The Best of George Michael*, though predictably No. 1 in the United Kingdom, had barely made the American Top 40. Another of its new tracks had become a source of pain. Shortly before his arrest, Michael had met Mary J. Blige, whom some considered an heir to Aretha Franklin. In two major hit albums, *What's the 411?* and *My Life*, Blige's raspy-toned singing merged hip-hop, soul, and the scars of a tough childhood, replete with sexual abuse. Michael, she said, warmed her heart. "He was like: 'I love you! You're the greatest.' Just to be recognized by him was amazing." Then came the scandal. But according to Blige, a staunch Christian, it "never stopped me from loving him."

To record with Blige would give him as much street cred as his Franklin duet. She jumped at the chance. Michael chose "As," a love song from Stevie Wonder's *Songs in the Key of Life*. They taped their parts separately. Blige worked with Babyface, the hottest star producer in hip-hop and soul. But the finished track sounded all too clearly recorded in two different places. Michael delivered the tune straight, copying Wonder; Blige wailed like a gospel singer. There wasn't much chemistry, yet Michael thought it was her best work.

Then came an unforeseen blow. Blige's label, MCA/Universal, barred "As" from the U.S. edition of *Ladies and Gentlemen* and forbade its release as a single. Michael received only "wimpy excuses," he said, as to why; he was later told that Blige's management had dropped the ax. Joey Arbagey, program director of a San Francisco radio station, had begun playing the track; MCA asked him to stop. He refused. MCA declined comment.

The United States had once been the land of his dreams; now he called it a place of "wall-to-wall homophobia." In the States, he believed, he'd fallen "prey to one of these SWAT teams" that were "paid to nick guys who are looking for sex with one another." He was sure that Steve Payne's photos would not have been saleable unless he had been arrested first; undoubtedly the tabloids and the BHPD had jointly conspired against him. "I was a convenient celebrity to slap on the wrist because I'm not making money in America," he said, "so it's not damaging to the industry."

As much as he had liked Michael, Jim Moret could not back those claims. "I don't believe that anybody was out to get him," Moret said. But the singer wouldn't be swayed. His explanation for the events of April 7 grew ever more defensive. "I was so sick of the idea that people thought I was ashamed of being gay, that I think subconsciously I put myself in the most shameful position I could think of just to say to everyone, 'Look, you know, I'm really *not* ashamed.'"

After the publicity had died down, Michael got one more rude surprise. The officer he had charged with entrapment filed suit against him for slander and "emotional distress." Marcelo Rodriguez didn't get far. The court ruled "that Michael's statements were non-actionable, non-defamatory expressions of opinion." No slander had occurred—simply because Michael had not accused the officer of anything that fell beyond his duty. Rodriguez, read the judgment, "was given the responsibility to investigate complaints of lewd acts in the men's restroom and apprehend any wrongdoers; Michael's allegations, at most, suggest that Rodriguez did his job with a bit too much enthusiasm. Rodriguez did not injure his suspect, or frame him, or tamper with evidence." In other words, Rodriguez was innocent even if he had committed entrapment.

Years passed before the good of Michael's lewd-conduct episode came to light. By talking so openly, Michael had alerted millions of people to the existence of entrapment. In 2001, John Duran was elected to the West Hollywood City Council; he and his colleagues helped put an end to undercover sting operations in West Hollywood. "It spread from there," he said. "But what really put the death knell on it was Grindr and Scruff and the other social apps. Men who want to have sex with men now have the whole world at their fingertips and don't have to use restrooms or glory holes or adult bookstores any longer. Now all that is just ancient gay history."

But not for Michael. As with other cottagers, the thrills of the "outside" were in his blood, and in London, they were condoned. He had little left to hide; his fetish had been discussed all over the media. Journalists remained his inescapable bedfellows. They used him and he used them. Only anonymity could free him, but Michael wanted it all: privacy and fame; the power to drop titillating hints about his personal life and still be left alone. He even confessed to MTV's John Norris that he might never have come out to the press if he hadn't been caught. "They would have got me some way or another," he said. "This is how it ended up because I wouldn't give it."

CHAPTER TWENTY-ONE

THE ARREST AND ITS aftermath had swerved all focus from Michael's music. The *Daily Telegraph* termed him a "former pinup idol for teenage girls, best known for shoving shuttlecocks down his shorts for concerts while with Wham! . . . turned homosexual icon following drunken fumblings in a public toilet with an L.A. policeman." Bus tours of scandal sites in Los Angeles now included Will Rogers Memorial Park.

One day he and Niall Flynn headed up a busy London thoroughfare on their way to a restaurant. From out of a truck, someone yelled: "GEORGE! GEORGE!" Michael glanced over and said a cordial hello. The man shouted back: "FUCKIN' POOF!"

But there were plenty of reminders that he was still loved. On March 31, 1999, the Capital FM Radio Awards named him Favorite Male Vocalist. He was supposed to have won it a year earlier, but due to the arrest he couldn't make it. This time he showed up, albeit two hours late, in the ballroom of the Royal Lancaster hotel and offered a humble speech. "First I'd like to apologize for not being here last year," he said. "But as you probably know I was otherwise engaged." Laughter swept the room. "It wasn't a disaster," explained Michael, "because I found the strength and dignity through awards like this. I'd like to think that I received this award because I'm a singer and not a gay singer."

Still, his career had derailed, and he knew he needed to make another album, fast. He had no new songs; a CD of covers would have to do. Michael had performed other people's tunes all his life; maybe his singing alone would please his fans. He told the BBC's Jo Whiley: "I don't have a great deal to write about, being happy and balanced and feeling as good as I do. I have a fantastic relationship, things in my life that I thought I'd never have, so writing an album about me would be really boring."

Though DreamWorks SKG had let him go, Virgin still wanted him; and if his idea excited no one, he was George Michael, and the label wanted to keep him happy. Michael scratched out a list of songs. It included "Someone Saved My Life Tonight," by Elton John and Bernie Taupin; "Miss Sarajevo," by the U2-Brian Eno collaboration project Passengers; and "True Faith," by the British rock band New Order. He rented a drafty warehouse in East London and turned it into a recording studio where he could work with his musicians for as long as he wished. But even that simple plan proved beyond him. Michael would "pop in when he felt like it, which wasn't very often," said Phil Palmer. The singer seemed distracted and uninspired as he tried and discarded song after song. Palmer recommended Joni Mitchell's "Edith and the Kingpin"; Danny Cummings proposed "For the Love of You," a hit for the Isley Brothers. In the end, Michael liked only the slinky pop-jazz groove that he and his band had found for "Miss Sarajevo," which told of a beauty-contest winner during the Bosnian war for independence.

With nothing more to show for six weeks of recording, he switched gears. A slew of pop-rock singers in their commercial twilight—Sinéad O'Connor, Bryan Ferry, Carly Simon, Sheena Easton, Robert Palmer—were recording the Great American Songbook with lush orchestras; it seemed like a striving for maturity. Michael had rarely sung that music, but he wanted to try. He went straight to the top and hired Phil Ramone, whose work as a producer and recording engineer for the titans of adult pop had won him shelves-full of Grammys. Ramone's credits included Paul Simon's *Still Crazy After All These Years*, Billy Joel's *The Stranger*, and Frank Sinatra's blockbuster farewell albums, *Duets* and *Duets II*.

In the autumn of 1999, Michael, Ramone, and a combo of musicians settled into Right Track, a studio in Manhattan's theater district. A symphony-sized orchestra would later be dubbed onto certain tracks. There was no time to research songs and learn them off sheet music; Michael copied recordings he liked. He reproduced Billie Holiday's bent notes on a lament of dying love, "You've Changed." His swing version of a Rodgers & Hart ballad, "Where or When," echoed the American but England-based soul singer Madeline Bell's arrangement. In "The First Time Ever I Saw Your Face," he borrowed the snail's-pace tempo and hushed intensity of Roberta Flack's hit single. His slow-burning "Wild Is the Wind" mirrored a recording by Nina Simone. He replicated the shuffle rhythm Simone had used on a 1930 novelty, "My Baby Just Cares for Me." For years, some Doris Day fans had read a gay subtext into her 1954 ballad hit, "Secret Love." Michael sang it as his coming-out song, in a swing tempo lifted from Sinéad O'Connor's version. His most blatant appropriation involved Bjork. The frosty-toned Icelandic singer had recorded a World War II ballad, "I Remember You," in duo with the sugar-spun arpeggios of Corky Hale, a West Coast pop-jazz harpist. Michael had Ramone seek out Hale so that he could clone Bjork's performance.

Yet for all the mimicry, Michael sounded just like himself. And unlike most of his peers, he knew that classic-pop lyrics were meant to be sung like conversation, not declaimed to the back of an arena. Jazz bassist David Finck, who had played with Rosemary Clooney, Anita O'Day, and Tony Bennett, accompanied Michael on the album. "George's phrasing was never that dumb rock approach," said Finck. "The guy had a great groove and natural rhythm, but I was impressed by the balance he found between the sentence structure and the music." What puzzled Finck was Michael's insistence on recording to finished backup tracks rather than singing live with the band. It was the same safety-net approach he had always used—"but George didn't need to do that."

Nonetheless, Michael loved this new challenge. He was engaged, on time, and eager to learn. Jill Dell'Abate, Ramone's production coordinator, spent hours talking with Michael between takes. "You would never have known he was famous," she said. "He was very approachable and super-sweet."

Michael sometimes brought Kenny Goss, and the tone of the chitchat coarsened as the two men sat in the control room and dished closeted celebrities. To mark his outness, Michael had retained the male pronouns that Simone had used in "My Baby Just Cares for Me"; he even inserted the name of Ricky Martin, the shimmying Latin sex symbol whose breakthrough hit, "Livin' La Vida Loca," had millions of girls screaming. To mention him was Michael's inside joke. Out of Goss's earshot, he told Finck and Dell'Abate: "In case you're wondering if Ricky Martin is gay, ask Kenny!" Martin, said Michael, had been one of Goss's previous flings.

At other times, the jollity vanished. Between takes, Michael confided in Dell'Abate that his longing for his mother was at times unbearable. "He told me about a cat that had climbed in his window and sat on his lap," she said. "He felt it was his mom. He was sure she had come back to him."

Veteran jazz singer Helen Merrill, the wife of Torrie Zito, one of the album's arrangers, dropped by the studio. Michael seemed somber and removed; when she gave him two of her albums as a gift he frowned, then disappeared into the bathroom. "I saw right away that he was extremely shy," said Merrill. "That seemed unusual to me, because he was so handsome and talented." Phil Palmer had experienced Michael's aloof side for years. "He was a difficult man to be friendly with," said the guitarist. "I think we all tried. There were very few occasions where we sat down and had a drink or shared a cigarette; he always kept himself isolated and protected. He often made people feel quite unwelcome."

His loathing of what he saw in the mirror had not dimmed. The album-cover shoot was looming, and Michael again fretted about his weight and appearance—"although he looked incredible," Dell'Abate said. Though he was only thirty-six, signs of aging troubled him. The selected photo, taken by Andrew MacPherson, was overexposed to wipe out facial detail. By now Michael bore a wide-eyed look of surprise, exaggerated further by dramatically arched eyebrows, which suggested plastic surgery.

But there was no artifice in his singing. Songs about poverty touched him; despite his wealth, he could identify with the ache of those who had lost everything or never had it to lose. He had written about this in "Hand to Mouth"; now he sang the most searing lament of the Great Depression, "Brother, Can You Spare a Dime." In a bravura acting performance, Michael took on the role of a once-mighty man whom society and fate had tossed aside; he was reduced to begging for coins while trying to maintain a shred of dignity. The singer moved from pained humility to a show-offy swagger to a full-throated cry of desperation: "Say, don't you remember—*I'm your pal!*" Arranger Rob Mathes's orchestration started off as smoldering small-group jazz, then burst into Broadway-like crescendos.

Michael felt proud of that rendition, as he did of the whole album. He knew the dangers of shunning promotion, yet he still thought his name was enough to sell a record. Michael let Virgin know he would neither give interviews nor tour. "We only found out at the last minute that an album was going to happen, so all our promotion was booked late," said an exasperated company spokesman. Virgin couldn't do much more than mail out promo copies and buy ads. Michael did agree to chat with morning host Neil Fox on Capital FM, a station that had always been kind to him, but he barely mentioned the record. "The last century wasn't all about rock 'n' roll, you know, because mostly that's what it's going to be remembered for," he explained. "There are all kinds of fantastic things that were written before then, and a couple since then." Hence the disc's title, *Songs from the Last Century*.

Released on December 6, 1999, the album impressed Neil McCormick of the *Daily Telegraph*. Michael's "tone, range and timing," he wrote, were "impeccable," while the arrangements granted him "the flexibility to unleash a jazzy and curiously feminine quality previously only hinted at." Other critics were disappointed. They wanted new hit songs, not recycled curios. "It's such a dull album," said Chris Heath. "He's so into having this classy producer and it just doesn't have that thing that George Michael brought to records." Heath wished that Michael could have "sung those songs with the spirit of the soul records he loved."

Certain reviews reflected a sad fact: Much of the press saw Michael as a spoiled brat and a has-been, out of creative juice and constantly bad-mouthing them. In the *Philadelphia Inquirer*, Tom Moon, never a fan, came down harder on Michael than ever. "He evidently thinks that his tortured oversinging can improve a sturdy melody such as 'Secret Love' or 'You've Changed' . . . Michael mucks up the works with arrogance and a mannered approach to swing that clunks."

The one track for which he made a video, the Police hit "Roxanne," a love song to a prostitute, had little to do with the album's theme. The video strained for controversy by showing scantily-clad prostitutes waiting for customers in the red-light district of Amsterdam. Michael did not appear. MTV and VH1 paid little attention.

Despite the mixed response, *Songs from the Last Century* reached No. 2 in Britain—it couldn't displace Shania Twain's *Come on Over*—and made the Top 10 in a dozen other countries. But on the U.S. *Billboard* Top 200, it rose only to No. 157.

• • •

As the new millennium began, Michael was adrift; he burned to make himself relevant again, but how? First he had an urgent matter to resolve. His chronic back pain had grown so bad that doctors gave a warning: If he kept delaying surgery, he would wind up in a wheelchair. The operation was risky, but he finally consented. Surgeons removed two decayed vertebrae, which they rebuilt with bone from his hip. The procedure worked, but never again would Michael move with the same agility.

For now, he limited his appearances to benefits. On October 9, 1999, he performed in the biggest all-star music fundraiser since Live Aid. NetAid sought to do nothing less than conquer poverty, notably among refugees from war-torn Kosovo. Harvey Goldsmith, the British concert promoter, announced plans to present three separate arrays of stars—including David Bowie, Sting, Eurythmics, Robbie Williams, and Michael— at Wembley Stadium, Geneva's Palais des Nations, and Giants Stadium in New Jersey. MTV, VH1, and the BBC would air the proceedings worldwide.

Secretly, Michael donated a half-million pounds to the refugees. As usual, he didn't wish to take bows for his generosity, and it irked him whenever a reporter leaked the news. But he put the tabloids to use by striking a deal with the *Mirror*: If its writers would promote NetAid, he would answer any questions they had for him. Soon Michael was opening up about "everything from his love life to his choice of facial hair," wrote the happy editors. In a thank-you piece, "You've Got a Heart of Pure Gold, George," the newspaper declared: "Despite all his success, George showed he's still in touch with the important issues that affect all our lives. Above all, he's shown that he has clearly kept a great sense of humor."

Michael joined the lineup at Wembley. He was ten minutes late for his entrance, and the crowd began chanting, "GEORGE! GEORGE! GEORGE!" Ronan Keating, the young pop star, was sent out to kill time. Viewers didn't know that Michael was backstage, reeling from residual pain. He had taken medications, but they were slow to act. Finally, the band began "Fastlove." Onstage was the high-backed chair from the video; it had been turned away from the audience. Entering in darkness, Michael sat in it, then spun around to thunderous applause. Though still in agony, he rose up and even attempted some basic moves. "I'm certainly not gonna be wiggling about like I used to," he warned. He sat again for "Brother, Can You Spare a Dime," which he sang with even more fire than he had shown on the record. "I'm not sure I ever heard him sound that good again," said Danny Cummings, who played for him.

But his sporadic guest spots were only cementing his image as a faded elder statesman. Michael resolved to make an edgy album, one that would prove what many people doubted: that he cared about his fellow gays. "He wanted to connect to gay clubbing culture and their love of dance music and house music," said Johnny Douglas, whom he hired to produce.

It was a bold step, for Michael had mostly resisted involving himself in gay causes. On November 28, 1999, Michael uneasily agreed to join Elton John and Boy George at the Royal Albert Hall for a concert to honor the tenth anniversary of Stonewall, the British LGBT charity. Michael sang his gay revamp of "My Baby Just Cares for Me" and "I Remember You"; when a gaggle of boys in black briefs surrounded him and John onstage, Michael noticeably cringed.

He understood better than ever why so many celebrities had delayed coming out. Olympic diving champ Greg Louganis had done it in 1994, years after his sports career had ended. Only when her popular morning talk/variety show had ended in 2002 would Rosie O'Donnell confirm the longstanding rumors about her sexuality. Getting outed was still a threat, but a few younger gay stars stood up to it.

In 1999, Stephen Gately of the British band Boyzone came out upon learning that a security guard was trying to sell a story to the tabloids. "This is the most important day of my life," announced Gately. "From today I will have the freedom to finally be myself." The next year he had a No. 3 hit. "There's been no homophobia at all," he told the *Guardian*, "except the odd slagging from lads on the street, but let them." George Michael called Gately with congratulations.

Perhaps Michael envied him. Though forced, at least Gately had revealed the news himself. Michael insisted to one interviewer that he felt "totally part of gay culture now," yet he strained to justify his choices. "I think my ambiguity probably means I have attention from both sexes," he said. "I've really always aimed for everybody."

He did so yet again in his introductory and closing statements for *Staying Alive*, an MTV special for World AIDS Day. The short film was a grim cautionary piece about people who had seroconverted. A Ukrainian junkie is infected by shooting up; full of regret, he plans his death. Female prostitutes in Calcutta agree not to use condoms; young men in São Paulo have casual unprotected sex with girls. Clubby soundtrack music, with porn-like female moans added, magnified the story's depravity. Except for one gay man who sweats out the results of his HIV test after a condom had broken, *Staying Alive* emphasized heterosexuals in third-world countries. Its message: HIV was a death sentence. "Fourteen million people have died of AIDS," announced Michael. "There is no cure." No mention was made of the protease inhibitor drugs that had been introduced in 1998 and that had the power to block infection or, in HIV-positive individuals, to slow the virus's replication.

PR moves such as that appearance, and even his forced coming-out, were enough to make Michael seem like a proud leader of the flock. It wasn't what he wanted. "I don't really see myself as being a role model for anyone unless gay youth are looking for advice on how to get arrested, I suppose," he joked. In an article entitled "Heroes Are Hard to Find When They're Hiding," Ray Mark Rinaldi of the *St. Louis Post-Dispatch* called the singer "a dubious choice for gay hero, and it's a curiously forgiving subculture that is willing to turn him into one." Not everybody was, however. "There were people I knew, well-known figures in the gay community, who were very unhappy about him," said Judy Wieder.

But Michael felt little choice but to join rank. "What's an outed, macho-posturing, pop-culture hero to do now that his career is wheezing and mainstream audiences are no longer all that interested?" asked Rinaldi. "Play to the hungry gay crowds, of course. . . . Pick up the rainbow flag, appear at rallies, charge up the troops. And maybe, if all goes well, folks will forget that you came out by accident, that you kept it all conveniently murky when your star was peaking, and you can still cash in on celebrity."

The creators of Equality Rocks, an all-star benefit concert to be held at Washington, D.C.'s RFK Stadium, were thrilled when Michael signed on. It would take place on April 29, 2000, the eve of the LGBT Millennium March on the mall in front of the Capitol. The concert would raise funds for the Human Rights Campaign Foundation (HRC), the foremost LGBT advocacy group in the United States.

The cast included out pop stars—Melissa Etheridge, k.d. lang, the Pet Shop Boys (one half of whom, Neil Tennant, was openly gay), Michael—and the gay-friendly diva Chaka Khan. Out actors Nathan Lane, Ellen DeGeneres, and her partner Anne Heche would speak. Rapper Queen Latifah, widely rumored to be a lesbian (only in 2021 did she confirm it), was also announced. At the last minute, she canceled—"and we all knew why," said Wieder. The bigger surprise was that country singer Garth Brooks, a superstar in a field considered as anti-gay as hip-hop, had agreed to appear. But that wasn't as unlikely as it seemed. His half-sister was a lesbian, and in 1993, Brooks had won a GLAAD (Gay & Lesbian Alliance Against Defamation) Media Award for his song "We Shall Be Free." In it he imagined a time "when we're free to love anyone we choose / When this world's big enough for all different views."

Equality Rocks was the brainchild of Elizabeth Birch, the HRC's executive director; her girlfriend Hilary Rosen, an HRC lobbyist and the CEO of the Recording Industry Association of America (RIAA); and Etheridge's manager, Bill Leopold, who had helped tend the singer's coming-out. "No one had ever done a concert that was focused exclusively on LGBT rights," said Birch. "People would always say, it's for humanity or for peace. I said, 'We're not gonna candy-wrap this.' I wanted it to be a pure, unabashed celebration of LGBT people and culture, when we could shift a little bit from all the tears over HIV and AIDS and the horrible response of the U.S. government."

To lure Michael, Birch had turned to Wieder. As much as he liked her, he didn't go easy on her or anyone else when they made requests. "He would always say, 'No, I don't want to,'" explained Wieder. "An interview? 'No.' Could you do a photo session? 'No.' I would look at Kenny and he would signal, 'I'll handle this.' Either with his help or just persistence on my part, George would turn around and say, 'Okay, I thought about it. I like the idea. Where do I need to be?'"

Michael had never sung at an explicitly gay event, and he had not even performed in the States since Cover to Cover. But Equality Rocks was a high-level chance to show concern; he couldn't turn it down. He had demands, however. Michael wanted eleven people—musicians, backup singers, friends—to be flown in and put up at a cost of approximately $120,000. And he wanted to speak, not just sing. Finally, he insisted a video be shown. Michael had read a grim piece in *Attitude*; it concerned LGBT American youths whose parents had sent them to psychiatric hospitals for conversion therapy, including electroshock treatments. They fled, hiding in secret shelters known as safehouses. Touched by their plight, Michael sought out the reporter, Tomas Mournian, to make a short documentary, which Michael financed. Birch consented to everything.

Signing Brooks was no less difficult. The idea had come from his business partner Lisa Sanderson, one of the concert's executive producers and an out lesbian. Despite the star's apparent gay-friendliness, Sanderson struggled to talk him into appearing. She tried to blur the focus of the event; it didn't work. Finally, Birch spoke with him directly. "I told him, 'This is not about peace or human rights. It is an LGBT concert and it will be huge, it will be beautifully produced. Please do not come if you're not comfortable.' We went around and around for about a half an hour, and finally he said, 'You know, Elizabeth, I think I'm gonna do this.'" Part of the reason was that Brooks loved Michael's music.

Yet in her announcement to the press, Sanderson stressed that Brooks was not participating in order to make an LGBT statement. "Garth will always step up for children," she announced, alluding to the HRC's hate-crime activism. "Garth's gonna stand on that stage to try to make people hear that the violence with our children in *all* communities has gone way too far."

Etheridge's musicians served as the house band; Michael brought Danny Cummings, Chris Cameron, and his computer programmer Pete Gleadall. As often happened, Michael skipped the first rehearsal; Cummings sang his parts. While Cameron spent hours whipping the band into shape for Michael, annoyance grew. "We got on the bus and there was this terrible atmosphere," recalled Cummings. Responding to a sarcastic remark, the percussionist said firmly: "You've been made to work this hard for a reason, and when he walks in that room tomorrow, you're going to know what that reason is." Cummings was right: "They heard him sing, and they heard his criticisms of what was going on, and they came to me the next day and said they were sorry for giving me such a hard time. George was mighty, and you suddenly realized you were working with a special kind of creature who knew more than your average artist."

• • •

On the night of the show, a near-capacity crowd of 43,500 filed into the RFK Stadium. "A handful of anti-gay protesters waved signs and shouted slurs to the arriving audience, who mostly laughed and jeered," wrote a reporter. Nearly everyone onstage upheld the spirit of the night. k.d. lang greeted the crowd by shouting: "Hey, you homos!" As she crooned her seductive hit, "Constant Craving," lesbians danced together. Chaka Khan sang her trademark, "I'm Every Woman," to which countless gays had boogied in discos and countless drag queens had lip-synched. The Pet Shop Boys performed "New York City Boy," their anthem for young urban gays, joined by a male backup choir in sailor suits. Etheridge joined them on another of their hits, "What Have I Done to Deserve This?," subbing for the recently deceased Dusty Springfield, who had come out late in life. Nathan Lane made eye-rolling fun of closeted actor Kevin Spacey. Brooks, in his black cowboy hat, sang "We Shall Be Free." "I'm not here for gay, straight, black or white," he stressed. "I hope we can rise above these fences we've put up."

In the show's most heart-tugging moment, the parents of youngsters who had perished in hate crimes gathered onstage. The best-known couple was Judy and Dennis Shepard, whose gay son Matthew had been brutally murdered in 1998. There was a moment of silence. Afterward, Etheridge sang "Scarecrow," her song for Shepard. "We'd given out little flags," recalled Birch, "and the entire audience became a sea, swaying back and forth."

An appearance by Tipper Gore, wife of vice president Al Gore, was greeted skeptically. In 1987, the Parents Music Resource Center, cofounded by Gore, had targeted "I Want Your Sex" for its supposed obscenity. Thirteen years later, Gore was sharing a stage with Michael as she assisted her husband on the presidential campaign trail. According to the *San Francisco Chronicle,* both Gore and President Bill Clinton (whom the HRC had endorsed) had "declined invitations to speak" at the next day's march; Gore's wife stepped in at Equality Rocks. Tipper, wrote a reporter from the Louisville, Kentucky *Courier-Journal,* "tried to sew up the gay vote for her husband by shouting, 'We will stand with you!'" Later she was allowed to display her old high-school drumming behind Etheridge.

Well into the concert, down came a screen, and *Hiding Out,* the five-minute documentary that Michael had commissioned, ran. It was a sobering cautionary tale about what awaited certain young people who came out. The high spirits sank. "People were getting up and going to get a beer," said Judy Wieder.

At last, Michael appeared. With his Fu Manchu mustache, shiny gray designer jacket, AIDS lapel pin, and dark glasses, he was an awkward combination of pop star and clone. His brief set signaled the conflicting sides of his personality. In "Fastlove" he sang about no-strings cruising; "I Remember You" was all dewy-eyed love words. The secretive, homoerotic "Father Figure" was inflated into a Grammy Awards-style production number, complete with choir. Then came "Freedom! '90," an emancipation anthem from a man whose choices still shackled him. In the night's happiest surprise, out strode Brooks, who played guitar and traded off a few lines of the song with Michael's arm around his shoulders. Michael left the stage and came back in a matching cowboy hat. At the end, the two men from opposite worlds hugged.

Out front was a sea of lesbians and gays, rejoicing in themselves in ways that Michael couldn't. He looked back at them, said Birch, "as though they were America"—a place that had let him down. And in a six-minute monologue, he let them know it. "For any non-George Michael fans out there, and God knows there are a few of you, I hope you'll allow me to just tell you what I've been doing for a while," he began. With that, he reeled off his letdowns. The love of his life had died of AIDS, and while the British press had used that as one more excuse to out him, in America no one had cared enough to mention it. "By that time," explained Michael, "journalists in this country weren't really taking much notice of me." *Older*, his love letter to Anselmo, was a European hit with two smash singles—but "funnily enough, no one here played them." Two years later, he found himself "performing to what I thought was a gay audience of one in a Beverly Hills rest room"; in fact, he'd been duped by a cop who "was only *pretending* to be gay. Which got me into quite a lot of trouble." He went on to write "Outside," a song about a defiant gay man who'd come out of hiding—"but somehow, America decided not to touch it. So, I mean, you can draw your own conclusions." U.S. reporters, even gay ones, "seem to think that I have no career anymore," he declared, "and I'm here tonight to exploit the last remaining George Michael fans there are. Which actually is complete bullshit, because I'm here to say thank you, and to tell you that even though I know I've not been on the radio for the last nine years in the States, there are so many people in this stadium tonight that have stuck by me, and I really love them for that."

The audience seemed uneasy and confused as the biggest star of the night stood up in a stadium filled with lesbians and gays and told them how badly gay life had treated him. In the *Tampa Bay Times*, Gina Vivinetto wrote: "He bellyached. He whined. Though he attempted to temper his rant with humor, Michael came across as bitter. . . . Many were furious with the singer for making the benefit appearance all about him." Cummings was onstage, listening to the outcry of a man he had observed up close for fifteen years. "He knew that it was over for him in America; that upset him. He saw himself as a target. At least he had the courage of his convictions to try and fight back a little bit, rather than just let it fade away, which these things tend to do."

In the end, Michael's mere presence had been a gift to the cause. After expenses, Equality Rocks netted $1 million. But soon a dark cloud had fallen over the weekend. The next day's march wound up massively in debt, due largely to a mysterious theft of vendor proceeds from an accompanying fair. To help defray the loss, the HRC turned over half its proceeds.

Michael had declined to appear at the march. Before he left town, he and Judy Wieder met at a restaurant in West Hollywood. He was "crushed," she recalled, by the audience's indifference to *Hiding Out*. Wieder tried to explain that in the midst of a rock concert, "they couldn't just suddenly switch channels and watch this devastatingly painful video about kids that were being ruined." But he took their response as a personal blow.

The concert had been videotaped, and a few months later, VH1 aired an hour-long special of highlights. Both Michael and Garth Brooks had barred the use of their segments. "Michael never gave HRC a reason for his refusal," reported *Us Weekly*, "while Brooks's rep said the country crooner didn't sign off because the show was never intended for future television broadcasts. Michael's rep did not return our call."

CHAPTER TWENTY-TWO

MICHAEL HAD A NEW album to make, but he felt more blocked than ever, and he leaned on Johnny Douglas to feed him ideas. Douglas poured himself into the task of recording fragments that he hoped would jump-start Michael's imagination. Another producer in the singer's stable, James Jackman, did the same; Niall Flynn was on board as engineer. But depression kept getting in Michael's way, and his antidepressants were dragging him down. "You don't feel very creative," said Douglas. "You don't really feel anything, and this was trouble, because George wanted to make a dance-y, upbeat album." On days when he didn't take his medications, said the producer, "he became a bit of a monster."

More often he seemed vague and detached. Douglas would play him his latest loop of punchy dance music. "He'd go, 'Yeah, I like that,' then he'd start talking about what was on TV."

Smoking pot had gotten him through *Older*, but now it was making his lyric-writing "too introspective, too meandering," said Douglas. Often the words didn't make much sense. Michael told himself he couldn't bear to keep trying. But if he gave up, he said, he would be letting down "a whole generation of young gay kids." His new songs had little optimism to offer them, but in the best ones he managed to translate his depression into poetry. In "My Mother Had a Brother," he wrote about the gay uncle, "oversensitive and kind," who had killed himself. Though Michael seemed no less tortured, he wanted his uncle to know that at last, "freedom is here / I'm gonna taste it all for you, boy." The song, slow and mournful, was also for his mother, to tell her how happy he was, and that he forgave her. But the sadness in his voice belied all hope.

The even darker "Cars and Trains" was a rambling portrait of three suicidal souls, sung for six minutes over an incongruously perky synth background. Michael sang semi-autobiographically of "Johnny," whose two opiates, sex and pills, were leading him toward doom: "You won't find daddy /

When you're popping those pills / Oh Johnny, is the danger just part of the thrill?" Michael again alluded to "mama," whom he begs to throw out the "bastard" who "hurt you, used you in every way." The song starts as he calls the "Afterlife Message Center"—looking, perhaps, for Lesley—and hears a recorded greeting from a cold, automated female voice.

In 2000, he broke from his sessions to record a duet with Whitney Houston, whose superstardom was short-circuiting. Arista was about to release *Whitney: The Greatest Hits*. The album would include several newly made star duets. Houston was shattered when one of the proposed partners, Michael Jackson, turned her down. That was no surprise; years earlier, at the dawn of her success, she had declined his request to sing with him on his *Bad* album.

When Jackson's refusal came in, Davis suggested George Michael. The executive had tried to pair them in 1987 and Michael passed; years later, he still wasn't interested. "But Kenny was very, very adamant about George doing it," said Flynn. "He was like, 'It's gonna be huge!'" Houston's producer was Rodney Jerkins, the twenty-one-year-old who also produced Destiny's Child, Monica, and other R&B divas. Jerkins informed John Norris of *MTV News* that Houston's team had wanted Jackson but couldn't get him—"so George Michael was the next pick."

Michael agreed to meet Houston in a Los Angeles studio in March, when he flew into town to attend the Soul Train Awards. Houston would be there, too, nominated for *My Love Is Your Love*, the hit album that had shifted her focus from schmaltzy power ballads to tough, urban R&B. (She lost to Mary J. Blige.)

Yet Houston was falling apart. Like much of the world, Michael had read of her last-minute cancellations and no-shows, her alarming weight loss, her memory lapses. She had succumbed to a crack cocaine addiction she would never shake; it had frayed her voice and would ultimately destroy it. All the while she maintained an abusive, drug-fueled marriage to R&B singer Bobby Brown.

More distressing to Houston than the drug gossip was the rising drumbeat of rumors—even *Time* brought them up—about her sexuality. Her mother, the venerated soul singer Cissy Houston, stated on *Oprah* that it would "absolutely" distress her if her daughter were a lesbian. Whitney angrily denied the speculation. "I know what I am," she told Barry Walters in *Out*.

"I'm a mother. I'm a woman. I'm heterosexual. Period." In 2019, seven years after Houston had been found dead in a hotel bathtub, Robyn Crawford, her longtime best friend and assistant, released a memoir, *A Song for You: My Life with Whitney Houston*; in it she confirmed the most persistent rumor, that she and Houston had been lovers.

For Michael, a lot of Houston's story hit disturbingly close to home. Nonetheless, he reported, as promised, to the studio in Los Angeles—and Houston stood him up. That same week, she did it again. To apologize on her behalf, Crawford bought Michael an expensive black shirt. He accepted it politely and flew home.

Jerkins stepped in. He took an overlooked track from *My Love Is Your Love*, "If I Told You That," written by him and three collaborators, and erased lines of Houston's vocal so that Michael could fill them in. When Michael heard it, he wished all the more that he had never said yes. The lyric was nearly senseless ("I know that we're just friends / But what if I decide to bring something in, ooh yeah"), and the production already sounded dated. Yet Michael dutifully recorded his part. In the New York *Daily News*, Jerkins explained that he spent two months working on the track. He thought the singers sounded "very cool together. I mean, Whitney, to me, is a far better singer, but I balanced out the two, and it's great."

That wasn't how Michael and his team felt when they received the mix. "It sounded lousy," said Flynn. Michael took it to Johnny Douglas for emergency surgery. "George didn't like the programming for it; it was a bit out-of-time and clunky," said Douglas. "I had to take Rodney's track and tweak it, line stuff up a little differently, change the feel."

Douglas couldn't ease the track's electronic chill. Two of pop's most wondrous voices hummed with the machinelike, homogenizing sound of Auto-Tune. The duet held not even the illusion of chemistry; in the *Baltimore Sun*, J. D. Considine wrote that Houston was "faking attraction with George Michael."

There was even less of it in the video, which showed them seeking each other out in a crowded club and meeting on the dance floor. Arriving for the shoot, Michael saw a clearly drugged Houston in a chair, Brown beside her. Michael found it a headache to work with her; he hated the first cut and demanded edits. The results give a deceptive sense of two icons in peak form. Houston, in a green-feathered jacket, looks cool, sassy, and controlled; Michael is at his handsomest in a shiny black suit. But he was still annoyed with her behavior and had no intention of deferring. Out to kill, he revives his slickest pre-surgery disco moves as Houston stands and poses.

"If I Told You That" became a top-ten British hit, but the song did little for his career. At a time when he was trying to appear upbeat and healthy, it didn't help to be teamed with another scandal-ridden, faltering star. As much as he wanted to stay current, Michael's music had moved in other directions. The Houston duet was not how he wanted to sound.

•••

Buying expensive new homes had always lifted his spirits, at least for a while, and Michael kept acquiring them as though they were toys. He had sold the ones in Beverly Hills and Santa Barbara; in their place he had bought a house in Regent's Park, one of the Royal Parks of London, all of which had once been owned by British royalty. In 2001, he impulsively purchased what the *Times* called "the most expensive house in Britain"—a six-bedroom Victorian dwelling in The Boltons, a historic garden square in South Kensington. But he never moved in, and sold it the next year. He was much fonder of his sixteenth-century cottage in Goring, South Oxfordshire, on the bank of a stream that joined the River Thames.

Michael's entry into that quaint village had sparked a furor. He built a "Club Tropicana"-style pool overlooked by an eighteen-foot-high changing room on stilts; though the local District Council gave its approval, local conservation groups were irate. "The swimming pool will wreck a beautiful view that has not changed for hundreds of years," complained Norman Radley, chairman of the Goring Parish Council planning committee. Soon, neighbors saw a barge approaching on the Thames, weighted down with chestnut trees, shipped in to conceal the addition.

With that, he paid an estimated £1 million to build a recording studio on the grounds. The finishing touch came in October 2000, when he won, at auction, the walnut-cased spinet piano on which John Lennon had composed "Imagine." Michael paid £1.45 million. The precious instrument, with the ex-Beatle's cigarette burns on it, wound up in the Goring house's dampest room, steps from the stream. Over time, the piano was bounced from one of his homes to another; Michael marred it with his own burns.

The win drew heavy publicity, and Michael accepted an offer from the *Sunday Times* to write an article about it. He still knew how to trigger controversy. Said Michael of the piano: "I wanted to keep it out of tiny hands in Tokyo (xenophobic but true)"—a slap at Lennon's widow, Yoko Ono. To Michael, the object embodied "a zenith in the humanity of popular culture, a time when people expressed a naive belief that they could change the world with music and conviction. These people wrote their own songs, sang them with a variety of untrained voices, drank, took drugs, drowned, marched, looked ridiculous and made amazing, beautiful music. And, in my humble opinion, the best of that music was British."

Michael seethed as he mourned the "steady demise" of his country's pop. Kid bands had taken over, he wrote, groomed by an industry whose hands were in the pockets of eight-to-sixteen-year-olds. He announced to the music business: "Everyone over the age of six in this country is bored to death with your clumsy, cynical attempts to make money." His remarks struck many readers as bitter, and some took him to task: Michael, after all, had led the premiere British boy band of the eighties, one that had strutted in micro-length gym shorts and stuffed shuttlecocks in their flies.

Bono, though, chimed in with his agreement: "People are sick to the teeth of processed and hyped pop bands." The remark was wishful thinking: That music sold in huge numbers, and the *Daily Telegraph*'s Neil McCormick published an elegy. Pop, he wrote, "has become synonymous with everything that is contrived, formulaic and disposable. . . . Pop is a world of precision choreography and perfect teeth, with a sinister undercurrent of adolescent sexuality. Pop wears pigtails and push-up bras. It dances with bare-chested boys with six-pack stomachs."

A part of Michael envied them; it troubled him deeply to see himself replaced. Uncommercial as most of his recent work was, he pined for another big hit. "He was constantly struggling to find where he fit in, what kind of record to make," said Johnny Douglas. "His audience didn't want him to be cool, didn't want him to have the latest sound; they just wanted to hear him sing great melodies with great lyrics. He still could have sold records, just not with the glam and glitz of a hot new artist."

But that was what he wanted, even as he talked like a disapproving father. The creator of "I Want Your Sex" had now decided that online porn was a threat to children. "If I was twelve now," he said, "I'd fall asleep in all my lessons and my right wrist would be overdeveloped." In response he wrote and recorded "Freeek!," which he rushed out as the first single from an album he had not come close to completing.

The idea had sprung out of an instrumental track created by Niall Flynn and his co-engineer, Ruadhri Cushnan. In another effort to awaken Michael's creativity, they had crafted an instrumental track in the clanging-and-whooshing house-music style of Daft Punk, a star synthpop duo. They sweetened it with Marvin Gaye samples. The piece got Michael so excited that lyrics tumbled out of him, starting with, "I'll be your sexual freak of the week." Concern for the children vanished; in a nasty, electrified growl, he sang to "mama": "You got yourself an ass with a mind of its own."

Michael had struck a one-single deal with Polydor Records; he retained the right to give the company a whole album if he liked how they treated him. He had little doubt that "Freeek!" would hit No. 1, and apparently neither did Polydor, which footed the seven-figure cost of making the video. It would later be called the twentieth most expensive one in history. Michael had seen the video of Janet Jackson's No. 1 hit, "Doesn't Really Matter"; it showed a futuristic city much like the one in *The Matrix*, a recent sci-fi blockbuster. Michael hired Jackson's director, Joseph Kahn, to make lightning strike for him, too.

They whipped up a parody of a Times Square catapulted forward in time—a barrage of space-age sexual imagery, S&M superheroes, and garish neon. Michael appears as a smirking sex god in a blood-red cyborg suit. He unleashes four Dobermans that transform into dominatrixes. When Michael and a female cyborg grind their bodies together, the sexual spark makes Times Square explode.

On March 18, 2002, Polydor released "Freeek!" To Michael's delight, it was instantly controversial; *Top of the Pops* refused to air more than an excerpt. It premiered in its entirety on Britain's Channel 4. Advance buzz pumped up the viewership to an estimated million-and-a-half viewers.

The single reached No. 1 in Italy, Spain, and Denmark, but made only No. 7 in the United Kingdom; Polydor didn't bother releasing it in the States. Critics dismissed the video as nothing more than a crass effort to shock. The

Observer's Colin Paterson wrote wearily of an artist who was "so desperate to stay cutting-edge" that he had resorted to seminaked bondage scenes and a shot of humping dogs. "Somehow," wrote Paterson, "the shots of George holding four women on leashes no longer rings quite true."

Michael returned to his album, even heavier of heart than before. One day he made an announcement to Douglas. "Look, I'm just depressed. I need to take some time off and think about stuff." Douglas asked how long. "I don't know," said Michael. "Could be three months, could be a year, could be two years." And when did he wish to stop working? "Today."

Michael escaped for four months to Dallas, where he had bought yet another house for himself and Goss. There, some song ideas occurred, one of them inspired by Lennon's piano. In "John and Elvis Are Dead," a childhood friend wakes up from a coma and sees a world whose heroes have perished and whose truth-seekers haven't a chance. "If Jesus Christ is alive and well," he asks, "then how come John and Elvis are dead?"

Other songs took him even further from his plan to make a gay-friendly dance album. "Precious Box" became an eight-minute drone of numbed free association in which he revisits the theme of a lonely life at the top. "It's so freezing out here . . . Life keeps kicking my ass . . . People can go out of fashion," he sings while chill-wave electronica hummed and buzzed. In "Through," he sings in an aching voice: "What kind of fool would remain in this cheap gilded cage . . . Suddenly the audience is so cruel / I think I'm, I know I'm through." "Round Here" is an ode to his London youth, "when music fell like rain to the streets." He marvels at how things had worked out: "In this town, yes / I guess I got to be someone."

Michael booked Andy Morahan and Mike Southon to turn the song into a video, in which he agreed to star. During the shoot, Michael was hostile, depressed, and difficult. A trailer had been rented for him; the leasing company would later have to fumigate it, for pot smoke had permeated every crevice. "There was tension between Andy and George from the moment he walked on the set," said Southon. "You could tell Andy was controlling his anger." Michael would wind up replacing all the footage with black-and-white sequences of himself in the studio, singing of a gratitude he didn't seem to feel.

•••

Despite his occasional social commentary, Michael had seldom been political; he considered his views moderate. Back in 1997, though, the *Sunday Times* had called Michael "one of [Tony] Blair's newest and richest friends." The newly elected British Prime Minister and Labour Party leader had vowed to overhaul education, and Michael agreed to serve as spokesman for a project that would gain every pupil access to a laptop computer.

Now, in the summer of 2001, he was at SARM to work on a vaguely themed anti-war dance tune. On the afternoon of September 11, Douglas bolted into the studio, shouting, "*Turn on the TV!*" A passenger plane had crashed into the North Tower of the World Trade Center in New York. A second plane hit the South Tower. Thirty-four minutes later, a third one hit the U.S. Pentagon in Arlington, Virginia.

Everyone at SARM watched the disaster, stunned. By that night, the White House had learned that the attacks had been masterminded by al-Qaeda, the Islamic extremist group, and one of its founders, Osama bin Laden. American President George W. Bush swiftly launched the war on terror. On October 7, Bush led a U.S. invasion of Afghanistan, al-Qaeda's headquarters. Soon thereafter, he took his first steps toward invading Iraq, based on the unproven theory that Saddam Hussein, the country's genocidal president, possessed al-Qaeda ties and weapons of mass destruction (WMD). It appeared that Blair would follow the United States into war.

Michael listened as Niall Flynn and other friends discussed the matter. "He didn't seem to know a great deal about any of it," said Flynn. "But he learned about it very quickly—overnight." Michael paid close attention to a *Daily Mirror* cover story, "This War's a Fraud," by Australian journalist John Pilger. It helped convince the singer that Bush was a warmonger who, in tandem with the U.S. media, was lying about WMD—and that, if Blair got his way, Hussein might end up crushing England.

With music-making leaving him more frustrated than fulfilled, Michael was in need of a new cause. Within days, his dance tune "Shoot the Dog" took shape. Its gist: that Blair was Bush's pet on a leash, and that Hussein was sure to torpedo him and the country he ran.

High on pot, Michael went to work. He borrowed the hook from the 1981 hit "Love Action (I Believe in Love)" by the Human League, the British synthpop band. Michael tried to write cutting political satire, but his efforts were confusing: "Nine nine nine gettin' jiggy / People did you see that fire in the city?" (999 was Britain's emergency phone number; "gettin' jiggy" was drug vernacular for the shakes that come from withdrawal.) He added a suggestion that Blair was "dancing with Dubya"—that is, in bed with Bush, both literally and figuratively. In the recording booth, he adopted his oft-used, guttural sex growl.

Michael loved *2DTV*, a British cartoon series that lampooned the absurdities of world leaders, current events, and pop culture. One of the show's running gags skewered the vapid luxury lifestyles of three friends. Elton John was shown as a toupee-wearing stuffed shirt; Geri Halliwell as a bug-eyed idiot with a lemon-yellow bob; and Michael as a hirsute parody of a Castro clone. The show's director, Tim Searle, heard "that Elton John was quite upset." But Michael found his own characterization hilarious. He phoned an incredulous Searle and asked if he could hire him and his team to make a "Shoot the Dog" video in *2DTV* style.

Meetings began. The team, including Searle, head writer Georgia Pritchett, and producer Giles Pilbrow, sat in their office with Michael, who wore a gray hoodie and sweatpants. Moments after he had said hello, Michael asked: "Do you mind if I light up?" Of course not, they said. Spliff in hand, yet with a fervor verging on paranoia, he explained his fears about Blair and Bush. Then he played them a cassette of the song, the lyric of which they could barely comprehend; Michael had to explain it. He added that he needed the video in about three weeks. "Please, take the mickey out of me," he said. "Unrelentingly. Use all the eras of my past. Dress me up as a woman." He wanted Geri Halliwell to be singled out for special laughs; the former Spice Girl wouldn't leave him alone, and she was driving him crazy, as Niall Flynn could attest. "I remember times where George would say, 'Fuck! Geri's at the door. Tell her I'm not here!' "

Working around the clock, the *2DTV* team made their deadline. The cartoon starts with Bush seated in the Oval Office, looking not unlike Alfred E. Neuman, the jug-eared, vacantly grinning mascot of *Mad* magazine. A general tries in vain to brief him on world affairs; as a last resort he speaks through a sock puppet. "Shoot the Dog" starts playing. Michael steps out of the men's room in low-slung black pants and a V-neck T-shirt that exposes his hairy belly. Reaching into his crotch, yanks out a shuttlecock (Michael's idea), then stuffs the sock puppet into his pants. He breaks into his campiest disco moves; Bush and the general join in.

Out on the sidewalk, Michael—out of his stage garb and now bald and pudgy—is splashed with mud and knocked down by a passing muscleman's car. The scene shifts to a family of pouty-lipped George Michaels in the style of *The Simpsons*; they sit glued to the TV, watching three Michaels dancing in drag. Halliwell butts in on the act and gets elbowed aside. She pops out of the hair of one of the Georges, who flicks her away; she cuts a hole from underneath the floor and is stomped back down. (All this, too, was Michael's suggestion.) On the White House lawn, Blair turns into a poodle who chases a ball tossed by the president. Michael mounts a missile—an image borrowed from the 1964 cold-war comedy film *Dr. Strangelove*—and lands in bed with the Blairs; Bush pops up between them.

The cartoon cuts to a duet between the Michaels of Wham! and *Faith*; the dour, bespectacled singer from *Older* shuffles in and takes over. A royal soccer match starts on TV; Michael, wearing the peekaboo hairstyle of The Human League's Phil Oakey, dances in sync with Prince Charles, Queen Elizabeth II, and a dog. He strolls through the Iraqi battlefield, then strips down to a leopard thong and leaps into bed with Cherie Blair while her husband tosses a lasso around the Statue of Liberty and grins. Michael joins the Village People as Bush and Blair tango past.

The video thrilled Michael. "He was bang-up for every idea we had," said Pilbrow. The singer screened "Shoot the Dog" for Andy Stephens, to his lawyers, to executives at Polydor, to trusted friends and colleagues. Most of them had severe misgivings. With his career teetering, especially in the States, Michael's political opinions were a recipe for disaster. Radio probably wouldn't touch the song, which few people besides Michael considered good. And the media were not likely to accept the author of "Wake Me Up Before You Go-Go" as a pundit on world affairs.

But he was adamant. Piers Morgan, now editor of the *Daily Mirror*, gave him three pages to expound. Michael stressed that Saddam Hussein, though a terrorist, was "a hero to his people," a lot of whom lived in England. "If we corner him he is too dramatic not to go out with a bang," asserted Michael.

ITV premiered the video on July 2, 2002, after an episode of *2DTV*; from there it went to MTV. The single would follow; Michael hoped the video would catapult it to No. 1. But the blowback was instant. The *New York Post*'s Bill Hoffmann had gotten an advance listen to "Shoot the Dog," and he greeted it with a scathing attack. Hoffman blasted the "washed-up pervert pop star" for suggesting that Bush and Blair—"close allies in the war against terror"—were lovers. In a song full of frivolous gun references, he wrote, Michael had dared mock America "for defending itself against Osama bin Laden and his terrorist network." The song, predicted Hoffmann, might "end Michael's career in the United States."

The singer rushed to halt the video's American release and to send out a peacemaking statement. "I am definitely not anti-American," he insisted. "My feelings about George W. Bush, however, are a little different. And I know I'm not alone in fearing his politics, and in hoping that our man Tony can be a calming and rational influence on him." Soon Michael's face was on the cover of the *Sun* accompanied by the word COWARD—a term supplied by Simon Cowell, an acid-tongued judge on Britain's *Pop Idol* and its U.S. spinoff, *American Idol*. In an editorial, the *Sun* declared of Michael: "He's scared to release it in the States in case it offends those fans he still has left. What a cop-out." The *Sunday Times* had even less patience for the video. "After watching this puerile effort you might want to start your own campaign to Save the Dog and Shoot the Singer. What exactly do the pop gibberish lyrics of 'Shoot the Dog' add to global debate?" Branding Michael "a desperate self-publicist without principle," the *Times* concluded: "Here is a crass case of career before conscience."

In an attempt to defend himself, Michael turned back to CNN. On July 3, he phoned into the network's *Talkback Live*, where he spoke with callers. A few of them voiced support, but not a woman from Florida. "You can't tell me that you did not intend to slam our country when you slam our president," she hissed. "You can talk about your own family, but I'll be danged if I am going to let somebody else step in from the outside and talk about ours!" Some members of the studio audience cheered; others booed.

Celebrities chimed in. Film actor Woody Harrelson called Michael's effort "brave and brilliant," but Noel Gallagher (of the British band Oasis) labeled it "fucking laughable." Michael, he said, had "hid who he actually was from the public for twenty years. Now all of a sudden he's going to say something about the world."

The scandal left the team at *2DTV* reeling. "I was accused of killing his career," said Tim Searle.

On his website, Michael strained to explain himself further. Having lived with an American for years, he said, "I would never knowingly disrespect the feelings of a nation, which has suffered so much loss, so recently. . . . However irreverent I may be of Mr. Blair and Mr. Bush, my intentions are genuinely to do something, however small, to protect all of us, the people I love, and the people you love, from a disaster that we have the power to avoid."

The next few days found Michael at home in London, stoned and struggling to figure out what had just happened. Because Rupert Murdoch's News Corp owned both the *Sun* and that "fascist newspaper," the *New York Post*, Michael concluded that the conservative mogul had set out to punish him. Homophobia *had* to be the root cause. On July 12, he brought his conclusions to the ITV talk show *Tonight with Trevor McDonald*. "For some reason I don't have a right to talk about anything because I got caught four years ago in a Los Angeles toilet," he said. Americans, he said, were "very reactionary right now," and he could not risk going back there, even to see Kenny.

For all the fallout, the single made it to No. 12 in Britain; that summer, the video "was all over the place," said Searle. "Then suddenly—nothing. Independent radio stopped playing it, the BBC stopped playing it. I thought, someone, somewhere has got the ability to turn something off. It was quite scary."

Michael agreed. He took a measure of pride in having placed himself in the front line of dissent when colleagues of his had, he felt, clammed up to protect their careers. "You know, fucking Lou Reed walking out of an interview because they asked him about it," Michael snarled. Madonna had shot an anti-war video for her song "American Life"; milder by far than "Shoot the Dog," it shows her on a runway in military garb accompanied by dancers in camouflage. A grenade is thrown at a Bush look-alike. But "due to the volatile state of the world and out of sensitivity and respect to the armed forces," she said, she yanked it. To Michael, that was "worse than not doing it at all. . . . I stand up and say, 'I really think we need to do something about this,' and everyone goes, 'It's a career move.'"

As passionately as he spoke, friends wondered what had compelled him to take this career-threatening plunge. "He wasted so much time going from

TV show to TV show," said Flynn, "and I don't think he had that much belief in it." How strongly was Michael driven by career frustration that needed venting? By disgust with the media? By his persistent longing to be taken seriously? By his undeniable attraction to scandal as a means of getting attention?

One of Michael's fears did come true: Blair indeed followed Bush into war. But WMD did not exist, and Britain was not annihilated. Those developments, however, were still to come. As the Iraq War dawned, Michael agreed to appear on *HARDtalk*, a BBC one-to-one interview series known for posing tough questions on world issues. The host, Tim Sebastian, had faced down national leaders; now he sat opposite a pop star with flaring eyes and agitated body language. "I have absolutely no desire to be here today," contended Michael, but he had an urgent cause. "This is something that threatens the lives and the lifestyle of myself and the people I love," he explained, and he had taken a "big risk" in denouncing it.

"Particularly if your record sales are falling," observed Sebastian.

"My record sales are *not* falling!" insisted Michael. The problem, he said, is that the industry now pandered to a pubescent audience; radio wouldn't play him. And he refused to play the game: "I never do TV; I'm phobic about cameras. I have no interest in promoting my music beyond making videos." He was only concerned, he said, about potential retaliation from "the entire fundamentalist terrorist network around the world." As he kept referencing the atomic bomb, it seemed as if Michael, like Blair and Bush, believed in the existence of WMD.

And how exactly had "Shoot the Dog" helped? "It's called satire," he said. Only humor, he explained, could rouse the politically indifferent youth of Britain. Sebastian quoted the line in which Cherie, the wife of Tony Blair, infers that he and Bush were lovers. "What does *that* contribute?" the host asked. "I'll tell you what it contributes!" said Michael. "She's saying she's going to *withhold* sex because there's something about that Bush ain't right. Do you get the little joke in there—Bush? *It was to bring it to people's attention!*"

In the end, he concluded, "it was worth what I put up with, it was worth no one playing the record, no one playing the video. It was worth it because when I was attacked for doing it, it came into the mainstream. What were the precedents for this in entertainment? Who talked before me?"

Michael wasn't done speaking out. Asked to contribute a track to an all-star charity album, *Hope*, that would benefit the children of Iraq, he recalled a song he had heard at eight. "The Grave" was singer-songwriter Don McLean's Vietnam War-era lament for a doomed soldier of twenty, lingering in a trench "as he held to his rifle and prayed not to die." Even as a child, said Michael, he was struck by the "terror of war" etched into those lines.

Michael rushed to record it. Then he made a video, which showed images of battlefield scenes. Three days before MTV Europe premiered it, Michael went on *The Graham Norton Show*. Its host, a campy gay Irish comic, preferred to keep things light and goofy, and Michael played along. When Norton joked that they *had* to discuss the toilet incident, Michael fired back: "Which one? . . . The time I got caught, you mean? . . . I heard Elton's signature is in there somewhere."

Michael shifted the talk to Blair, Bush, and the Iraq War, which England would enter in a few days. "It would be great if either of them would hear this song and understand exactly what they're asking people to do for them," Michael said.

He moved to a stool, and with three musicians behind him he sat in profile, head tilted down, and talk-sang in a fragile, defeated voice about the burial of that soldier. In a full-throated wail, he cried out the youth's last words: "*They can't let me die here!*"

Two weeks later, Michael returned to *Top of the Pops* for the first time since Wham! to sing "The Grave." Advance word had reached Britain's shadow defense minister, Gerald Howarth, who wasted no time in denouncing Michael. "We should be supporting our troops, not undermining them," he announced, adding: "The BBC is making a mistake and should reconsider."

It didn't. Michael had not only the producers but the song's creator on his side. "I am proud of George Michael for standing up for life and sanity," said McLean. "I am delighted that he chose a song of mine to express these feelings. We must remember that the Wizard is really a cowardly old man hiding behind a curtain with a loud microphone. It takes courage and a song to pull the curtain open and expose him. Good luck, George."

•••

Michael needed it. The responses to "Freeek!" and "Shoot the Dog" had seriously dashed his confidence, and again he felt blocked. His album had turned into a hodgepodge of unrelated material, and no one knew when he would finish. "It went around in circles for a long time," said Flynn. "It was hard for him to have any sort of clarity."

One more distraction came in 2002, when he paid £2 million for what he considered his dream home. The neighborhood was Highgate, the exclusive North London hilltop suburb where Charles Dickens, John Keats, and Samuel Taylor Coleridge had once lived. At Michael's new address—5, The Grove—stood a seventeenth-century, vine-covered red-brick house. It wasn't flashy and had no garage; Michael parked his Range Rover out front. But everything about it charmed him. There was a huge garden and swimming pool out back, and he owned a tiny square that faced the house. Michael used the house to throw lavish catered parties. "Some of them would end up like a Fellini film," recalled a frequent guest. "It was incredible, some of the stuff that was going on. The expression free love comes to mind. Certainly free drugs."

Highgate's "café and shop owners could count on a smile and a wave" as Michael passed, wrote journalist Thomas Andrei; still, the locals gave him his space. At the nearby Côte Brasserie, he ate at a favorite table near a bay window. "Everyone could see him, but nobody bothered him," said Andrei. Once more, however, the man who craved privacy had left himself exposed. Anyone could see his front door through a gate, and fans and paparazzi lurked outside.

He had kept his house in Hampstead, but no security system seemed to protect him there. While he was traveling, thieves robbed the home of a sports car, jewelry, paintings, and clothes. Months later, a female stalker hid beneath the floorboards. "She leapt out, sending the former Wham! star reeling in horror after yelling out his name," reported the *Mirror*. Michael phoned the police, who came and arrested her, but somehow she kept breaking in. He wondered if he would end up like John Lennon, shot dead outside his luxury apartment building, the Dakota, in New York. Another stalker managed to enter and steal an address book that contained his email address. Soon Michael's inbox held "a flood of deranged messages," reported the *Mirror*. The police's indifference enraged him.

Fate, he was sure, was out to get him; the Goring house also seemed cursed. Michael had bought a Labrador puppy for companionship, and it drowned in the Thames. Then, in the winter of 2003, the river overflowed for the first time in decades. Fearing the worst, Niall Flynn opened the door to Michael's home studio, which stood down a path, below ground level. "The sofa was floating across the room," he said. "The studio was totally destroyed."

Luckily, Flynn had stored the recent recordings elsewhere. But the mess delayed the project by several more months. Through it all, Michael kept pushing to produce. Two new songs glorified his relationship with Goss. Douglas spent months working with him on "Amazing," an eighties-style dance track that came closer to anything on the album to honoring his original club-music theme. "I thought, oh, good, we've finally got a nice, straight-up, simple pop song," said the producer. Sang Michael: "I never thought that my savior would come . . . I think it's amazing / The way that love can set you free." The song convinced him he had recaptured the joy of Wham!. In a gauzy chillwave track, "American Angel," cowritten with Flynn, Michael rhapsodized about his "horny cowboy . . . with that Texan smile." But the lyric took a dark turn: "I don't think that I could love and lose again / I don't think I have the strength."

Some onlookers wondered how happy the relationship was. "I sensed there was a resentment from Kenny toward George," said Phil Palmer, who overheard "a lot of bickering" between them. Billy Masters had observed them together at numerous events. "I never got a feeling of passion between them," he said.

A key line in "Amazing" did not suggest a stable rapport: "We're like victims of the same disease." Later he confessed they had not been monogamous for years. "No jealousy," he explained. "We had our couple of years of that bliss, and we have to mix that up with the desire for newness, with the desire for the unknown. Which is what drives men's sexuality." Anyone who disapproved, he declared, could "stick it up their ass. . . . It's time we accepted gay men for what they are as opposed to a tea-and-biscuit version."

Michael preferred to meet strangers in Hampstead Heath, the spacious park, just down a curving hill from his Highgate house, that had become home base for London cottagers. On many a late night he hopped in his car, parked near the West Heath, and wandered into the cruising area: about an acre of overgrown bushes and trees that hid a maze of trails. At peak night-time hours it was packed with men, "sitting on every available horizontal plane, leaning against every tree," wrote John O'Brien in the *Independent*. Many visitors were lit by the pale glow of cigarettes; all had furtive, darting eyes. Some, like Michael, brought their dogs. "After dark there can even by a naked man walking about, pale and ghostly," O'Brien explained. "And the pace is slow. So slow it can look like that scene from *Night of the Living Dead* when all the zombies emerge from out of the darkness."

Michael was not hard to recognize, but the fact that most of the men he met "were either married or in the closet," he said, made him feel safe. "If you're a suburban cruiser like my good self and you like guys that are really straight-acting, then most of the people you pick up, whether you take them home or do it there and then, are not going to tell your secret because they've got one themselves."

His nocturnal habits—often he got home shortly before dawn, slept just a few hours, then went to the studio—had not helped his productivity. His health was another matter of concern. Michael's smoking habit, both pot and Marlboro Lights, worried friends, who feared the damage it would cause to his voice. Then there was the issue of safe sex. Michael claimed that he and Goss had used condoms early in their relationship, then stopped when they vowed monogamy; once they had lifted that rule, he said, he had always insisted on them. His one HIV test following Anselmo's death had come back negative, but that was years ago; the thought of what he might learn in the next one scared him.

•••

For now, he was more concerned about how to make himself timely. In 2003, Michael watched Madonna and Britney Spears perform a staged lip-lock on the MTV Video Music Awards. A camera cut to the seemingly shocked face of Spears's ex, twenty-two-year-old Justin Timberlake, who had inherited Michael's crown as a purveyor of blue-eyed soul and urban music. Michael let the *Mirror* know he was game for an on-camera, cross-generational kiss with Timberlake. "I've already called Justin," explained Michael, "but unfortunately he hasn't called back." A columnist at Montreal's *The Gazette* advised: "Don't hold your breath, George."

The real surprise came when he announced who would be releasing his album. Having sworn he would never let Sony have another note of his music, he returned to Epic in late 2003; Michael had signed a one-album contract. Money talked: they "gave me the most amazing deal," he said.

He had finally accumulated enough tunes to fill an album. "I really think it's some of my best work for a long time," he told Piers Morgan. There were enough dance tracks to give the album some energy. "Flawless (Go to the City)" had come from the Ones, a popular electronica trio in the New York gay club scene. The song, a takeoff on club culture and the obsession with fabulousness, had landed on a U.K. Revlon commercial. Michael sampled the original, with its Auto-Tuned, druggy disco sound. It had hardly any words, so he wrote a lyric that took a dark view of club life—"I think you know that you are more than just / Some fucked-up piece of ass." Michael proudly called the track his "first proper queen's record," adding: "I think there will be people dancing around their handbags to this one. . . . It's supposed to be about that *Pop Idol* mentality applied to a young gay man. That idea of getting out of the dull-as-dishwater town you're in and to London or whatever. But I wanted to camp it a bit more."

No longer did he feel the need to bury each vocal in reverb. On several tracks, his voice is front, center, and unenhanced. Never had he exposed it more starkly than in "Patience," one of the last songs he recorded for the album. He sang its freeform lyric with just piano. Slow and elegiac, it summed up his forlorn world view, in which even the elderly were left to fend for themselves. He begged the listener to show compassion: "Look into the eyes of any patient man / Whether they be amber, green, or blue / There's a piece of God staring back at you."

Michael had spent hours drafting the lyric on paper, which was rare for him. He sat in the studio even longer, working out a piano part. From there he recorded it quickly, and made it the opening track. All told, the album had taken him five years to complete. "That's why he called it *Patience*," said Douglas.

CHAPTER TWENTY-THREE

IN MARCH 2004, EPIC RECORDS released *Patience* everywhere but in the United States and Canada; those editions would come out in May, shorn of "Shoot the Dog." Michael soon learned that most English critics had lost patience with him. The title, wrote Peter Paphides in the *Times*, "suggests that we sat here all this time, anticipating George's next dispatch." Paul Connolly, another *Times* critic, called the songs "often angry and bitter, sometimes a little self-pitying. . . . The chubby lad who hated parties and being an outsider still craves validation." David Thomas of the *Daily Mail* was even harsher. "For years," he wrote, "they've been saying that George Michael's new records are such rubbish, you can't give them away. . . . For a man blessed with one of the finest voices in pop and a once-infallible gift for hit-making, George's creative and commercial decline was pathetic to behold. Yet his mighty ego and craving for success remained undiminished."

But Alexis Petridis, the *Guardian*'s young music reviewer, heard *Patience* sympathetically. "It gives the listener an awful lot to plough through," he wrote, "but anyone willing to persevere will find George Michael's finest work is buried within it." Even so, wrote Petridis, Michael's artistic vision had scarcely advanced since *Faith*. To the *Independent*'s Andy Gill, Michael was copying himself: "The bits that don't sound like *Older* sound like 'Fastlove,' or even 'Freedom! '90.' "

Even so, Gill gave Michael four stars. "*Patience*, he wrote, "is a thoughtful, sophisticated work that flip-flops back and forth between, on the one hand, intense ballads dealing with serious matters—societal ills, the failure of faith (the belief, not the album), suicide, and George's own life; and on the other, pounding disco anthems celebrating shameless hedonism."

In England, *Patience* lurched to No. 1. "Amazing" hit No. 4 there and No. 1 in Italy and Spain. London's Radio Academy proclaimed him the most frequently spun artist on British airwaves since the eighties, beyond even Elton John. "I can't believe it!" exclaimed Michael. "I've only made six albums in twenty-two years, so I don't know how this happened. I'm the luckiest writer on earth."

As much as he pretended not to care, he dreamed of a grand reemergence in the States. But he still couldn't bear the thought of touring nor of interacting with the American press. Without that, *Patience* would be just another album, and Michael an old-timer in a pop world ruled by Usher, Beyoncé, Kanye West, and Britney Spears. Once the U.S. issue had appeared, coverage was sparse and unimpressed. "This isn't the dance-friendly George you know and love," announced Christy Lemire of the Associated Press. "This is, instead, a kinder, gentler Michael—and an increasingly irrelevant one." The disco tunes, she wrote, "sound like the breathy Europop you'd hear while shopping for sweaters at Express. 'Flawless (Go to the City)' and 'Precious Box,' meanwhile, are generic gay-bar electronica." Mary Lamey of Montreal's *The Gazette* listened with a groan. "George Michael is officially incapable of releasing a simple pop album anymore. Everything is freighted with meaning: homophobia and suicide, spiritual doubt, AIDS."

Never again, resolved Michael, would he make another album. He dreaded putting himself on display in the American media, but he appeared reluctantly on a few TV shows. The four female hosts of ABC's *The View* dredged-up tired talking points—the Sony lawsuit, the arrest, his years in the closet—and asked nothing about his new music, although he sang "Amazing." In a brief appearance on *Today* he performed "Father Figure," which scarcely helped *Patience*.

But in a coup that heartened Sony, *Oprah* booked him for a full hour, to be aired on May 26. His appearance was promoted in leering tabloid style as "George's Michael's Darkest Secrets." The ad copy framed him as a disgraced has-been. "Eighties music sensation George Michael breaks his ten-year silence," it boasted; *Oprah* viewers would be the first to hear the "intimate details about his fall from fame"—this despite the fact that he had already discussed that in countless interviews.

Winfrey began by reeling off a list of Michael's past successes and scandals, while adding her familiar redemptive spin, which cast *Patience* as the epiphany of an embattled man who had finally found peace. Now, she proclaimed, he could even laugh off his humiliating arrest. So could Goss, who waved and grinned from the front row and seemed thrilled to speak on camera.

Winfrey asked Michael if he worried over whether his American fans accepted him as a gay artist. He gave a poised response. "I'm not really interested in selling records to people who are homophobic," he said. "I'm a very lucky man. I'm forty years old; I live with a man I love dearly; I have more love and success and security in my life than I could have ever dreamed of. So really, I don't need the approval of people who don't approve of me."

Michael wanted his fans to know that personal crises behind his control had kept him in hiding. "It wasn't that I didn't care," he said. "It was just because I didn't have the emotional energy to face what would have been an uphill struggle. And now that I feel great again and my writing ability has come back, I just wanna touch base with them again and say, I'm kind of fighting fit now, and if you're interested, I'm here again." With that, Winfrey showed a prerecorded tour of Michael's house in Goring. The singer demonstrated his most expensive toy, the Lennon piano.

The *Oprah* hour helped boost *Patience* to No. 12 in the United States, although it soon plummeted. "Flawless (Go to the City)," already a top-ten U.K. hit, reached No. 1 on *Billboard* Hot Dance Club Songs; so did "Amazing." But that chart was a minor sub-category of the coveted Hot 100. Ultimately, *Patience* sold 381,100 copies in the States and four million worldwide—a success by almost anyone's standards but his. The album had dominated his life for five years; he wanted more from it. In a BBC interview with program host Jo Whiley, he announced that in the future he would record only occasional tracks and offer them on his website for a requested donation to his favorite charities.

That news sparked dozens of newspaper stories and a fair amount of sarcasm. "George Michael, forgotten but not gone, has announced his retirement from the music business," cracked Doug Camilli in *The Gazette*. "I mean, George Michael? The guy has been old news for a decade now."

• • •

Without music-making to propel him, Michael's world shrank. He stayed mostly home, watching TV and rolling spliffs, a container of Häagen-Dazs at hand. Amid a cloud of smoke, he stayed glued to *Coronation Street*, the long-running British primetime soap opera about working-class Brits. He loved the storyline about Todd Grimshaw, the show's handsome, brooding, sexually confused character whose first gay kiss drew fourteen million viewers. Michael's other favorite soap, *EastEnders*, gave him a special kick. One of its characters, the square and frowsy Heather Trott, was so obsessed with the star that she tried to climb the wall of his house; after a male escort had impregnated her, she named the baby George Michael.

Giving away money still brought him joy. By now Michael had quietly donated over £20 million to charity. One cause touched him enough to get him back on TV. When he heard that Ronan Keating, a former member of Boyzone, was about to appear on the game show *Who Wants to Be a Millionaire?* to earn money for cancer, Michael volunteered to join him. Both men had lost their mothers to the disease within the same twelve months. Michael's win would benefit Macmillan Cancer Support, which had provided the nurse who cared for his mother. Charming and relaxed, he helped Keating answer multiple-choice questions and raised £32,000.

But at home, he lived in a state of growing paranoia, a common side effect of heavy marijuana use. Michael confessed to Johann Hari of the *Independent* that it "terrified" him to hear his name on TV. "I have to change the channel," he said. He had banned newspapers in his homes for fear of reading something unflattering about himself. Michael turned to the chat room on his website, a place where he could surely bask in his fans' unconditional love. Instead, many of their remarks incensed him. He was fat, he looked old, they didn't like his recent songs, and why wasn't he out promoting *Patience?* Feelings hurt, he shut the chat room down. "Those of you that want to carry on the media's work will have to do it somewhere else," he announced. "Sorry, guys, but that's the way it goes. Peace and love . . . or nothing at all."

Michael dealt with his personal relationships in much the same way; to tell him something he didn't want to hear about himself could result in instant expulsion. Most friends didn't risk it. Michael, wrote the *Independent*'s Janet Street-Porter, was "surrounded by loyal sycophants who pander to his whims." Andros's published disapproval of Michael's men's-room fetish had helped end their lifelong friendship; now, mostly unemployed and broke, he mined their shared past for every pound he could squeeze out of it. He announced he was shopping a book. "I know all about the dark side of George Michael and for the right money"—he wanted millions—"I will tell everything. George thinks he can do anything he wants to do. . . . and I was left to carry the weight. It's time the truth came out."

No one would give him the deal he wanted. In the end, Andros self-published his book, which he called *Rock: The Luckiest Man in Pop*. It earned him almost nothing, but he stayed available to the press as a paid Michael informant. Recordings and memorabilia from the Ægean years kept turning up on eBay. "He betrayed George, selling photographs to the press of Anselmo and George's mum," said Danny Cummings. Andros claimed he had no other choice; he was dead broke and unable to provide for his family. Years later, in a pleading letter to Michael, Andros wrote: "I am sorry that I let [my wife] Jackie sell off some memorabilia that you GAVE to ME."

The singer's friendship with Elton John had also crumbled. Its combative swirl of feelings had included hero worship on Michael's part, jealousy on John's, constant competitiveness, and, underneath it all, true affection. Although both had long-term partners, their lives had diverged dramatically. As addictions seized hold of Michael, John aggressively advocated rehab, which had cured him of his cocaine and alcohol habits. Yet his craving for attention still raged, and he used the media to gossip about friends and colleagues, criticize their choices, and air grievances.

In the November 2004 issue of the British celebrity-news magazine *Heat*, John called Michael's current lifestyle "disappointing." What he said would normally have stayed between friends, except that Michael wouldn't listen. "George is in a strange place," John observed. "It upsets me because he won't perform live. . . . There seems to be a deep-rooted unhappiness in his life and it shows on the album. All I would say to George is: You should get out more."

Heat was glad to publish Michael's eviscerating response. He and John had *never* been close, he insisted, and had barely seen each other in years. "We have never discussed my private life," he claimed. "Ever." John and his friends, Michael said, comprised "the busiest rumor mill in town"; they loved to dish him and spread rumors on the "gay grapevine." Aside from that, wrote Michael, "he knows that I don't like to tour, that I smoke too much pot, and that my albums still have a habit of going to No. 1. In other words, he knows as much as most of my fans do. If I stay at home too much, if anything it is because I am too contented right now. I have earned the right to a quiet life, which I truly love, and maybe Elton just can't relate to that. He makes millions playing those old classics day-in and day-out, whereas my drive and passion is still about the future, and the songs I have yet to write."

But Michael had almost no motivation to work. He admitted that marijuana—especially when smoked to excess—"chills you out to such a degree you could lose your ambitions." The New Year brought a chance to collaborate with Daft Punk, whose state-of-the-art electropop had inspired "Freeek!" The group's two members, Thomas Bangalter and Guy-Manuel De Homem-Christo, sent Michael some demos of instrumental tracks for their new album; they hoped he would provide lyrics. It was just the sort of project Michael needed to step inside the radar of a younger, cooler audience. He visited the duo in Paris. Michael reportedly sat on a beanbag chair, munching M&Ms and offering vague ideas that led to nothing.

More than ever, he felt compelled to tell his story in hopes of showing the public the George Michael he wanted them to see. In 2004 he teamed with British director Southan Morris, head of a small production company, Scream Films, to make a new documentary about the real George. A star who felt chronically misunderstood was not about to leave any filmmaker in charge. According to Janet Street-Porter, Michael so hated Morris's rough cut that he got hold of it and re-edited it as he pleased; after all, he had bankrolled the project. *George Michael: A Different Story* included fawning testimonials from Shirlie and Pepsi, Geri Halliwell, and other Michael loyalists; careful statements from Elton John; gush from Mariah Carey; and dubious history by Goss: "The way we actually met was at this really famous spa. It's not gay or anything. . . . I wasn't sure it was him."

Seated on a sofa and on a private plane, Michael recounted his every grievance: the pains of superstardom, his hatred of doing publicity, his resentment of audiences who couldn't see past his eighties image, the cruelty of Anselmo's death, Sony's mistreatment of him, the homophobia of the United States, the conniving of the tabloids that had framed him in Beverly Hills. He jabbed at his father for his early discouragement ("He just thought I was a dreamer") and for his callous treatment of Lesley. Through it all, Michael still felt the need to convince viewers, and himself, of how special he was: "I was doing something remarkable as a twenty-year-old kid! . . . When I look back I still think it's kind of stunning."

The film had a few flashes of the humor his friends loved, notably a memory of Wham!: "It was, oh my god, I'm a massive star . . . and I think I may be a poof. What am I gonna do? This is not gonna end well."

In the most talked-about part of the film, he reminisced with Andrew Ridgeley, who had agreed, with obvious reluctance, to give his first interview about Wham! in many years. For years they had barely seen each other. Ridgeley existed largely on royalties from "Careless Whisper"; he continued to live in his modest farmhouse down a winding path in Cornwall. History did not remember him kindly. In a forthcoming film, *Music and Lyrics*, Hugh Grant would play a fallen eighties band member of dubious gifts—a character clearly inspired by Ridgeley.

Whatever his regrets, Michael's ex-partner had cut the past dead. "These days he's grey and bald and his nickname on the golf course is Osama bin Laden," said his girlfriend Keren Woodward. "Our neighbors protect us from anyone who tries to drag us back into the public eye. Anyone who asks the wrong kind of questions about us gets thrown out of the local pub." Ridgeley, said Michael, "spends half his time pissed out of his head." Incredulously, the singer added: "He really enjoys his life."

As Ridgeley sat in an armchair before the camera, Michael poured out lighthearted Wham! stories, delighted to relive his happiest days alongside the man who had made them possible. Ridgeley held a frozen smile and said little. Michael prodded him: Which of their lives would he have rather led? Ridgeley smiled enigmatically. "No one who watched that film saw a trace of regret in him," wrote Cheryl Stonehouse in the *Daily Mirror*. Certainly Ridgeley knew what his former best mate's rabid quest for stardom and the love of millions had done to him.

Finally, he spoke. "Do I think perhaps I've missed out in not pursuing music as a lifelong career? May have. But, um . . ." Michael cut in, awkwardly trying to save face. "Well, put it this way, *I* know whose life I would rather have led. I think anybody would. I'm very blessed in different ways but ultimately I think, touch wood and thank God, you've had a really good life."

The exchange with his onetime soul brother haunted him. Later he complained to the *Guardian*'s Simon Hattenstone that Ridgeley "hasn't experienced loss. I wanted to say to him, 'You don't understand. Twelve years of my life disappeared into darkness.'"

The gloom had gone on longer than that; Michael said he hoped the film would spell closure to "twenty-two years of stress"—a bleak assessment of a mostly stunning career. Michael claimed no regrets for having stayed in the closet as long as he did; otherwise, he said, "I probably wouldn't have got to sing with Aretha Franklin, or to rise that high." In his most revealing statement, he explained: "It's very hard to be proud of your sexuality when it hasn't given you any joy."

On February 16, 2005, *A Different Story* premiered at the Berlin International Film Festival. Michael flew in to give a press conference. Southan Morris shared a panel with him as well as executive producer Andy Stephens, but all eyes were on Michael. "I just thought it was very important to explain myself before I disappear," he told his admirers. Sticking around seemed pointless: "My genre is dead. It doesn't want to hear intelligent pop music anymore. . . . I'm really not that interested in sparring with Robbie Williams or Will Young or Rachel Stevens." As for future plans, he just didn't know. "I have got to find ways to make music and enjoy it the way I used to," he said.

Sympathy among the press ran low. "He's had tough times over the last decade," acknowledged Street-Porter. "But all cushioned by tremendous material gain, and no more sorrow than thousands of less fortunate gay men." Michael, she concluded, "still hasn't reached maturity."

Even so, his views on legalized gay unions—a hot topic in 2005—were remarkably clear-eyed. The United Kingdom had trailed far behind much of the world in allowing same-sex civil partnerships, but on December 5, the first one in England took place. The country would not sanction gay marriage until 2013, but Michael was in no hurry; as long as gays had full legal protections, he argued, why obsess over a word? "I absolutely believe that the nature of marriage is designed for children and that it doesn't appeal to me," he told Adam Mattera.

But when Elton John and his partner, David Furnish, scheduled their civil partnership, Michael decided that he and Kenny Goss would tie the knot in June 2006. "I could get hit by a bus and the poor man could have nothing," he explained. "I think we'll just do the formal legal thing, and then we'll have a party. But no one's going to be getting into a dress. Neither of us has the body for it, you know."

The union kept getting postponed, raising questions about how much either partner truly wanted it. The relationship provided Goss with limitless financial bounty and reflected celebrity glow; both men could do whatever they wished on the side. Michael made it known in interview after interview that no-strings sex, not romance, was his priority. "I'm a dirty, filthy fucker and if you can't deal with it, you can't deal with it," he informed Simon Hattenstone. Michael told Johann Hari of the *Independent* that he had a "huge amount" of tricks, many of them rent boys. "You don't pay an escort for sex," he explained. "What you really pay an escort for is to leave after the sex."

One of those men had helped pave the way to a disturbing new phase of his life. Paul Stag, as he called himself, was a British adult film actor and producer and an escort with whom Michael had begun an on-and-off nine-year relationship. Michael paid him both for sex and for procuring his new drug of choice, GHB. In text messages, they called it "champagne." "George was mad on G," Stag told the *Sun* years later. "He was incredibly sexually active, and in his mind drugs equaled sex and sex equaled drugs."

GHB (gamma hydroxybutyrate) and its two variants, GBL (gamma butyrolactone) and BD (1,4-butanediol), now vied with methamphetamine (crystal meth) as the most popular party drug on the gay scene. G, as all its brands were known, has been dubbed "Liquid Ecstasy," but its effects are far stronger. One dose of that oily, salty liquid, mixed with juice or taken in drops, opens a floodgate of dopamine and serotonin, bringing intense euphoria. G is also a powerful aphrodisiac, inducing users to act out sexually in unimagined ways. One longtime user, Craig,* explained how: "You and I could be having a conversation," he said, "and I can dose myself and you, and within thirty minutes we'd be naked and fucking. The mind will go to places it normally wouldn't go. Kinks, perversions—they all bubble up, and there's no longer any inhibition. Plus, it's so convenient. You can put any of the three compounds in a small dispenser bottle and keep it in your pocket." G lacked the stigma of crystal meth, whose dangers were far more publicized. "Your teeth are not gonna fall out; you're not gonna have this look of falling apart," Craig noted. "It just makes you feel so goddamn good."

* Name changed

For Michael, G seemed heaven-sent. Apart from fueling his sexual compulsiveness, it made a depressed and self-loathing man feel attractive; it brought joy where there was little. G gave him confidence on Hampstead Heath and with the most intimidatingly sexy escorts. But it also took him to a frightening new level of self-destruction. G is more addictive than meth, and riskier in all varieties. GBL, which has a gasoline taste, triggers a rocket ship high followed by a crash, which makes the body want more. BD, used normally as a cleaning solvent, is legal to carry; once ingested, it converts to GHB in the body. Processed GHB brings a gradual and more consistent high.

The drug's strength varies from batch to batch, as does an individual's sensitivity to it; a manageable dose for one user can make another one black out. G is often taken hourly to sustain the high throughout a night or a weekend of clubbing. But unlike most drugs it lingers in the system; repeated intakes can cause an overdose. For that reason, many gay men team up with a friend to take G—a bonding ritual but also a safety precaution.

When used in moderation, the effects go unnoticed. Anything more can cause slurring of words, darting and protruding eyes, and loud, babbling speech—all of which were observed in Michael. One can nod off in the middle of a conversation or start hallucinating. Most commonly, users can slide into a "G-hole": They slump over, even while standing on a dance floor. Quitting the drug is hard because of the severe chemical dependency it causes; users need it just to feel normal. Withdrawal can bring unbearable depression; many addicts would rather keep risking their lives than quit. "They don't care," said Craig. "They just want the pain to stop."

Stag delivered the drug in travel-size shampoo bottles to Michael, who took it on the spot, mixed into a glass of Coke. The singer would begin making small talk—"endless drivel, waiting for the G to kick in," recalled Stag. All of a sudden, Michael would announce: "I'm ready now. Let's go and have sex." Often he took too much G. "I saw him collapse many, many times," said Stag. "I had to take his clothes off, put him to bed, switch everything off in the house."

Michael also dosed up alone, sometimes combining G with other substances. The repercussions were alarming. On Saturday, February 25, 2006, he ventured out at night to a club in London. By one A.M. he was back in his car, driving toward Hyde Park Corner, less than two miles from his Regent's

Park home. Around one-thirty, a passerby saw a Mercedes stalled diagonally across a traffic lane. Its driver was slumped over the wheel. The witness phoned emergency. Paramedics and police arrived; a cop banged on the window. George Michael opened the door, semiconscious and mumbling.

Police did a search and found marijuana and GHB in his possession. A source involved in the investigation leaked word to the *Daily Mirror* that officers had also discovered "sex toys," including a studded black-leather fetish mask with headlight eyes and a zipper mouth. For a man who termed his sexual tastes as "vanilla," the mask—pictured in the *Mirror*—was a surprise, except to those who knew of his G habit.

Michael was taken to Charing Cross station and detained for three hours. "I don't know how it happened," he explained. "I was at the lights with my foot still on the brake and I must have nodded off." Despite his drug possession and a dangerous traffic violation, police gave Michael a warning and released him uncharged. A duty solicitor drove him home.

He didn't stay there. Just after five A.M. at the nearby Hilton London Metropole Hotel, a guest awoke to a banging on his door. Opening it, he saw a man in a ski mask, muttering and making little sense. He slammed the door and phoned security. Guards searched for the intruder, who had wandered off. They discovered Michael, who asked, "Is this the Hilton?" He told them he was looking for a man he had met that night and who had given him that room number. They escorted him out.

Michael didn't have much time to sleep off the effects of the drugs. That day was his family's annual memorial for Lesley. Saturday had been the ninth anniversary of her death—an occasion that often plunged Michael into depression and overindulgence. Somehow, he made the memorial.

By Monday, his exploits were on the cover of several British newspapers; from there, the story spread worldwide. In a response sent out by his publicist, Michael wielded his familiar self-deprecation—"It's my own stupid fault, as usual"—while sidestepping responsibility: "It's quite easy to fall asleep at the Hyde Park lights. Momentarily I put my foot on the brake and I must have nodded off." He threw in a stab at humor: "I promise I won't make a record out of this one—even though it is tempting."

But soon he was back in the tabloids. On April 16, at eight A.M., residents of Hornsey Lane, less than a mile from Michael's home in Highgate, heard a crash. They rushed outside or peered through their windows to see a navy Range Rover, its front end mangled. A man sat at the wheel, staring at a banged-up Ford Fiesta parked a few feet away. One neighbor was stunned to recognize the driver as Michael. "He didn't look too good for that time on a Sunday morning," the witness said. Michael drove off—then returned seconds later and hit the back of a white Peugeot, tearing off its bumper. The Peugeot lunged forward into a green Rover. "There was another almighty crash," said the neighbor, "then he just drove off again. It was really bizarre. No one could quite believe what they were seeing."

Someone called the police, naming him. Officers drove to the Highgate house and found the Rover parked out front; his front door went unanswered. Within hours, a man showed up on Hornsey Lane and rang the bells of homes near the collisions; he hoped to find the car owners "to sort out repairs," reported the *Daily Express*. "The man declined to reveal his identity but he was later spotted at George's home."

Michael had spent a drugged night with a trick who lived on Hornsey Lane—this despite the fact that on that very afternoon he was due at Abbey Road, the legendary London recording studio, to sing with the last surviving king of classic pop, Tony Bennett, who would soon turn eighty. Phil Ramone was producing *Duets: An American Classic*, Bennett's first volume of collaborations with pop stars. Several of them—Paul McCartney, Stevie Wonder, Elton John—had been Michael's heroes. The song chosen for him to sing with Bennett was "How Do You Keep the Music Playing?," Michel Legrand and Alan & Marilyn Bergman's Oscar-nominated expression of fear over the inevitable fading of a longtime love. Word of Michael's calamity had reached Abbey Road; Bennett's pianist, Lee Musiker, recalled "a lot of hush-hush about it from the Tony camp." Michael arrived on time, a baseball cap on his head, prepared but very nervous. He sounded fine, although as he and Bennett randomly traded lines of the song, they seemed, unintentionally, to be pledging their love to each other ("I know the way I feel for you is now or never . . .").

Michael promptly went on *Parkinson* to play down his latest embarrassment. "It was nothing, really, but again it becomes this massive drama," he said, blaming the tabloids. "I literally had a parking accident." He implicated Elton John for having told *Heat* how unhappy he was—thus sending the media on the lookout for proof. "The subtext to it is, he was all right before he came out and now he lives this depraved gay life and he's miserable and fat," complained Michael. In fact, he claimed, he had never felt better.

John fired back in the *Mirror*. "Did I crash George's car? No. Was I found slumped over the wheel in Hyde Park? No . . . Poor George. I struck a nerve and he took it the wrong way. I'd like to resolve it. I've been where George is and I'm concerned. If something happens, I want to be there because under these huge egos, we're all human."

Michael wasn't interested. And the *Parkinson* appearance had done little to ease people's worries. The British were baffled at the unraveling of one of their favorite sons, once famous for his steely control. "This is not the kind of behavior the public expect of multi-millionaire pop icons," wrote the *Telegraph*'s Craig McLean. "He was never a grungy rock star." Even the *Mirror* expressed concern. "Just What *Is* the Matter with Him?" read a headline. "Get Help, George," pleaded another one.

ITV questioned a frighteningly unhinged Michael at home. "Believe me, I don't want to do this interview," he spewed, eyes flaring. Yet there he was, railing at the "complete lies" the press had flung at him. "The *only* thing that's wrong with my life," he snapped, "is that I have *lived* with *photographers* outside my house and following me around twenty-four hours a day!"

Theories about his drug use abounded, but despite the fact that he had been found with GHB, the drug was obscure to almost everyone except partying gays, and no one in the media connected it to his troubles. Neil McCormick circled around the truth: "I think he is tired of being a celebrity and subconsciously wants to destroy it." Brian Reade of the *Mirror* had no sympathy. He branded Michael "a sad, tortured porker screaming to be loved and noticed. Georgie, mate, to make it on to the front pages once for bizarre solo doped-up, nocturnal activities in a car is unfortunate. To make it twice in a matter of weeks is a full-blown scream to be back on those front pages."

In the *Express*, a music executive expressed "the fear that one day—when everyone least expects it—one of these blips might turn into a serious attempt to end it all."

Many observers wondered: Why wasn't his inner circle trying to help? Michael, said Phil Palmer, "surrounded himself with people who were there to bolster his ego and to support his lifestyle. The proper friends around him should have been more protective of him, I think."

Niall Flynn had known the star through several crises. "Suggesting that his friends didn't give a shit is wrong, because we did. He didn't listen to anybody. His family didn't really say anything. People like me were depending on him for our salaries, even though for long periods of time we weren't working because of all the rubbish that was going on. When you're in that situation it feels a bit difficult to stand up and say, 'You know what, I don't agree with what you're doing.' I saw him just walk off, pissed off that you'd had a conversation with him about it. And you'd be left feeling, where do I stand?"

But the bad press had stung, and it spurred Michael to prove he wasn't washed-up. Sony was about to release a silver anniversary best-of, *Twenty Five*. To entice old fans into buying it, Michael recorded three new tracks. He called in twenty-one-year-old Mutya Buena, a copiously tattooed, Irish-Filipino R&B singer, formerly of a British girl trio, Sugababes, who had scored six No. 1 U.K. hits. Although she couldn't lift Michael to that peak, their duet, "This Is Not Real Love," a Quiet Storm ballad that he cowrote, rose to No. 15. "I was star-struck," Buena said, "but he was so lovely." On the day of her first solo gig, recalled the singer, he treated her with fatherly concern: "He was on the phone to me all day trying to calm my nerves."

Much excitement had greeted the news that Paul McCartney had agreed to join him on a remake of "Heal the Pain," which the ex-Beatle had inspired. The stars recorded together at London's AIR Studios; McCartney played bass as well as sang. But the track had none of the anticipated magic. "The sappy duet has got to go," wrote Heath McCoy in the *Calgary Herald*. "An Easier Affair" meant more to him. It was his first coming-out anthem, with music and beats provided by Flynn and Ruadhri Cushnan, and Michael hoped it would have young gay clubgoers dancing to his message of freedom: "I told myself I was straight / But I shouldn't have worried / 'Cos my maker had a better plan for me."

Few of them heard it; deejays had moved on from George Michael. But at least the new songs gave a sense that he was still productive. Michael had shunned the road since 1991, but a *Twenty Five* tour, stuffed with the songs his fans wanted to hear, made sense. "I want to say thank you to people," he explained humbly. "I want it to be a show that they never forget." Thinking it would be his last time on the road, he agreed to play over a hundred arena shows, broken into three annual legs, starting in September 2006.

The first one would cover much of Europe. Once it was announced, over six hundred thousand tickets sold out.

•••

His all-night binges of drugs and sex went on. *News of the World* knew it could catch him in a compromising situation in the Heath. In the summer of 2006, the paper's photographers and reporters lurked there in the midnight hours, poised to strike. Sure enough, on July 18, out walked Michael from behind some bushes. Another man followed; *News of the World* identified him later as "a pot-bellied, fifty-eight-year-old, jobless van driver." He headed for his van while Michael walked to his Mercedes. A photographer's flashbulb began popping. The pictures caught a shocked and enraged Michael at the wheel, irises like pinwheels. "I DON'T FUCKING BELIEVE IT!" he sputtered. "Are you gay? No? Then fuck off! If you put those pictures in the paper, I'll sue!" He turned the key in the ignition and sped off.

In his article, "George's Sex Shame," Neville Thurlbeck wrote: "Mega-rich pop superstar George Michael this week sank to new levels of depravity—trawling for illegal gay sex thrills in a London park." Thurlbeck reported trailing Michael's alleged trick sixty miles to his "squalid flat" in Brighton, where he "answered the door naked—pulling on grimy shorts as he invited us in." He was quoted as saying: "I don't even like George Michael. And I didn't recognize him immediately. He told me I could contact him on the Gaydar website and we just started kissing. . . . Then it was fondling and mutual pleasuring. It wasn't full sex but it was fantastic."

Michael later claimed that the man had been blackmailed into making false statements. Nonetheless, the story sent other reporters to Michael's front door. Goss answered. "George is not going to say anything today," he announced, clearly weary of having to make excuses. "This is behind us. We are getting on with the rest of our lives."

Michael stayed inside, where he rushed to his own defense. He phoned into the popular morning TV show *Richard & Judy*, hosted by a perky married couple, Richard Madeley and Judy Finnigan. They were predisposed to be sympathetic to Michael, who had once given £50,000 to a children's charity they had promoted. On the air, he tried making light of his latest scandal: "I mean, as much as I don't want to be ageist or fattist, it's dark out there but it's not *that* dark. I've no idea who that guy was."

In general, however, Michael knew he was being judged, and it made his blood boil. "He now conducts himself with an almost belligerent candor," wrote Neil McCormick, "and an insistence that he will not allow celebrity to compromise how he wants to live." As he had blurted out in the Heath: "I'm not doing anything illegal. I'm a free man. I'm not harming anyone." But even the sympathetic Michael Parkinson could no longer hide his dismay. He spoke to the singer like a perplexed grandfather, reminding him that he was adored, successful, and in his prime. What was the problem?

"I don't have a problem," Michael answered. "The problem is that we have a very, very inquisitive media and I seem to meet a lot of different requirements in terms of people's interests." But why the unhappiness? Michael bristled. "You can get arrested and you can pass out without being unhappy, you know?" Because of "this constant surveillance," he said, he was strongly considering leaving England. The audience gasped.

When Parkinson suggested that stars ought to be more discreet, Michael turned angry. "*Why? Why?* What do you suggest, I don't live my life? Believe me, I think the sex that I have is worth being in the paper for."

CHAPTER TWENTY-FOUR

SINCE THE MID-NINETIES, DEPRESSION and drugs had wreaked havoc on Michael's ability to finish almost anything. But the new tour, 25 Live, fired him up again. The production would involve sixteen musicians (led by Chris Cameron) and six backup singers, arranged on a six-level stage. Michael would stand on an enormous screen that hung like a scroll, curled onto the stage and hung over the rim; video projections seemed to slide down it. A runway reached far into the audience. The equipment would require forty trucks.

Holed up in Dallas, he planned the show. Its theme was nostalgia; he had few new songs to offer. Yet amid the hits—"They will get 'Careless Whisper,' which I don't particularly enjoy singing," he told the *Express*—Michael programmed in at least twenty minutes of slow, sad ballads: "My Mother Had a Brother," "Jesus to a Child," "Praying for Time," "You Have Been Loved."

He had set big physical demands for himself, and he worked with a trainer to get in shape. What exercise wouldn't fix, he addressed with liposuction. He also had to deal with the changes in his voice. Michael had lost the upper range of his youth, and the keys to several songs were dropped. Otherwise, said Phil Palmer, one of the show's three guitarists, "he was uncompromising on every level. Not only with the music—the stage effects, the choreography. He would keep the band on the stage for eight, nine hours while he went through stuff that didn't necessarily involve us. You would see George dictating what the lights should be doing and how the backdrop should work. If something didn't work he'd be slamming into people: Get it right or get off."

But in a move that dismayed his band, Michael had most of the accompaniment prerecorded and played back on Pro Tools, a digital audio software. The musicians played along, pretended to, or did nothing. Michael had told Danny Cummings that he'd gotten the idea for all this when he saw Madonna at Wembley. As one of her hits began, the audience heard a prerecorded backing track that was identical to the famous version. Fans sighed in approval. "George just wanted happy audiences," Cummings explained. "But suddenly, it mattered a lot less who was on the stage playing."

On September 23, 2006, eighteen thousand fans greeted the premiere of 25 Live at Palau Sant Jordi in Barcelona, Spain. That day Michael had written in wonderment on his website: "I truly believed that tonight would never happen, that I would never sing these songs to you again. But then, I'm a fool, which you've probably worked out by now."

The performance suffered from false starts and technical glitches. Yet the city's main newspaper, La Vanguardia, reported that an arena packed with "fervent fans" had turned into a hot bed of delirium. As the show opened, the audience saw projections of stars in the night sky. Michael's voice floated from the darkness, singing "Waiting (Reprise)," the last track of Listen Without Prejudice. "Here I am . . . Is it too late to try again?" he pleaded, as acoustic guitars strummed and backup vocalists softly doop-do-doo'd. A door in the onstage screen swung open; through it walked Michael to a thunderous roar.

In three decades, his look had changed from that of a hot young biker to an aging, upscale sex symbol; graying stubble set off his black-on-black Armani. He moved more gingerly than before, but his presence, like Frank Sinatra's, had grown with his history. By now it was common practice for pop stars to lip-synch to their own vocal tracks; many of the younger ones couldn't reproduce the fabricated sound on their records, while some older performers had lost their stamina. Synchronized dancers, crisscrossing laser beams, and trapeze artists provided distraction.

But if most of his accompaniment was canned, Michael's singing never was. Unlike Sinatra, who tampered with his timeworn hits out of boredom, Michael honored his audiences' memories. His fans rewarded him with floods of affection, and he returned it. He strolled down the runway and shook every outstretched hand he could reach; thousands sang along even without prompting. Michael surrendered good-naturedly to his age. "If you're lucky enough to be young enough not to remember 1984," he said, "then just turn and look at the person next to you. Imagine them with four or five times more hair, and you have the eighties."

But for anyone who had seen the closeted star of the Faith Tour, this new show was full of surprises. He had written "Amazing," he revealed, "for my partner Kenny—can I hear it for Kenny?" Of "Flawless," he declared: "Apparently this is the gayest record ever made!" In "Freedom! '90," he danced in front of rainbow projections; for "Outside" he donned his gay-cop look as the video played behind him. Singing "you were the perfect girl for me" in his favorite Wham! song, "Everything She Wants," he added with a snicker, "Yeah, right!"

The female fans of his Wham! and *Faith* days—now two decades older—were still there screaming. One yelled out, "I WANT YOUR BABIES!" Having lived through all the bygone concealment of Michael's sexuality, Simon Napier-Bell was amused: "The fact that he'd said he was gay was not a big problem, because girls always think they can turn you straight." But when Michael shouted, "K, I wanna hear it from my gay boys now," he heard no comparable noise. "There has never been overwhelming 'gay' interest in Michael in or out of the closet," observed Tim Teeman in the *Times*. He sang his AIDS-inspired song "Spinning the Wheel," but his old reticence resurfaced. Michael had audiences incongruously sway their arms in the air as if the song were "Imagine"; projections of Marilyn Monroe, Elizabeth Taylor, and Lennon and Yoko Ono further clouded the meaning.

Yet he seemed more comfortable than ever pouring out his heart to strangers. Michael sang "You Have Been Loved" for his mother while seated on a tall chair in front of a montage of family photos. "I'm so scared, I'm so scared," he told the audience in "A Different Corner," a shiver in his voice.

Michael was still determined to have the last word on "Shoot the Dog." Fans were dazzled by the sight of a slowly inflating, fifty-foot blowup of the creepily leering George Bush seen in the video—followed by a second one of a bulldog wearing the British flag and a leash around its neck, held by Michael. As the dog grew to full-size it wobbled against the Bush figure; to Michael's delight, the bulldog seemed to be fellating the president. His European audiences cheered as he blamed Bush for turning the world into a "much more dangerous place" and called Tony Blair a "wanker."

Throughout the show, said Palmer, "George was dancing and laughing and interacting with the audience. It surprised everyone how much he enjoyed it. I think it surprised him." Near the end, he shouted: "Thank you for twenty-five fucking *amazing* years!" Madrid's *El País* called him "a George Michael in full artistic maturity." At last, he realized, his fans had adored the real him.

• • •

That still wasn't enough. On October 1, hours after leaving a stage in Toulon, France, his fourth stop, Michael was back in London with one day off. Throughout the tour he would fly a private jet home whenever possible; ostensibly he wanted to sleep in his own bed, but it was also safer not to cross borders with drugs. Though exhausted, he did not go to bed. Instead, he ingested a dangerous combination of GHB, the sleeping medication Zolpidem, and Effexor, an antidepressant that can induce drowsiness. He smoked pot. Then he got in his car.

Close to Hampstead Heath, late-night travelers saw a Mercedes weaving in and out of the wrong side of the road. Its driver kept nodding off at the steering wheel, sometimes staying put through several changes of the traffic light. At one point the car went into reverse. Finally, it halted at a junction in nearby Cricklewood.

When the cops came, Michael was slumped over the wheel, drooling and barely conscious. They searched him and found only marijuana. At 3:22 A.M. they took him to the hospital, then to the police station. Blood tests were done. As the sun rose, he was released on bail. A judge would decide his fate in court.

The following afternoon, Michael, in dark glasses, stepped out of his Highgate home accompanied by Goss and a handler. They were headed to his private plane; Michael had a show that night in Lyon, France. He raised his fingers in a peace sign and smiled at cameras. Asked for comment on the arrest, he declared: "I had no drink or drugs in my body. I have *not* got a problem with drugs."

After three such incidents in a year, road safety advocates were incensed that Michael had once more walked away with his driver's license intact. In the *Mirror*, Fiona Phillips denounced Michael's paid enablers for constantly helping to cover up his messes. "They cocoon him in a world which is increasingly distanced from the one in which the rest of us live," she wrote.

Like others in his inner circle, Niall Flynn had been warned by members of Michael's team not to divulge anything. "I felt many times like leaving George because of what I knew," he said. Incidents were piling up, not all of which had made the papers. "The police were doing their best to figure out what the hell was going on but no one would talk," said Flynn. "There was a huge book they wanted to throw at George."

Ultimately he was charged with drug possession and driving under the influence. Ignoring his lawyers' advice, Michael, as usual, told his version of things to reporters. Just after the incident, he met Craig McLean of the *Telegraph* at an Italian restaurant in Highgate. For four hours, Michael poured out his heart and his rage to another stranger with a tape recorder. "He was charming, self-deprecating, and honest," wrote McLean, "but full of fantastical conspiracy theories and paranoia about the media and the music industry—everyone was out to get George Michael. He was cross about everyone from George Bush to Cliff Richard. He was coherent yet he was loony. His eyes were boggling, and so were mine, although perhaps for different reasons."

Few celebrities scored a second episode of *South Bank Show*, but at the end of October, Michael got one. His earlier installment, from 1990, was a calculated display of his newfound maturity as an artist and his cunning control over every aspect of his career. At his insistence, the new edition began with a statement flashed on a black screen: "George Michael wishes to inform viewers that he has never tested positive for drink or drugs whilst driving"—this despite the fact that the show contained no mention of his DUIs. From there, the program showed him preparing for his concert in Madrid. In a sequence that would make the cover of the *Mirror*, Michael lights up a spliff and holds it aloft, a wine glass in the other hand. "This stuff keeps me sane and happy," he explains of the joint. "I could write without it . . . if I were sane and happy. I'd say it's a great drug—but obviously it's not very healthy. You can't afford to smoke it if you've got anything to do."

In place of another probing demonstration of his art, Michael complained about the "Shoot the Dog" fallout, Rupert Murdoch's seeming vendetta against him, and the apparent indifference of his fellow gays. "They're only interested when you're in the closet," he said. "Once you're out, they don't give a toss." Yet he insisted he'd found peace. "I live in the house of my dreams with the man of my dreams," he said. "I'm happy with the music I'm making—and I'm still loaded." As for his future dreams, Michael offered: "I hope I learn to shut my mouth. If I did, I would probably have all the sex I like. Which I do anyway, to be honest with you."

The episode earned a scathing review from Tim Teeman, who called it a "ridiculously shallow portrait of a celebrity." He slammed the "shameful" performance of host Melvyn Bragg. "Michael's sentences started in one place, drifted, didn't scan. Bragg just nodded away." But Michael, wrote Teeman, was equally to blame. "If he's so down on the tabloids, why light up a joint on national television, which will inevitably attract even more headlines? His hypocrisy—look-at-me-no-don't-look-at-me—was laughable." Michael's declarations about pot, illustrated by freeze-frames of him smoking in Spain, got him on the cover of the *Mirror*; the double-entendre headline read GEORGE MICHAEL ON DRUGS.

But nothing could make his European fans love him any less. In November 2006, he reached the United Kingdom for seventeen shows. At the opening of a three-night run at Manchester Arena, he was overwhelmed to hear over twenty thousand fans chanting his name. Everything he said and sang evoked deafening cheers, including a reference to his fateful night in Hampstead Heath: "I did *not* have sexual relations with that van driver!"

None of this surprised Johnny Douglas. "Every time he messed up," observed the producer, "I think that endeared him to people in the U.K. even more, because hey, we can all fuck up. In that period, with untouchable pop stars behind big gates, he was doing something a little bit naughty. In the U.K. we love keeping it real; we don't like that Hollywood veneer."

One of the loudest ovations followed Michael's news that the *Twenty Five* CD would hit No. 1 that Sunday. In the *Independent*, Chris Mugan told readers exactly what Michael wanted them to read: "Trim and in rude health, he makes a mockery of press insinuations that he has been on a self-destructive path. . . . The only effect a series of tabloid stories seems to have had on his middle-aged fan base is to make its support even more vociferous." Chris Goodman of the *Daily Express* hailed Michael as both human and victorious. "He wears his flaws as badges of honor. As an exercise in reminding us that he is more than a gay drug user, this was mission accomplished."

Michael's London shows included a night at the Roundhouse, a domelike venue in the city's north end. It seated only 1,700, but Michael had chosen it for a reason: His mother's birthday (December 24) was just days away, and he wanted to invite the National Health Service nurses who had cared for her on her deathbed. He seldom performed "Last Christmas," but on this night he did, and everyone sang with him.

His feelings about his father remained conflicted. Often Jack showed up backstage, a white-bearded bear, hugging Michael and bursting with bonhomie. The singer commented to Flynn that his father had aged into a rather sweet old man. But Michael refused to forget his father's brutal discouragement; Jack had only changed his mind, said Michael, "because ultimately he is pretty much overwhelmed by the power that I have managed to get for myself."

• • •

Just before Christmas, Michael closed the first rung of the tour. Five months of rest lay ahead, interrupted by his court appearance for the Cricklewood car incident. Michael's lawyers had postponed the hearing four times, and there could be no more delays. The singer had been charged with driving under the influence of drugs. His defense lawyer, Brian Spiro, had persuaded him to plead guilty. But despite the pot and GHB that police had found on Michael, Spiro would try to blame him passing-out at the wheel on sleeping pills. Depending on the verdict, Michael might lose his U.S. work visa and have to cancel the American leg of his tour.

On May 8, 2007, four days before 25 Live would resume in Portugal, Michael stepped out of a car in front of Brent Magistrates Court in northwest London. A few reporters had come to dutifully cover the event, but hardly anyone else had gathered; a George Michael court date was no longer an event. He said half-jokingly to Spiro: "Did they tell everyone where it was?"

The judge, Katherine Marshall, seemed wary as she faced a seemingly disoriented star. He sat with Spiro at the defense counsel's side bench, not in his required place, the "dock" (the defendant's chair) in front of her. Marshall instructed him to move, then asked him to rise and enter his plea. He stood and answered: "Not guilty!"

Spiro looked alarmed. "*No!*" he whispered loudly at Michael. "*Guilty!*"

"Guilty?" said Michael.

The lawyer hurried over for a quick, hushed exchange. Michael's next statement again made Spiro cringe. "My point was a different point, Your

Honor. I'm sorry. I plead guilty due to tiredness and prescribed drugs."
Marshall told him to plead guilty or not guilty—period.

"So I should just say one word? Okay. Guilty."

He asked if he could make a comment. Marshall consented—and heard a
rambling, blurry plea for sympathy. "I did something very stupid and I've been
ashamed ever since," he told her. "I have been in a combination of mischief
and shame for about eight months. I really have been very distressed by this
whole thing because I was perfectly aware that I did something very wrong
when I got into my car when I was unfit to drive. I was not in my normal
physical state and I'm totally prepared to accept the punishment."

Spiro attempted to clarify. Michael, he argued, had just flown home after
a concert in France; exhausted, he had overmedicated himself on sleeping
pills. The lawyer did not attempt to explain why Michael had needed sleeping
pills when he was already dead-tired.

Andrew Torrington, the prosecutor, was skeptical. He asked that the
hearing be adjourned until the physician who had tested Michael's blood at
the time of his arrest had supplied a list of all detected medications.

On May 30, court reconvened. Michael's blood test had revealed his
use of marijuana, Zolpidem, Effexor—and GHB. With that information at
hand, sentencing was scheduled for June 8. Spiro again tried to postpone,
for Michael would be on tour. Marshall wouldn't bend. The day after, she
pointed out, Michael was playing Wembley Stadium. "I do not think he will
have any difficulty in being here on June 8," stated Marshall curtly.

That day, Michael returned to court. Shock crossed his face as Marshall
told him she had considered a jail sentence or a curfew order—but those
penalties would "cause havoc" with his tour. She sentenced Michael to a
hundred hours of community service, fined him £2,000, and banned him
from driving for two years. His U.S. work visa was safe.

Afterward, Michael stressed to reporters that "tiredness and prescription
medicines" were to blame; for some reason, no one mentioned GHB. "I'm
glad to put this behind me," he concluded. "Now I'm off to do the biggest
show of my life."

In fact, the Wembley appearance was a two-night stand, and both
shows had sold out. The Stadium had recently reopened after a five-year
renovation; Michael had approached the board and told them he wanted to

be the first musical artist to rechristen it. Audiences greeted him with the same hysteria he recalled from the Faith Tour. It astounded him. "I think in a strange way that I've spent much of the last fifteen or twenty years trying to derail my own career because it never seems to suffer," he observed. "My career always seems to right itself like a plastic duck in a bath. And I think in some ways I resent that."

By August, however, he was on his hands and knees, scrubbing the filthy walls and floors of St. Mungo's, a hostel for London's homeless. Management had expected a swarm of press to greet him, but only a couple of newsmen, including Paul Keilthy of *Camden New Journal*, had shown up. Arriving in a baseball cap and jogging suit, he went unrecognized by the residents. One of them, Andrew Gilmour, had trouble believing this was George Michael. "He spoke to anyone and everyone and didn't act special," he told Keilthy. Michael gave the dwellers a class in songwriting, urging them to draw upon their life stories. He also cooked for them and signed memorabilia for all who asked.

The more he was humbled publicly, the more empathy he seemed to have, even as his station in life drifted ever upward. Thanks to 25 Live, millions of pounds were flooding in. On New Year's Eve, a Russian billionaire even paid him a £1.5 million to do a one-hour show at his estate near Moscow.

Michael wound up funneling a sizable chunk of that money into helping build a new career for his boyfriend. Goss had an interest in contemporary art, and they socialized with some of its flashiest British stars. Installation artist and painter Damien Hirst, a superstar in his field, shared Michael's flair for exploiting shock value. Hirst was known for preserving dead animals and ascribing religious and social themes to them. He knew how to throw verbal hand grenades; Hirst called 9/11 "kind of like an artwork in its own right." Tracey Emin could do the same. The multi-media provocateur had scored her own hour on *South Bank Show*; her works included her unmade and filthy bed, which she littered with bloodied panties and used condoms.

In Emin's and Hirst's world, Goss—with George Michael as his partner and patron—was sure to get noticed. In June 2007, the Dallas social scene heralded the launch of the Goss-Michael Foundation, a gallery, bankrolled by Michael, that lionized Britain's most daring young artists. For the next few years, the couple went on an exorbitantly costly acquisition spree. Most of the

hundreds of works they bought—some auction items, others commissions—
were chosen by Goss.

Collectively, however, the art captured Michael's mountingly cynical
world view. Much of it was macabre and disturbing, dealing with themes of
pain, death, emotional turmoil, and coldly commercialized sex. Goss and
Michael bought Hirst's most notorious (though far from his grisliest) piece,
Saint Sebastian, Exquisite Pain: a fifteen-foot-high, blue-tinted tank of form-
aldehyde in which an actual bull, roped to a post and pierced with dozens of
arrows, stared out with helpless eyes. The work was based on the myth of a
young Catholic martyr who was persecuted in ancient Rome by being tied
naked to a tree and shot with arrows. Because of his beauty, Saint Sebastian
was an iconic gay figure; now a bull who bore his name was set on display
for gawking eyes. It was a victim image to which Michael could relate. Goss
surely did. He told Jamie Stengle of Associated Press: "Most people initially
freak a little bit about Sebastian, then they stare and stare at it and they say,
'That's the most beautiful thing I've ever seen.'"

The pieces by Emin included a garish pink-and-red neon sign that
read, "Fuck Off and Die You Slag." An installation by Tim Noble and Sue
Webster, *Metal Fucking Rats (Version Four)*, showed a projected silhouette
of one rat mounting another behind a jagged blob of scrap metal. Harland
Miller painted somber takeoffs on the covers of Penguin Classics, the mass-
market paperback series of literary milestones. One of Miller's "covers" read,
"Incurable Romantic Seeks Dirty Filthy Whore"; another was titled, *DEATH:
What's In It for Me?* Jake and Dinos Chapman contributed *Platinum Joey*, a
life-size, unclothed doll of a child that had sprouted two adult blonde heads,
both looking dazed or perhaps dead. On their shared neck is a vagina with a
penis entering it from behind. The figure wore black-and-white tennis shoes.
Sarah Lucas's *New Religion* was a three-dimensional outline of a coffin, made
from neon tubing and fixed on a lavender base.

The singer paid to have himself immortalized, sometimes satirically.
Michael Craig-Martin's Warhol-like painting *Untitled (God)* shows a urinal
in clashing candy colors; the artist did a similar painting of handcuffs. In Jim
Lambie's intricately detailed oil, *Careless Whisper*, Michael's eyes are wreathed
in colorful flowers, as though he were laid in a casket.

Michael and Goss displayed some of these creations in their homes, where the work radiated a dark, menacing energy. Most pieces went to the foundation, forming the basis for fashionable gallery shows. Goss now had a role in life beyond that of Mr. George Michael. But he continued to act as gatekeeper, approached by many who wanted his boyfriend's participation in projects. If he liked an idea, Goss would present it to Michael, whose first answer was invariably no. Goss would try to change his mind. Often Michael would have a sudden change of heart and command whoever had made the request to drop everything and fly wherever Michael specified, sometimes the next day.

In the spring of 2007, Goss was contacted by Stephen Fry, the revered British film actor, writer, voiceover artist, and witty intellectual voice of authority on a thousand talk show panels. Fry was also openly gay, without ever having made a fuss over it. He was now producing a two-hour documentary for the BBC, *Stephen Fry: HIV & Me*. Its goal was to shake the British public out of a growing ennui about a crisis that was far from over, especially with the rise in unprotected sex. The film showed him roaming the world, interviewing ordinary people; he even took an HIV test on camera (it was negative).

Fry knew that Michael had lost a lover to AIDS and that he had a lot to say. Would he talk?

The singer had been helpful before. Years earlier, as head of fundraising for the Terrence Higgins Trust, Europe's flagship HIV/AIDS charity, Fry had held an exclusive charity dinner. Several guests wrote checks on the spot. Michael took Fry aside. *Ladies and Gentleman: The Best of George Michael* was about to come out. "How about if all the U.K. rights for that went to you?" he said. "But keep it just between ourselves."

Fry was stunned—not only at Michael's generosity, but at his refusal to take bows for it. "Sometimes people insist on anonymity because they don't want the world to think they're an open spigot, but in his case I knew it really was modesty. For all the cockiness, swagger, and mouthiness, George was very insecure and sweetly shy."

Donating money came easily for him, but speaking on TV about HIV was another matter. He refused. But there was no predicting his changes of mood, especially under the influence of drugs. Fry and his crew were shooting in San Francisco when Goss called. Michael, he said, would do the interview. Would Fry come to Dallas the next day?

While en route, his phone rang. "Stephen," said Michael, "my makeup artist can't come this morning, so I'm going to have to use yours."

"George," said Fry, "I don't *have* a makeup artist. This is a documentary. You always look great. I'm sure you won't need anything."

"There was an incredibly long pause. 'Okay,' he said, with the gusty sigh of a man on whom all the sorrows of the world have been heaped. 'I'll make some calls.'"

Once at the house, Fry and his crew waited for hours for a makeup artist to arrive, then to work on Michael. "As far as I could tell he didn't look any different," said Fry, "but he was certainly cheerier and sparklier." Then Michael announced, "Your turn, Stephen! It's on me." Fry tried to announce that he wore no makeup on any of the shoots. "George shook his head sorrowfully and we sat for the interview." He begged Fry: "Please, if you find something in the edit that is going to bite me in the arse, cut it."

To appease him, Fry promised approval rights over his segment, and the questioning began. "He was brilliant, of course. Funny, poignant, truthful, honest, raw. There was nothing revolutionary in his views on AIDS or on gay life and culture, but he instinctively had the authenticity and candor to know that life and people are complicated and contradictory. The idea of a holy 'gay community' didn't appeal to him at all. He knew that individuals are individuals."

Fry asked the big question: Had he been tested for HIV? Not since at least 2004, Michael confessed; the wait for the answer was too nerve-wracking. Fry challenged him, stating that a third to a half of HIV-positive people in Britain didn't know they were infected.

Michael clammed up, and the interview ended. Fry had a flight to London to catch, but the singer wasn't through. "He opened a huge box containing every strain of weed you could imagine. 'Have a smoke before you go?'" The singer was disappointed when Fry declined. Michael's response had a verbal dexterity that Fry found dazzling: "He won't make up, and he won't skin up," chaffed Michael. "No slap, no smoke. No mascara, no marijuana. No kief, no coif. No bhang, no bangs."

Weeks later, Fry sent Michael a cut of the film. Word came back through Goss: Michael wanted his part cut entirely. He wouldn't budge.

Fry had no choice but to comply. The BBC was sufficiently disappointed to leak the story to the *Times*. Adam Sherwin's report included a statement from the Michael camp: "On reflection, he felt it was too close and too personal a journey." Moreover, the singer didn't want to infringe on the privacy of Anselmo's family. "I couldn't tell those who came up to me grumbling about George," said Fry, "and calling him a traitor to the cause, about his single stunning act of generosity toward the Terrence Higgins Trust—which that year, ironically, had been pursuing a highly successful campaign to increase testing and creating one-stop, anonymous testing centers all over Britain, much of it paid for by him."

But Michael had no safe-sex message to offer. Instead, he defiantly kept telling the world of his trips to the Heath and of the escorts he hired. "I've decided just to admit everything so people can't expose me for it," said Michael with a laugh. All the while he stayed hooked on a drug that made sexual caution vanish.

That didn't mean he had no room for reflection. Shortly after the Fry incident, he appeared on *Desert Island Discs*, the decades-old BBC radio series that the *Financial Times* called a "part of the vocabulary of middle-class Britain." Celebrities brought their favorite recordings and discussed them with the show's Scottish host, Kirsty Young, whom Michael adored. Young conversed eloquently in low, plush BBC tones; her dignified air enabled her to coax surprisingly frank revelations from her guests, all tied in with their chosen music. In her presence, Michael voiced poignant regrets. "I'd been out to a lot of people since nineteen," he said. "I wish to God it had happened then. I don't think I would have had the same career—my ego might not have been satisfied in some areas—but I think I would have been a happier man."

The records he had picked revealed a man whose ears were still wide-open. He brought Kanye West's "Gold Digger"; "Paper Bag" by the British electronic duo Goldfrapp; and "Crazy," a recent No. 1 British hit by Gnarls Barkley, an American duo who revived the sounds of sixties soul. Michael called Nirvana's ode to youthful rebellion, "Smells Like Teen Spirit," the "best-produced record in the history of rock." AIDS entered the discussion when Michael played the Pet Shop Boys' "Being Boring," a look back at carefree days that the disease had cut short. "All the people I was kissing / Some are here and some are missing," went the song, which touched Michael for obvious reasons.

But for him, no one could top Amy Winehouse, then twenty-three and steeped in the retro soul that Michael adored. In the song he chose, "Love Is a Losing Game," Winehouse made an end-of-life statement—"Oh what a mess we made . . . and now the final frame"—while masking it in funky sixties R&B. "This is the best female vocalist I've heard in my entire career," said Michael. "And one of the best writers." But already she had begun a painful unraveling due to alcohol and drugs. On *Desert Island Discs*, Michael said to her what others had tried telling him: "Please, please understand how brilliant you are."

Young asked if he thought he himself had a drug problem. "I'm constantly trying to smoke less," he allowed. "To that degree it's a problem, yes. . . . Is it getting in the way of my life in any way? I don't think so . . . I really don't think so."

CHAPTER TWENTY-FIVE

MICHAEL'S UPCOMING U.S. TOUR rekindled a bonfire of mixed emotions. Never would he stop resenting the country for how it had treated him; yet still he hoped to regain some of his past American glory. Michael would visit eighteen cities; if the shows sold out, maybe he could come back and do a tour of superstar proportions.

He knew that many there perceived him as a has-been who had lapsed into scandal and camp. But Michael had learned to laugh at himself. In 2006, he roared as he watched himself lambasted on *Star Stories*, the British TV series that offered scathing celebrity parodies. "Watch Without Prejudice Vol. 1" begins with Michael, played by actor Kevin Bishop, crashing his Range Rover into a tree. From there, Bishop lisps and swishes his way through the Michael saga. "I was a nervous, shy child," he explains. "So different to the man who can now so confidently walk into a public toilet and have my gay fun."

The young George sleeps in a pink bedroom papered with Elton John magazine photos. "Elton bloody John is a poof, Georgios!" yowls Jack in a comical Greek accent. "No, father, you're wrong!" whines Bishop. "Elton John's for everyone—not just for gay and poof men!" After Wham!'s debut on *Top of the Pops*, Boy George, depicted as the Wicked Witch of the West, appears backstage, cackling: "I can detect the scent of a homosexual from a mile off!" Years later, Michael stands at a public urinal alongside an undercover cop, out of whose unzipped fly comes a golden light. "Staring at the gentleman's knob, I realized something—I was a gay after all!"

Self-effacement, Michael found, could be the best defense. On December 16, 2007, HBO viewers watched the final episode of *Extras*, the British sitcom about a dead-ended TV bit-role actor, played by the show's co-creator, Ricky Gervais. In one scene, Gervais's character walks through Hampstead Heath and finds himself on a bench next to the real George Michael, dragging on a joint and hoping to score. His latest bust, he explains, had been unrelated to sex; he'd been helping Annie Lennox clear out her refrigerator, and they were nabbed for illegal trash disposal. "Sting called the fucking council because he's a fucking do-gooder," complains Michael. He leaves the bench to continue cruising. "Keep an eye out for paparazzi," he tells Gervais.

"I was really knocked out at how good an actor he was," said the comedian. "And such a sport." Explained Michael: "I was prepared to go as far as it took to let everybody know that this was someone who understood how badly he'd fucked up and how easy it was to laugh at him." When the British Comedy Awards honored Gervais for the *Extras* special, a video was shown of him in bed, thanking Michael for having played "a hairy kabob-eating, drug-taking pop star who likes to look for cock in the bushes. Where *do* I get my ideas from?" The camera panned to Michael at his side, reading the *Sun*.

The singer had found himself a new sideline. On the 2007 Christmas edition of *The Catherine Tate Show*, the British comedienne appeared in one of her most famous guises, the bumbling, sex-crazed Nurse Bernie. At someone's bedside, she bursts into "Wake Me Up Before You Go-Go." In walks Michael in striped pajamas. "Shut the fuck up!" he says. The stunned nurse pleads: "D'ya want my sex?"

"Y'don't read the papers, love," he answers.

But to Greg Berlanti, the thirty-five-year-old writer and executive producer of several acclaimed TV shows (*Everwood, Brothers & Sisters, Dirty Sexy Money*), Michael was no joke; he was eternal cool, and his persona held a key to what freedom meant. "I grew up a closeted gay boy in a Catholic family," explained Berlanti. "I think I was identifying with him and didn't really know why. The way he wore his sexuality was as close as I could get at the time to a sense of being myself. I think many of my generation connected with it, even though he didn't say it explicitly."

Berlanti went on to work as a high-profile, openly gay man in an industry where few others did the same. Early in 2007, he wrote the pilot for *Eli Stone*, a comedy-drama series about a hotshot San Francisco lawyer (played by Jonny Lee Miller) plagued by hallucinations. Stone has a brain aneurysm but doesn't know it; his visions, he decides, are meant to reroute him from cold corporate life to the service of others in need. The pilot shows Stone in bed with his fiancée. He thinks he hears George Michael singing "Faith." Stone bolts into the living room and sees Michael dancing on his coffee table, microphone in hand. Later on, the lawyer exits his building's elevator, and there's Michael again, performing "Faith" for a lobby full of boogying employees. Michael becomes Stone's imaginary angel.

ABC green-lit the pilot, but Michael had not signed on yet, and everyone assured Berlanti he would never say yes. Berlanti didn't know that the star was then at risk of losing his U.S. work visa, pending a decision on the Hyde Park bust.

Luckily for Berlanti and his co-producer and writer, Marc Guggenheim, the script tickled Michael, who sensed that *Eli Stone* might help re-endear him to the U.S. public. What's more, Michael knew that Elton John had recently produced a failed ABC pilot, *Him and Us*, about a campy, over-the-hill gay rock star and his manager. It would have pleased Michael to succeed on TV after John had failed.

Berlanti received word that Michael wanted him to fly to Dallas for a meeting.

He arrived at the house at one P.M. for lunch. Goss and an entourage greeted him. George Michael records were playing, but the star was still in bed. Around two o'clock, Michael came downstairs. To Berlanti, he exuded rock-star energy, the kind that shone from a deity who could electrify a stadium. But the Michael who greeted him was a "sweet, gentle person," not a diva. "He was definitely catty, which I loved," said Berlanti. "He was a gay guy; he was a little bitchy, but very smart. And very shy." That didn't stop Michael from rolling a joint in front of him during the sales pitch. Berlanti spoke of his dreams for the series, but the singer had already decided to say yes. "It's a very charming show," he said. "It's genuinely funny and genuinely sad."

For now, he had to go back to London; his court case as well as Wembley awaited him. Michael shot his pilot scenes there. Once it was known that his U.S. work visa had survived, Berlanti moved on with his plans. Michael would appear in three more episodes of Season One; all thirteen would have Michael songs as themes. Once he was through touring, Michael would fly to Los Angeles to shoot. Berlanti kept writing, intent upon getting a new gay generation excited about his hero.

This second phase of the tour took Michael all over Scandinavia and Eastern Europe, with further stops in Greece, Austria, Ireland, and elsewhere. To Mark Kavanagh of Dublin's *Hot Press*, the show was an oldies act. "It seemed like the entire thirtysomething female population of south Dublin came out to the RDS Arena to greet the former teen idol," he wrote. "George was their fantasy sex god all over again."

Yet virtually every ticket of the three-month leg had sold. The next time Berlanti saw Michael, he was in Los Angeles, ready to shoot *Eli Stone*. He feared he had been dreadful on the pilot— "I had to watch it from the other end of the room because I really couldn't bear it"—yet he loved these stabs at acting, and in fact, he was a natural with a script. In one scene, Stone is visited in his office by the ghost of Michael, slickly dressed and flashing a dazzling smile. Stone touches him in disbelief. "Would you mind not poking me, please?" asks Michael, deadpan. He shows the attorney a newspaper article about a high-school girl who has gotten expelled for playing "I Want Your Sex" during an abstinence assembly, and asks Stone to rep her at his expense. In the brief scene he seems expressive and relaxed; he smirks, laughs, rolls his eyes, and finally turns serious. "The other night I had a dream," he explains. "And in the dream I was completely lost, when someone told me I needed to find a lawyer. Named"—Michael bows his head and looks deep into Miller's eyes—"Eli Stone."

The singer was prominent in the Season One finale where Stone is in the hospital, unconscious and on oxygen. He sees Michael in a dark, windy abyss. "George . . . Oh man, are you God?"

"Well, some men have said so."

With that, Michael sings "Feeling Good," a 1960s British showtune, written by Anthony Newley and Leslie Bricusse, that Nina Simone had transformed into a civil-rights anthem. As with the Simone tunes he had borrowed in the past, his version was an almost identical copy of Simone's, complete with a searing big-band arrangement. Stone hears Michael and his life passes before his eyes.

Prior to the shoot, the Writers Guild of America had called a strike. Berlanti and Guggenheim couldn't go to the set, but Michael invited them to Hollywood's fabled Capitol Records, the cylindrical white tower where Frank Sinatra, Peggy Lee, and Nat King Cole had made most of their greatest recordings. If the two partners couldn't watch the shoot, at least they could see Michael record "Feeling Good" with a prerecorded orchestral track. Berlanti and Guggenheim arrived, and they waited, and waited. Three hours passed.

"Feeling Good" had been written into the episode. If Michael didn't show up they were in trouble; because of the strike, the script could not be touched.

With about a half-hour of session time left, he arrived. Lighting a joint, he chatted casually as the two writers squirmed. Then he stepped inside the recording booth and delivered a single, perfect take. "When he opened up his mouth to sing it just poured out of him," said Berlanti. "That moment will live with me forever."

The response to his first presence on *Eli Stone*, which had premiered on January 31, 2008, was closer to indifference. "Yes, *that* George Michael," wrote a critic. Another referred to him as "the ex-Wham! star." Some reviews didn't mention him at all. Twenty years earlier, Michael's involvement might have fueled the show for a long life, but *Eli Stone* lasted just two seasons. Michael did not appear in the second; he had to go back on the road.

• • •

Michael's twenty U.S. concert dates included two nights at Madison Square Garden. Once more he would only do limited press, and it hurt his ego to learn that in most venues only 75 percent or less of the tickets had sold. In May 2008, the month before his first U.S. show, he joined a parade of senior pop stars—Graham Nash, Bryan Adams, Donna Summer—on the season finale of *American Idol*. He slowly descended a huge expanse of stairs then sang "Praying for Time." The top twelve finalists sang a medley of his hits. Observed Randy Cordova of *Gannett*: "One imagines a good number of twelve-year-olds asking their moms who was the old guy in the sunglasses."

On June 17, a less-than-sellout audience at San Diego Sports Arena welcomed him back to the States. Just before showtime, Michael spoke with a reporter from *Access Hollywood*. "I really don't know what to expect," he admitted.

Michael kept a teleprompter running, just in case. "He was out of it most of the time," said Phil Palmer. Yet he seemed genuinely touched by the loyalty of those who had come. "Lord knows it's not always easy being a George Michael fan," he told them. "Hopefully by the end of the evening you will forgive me for having stayed away so long."

The city's main newspaper, the *San Diego Union-Tribune*, didn't cover this newsworthy comeback. Elsewhere, the critical response seesawed dramatically. Reviewing him at Philadelphia's Wachovia Center, A.D. Amorosi of the *Philadelphia Inquirer* wrote that Michael "performed gorgeously . . . you realized how much time he wasted *not* engaging his talents." But to Jim Farber of the New York *Daily News*, the Madison Square Garden show "had little sense of momentum, and much of the material hasn't aged well." Numerous shows began late, sometimes by as much as an hour; Michael made excuses onstage while apologizing profusely.

In the States, his political diatribes as well as "Shoot the Dog" fell on colder ears; not everyone wanted to hear an Englishman pontificate about American politics. Palmer felt stirrings of resentment: "He used to frighten us as a band, doing that stuff in America."

At the Forum in Inglewood, California, he celebrated his forty-fifth birthday by having Bo Derek, the seminaked star of such panned eighties films as *Tarzan the Ape Man* and *Bolero*, wheel out a giant cake. Watching from prime seats were two of Michael's closest companions of the *Faith* days, Bret Witke and Kathy Jeung. The singer had fallen out of touch with the woman from whom he had once been inseparable. "She had reached out a couple of times—no contact back," said Witke.

The former club owner, by now an interior designer, watched Michael in dismay. "Nothing felt the same," said Witke. "He was just doing an act." Afterward, the two friends went backstage. Spotting them, Michael walked over. "I tried to talk to him and somebody dragged him away," recalled Witke. "He didn't look great. You looked in his eyes, you didn't see anybody." Witke knew the telltale signs of drug use, and he couldn't help but recall how Michael had written "Monkey" to warn Jeung of her friends' bad influence. Now all of them were clean, and Michael was deep in the throes of drugs. "It broke my heart," Witke said.

The tour's last week found Michael in Florida, playing the BankAtlantic Center in the town of Sunrise. He was an hour late and in fragile voice. "Sick as a dog" with a cold, he explained, Michael avoided most high notes and cracked on others. Even so, wrote Leslie Gray Streeter of the *Palm Beach Post*, Michael's singing "powerfully and confidently" filled the arena.

But Michael was burned out. He was through playing stadiums; the joy had gone out of it. Once home in London, he told the BBC it was time he made room for the young. On August 24 and 25, 2008, he gave two farewell shows at Earls Court. Subtitled The Final Two, they drew thirty-two thousand fans who couldn't bear the thought of not seeing him again.

Those shows, in fact, were not the end; 25 Live concluded officially in Copenhagen. Even then, promoters kept throwing money at him to come back. Off he flew to Abu Dhabi to play the forty-five-thousand-seat Zayed Sports City Stadium—the biggest concert ever held in the Emirates. While there, he accepted a reported £1 million to perform for a billionaire and his friends.

• • •

Overall, the 25 Live Tour had been a commercial triumph. Back home in London, however, Michael lived in a haze. He slept until mid-afternoon, then stayed high on pot for almost every waking moment. He sat at his computer playing video games, binge-watched TV, arranged GHB-fueled trysts, and took midnight jaunts to the Heath. "I do get anyone I want," he told Piers Morgan with a laugh. "But I like a bit of everything. I have friends up there; I have a laugh."

Friends dropped by; some, like Kate Moss, shared some of his worst habits. The troubled supermodel had bought a house a few doors from Michael in Highgate village. It had once belonged to Samuel Taylor Coleridge, the British romantic poet. But Moss's reputation was less refined. She had popularized a pale, emaciated look known as "heroin chic." Moss denied using that particular drug, but in 2005 she had made the cover of the Mirror with the headline "COCAINE KATE: Supermodel Kate Moss Snorts Line After Line." It showed stills from a video in which Moss seemed to be doing just that at a recording date of her boyfriend, British musician Pete Doherty, whose heroin, cocaine, and crack use were all over the tabloids.

It was exactly the kind of influence Michael didn't need. But depression had again consumed him, and he craved any quick fixes he could find. On Friday afternoon, September 19, 2008, Michael was in the Heath, lurking in an underground men's room. His loitering and body language suggested a man who was either selling drugs or looking to buy them. Who reported him wasn't clear, but the police arrived. Searching Michael, they found marijuana and crack cocaine. They arrested him.

By now the press coverage of his arrests had shrunken; they were hardly breaking news. In a short article, the *Sun* dutifully noted this latest misstep by "the gay 'Careless Whisper' star." According to an unnamed source, Michael had begged the police not to charge him, claiming tearfully that this could get him banned from the United States, where he was due to sing at an AIDS benefit. "His sob story worked," claimed the source. "He was even chauffeured home."

By the time word had gotten out, Michael had posted a message on his website. "I apologize to my fans for screwing up again and promise I'll sort myself out," he said, adding a mea culpa "just for boring them." But some observers were furious that police had once more set him free. "He should have been prosecuted," said John O'Connor, a former official from Scotland Yard. "He's clearly out of control. What does he have to do to be dealt with properly?"

Even the *Sun* took the high ground. "It seems there's one law for the rich and famous and another for the rest of us," wrote the editors. "Michael, like sleazy Kate Moss, has learned there is no limit to police tolerance of celebrity druggies. . . . The police might as well put up a sign saying, 'Just Do It.'"

The greatest show of outrage came in the *Mirror*. Michael had not spoken to Tony Parsons, coauthor of his 1990 memoir *Bare* and conductor of numerous in-depth Michael interviews, in years. Parsons had boasted of their close friendship—Michael never did—but ever since the columnist had begun revealing too much about him in print, the star had erased him from his life.

Parsons had nothing to lose, and in a *Mirror* column he gave Michael the most scabrous indictment he had ever received in print. The article, "Don't Go Down the Pan, George," opened with a cartoon of a hunched-over, pot-bellied, gray-bearded Michael skulking into a men's room. A bubble contained the words of an unseen loiterer: "Oh no! Here comes George Michael again!"

"Somewhere inside that fat, sleazy, bloated old geezer is the George Michael I used to know," wrote Parsons. "That kid was smart, funny, and he had a heart of gold." The apology he'd just posted to his website, Parsons added, was sad: "He knows the world is bored sick of hearing about him getting caught with his, metaphorically speaking, trousers down, and sometimes not so metaphorically. How many times does he intend to get caught, go on *Parky* [*Parkinson*], and ask for forgiveness from the people who bought 'Careless Whisper'?" Today, Parsons said, Michael "would rather appear in a toilet than on a stage." His fans were "giving up on him. This scandal has proved a toilet too far."

For twelve years, Michael could at least point to his relationship with Kenny Goss as a sign of stability. Having the Texan on his arm and in his homes gave assurance to the world, and perhaps to Michael himself, that he had found peace as a gay man. "I think there was a lot of love there, a lot of grounding," said Johnny Douglas. Certainly, Goss had benefited enormously from the relationship. He had lived a jet-setting life on the arm of a superstar who had sung and talked about him to millions. The Goss-Michael Foundation had made its founder a celebrity in Dallas. He could boast of friendships with celebrities in his partner's circle, such as Geri Halliwell. But some of Michael's less famous companions had grown sick of Goss's brushoffs. "It pissed George off because Kenny was rude to his friends," said Niall Flynn.

Although no civil union had happened between them, Michael had long given Goss a £15,000-per-month allowance, enough for him to buy almost every treasure his heart desired. It was the culmination, beyond his wildest dreams, of all he had left Texas to find.

But his joyride had degenerated into a string of public humiliations, which he was expected to whitewash to the press. More than once, Michael had sworn he'd quit drugs; Goss would find a hidden stash and flush it down the toilet. Along the way, Goss had developed his own problem with alcohol. Michael had pleaded with him to go to rehab, which he ultimately did.

It didn't save the relationship. Around the end of 2008, Michael dropped him. But Goss would not be out of the picture anytime soon. They stayed tied financially because of the art foundation, which Michael had paid for. "He just wouldn't give up what he got from being George's husband," said Flynn. The Texan didn't lack encouragement: Michael kept him around, and would deny the breakup publicly for at least two years. Thereafter, he waxed romantic about the loss of his "horny cowboy."

•••

Michael's songwriting had dwindled to almost nothing, but he hoped his voice could lead him down the path of currency. Over the years he had sung with the hottest soul divas of the moment—Aretha Franklin, Mary J. Blige, Whitney Houston. Now he set his sights on pop's statuesque reigning goddess, Beyoncé. With her shrewd grasp of trends and merchandising, the singer had wrested the crown of "Material Girl" from Madonna. On June 9, 2009, Beyoncé brought her I Am . . . World Tour to London's O2 Arena. Michael learned that her creative advisor was his old nemesis Thierry Mugler. On the day of the show, the designer was amused to receive his first note from Michael since the "Too Funky" debacle. Mugler paraphrased Michael's words with a sarcastic spin: "Hi Thierry, it's George, the poor English queen manipulated by his managers in Los Angeles. . . . But all that's behind us now. You made the most beautiful video of my career . . . And my dream now is to appear on stage with Beyoncé tonight."

Seeing a chance for backhanded revenge, Mugler phoned Beyoncé. "Okay, Miss B, we'll say yes to George on one condition: that he sings 'If I Were a Boy' in a duet with you!" That song, from her latest album, was a brokenhearted woman's lament about how much easier men had it in affairs of the heart. With a stab of effeminizing gay bitchery, Mugler told a reporter: "The poor guy was busted in public toilets in L.A. and had been forced to come out, so I thought that track was very appropriate."

That night, Beyoncé, in a short leather combat-style dress designed by Mugler, sang the song once through. Suddenly George Michael walked toward her, unannounced, in a white jacket. She was twenty-eight, he forty-six, and most of her fans were too young to have grown up hearing him; not all of them knew who he was. Michael did his chorus accompanied by a few moves. Beyoncé took over with hand on hip, defiant and pouty. She easily outsang him. The pair showed no chemistry; their odd meeting lasted only two minutes.

When Andy Stephens heard about it, he was flummoxed; Michael had never told him. Stephens had long since passed the breaking point of frustration. Years earlier, said Judy Wieder, the manager had asked her to come and work for him. "I said, 'Are you kidding? Why?' He said, 'Because you can get him to do things I can't.'" Stephens had spent much of their relationship pleading with the contrary singer to make wiser choices and avoid self-sabotage, but it was a lost cause. "Nobody knew what was going on in George's life—even the people who seemed to be closest to him, like Kenny," said Niall Flynn. "Everybody was a bit paranoid because they had no fucking idea what was going on in his head."

Michael seemed creatively paralyzed, and drug use had made him almost unmanageable. A 25 Live DVD, recorded at Earls Court, should have come out the previous December. The singer insisted on approving every frame, but he hated how he looked and couldn't bear to watch.

A much bigger project was on the verge of falling through. In January of 2008, HarperCollins, a major book publisher, had announced plans to publish a George Michael memoir, signed at a staggering $7 million advance. The sum virtually required that the book become a No. 1 bestseller—a likelihood in the United Kingdom, but not in the States. Stephens, who had helped broker the deal, did his best to release a tantalizing announcement. "George has promised HarperCollins a no-holds-barred biography, and it's certain to be just that," he promised. There would be no coauthor; HarperCollins had been assured that Michael had the discipline to write it himself.

He didn't. On December 4, 2009, staffers at HarperCollins read in the *Guardian* that Michael was planning to break the deal. He gave journalist Simon Hattenstone an excuse: When he signed the contract, he hadn't known that HarperCollins was owned by "the devil," as he called Rupert Murdoch. Michael had begun the book, but he never got far, and the project faded away. Its death was one more blow to Stephens. In 1995, when Michael hired him, he had told the manager that he knew he could depend on his unedited honesty. Now, said Chris Cameron, "George didn't want anyone around him who was gonna tell him the truth—nobody." In the summer of 2009, Michael fired Stephens. Previously he had engaged Michael Lippman, who had co-managed him with Rob Kahane in the late eighties, to handle the American third of 25 Live. Lippman would now take over worldwide duties, but there didn't seem much work ahead to manage.

Instead, his handlers focused on cleaning up further scandals. After midnight on Friday, August 14, 2009, Lawrie Bowe, a lorry driver, was heading down the A34 motorway west of London. In his rearview mirror, he spied a silver Range Rover weaving back and forth between two lanes. Its driver picked up speed, and Bowe felt a bump. The Rover had hooked into the truck's rear axle; Bowe realized he was dragging it behind him. He screeched to a stop.

Amazingly, he escaped uninjured, as did the other driver. Bowe leapt out of his truck and saw a dazed George Michael in the Rover. According to one report, Michael tried to step inside Bowe's truck, saying he needed a lift. The driver refused, and Michael wandered up the motorway. He took a small object out of his pocket—perhaps a bottle of GHB—and tossed it over the guardrail.

His two-year driving ban had ended just three months before. Police arrested Michael and held him for five hours. He passed a breath test for alcohol; whether or not he had a blood test for drugs was unclear. Once more he was released. "Neither of us was charged because we were both stone-cold sober," he told a reporter. But the press was no longer buying it. "The fact that George hasn't killed anyone—or himself—is pure good fortune," wrote Simon Price in the *Independent*. "George, for God's sake get a chauffeur."

The *Sun* couldn't resist having a laugh at Michael's expense. Its cover story was headlined: "George Michael Shunts Trucker in the Rear."

As self-satirizing as he was, Michael found no wit in old stereotypes. He liked Graham Norton, but cited him as the kind of gay cliché that was keeping public attitudes in the stone age. "Why should this generation of gay children have to accept that their sexuality is laughable?" he asked Hattenstone. "You only have to turn on the television to see the whole of British society being comforted by gay men who are so clearly gay and so obviously sexually unthreatening."

Yet a new wave of young gay singers were living a lot more openly than he had at their age. In June 2009, Joanna Weiss of the *Boston Globe* extolled "the überconfident *Idol* contestant with the painted nails and wailing high notes." Adam Lambert, a twenty-seven-year-old Goth boy, rose through *American Idol*'s ranks by singing "Bohemian Rhapsody," Motown, and other music that Michael had memorized in his teens. Though he came in second, Lambert—who later talked of Michael's "God-gifted voice from the heavens"—became one of *Idol*'s great finds. He quickly came out in a *Rolling Stone* cover story.

That December, finalists on *The X Factor UK*, an *Idol* spinoff, included Joe McElderry, a clean-cut, boyish seventeen-year-old. He and his mother worshipped Michael; in an early round of the show, he had sung "Praying for Time." Michael considered the show's creator, *Idol* judge Simon Cowell, a "genius," and he agreed to join McElderry in a duet.

Backstage, Michael spent a half hour with the starstruck youth. During the taping, McElderry began "Don't Let the Sun Go Down on Me" alone. Then he spoke the magic words: "I can't actually believe I'm gonna introduce this man on the stage. The one and only *George Michael!*" Out came his hero. Touching the young man's shoulder, Michael joined in on the song. McElderry won first place, and the star thrilled him again by sending a bottle of champagne and a card. Not long after, the teenager confirmed a rumor he had previously denied: He was gay. He went on to record three top-ten albums.

Michael loved knowing he'd inspired these young men, while realizing he'd fallen short as their role model. But as Christmastime of 2009 approached, Michael took great pride in two gifts he had for his fans. At last came the 25 Live DVD, entitled *Live in London*. A bonus road documentary by David Austin showed Michael as a trim, vigorous, self-deprecating picture of health, dazzling audiences worldwide. Michael's second stocking-stuffer was a single, "December Song (I Dreamed of Christmas)," released on Island Records. He had briefly offered it as a free download the previous Christmas, and he wanted to give it a proper life.

Michael had written two versions in the studio. "I really liked the earlier one, which seemed old-Christmasy, but George thought it was a little too cheesy," said Niall Flynn, who did the engineering. "He decided to make something a bit more grown up." Now, guitar, strings, and choir—all synthesized—sweetened a lyric about a little boy who yearned for Christmas, when "snow would fall upon my bed / White sugar from Jesus." The day after his Joe McElderry taping, Michael had gone back to *The X Factor* to tape "December Song." He lip-synched the song in front of a choir that wore white robes and held candles. The exposure pushed "December Song" to No. 14 in the United Kingdom, despite a pan in the *Financial Times*, whose reviewer opined: "One can only assume a single as bland as this . . . represents a deliberate attempt to reposition him back in the middle of the road, not crashed out on the side clutching a crack pipe."

For the video, an offer went out to Yibi Hu and Joe Marshall, partners at Moving Image Exchange (MIE), a London-based animation production company. Michael wanted to employ the stop-motion animation style of the 1964 TV special *Rudolph the Red-Nosed Reindeer*, in which clay and wooden figurines were manipulated and photographed a frame at a time. The results were touchingly lifelike; they could now, of course, be simulated digitally.

Hu heard the song and whipped up a treatment. It involved a boy's lonely Christmas without his father, who has gone to war in the Middle East. In his sleep, he envisions himself inside the holiday paradise he is sure he won't experience. But he does: On Christmas Day, his father returns.

The singer read Hu's pitch and called to discuss it. Michael saw himself in that little boy, he said, but the details had to change. He told Hu about his beloved mother, whose birthday was on Christmas Eve. "He said he wanted to make this special moment about her—not about his father."

Hu rewrote the story, and he and Joe Marshall rushed to create the cartoon in time for the holidays. Back in London, he and Marshall went to Michael's Regent's Park home to screen it for him. The singer rolled a joint and watched. He saw a sad little animated boy in his room with only the company of a hamster spinning in a cage. Nodding off to sleep, the boy dreams that he and his pet have crawled inside a TV that shows a snowy, enchanted forest. A moving bed of Christmas-tree bulbs sweeps them into Santa's workshop, alive with bouncing toys. Finally, the boy smiles. He awakens in his room to find his mother by his side, cradling his head in her lap. Michael loved it. The video was his and his mother's love story.

European MTV aired the "December Song" video; it appeared with the song on an EP. But people weren't much interested in a George Michael video anymore. Hu and Marshall's representative used it to shop their services at ad agencies. "No one wanted to hear about him," said Hu. "This is how biased the world is when all the publicity is against you. Anytime we mentioned George Michael, people would perceive you as uncool. Same thing with Elton John. But I still love George's video."

● ● ●

Reclusive as Michael was, in December he welcomed Simon Hattenstone into his Highgate home. The *Guardian* contributor, whom Michael trusted, didn't shirk tough questions, some about the star's sex life and drug use; Michael revealed himself in all his contradictions.

As he and Hattenstone sat near the fireplace, a table stood within the star's reach. On it was a Tupperware container of pot, which filled the air with a smell as biting as body odor; rolling papers; numerous pills (to stave off back pain and smoking pangs, he said, although he hadn't quit); and several rolled joints. He had cut back to seven or eight a day, he explained. Asked about his musical projects, he responded vaguely; Michael preferred talking about his personal life. Describing a typical day, he listed some mundane details—emailing, Starbucks—after which, he said, he would usually "go off and have a shag or have someone come here and have a shag." Did he mean Kenny? "If it was shagging with Kenny, I wouldn't have to invite him 'round, would I?" countered the singer. He quickly backtracked: "Kenny gets his, believe me."

Hattenstone brought up the bust for crack cocaine. Was he still smoking it? Michael swore he wasn't, insisting he had only done so "once or twice." And when was the last time? He declined to answer. "But I am going to tell you, whatever I do, I did a hundred and five really good performances, and none of my musicians can ever say they've seen me wasted."

"I'm feeling more parental by the second," wrote Hattenstone. "It's hard not to worry about Michael—for all his paranoia, recklessness, and self-absorption, he exudes intelligence, warmth and generosity."

Asking him intimate questions was fine, so long as no one lectured him or even voiced concern. He mentioned that Bono, whom he barely knew, had asked Geri Halliwell what they could do to save him. "As if Bono gives a shit what I do with my private life," he snarled. Michael reminded Elton John now, via the *Guardian*, that he was sick of his meddling. "Elton just needs to shut his mouth and get on with his own life. He will not be happy until I bang on his door saying, 'Please, please help me, Elton. Take me to rehab.' It's not going to happen."

That April, Michael had drawn up his will. If one of his missteps were to kill him he would die contented, he told Hattenstone, knowing how much beautiful work he had left behind. "My ego is sated," he said.

CHAPTER TWENTY-SIX

FOR MICHAEL AND THE pop stars he had grown up worshipping, record studios were a second home; none of those artists could have imagined an age of do-it-yourself recording, untied to producers, budgets, or company approval. But audio software such as GarageBand had turned bedrooms and basements into studios and laptops into consoles. None of this seemed revolutionary to Michael, who was creating homemade tracks on cassette in 1981. In the summer of 2010, he sat in his home studio and tinkered with a vocoder, a vocal synthesizer that had been integral to electronic pop for decades. Controlled by knobs and a keyboard, it added a plethora of whirring, mechanical sounds to a voice.

Michael had been asked to contribute a video to Red Nose Day, the BBC's starry biannual telethon for Comic Relief, which raised funds to fight poverty. The show would not air until March, but Michael had time on his hands, and he got to work. Before he could make a video, he needed a song. He dug an old, unfinished track, New Order's "True Faith," out of the archives. It had a theme of emerging from darkness: "My morning sun is the drug that brings me near / To the childhood I lost, replaced by fear."

To Michael, it sounded like an anthem for a new gay generation. According to Matthew Todd, editor of *Attitude*, they had more in common with him than they knew. "George Michael reflects the experiences of a lot of gay men," Todd told the *Independent*'s Adam Sherwin. "There is a higher level of drink and drug abuse because of what they go through growing up."

On Saturday, July 3, Michael joined the multitudes at London's Gay Pride Parade. A huge costume pageant, it culminated in front of City Hall in Trafalgar Square, which became a sea of rainbow flags, tank tops, and grinning faces. One of the latter—adorned by a graying buzzcut, a goatee, and sunglasses—belonged to George Michael. Nightfall brought Liberation, a drug-fueled after-party in Hampstead.

Past three A.M., police got a call about a car accident in front of the Hampstead location of Snappy Snaps, a photo-developing chain. Officers pulled up to the tiny corner shop to find that a Range Rover had crashed into the store's yellow façade. The engine was still running, and inside was the driver, seemingly uninjured but in a daze. One of the officers banged on the window to rouse him—and George Michael turned his head, staring blankly. He was drenched in sweat and had the same gaping eyes and dilated pupils caught by *News of the World* in Hampstead Heath.

Michael was told to step out of his car. He needed help to stand up and didn't seem to know where he was. Told he had crashed into a storefront, Michael murmured, "No, I didn't. I didn't crash into anything." A search of the car uncovered two joints.

For the seventh time in twelve years, Michael was arrested. At Camden station, the singer, now more lucid, argued that he had smoked only "a small quantity" of pot and had taken a new antidepressant, amitriptyline. He left the station on bail. On Monday morning, the Snappy Snaps at Willoughby Road and Rosslyn Hill was all over the news. In the middle of the bashed-in section of wood beside the front door, someone had written WHAM.

The court charged him with possession of marijuana and with driving in an unfit state, and there wasn't much he could say in his defense. On August 24, Michael arrived with four security guards in a chauffeured car at Highbury Corner Magistrates' Court. A new lawyer, Mukul Chawla, pleaded his case. Michael, he said, wanted to express his "profound shame and horror" at what he'd done. Chawla added that his client had reimbursed the shop owner for the damage. But District Judge John Perkins was not moved. Jail time, he declared, was likely. He would see Michael in three weeks for sentencing.

The possibility of prison threw Michael into a panic. A day later, he did what a few friends had long begged him to do: He checked into a clinic. There he underwent two weeks of detox. Both he and his attorney hoped it might reduce whatever punishment lay ahead. On September 14, Michael returned to court. Kenny Goss had come to provide a shoulder. Both men trembled as Perkins delivered the news. "It does not appear that you took proper steps to deal with what is clearly an addiction to cannabis. That's a mistake that puts you and, on this occasion, the public at risk." He brought up the "dangerous and unpredictable mix" of pot and prescription drugs Michael had taken. Once again, no mention was made of GHB, whose telltale effects had been all too clear in his behavior that night.

Still, Perkins came down harder on Michael than any other judge had. He placed a five-year block on Michael's driver's license, ordered him to pay a £1,250 fine—and sentenced him to four weeks in jail and four on probation. Sky News Australia reported what happened next: "There were gasps and tears from fans within the court's public gallery. George Michael smirked in utter disbelief." Goss lowered his face into his hands.

Michael would go straight to prison. Two security guards escorted him, unhandcuffed, to a large white van on the street. As it drove off, photographers ran alongside it, holding cameras up to porthole-like windows. Michael was brought to Pentonville, a notoriously crowded, violent, and drug-infested men's prison, for the first three nights of his sentence.

Upon admission, he was handed a prison uniform. Before he donned it, he was strip-searched for weapons and drugs. Michael was brought to a cell in the A Wing, known as the "Reception, First Night Centre and Induction." For a star who had spent most of his life in expensive homes and five-star hotels, Pentonville was a shock. "I thought, 'Oh my God, this place is absolutely filthy,'" he said later. An internal report described the basement space as a pit of "cockroaches, mice, and offensive smells."

Things got worse. Michael was next taken to G1, the Vulnerable Prisoners' Unit—"for sex offenders and people who have committed serious crimes." Word that he was coming had spread among the section's convicts; before his arrival some had chanted, "Where's George Michael? Bring George Michael!"

Michael lingered in his cell, crying. The next morning, reported Sena, he heard inmates taunting him by singing, "Guilty George has got no freedom!" to the tune of "Careless Whisper."

Once his three days had passed, Michael rode in a prison vehicle for about two hours to Suffolk, where he moved into Highpoint Prison. Highpoint was a lot less threatening than Pentonville. Michael wore a uniform of jeans and a blue-and-white striped shirt, and he slept in a cell in the "good behavior" wing. For the next three and a half weeks he was cheered by letters from friends and supporters, among them Elton John and Paul McCartney; even Boy George wrote with good wishes. Michael played pool, and Goss visited.

No one could deny the scene's strangeness. Michael had gone from black Armani to prison blue, from Wembley and Ibiza to a cot in a cell. He could have employed a full-time chauffeur and avoided several embarrassing scandals, but he didn't want to; now he would have no choice. Gay fans laughed as they envisioned Michael in a porno fantasy of communal showers and tattooed brutes: Would he ever want to leave?

But his last night at Highpoint came, and Michael went so far as to call it "great." He signed an autograph, he said, for "every single staff member" and convict, using prison paper. The next day, Monday, October 11, Goss drove Michael home to Highgate. Predictably, a horde of press waited. Michael was so relieved to be home that he seemed glad to talk to them. "I'm going to try to stop running away from you guys," he said with a smile. "You'll see me about."

The Michael they encountered was double-chinned but looked healthier; for four weeks he had not been able to smoke or do drugs. "I just want to start again," he told the flock. "I just want to thank everybody who supported me. It was quite inspirational." He would undergo therapy for his drug addictions; he even promised to cut back on smoking pot.

Once settled in, Michael had time to philosophize. "Karmically, I felt like I had a bill to pay," he told a reporter. "It's so much easier to take any form of punishment if you believe you actually deserve it, and I did." But he couldn't shake the sense that he'd been targeted again. Why? "I'm George Michael," he said, "and the poster boy for cannabis."

●●●

For all his troubles, he felt "reinvigorated musically," he said, and began "writing like a demon." Despite having sworn he would never make another album, an idea for one had gelled in prison. But it wasn't new. Having let down the gays once again, he felt, Michael had decided to give them the dance album that *Patience* was supposed to have been. He explained it all to Will Hodgkinson of the *Times*. "House music has been the staple of the gay world since it was invented," he said. "I'm going to be working with either gay or gay-friendly artists, and it'll be a mixture of tracks sung by me and others by young gay artists—possibly unknown ones." The album would raise a middle finger to homophobes; some of its lyrics, he warned, would be "gay enough to alienate a lot of people."

Meanwhile, he forged ahead on the "True Faith" video. Weeks after he had regained his freedom, he summoned Yibi Hu and Joe Marshall to Highgate.

As they approached his house, the young men saw his smashed Range Rover out front. Michael answered the door. All the window shades were drawn—"because he thought the paparazzi were trying to take photos of him," said Hu. Michael's pledges to quit hiding from the press and to ease up on marijuana had vanished in a puff of smoke: To Hu, the singer seemed even more stoned than he had in their last meeting.

Even so, he had ideas. Michael loved Tom of Finland, the Finnish illustrator whose post-World War II homoerotic drawings depicted an underworld of hypermasculine men in skintight jeans and biker gear—the blueprint for the clone look. Perhaps, suggested Michael, the video could show an animated band of Tom-like figures. "He wanted to be the drummer," said Hu. "He thought drummers were the sexiest."

But Michael's backup plan won out. It involved dancing figures who emerged out of pot smoke. He was even willing to appear on camera. Michael asked Hu to direct as well as coproduce, but the young man was too busy; Michael planned to do the filming in Sydney, where he had been spending increasing amounts of time. Now that he was "on the market again," as he put it, he relished his time in that alluringly gay metropolis. There he could cruise and use gay hookup apps without fear of the London snoops.

On one of his Australian trips, he arranged to be filmed lip-synching to "True Faith." Wearing a black shirt and a near-skinhead haircut, Michael looked younger and more menacingly sexy than he had since "Outside." The animation was superimposed. It showed him flanked by white clouds of marijuana smoke streaked with red, gold, and blue. They grow slowly like atomic bombs, then morph into a balletic couple. Michael becomes a godlike face in the clouds.

"True Faith" was slated for a prime spot in Red Nose Day, but that wasn't all Michael contributed. One of that year's hosts was the young British comic actor James Corden. In *Gavin & Stacey*, a smash sitcom, Corden played Smithy, the stout, oafish best friend of married man Gavin. Knowing Michael was game for self-satire, Corden offered him a sketch that began with Smithy giving him a lift home from prison. Michael vetoed the bit. "When it came to the car thing, I did something wrong," he explained. "When it came to the Hampstead Heath thing, fuck off!"

Corden adjusted the script, and the scene was shot. Talking on his phone to a friend as he drives, Smithy explains that he's "spendin' the day with my mate; he's been away for a while." Corden is headed to a Red Nose Day production meeting, but he hasn't invited Michael. The singer begs to come, and when Smithy refuses, Michael turns petulant. "Let's be honest," he says, pouting. You don't want me to come to Comic Relief because you don't want to be seen with a *gay man*!" Michael imitates Smithy's doltish North London accent. Finally, Smithy breaks the truth about why he can't come: "Because you're a joke, George! It's embarrassing! I can't walk into Comic Relief with you! Comic Relief's about *helping* people like you!" Tearfully, Michael turns his head away. Smithy tries to cheers him up by playing "I'm Your Man" on the car stereo. He starts singing along. Michael can't resist joining in, and the two of them belt the old Wham! hit at the top of their lungs.

The spot—which Michael later tried to cancel—was the most talked-about segment on that year's Red Nose Day. The fundraiser broke its own record, raising £74 million. Corden got a bonus. In 2015, he broke through on American TV as host of *The Late Late Show*. One of its running gags, "Carpool Karaoke," was modeled on the Michael sketch; it found Adele, Elton John, Paul McCartney, Madonna, and dozens more pop stars in the car with Corden, singing along with their own hits.

Red Nose Day gave "True Faith" a modest bump to No. 27 in the United Kingdom. Michael had hoped for more, and on Twitter, he asked fans to please buy his single. Having recently opened an account there, he was now hooked. One day he posted twenty-seven tweets. Like other stars, he loved having the power to bypass the press by speaking directly to "my lovelies," as he called them.

Some of his tweets were funny: "OOOh, look, I'm on the cusp of 400 thousand lovelies! Let me think of something profound to say . . . erm . . . what usually works on here? . . . Fuck, fuck, fuckety fuck cock piss bastard." Others were barbed. When Jeremy Clarkson, host of the TV automotive show *Top Gear*, said of a Jaguar, "In the corner it will get its tail out more readily than George Michael," Michael had a handy forum to call Clarkson a "pig-ugly homophobic twat." Michael held forth on politics, needled colleagues ("Just saw the Madonna video, she looks great. As for the song, err. . . . don't really think I should comment"), and self-deprecated endlessly ("Every radio request from you guys is much appreciated . . . . Help the Aged"). Intima-cies normally reserved for friends flooded out to strangers. Posting a link to a photo of a handsome man, Michael posted: "Quite a good shag but not very friendly."

Sometimes he tweeted while stoned and in front of the TV, watching news shows that made him reel in anger. A string of tweets, some barely comprehensible, concerned "Murdoch's attempts to destroy me." Michael rejoiced at the 2011 demise of Murdoch's *News of the World*, which had come under fire for hacking the phones of celebrities and political figures. Several editors were arrested; Michael tweeted for days about one of them, Rebekah Brooks. She had "sat two feet from me in my own home," he wrote, and explained the paper's dirty methods.

Michael's philanthropy rolled on. Britain's Prince William was about to take a wife, Kate Middleton. As a wedding gift, Michael recorded the Stevie Wonder love song "You and I." He announced that he would offer it on his website, asking only that downloaders donate to the couple's Royal Wedding Charitable Gift Fund, which endowed a variety of causes. Wonder agreed to waive his share of the rights.

Michael was driven partly by guilt. In 1990, William's mother, Diana, had invited the singer to a small Christmas party at Buckingham Palace. The prince, then eight, approached him. "Would you sing a song and Uncle Elton play the piano?" Michael declined; he *hated* singing for small groups of mostly strangers. "His little Christmas smile disappeared," recalled Michael. "I bloody said no to the future king of my country . . . oh, the shame." He would not attend the wedding. The royal couple, he explained, should be "surrounded by people they love, not dodgy ex-con pop stars."

His "You and I" had a homemade simplicity, just keyboards and voice. The recording should have been simple, but for Chris Cameron, whom he asked to play, the experience was "painful." Cameron arrived in the studio at the appointed hour of noon. "At four o'clock he bounded in, spliff that long," said Cameron. They worked out a key and Michael went home. He didn't return until eight. "Now he's got the dark glasses on. *Completely* different man. Cold. I don't know what he had taken." As they ran through the song, Michael was hostile and combative. " 'No, no, no, I want it like *that!*' Scary. I got home at four that morning. I thought, I don't want to be doing this anymore."

Whatever buzz that surrounded the recording was quickly silenced by a news flash: Michael was going back on tour. The decision was a surprise. He had hardly any new material; most of the songs from his post-prison writing binge had gone unfinished. He couldn't do another concert of covers or his greatest hits. But one possibility remained: "to make a show really about my voice." Recently he had seen Tony Bennett with a symphony orchestra; it occurred to him that he could do that, too. Michael had always regretted his failure to promote *Songs from the Last Century*, an album he loved but had let die. Now, he decided, he would hit the road with an orchestra of the same size and give those lavishly arranged songs a second chance.

He called the record's producer, Phil Ramone. It so happened that Ramone was coming to London soon with Bennett. Now eighty-four, the singer was making a second volume of duets, produced by Ramone; Bennett was about to record "Body and Soul" at Abbey Road studios with Amy Winehouse. With David Austin in tow, Michael went there for the session. There they hashed out ideas for the show, to be called Symphonica, and a live album, which Ramone would produce.

All creative choices, of course, would be Michael's. He felt no obligation to make people dance. "He even said, 'I don't care if it's all ballads—this is what I want,'" recalled Ben Butler, who would be joining him on guitar. The cost of traveling with over forty musicians and a huge crew would be exorbitant; Michael didn't care.

Over seventy dates were booked, from the fall to just before Christmas of 2011. Conspicuously absent from the schedule was North America. Michael's jail sentence had finally lost him his American work visa. But Ramone and his contractor, Jill Dell'Abate, arranged for him to carry the States with him in the form of an intimidatingly accomplished New York rhythm section. Henry Hey, Michael's new pianist and musical director, had worked with Rod Stewart and David Bowie. David Finck, the jazz bassist on *Songs from the Last Century*, had returned, having played for years with

Sir André Previn. Butler toured with Sting; drummer Mark McLean had worked with Gladys Knight. "I think George was a little bit in awe of these guys," said Phil Palmer. "He wasn't really equipped to understand what they were doing musically."

The project terrified him—"which is not normally the case," he confessed, "but it's such a different show to any I've done before." He had more fears than that. Although his vocal texture remained cloudless and sweet, years of smoking had taken a toll on his range and lung power. "I'm not ready to be a crooner yet," he noted uncomfortably at a May 11 press conference.

That week he texted Paul Stag, his steady escort and GHB connection. "I'm in need fella," he typed. "After the tour conference Kenny arrived unannounced and totally fucked with my head for an hour straight. He's turned up every day and I'm so scared I need champagne. Any chance? X." Around that time, Michael spoke by phone with Rufus Wainwright, whose song "Going to a Town" was on the set list. Michael was so stoned he nodded off.

But once he showed up at AIR Studios to start singing with the orchestra, the "control freak" in him snapped back. Michael would be singing to arrangements from *Songs from the Last Century*; Henry Hey and others had orchestrated additional songs. Michael assessed each one to make sure it fit his current vocal state. "We stripped a lot away," said Hey. As always, everything that happened onstage had to be set in stone. "He was the opposite of a jazz musician who's comfortable with spontaneity, changing things on the fly, working with different musicians and improvising," said Butler.

Due to Michael's perfectionism or to his insecurity, the "live" *Symphonica* album would be only half-live. Plans had been made to record the orchestra at AIR and the vocals in concert; those would be spliced together phrase by phrase, if need be, from dozens of performances. It was a tricky process, and Steve Sidwell, the trumpeter and conductor who had played with Michael on and off since Wham!, was there to coordinate it all.

Obviously no album could be released during the tour, but Michael didn't care; he was more concerned with the shows. He took command of the entire production: the stage design, the mix, the amount of reverb on his voice, and most of all the video. Abstract, kaleidoscopic figures would shift slowly behind him; they evoked an LSD trip. Deep red and blue washes would underscore the moodiness of the event.

For all this hands-on involvement, Michael seemed more distant and protected than ever. The brass section included trumpeter Paul Spong, who had last played with Michael in Wham!. He witnessed "an absolutely different man" than the one he remembered. "Early on, you could just talk to George. He was the same as you and me. But in 2011, there were so many people around him, terrified of what you were gonna say to him. I felt really sorry for him. I thought, 'Nobody's gonna be able to tell you whether that shirt looks stupid on you today.'"

At one rehearsal, Spong managed to hug him and exchange a few words. "I said, 'I'm so sorry to hear about all the shit you've been dealing with the past few years.'"

Michael looked at him with a glint in his eye and answered, "Which bit of shit in particular, Paul?"

At that moment, said Spong, "I knew Yog was there, inside."

•••

At the final Symphonica rehearsals, a happy Michael delivered love songs into the face of a swarthy, bearded, muscular beau with brooding eyes. "My lovely new man," as Michael called him, was Fadi Fawaz, a Lebanese hairdresser who had been raised in Australia. He wasn't exactly new in Michael's life, though. According to the singer, they had hooked up in 2008, before he left Kenny; Fawaz would later claim that Michael's penchant for GHB had put him off. Two years later, he didn't seem to mind it.

Whereas the clean-cut Goss had been far from Michael's type, Fawaz, thirteen years his junior, was physically his ideal. To add to the allure, Fawaz had done gay porn under a pseudonym, Isaac Mazar, for Cazzo, a Berlin-based company. Jazz singer Caesar Gergess, who was also Lebanese, worked briefly in the office. Fawaz, he said, "was like George's escort, or gigolo. I think Fadi took advantage of that and liked it. Who would say no to going out with George Michael?"

Although labeled a "fine art photographer," there is scant public record of it; Fawaz was, in fact, a skilled hairdresser with numerous celebrity clients at a top London salon, Daniel Mikhael Haute Coiffure. Once word had leaked that he was George Michael's new man, fans reportedly began showing up at the salon to gawk and ask questions, and Michael encouraged him to quit. Soon he would give his lover a credit card, which meant that Fawaz had little motivation to work.

Now he was arm candy for an aging star; Michael even took him to meet Madonna. The singer tweeted beefcake photos of Fawaz along with breathless captions. One picture, taken on a beach, appeared with the exclamation: "Sun, sand, and a bit of this doesn't hurt either :) !!" Alongside the impeccably well-mannered singer, Fawaz struck most of Michael's intimates as gauche and often rude. Niall Flynn tried to be friendly, but it was hard. "George was obviously a smart man, and enjoyed having conversations with people where he'd get something out of it. With Fadi it was just blank."

But Michael wanted to believe he'd found love. He even told Paul Stag goodbye, although he later changed his mind.

Regardless of that, Fawaz remained Michael's boyfriend, and he served as a security blanket as *Symphonica* took wing. His cocky self-confidence seemed far in the past. "I'm looking a little less bloated," he said wryly to Morten Resen, a Danish TV host. But he seemed less comfortable in his skin than ever. For his whole adult life, he had "wished I was someone else," he confessed. "I haven't been happy with fame since I was twenty-two. I hate the effect it has on friendships, on relationships, on your privacy—I hate it. All of it."

Even so, Michael would open his latest giant tour at the Prague State Opera House on August 22, 2011. The venue held only 1,041, a fraction of the viewers who would fill the arenas ahead, but that didn't comfort him. "I've got to admit I'm shitting myself," he said that night. Backstage, Michael kept the marijuana burning. "I could smell it from his dressing room," said David Finck. Before showtime, his four backup singers dropped by for a nightly ritual: They and Michael would warm up together by harmonizing on an old spiritual, "This Little Light of Mine."

A few minutes later they left to take their place onstage. Escorted by security, Michael walked to the shadows beneath the center LED screen and waited. The orchestra, bathed in blue, began playing music that would have fit the memorial of a deceased president. Michael appeared in silhouette, singing a few lines from one of the bleakest songs on *Patience*, "Through": "I think it's over . . . No one else to blame for where I stand today."

He emerged from the darkness, wearing a purple-lapeled black Armani suit. "He was not a big guy," said Finck, "but I thought, Jesus Christ, this guy is bigger than life." As Michael sang, a red geometric shape unfolded behind him like a pulsing heart.

Audiences were not prepared for the somberness of Symphonica. Michael had aged into a fragile treasure who sat for many songs. Without his old breath control, his singing had become conversational. Michael *was* a crooner now, and his vulnerability made Symphonica intensely poignant. "I'm gonna do my best for you," he told the audience.

Over the next two hours, he gave a sober summation of his life. The prevailing theme was disappointment. "Praying for Time" had taken on an end-of-the-world resignation. "John and Elvis Are Dead" acknowledged what Michael had never considered in his youth: that even the immortal gods of pop were destined to die just like everyone else. In Rihanna's "Russian Roulette," Michael sang: "As my life flashes before my eyes, I'm wondering, will I ever see another sunrise?" A galloping rhythm behind him seemed like a march toward doom; the song ended with a gunshot sound. "You've Changed," one of the last songs Billie Holiday recorded, described the heartbreak of watching the spark fade from a loved one's eyes. Decades later Michael had written "Cowboys and Angels," an expression, in waltz time, of never feeling worthy of love. Henry Hey opened with a piano solo that evoked the saddest of Chopin's preludes; Mark McLean's whispery drumming made the song spin in mid-air. Every now and then, a cold shiver of strings blew in.

The show eulogized many of Michael's losses. He kissed off the United States for good in "Going to a Town." The song, he explained, told of "the terrible, terrible effect of the religious right on gay rights in America," but it was he who felt victimized. "I'm so tired of you, America," he sang. "Do you really think you go to hell for having loved?" On the center screen, a burning cross metamorphosed into the word LOVE. Introducing "You Have Been Loved," Michael said simply: "This song is for my mother." Soon he would add Anselmo to that dedication. On July 23 of that year, Amy Winehouse had died at twenty-seven, felled by alcohol poisoning and heavy drug use. With Winehouse projected behind him, Michael sang one of her darkest songs, "Love Is a Losing Game."

Occasionally, a bit of self-deprecating wit leavened the mood. "True Faith," he said was about "the nature of addiction . . . about which I know zero." Otherwise, Michael leaned on the audience for energy, asking them to clap along with "My Baby Just Cares for Me" and to snap on "Father Figure." He didn't dance during the swaggering Nina Simone big-band arrangement of "Feeling Good"; he left that to his friend Dita Von Teese, a burlesque idol, who smiled, bumped, and twirled on video. Michael loved Rob Mathes's arrangement of "Brother, Can You Spare a Dime"; now he let it carry him. He shirked the high notes or released them quickly, and couldn't manage his former big ending. Now the beggar in the song had weariness as well as braggadocio; the effect was more dramatic than ever.

Throughout the show, he poured out his heart to the audience as though they were his most trusted mates. Sometimes he fought back tears. For all his rhapsodizing about Fadi, onstage he sang to the ghost of Anselmo and pined for Kenny. "This man," he confessed, "has brought me a lot of joy and a lot of pain." With that in mind, he unveiled one of the show's only new songs, "Where I Hope You Are." He had written it for Goss, he noted. The song meandered tunelessly but made its point: "Oh, but there was a time / All I had to do was look at you / The world was mine."

Each song earned the response he had hoped it would. "If I took the in-ear monitors out, all I heard was screaming," said Finck. Fans shouted, I LOVE YOU! Michael seemed genuinely touched. "You've been so gracious," he said humbly.

To close, he gave them three of the songs they wanted. In a medley of "Amazing," "I'm Your Man," and "Freedom! '90," his core band joined him at the rim of the stage. As soon as he started, the audience stood and began swaying. Michael let the backup singers and audience do most of the singing. His encore was "I Remember You," backed only by harp. "When my life is through / And the angels ask me to recall the thrill of them all . . ." he sang in a voice that suddenly sounded no older than it had in his teens. Yet Symphonica was the mature George Michael. The man whom he had longed to show the world in 1990 had at last arrived.

The concerts sold out, unaffected by a string of mostly two- and three-star reviews. This wasn't the Michael critics preferred. "Come on, cheer up, George," wrote the *Independent*'s Ben Walsh. Ludovic Hunter-Tilney of

Financial Times was puzzled by the minimal presence of the much-touted symphony orchestra. "It murmured background blandishments," he wrote, "as wallpaper-like as the patterns blossoming on an LED light screen behind the stage." Gregory Katz of Associated Press missed the "swagger and 'come and get it' sexuality" of the young Michael; the current one, he wrote, was "a more subtle singer happy to pay homage to Nina Simone, Marvin Gaye and other giants. . . . But the quality of the singing puts Michael head and shoulders ahead of the other older English rockers looking to the Great American Songbook for inspiration."

Most of the notices depressed him, but his audiences' love got him through. "I have a huge family of friends in the people I sing for," he tweeted. He wanted to give them a heartfelt token of what they'd seen. Following his night at the Prague Opera House, Michael had almost a week off. At huge cost, he rented out the theater for several days in order to tape a performance video of "Where I Hope You Are" before an invited audience. Michael flew in Andy Morahan and Mike Southon. On the day of shooting, they and the crew waited patiently for Michael. At last he showed up, but he vanished promptly into his dressing room. When he emerged, said Southon, "he was smelling of weed, a lot." Michael had demanded a monitor and a mirror by the stage so he could see how he looked at all times. "He kept saying, 'I want it slightly to the left . . . slightly to the right,' and he was getting very fidgety," Southon recalled. At the sight of one closeup he let out a pained groan. He confessed to Southon that he thought he looked old. "Come on, it happens to all of us, George," said the videographer. "There's not gonna be a single fan who gives a damn. You're a great singer." But Michael seemed inconsolable, and the video was shelved.

On he went with the tour, stopping in Denmark, Germany, Italy, France, Spain, Poland, and elsewhere. "My voice is getting stronger show by show, which I think means I can relax into the songs more," he tweeted. Wherever Symphonica played, Michael dazzled his musicians. "It was beautiful," said Paul Spong. "He lifted us up every night to perform better and better." Finck marveled at his consistency: "He never phoned it in or screwed it up."

The show was becoming even more darkly autobiographical. Michael's tender "Kissing a Fool" was out, replaced by "The Recluse," an angry rant by the British singer-rapper Benjamin Paul Balance-Drew, who called himself

Plan B. Michael could have written it himself; it depicted a man who hated what lay outside his front door. "Why don't you leave me alone?" he sang. "I ain't hurtin' nobody, why you up in my face?" The song gave him his one chance of the night to rock out; his dance-club body language made a surprise return. From his teenage record collection he exhumed "Idol" by Elton John and Bernie Taupin. Michael sang about the faded star he had become: "His face has changed, he's not the same no more. . . . I like the way his music sounded before." The memory of Anselmo haunted "Song to the Siren," written by Tim Buckley, a mythic folk-rock artist who had died of a heroin overdose at twenty-eight. Funereal, organ-like strains enveloped him as he sang about a mirage that had appeared to him at sea, much like his vision of Anselmo in that massive crowd in Rio: "And you sang, sail to me, sail to me, let me enfold you / Here I am, here I am, waiting to hold you."

Night after night he opened his heart ever wider to strangers. Then, after the show, his security detail ensured that there would be little mingling with the star. A guard whisked him to the car that would take him to a private jet headed to London. No matter how reclusive he grew, an inner core of sycophants clung on. The proof resides in a two-hour BBC radio documentary, *Up Close with George Michael*, produced during the tour and hosted by Vicki Wickham, the longtime manager of Dusty Spring-field. Authorized by Michael to speak, friends effused like talking heads in an infomercial: "one of the great voices of the last two decades!" . . . "undoubtedly handsome" . . . "extremely well-disciplined." Declared one informant: "He never once said, 'I want to be famous.' " Friends proclaimed him "incredible," "amazing."

His musicians barely saw him, but in early November, when Symphonica reached Dublin, a group of them invited Michael to dinner at a private dining room in an Italian restaurant. To their delight, he accepted. Michael loved their company; the night left them loving him even more. "George's food came first and he wouldn't touch it until everyone was served," said Finck. "He was a gentleman in every way." Michael regaled them with stories. He spoke of his first encounter with Michael Jackson at the pop star's home—"a bizarre experience for him," recalled Mark McLean. "And he talked about meeting Liza Minnelli for the first time and what a big fan he was." Quipped Michael: "I didn't know I was gay then. But it makes sense now." The next day he tweeted happily: "Went for an Italian with the band last night, stuffed my face and laughed till my sides hurt."

A week later, Symphonica reached Milan. In a throwback to the *Faith* days, Michael rented out a portion of a nightclub and threw a party for his whole touring ensemble. "He was on the dance floor," said McLean. "There were paparazzi everywhere. He had a good time."

Michael spent many of his other nights off partying with Fadi, often in glamorous island getaways. "New George Michael toyboy flexes his muscles in Venice," wrote *Vogue Italia*; Michael tweeted the headline to his fans. The article continued: "The topless twosome hung out on the balcony of a private suite, where they chatted, smoked, and took in the surrounding scenery. After stepping away from the balcony, the singer and his companion left their hotel and jumped onto a boat to navigate Venice's many canals."

Michael's GHB use continued, and he inhaled various forms of smoke relentlessly. "He seemed to have no respect for his body," said Phil Palmer. In late October, Michael came to London's Royal Albert Hall for four shows. During the first, his head and back were in agony and his heart pounded; he also had a temperature. Michael told himself he had probably caught the bug that had stricken several members of the company. The next day he felt no better, and had to cancel. A day later he tweeted: "It's such a horrific thought that people turn up and are turned away . . . The guilt is overwhelming, but this time I had absolutely no choice. Was feverish yesterday but feeling better today." Without seeing a doctor, he resumed his Albert Hall run and kept touring. At one performance, he looked down at Elton John, sound asleep in a prime seat. Afterward, John told Michael that his voice had sounded below par. Later Michael exploded: "*That fucking asshole! That fucking bastard! Sleeping during the fucking concert!*"

On November 17, Symphonica played Olympiahalle in Munich. At lunchtime, Michael needed to lie down; he felt odd. That night, said Palmer, "you could sense there was something not right. And you could sense that he was not happy." Four days later he flew into Vienna to play the Stadthalle—the forty-eighth show of the tour. A photographer snapped him and Fadi on the balcony of the Hotel Imperial, smoking. By six P.M. the stage was set and the musicians were at dinner. None of them knew that Michael would not be performing. That day, in his suite, he had begun suffering from chest pains. He was coughing, and by dinnertime he could barely breathe. A doctor was called. The news was disturbing: Michael had to head straight to the hospital. He fought it; he wanted to do the show first. But his advisors demanded he cancel.

With fans already milling outside Stadthalle, a tour manager told the orchestra and crew that there would be no show. "The details were very vague," said Ben Butler. "We heard, 'He's not well.' That could have been anything."

An ambulance took Michael to nearby Rudolfinerhaus, the most respected private clinic in Vienna. Doctors diagnosed him with streptococcus pneumonia—an alarming bacterial form of the illness. From there, Michael was rushed to intensive care at Vienna General Hospital.

What about the tour? His management scrambled to throw together a plan. The whole company was sent to Strasbourg, France, for the next show, on November 23. For insurance purposes, everyone had to go through the motions of setting up and preparing to play. They were kept in the dark about Michael's condition; for the moment, no one knew the fate of Symphonica. Before showtime, the company learned that Strasbourg, too, was off. The next day they were sent to Cardiff, Wales, where Symphonica was slated for two shows. On November 25, the day before the first one, they got the news: The remaining fourteen shows had been canceled. Everyone but Michael was going home. "That's when we realized that he was very sick—worse than any of us knew," Butler said.

CHAPTER TWENTY-SEVEN

DR. CHRISTOPH ZIELINSKI, THE chairman of Rudolfinerhaus, and Thomas Staudinger, another of Michael's physicians, announced that the singer had "severe community-acquired pneumonia." Speaking to the BBC, David Austin blamed it on the arenas—"germs are flying around there"—and on Michael's exhaustion. But the real cause, said a close friend of Michael's, was "partying too hard."

The rumor began instantly that Michael had AIDS. Connie Filippello rushed to refute it: "George Michael is ill with pneumonia; any other speculation regarding his illness is unfounded and untrue." But the suspicion was not unfounded. Streptococcus pneumonia was thirteen times more common in HIV-positive people, whose compromised immune systems can fail at fighting the bacteria. The statistic rose among smokers.

For now, all that mattered was saving Michael's life. Doctors shot him full of antibiotics, but his family was informed he might die. Soon his father and sisters, along with Fadi, had gathered at his bedside. Michael's lungs had filled with fluid; he needed an emergency tracheotomy—the insertion of a breathing tube, attached to a ventilator, into the windpipe through an incision in the lower throat. Though the cutting occurred below the voice box, the resultant scarring could endanger his singing. But doctors saw no choice. The tube would be almost unendurable unless he were placed in a medically induced coma—a risky process in itself, for it lowers blood pressure and reduces blood flow to parts of the brain. Nonetheless, an anesthesiologist put him out with an infusion of powerful sedatives; it would continue for as long as needed. From there, the tracheotomy was performed.

It went well, but Michael was still wracked with a potentially deadly infection. For the next three weeks, doctors struggled to quell the pneumonia. In mid-December, they deemed him well enough to regain consciousness. He awakened slowly, recalling nothing of what happened to him and barely knowing who or where he was. "Apparently I did about two days of standup comedy," he said later. It spilled out of him in a "vaguely Bristolian" accent—rural British bumpkin-talk, mimicked by comics. Once he was lucid, he felt like a "feeble old man." Michael, said a friend, "was like a skeleton." His muscles had atrophied, and he could not stand up unassisted: "I literally had to learn to walk again."

One thing he knew for sure: He did *not* want to spend Christmas in this hospital. His release before the holidays was approved. Before doctors sent him home, they strongly urged him to take 2012 off to allow his extremely compromised lungs to mend. Smoking could kill him. Post-traumatic stress disorder (PTSD) often followed comas and near-death experiences, and Michael was urged to seek counseling.

On Friday, December 23, 2011, he flew home to London, accompanied by Fawaz. The press awaited him in Highgate. Finally, a car pulled up, and into the freezing air stepped Michael in a black overcoat. Ashen and gaunt, he wobbled as he walked a few steps, carrying a potted rose plant he'd received as a gift. The black-and-gray scarf around his neck covered his scar.

Michael and the press had crossed swords for three decades. But on this day they could not help but look at him in sympathy. He stood in front of a lush Christmas tree that he paid every year to have installed in the tiny park in front of his house. Though gasping for breath, he talked, fighting back tears, for ten minutes. He confirmed that he had nearly died, although his PR, he said, had tried to deny it. "I'm very weak," he confessed, "but I feel amazing. This has changed my life. I'm a new man." Thank-yous poured out of him: to "everybody in that IC unit that made sure I'm still here today"; to his family, friends, and fans for caring.

Already he had decided to ignore a part of the doctors' orders. He would go back on the road in September, he said, to make up the canceled shows. "Absolutely without question," he said, "the plan is to play to every single person who had a ticket." He vowed to stop taking his good fortune for granted. "If I wasn't spiritual enough before the last four, five weeks," he reflected, "then I certainly am now. . . . I have to believe that somebody up there thinks I've still got some work to do." Michael wished "a very, very, very, very, *very* Merry Christmas to everyone." And he went inside.

That day, he began jubilantly tweeting. "Hey everyone, your favorite homo is home :)))" . . . "I'm back and I'm proud, though not very loud . . . . . ."

(which, I assure you, will be temporary!) MERRY XMAS TO ALL OF YOU! ISN'T LIFE GRAND !! X."

Two days later, he enjoyed the "best Christmas I can remember, surrounded by the people I love." They included his sisters, Fawaz, and so many others that he boasted of having "a house full of sleeping guests"; more were coming the next day. "We stuffed and laughed ourselves silly," he said. "And knowing that Christmas could have been very different this year for everyone at that table . . . I'm such a lucky man." Fawaz did his own tweeting: "I cannot stop smiling, the best day ever. He is getting better and better. Nothing to worry about, happy days."

• • •

Michael's heart did not stay light for long. To quit marijuana had meant tossing away his daily crutch of almost twenty years; the anxiety it caused was almost unbearable. His mood turned even bleaker when he learned that a member of a radical group, Christians for a Moral America, had sent out a series of chilling tweets about him. "Pray for George Michael's demise. He has chosen a satanic lifestyle and must meet an appropriate end. . . . Apparently George Michael has AIDS. Figures since he's a homosexual and it goes with the territory. Another sodomite bites the dust?"

Michael retweeted the morbid pronouncements. While noting how many kindhearted Christians he knew, he branded the people who had wished him dead as "totally fucked up cocksucking bastards. And not in a good way . . . . . . !"

Most of the time he sat around the house, bored. When a doctor told him he was recovering nicely, he rushed to book a beach vacation for himself and Fawaz. In late January, he tweeted: "First real holiday in many years. Bliss. Not the slightest chance of controversy. I may have to flash room service."

While they were away, another star's life met a tragic end. On the night of February 11, 2012, he and Fawaz were in their hotel room, watching TV. Suddenly they found themselves watching an ambulance carry the dead body of Whitney Houston out of the Beverly Hilton Hotel. The singer had been due at a pre-Grammy party in the same hotel, hosted by Clive Davis, who had signed her to her breakthrough record deal. By the end, Houston's voice had been ravaged by crack cocaine, which Michael had smoked for years. The Davis event had already begun when word came that a heavily drugged Houston, who suffered from heart disease, had drowned in the tub. Photographers encircled the tall vehicle that drove her corpse away; they held their cameras high and jumped, trying to get a shot of the singer's body through the windows.

Michael was in shock. *"Change the channel!"* he blurted to Fadi.

"Why?"

"Why d'ya think?"

The irony of the moment chilled him. He and Houston had become stars at the same time—and he could well have died within three months of her.

It was a rude awakening, and it reminded him of his reason for living. "I needed to throw myself into music, and thank God that I did," he told the BBC's Chris Evans. His gay dance-music project had lain dormant for months, but now, he said, "I've been working seven days a week, and so far I'm thrilled with it." His *Patience* team—Johnny Douglas, James Jackman, and Niall Flynn—were back; once more he leaned on them to inspire him. "We would throw ideas at George, some chords and a groove," said Flynn. "George would be sitting at home and he'd come down to his computer and write little ideas over them. Some were pretty weird, and some were fucking awful."

But two tracks, based on fragments from Jackman, stood out. Both of them suggested that the source of so much of Michael's pain—his youthful relationship with his father—continued to gnaw at him. "The Fag and White Minstrel Show" (later retitled "Alone") took the form of a letter from a dad to his estranged gay son, who pours out regrets for the family's hurtful words and pleads for a visit. "So sorry for believing in the fag and white minstrel show," says the father, referring to old gay stereotypes and epithets. An insistent, pounding beat evoked stoned nights on the dance floor and pained memories that no music could drown out. In "This Is How (We Want You to Get High)," a son lashes out at a father's cruelty: "I never picked a fight in my life / Or raised a hand to my wife / Or saw my children as things to bully." He had intended to give young gays something to dance about, but gay life, as he'd said before, had not been something to celebrate, and he couldn't hide it.

The rescheduled Symphonica shows lay ahead in September and October, and the live album needed his attention, too. Phil Ramone's health was failing;

soon he would die of an aortic aneurysm. With Michael also ill, confusion had reigned. Niall Flynn had been traveling with the show, and he flew home with hard drives full of recordings. He began piecing together vocal tracks phrase by phrase, in search of the perfection Michael craved. In "Praying for Time," Flynn recalled editing "like, a hundred bits." Not everything fit the orchestral prerecordings; on the road, Michael had tinkered with the arrangements, as had David Austin, who, as his friend grew weaker, had assumed the role of majordomo. "David had a lot of opinions about what should happen with George's music," said Henry Hey. "Often David would try to make changes that weren't necessarily cleared with George." Hey would inform Michael, who okayed some of Austin's commands and retracted others.

It was up to Ramone to weave all the chaos into an album. "It became a huge mess," said Jill Dell'Abate. "Even the engineer couldn't keep track, and Phil was losing his mind. He was getting yelled at all the time by managers. He felt like he was being given an impossible task." According to Flynn, Ramone "was sending stuff to his son, who was Auto-Tuning it. George didn't like it."

The project would not be released for nearly two years. In the meantime, Michael got a lightning flash. He decided to turn catastrophe into art, as he had with "Outside." In April 2012 he wrote a song, "White Light," about having beaten death. Sitting at home with a synthesizer and vocoder, Michael detailed his survival. "I'm not through . . . I'm alive, I'm alive," he sang, although the track's droning hum and thumping beats made him sound more robotic than human. One line, "Change that channel, that could have been me," recalled the night he had seen Houston wheeled into an ambulance on TV—although without the back story, no one would know what he meant.

But Michael was immensely pleased with "White Light," and planned to release it in June on the thirtieth anniversary of "Wham Rap!" "I love that something so disturbing can be turned into something that has people dancing all over the summer, I hope," he told Chris Evans.

To boost sales, he undertook a video that he hoped would be his hottest since "Freedom! '90." Its director, Ryan Hope, had released an arty documentary, *Skin*, in which Damien Hirst and other artists glorified tattoo culture. The "White Light" video was equally high-flown. It starred Michael, Kate Moss, flocks of black ravens and white doves, and a swarm of sexy men in an elaborately metaphorical saga of endurance. A car accident occurs at night;

hospital imagery—a needle in closeup, a surgeon's masked face—suggests a fight to save a life. Michael appears, clothed in black and peering forebodingly. A zebra strolls past him in a dark, deserted field. Nineties-style MTV devices are cut in: Shirtless male models writhe and preen; Moss whips her hair and pouts dramatically. A policeman points a gun at Michael. Moss flips a coin in slow motion, then the gun is fired. Michael falls in slow motion. The coin is apparently heads, for he lives.

Having narrowly escaped the fate of Houston and Michael Jackson, Michael wanted the world to know it. He agreed to sing at the closing ceremony of the 2012 Olympics, to be held on August 12 at London's Olympic Stadium. His first appearance in nine months, it placed him before his biggest audience since Live Aid: 750 million TV viewers. A £20 million marathon of grandiosity, the show extolled British culture, from Shakespeare to the Spice Girls. An actor portraying Winston Churchill stood atop Big Ben; a gymnastic troupe from *Britain's Got Talent* twirled and flexed to the Beatles; an array of supermodels, including Moss, strutted in British couture; the Pet Shop Boys barreled in on rickshaws. For a segment entitled "A Symphony of British Music," Annie Lennox, the Who, Take That, and Michael had all been asked to sing one of their hits. Michael was asked to do "Freedom! '90." He said yes—but only if he could perform "White Light," too. Reluctantly, the producers consented.

Rarely had Michael been so nervous, especially over how he would sound. Prior to his entrance, he gulped two glasses of wine, then took his place in the center of a blue-lit sunburst of runways. He opened with "Freedom! '90." Although his pitch remained almost flawless, he had insisted on using Auto-Tune, and Niall Flynn, whom Michael had brought, cringed at what he heard: "They were hitting the tuner too hard and it was pushing his voice all over the place." As he sang one of the defining lyrics of his career, with its pivotal line, "Sometimes the clothes do not make the man," he swiveled around wearing a version of his *Faith* clone garb. But a graying handlebar mustache and soul patch and his spinal impairment made him look as strained as an oldies act.

Then his recording of "White Light" was cued. With his band and backup singers in place and going through the motions, Michael lip-synched to his vocoder-processed vocal. Amid all the arena noise and echo, the words, which were already hard to comprehend, went for nothing. Why, many wondered, was he singing this?

While Michael was onstage, a blowout party of his own planning had begun at his home in Highgate. "Everywhere you looked," said Johnny Douglas, "was another face you recognized"—Moss, the Spice Girls, Liam Gallagher. Guests visited a luxury spread of food and alcohol; some did drugs in the darker corners. In the garden, a group of people gathered in front of a large TV screen to cheer on their host's shaky performance.

Around midnight, Michael arrived—"quite pissed off," said Douglas. Friends flocked to him to gush over his performance, but he knew it had not gone well. Danny Cummings, who had played with him that night, had barely gotten to talk with Michael, and there was little chance of it now. Finally, the percussionist caught him at a free moment and said good night. "We stood for a minute and talked. I gave him a hug and told him I loved him." It was the last time they would ever speak.

Michael made a few trips to a dance floor created inside; thereafter he went upstairs. "Normally he would have been all over that party," said Douglas. At nine A.M., Douglas and Flynn lingered along with Moss, Gallagher, and a few others. When Michael emerged, Douglas, too, saw his beloved employer for the last time.

That day, Michael found himself panned by the press for having forced his low-fi dance tune on a jubilee of the best of Britain. Steve Anderson, musical director for Kylie Minogue, observed on the BBC News that the occasion was "not the time for new single promo. I'm genuinely surprised he was allowed to do this." *New Musical Express* posted Seth Abramovitch's review of the song. "'White Light,'" he wrote, "could do for George what 'Believe' did for Cher—make him cool again for five minutes before relegating him to a life in Vegas." The track did not even achieve that. "White Light" hit No. 15 in England and faded quickly. It would be the last commercially issued single in his lifetime. Michael hated the naysayers—"Please join me in telling them to fuck off!" he tweeted—but he was more hurt than angry. "It's not a piece of shit," he told Flynn. "Why have people got a problem with it?"

•••

On September 4 and 6, more than thirty thousand Austrians filled the Wiener Stadthalle in Vienna. Symphonica was back on tour, starting with the city whose doctors had saved his life. As a thank-you, a thousand local medical workers attended as his guests. The show found Michael back on track after the Olympics debacle; he looked rested and trim and sang with an almost dulcet clarity, thanks to his hiatus from smoking. Several of the slowest songs had been cut; he added "Father Figure," which made the crowds happier. "Doesn't it feel good to be alive?" he exclaimed.

By the time he reached the United Kingdom for a series of fifteen shows, he had yanked "White Light" from the setlist. The audiences were as enraptured with him as ever, but, as before, most critics greeted this solemn and dignified Michael with low enthusiasm. To David Sinclair of the *Times*, Michael had "reinvented himself as a superstar cabaret singer."

Hardly anyone knew how tortured he was. He later spoke of "the major anxiety that has plagued me since I left Austria last December." Michael showed many of the symptoms of PTSD—dark, recurring thoughts about his trauma, nightmares, and a compulsion to withdraw. He had hoped performing would heal him; it hadn't, and he made a bleak admission to Chris Evans: "That feeling, I'm glad to be alive—I'd love to say that that lasts for months and months but it doesn't. You soon take for granted that you're alive again."

For years, he had certainly taken his voice for granted. But pneumonia had weakened his remaining stamina. Now singing was work, and he had to pace himself carefully. "I have a feeling he was concerned that his voice was not gonna stay strong," said Henry Hey.

Michael had hoped Symphonica might find its way to the States, but that wasn't to be. On September 30, 2012, he released a statement on his website. The tour would end there in England, minus its Australian finale—"which breaks my heart," he said. "Unfortunately I seriously underestimated how difficult this year would be. All that's left for me to do is apologize to my wonderful Australian fan base and to promise faithfully that as soon as I complete these shows here in the U.K. I will receive the treatment which is so long overdue." He gave no hint of ever returning.

Elton John agreed to sub for him at the Perth Arena, the first of the canceled stops. On Symphonica's closing night, October 17, 2012, at Earls Court, he threw a party for the company and "gave everybody a hug goodbye," said David Finck. He made sure his musicians would be paid for the missed shows.

Once home, he returned, with faltering confidence, to the dance album. Fans had filed it away among the many projects that Michael had "said were coming that never came," noted Chris Heath. All he had was a handful of tracks in varying stages of completion. Most sounded dated and derivative. His obsession with the vocoder, by now a dated tool, mystified a lot of listeners.

Near the start of the project, he had promised a track that would make his straight listeners squirm. "Every Other Lover" began with the line: "You say, shut your mouth and suck me"; from there, it sounded like a drugged effort whose lyrics defied comprehension. "All those one-track minds, well, it turns out that they're in luck / in the capital city of cock." Which city that was, he didn't say. Like many of the other tracks, "Every Other Lover" was set to nineties-style house music, replete with cliché chord progressions and electronics.

One song showed promise. Michael had written "This Kind of Love" for Elton John to sing in *Trojan Souls,* his aborted all-star album effort of the nineties. It seemed to fit the album's gay-empowerment theme. "You don't have to be so scared. . . . You just have to believe in this kind of love," sang Michael over a slow-burning, seventies-style soul groove. His voice, minimally processed, sounded raspy and deep—a sultry sound, but not one he had adopted for the occasion; it was all he had left.

Michael hoped he had created something worth hearing, but Douglas had doubts. "George wasn't a dance producer; he was a soulful, classy singer-songwriter. The only thing he wasn't good at was doing cool shit. It all went very cheesy because that's not his world." Universal Music U.K. had given Michael an advance for the album, but the relationship collapsed, leaving the project officially dead.

A few tracks leaked onto the internet. A chat group on the website Popjustice debated them. The participants included a few George Michael defenders ("I don't think Kate Bush is ever slagged off for taking 10 years between albums") and others who seemed to have given up on him. One of them posted: "I've reconciled myself to the fact that his peak years have long gone. Now if his records are listenable it's almost a triumph." A fellow contributor lamented: "I'm afraid I can't trust George's own quality control anymore. Nothing he's done in the last decade shows that he knows best." Amid these caveats was the saddest comment of all: "Can't believe there was a time when I considered him to be my all time favourite popstar."

With his two greatest gifts—his songwriting and his voice—in seeming decline, Michael's incentive was broken. In 2013, Flynn saw him in a recording studio (AIR) for the last time. "We were in the middle of doing this record and he just kind of stopped," said Flynn.

Michael had continued to exchange occasional emails with his old friend Judy Wieder. He confided that he felt lost. "I think he was trying to recover himself—find out what he wanted to do," she said.

● ● ●

Michael's five-year driving ban had about two years to run; Alex Georgiou, Andros's cousin, with whom the singer was close, sometimes served as chauffeur. For Michael, not driving meant a loss of independence, and also made it harder for him to get to Hampstead Heath. Now he relied mainly on indoor, sometimes weekend-long drug-fueled binges with escorts. Not all of them were discreet; Piers Morgan would later report that Michael had been blackmailed by a French one. The singer's relationship with Paul Stag temporarily resumed; always he asked Stag via text to bring the "champagne" or "champers." Michael now relied on GHB to buffer almost every responsibility, from mixing sessions to meetings with his lawyers. After Stag was gone, he found other suppliers. He was also smoking crystal meth.

Frequently he stayed up all night and slept the day away. Fawaz would come downstairs to find his boyfriend "passed out in the chair." Sometimes Michael nodded off in restaurants, at parties, even in the studio.

The incident that boded worst for his future happened on the afternoon of May 16, 2013. Michael's Range Rover was barreling down the northbound side of the M1 motorway, on the fourth lane, near the center. His car had left London and was passing through Hertfordshire, north of the city. A friend of Michael's drove; next to him sat one of the singer's physicians. Michael was behind the driver's seat. He had not fastened his seat belt.

Suddenly Michael wrenched open the door and tumbled onto the third lane. "He bounced several times as drivers swerved frantically to avoid him," noted the *Daily Mail*. One of the cars belonged to Katherine Fox, a young nanny. Fox slammed on her breaks and blocked the lane with her car to shield him from other drivers.

"I saw blood everywhere," she said. It poured from the back of his head and from his forehead and ran onto his teeth. Michael's black-and-gold Adidas sweat suit was shredded; his sneakers had been wrenched off. "His sunglasses were also in the road," said Fox. "I could hear the crunch as cars drove over them." Michael lay on the ground, speechless and in shock. "Even if I had known who it was I probably wouldn't have recognized him," said Fox, who had called for emergency help. "The guy holding him was quite scared. He kept saying to George, 'Are you all right, mate?'"

When paramedics arrived, they carried Michael to the east side of the motorway. The northbound M1 was blocked off, halting traffic for miles. Finally, Michael was airlifted to a trauma center in London. He stayed hospitalized for a week and a half. During that time, his team rushed to deny the accident was related to anything suicidal. An unnamed "friend" told the *Mirror*: "There is no mystery—he was just trying to shut the door. George has been perfectly happy and in a great place." Connie Filippello issued a statement: "He's being treated for superficial cuts and bruises but is fine. We have no further comment."

A reporter rang Michael's bell in Highgate. Fadi said through the intercom: "He's perfectly fine. . . . He suffered a few bruises, but it's nothing to worry about. . . . I've no idea what happened."

Auto experts knew that a Range Rover's doors have a highly secure electronic locking system, making it virtually impossible for them to open accidentally. But the investigation was closed, and Hertfordshire police announced that to prosecute Michael for not having worn a seat belt would go against "public interest."

Michael neither confirmed nor denied the suicide rumors. But Fawaz would later insist that his partner had, in fact, tried to kill himself. He recalled asking Michael: "Aren't you glad May 16 didn't happen?"

"No," said Michael.

"He wanted to die so badly," claimed Fawaz. "I think life stopped for him a long time ago. Everyone wanted him because of what and who he is. 'Everyone wants me alive,' is what he would say." Around that time, Michael was found in his pool at Highgate, hypothermic after having been in the water all night. According to a friend, he had set up a little shrine of framed photos of his loved ones. Chris Cameron didn't doubt that Michael wanted to move on. "It was almost like, Mum is there, Anselmo is there—this is where I'm going to have to be." Michael said as much to Chris Evans: "I'd love to believe somehow there's an afterlife. Because I've lost people."

CHAPTER TWENTY-EIGHT

THE M1 INCIDENT MADE Michael withdraw even further. In late 2013, fans found his website shut down, although a statement was released, promising a big year ahead. It would include the long-awaited release of the *Symphonica* album as well as a video to accompany its first single, "Let Her Down Easy," Terence Trent D'Arby's ballad about a vulnerable young woman's coming of age.

Brainstorming for a concept, Michael envisioned its heroine as a shy performer in a circus—a stranger in a strange land. "We found a really old family-run circus that was based in Barcelona on the waterfront," said Vaughan Arnell, who directed. "We went over there. All the cast were members of the family." One exception was Hannah Janes, a winsome British model, age twenty. The singer had chosen her out of a large group of auditioners. He himself would not appear. Michael felt more self-conscious about his appearance than ever, and he told Arnell: "I don't want people to look at me. I want the music to speak for itself." He sat out the filming—a first for him—and Skyped from home to check up on things.

Made in black-and-white, the video looks as stylized and glamorous as a *Vanity Fair* fashion spread. On a bare theater-in-the-round stage, a sad clown plays accordion. Two dancers perform a smoldering pas de deux. Janes enters in silhouette through billowing curtains and catches the eye of the circus heartthrob. The video concludes in R-rated territory: Janes drops her filmy white robe and stands naked, her pubic area hidden by a glittery white triangle.

Hoping to add a touch of the profound, Michael had Arnell open the video by displaying a quote from Voltaire.

It is an infantile superstition of the human spirit
That virginity would be thought a virtue
And not the barrier that separates ignorance from knowledge

Those words could have applied to "I Want Your Sex," "Father Figure," "Fastlove," or "Outside," all of which were based on the theme that "sex is natural, sex is good." But Michael's vision of sex had always had much to do with anger, shame, and transgression. He had been making music videos almost since the dawn of the art; some had sparked as much controversy as anything on MTV. But in three decades the genre had changed radically; Hollywood-style productions with huge budgets had given way to cheaply-made attention-grabbers, designed for viewing on a smartphone. "It's a very different mentality and approach," said Yibi Hu. "Videos now have less depth, and the musicality's terrible; however, a really badly-produced one can have, like, fourteen million views in a week. Visually they need to be more sexual, more violent, more outrageous. The old-school way of storytelling—no one has the patience to sit through it anymore."

Michael, said Hu, was at a special disadvantage. "Whatever you do when you are winding down, nobody gives a shit. No one pays attention to a dying star." By this time, Hu added, "his news was all about driving his car and hitting a shop. Or jumping out of a high-speed car. He wasn't really known for his music."

The "Let Her Down Easy" video caused barely a ripple, but Michael had one more hit left in him. The *Symphonica* album was finally released on March 14, 2014. Excessive editing and corrections had stripped much of the life from it, but he and Ramone had still turned out a class project, and it debuted at No. 1 on the U.K. chart.

Whatever joy this brought him was short-lived. Panic attacks plagued him. He downed Valium daily. It dismayed his friends to see him smoking cigarettes and pot again and looking unhealthily bloated from overeating and drinking. On May 30, the *Times* reported that "the former Wham! singer" had been taken by ambulance to the hospital "for an undisclosed ailment." The *Sun* dug deeper, and found that Michael's darkest fears about ending up like Whitney Houston had nearly come true. An unidentified person found him unconscious in his bathtub in Highgate. The mysterious "ailment" was revealed to have been a GHB overdose.

This was not his first OD, but the nature of it hinted at how reckless he'd become with a drug that made overdosing easy. Creatively it had paralyzed him. Niall Flynn had moved to Thailand, and Michael asked him to fly in to work with him on the dance album. Flynn rented a flat in London at his own expense. "I'd go around George's house," Flynn said. "He wouldn't be able to look at you or talk to you." Michael didn't work a single day. Finally, the engineer went home, broke.

A friend of the guitarist and songwriter Barry Reynolds was corresponding with Michael. "He would occasionally send her cards saying he wasn't really interested in life, that there was nothing there for him," recalled Reynolds. Friends begged Michael to go back to rehab; ultimately a psychiatrist talked him into it. The place chosen for him, the Kusnacht Practice, was the addict's equivalent of a five-star continental resort.

Located on the shore of Lake Zürich, the center cost $130,000 and upward per week; it paid a finder's fee to doctors who sent patients there. Often they stayed for months, during which they received constant supervision. Treatment was sugar-pilled in the most extravagant ways; patients had butlers, trainers, and shoppers and lived in private villas that faced the Alps. They could play tennis, ride horses, even charter a yacht and cruise the lake. But for Michael, what really mattered at Kusnacht was its clinical director, David Smallwood, an expert in gay-related depression rooted in childhood.

In June 2015, a chauffeur picked him up at the Zürich airport and took him on the lushly scenic drive to Kusnacht. Michael's villa had a baby-grand piano and a spacious balcony. Once he settled in, he underwent the center's much-touted induction: the creation of a two-hundred-page dossier on his "unique body and brain chemistry." From there, Kusnacht offered a "biochemical restoration program" that aimed to make the brain function normally without drugs.

But Michael needed to talk, and Smallwood seemed uniquely attuned to his issues. "What we show is: 'I'm proud to be gay,'" explained the clinician. "Underneath that, we might be dying inside." Required reading was the Bible of gay dysfunction: *The Velvet Rage: Overcoming the Pain of Growing Up Gay in a Straight Man's World*, written by Alan Downs, a West Hollywood therapist. Michael related deeply to what Downs called "the deep and abiding anger that results from growing up in an environment when I learn that who I am as a gay person is unacceptable, perhaps even unlovable. . . . This anger pushes me at times to overcompensate and try to earn love and acceptance by being more, better, beautiful, more sexy—in short, to become something I believe will make me more acceptable and loved."

Michael's reps had hoped to hide his whereabouts from the press; friends who knew of it were sworn to secrecy. But there was always someone around to leak his secrets. In this case, it was Jackie Georgiou, the wife of Andros. The couple maintained ties to his circle and kept up with the gossip. In the article "George Is a Crack Addict," Jackie informed the *Sun* that Michael had been shipped off to rehab for that reason, not to mention his abuse of pot (which no one could deny) and cocaine (a drug Michael had never liked). "There were parties where he was taking drugs and collapsing and being picked up off the floor. Waking up in vomit, horrible things. He was so thin, so ill. . . . He was going to end up locked or dead."

News of the article reached Michael on the day it ran. From Switzerland he tweeted: "To my lovelies, do not believe this rubbish in the papers by someone I haven't seen for nearly 18 years. . . . I am perfectly fine. Love, The Singing Greek xxx."

But word about his rehab was greeted mostly with relief. Michael stayed in Switzerland for the better part of a year; for several months he lived at Kusnacht, then continued on as an outpatient. Yacht rides and doting butlers, though, did not go far in grounding rich patients in reality. And Michael's detox did not extend to smoking. He was photographed walking around Zürich, one hand in Fadi's, the other holding a cigarette. Fadi would later claim that Michael had tried to stab himself twenty-five times in rehab—an outlandish claim, but one that obviously revealed a man in turmoil.

In the end, Kusnacht cost him an estimated £1.5 million. While it was widely assumed that his wealth was limitless, his glamorous lifestyle—including multiple homes and hefty "allowances" to boyfriends—was draining his cash. The costly Symphonica tour had netted him little. Michael seemed stubbornly unaware. The star known for his abundant generosity could also be tight with his wallet; friends talked of how he had employed the same housekeeper for over two decades and never given her a raise. Loyal staff members received no health insurance. During Michael's rehab, Austin had reportedly tried to cut corners. Salaries were halved, retainers canceled, houses remortgaged. "It's not that George couldn't have made the money back," said Flynn. "He could have gone out on tour again. I think he was just tired."

• • •

Midway through 2016, Michael went home. The old habits returned, and there would be no more attempts at rehab. "Much stronger forces were at work—too strong, really, for someone to sort out for him," said Danny Cummings.

Still, Johnny Douglas kept trying to nudge him forward. The producer had dug up some old, unfinished songs and had ideas for reworking them. Earlier on it had been easy to call or text Michael. Now, said Douglas, "it was impossible to get hold of him. You'd have to contact his lawyer and say, 'Can you speak to George for me? I've got something that I want to play him.' And the lawyer would just cut it down." Even close longtime friends found their access barred. "Even if George agreed to have dinner," said one of them, "David would intercept the message then make sure he was around." Even Michael's family saw little of him.

Barry Reynolds, who was in recovery, knew the danger signs. "When someone's addicted like that, no one can save them but themselves. They've really got to want to be straight. The opposite of addiction is connection. When you go so deep inside yourself, it's never-ending. I think that's what happened with him. He couldn't climb his way out." Sasha Gretsay, a neighbor in Highgate, got a troubling glimpse of Michael outside his house. "I remember thinking that he looked unwell. He looked worried and older than my friend who was fifty-seven."

For most of his life, Michael had feared getting fat—a problem that had overtaken his father and his sister Melanie. "George didn't really eat a lot for years," said Flynn. "He just picked at things, drank too many Diet Cokes, to keep his weight down." But GHB is known for making users binge-eat, particularly greasy and sugary comfort foods. All of these, and the resultant weight gain, were dangerous to those afflicted with fatty liver disease, a condition Michael had developed.

He had stopped fighting excess pounds—a sign of giving up. One night he ventured out with Fadi to an Italian restaurant, Rossini, near his Goring home. As waiters circulated, carrying plates of rich pasta, fellow diners spotted Michael and gasped. Though dressed in concealing black, he was so round and bloated that he was almost unrecognizable as the George Michael of the nineties or even of Symphonica. A customer took furtive cell phone shots; they were quickly leaked to the press.

Flynn had not seen Michael since before he had gone to Kusnacht. But in September 2016, the singer summoned him to Highgate, along with James Jackman and David Austin, for a meeting. Flynn was startled at his friend's size, but Michael seemed unashamed: "He still got into his swimming trunks and went into the pool."

Michael, said Flynn, "had plans. He was talking about the work that was ahead. And he was serious about it." Most of it involved tending his legacy. An expanded reissue of *Listen Without Prejudice Vol. 1* was in the works; there was even talk of a *Mamma Mia!*-style jukebox musical, which excited him. As for the dance album, it remained in complete disarray. Michael brought up "The Fag and White Minstrel Show" and "This Is How (We Want You to Get High)," both of them collaborations with Jackman. "He said, 'I don't want those two songs released,'" recalled Flynn. Why he didn't was unclear; he may have considered them too damning of his father. Michael also nixed the ostensibly scandalous "Every Other Lover," with its mention of the "capital city of cock." Flynn thought he might be worried about embarrassing his family.

There was an additional project underway. Michael and Austin had spent months working on yet another autobiographical documentary, *Freedom*. It would focus on his love affair with Anselmo and the Sony lawsuit. One thing was certain: He did not want to be seen onscreen as he looked now. Michael had recorded narration, but it sounded stiff. Then he remembered Kirsty Young, the hostess of *Desert Island Discs*, whose interviewing he loved. He called her. Almost apologetically, he said, "I've got a strange thing to ask you." Would she come to the house and interview him—audio only—for *Freedom*? She didn't hesitate to say yes.

A representative of Michael's called her agent and asked her to name a fee. Nothing, she said—it was enough just to see him again. But Michael insisted, and Young suggested he send a donation to UNICEF, for she was its U.K. president. A day later, Michael gave the charity £50,000. "He felt that connection with vulnerable children," said Young, "because in his own middle-class way he was a vulnerable little kid."

Michael sent her a cut of the film. Around the beginning of October, she went to Goring with no formal interview prepared, just a sense of which topics to bring up. The front door opened, and there was Michael—not an assistant. A sound engineer and Austin waited inside. "It was not some brittle, flashy rock-star house," she said. "It had a Labrador and real tiles in the kitchen—very chic and stylish, with a beautiful garden."

The singer himself did not look well, and she sensed his self-consciousness. Several times that afternoon, Michael, who was then fifty-three, referred to himself as old. Indeed, he sounded like a senior Englishman; his voice was worn and graveled, and he spoke at a slow, deliberate pace, casting serious doubt as to whether he could still sing.

But with Young to guide him, Michael gave the interview of a lifetime. It touched on almost every issue of importance and every regret, of which he named many. He sounded drugged, yet looked back at his life with unprecedented clarity. Michael spoke longingly of the Wham! years; never again would he have such fun or feel so free, although he had been too fixated on success to realize it. Nor had he ever managed to feel attractive; his father's cruel early comments about his looks had left too deep a scar. Now, said Michael, he looked back at old images from his twenties and thought, "My God, you were gorgeous!"

He still worshipped his mother. It was to protect her, he said, that he had tried to hide his sexuality—"and I would do it again." But worldwide adulation had only brought a sad truth into focus: "I was still desperately lonely. . . . I had millions of lovers that I never saw, but I still deserved one, just one of them, for me." Michael broke down in tears as he recalled Anselmo: "such a beautiful companion, such an amazing person. . . . I was so proud that this was my destiny."

Time had not made him feel any less the victim over Anselmo's death, nor over his lost battle against Sony. Now, he felt, labels were exploiting artists even more ruthlessly. Michael flagged one star for having helped them do their dirty work. In 2002, Robbie Williams had signed a six-album contract deal with EMI for a reported £80 million pounds—an unprecedented payout in the United Kingdom. "I'm rich beyond my wildest dreams!" he boasted. In exchange, fumed Michael, Williams had "totally robbed everyone that came after" of the chance of getting fair terms. Williams had helped pioneer what became the industry norm: the "360 deal," in which artists who sign with a label have to turn over a considerable chunk of their income from concerts, TV specials, merchandising, publishing, sponsorship, and everything else related to performing. (Williams would later apologize for that comment; he, too, would turn cold on the label that had made him a tycoon.)

Young went on to ask Michael why he thought so many pop stars died young. That April, Prince had died at fifty-seven by overdosing on fentanyl, a pain-relieving opioid. Michael's response suggested a canny view of the downfalls of others; concerning his own, he stayed in denial. "People who are rich enough and independent enough to demand too many drugs are given them," he explained, while sidestepping inclusion in that group. Michael cited the "four video legends, as it were": Michael Jackson, Prince, Madonna, and himself. He had long believed that he and Madonna would survive the longest—"because we're sane," he said. "Not because we're the most talented." Jackson and Prince, he said, were "incredibly vulnerable, because their world view was so overshadowed by their self-obsession and their self-absorption." But that didn't apply to him, he said: "I've had my own battles, but my battles have never been extreme."

Later on, Young would ponder that answer. "We minimize our worst behaviors because it's the only way we can deal with them," she observed. "It's like, other people are alcoholics or drug addicts or beat their wives. George was a high-functioning addict; he wasn't in the gutter, so I think he had convinced himself that his story was true."

But their discussion ended on a hopeful note. "Even when I've really hit rock-bottom," he told her, "I believe that this period of down time will result in something spectacular. . . . It has to."

The recorder was switched off. Michael and Young visited for another hour or so. "We had a couple of glasses of wine and he showed me his garden and things he was gonna change. Then he said, which made me optimistic: 'The best is yet to come.'"

•••

Many of Michael's closest associates wished he would cut Fadi Fawaz from that future. "I just had dodgy feelings about that guy," said Johnny Douglas.

He wished he could tell Fawaz: "You're unemployed, you're just bumming around. You hooked up with George. He's a meal ticket." In years to come, Fawaz talked of having scolded Michael over his drug use. Yet a few years later, according to the *Daily Mail*, London police reported finding Fawaz in possession of Class A drugs, the most dangerous group.

Although he still had access to Michael's bounty, they had been sleeping in separate bedrooms and fighting a lot. "George had tried to finish the relationship many times," argued Flynn. "But he found it impossible to confront people. When you haven't said bye-bye and that person's still living in your house"—the one in Goring—"it's very hard to say, 'Out you go.'"

In the fall of 2016, however, he had his documentary and other projects to distract him. On December 9, an Italian fan got a glimpse, through a window, of Michael in the studio of his Highgate house. A cell phone video caught the singer watching what appeared to be his documentary. He rocked gently in his chair to the beat of a song and smoked an e-cigarette. David Austin helped shepherd one more recycling of the singer's past. Nile Rodgers, cofounder of the 1970s band Chic and a gigantically successful producer of disco, funk, and soul artists, was hired to create a remix of "Fantasy," an obscure Michael B-side from 1990. It would be added to the *Listen Without Prejudice* reissue and released as the first single. On the morning of Friday, December 23, Rodgers stopped by the Goring house for a business meeting.

The town glowed with holiday cheer, along with a melancholy touch, as "Last Christmas" played on the radio and in department stores, restaurants, and shops.

For Michael, the holiday was traditionally a family event. Yet this time his only company was Fawaz, who joined him in Goring on the twenty-third and told others of their plans for a Christmas lunch for two. The scenario confused some of Michael's friends, who believed the couple had split up. For Michael, it may have simply been an antidote to loneliness, although he could have spent those days with almost anyone he wanted. Christmas Eve had been his mother's birthday, and that always made him miss her even more. Normally he attended midnight mass at a local church, but not in 2016. Michael had also loved Goring's annual Christmas Eve procession, in which thousands of people held lit torches and sang carols as they paraded through the streets. From his window, Michael would watch the parade and gaze at one of his annual gifts to the neighborhood: a big fir tree, decorated with English gentility and placed in the square opposite his front door. But this December no passerby would glimpse George Michael.

From the night of the twenty-third until Christmas afternoon, the only known witness to what occurred at Michael's home was Fawaz. As he gave a series of accounts, fans on social media and reporters for various news outlets, including the *Daily Mail*, pointed out multiple inconsistencies and contradictions. Either on the twenty-third or twenty-fourth, Fawaz said, the two men "upset each other," and Michael retired to his room. At first he claimed he didn't see Michael at all on Christmas Eve. Instead, said Fawaz, he napped the afternoon away, then glanced a few times at Michael's door, which was slightly ajar, but didn't check on him—this despite his claim that he had often feared his partner would die in bed of an overdose.

The mystery grew when Fawaz claimed that he slept in his car on Christmas Eve. He told of having considered driving back to London, then changing his mind—but why? Robert Sepúlveda, Jr., a Puerto Rican model and reality-show performer, had an explanation. "I know them both," he said. "They were drinking and smoking a lot on Christmas Eve and had a terrible row. Fadi stormed off, saying he was leaving and driving down to London, but he soon realized he was too high to drive and so settled on sleeping in his car." Later Fawaz changed his story, asserting that he had actually slept in his bedroom in the Goring house.

On Christmas Day, he said, he woke up—"I have no idea what time"—and finally opened the door to Michael's room. The singer lay under the covers, face pressed against his fist. All the shades were drawn—Michael liked complete darkness when he slept—and a fan blew on him. "I touched him," said Fawaz, "but he was cold." Then he saw that Michael's fingers were blue. "I was shaking him and saying 'George, George,' but he was dead."

Rather than phoning 999, Fawaz claimed he spent an hour trying to revive Michael. Around one-forty-five, he said, he began making calls—to his niece, to a friend, to David Austin. "He said to put water on George but I said, 'I'm not doing that. He is dead.'" Austin, he said, directed him to call 999."

All emergency calls are recorded, and the *Sun* managed to procure the tape of this one. The female operator remained calm and professional; Fawaz spoke to her with chilling matter-of-factness.

"Is the patient conscious and breathing?" she asked.

"Nah, it's George Michael," said Fawaz. "He's in bed, dead."

She asked for the address. He couldn't name it. There was a long pause as he flipped through papers, looking to find it.

"Okay. Is he cold?"

"He's cold and he's blue."

"And is he stiff?"

"He's stiff, yes, he's very stiff."

"Do you think he's beyond any help at the moment?"

"Yes, he's beyond any help. He's gone. He's blue."

"Was it an expected death?"

"No, no, nooo. . . . I went to wake him up and he was gone. . . . Somebody's coming, right?"

"We've got someone on the way, okay. What's his name?"

"It's George Michael, you know, the singer?"

If she recognized the name, she didn't let on. She asked for Michael's date of birth. "I think it's . . . the twenty-fifth of July? Sixty or something. . . . Can I hang up?"

An ambulance arrived, and a paramedic examined the body. Michael, she remarked, had been dead for some time.

Within hours, Connie Filippello's statement had appeared. "It is with great sadness that we can confirm our beloved son, brother, and friend George passed away peacefully at home over the Christmas period. The family would ask that their privacy be respected at this difficult and emotional time. There will be no further comment at this stage." Pending an autopsy, no cause of death was noted.

The BBC broke the news. Its incredible poignancy was widely noted: At fifty-three, Michael had died alone at Christmas, while his twenty-one-year-old voice was in the air all over England, singing wistfully of a broken heart.

Almost immediately, fans in overcoats, winter hats, and gloves began making sad pilgrimages to his homes, carrying offerings. At the twin black doors that stood a few feet outside his Goring home, mementos piled up: countless bouquets of flowers, candles, drawings, handwritten tributes. On one of the doors, someone hung a CHOOSE LIFE T-shirt. People kneeled before the display as though it were an altar; tears streamed down cheeks that were freezing from the cold. The same rituals occurred in Highgate, where "the entire neighborhood was in shock," wrote Thomas Andrei. "The sadness was overwhelming."

Intense speculation about Michael's death was brewing. But for now, all his friends and fans could think about was the unbearable loss. Kirsty Young was in her kitchen on Christmas when word came over the radio. She flashed on her visit with Michael less than three months earlier, when he had promised great things ahead. "That's what I had chosen to hear," she said, "even though I was standing with him and I thought, you don't look great, you don't seem quite yourself." Christmas, she said, "was a sad, sad day."

Danny Cummings had been napping on Christmas night when his stepson William woke him up with the news. "I was in disbelief," Cummings said. The following night, he watched some videos of their performances together, and the tears came. "I'd thought he had a tremendous capability for bouncing back, which is why it puzzled me, the deterioration marked by various accidents. He could be such a good judge of character, and yet, look at who he surrounded himself with. I think the company he kept is what tipped the scales the wrong way."

Others had long expected fate to swoop down on Michael; the only question was when. Dee C. Lee had not seen her former employer in years, but reports of his decline had made her fear the worst. "I thought, any day I'm gonna get the news. It breaks my heart that after everything he had been through, everything he had achieved, he died alone on Christmas."

Even in the eighties, Rob Kahane had sensed trouble ahead. "George used to tell me all the time: 'I think I'm gonna die young.' I said, 'Why?' He said, 'I don't know, I just always thought I was gonna die young. I'm okay with it.' I said, 'Well, I'm not okay with it. Why would you talk that way?'"

Shortly after the singer's death, Elton John inflamed Michael's sister Melanie by suggesting that, even after all of his out-and-proud assertions, Michael had never come to terms with being gay; as addiction seized him, he just couldn't feel he was worth saving.

"I wanted to live," said John. "Poor George didn't want it." Michael Pagnotta had sensed the self-loathing in one of pop's most beloved men. "I always felt that the last fifteen years or so of his life were about him trying to punish himself," Pagnotta said.

CHAPTER TWENTY-NINE

IN 2016, THE DEATHS of David Bowie, Prince, Leonard Cohen, and finally, George Michael, had kept the pop world in mourning. In the United Kingdom and throughout Europe, Michael was now a fallen king—"4ever loved," as Andrew Ridgeley tweeted. "Heartbroken at the loss of my beloved friend Yog," he added. A *Daily Mirror* headline proclaimed Michael "a kind and gentle genius." British comic and TV host David Baddiel recalled having emailed Michael to ask if he could use "Faith" in *The Infidel*, a 2010 film comedy that Baddiel had written. He had embarrassingly little money to offer. "My pleasure," answered Michael. "I remember having a long chat with you years back so I know you are fond of the record. I'd love a copy when it's done." Remarked Baddiel: "What a lovely bloke."

Michael's passing made front pages in the United States and brought a predictable flood of tearful celebrity tweets from the likes of Miley Cyrus and Lady Gaga. But whereas Bowie, Cohen, and Prince had all been portrayed as icons of timeless cool, most of his obituaries depicted Michael as a nostalgic figure whose art had been usurped by scandal.

Among his superstar contemporaries, Madonna seemed indomitable. But there was no Symphonica in her maturity; at fifty-eight, she clung to the same kind of shock tactics she had used in her twenties. Michael had always had mixed feelings about her, and the two had never been close. Yet his death prompted her to make an Instagram post designed for quoting: "I've lost a beloved friend—the kindest, most generous soul and a brilliant artist. . . . Farewell My Friend! Another Great Artist leaves us. Can 2016 Fuck Off NOW?"

In England, Michael's death was one of the biggest mysteries of the day. An investigation had begun, and every tidbit of information spawned articles and speculation. The media pressured his camp for answers. Michael Lippman cited cardiac arrest as the likely cause of death, but that explanation appeased no one. The Thames Valley Police did a full probe of the death scene and searched the house for drugs. They termed Michael's passing "non-suspicious" but "unexplained," although a comment from a spokesman revealed suspicions: "Where someone dies of a drug overdose, we would seek to establish who supplied those drugs." Learning that shutterbugs from the Flynet photo agency had been stationed outside Michael's homes in his last days, police demanded all images.

Meanwhile, they quizzed neighbors, friends, family, his housekeeper, and most of all Fawaz, to try and piece together what had happened in Michael's last week. Michael's last partner was judged innocent of wrongdoing, but tabloid writers and Twitter followers pummeled him with questions. Why had he slept in his car on Christmas Eve? How could he have delayed calling 999 for an hour? What role had drugs played in all of this? "FUCK YOU," he tweeted.

In a *Mirror* feature, "I Found My Tragic George Dead in Bed," Fawaz told a more polished version of his story. "I went to wake him up and he was just gone, lying peacefully in bed. Everything had been very complicated recently, but George was looking forward to Christmas, and so was I. Now everything is ruined."

His life whirled into chaos. Just after New Year's Eve had turned to 2017, Fawaz began a Twitter spree that sent the tabloids into a frenzy. A few of his tweets wound up deleted; as for certain others, he claimed that someone had hacked his account. "The only thing George wanted is to DIE," read one tweet. "He tired [*sic*] numbers of time [*sic*] to kill himself many times . . . and finally he managed . . ."

All conclusions about Michael's death would hinge on the medical reports. The first autopsy had proven inconclusive, and many further steps were needed—crucially, the toxicology tests. Typically, they drag on for weeks, as multiple labs and experts test urine, blood drawn from different parts of the body, and tissue samples from various organs. Medical records are analyzed. Michael's case was complex, for he had a long and public history with illegal drugs, marijuana, and antidepressants.

During the process, no interment could take place, which reportedly "devastated" his father. Greek Orthodox burials occur quickly, and Jack had taken a firm hand in the arrangements, even inviting pallbearers from Cyprus. It was announced that Jack would include Kenny Goss in the proceedings as an acknowledgment of his son's sexuality. "It is not acceptable in our community to be homosexual," said one of Jack's Greek relatives, "so that was very hard for George's father, but we accepted George as he was." The snub of Fawaz said much about the family's opinion of him.

Winter wore on with no definitive answers. Theories about an overdose ran rampant; family members scrambled to deny it. Kyriakos Pourikou, the husband of Michael's cousin Katerina, told the *Mirror*: "Did I ever see him on drugs? Not while we've been together." But several people who had known him thought otherwise. "I just think he took too much of something, mixed with antidepressants and other drugs he was on, with alcohol," said Andros in the *Sun*. "I think his heart just stopped beating." Paul Stag brought up GHB: "Any pretense that he didn't have any on Christmas Eve is ridiculous to me. He was mad on G. He loved it." Goss offered a credible explanation: "I think his body just gave up. All these years, it was just weak."

After months of agonized waiting, a death certificate was released on March 9, 2017. It gave the unsatisfying news that Michael had died of "natural causes" stemming from a fatty liver and cardiomyopathy, in which one of the heart ventricles is so stretched and weakened that blood doesn't pump properly. At the family's request, the coroner withheld the results of the toxicology tests.

Fans, media, and even Michael's friends knew they weren't getting the whole truth. If his system had tested drug-free, it seemed likely that his family would have wanted the world to know. The nature of his conditions held clues. Cardiomyopathy can result from severe infection, such as Michael had suffered in Vienna. It is also associated with drug abuse, especially coke; Michael's crack cocaine use was no secret. Overuse of antidepressants and smoking can also play a role. But one of the leading causes of cardiomyopathy is HIV—and on this point his team would not comment. It would go unaddressed for some time to come.

As for Michael's fatty liver, that ailment was a common byproduct of alcoholism. GHB, however, metabolizes mostly in the liver, and the drug can wreak havoc on that organ. It also slows the heart rate, which can contribute to cardiac arrest. Had he, in fact, committed suicide? Perhaps not consciously, despite prior efforts. But anyone who remembered Michael's belief that he had set himself up passive-aggressively to be outed in 1998 had cause to wonder if he taken steps to set his own death in motion.

Fawaz had other concerns. "I am very happy," he told the press. "The truth is out and I am not getting doubted any more from the world." That changed as he continued to drop hints about what he knew and to contradict more of his old claims. One of them concerned the time of Michael's death. The plaque on his coffin would read December 25, 2016, but Fawaz denied it. "George died on his mother's birthday," he declared, "so that might answer a few questions. Not to mention it took five attempts to manage to end his life."

A "family source" rushed to refute suggestions of suicide. As far as Jack and his family were concerned, Fawaz's claim *had* to be denied. In the Greek Orthodox religion, suicide is a heinous sin, and it precludes a church burial.

As for the day on which Michael had died, this, too, stayed mysterious. Friends knew how Michael's spirits could crash on the twenty-fourth, as memories of his mother filled his thoughts. "It's impossible to know exactly what went on at the end," said one of his close colleagues. "There's only one piece of info you need to know: George's mother was born on the twenty-fourth of December. George didn't die on Christmas Day. He died on Christmas Eve. But I didn't say that."

Johnny Douglas had his own opinions. "I'm not buying a word of what I am told in the official narrative," he said. Douglas had not heard Michael sing in at least three years, and he was aware of the likelihood that the singer had suffered vocal damage. He had also watched the downfall of his friend's songwriting ability. "I knew this man. I watched him mentally decline. If he thought he couldn't sing or write anymore, that would probably be the biggest killer for him." Michael's demise remained mysterious even to Andrew Ridgeley. "We may never know what really happened," he said.

The release of Michael's death certificate meant that the funeral could finally take place. It was scheduled for Wednesday, March 29, 2017, at two P.M. in the tiny Chapel of Rest in Highgate Cemetery, where Michael would be buried. Every attempt had been made to keep the media in the dark.

Word about the funeral got out anyway. Only around forty people—the chapel's capacity—were invited. Elton John, Geri Halliwell, and Kate Moss were reportedly asked not to attend, for their presence would attract unwanted attention. Photographers caught the arrivals of several somber guests, dressed in black: Ridgeley, Goss, Pepsi DeMacque, Shirlie and Martin Kemp and their children, Roman and Harley. One picture shows Melanie in dark glasses as she gazes out a car window, looking desperately sad. She, Yioda, Jack (then eighty), David Austin, and Niall Flynn shuffled past the security guard. Family members of Jack's—including "a lot of bearded old ladies," said one attendee—had flown in from Greece. Phones were held at the entrance so no one could take pictures. No one could have photographed Deon Estus, Chris Porter, Chris Cameron, Kathy Jeung, or Andy Morahan; according to Andros, neither he nor any of them had been invited.

Inside, the chapel was a wash of white, from the chairs—just a few on each side with an aisle in between—to the candles up front to the elaborate floral arrangements, chosen by Melanie. One cluster lay on top of the closed coffin. White was the traditional color of a Greek Orthodox funeral; in this case it implied the cleansing of a son whose life, according to the religion's harsh tenets, had been alarmingly sinful. As the mourners entered they filed past the coffin; many of them touched it. A Greek minister swung an urn of incense, and the ceremony, meticulously planned by the sisters, was underway.

"Then the door opened," recalled Flynn, "and in walked Fadi up the center of the church with his sunglasses on, like some kind of rock star. Everybody turned around, like, 'What the fuck?' It was hugely disrespectful."

Fawaz, who that month had claimed he hadn't been invited, sat far from the family and the funeral proceeded. Jack didn't speak, but the minister conveyed his thoughts: Never had he thought his son would be so successful, but George had made him proud. Melanie took the lectern, acknowledging other guests and their importance to Michael. She noted Goss as though he were the widower; nobody mentioned the real one. She spoke of the family commitment to do right by Michael's legacy. The ceremony lasted barely an hour. Fawaz left quickly.

Then came the burial, in the west section of the cemetery. Michael had bought a plot for his family; there he was laid in the ground alongside his mother. A white-rose arrangement in the shape of a large heart was placed on Lesley's grave. Guests proceeded to a reception in Highgate.

A few weeks later, Goss's account of the funeral showed up in the *Sun*. Though respectful, his interview was seen by those closest to Michael as a betrayal. The piece stressed that Goss had not been paid for this information directly; instead, the *Sun* had made a "donation" to the Goss-Michael Foundation.

Per the family's wishes, Michael's final resting place bore an unmarked headstone. The reason, ostensibly, was to prevent a barrage of fans, yet until 2020, that part of the cemetery was restricted to those on guided tours. Finally a marked stone was lain on the ground close to the burial places of his mother and sister. It bore the singer's name in Greek; the dates of his birth and death; and the phrase, "Beloved Son, Brother, Friend." Nothing more seemed necessary.

•••

The family's problems with Fawaz had barely begun; soon they escalated into what Melanie termed a nightmare. Since well before Michael's death, Fawaz had been living in the Regent's Park house. He claimed that Michael had told him he could stay as long as he wanted, which may well have been true. Fawaz seemed to be hoping that Michael had left him the house in his will, whose details had not yet been disclosed. In fact, he had not inherited it—and while some American states granted ownership rights to common-law partners, the United Kingdom did not.

Nonetheless, Fawaz had no intention of leaving "my place." Fawaz's Twitter followers read his angry announcement that the credit cards Michael had given him had been canceled. With that, he began waging war. "An eye for an eye, a tooth for a tooth," he wrote. Often he spoke directly to his dead boyfriend, whose extreme financial generosity should have left him comfortable for a long time. "George I am starving," Fawaz wrote. "The icon partner"—as he called himself—"refused to sell stories worth millions when he was hungry. . . . Lunchtime I didn't sell a story I searched my car for a pound here and a pound there so I could buy my double cheese burger."

He found a short-term solution: "Goerge Micheal [*sic*] Items for sale if you interested please let me know." He also offered the Range Rover Michael had given him one Christmas. "It's a way so I can survive till we solve the problems with his family and lawyer. Since I'm left with no help and since no one is human anymore." Fawaz thanked Michael for having gifted him with an unreleased album; which one wasn't clear. "I feel so special," he wrote. "I love you George." Of course, he owned no rights—and when he posted a link to a track on Twitter, Michael's lawyers demanded he remove it.

According to Fawaz, in the winter of 2018 lawyers sent him a letter, insisting he vacate the house. He stepped up his attacks on Michael's inner circle, calling them "savages" and "deadly creatures"; to Michael, he complained: "They even accused me I had something to do with your death." Word had spread that Fawaz was planning a tell-all book; for now he tweeted: "To every news papers in the world please get in touch I'm ready to talk." Undoubtedly he knew things that the family did not want revealed. Reports followed that they were considering a £250,000 payoff to hush him up and get him out.

They could have afforded it. Despite the recent concerns over his cash flow, Michael had owned an abundance of assets, and the estate was valued at £95 to £105 million. Finally, after eighteen months of probate, the contents were revealed. Most of Michael's fortune would go to his sisters, neither of whom had married. Yioda, who was far tougher than the growingly fragile Melanie, would serve as co-executor along with one of Michael's lawyers. The singer had expected her to keep supporting his favorite charities and to bestow other funds where she saw fit. He directed that his artwork and antiques—including the Lennon piano—be sold and the funds poured into the philanthropic organization he had created, the Mill Charitable Trust.

To his father, Michael left the racehorse stud farm, located in Hertfordshire, that he had bought for him. Since Jack already lived there, it was a redundant gift. A short list of true-blue friends such as David Austin and Shirlie Kemp and a handful of loyal employees, including Connie Filippello, would be rewarded in amounts to be determined by Yioda.

"All of these people had one thing in common," wrote Amanda Platell in the *Mirror*. "They were there for him through good times and bad. . . . The friends never betrayed him, but instead supported and defended him at every turn."

The omissions were more telling. They included such close pals as Geri Halliwell and Kate Moss, although both women had plenty of their own money; his faithful studio colleagues Johnny Douglas and Niall Flynn; Andrew Ridgeley, who admittedly had been well compensated through "Careless Whisper"; Pepsi DeMacque, Shirlie's fellow backup singer from Wham!; and his last two partners, Goss and Fawaz, who of course had reaped lavish rewards already. Fawaz's Twitter followers read a brutal response: "George I hate you. Your power proved to me you could turn friends, family and strangers into liars, cowards and very much inhuman and yet this mega power can't make or keep someone KIND or LOVING."

Fawaz was no more the muscley hunk whom Michael had shown off to the world on Twitter. In July 2019, photographers snapped him shirtless on the balcony of the Regent's Park house, belly hanging over his waistband and a cigarette in his mouth. Behind him, the glass panels of the French doors were smashed. Battered walls were visible inside. On Facebook, Fawaz posted a photo of a broken window with his fist held in front of it in silhouette; his middle finger was raised. Questioned by a *Sun* reporter, he said he was "renovating." In fact, the family had upped its pressure to expel him.

Later that month, a neighbor reported that Fawaz had gone "absolutely berserk" and that there was "glass flying everywhere." Others told of seeing Fawaz on the roof, pitching items that crashed into their gardens. Water gushed out the house's front door. On the night of July 23, the police and fire department were called. As they entered, a shocking sight awaited them. "Every fixture and fitting, every door and window, everything George left in there—it's all completely destroyed," said a neighbor. "Even the toilets and sinks have been smashed. There's major damage to the walls and even the ceilings." Three young policemen in black-and-white uniforms escorted him out, handcuffed, and arrested him on suspicion of aggravated criminal damage. They drove him to the station, where he was held for approximately twenty-four hours.

The family had the locks changed and windows barred. Fawaz was finally out. He moved into a forty-nine-pound-per-night Travelodge; then, he said, he began "sleeping in the street in Covent Garden instead of being in my home . . . What a cheap ikon [*sic*] this George fucking Michael is." Numerous photos were shot of him wandering the streets and sitting on stoops.

He got his revenge. On October 30, 2019, Fawaz addressed years of speculation in a single tweet. "George Michael was HIV+," he wrote. "We found out in Vienna after his illness." His representatives did not respond. Given Michael's near-death of pneumonia and his notorious reputation for promiscuity and hard drug use, the claim caused hardly a ripple.

Fawaz wasn't through. Later that day he posted: "He never wrote his own music. He paid other people to make the music for him and pretended it was him. Not so talented after all." Michael, he added, was "extremely boring" in bed. He claimed he had taken photos of the dead body, although they didn't surface. In August 2020, Fawaz was videotaped wandering around the neighborhood of Bethnal Green and bashing parked cars with a hammer. Police were called; they searched him, then reported finding Class A drugs in his possession. According to the *New York Post*, the officers on the scene "said that a man in his forties was 'taken into custody and subsequently released under investigation.'"

Other tabloid-worthy incidents followed. No matter how low he sank, he held fast to his declaration: "I will revenge till the last breath of my life. . . . And no I won't get a job."

• • •

The side of Michael that had made every good thing possible—his artistry— still shone in the best of his catalog. On his website, his sisters posted their vow to carry on Michael's creative legacy "exactly as Yog would have wanted." With that in mind, they appointed David Austin as adviser. Austin had spent the better part of his life in the shadow of his overwhelmingly charismatic best mate; he had served as caretaker, gofer, and occasional songwriting assistant. But according to Andros—who, in his memoirs, wrote of an amicable reunion call with his former friend shortly before his death—Michael had confided plans to cut Austin off after the New Year; it had to do with his annoyance over "David trying to take control."

Now, all decisions as to his famous friend's body of work would be made by lawyers, with input from Austin. What would Michael have thought? "George was really anti-corporate," said Flynn. "He was constantly cursing his lawyers and now they're running it the way they want to run it."

Several deluxe reissues of his albums were produced. But having heard about a wealth of unreleased material, fans and writers awaited a stream of discoveries. Johnny Douglas was eager to help. Michael's trusted producer for twenty years had retained outtakes and song fragments going back to 1995. Some showed promise, and he went about finishing them, but their release was blocked. "I said, 'I've got these tunes, I've been working on them, these could be huge.' No."

September 2017 saw the premiere of the Nile Rodgers remix of "Fantasy" on BBC Radio 2. The release of Michael's first posthumous single, revamped by a flashy producer, was news. Rodgers had given the old track a funk groove; he had also added sped-up samples of Michael's vocals—a throwback to *Faith*, where Michael had copied Prince's electronically created alter ego, Camille. On the website Queerty, David Grant compared the sound to that of a "choir of bipolar chipmunks." Deon Estus was no more restrained. "It's absolute fucking shit," he said of the remix. "I love Nile. But it's crap. George would turn in his grave!"

Michael's last big project, the *Freedom* documentary, was almost certainly what he had wanted it to be. The star renowned for wanting his privacy had shown an almost pathological compulsion to explain himself, spelling out the what, how, and why of his every move, while assuring viewers of how happy he was. *Freedom*, which credited Michael and Austin as codirectors, zeroed in on his sense of victimization. Most of the gems of self-assessment from his talk with Kirsty Young did not appear; nor did the Michael of 2016, as least visually. Instead, a British actor, Simon Rutter, played a young and beautiful George. The glamour quotient was upped by a profusion of celebrity talking heads (Clive Davis, Stevie Wonder, Naomi Campbell, Ricky Gervais, Mary J. Blige, Tony Bennett, James Corden) who had barely known him; they and a few who had (Kate Moss, Elton John, Tracey Emin) either fawned over Michael or tiptoed around the truth.

In the *Los Angeles Times*, Mikael Wood called *Freedom* "essentially a glorified sizzle reel" that "does little to deepen our understanding of Michael or his music; it sheds no fresh light on why he made the artistic choices he did or how he carried them out." Most of the starry commentators, he wrote, praised the star in "bland generalities that could be easily swapped into a film about Freddie Mercury or Amy Winehouse. . . . A film as shallow as this one doesn't deserve anyone's time."

Another movie, long in the works, emerged in the 2019 holiday season. The romantic comedy *Last Christmas* featured a script that Emma Thompson, the esteemed British actress, had cowritten. Four years earlier, Thompson had visited Michael to propose a film that would flesh out the story in Wham!'s yuletide evergreen. He was amenable. Then he died, and Austin stepped in, receiving an associate producer credit. One Michael song burgeoned into a soundtrack of fifteen; according to one report, about a fifth of the $25–30 million budget went for the songs.

Emilia Clarke plays Kate, an aspiring singer who works in a Christmas store. She embarks on a romance with a mysterious man, Tom (played by Henry Golding), to whom she reveals she had a heart transplant. Her selfish behavior alienates him and he disappears. Only later does she learn that she had imagined their affair; Tom had died some time before in an accident, and she had received his donated heart. Armed with this knowledge, Kate becomes a force for good. She organizes a benefit talent show at the home-less shelter where, in her hallucinations, her mythical angel had volunteered. Joined by the residents, she sings "Last Christmas" ("I gave you my heart . . ."). In a flash cameo, Andrew Ridgeley is in the audience.

Though a box-office success in England, *Last Christmas* earned mostly scathing reviews. *Rolling Stone*'s David Fear called it "incredibly, shockingly, monumentally bad. The kind of bad that falls somewhere between finding a lump of coal in your stocking and discovering one painfully lodged in your rectum."

Seeing the finished film, Niall Flynn shuddered at the use of "fifteen of George's songs in this appalling movie" and on a soundtrack album. "George made money but he was never about money," Flynn said. "The whole idea was to do the best for George's legacy so he would be remembered as an artist of the stature he deserved. Once he had seen this film he would have said, 'You can use 'Last Christmas' but I'm not putting any more of my songs in it.'" Among the inclusions was "This Is How (We Want You to Get High)" from the unfinished disco album. Flynn flashed back to his last visit with Michael in 2016, when his friend had instructed him, Austin, and James Jackman that the track had to be shelved.

The feeding frenzy that had encircled him since Wham! showed no signs of dying off. That March, Michael's art collection—nearly two hundred pieces—had been auctioned off at Christie's in London to benefit his pet causes. Nearly every item except the ones by Damien Hirst—whose shock value had waned—had proven a good investment on Michael's part, with winning bids exceeding estimates. According to Christie's, the proceeds topped $12.3 million.

Every bang of the auctioneer's gavel occurred "under the watchful eye of George's ex, Kenny Goss," the *Sun* reported. Even though Michael had paid for the whole collection, Goss had claimed rights to it, which led to a nasty dispute. Ostensibly, Michael had purchased most of the works for the Goss-Michael Foundation, which had continued to house them. For Michael's estate to reclaim the art had not been easy.

Goss retaliated. Clearly, he announced, Michael had not been "in his right mind" in 2013, when he had last revised his will. During their relationship, Goss had gotten used to receiving his £15,000-a-month allowance. In October 2020, the family was stunned to learn that Goss was suing them. After all he had done for Michael, argued Goss, he deserved to keep living in the style to which his ex had made him accustomed. In 2021, the estate settled with him for an undisclosed sum.

By this time, the family had suffered one more tremendous blow. Ever since Michael's death, Christmas had been especially bleak for Melanie, the sister to whom he had been closest. She was one of the first people to whom he had come out; from then on she had been second only to their mother as his adoring cheerleader and support system. That hadn't stopped her from pleading with him for years to seek help for his addictions. For his last several years he saw as little of Melanie as possible.

His death devastated her. Agonizing over what more she might have done to save him, she fell into an intense depression. Melanie had moved into the Hampstead house, where memories of her brother were constant. Now a recluse, she ate herself to a state of morbid obesity and developed diabetes and heart disease. On the day before Christmas Eve of 2019, she joined with her sister, father, and Austin in posting a valiant message on social media: "We will be swerving the bad and enjoying the good as much as we can this coming year."

On Christmas Day, Melanie was found dead at the house. At fifty-five, she had lapsed into a coma triggered by diabetic ketoacidosis, a condition marked by low insulin and skyrocketing blood sugar. She had also had bronchopneumonia, a condition not unlike Michael's in 2011. The fact that Melanie had died three years to the day after the published date of her brother's loss seemed no coincidence. Now Jack would have to bury another child. Melanie's funeral was a near-replica of Michael's, down to the chapel and the white flowers. She was laid to rest in the family plot alongside her mother and brother.

•••

The man who had written two anthems called "Freedom" had known little of it; even in death he had not found peace. In his final months he had talked to Kirsty Young about his trademark sunglasses, behind which he had long hidden. "I think the glasses were probably very much a first sign that my place in life had begun to become a heavy thing for me to carry," he said. "Something I didn't truly believe in." Michael recalled how much he had longed for one special person to make him feel complete, but the battle for self-love had been his toughest, and in the end he had lost. His feelings at the peak of *Faith* gave a clue as to what lay ahead. He was "adored by millions," he said, "but couldn't work out why."

EPILOGUE

ON APRIL 8, 2017, THE sun shone on a crowd of revelers in the cruising section of Hampstead Heath. Some were there for sex, others to dance; a few played bongos or sang. The party was hosted by Queer Tours of London, an activist group that hosted excursions through the byways of British LGBT history. A rainbow of genders, ages, and types had gathered in the park—some tattooed and pierced, others looking like people one might encounter at the office. Several wore white T-shirts that said CHOOSE LIFE. A few reached into baskets of condoms and ventured behind the bushes.

Blue and lavender ribbons were tied around trees, many of which had flyers Scotch-taped to them. They showed a drawing of an unmistakable man in a leather jacket and tight jeans, peering over his shoulder. GEORGE MICHAEL WANTS YOU . . . LET'S GO OUTSIDE, it said. "We are here to celebrate George Michael!" announced Dan Glass, QT's bearded, platinum-haired organizer. The crowd cheered. A couple of bemused policemen stood by as gay men dressed like them danced to Wham!'s "Freedom." All this, said one participant, was a salute to Michael's "stance on freedom of choice and freedom to live your life as you want."

It had been fifty years since the limited decriminalization of homosexuality in England and Wales. According to Glass, Michael fit right in with that milestone, having sent a message of "screw you" to every societal force that had shrouded gay men in shame. "We wanted to highlight his response to the homophobic oppression that he dealt with in such a pioneering, fierce, beautiful way," Glass said. Many had wondered how a star like Michael could have cruised and cottaged so blatantly; but for Glass, "that was one of the great things about George. He carried on showing his raw sexual desire on a human level, rather than thinking he was too big for that."

A redheaded man in the Heath had his own words of thanks: "So many people have benefited from what happened to him, who he was, and what he represented." To the hippie boyfriend at his side, Michael symbolized "that vulnerability" that comes with growing up gay.

He also embodied danger, starting in the days when his sexually coded videos had sent tingles through many a gay viewer. Then, in 1998, Michael was suddenly out, with a temerity that almost no star had shown. "I think he challenged the stereotype of the gay man and what was acceptable," said Ricky Gervais. Unlike the "safe, sexless," benignly amusing gay males who adorned the media, Michael showed the public a bit of what it hadn't wished to see. "George went, 'I've got a cock!'" said the comedian. "That frightened some people."

In time, it also overpowered a relatively slim body of work. Debate arose over where Michael stood in the galaxy of pop superstars. Wrote an unnamed essayist in the *Observer*: "For all his enormous success, he has never been a revolutionary in the manner of a Presley, Dylan, or Bowie; aspiring to become a classic songwriter in the mould of past masters, he has left the course of popular music largely unchanged."

But if pop is ephemeral by nature, Michael touched hearts in ways that haven't faded. The 2017 Grammys contained a vivid example. To commemorate him months after his death, "Fastlove" was sung by that year's five-time winner, Adele, whose acoustic music-making and unprocessed vocals had made her a unicorn in the Auto-Tuned pop world of her day. She sang Michael's disco-fied hymn to no-strings-attached sex at a snail's pace while he danced on a screen behind her in ghostly slow-motion. Overcome by emotion, she fell out of tune and couldn't find her way back. Finally, on live TV, Adele murmured, "Fuck!" and stopped. "Can we please start it again? I'm sorry, I can't mess this up for him." She kept apologizing tearfully, then began the song again, almost perfectly on key.

It was a moment whose honesty Michael would have respected. From Wham! through Symphonica, he had stood onstage in hundreds of arenas, singing in real time with all his humanity on show. In pop, this tradition had grown rare. Ellyn Solis, Epic Records' U.S. head of publicity in the Michael era, had seen the change. "Pop singers today get lauded if they can deliver a real performance," she said. "Peggy Lee didn't get lauded for that; she got lauded because she never *didn't* deliver a real performance. There was no other way to do it. If you sing, get up and sing."

Neither Michael nor Adele, beloved as they were, had triggered a renaissance of that style. Johnny Douglas, who had helped nurtured some of Michael's best songs, looked around in despair. "I find that modern pop music is such a narcissistic wankfest of people doing it mainly for money and fame," he said. "It's so dumbed-down, just four chords on a loop going around. Chuck it out there and if it doesn't work, that's fine; they've got twenty others lined up. George's intention was to craft masterpieces, and for people to hold them in their hearts. He kept rewriting and rewriting, pushing— 'That's not good enough. I'm gonna do it again.'" Even though Michael was just twenty-two when he wrote it, "Last Christmas" bore out Douglas's view. In December 2018, thirty-three years after its release, that naive confession of holiday loss hit the American Top 40 for the first time.

Michael had made a case for pop music as an art form worth celebrating—a soundtrack of the present, shot through with youthful good feelings. As he had once told *Rolling Stone*: "Somewhere along the way, pop lost all its respect. And I think I kind of stubbornly stick up for all of that."

Along the way, he had passed through one cultural phenomenon after another—the rise of MTV, the aggressive sexualizing of pop culture, the heyday of the tabloids, the AIDS crisis, the downfall of record-label sovereignty, the breakdown of the celebrity closet—and left his mark on all of them. Following his death, Julianne Escobedo Shepherd of the online feminist magazine *Jezebel* noted the "culture of fear and repression that made the openness and virility in his songs so much more appealing."

Michael had watched that climate shift dramatically. "When I meet gay artists now who are starting their careers, they've been out since they were ten or twelve," said Billy Masters. "They didn't have to go through any transition of private versus public life. Even when George was totally open he was still a product of where he came from."

That may be why, in his last years, he wanted so much to connect with young gay generations. The year before he died, Michael had taken notice of a singer whom the *Philadelphia Inquirer* called "British blue-eyed pop-soul's voice du jour." In 2015, Sam Smith, then twenty-two, came out as gay upon the release of his debut album, *In the Lonely Hour*, which followed a few hit singles. The album went platinum. "He sent me flowers," Smith told the AP, "and he was in touch a few times and said that he liked what I did. He was the reason I decided I wanted to do pop music. I just loved how human he was."

His flaws and foibles had only made him seem more so. But to Craig* a young gay Texan who had also battled an addiction to GHB, Michael's death, and the evasiveness that followed, spelled a lost opportunity to open a discussion as to why so many gays had shared Michael's struggle. "I wish our community would understand that people are in pain. Someone is broken and needs support. Comes the point where we do every drug known to man to make it go away. To make us, for this hour, these two hours, these ten hours, not be in constant pain." In Michael's case, Craig sensed the root cause: "Is there nothing more horrible than to believe that we're just not good enough? That's the strongest thing that gay men have in common. We constantly believe there's something wrong with us. We know we have to strive to try harder. Be more masculine, be smarter, better-looking, better at sports—whatever."

Others had their own theories about what had gone so terribly wrong in the life of a man who had surpassed his every childhood dream. "We can all play amateur psychologist and try to analyze why he was so uncomfortable under the mantle of such charm, wit, talent, and popularity," said Stephen Fry. "George did seem to have a will to wreck everything about him that was stable and lasting. But he was always one of those people whose presence in a room cause you to light up and feel happier."

The same was true of his records. On more than one Saturday night in Fire Island Pines, the world's most fashionable gay resort town, located near the south shore of Long Island, New York, "Freedom! '90" blasted from the Pavilion, the main dance club, and into the balmy night air of the harbor outside. Decades after the song had been on the radio, few of the gays dancing to it had a clue about Michael's professional identity crisis, nor his issues with Sony. But the song's essence—a call to break free from one's cage and live in truth—still held power.

---

* Name changed

Deejay Will Automagic had often used the track as a closing tune—"the emotional one that you want to leave everyone with the memory of at the end of the night." As soon as they recognized it, a glow would spread across many of their faces. "That song means a lot to a lot of people," he said. "When the chorus hits, they're crying on the dance floor."

• • •

Michael made the news yet again in June 2021, when Lorde, the New Zealand-born electropop superstar born in 1996, released a new hit single, "Solar Power." Fans and critics rushed to scold her over its similarities to "Freedom! '90," particularly the chord sequence and groove of the refrain. She denied it; her real influence, she said, had been Primal Scream's less-famous single "Loaded," Michael's blueprint for "Freedom! '90." The issue revived a few old jeers about all the appropriation he had done as a songwriter, but for Danny Cummings, to single out Michael was silly. "Loaded," he observed, sounded quite a bit like "Sympathy for the Devil," a 1968 Rolling Stones classic; the chord sequence had appeared in countless songs. "Pop music after the seventies is often one shameless plagiarization after another, whether deliberate or unwitting. Everything is borrowed, sometimes copied, but there is nothing new under the sun. George listened with a keen ear to everybody. He was a pop musician; he tapped into many different styles and feels, none of which he had created. But the content of some and the silken self-expression were undoubtedly his own."

For years, Michael had been defined largely by stories about his wealth, his luxury homes, and his friendships with royalty and fellow superstars. But that didn't capture the man whom Barb Jungr, the British cabaret singer, had long observed from afar. "Maybe it's a good idea to think of him in the context of Princess Diana," she said. "There was something about him that touched ordinary people."

NOTES

PROLOGUE

viii   **"It had a"**: Danny Cummings to JG, May 26, 2018.

viii   **"an everyman"**: Lynda Hayes to JG, June 1, 2018.

viii   **"I sensed"**: Ben Butler to JG, Feb. 5, 2018.

viii   **"No one"**: Steve Pond, "George Michael, Seriously," *Rolling Stone*, Jan. 28, 1988.

viii   **"When you"**: Dan Aquilante, *New York Post*, Apr. 9, 1998.

ix   **"the most"**: Johnny Douglas to JG, July 10, 2019.

ix   **"He pops"**: Ron Tannenbaum, "George Michael—Artist or Airhead?," *Musician*, Jan. 1988.

ix   **"He always"**: Richard Smith, "George Michael—A Single Man?," *Gay Times*, May 1996.

ix   **"a songwriter"**: Jim White, "My Kind of Guy," *Guardian*, Apr. 15, 1998.

ix   **"He never"**: David Geffen to JG, Sept. 5, 2017.

ix   **"It was impossible"**: David Bartolomi to JG, Feb. 1, 2020.

x   ***"Stop trying"***: Chris Cameron to JG, June 3, 2018.

CHAPTER ONE

2   **"I grew up"**: GM, *Desert Island Discs*, BBC Radio 4, Sept. 30, 2007

2   **"He was a mean"**: Andros Georgiou, *Rock: The Luckiest Man in Pop* (2012), 51.

2   **"You could"**: Georgiou, 68.

2   **"a great coffin"**: Simon Napier-Bell to JG, Sept. 7, 2018.

2   **"extremely"**: *George Michael: A Different Story* (documentary), 2005.

3 "Depression" . . . "quiet boy": *George Michael: A Different Story.*

3 "I was never": Johann Hari, "Talk Without Prejudice," *Independent,* Dec. 9, 2005.

3 "Conceit": Elias Leight, "George Michael Doc 'Freedom,'" *Rolling Stone,* Oct. 20, 2017.

3 "A few things": *The Red Line,* Pt. 1, BBC Radio 2, Nov. 1, 2017.

3 "all I wanted": George Michael & Tony Parsons, *Bare* (Michael Joseph, 1990), 41.

6 "I feel burnt": Maeve Walsh, "Crushed to Death at a David Cassidy Concert," *Independent,* May 23, 1999.

6 "I didn't want": *Parkinson,* BBC1, Dec. 5, 1998.

6 "It was feeling": *Parkinson,* Dec. 5, 1998.

6 "Jack hated": Andros Georgiou, *Rock: The Luckiest Man in Pop,* 81.

6 "People absolutely": Michael Mavros to JG, Dec. 17, 2017.

6 "always trying": Georgiou, 53–54.

6 "For the old": Danny Cummings to JG, May 26, 2018.

7 "I was fat": David Thomas, "I Was Ugly, but I Always Knew I'd Be a Star," source unknown, Sept. 1990.

7 "clichéd": Adam Mattera, "George Michael: Days of the Open Hand," *Attitude,* May 2004.

7 "in between": Chris Evans, "An Audience with George Michael," BBC Radio 1, Dec. 8, 1996.

8 "You inspired": John Altman to JG, July 29, 2017.

9 "cherry silk": Richard Smith & Steve Pafford, "George Talks: His Frankest Interview Ever," *Gay Times,* July 2007.

9 "cerise satin": *Bare,* 41.

9 "just oozed": GM, *Desert Island Discs.*

9 "ordered me": Louise Gannon, "Mum Hid Gay Uncle from Me," *Daily Mirror,* June 8, 2007.

9 "They were so": *George Michael: A Different Story.*

10 "Everyone called": "Starwears," *No. 1,* May 21, 1983.

10 "No one": Chris Heath, "George Michael: The Story So Far," *Smash Hits,* Apr. 9-22, 1986.

10 "lots of": *Parkinson,* BBC1, Dec. 5, 1998.

10   **"They had such":** *Bare*, 59.

10   **"lived for":** GM, *Desert Island Discs*.

11   **"The whole":** Robert Christgau, "Elton John: The Little Hooker That Could," *Village Voice*, Nov. 24, 1975.

11   **"living a lie":** Julie Miller, "*Rocketman*: Elton John's Forgotten 1984 Wedding to Renate Blauel," *Vanity Fair*, May 31, 2019.

11   **"because I":** Mark Allen, "George Michael Unzipped," *Marie Claire*, Oct. 2004.

12   **"He had such":** Greg Kot, "Queen Back on the Throne," *Chicago Tribune*, Apr. 14, 1992.

12   **"wasn't manly":** Adam Mattera, "George Michael: Days of the Open Hand."

12   **"This man":** Joseph Curtis, "George Michael Was So Haunted . . .," *Daily Mail Online*, Jan. 5, 2017.

12   **"supposedly":** Adam Mattera, "George Michael: Days of the Open Hand."

13   **"poof":** Mattera.

13   **"in case":** Richard Smith & Steve Pafford, "George Talks: His Frankest Interview Ever."

13   **"Deep down":** Simon Hattenstone, "There Was So Much Death," *Guardian*, Dec. 8, 2005.

14   **"having a tantrum":** Andros Georgiou, *Rock: The Luckiest Man in Pop*, 87.

14   **"I always":** *George Michael: A Different Story*.

14   **"As a young":** *Up Close with George Michael*, Pt. 2, BBC Radio 2, Mar. 25, 2014.

15   **"There was":** Scott Leaver, "Andrew Leaver," arcaleaver.co.uk.

15   **"Don't worry":** Leaver.

15–17   **"You either"** . . . **"throat open":** James Sullivan to JG, Mar. 18, 2018.

17   **"Dad was":** Chris Heath, "George Michael: The Story So Far," *Smash Hits*.

17   **"useless band":** U.S. interview, *George Michael: The Unauthorized Edition* CD, 1985.

17   **"The fact"**: Johann Hari, "Talk Without Prejudice."

18   **"I had a"**: GM, *Desert Island Discs.*

18   **"on the dole"**: *Bare*, 54.

18   **"Good evening"**: *Parkinson*, Dec. 5, 1998.

18   **"It was so"**: Chris Evans, *An Audience with George Michael.*

19   **"and the floor"**: Sue Evison, "George and Andrew Had a Dream . . . They Would Be Famous," *Sun*, Apr. 9, 1998.

20   **"I knew that"**: James Sullivan to JG.

20   **"rare cancer"**: Lawrence K. Altman, "Rare Cancer Seen in 41 Homosexuals," *New York Times*, July 3, 1981.

20   **"You know"**: Patricia Morrisroe, *Mapplethorpe: A Biography* (Random House, 1995), 270.

20   **"What happens?"** . . . **"fucking disease"**: James Sullivan to JG.

CHAPTER TWO

21   **"He told me"**: James Spencer to JG, Oct. 8, 2017.

21   **"George used"**: Louise Jury, "How We Met: Pepsi and Shirlie," *Independent*, Nov. 23, 1997.

22   **"Wham! Bam!"**: Andrew Ridgeley, *Wham! George & Me* (Penguin, 2019), 122.

22   **"That's a great name for a band"**: James Spencer to JG.

22   **"It's very much"**: *The Graham Norton Show*, Channel 4 (U.K.), Feb. 28, 2003.

23   **"Now go home"**: *George Michael: A Different Story* (documentary), 2005.

23   **"I don't know"**: David Wigg, "Wham! The Making of a Supergroup," *Daily Express*, Dec. 2, 1986.

23   **"I would say"**: David Chidekel to JG, Jan. 10, 2019.

24   **"It was just"**: Wham! at Miraval, Historic Films, Aug. 1984.

24   **"He did his best"**: Paul Russell to JG, Dec. 22, 2018.

24   **"as though"**: GM, *Desert Island Discs*, BBC Radio 4, Sept. 30, 2007.

25   **"Remember that"**: David Geffen to JG, Sept. 5, 2017.

25   "You ever": *Aspel & Company*, ITV, Mar. 1, 1986.

25   "George had a plan": dhvinyl, "A Personal History of the British Records Business—Dick Leahy, Pt. 3," *vinylmemories* (blog), 1999.

25   "George would play": Rob Kahane to JG, Sept. 28, 2018.

26   "came bouncing . . . these things": Chris Porter to JG, June 2, 2018.

27   "I thought": Dee C. Lee to JG, Feb. 10, 2021.

27   "I was blown": Dave Novik to JG, Dec. 7, 2017.

28   "We were all": Richard Tay to JG. Sept. 27, 2020.

28   "The little dance": Dee C. Lee to JG.

28   "I think everyone": Stephen BLN, harringayonline.com, Comment: 947449, Dec. 29, 2016.

28   "If you listen": James Spencer to JG.

28   "The boys": Dee C. Lee to JG.

29   "It was all": Adrian Deevoy, "The Lone Star State," *Q*, June 1988.

29   "She was a": Dee C. Lee to JG.

29   "really sweet girl": Adam Mattera, "George Michael: Days of the Open Hand," *Attitude*, May 2004.

29–30   "There were these . . . be done": Debbie Samuelson to JG, June 13, 2017.

30   "I hate": Monique Freedlander and Chloe Lee-Longhetti, "After THAT Private Jet Meltdown," *Daily Mail Australia*, Dec. 9, 2019.

30   "Isn't that": *Saturday Superstore*, BBC1, Nov. 10, 1984.

30   "The video": Michael Pagnotta to JG, July 10, 2017.

30   "I wasn't that": Dee C. Lee to JG.

31   "George was . . . that song": Lynda Hayes to JG, June 1, 2018.

32   "almost suicidal": Andrew Ridgeley, *Wham! George Michael & Me* (Penguin, 2019), 164.

32   "It would have": Jennifer Ruby, "George Michael Hid Being Gay to Protect His Career," *Daily Mail*, Oct. 4, 2019.

32   "I was sitting": GM, "Terrible" radio interview, source unknown, c.1988.

33   "I was on . . . miming to me": Lynda Hayes to JG, June 1, 2018.

34   "**Wham! What a**" . . . "**luminous**": Jazz Summers, *Big Life* (Quartet Books, 2013), 88–89.

35   "**I crossed**": Summers, 93.

35   "**He could shoot**": Simon Napier-Bell, *I'm Coming to Take You to Lunch* (Ebury Press, 2005), 12.

35   "**Our ambition**": John Blake, "George's Erotic Bedroom Secrets," *Daily Mirror*, Dec. 17, 1985.

35   "**awful**": Jazz Summers, *Big Life*, 96–97.

32   "**how crummy**": *The Last Resort with Jonathan Ross*, Channel 4 (U.K.), June 19, 1987.

36   "**At least**": Simon Napier-Bell to JG, Sept. 7, 2018.

36   "**macho enough**": James Spencer to JG.

36   "**not having**" . . . "**mangy ear**": Mark Allen, "George Michael Unzipped," *Marie Claire*, Oct. 2004.

37   "**a real Andrew**": Simon Napier-Bell to JG.

CHAPTER THREE

38   "**There's these**": U.S. interview, *George Michael: The Unauthorized Edition* CD, 1985.

38   "**the center**": Danny Cummings to JG, May 26, 2018.

38   "**He seemed**": Chris Heath to JG, July 10, 2017.

38   "**You couldn't**": Jazz Summers, *Big Life* (Quartet Books, 2013),115.

38   "**couldn't get**": "Seventies Teen Mag My Guy Gets One-Off Relaunch," *Daily Mail*, Oct. 23, 2006.

39   "**weren't negotiable**": Paul Gomersall to JG, Apr. 4, 2020.

39   "**George was a**": Henry Hey to JG, Feb. 5, 2018.

39   "**We were like**" . . . "**beautiful**": Deon Estus to JG, May 2, 2019.

39   "**It was to**": Chris Porter to JG, June 2, 2018.

39   "**I've stopped**": Andrew Barr, "Wham Coy About Coming to Phone," *Age* (Melbourne), Jan. 18, 1985.

40   "**There's not much**": Greg Placek, "Critics Wish Wham! Ham Would Scram," *Fort Lauderdale News/Sun-Sentinel*, Sept. 6, 1985.

40   "**I remember**": James Spencer to JG, Oct. 8, 2017.

41   "**You don't**" . . . "**this way**": Dee C. Lee to JG, Feb. 10, 2021.

41–42   "the best" . . . "cocaine": "Tony Pike: Sex & Drugs in Ibiza" (video), Aug. 10, 2018.

42   "an exorcism": Mick Brown, "Going Out with a Wham!," *Sunday Times*, June 22, 1986.

42   "I had silver": Barb Jungr to JG, June 7, 2018.

43   "that communicates": Chris Heath to JG.

43   "the Thatcherite" . . . "are going": Roland Gribben, "The Sixties Idealists Have Produced a Generation of Utterly Pragmatic Realists," *Daily Telegraph*, May 11, 1988.

43   "They danced": Barb Jungr to JG.

43   "the slightest": Simon Price, "We Love You, George, but You Don't Make It Easy for Us," *Independent*, Aug. 16, 2009.

43   "I said, 'Oh'": James Spencer to JG.

43   "tone": Marc Almond, *Tainted Life* (Sidgwick & Jackson, 1995), 119.

43   "Any queers?": Boy George (with Spencer Bright), *Take It Like a Man* (!t Books, 1995), 94.

44   "I'm not gay" . . . "movements": Martin Dunn, "Gay? Not Me, Says Michael Jackson," *Sun*, Jan. 24, 1984.

44   "Good on": Jackie Jackson, "Elton John's Someone Saved My Life Tonight," *Jaquo*, date not listed.

44   "Are you gay?" Dee C. Lee to JG.

44   "tender": Jon Lockett, "The Party's Over," *Sun*, Feb. 26, 2019.

44   "I didn't know": James Brinsford, "Andrew Ridgeley 'Had No Idea George Michael Was Gay,'" *Daily Mirror*, Oct. 9, 2019.

44   "the three": Mara Reinstein, "Sex, Insecurity and Careless Whispers," *Billboard*, Oct. 8, 2019.

44   "and of course": *George Michael: A Different Story* (documentary), 2005.

45   "cool-looking": Dee C. Lee to JG.

45   "the worst": Sheryl Garratt, "A Double Whammy," *Sunday Times*, Nov. 16, 1997.

45   "We were always": Garratt.

45   "Fuck you": Jazz Summers, *Big Life* (Quartet Books, 2013), 99.

46   "If you are": *Bare*, George Michael & Tony Parsons, *Bare* (Michael Joseph, 1990), 105.

46   "effete": Ian Gill, "Beware, Faint Hearts," *Vancouver Sun*, Aug. 20, 1983.

46   "a skilled": Judgment of the Hon. Mr. Justice Jonathan Parker, George Michael vs. Sony, June 1994, 14.

46   "Tony Russell might": Jazz Summers, *Big Life*, 98.

47   "This band": Simon Napier-Bell to JG, Sept. 7, 2018.

47   "Wham! was": Danny Cummings to JG.

47   "Danny was": Phil Palmer to JG, Apr. 10, 2018.

48   "It has to": Simon Napier-Bell, *I'm Coming to Take You to Lunch*, 43.

48   "like Europop": Chris Porter to JG.

49   "Smoke": Danny Cummings to JG.

49   "A Wham!": Billy Masters to JG, June 13, 2018.

49   "alternately": Max Bell, "Wham! Hammersmith Odeon," *Times*, Oct. 31, 1983.

50   "was a lovely": "Meet the Old Boss," *MBUK*, date unknown.

50   "In the record": Simon Napier-Bell to JG.

50   "CBS behaved": Napier-Bell.

51   "for the simple": Paul Russell to JG, Dec. 22, 2018.

51   "He was definitely": David Chidekel to JG, Jan. 10, 2019

51   "because otherwise": Chris Evans, "An Audience with George Michael," BBC Radio 1, Dec. 8, 1996.

51   "just magical": GM, *Desert Island Discs*, BBC Radio 4, Sept. 30, 2007.

51   "Everyone feels": Chris Evans, "An Audience with George Michael."

51   "If he was": Andrew Harvey, "They're Not Just a One-Wham Band," *Daily Express*, May 24, 1984.

51   "always seemed": Paul Spong to JG, Apr. 14, 2020.

52   "George never": Bret Witke to JG, May 1, 2020.

52   "I was thrilled": David Wigg, "My Bed Hopping Days Are Over, Says George," *Daily Express*, Apr. 13, 1988.

52   "I was supremely": GM, *Desert Island Discs*.

52   "It kept coming": U.S. interview, *George Michael: The Unauthorized Edition* CD, 1985.

53   "I was intrigued": Paul Spong to JG.

53   "To rule": *American Bandstand*, ABC, Jan. 14, 1984.

53   "That's what": Bryan Appleyard, "The Puppet Who Pulled the Strings," *Times*, Sept. 8, 1990.

54   "It was such": Louise Jury, "How We Met: Pepsi and Shirlie," *Independent*, Nov. 23, 1997.

54   "I thought": Jazz Summers, *Big Life*, 201.

54   "If you took": Kenny Mellman to JG, July 7, 2017.

55   "I love": Recording, Doris Day fan convention, Carmel Valley, CA, 1987.

CHAPTER FOUR

56   "Dahlinks": Simon Napier-Bell, *I'm Coming to Take You to Lunch*, 12.

56   "never, ever": Simon Napier-Bell to JG, Sept. 7 2018.

57   "a fairly": Iain Blair, "How Wham! Became Teenage Idols . . . or, the Tale of the $60,000 Haircut," *Chicago Tribune*, Aug. 18, 1985.

57   "It's dreadful": Simon Napier-Bell, *I'm Coming to Take You to Lunch*, 115.

57   "I totally": Rob Tannenbaum, "Artist or Airhead?," *Musician*, January 1988.

57   "they were": Tannenbaum.

58   "All right": Paul Spong to JG, Apr. 14, 2020.

58   "has a vestigial": Stephen Holden, "George Michael Tour Brings 'Bad'-Like Frenzy," *New York Times*, Sept. 9, 1988.

58   "He's going": Jamie James, "This Pair Has a Right to Be a Little Cocky," *San Francisco Examiner*, Aug. 25, 1985.

59   "From my": David Geffen to JG, Sept. 5, 2017.

59   "I've got": Paul Gomersall to JG, Apr. 4, 2020.

59   "embittered": Simon Price, "We Love You, George, but You Don't Make It Easy for Us," *Independent*, Aug. 16, 2009.

60   "We wanted . . . rid of him": Chris Porter to JG, June 2, 2018.

60   "I think . . . That's real": Steve Gregory to JG, Apr. 15, 2020.

60   "Technically": Andrew D'Angelo to JG, Dec. 6, 2020.

61   "The fact": Allen Mezquida to JG, Jan. 12, 2021.

61   **"I was a bit . . . the record"**: Steve Gregory to JG.

61   **"We sat"**: Paul Spong to JG.

61   **"Wham! was"**: Ellyn Solis to JG, May 23, 2017.

61   **"Don't be"**: Simon Napier-Bell, *I'm Coming to Take You to Lunch*, 221.

62   **"They were . . . crazy"**: Howard Thompson to JG, Aug. 10, 2018.

62   **"George struck"**: Debbie Samuelson to JG, June 13, 2017.

62   **"beyond a joke"**: "Wham! Star Lashes 'Old Man' Mick," *Daily Mail*, June 17, 1986.

63   **"Andrew wanted"**: Paul Spong to JG.

63   **"Randy Andy . . . fabrication"**: Phil Dampier, "Andy's Antics," *Sun*, Mar. 28, 1985.

63   **"I'm twenty-one"**: David Thomas & Greg Placek, "George Michael: Wham!'s Biggest Fan," *Los Angeles Times*, June 28, 1985.

63   **"We take"**: "Chart War Winners," *Daily Mirror*, Oct. 20, 1984.

63   **"Well, let's"**: Dennis Hunt, "Wham's Singer an Arrogant Chap," *Los Angeles Times*, Nov. 9, 1984.

63   **"His songwriting"**: Lesley-Ann Jones, "What's Wrong with Today's Pop Stars," *Daily Mail*, June 3, 1986.

64   **"was the best"**: Caroline Graham to JG, Nov. 27, 2018.

64   **"The music business"**: "Boy George Dumps on His Pop Pals," *Sun*, Feb. 8, 1985.

64   **"always so snotty"**: Boy George (with Spencer Bright), *Take It Like a Man* (!t Books, 1995) 446.

65   **"camp"**: George (Bright), 257.

65   **"AIDS Blood"**: "AIDS Blood Donor Who Infected 41 People Dies," *Sun*, Feb. 11, 1985.

65   **"AIDS Panic"**: John Kay, "AIDS Panic at British Airways," *Sun*, Feb. 22, 1985.

65   **"AIDS Is"**: Hugh Whittow, "AIDS Is the Wrath of God, Says Vicar," *Sun*, Feb. 7, 1985.

65   **"Don't Sleep"**: Peter Bond, "Don't Sleep Around, Gays Told," *Sun*, Feb. 7, 1985.

65   **"The health"**: Charles Rae, "Boot Out Gays' Call to Union!," *Sun*, May 1, 1985.

65   **"gay sex drug"**: *Sun*, spring 1985.

65   **"high-pitched"**: Julie Burchill, "Standing in a Different Corner," *Times*, May 5, 1986.

65   **"I don't think"**: Danny Kelly, "Idoling Away the Years," *New Musical Express*, Nov. 16, 1985.

66   **"*Do you find*"**: GM, *The Tube*, c.1985.

67   **"I gorged"**: "Wham! Star George Went on Sex Spree," *Daily Mail*, June 24, 1986.

67   **"so that"**: Paul Gomersall to JG.

67   **"I can't"**: *George Michael: A Different Story* (documentary), 2005.

67   **"career was . . . profile"**: Midge Ure, "My Live Aid Nightmare," *Daily Mail*, Oct. 4, 2004.

67   **"There's nothing"**: Bill Hagerty, "Wise at 21 . . . with Dreams of More Than Cash & Looks," *Daily Mirror*, Dec. 28, 2016.

68   **"One day"**: Simon Napier-Bell to JG.

68   **"A lot of"** . . . **"wanker"**: Mick Brown, "Going Out with a Wham!," *Sunday Times*, June 22, 1986.

68   **"*I'll tell*"**: Midge Ure, "My Live Aid Nightmare."

68   **"was one"**: *Rock: The Luckiest Man in Pop* (2012), 153.

69   **"Don't be"**: Craig Marks & Rob Tannenbaum, *I Want My MTV* (Dutton, 2011), 246.

69   **"That didn't"**: David Thomas & Greg Placek, "George Michael: Wham!'s Biggest Fan."

70   **"a floor"**: Rebecca Batties, "All-Action Wham Are a Pleasant Surprise," *Age* (Melbourne), Jan. 24, 1985.

70   **"wind noise"**: Paul Spong to JG.

70   **"George Michael's"**: Mick Brown, "Wembley: Wham," *Guardian*, Dec. 28, 1984.

70   **"reduced to"**: Mark Ellen, " 'He Sat at the Piano and Rolled Endless Spliffs,' " *Times*, Sept. 18, 2010.

70   **"It was difficult"**: Rebecca Batties, "All-Action Wham Are a Pleasant Surprise."

71   **"It's all"**: David Wigg, "Wham Slam from George," *Daily Express*, Dec. 6, 1984.

71   **"I think"**: David Thomas, "Wham! Why They're the Heartthrobs of American Teens," *Boston Globe*, Feb. 7, 1985.

72   "You really": Steve Morse, "Wham! Powderpuff Pop and Pretty-Boy Posing," *Boston Globe*, Dec. 18, 1985.

72–73   "was not much . . . very often": Billy Masters to JG, June 13, 2018.

73   "the greatest" . . . "to me": Nick Ferrari, "Wham Weeps," *Sun*, Mar. 14, 1985.

73   "Messing": Simon Napier-Bell, *I'm Coming to Take You to Lunch*, 52.

73   "Everyone looked": Andrew Jacobs to JG, Mar. 18, 2019.

74   "the prized": Willy Newlands, "Pop! Goes the Peking Hard Line," *Sydney Sun-Herald*, Mar. 31, 1985.

CHAPTER FIVE

75   "grim": Simon Napier-Bell, *I'm Coming to Take You to Lunch*, vii.

75   "all you could": Danny Cummings to JG, May 26, 2018.

75   "I can't imagine": Sam Neville, "East Meets Wham!, and Another Great Wall Comes Down," *Chicago Tribune*, Apr. 28, 1985.

75   "It was all": Paul Spong to JG, Apr. 14, 2020.

75   "a cultural": Sam Neville, "East Meets Wham!."

75   "I had a": Deon Estus to JG, May 2, 2019.

76   "a landmark": "*If . . .*," Critics Consensus, *Rotten Tomatoes*.

76   "If we react": "The Rock Age: Wham! Shakes Peking," New York *Daily News*, Apr. 8, 1985.

76   "Stay in": Simon Napier-Bell, *I'm Coming to Take You to Lunch*, 198.

76   "We walked": Paul Spong to JG.

77   "This was mortifying": Craig Peikin to JG, Apr. 10, 2018.

77   "One guy": Danny Cummings to JG.

77   "much better": "The Rock Age: Wham! Shakes Peking."

77   "If all": Yibi Hu to JG, Sept. 24, 2020.

78   "screaming": Sam Neville, "East Meets Wham!."

78   "Had he used . . . anybody": Paul Spong to JG.

78   "We knew": "From Wham! to Tiananmen Square? It Makes Sense to Me," *Independent*, Apr. 11, 2015.

78   "I am not": "Mixed Reactions," *Philadelphia Inquirer*, Apr. 16, 1985.

78   "I'd never": "Once Is Enough," *Orlando Sentinel*, Oct. 4, 1985.

78   "There's a general": "China Bans Pop Stars," *Daily Mirror*, Oct. 4, 1985.

79   "He'd made": Simon Napier-Bell, *I'm Coming to Take You to Lunch*, 240.

79   "Jazz and Simon": Lindsay Anderson to GM, Letter, Oct. 2, 1985.

79   "a fearful idiot" . . . "execute": Letter, Lindsay Anderson to Dave, Jan. 10, 1986.

79   "pretty": John Peel, "Wham! Bam, Thank You," *Observer*, July 6, 1986.

80   "I can write": Dennis Hunt, "Wham!'s Singer an Arrogant Chap," *Los Angeles Times*, Nov. 9, 1984.

80   "relieved": Boy George (with Spencer Bright), *Take It Like a Man*, (!t Books, 1995), 290.

80   "The Stevie thing": Rob Tannenbaum, "George Michael—Artist or Airhead?," *Musician*, Jan. 1988.

81   "There's something": Simon Napier-Bell to JG, Sep 7, 2018.

81   "it was a bit": Gill Pringle to JG, June 23, 2018.

82   "very gorgeous": Gill Pringle & Reginald White, "Gorgeous George by Di the Royal Wham Fan," *Daily Mirror*, Jan. 30, 1986.

84   "Are you horny?": James Spencer to JG, Oct. 8, 2017.

84   "Good evening": Randy Lewis, "Wham!—Specks in a Spectacle," *Los Angeles Times*, Sept. 2, 1985.

84   "It was a": James Spencer to JG.

84   "decent-enough": Anne Hull, "Wham! Delivers Slick Package to Euphoric Fans," *St. Petersburg Times*, Sept. 9, 1985.

84   "more derivative": Scott Benarde, "Duo Wham! Jams Well at Razzle-Dazzle Show," *South Florida Sun-Sentinel*, Sept. 9, 1985.

84   "Will he be": Iain Blair, "How Wham! Became Teenage Idols," *Chicago Tribune*, August 18, 1985.

84   "It's going": David Wigg, "Wham! Bam! Thank You Fans!," *Daily Mirror*, June 28, 1986.

85   "Yeah, I'm": Craig Peikin to JG, Apr. 10, 2018.

85   "I don't care . . . huge": Carolyn Montgomery to JG, Aug. 17, 2020.

85   "An hour ago": Lesley-Ann Jones, "Is There Life After Wham?," *Daily Mail*, Nov. 19, 1986.

86   **"dusky"**: Lesley-Ann Jones, "A Record Booze-Up," *Sun*, February 16, 1985.

86   **"I announced"**: Adam Mattera, "George Michael: Days of the Open Hand," *Attitude*, May 2004.

86   **"How Pat"**: Boy George (with Spencer Bright), *Take It Like a Man*, 446.

86   **"silly drugs"**: Bryan Appleyard, "The Puppet Who Pulled the Strings." *Times*, Sept. 8, 1990.

86   **"Kathy looked"**: Bret Witke to JG, May 1, 2020.

86   **"found happiness"**: Gill Pringle & Lesley Johnson, "Wham's Sunshine Reunion," *Daily Mirror*, Aug. 20, 1986.

87   **"passionate affair"**: Roger Tavener, "Wham! George Broke My Heart," *Daily Express*, June 16, 1988.

87   **"Brooke Shields"**: Simon Napier-Bell to JG.

87   **"We hear"**: "Brooke and George Make a Beautiful Couple," *Rolling Stone*, Dec. 27, 1985.

87   **"I think"**: Roger Tavener, "Wham! George Broke My Heart," *Daily Express*, June 16, 1988.

87   **"You get"**: Patrick Goldstein, "Rod Stewart Sounds an Echo of Dylan," *Los Angeles Times*, June 26, 1988.

87   **"He was such"**: Brooke Shields, *The Wendy Williams Show*, Oct. 6, 2011.

88   **"I just never"**: *Careless Whiskers: The Unseen George Michael* (documentary), 2006.

CHAPTER SIX

89   **"It's not"**: Danny Cummings to JG, May 26, 2018.

90   **"You've been"**: Rob Kahane to JG, Sept. 28, 2018.

90   **"He had let"**: Simon Napier-Bell to JG, Sept. 7, 2018.

90   **"He desperately"**: Paul Spong to JG, Apr. 14, 2020.

90   **"bloke prancing"**: David Wigg, "Wham! Was Sham, Says Fed-Up Star George," *Daily Express*, June 18, 1986.

90   **"This Thatcherite"**: Phil Shaw, "Sweet Soul Music Man," *Guardian*, Nov. 22, 1985.

91   **"You were meant"**: Simon Napier-Bell, *I'm Coming to Take You to Lunch*, 264.

92   **"Motor racing"**: Roger Tavener, "Why My Bad Boy Days Are Over, by Wham! Star," *Daily Express*, Aug. 1, 1986.

93   **"He said"**: Simon Napier-Bell to JG.

93   **"personal decision"**: Gill Pringle, "Wham Stars Split!," *Daily Mirror*, Feb. 22, 1986.

93   **"finished"**: Simon Napier-Bell to JG.

93   **"By the end"**: Roger Tavener, "So You Think the Wild Man of Wham! Is All Washed Up . . . ," *Daily Express*, Apr. 14, 1986.

93   **"Andrew is"**: John Blake, "Dumped Again," *Daily Mirror*, Feb. 28, 1986.

93   **"discussed"**: "Wham! Goes Boom! As George Michael Dumps His Bitter Half, Andrew Ridgeley," *People*, Mar. 10, 1986.

93   **"ignoring"**: Lesley-Ann Jones, "Is There Life After Wham?," *Daily Mail*, Nov. 19, 1986.

94   **"I thought"**: Daniel Martin, "Wham! Singer Andrew Ridgeley Slams X Factor," *Daily Mail*, Oct. 13, 2019.

94   **"George had"**: Danny Cummings to JG.

94   **"Ten years"**: Adam Sweeting, "Clash of Values," *Guardian*, Mar. 11, 1988.

94   **"really filthy"**: Bryan Appleyard, "The Puppet Who Pulled the Strings." *Times*, Sept. 8, 1990.

95   **"presented"**: Anne Barrowclough, "Wake Me Up When It's Time to Go-Go!," *Daily Mail*, June 16, 1986.

96   **"He reckoned"**: George Michael & Tony Parsons, *Bare* (Michael Joseph, 1990),181.

96   **"They'd say"**: Rob Kahane to JG.

96   **"She wasn't"**: Rob Tannenbaum, "George Michael—Artist or Airhead?" *Musician*, Jan. 1988.

96   **"She'd put"**: Rob Kahane to JG.

97   **"Hey, man . . . Franklin"**: Mike Southon to JG, May 7, 2020.

97   **"I don't"**: John Blake, "Pro George Soldiers On," *Daily Mirror*, June 13, 1986.

98   **"We were all"**: Danny Cummings to JG.

98   "finally": Antony Thorncroft, "Wham/Wembley Stadium," *Financial Times*, July 1, 1986.

99   "a doomed": John Peel, "Wham! Bam, Thank You," *Observer*, July 6, 1986.

99   "like two": "Wham! The Final Concert," *Daily Mirror*, June 30, 1986.

99   "the best": Jim White, "My Kind of Guy," *Guardian*, Apr. 15, 1998.

99   "exactly the": Julie Burchill, "Standing in a Different Corner," *Times*, May 5, 1986.

99   "I couldn't": Simon Napier-Bell to JG.

100   "My son": John Blake, "Dishy Enough to Eat!," *Daily Mirror*, Oct. 22, 1986.

100   "was telling": Chris Evans, "An Audience with George Michael," BBC Radio 1, Dec. 8, 1996.

100   "his mother": Deon Estus to JG, May 2, 2019.

100   "She was as": Rob Kahane to JG.

100   "I suspect": Judy Wieder to JG, Mar. 23, 2018.

CHAPTER SEVEN

101   "I'm mad": Stefan Kyriazis, "Freddie Mercury's Cheeky George Michael Comment," *Express*, Sept. 22, 2019.

102   "for the very": GM to Mark Goodier, *Faith*, Legacy Edition 2010.

102   "couldn't get": Richard Smith & Steve Pafford, "George Talks: His Frankest Interview Ever," *Gay Times*, July 2007.

102   "tired": Smith & Pafford.

102   "David called": Simon Napier-Bell to JG, Sept. 7, 2018.

103   "one-man" Henrik Tuxen, "Gold from the Savings: The Story of George Michael," *Gaffa*, Apr. 13, 2020.

103   "massively": GM to Mark Goodier, *Faith* Legacy Edition, 2010.

103   "He always had": Steve Sidwell to JG, Apr. 7, 2020.

103   "George, you": Paul Spong to JG, April 14, 2020.

104   "George, tell": Spong.

104   "He manages": Baz Bamigboye, "The Gender Pretenders," *Daily Mail*, Aug. 2, 1984.

104   "It was convenience": Danny Cummings to JG. May 26, 2018.

105   "I want it": Chris Porter to JG, June 2, 2018.

105   "songwriting": Stephen Holden, "George Michael: He'll Last," *New York Times*, 1988.

105   "I always imagined": "Boy George Has an Unreleased George Michael Duet," *Celebratainment*, Oct. 26, 2017.

105   "a semicomplete": Danny Cummings to JG.

105   "Because of": Chris Cameron to JG, June 2, 2018.

106   "George couldn't": Rob Kahane to JG, Sept. 28, 2018.

106   "he would come": Chris Porter to JG.

106   "I started": Chris Cameron to JG, June 2, 2018

106   "this thing": Paul Gomersall to JG. Apr. 4, 2020.

106   "just because": "The Faith Interview" (U.S. radio), 1987.

107   "We were": Bret Witke to JG.

107   "the way": Lucas Cava, "Creating Without Prejudice," *lucascava. medium*, Sept. 28, 2019.

107   "the nearest thing": Danny Cummings to JG.

108   "each take": John Altman to JG, July 29, 2017.

108   "Personally": Paul Spong to JG.

108   "this horrible": Craig Rosen, *The Billboard Book of Number One Albums*, Watson-Guptill, 1996.

109   "I remember": Chris Cameron to JG, June 2, 2018.

109   "George Michael, by": "George Michael Headlines Rather Splendid AIDS Benefit," *Smash Hits*, Feb. 25-Mar. 10, 1987.

110   "ecstatic": "Wham! Back," *Daily Mail*, Apr. 2, 1987.

110   "I was standing": Chris Heath to JG, July 10, 2017.

110   "He wasn't happy": "Boy George Has an Unreleased George Michael Duet," *Celebratainment*, Oct. 26, 2017.

111   "I'm afraid": Hugh Muir, "George Michael's Sex Appeal in Court," *Daily Telegraph*, Oct. 29, 1993.

111   "George knew": Mike Southon to JG, May 7, 2020.

111   "Personally": Craig Marks & Rob Tannenbaum, *I Want My MTV* (Dutton, 2011), 310.

111   "Andy": Marks & Tannenbaum.

112 **"nervy"**: Cliff Radel, "It's Easy to Say No to 'Sex,'" *Cincinnati Enquirer*, June 6, 1987.

112 **"I remember"**: Trevor Dann to JG, June 23, 2021.

112 **"At a time"**: Stephen Holden, "Sign of the Times," *New York Times*, Jun. 11, 1987.

112 **"child sexual molestation"** . . . **"nation today"**: Tracey Buchanan, "Teens Like It, but Readers Say Don't Play Sex Song," *Paducah Sun*, June 26, 1987.

112 **"blatant"**: Susan Whitall, "Barry White: 'The Man Is Back,'" *Gannett Westchester Newspapers*, June 18, 1990.

112 **"I'll be perfectly"**: "Stardom" radio interview, 1987.

113 **"I find that"**: "George's Sexy Song Attacked by Angry Cliff," *Daily Mail*, Oct. 5, 1987.

113 **"Kids aren't"**: Chris Heath, "Love, Sex and Stupid Wigs," *Smash Hits*, June 3–16, 1987.

113 **"In no way"**: J. D. Considine, "Is Michael's Sex Naughty or Not?," *Baltimore Sun*, Aug. 16, 1987.

113 **"per the"**: Chris Willman, "Sex! Sweeps! Philosophy!?," *Los Angeles Times*, June 28, 1987.

114 **"started writing"**: Heath, "Love, Sex and Stupid Wigs," *Smash Hits*, 1987.

114 **"I didn't have"**: Smith & Pafford, "George Talks: His Frankest Interview Ever," *Gay Times*, 2007.

114 **"accommodate:"** Heath, "Love, Sex and Stupid Wigs," *Smash Hits*, 1987.

114 **"contrived"**: Chris Willman, "Sex! Sweeps! Philosophy!?"

114 **"snowballed"**: Paul Grein, "George Michael's Got 'Faith' and Lots More," *Los Angeles Times*, Nov. 4, 1988.

114 **"No doubt"**: "A Salty Album Cleans Up," *Courier-Journal* (Louisville, KY), Mar. 11, 1988.

115 **"fairly obvious"**: *The Last Resort with Jonathan Ross*, July 19, 1987.

115 **"That places"**: Jeff Davis, "MTV Connoisseurs Respond to 'Hot' Video with Yawns," *Press & Sun-Bulletin* (Binghamton, NY), June 23, 1987.

115   "Musically": Adrian Deevoy, "Sex, Drugs and Sony," *Big Issue*, Nov. 11–17, 1996.

115   "I'm very": *The Last Resort with Jonathan Ross*.

CHAPTER EIGHT

116   "When George": Bret Witke to JG, May 1, 2020.

116   "I didn't want": Rob Kahane to JG, Sept. 28, 2018.

116   "But they": Phillip Zonkel, "George Michael's Publicist During 'Faith' Album, Tour Remembers the Pop Icon," *Q Voice News*, Jan. 23, 2017.

116   "basically": Adam Mattera, "George Michael: Days of the Open Hand," *Attitude*, May 2004.

116–17   "She was like . . . playing": Bret Witke to JG.

117   "He thought": Rob Kahane to JG.

117–18   "the industry's": Beth Landman & Alex Williams, "Reversal of Fortune," *New York*, July 30, 2001.

118   "to become": "The Faith Interview" (U.S. radio), 1987.

118   "a star": "Figure Head," *Daily Mirror* Jan. 7, 1988.

119   "George always": Jane Berk to JG, May 30, 2017.

119   "We were all": Dave Novik to JG, Dec. 7, 2017.

119   "I'm gonna": "The Faith Interview" (U.S. radio), 1987.

120   "I've been accused": *South Bank Show*, ITV, Sept. 2, 1990.

120   "a middle-class": Mick Brown, "Wham! Torment Hits a Middle-Class Soul," *Sunday Times*, June 19, 1988.

120   "It was a": Bret Witke to JG.

120   "I somehow": GM to Mark Goodier, *Faith Legacy Edition*, 2010.

121   "that strange": *The Red Line*, Pt. 1, BBC Radio 2.

121   "He was probably": Judy Wieder to JG, March 23, 2018.

121   "What does": Jane Berk to JG, May 30, 2017.

121   "a very intelligent": Marc T. Nobleman, "The Girl in the Video: 'Father Figure' (1988), *Noblemania*, July 25, 2014.

121   "If you said": Bret Witke to JG.

121   "It never": Howard Thompson to JG, Aug. 10, 2018.

121   **"If I turn"**: GM, "The Faith Interview" (U.S. radio), 1987.

122   **"I don't want"**: Bobby Hankinson, "A Little Respect for Erasure's Andy Bell," *Towleroad*, Jan. 31, 2014.

122   **"I'm sure"**: Michael Pagnotta to JG, July 10, 2017.

122   **"none true"**: Rob Kahane to JG.

122   **"on the town"**: John Blake, "Brilliant June," *Daily Mirror*, Feb. 5, 1987.

122   **"with a French"**: "Hellraiser George and His French Connection," *Daily Mail*, July 15, 1989.

122   **"reported"**: "Hellraiser George and His French Connection."

123   **"appeared to"**: Jim White, "My Kind of Guy," *Guardian*, Apr. 15, 1998.

123   **"I was stunned"**: Andros Georgiou, "The Day I Told George Michael His Lover Had Died of AIDS," *Sun*, Nov. 12, 2012.

123   **"met that person"**: "The Crisis Tearing George Michael Apart," *Daily Mail*, May 10, 1988.

123   **"about my"**: Chris Heath, "Love, Sex and Stupid Wigs," *Smash Hits*, June 3–16, 1987.

123   **"These days"**: Garry Jenkins, "The New Me, by George Michael," *Daily Mail*, Apr. 13, 1988.

123   **"he had arrived"**: Danny Cummings to JG, May 26, 2018.

124   **"At twenty-four"**: Stephen Holden, "George Michael: He'll Last," *New York Times*, 1988.

124   **"a startling"**: Paul Grein, "George Michael's Got 'Faith' and Lots More," *Los Angeles Times*, Nov. 4, 1988.

124   **"one of pop's"**: Mark Coleman, "Faith," *Rolling Stone*, Jan. 14, 1988.

124   **"a collection"**: Tom Moon, "Recreating George Michael," *Philadelphia Inquirer*, Aug. 7, 1988.

124   **"less of a"**: Marcus Berkmann, "It's No Laughing Matter When Pop Stars Are Hit by Those Moody Blues," *Daily Mail*, Nov. 2, 1987.

124   **"George was in"**: Dave Bitelli to JG, June 3, 2018.

125   **"a pastiche"**: Dave Hill, "Reaching for the Dimmer Switch," *Independent*, June 13, 1987.

125   **"an anonymous"**: Robert Hilburn, "George Michael's Case Against Fame," *Los Angeles Times*, Sept. 9, 1990.

125 **"work of genius"**: Rick Sky, "George Loses Faith with the Critics," *Sun*, Nov. 30, 1987.

125 **"I resent"**: Adrian Deevoy, "The Lone Star State," *Q*, June 1988.

125 **"I really think"**: Steve Pond, "George Michael, Seriously," *Rolling Stone*, Jan. 28, 1988.

126 **"the highlight"**: Stephen Holden, "The Pop Life," *New York Times*, Aug. 31, 1988.

126 **"He was so"**: Rob Kahane to JG.

126 **"You have to"**: Barbara Jaeger, "Crossover: Black, White, and Heard All Over," *Record* (Hackensack, NJ), Apr. 14, 1989.

126 **"Who does"**: Dennis Hunt, "Freddie Jackson Won't Sell His Soul for a Pop Hit," *Los Angeles Times*, Jun. 26, 1988.

127 **"unbelievably"**: George Michael vs. Sony, June 1994, 81.

127 **"You don't even"**: George Michael vs. Sony, June 1994, 84.

CHAPTER NINE

130 **"They were making"**: Deon Estus to JG, May 2, 2019.

130 **"All the really"**: "The Faith Interview" (U.S. radio), 1987.

130 **"constantly"**: Ben Rimalower to JG, June 7, 2019.

131 **"I had to be"**: Rob Kahane to JG, 28, 2018.

131 **"They want"**: Adrian Deevoy, "The Lone Star State," *Q*, June 1988.

131 **"You're a great"**: Chris Cameron to JG, June 2, 2018.

132 **"All these"**: Rob Kahane to JG.

132 **"the most"**: Marcus Berkmann, "George Michael Beards Reluctant Audience," *Daily Mail*, June 11, 1988.

133 **"He chases"**: Antony Thorncroft, "George Michael/Earls Court," *Financial Times,* June 16, 1988.

133 **"We couldn't"**: Chris Cameron to JG, June 2, 2018.

133 **"His most"**: Jon Bowermaster, "Michael Unmasked," *Chicago Tribune*, Sept. 4, 1988.

133 **"meant"**: *The Red Line*, Pt. 1, BBC Radio 2.

134 **"Self-loathing"**: David Geffen to JG, Sept. 5, 2017.

134 **"same"** . . . **"environment"**: Chris Cameron to JG, May 27, 2021.

134 **"Where Whitney"**: Adam Sweeting, "Right-On George in Shape for the 90s," *Guardian*, Jun. 14, 1988.

134 **"You have to"**: Garry Jenkins, "The Crisis Tearing George Michael Apart," *Daily Mail*, May 10, 1988.

134 **"believe me"**: *The Red Line*, Pt. 1, BBC Radio 2.

134 **"There is twice"**: Garry Jenkins, "The Crisis Tearing George Michael Apart."

134 **"The more people . . . bother me"**: Adrian Deevoy, "The Lone Star State," *Q*, June 1988.

135 **"What's the point"**: Chris Heath, "Love, Sex and Stupid Wigs," *Smash Hits*, June 3–16, 1987.

135 **"I thought it" . . . "real man"**: Jeff McMullen to JG, March 16, 2020.

136 **"George, are" . . . "year's time"**: "Gorgeous George," *60 Minutes* (AU), March 16, 1988.

136 **"Why did" . . . "explore"**: Jeff McMullen to JG.

137 **"video"**: Patrick Goldstein, "The 'George, Are You Gay?' Scandal," *Los Angeles Times*, Sept. 18, 1988.

137 **"I had a"**: Jeff McMullen to JG.

138 **"feminine-looking"**: Adrian Deevoy, "The Lone Star State," *Q*, June 1988.

138 **"George went"**: Gill Pringle, "Belt Up George," *Daily Mirror*, Mar. 22, 1988.

138 **"He sprained"**: Gill Pringle, "George Lets the Fans Down Again," *Daily Mirror*, Mar. 31, 1988.

138 **"a satellite"**: Louise Court, "Riding George's Dream Machine," *Daily Express*, Apr. 20, 1988.

138 **"Sensible questions . . . teeth"**: Adrian Deevoy, "The Lone Star State."

139 **"What I'm not"**: Richard Smith, "George Michael—A Single Man?," *Gay Times*, May 1996.

139 **"Have you"**: Adrian Deevoy, "The Lone Star State."

139 **"I was very"**: Robert Hilburn, "George Michael's Case Against Fame," *Los Angeles Times*, Sept. 9, 1990.

139   "The people": Gill Pringle, "Too Many Gigs," *Daily Mirror*, May 30, 1988.

139   "People thought": Hilburn, "George Michael's Case Against Fame."

140   "This country's": Adam Sweeting, "Right-On George in Shape for the 90s," *Guardian*, Jun. 14, 1988.

140   "A sorry": Peter Watrous, "Political Moments Only Spark in 'Freedomfest,' " *New York Times*, June 14, 1988.

140   "narcissistic": Marcus Berkmann, "George Michael Beards Reluctant Audience," *Daily Mail*, June 11, 1988.

140   "mechanically": Antony Thorncroft, "George Michael/Earls Court," *Financial Times,* June 16, 1988.

141   "I feel" . . . "rather sad": Mick Brown, "Wham! Torment Hits a Middle-Class Soul," *Sunday Times*, June 19, 1988.

141   "Normally": Gary Graff, "Queen Sees More Duets," *Detroit Free Press*, Aug. 31, 1988.

141   "No bullshit": Gary Graff, "Michael Wows Crowd and Aretha," *Detroit Free Press*, Aug. 31, 1988.

141–42   "It was wonderful . . . great": Graff.

142   "He's very": "Queen Sees More Duets," *Detroit Free Press*, Aug. 31, 1988.

142   "Michael exuberantly": Dennis Hunt, "The Seductive Style of George Michael," *Los Angeles Times*, Oct. 4, 1988.

142   "I can honestly": *Sunday Correspondent* (U.K.), 1990.

CHAPTER TEN

143   "When he talks": Bryan Appleyard, "The Puppet Who Pulled the Strings," *Times*, Sept. 8, 1990.

143   "There's good": Rick Sylvain, "Carmen McRae Is a Living Jazz Legend," *Detroit Free Press*, Sept. 2, 1988.

143   "I had my": *Battle Creek Enquirer*, Dec. 9, 1988.

143   "the most": Rob Kahane to JG, 28, 2018.

143   "Everyone owes": Adrian Deevoy, "The Lone Star State," *Q*, June 1988.

144   **"His homes"**: Danny Cummings to JG, May 26, 2018.

144   **"Like that"**: Richard Smith, "George Michael—A Single Man?" May 1996.

144   **"Whatever"**: "Billy Joel Faces Money Woes," AP (*Longview News Journal*), Nov. 23, 1990.

145   **"Is he"**: Barbara Lippert, *Matadors of Music*, Feb. 10, 1989.

146   **"outsider"**: *South Bank Show*, ITV, Sept. 2, 1990.

146   **"It's a puzzle"**: "Dionne Warwick Is Not Happy with Dick Clark," *TV Guide*, Apr. 8, 1989.

146   **"This being"**: "Dionne Warwick Is Not Happy with Dick Clark."

146   **"I didn't ask"**: *South Bank Show*, Sept. 2, 1990.

146   **"Before we"**: *Saturday Night Live*, NBC, Feb. 11, 1989.

147   **"because he"**: Rob Kahane to JG.

147   **"reportedly"**: David Browne, "Don't Worry, Be Happy," New York *Daily News*, Feb. 19, 1989.

147   **"surprise"**: Robert Hilburn, "McFerrin's 'Don't Worry' Wins Top Single Grammy," *Los Angeles Times*, Feb. 23, 1989.

147   **"an album"**: Richard De Atley, "Bobby's Happy," AP (*Fort Worth Star-Telegram*), Feb. 23, 1989.

147   **"I am completely"**: Jane Oddy, "I'm So Pissed," *Daily Mirror*, Apr. 5, 1989.

148–49   **"I think"**: Stephen Holden, "Image Gets in Way of George Michael's Music," *New York Times*, Sept. 8, 1988.

149   **"I'm not prolific"**: Rob Kahane to JG.

149   **"he was often"** . . . **"few days"**: Phil Palmer to JG.

149   **"He would do"**: Chris Cameron to JG, June 2, 2018.

149   **"It was a"**: Phil Palmer to JG.

149   **"to bring"**: Danny Cummings to JG.

149   **"distracting"** . . . **"the song"**: Phil Palmer to JG.

150   **"It's like"**: Will Automagic to JG, July 19, 2019.

150   **"to show"**: Mikael Wood, "Little More Than a Careless Whisper," *Los Angeles Times*, Oct. 21, 2017.

151   **"the Paul"**: Adam Sweeting, "Now George Wants Your Cheques," *Guardian*, Aug. 30, 1990.

152   **"Can you"**: Danny Cummings to JG.

152   **"All you have"**: Rob Kahane to JG.

152   **"stunned"**: Andros Georgiou, *The Luckiest Man in Pop*, 253.

152   **"If I take"**: *The Red Line*, Pt. 1, BBC Radio 2.

153   **"His eyes"** . . . **"onstage"**: Rob Kahane to JG.

153   **"and it ended"**: Chris Cameron to JG, May 27, 2021.

CHAPTER ELEVEN

154   **"He was pretty"**: Adrian Deevoy, "Strictly No Admittance: The Privatisation of George Michael," *Q*, Nov. 1990.

154   **"This album"**: Robert Hilburn, "The Hot 'Tag Team' of Rock Management," *Los Angeles Times*, Apr. 8, 1990.

154   **"very macho"**: Chrissy Iley, "How I've Made It on Wham, Women and Song," *Daily Mail*, Apr. 6, 1990.

155   **"super-suspicious"**: Chris Heath to JG, July 10, 2017.

155   **"breezy"**: Chrissy Iley, "How I've Made It on Wham, Women and Song," *Daily Mail*, Apr. 6, 1990.

155   **"fake-raunchy"**: Greg Sandow, "Son of Albert," *Entertainment Weekly*, June 1, 1990.

155   **"I'd never have"**: Adrian Deevoy, "Strictly No Admittance."

156   **"transformation"**: John Davison & Alexandra Frean, "By George: Mr. Michael Stays Cool Over His Lost Memoirs," *Sunday Times*, Sept. 2, 1990.

156   **"a bright"**: Kevin Jackson, "Bright-Eyed and Bushey-Tailed Pop," *Independent*, Sept. 3, 1990.

156   **"considerable"**: Chris Heath, "Baring the Pain of Success," *Daily Telegraph*, Sept. 8, 1990.

156   **"I don't believe"**: *South Bank Show*, Sept. 2, 1990.

156   **"had become"**: Tony Parsons, "In the Court of King George," *Daily Telegraph*, July 13, 1991.

157   **"superficial"**: Rob Kahane to JG, 28, 2018.

157   **"everything that"**: George Michael & Tony Parsons, *Bare* (Michael Joseph, 1990), 135.

157   **"I've settled"**: *Bare*, 229–230.

157   **"It wouldn't matter"**: *Bare*, 230.

157   **"that someone's"**: Adrian Deevoy, "Strictly No Admittance."

157   **"They immediately"**: Billy Masters to JG, June 13, 2018.

157   **"kind of"**: Mike Ellison, Mike, "The Day the Music Died for a Pop Icon," *Guardian*, June 23, 1994.

157   **"Very little"**: "Hyperactive Singer Has Clothes to Prove It," *Index-Journal* (Greenwood, SC), Sept. 12, 1990.

158   **"He was just"**: Rob Kahane to JG.

158   **"sharp drop"**: George Michael vs. Sony, June 1994, 53.

158   **"very brash"**: Dave Novik to JG, Dec. 7, 2017.

158   **"Our job"**: Chuck Philips, "Michael's Pact with Sony is Upheld," *Los Angeles Times*, June 22, 1994.

159   **"I was extremely"**: George Michael vs. Sony, June 1994, 53.

159   **"disappear"**: Adrian Deevoy, "Strictly No Admittance: The Privatisation of George Michael," Oct. 1990.

159   **"If my life"**: Robert Hilburn, "George Michael's Case Against Fame," *Los Angeles Times*, Sept. 9, 1990.

159   **"It was very"**: Rob Kahane to JG.

159   **"If you bought"**: Jerry Blair to JG, July 31, 2017.

159   **"lot of"**: "Hyperactive Singer Has Clothes to Prove It," *Index-Journal* (Greenwood, SC), Sept. 12, 1990.

159   **"I told George"**: George Michael vs. Sony, June 1994, 54.

160   **"Nothing on"**: Jay Landers to JG, Apr. 26, 2023.

160   **"driven by"**: Rick Sky, "So What if They Say I'm Gay," *Daily Mirror*, Apr. 22, 1993.

160   **"I can't see"**: Bryan Appleyard, "The Puppet Who Pulled the Strings," *Times*, Sept. 8, 1990.

160   **"I'm not stupid"**: Robert Hilburn, "George Michael's Case Against Fame," *Los Angeles Times*, Sept. 9, 1990.

160   **"doesn't seem"**: Gary Graff, "Some Rockers Would Rather Sing the Blues," *Detroit Free Press*, Feb. 10, 1991.

161   **"Come on, George"**: Letter, Frank Sinatra to GM, Sept. 9, 1990.

161   **"I think that"**: Ægean Records online chat, July 21, 1998.

161   **"merely voiced"**: Marcus Dunk, "He's Back—but Will George

Michael's New Album Be His Goodbye Note?" *Daily Express*, Mar. 6, 2004.

161 **"he was as"**: Rob Kahane to JG.

161 **"hot pursuit"**: Robert Sandall, "Now You See Him, Now You . . ." *Sunday Times*, Jan. 20, 1991.

162 **"gone from"**: Tom Moon, "George Michael's 'Listen,'" *Philadelphia Inquirer*, Sept. 11, 1990.

162 **"Singing pop"**: Chris Heath, "Baring the Pain of Success," *Daily Telegraph*, Sept. 8, 1990.

162 **"In reinventing"**: Deborah Wilker, "Michael Plays It Seriously," *South Florida Sun-Sentinel*, Sept. 11, 1990.

162 **"That the eloquent"**: Bruce Britt, "Album Deserves a 'Listen,'" *Los Angeles Daily News*, Sept. 16, 1990.

162 **"George may"**: Marcus Berkmann, "Here at Last, the 1990 Show!," *Daily Mail*, Dec. 18, 1990.

162 **"for the most"**: James Hunter, "Listen Without Prejudice Vol. 1," *Rolling Stone*, Oct. 4, 1990.

162 **"We don't get"**: David Munk to JG, Mar. 18, 2018.

163 **"Long before"**: Spencer Day to JG, Mar. 14, 2021.

163 **"fixated"**: Craig Marks & Rob Tannenbaum, *I Want My MTV* (Dutton, 2011), 486

163 **"We have this"**: "Can the World's Two Top Models Really Be Best Friends?," *Vogue*, Oct. 1990.

163 **"Look deep"**: Louise Gannon, "Vision on Video," *Daily Express*, June 20, 1992.

164 **"He thought it"**: Patrick Rogers, "Looking Back: George Michael's 'Freedom' Music Video," *Allure*, Aug. 2015.

164 **"Convincing"**: Rob Kahane to JG.

164 **"Apparently"** . . . **"happy"**: Mike Southon to JG, May 7, 2020.

165 **"It was a"**: Adam Mattera, "George Michael: Days of the Open Hand," *Attitude*, May 2004.

165 **"Little did"**: Rogers, "Looking Back: George Michael's 'Freedom' Music Video."

166 **"Selling"**: *The Red Line*, Pt. 1, BBC Radio 2.

166 **"He figured"**: Phil Palmer to JG.

166 "The white-hotness": Jerry Blair to JG, July 31, 2017.

166 "Music had": Reed McGowan to JG, Oct. 31, 2018.

167 "Every artist": Mickey Schulhof to JG, Mar. 26, 2018.

167 "Where's my": George Michael vs. Sony, June 1994, 220.

167 "did *not*": Jay Landers to JG, Apr. 26, 2023.

167 "I heard": *The Red Line*, Pt. 1, BBC Radio 2.

CHAPTER TWELVE

168 "Like most": Chris Heath, "George Michael," *Sunday Telegraph*, Mar. 17, 1991.

168 "I make": Neal Karlen, "Prince Talks," *Rolling Stone*, Oct. 18, 1990.

168 "No, I'm": Michael Pagnotta to JG, July 10, 2017.

169 "The pressure": Danny Cummings to JG, May 26, 2018.

169 "a spotlit": Jasper Rees, "George Michael/NEC Birmingham," *Sunday Times*, Jan. 17, 1991.

169 "Obsessive": Adam Sweeting, "Feeble Cover Drive," *Guardian*, Jan. 17, 1991.

170 "there was" . . . "self-discovery": "Will the Real George Please Sing Up?," *Daily Mail*, Jan. 16, 1991.

170 "You were about": James Rampton, "A Legend of His Own Making," *Independent*, Jan. 20, 1991.

170 "the George": Rob Kahane to JG, 28, 2018.

170 "All these": Michael Pagnotta to JG, July 10, 2017.

170 "I felt": *The Red Line*, Pt. 1, BBC Radio 2.

170 "If you tell": Matthew Parris, "What's George Done That Is So Dreadful?," *Sun*, Apr. 11, 1998.

171 "lemon-bleached" . . . "certainly do": Sarah Boseley, "Expensive Outing Could Smother The Face," *Guardian*, Apr. 4, 1992.

172–73 "it was stressful" . . . "each other": Rob Kahane to JG.

173 "He looked": Michael Snyder, "The Girls Still Squeal at George Michael," *San Francisco Chronicle*, Oct. 6, 1991.

173 "I think": Luiz Felipe Carneiro to JG, Apr. 18, 2019.

173 "The stadium": Danny Cummings to JG.

173 "I'm a football": Chris Cameron to JG, June 2, 2018.

173 **"I don't think"**: Luiz Felipe Carneiro to JG.

174 **"He's beautiful"** . . . **"went crazy"**: Rosa Fernandes to JG, May 31, 2019.

174 **"I saw him"**: *The Red Line*, Pt. 1, BBC Radio 2.

174 **"I have to go!"**: Lucia Guanabara to JG, Apr. 18, 2019.

174 **"merry throng"**: Danny Cummings to JG.

175 **"We split"**: Lucia Guanabara to JG.

175 **"He'd followed"**: Richard Smith & Steve Pafford, "George Talks: His Frankest Interview Ever," *Gay Times*, July 2007.

175 **"this angel"** . . . **"at me"**: *The Red Line*, Pt. 1, BBC Radio 2.

175 **"and he was"**: Smith & Pafford, "George Talks: His Frankest Interview Ever," *Gay Times*, 2007.

175 **"walked up"**: *The Red Line*, Pt. 1, BBC Radio 2.

175 **"was a dream"**: Rosa Fernandes to JG.

CHAPTER THIRTEEN

176 **"was such"**: Tony Parsons, "I Was Very Lucky to Have Had Anselmo in My Life," *Daily Mirror*, Nov. 10, 1997.

176 **"Everybody"**: Lucia Guanabara to JG, Apr. 18, 2019.

176 **"Life is"**: Parsons, "I Was Very Lucky to Have Had Anselmo in My Life," *Daily Mirror*, 1997.

176 **"Petrópolis"**: Marcelo Lago to JG, Nov. 14, 2017.

176 **"extremely"**: Sylvynho to JG, Nov. 15, 2017.

176 **"He was very"** . . . **"relieved"**: Marcelo Lago to JG.

177 **"From that time"**: Lucia Guanabara to JG.

177 **"He would"**: Sylvynho to JG.

177 **"We were"**: Patricia Agressot to JG, July 23, 2018.

177 **"Anselmo was"**: Rosa Fernandes to JG, May 31, 2019.

178 **"This was the"**: *The Red Line*, Pt. 2, BBC Radio 2, Nov. 8, 2017.

178 **"I'm here"**: Lucia Guanabara to JG.

178 **"This is my"**: Chris Porter to JG, June 2, 2018.

178 **"Everything was"**: Patricia Agressot to JG.

179 **"George turned"**: Jonathan King to JG, May 23, 2019.

179 **"Actually I've"**: *The 1991 BRIT Awards*, BBC, Feb. 10, 1991.

179   **"pompous"**: Deborah Wilker, "Michael Plays It Serious," *South Florida Sun Sentinel*, Sept. 11, 1990.

179   **"self-absorbed"**: Michael MacCambridge, "Michael Strives to Be Serious," *Austin American-Statesman*, Sept. 27, 1990.

179   **"It just"**: "The Faith Interview" (U.S. radio), 1987.

180   **"Luther doesn't"**: John Carlin to JG, Nov. 16, 2020.

181   **"emotional"**: Richard Cromelin, "George Michael Concert Has the Faithful Cheering," *Los Angeles Times*, Oct. 7, 1991.

181   **"Dropping"**: Barry Walters, "Inspired Interpreter," *San Francisco Examiner*, Oct. 2, 1991.

182   **"Elton wanted"** . . . **"Ecstasy"**: Rob Kahane to JG, 28, 2018.

183   **"Donnie was"**: Dave Novik to JG, Dec. 7, 2017.

183   **"overheard"**: Bruce Haring, *Off the Charts* (Birch Lane Press, 1996), 216.

183   **"I think that"**: George Michael vs. Sony, June 1994, 218–219.

183   **"Mr. Michael's"**: George Michael vs. Sony, 9–10.

183   **"deep trouble"**: George Michael vs. Sony, 220.

184   **"Please pass"**: George Michael vs. Sony, 221.

184   **"If further"**: George Michael vs. Sony, 222.

184   **"the straw"**: George Michael vs. Sony, 60.

184   **"looking at"**: *George Michael: A Different Story* (documentary), 2005.

185   **"He didn't want"**: Lucia Guanabara to JG.

185   **"the first love"**: GM, *Desert Island Discs*, BBC Radio 4, Sept. 30, 2007.

185   **"Have you"**: Andros Georgiou, "The Day I Told George Michael His Lover Had Died of AIDS," *Sun*, Nov. 12, 2012.

185   **"knew I"**: Richard Smith & Steve Pafford, "George Talks: His Frankest Interview Ever," *Gay Times*, July 2007.

CHAPTER FOURTEEN

186   **"My privacy"**: Daniel Ross, *Queen FAQ: All That's Left to Know About Britain's Most Eccentric Band*, Rowman & Littlefield, 2020, 204.

186   "warbling": Jim Farber, "Queen Back on the Throne," New York *Daily News*, Apr. 14, 1992.

187   "sidestepped": David A. Keeps, "AIDS and Pop: An Uneasy Alliance," *New York Times*, Aug. 14, 1992.

187   "I don't care": Rick Sky, "So What if They Say I'm Gay," *Daily Mirror*, Apr. 22, 1993.

187   "I was just": *George Michael: The Road to Wembley* (documentary), 2007.

187   "Everybody is": Sky, "So What if They Say I'm Gay."

187   "childhood fantasy": *George Michael and Brian May: A Conversation*, MTV, 1993.

187   "It was probably": Sky, "So What if They Say I'm Gay."

188   "That's probably" . . . "crazy": Johann Hari, "Talk Without Prejudice," *Independent*, Dec. 9, 2005.

189   "obsessed with" . . . "darling": "Thierry Mugler," *Vice Blog*, Apr. 6, 2010

190   "I think Thierry": Laird Borrelli-Persson, "Moulin Rouge Meets Vegas!," *Vogue*, Dec. 25, 2016.

190   "Well, it's": Mike Southon to JG, May 7, 2020.

190   "fashion heaven": Chris Heath, "George Michael's Disappearing Act," *Daily Telegraph*, June 19, 1992.

190   "Oh, it's": Joey Arias to JG, June 29, 2017.

191   "*Nothing*" . . . "you want!": Chris Heath, "George Michael's Disappearing Act."

191   "hundreds": Joey Arias to JG.

191   "*Nobody*" . . . "to eye": Mike Southon to JG.

191   "I knew he": Philip Utz, "The Confessions of Manfred Thierry Mugler," *Numéro Homme*, Oct. 12, 2017.

191–92 "Okay, Mistress" . . . "perfection": Joey Arias to JG.

192   "That's what": *The Red Line*, Pt. 2, BBC Radio 2.

192   "*What are*": Richard Johnson, "Rose Has an Axl to Grind with Beatty," *New York Daily News*, June 9, 1992.

192   "Thierry": *The Red Line*, Pt. 2, BBC Radio 2.

192   "hysteria": Laird Borrelli-Persson, "Moulin Rouge Meets Vegas!," *Vogue*, Dec. 25, 2016.

192   **"I don't"**: Joey Arias to JG.

192   **"There were"**: Mike Southon to JG.

192   **"*I'm* the one"**: Joey Arias to JG.

192   **"a deathly"** . . . **"throw me out"**: Philip Utz, "The Confessions of Manfred Thierry Mugler."

192   **"You know what?"**: Laird Borrelli-Persson, "Moulin Rouge Meets Vegas!"

193   **"He completely"**: Philip Utz, "The Confessions of Manfred Thierry Mugler."

194   **"complete joke"**: George Michael vs. Sony, June 1994, 222.

194   **"George immediately"**: John Carlin to JG, Nov. 16, 2020.

194   **"basically"**: Sylvia Coleman to JG, Mar. 20, 2018.

194   **"I told him"**: George Michael vs. Sony, June 1994, 98.

195   **"as a matter"**: George Michael vs. Sony, 67.

195   **"irreconcilable"** . . . **"is yours"**: George Michael vs. Sony, 69.

195   **"Norio"**: Mickey Schulhof to JG.

195   **"Mr. Schulhof"**: George Michael vs. Sony, June 1994, 68–69.

195   **"Threats"**: Mickey Schulhof to JG.

196   **"He didn't"**: Simon Garfield, "George's Last Wham!," *Independent*, Dec. 4, 1992.

196   **"set in motion"**: Mike Ellison, "The Day the Music Died for a Pop Icon," *Guardian*, June 23, 1994.

196   **"I think"**: Mickey Schulhof to JG.

196   **"Had Anselmo"** . . . **"from me"**: *The Red Line*, Pt. 1, BBC Radio 2.

197   **"I think"**: Rob Kahane to JG, 28, 2018.

CHAPTER FIFTEEN

198   **"He bought"**: Don Goldstone to JG, Nov. 29, 2017.

198   **"He is a"**: Tony Parsons, "I Was Very Lucky to Have Had Anselmo in My Life," *Daily Mirror*, Nov. 10, 1997.

198   **"He was so"** . . . **"come home"**: Rosa Fernandes to JG, May 31, 2019.

198   **"He was reticent"**: Rob Kahane to JG, 28, 2018.

199   **"I was absolutely"**: GM, *Desert Island Discs*, BBC Radio 4, Sept. 30, 2007.

199 **"I thought"**: *The Red Line*, Pt. 2, BBC Radio 2.

199 **"He's not"**: "George Takes on the System," *Sun*, Oct. 1993.

199 **"so comically"**: Dorian Lynskey, "The 10 Best Legal Wrangles in Pop—In Pictures," *Guardian*, Aug. 10, 2013.

199 **"We are saddened"**: Spencer Bright, "Why George May Never Record Again," *Daily Mail*, Nov. 27, 1992.

199 **"George wasn't"**: Chris Cameron to JG, June 2, 2018.

200 **"Our plan"**: Piers Morgan, "George Hits Hollywood," *Sun*, Sept. 8, 1993.

200 **"A million"**: Rob Kahane to JG.

200 **"He preferred"**: Rosa Fernandes to JG.

200 **"He's not"**: Patricia Agressot to JG, July 23, 2018.

200 **"He was really"**: Sylvynho to JG, Nov. 15, 2017.

201 **"Yog wanted"** . . . **"to L.A."**: Andros Georgiou, *Rock: The Luckiest Man in Pop*, 347.

201 **"YOG!"**: Georgiou, 348.

201 **"He got"**: Andros Georgiou, "The Day I Told George Michael His Lover Had Died of AIDS," *Sun*, Nov. 12, 2012.

201 **"There was"** . . . **"was there"**: Lucia Guanabara to JG, Apr. 18, 2019.

201 **"We cannot"**: Caroline Graham, "The Cop George Fancied," *Sun*, Apr. 14, 1998.

201 **"Maybe George"**: Howard Sounes, "This Man Changed the Way I Look at My Life," *Daily Mirror*, May 15, 1996

201 **"with the right"**: Adam Mattera, "George Michael: Days of the Open Hand," *Attitude*, May 2004.

201 **"was the most"**: *The Red Line*, Pt. 1, BBC Radio 2.

202 **"If you'd been"**: Chris Porter to JG, June 2, 2018.

202 **"It was the"**: Smith & Pafford, "George Talks: His Frankest Interview Ever," *Gay Times*, 2007.

202 **"But his dad"**: Deon Estus to JG, May 2, 2019.

202 **"If his goal"**: Rob Kahane to JG.

202 **"threatens"**: Paul Fuller, "George Michael Earned £100m but Kept £7.3m," *Daily Express*, Oct. 19, 1993.

202   **"I've got more"**: Adrian Deevoy, "Strictly No Admittance: The Privatisation of George Michael," *Q*, Nov. 1990."

202   **"I would have"**: "Oh Lord, Please Don't Let Me Be Misunderstood," *Sunday Times*, Oct. 24, 1993.

203   **"Hardly"**: Dan Conaghan, "Pop World in a Spin as Singer Seeks to End Record Contract," *Daily Telegraph*, Oct. 18, 1993.

203   **"The record"**: Mark Lepage, "George Michael Is Unlikely Hero as He Takes on Corporate Music Giant," *Gazette* (Montreal), Dec. 17, 1992.

203   **"could signal"**: "Why George May Never Record Again," *Daily Mail*, Nov. 27, 1992.

203   **"Bastards!"**: David Thomas, "Taking the Michael!," *Daily Mail*, Mar. 12, 2004.

203   **"more prurient"**: Melissa Wittstock, "Losing Faith," *Times*, Oct. 2, 1993.

203   **"Only his"**: "Sony Faces a Test of Faith," *Independent*, Oct. 24, 1993.

204   **"Based upon"**: Michael Pagnotta to JG, July 10, 2017.

204   **"George thinks"** . . . **"used to"**: Nigel Cope, "Sony Faces a Test of Faith," *Independent*, Oct. 24, 1993.

204   **"the Bruiser"**: Phil Davison, "Obituary: Gordon Pollock, Barrister Known as 'the Bruiser,'" *Herald Scotland*, May 29, 2019.

204   **"like Moses"**: Rob Kahane to JG.

204   ***"Ah Love!"***: George Michael vs. Sony, June 1994, 164–165.

205   **"a man"**: Jeff Randall, "It Looks Bleak for Deloitte," *Daily Telegraph*, Apr. 14, 2006.

205   **"the wish"**: George Michael vs. Sony, June 1994, 70.

205   **"almost no"**: Paul Harris, "Why I Need to Take Charge of My Career," *Daily Mail*, Oct. 19, 1993.

206   **"I have a"**: Sylvia Coleman to JG, Mar. 20, 2018.

206   **"This court"**: Hugh Muir, "Courtroom Blues for the Star Who Changed His Tune," *Daily Telegraph*, June 22, 1994.

206   **"Would you agree"** . . . **"my work"**: Michael vs. Sony, June 1994, 71.

207   **"strong impression"**: Michael vs. Sony, 218.

207   **"You are saying"**: "I'm Not Too Grand, Says George Michael," *Daily Mail*, Oct. 30, 1993.

207   **"Yes. In"**: Joe Joseph, "Singer Claims Sony Misused Peace Song," *Times*, Oct. 30, 1993.

207   **"It may be"**: Hugh Muir, "Courtroom Blues for the Star Who Changed His Tune," *Daily Telegraph*, June 22, 1994.

207   **"Although I"**: Michael Skapinker, "Sony 'Killed' Album, Singer Says," *Financial Times*, Oct. 29, 1993.

207   **"So, this"** . . . **"Yes"**: Andrew Pierce, "Singer Denies He Broke Promises to Get His Own Way," *Times*, Oct. 29, 1993.

207   **"You have got"**: Michael Skapinker, "Sony 'Killed' Album, Singer Says," *Financial Times*, Oct. 29, 1993.

207   **"I think you"**: Hugh Muir, "George Michael's Sex Appeal in Court," *Daily Telegraph*, Oct. 29, 1993.

207   **"Give us"**: Andrew Pierce, "Singer Denies He Broke Promises to Get His Own Way," *Times*, Oct. 29, 1993.

207   **"Do I"** . . . **"decimal point"**: Paul Fuller, "George: Do I Really Have to Tell You All How Wealthy I Am?," *Daily Express*, Oct. 29, 1993.

208   **"image of"** . . . **"chest"**: Hugh Muir, "George Michael's Sex Appeal in Court," *Daily Telegraph*, Oct. 29, 1993.

208   **"I was very"**: Michael Skapinker, "Designer Stubble That Got Burnt," *Financial Times*, June 22, 1994.

208   **"that if I"**: George Michael vs. Sony, June 1994, 90.

208   **"CBS"**: George Michael vs. Sony, 35.

209   **"Anyone can"**: Carol Midgley, "I Wasn't Sexy Enough for My Video, Says George," *Daily Mirror*, Oct. 29, 1993.

209   **"It was difficult"**: Michael Skapinker, "Designer Stubble That Got Burnt," *Financial Times*, June 22, 1994.

209   **"detail freak"**: Giles Smith, "What Did George Know?," *Independent*, June 23, 1994.

209   **"desperately needed"**: George Michael vs. Sony, June 1994, 220.

209   **"I am satisfied"**: George Michael vs. Sony, 221.

209   **"a scary guy"** . . . **"*Godfather*"**: George Michael vs. Sony, 93–94.

209   **"I was afraid"**: Doug Camilli, "Pearl Jam Achieves Celebrity Status," *Gazette* (Montreal), Nov. 17, 1993.

209   *"Answer"*: Rob Kahane to JG.

210   **"whatever made"**: George Michael vs. Sony, June 1994, 48.

210   **"which I had"** . . . **"divisive"**: George Michael vs. Sony, 96.

210   **"could ever"**: George Michael vs. Sony, 75.

CHAPTER SIXTEEN

211   **"I was expecting"**: Chris Evans, An Audience with George Michael, BBC Radio 1, Dec. 8, 1996.

211   **"A wave"**: Imogen Edwards-Jones, "I Want Your Specs," *Sunday Times*, Nov. 7, 1993.

211   **"Stars get"** . . . **"hilarious"**: Tony Parsons, "As Rockers Take to the Courts—The Real Scandal," *Daily Telegraph*, Nov. 11, 1993.

211   **"my darling"**: GM to Princess Diana, recorded conversation, July 1996.

211   **"I think"**: Gill Pringle to JG, June 23, 2018.

212   **"lonely"**: "I Bawled My Eyes Out at Diana's Funeral," *Daily Mirror*, Nov. 11, 1997.

212   **"tittered"**: "Are Diana's Secrets Safe?," *Daily Telegraph*, Jan. 9, 1998.

213   **"I did"**: Ed Condran, "Bi-Coastal k.d. lang," *Central New Jersey Home News*, May 8, 2004.

213   **"looked absolutely"**: Danny Cummings to JG, May 26, 2018.

213   **"George demanded"**: Janet Street-Porter, "Back in the Closet, George. We Only Want Your Songs," *Independent*, Dec. 11, 2005.

214   **"The person"**: "Singer's Contract Defended," *Financial Times*, Feb. 22, 1994.

215   **"kill off"** . . . **"It would"**: George Michael vs. Sony, June 1994, 223–224.

215   **"On the contrary"** . . . **"He cannot"**: George Michael vs. Sony, 225–226.

215   **"most impressive"**: George Michael vs. Sony, 97.

216   **"a thoroughly"**: George Michael vs. Sony, 5.

216   **"that Sony"**: George Michael vs. Sony, 222.

216   **"negotiating tactics"**: George Michael vs. Sony, 97.

216   **"angry and"**: George Michael vs. Sony, 10.

216   **"without raising"**: George Michael vs. Sony, 99.

216   **"legal battle"**: "Wham Goes George's Glittering Pop Career," *Daily Express*, June 29, 1994.

216   **"proceeded on"**: George Michael vs. Sony, June 1994, 226.

216   **"would lead to"**: George Michael vs. Sony, app. 3/12.

216   **"I am satisfied"** . . . **"I conclude that"**: Giles Smith, " 'Pop Slave' George Michael to Fight On," *Independent*, June 22, 1994.

216   **"What can"**: "Wham Goes George's Glittering Pop Career," *Daily Express*, June 22, 1994.

216   **"I am stunned"**: Giles Smith, "What Did George Know?," *Independent*, June 23, 1994.

217   **"When they"**: Joe Joseph, "Fans' Careless Screams Show Their Faith in Singer," *Times*, June 22, 1994.

217   **"I am shocked** . . . **appeal"**: Hugh Muir, "I Fight On, Says George Michael After Losing £3mil Battle," *Daily Telegraph*, June 22, 1994.

217   **"George was very"**: Rob Kahane to JG, 28, 2018.

217   **"due to** . . . **friendship"**: Linda Stasi, "Faith and Freedom," New York *Daily News*, Oct. 9, 1994.

217   **"I remember"** . . . **"own ship"**: Rob Kahane to JG.

218   **"Usually guys"**: Michael Pagnotta to JG, July 10, 2017.

218   **"great day"**: "Wham Goes George's Glittering Pop Career," *Daily Express*, June 22, 1994.

218   **"Who feels"**: "I Don't Want Your Freedom . . . ," *Q*, July 1994.

218   **"When Mr. Michael"**: "You Let Them Buy You So Stop Wingeing and Grow Up, George," *Daily Mail*, June 22, 1994.

218   **"There are just"**: Sylvia Coleman to JG Mar. 20, 2018.

218   **"A skillful"**: "George Michael Returns to Millionaire Slavery," *Independent*, June 22, 1994.

218   **"We have great"**: Hugh Muir, "I Fight On."

218-19   **"It's a ridiculous"** . . . **"pride"**: *Breakfast with Frost*, BBC1, July 2, 1994.

219   **"Millions"**: "George Michael Denied Speedy Appeal Hearing," *Financial Times*, Dec. 13, 1994.

219   **"no longer"**: Philips, Chuck, "EMI Offer Intensifies Henley Feud with Geffen," *Los Angeles Times*, April 29, 1993.

220   **"Prince was"**: Michael Pagnotta to JG.

220   **"enormous"**: Jonathan King, "You Let Them Buy You So Stop Wingeing and Grow Up, George," *Daily Mail*, June 22, 1994.

220   **"A lot of"**: Anthea Benton to JG, Dec. 4, 2017.

220   **"Did all"**: Michael Pagnotta to JG.

CHAPTER SEVENTEEN

221   **"George has"**: Jonathan King, "It's the End of the Incredible Sulk," *Daily Mail*, June 28, 1995.

221   **"Talk to"**: "Stubble and Strife," *Observer*, May 12, 1996.

221   **"I kept"**: David Geffen to JG, Sept. 5, 2017.

222   **"I'll take"** . . . **"tell you?"**: Geffen.

223   **"He had a"**: Geffen.

223   **"It's always"**: Matthew Lynn & Rufus Olins, "Harmony Restored as Michael Sheds Sony," *Sunday Times*, July 16, 1995.

223   **"late-night"**: Patrick M. Reilly, "Despite Criticism, the Beat Goes On for EMI Group's Powerful Couple," *Wall Street Journal*, Feb. 25, 1998.

223   **"was a huge"**: David Geffen to JG.

224   **"Nobody is"**: Simon Garfield, "The Battle for George Michael," *Independent*, July 15, 1995.

224   **"the biggest"**: Matthew Lynn & Rufus Olins, "Harmony Restored as Michael Sheds Sony."

224   **"I haven't**: Andrew Smith, "Can We Listen Without Prejudice?," *Sunday Times*, Jan. 7, 1996.

225   **"camping"**: Miranda Sawyer, "Breaking Up Is Hard to Do," *Observer*, July 28, 1996.

225   **"new George . . . to George"**: "Gary Barlow on . . . Why I Love George Michael," *Daily Express*, Oct. 18, 1996.

225   **"I used"**: "Gary's Taking the Michael . . ." *Daily Mirror*, 1996.

225   **"I'm not sure"** . . . **"aggressive"**: David Geffen to JG.

226   **"If you have"**: Tony Parsons, "I Was Very Lucky to Have Had Anselmo in My Life," *Daily Mirror*, Nov. 10, 1997.

226   **"total"**: *The Red Line*, Pt. 2, BBC Radio 2.

226   **"No, that's"**: Johnny Douglas to JG, July 10, 2019.

227   **"I just need"**: Chris Porter to JG, June 2, 2018.

227   **"We'd do"**: Chris Cameron to JG, June 2, 2018.

227   **"Not only"**: Chris Porter to JG.

227   **"Oh my God"** . . . **"for me"**: *The Red Line*, Pt. 2, BBC Radio 2.

228   **"George Michael"**: Sheryl Garratt, "Et tu, George?," *Sunday Times*, Jan. 14, 1996.

229   **"George pretty"**: Niall Flynn to JG, Apr. 7, 2020.

230   **"very hick"**: Johnny Douglas to JG.

230   **"dirty sexy"** . . . **"this silly"**: Douglas.

231   **"I didn't see"**: Douglas.

231   **"Because I"**: Andy Stephens to JG, May 3, 2021.

231   **"I didn't have"**: David Geffen to JG.

232   **"George wanted"**: Geffen.

232   **"use of his"**: Andros Georgiou, *Rock: The Luckiest Man in Pop*, 405.

233   **"Look, this"**: Anthea Benton to JG, Dec. 4, 2017.

233   **"He was really"** . . . **"angle"**: Vaughan Arnell to JG, Dec. 4, 2017.

234   **"hairy"**: Tony Parsons, "The Price of George Michael's Freedom," *Daily Telegraph*, July 13, 1995.

234   **"the look of"**: Stephen Holden, "A Guide to Pop Albums for Adults," *New York Times*, Nov. 29, 1996.

234   **"the perfect"**: Richard Smith, "George Michael—A Single Man?," *Gay Times*, May 1996.

235   **"increasingly"**: David Sinclair, "Pop Single," *Times*, Dec. 23, 1995.

235   **"Five years"**: Jim White, "He'll Need More Than Faith This Time," *Independent*, Jan. 5, 1996.

236   **"For this"**: Nicholas Barber, "Records," *Independent*, May 12, 1996.

236   **"crashing"**: Tom Moon, "Finally, a New Album from the New George Michael," *Philadelphia Inquirer*, May 16, 1996.

236   **"George Michael returns"**: "'Older' George Michael Isn't Much Fun," *San Bernardino County Sun*, May 19, 1996.

236 **"a comedian"**: Jim White, "My Kind of Guy," *Guardian*, Apr. 15, 1998.

236 **"This is a"**: Andrew Smith, "Record Check," *Times*, May 12, 1996.

237 **"mature"**: Dan Aquilante, *New York Post*, Apr. 9, 1998.

237 **"gorgeous"**: "Serious George Is Back," *Newsweek*, May 20, 1996.

237 **"Anselmo was"**: Howard Sounes, "This Man Changed the Way I Look at My Life," *Daily Mirror*, May 15, 1996.

237 **"For anyone"**: *The Red Line*, Pt. 1, BBC Radio 2.

237 **"overtly"**: Howard Sounes, "This Man Changed the Way I Look at My Life," *Daily Mirror*, May 15, 1996.

237 **"Madonna"**: Reed McGowan to JG, Oct. 31, 2018.

238 **"He ended" . . . "said that"**: David Geffen to JG.

238 **"A lot of" . . . "smoked"**: Johnny Douglas to JG.

238 **"My next" . . . "my life"**: Tony Parsons, "I Smoked 25 Cannabis Joints Every Day as I Grieved for the Man I Loved," *Daily Mirror*, Nov. 10, 1997.

238 **"I don't ever"**: *The Red Line*, Pt. 2, BBC Radio 2.

CHAPTER EIGHTEEN

239 **"personal interest"**: Mark Jefferies & Nicola Bartlett, "George Hadn't Taken Heroin Before He Died," *Daily Mirror*, Dec. 28, 2016.

239 **"The funniest"**: "Soup-erstar George Feeds Homeless," *Daily Mirror*, Jan. 27, 1997.

241 **"Let's start"**: Andros Georgiou, *Rock: The Luckiest Man in Pop*, 396.

241 **"I can't help"**: Ægean Records online chat, July 21, 1998.

241 **"It wasn't the"**: *Autopsy: The Last Hours of George Michael* (documentary), Reelz, 2018.

242 **"He knows"**: "George Michael TV," MTV, Nov. 4, 1998.

242 **"I think he"**: Johnny Douglas to JG, July 10, 2019.

242 **"demanded"**: Phil Palmer to JG.

242 **"It would have"**: Andros Georgiou, *Rock: The Luckiest Man in Pop*, 437.

242 **"this fantastic"**: Richard Smith & Steve Pafford, "George Talks: His Frankest Interview Ever," *Gay Times*, July 2007.

242   **"a completely"**: Martin Phillips, "My Misery Over Mum," *Sun*, Apr. 9, 1998.

242   **"Lesley was"**: Andros Georgiou, *Rock: The Luckiest Man in Pop*, 422.

243   **"We slept"**: Georgiou, 417.

243   **"He never"**: Phil Palmer to JG.

244   **"George would"**: Martin Fricker, "Wasted," *Daily Mirror*, Apr. 19, 2006.

244   **"Sometimes"**: Andros Georgiou, *Rock: The Luckiest Man in Pop*, 420.

244   **"I didn't think"**: Jason Solomons, "Charity Given a £1m Lift, by George," *Daily Express*, March 31, 1997.

245   **"rock 'n' roll's"**: Ray Richmond, "Michael Surprises VH1 Do," *Variety*, Apr. 11, 1997.

246   **"For the first"**: *4th Annual VH1 Honors*, Apr. 12, 1997.

246   **"It seemed"**: Andros Georgiou, *Rock: The Luckiest Man in Pop*, 421.

246   **"We could do"**: Martin Fricker, "Exclusive: Drugs Could Kill George Michael," *Daily Mirror*, Apr. 19, 2006.

247   **"throw around"**: Niall Flynn, essay, "Ægean: The Building of an Empire," 2020.

247   **"shadows"**: Danny Cummings to JG, May 26, 2018.

247   **"George was a"**: Phil Palmer to JG.

247   **"One minute"**: "My Week: Geri Halliwell," *Times*, Apr. 14, 2007.

247   **"When I"**: Caroline Overington, "Geri Finds Caring Is the Spice of Life," *Age* (Melbourne), Apr. 15, 1999.

247   **"Geri Halliwell"**: Tanith Carey, "George and Geri, the Oddest Couple in Town," *Daily Mirror*, Aug. 8, 1998.

248   **"All she"**: Cassandra Jardine, "Are Diana's Secrets Safe?," *Daily Telegraph*, Jan. 9, 1998.

248   **"How are you"**: GM to Princess Diana, recorded conversation, July 1996.

249   **"Leave me"**: John Thordahlburg, "Diana Made Plea to 'Leave Me Alone,'" *Los Angeles Times*, Sept. 10, 1997.

249   **"I think she"**: Tony Parsons, "I Bawled My Eyes Out at Diana's Funeral," *Daily Mirror*, Nov. 11, 1997.

250   **"I think he"**: Danny Cummings to JG.

250   **"deep-seated"**: Martin Fricker, "Wasted," *Daily Mirror*, Apr. 19, 2006.

250   **"If there's"**: Chris Evans, An Audience with George Michael, BBC Radio 1, Dec. 8, 1996.

250   **"I can sue"**: Richard Smith, "George Michael—A Single Man?," *Gay Times.*

250   **"George Michael"**: James Collard, "When Will George Michael Come Out to Play?," *Daily Express*, Aug. 9, 1996.

251   **"desperate"**: Tom Leonard, "George Pays the Price for Being a Show-Off," *Daily Telegraph*, Apr. 10, 1998.

251   **"would have killed"**: Daniel Reynolds, "Barry Manilow: Coming Out Sooner 'Would Have Killed My Career," *Advocate,* May 15, 2019.

251   **"I said, 'Don't"**: Ellyn Solis to JG.

251   **"Would I"**: Elizabeth Daley, "WATCH: Ellen DeGeneres Teaches *Oprah's Master Class* on Coming Out," *Advocate*, Oct. 26, 2015.

251   **"Yep"**: Lily Rothman, "Yep, I'm Gay," *Time*, Apr. 13, 2017.

252   **"promoting"**: Trish Bendix, "Backlash: What Happened to Ellen DeGeneres AFTER She Came Out?," *NewNowNext*, Apr. 27, 2017.

252   **"ostentatious"**: "Ellen and 'Ellen' Come Out," *New York Times*, May 1, 1997.

252–53 **"Everyone" . . . "myself:** Chris Evans, "An Audience with George Michael."

253   **"George says"**: "Outside Edge: Boy George," *Daily Express*, Nov. 13, 1996.

253   **"discreetly"**: Chris Boffey & Ciaran Byrne, "I Am Not Ashamed That I'm Gay, Says George Michael," *Sunday Telegraph*, Apr. 12, 1998.

CHAPTER NINETEEN

254   **"I really"**: Melissa Etheridge to JG, Oct. 20, 1993.

254   **"Andy would"**: Judy Wieder to JG, March 23, 2018.

254   **"the good-looking"**: Tony Parsons, "I Was Lucky to Have Had Anselmo in My Life," *Daily Mirror*, Nov. 10, 1997.

255   **"He was a"**: Don Goldstone to JG, Nov. 29, 2017.

255   **"People want"**: Catherine Pepinster, "Focus: Who's Looking for What on Clapham Common," *Independent*, Oct. 23, 2011.

255   "an ersatz": Bradley Jones to JG, June 26, 2019.

256   "He comes": Nick Hopkins & David Gardner, "Michael's Photo Trap," *Daily Mail*, Apr. 10, 1998.

256   "that they": John South & Darryl Wrobel, "How AIDS Tragedy Drove George Michael to Public Shame," *National Enquirer*, Apr. 28, 1998.

256   "As a person": J. T. Anderson to JG, Dec. 21, 2017.

256   "potty patrol": John Blosser, "Potty Patrol—The Job Cops Hate," *National Enquirer*, Apr. 28, 1998.

257   "It was common": John Duran to JG, Nov. 29, 2017.

257   "He kept": J. T. Anderson to JG.

258   "if they": Richard Smith & Steve Pafford, "George Talks: His Frankest Interview Ever," *Gay Times*, July 2007.

258   "This megastar": Janet Charlton, *Star*, Apr. 28, 1998.

258   "I gave": J. T. Anderson to JG.

258–59 "limp-wristed" . . . "dinners": Tony Parsons, "A Real Man, and a Vain, Spiteful Boy," *Daily Mirror*, Apr. 6, 1998.

259   "I hung up": Jay Landers to JG, Apr. 26, 2023.

259   "six-foot": Bill Coles, "Arrest Cop Is a Hunk," *Sun*, Apr. 11, 1998.

260   "This is ridiculous!": Judy Wieder, "George Michael: All the Way Out," *Advocate*, Jan. 19, 1999.

260   "visibly": Caroline Graham, "Led Away in Handcuffs," *Sun*, Apr. 9, 1998.

260   "Georgios": Brendan Bourne, Robin Gregg, Tracy Connor, "Lewd Star Busted in Boys' Room," source unknown, Apr. 1998.

260   "I left": Judy Wieder, "George Michael" All the Way Out," *Advocate*, Jan. 19, 1999.

261   "I've just": Caroline Graham to JG, Nov. 27, 2018.

261   "the singer": Ltd. Edward Kreins, press conference, Beverly Hills, Apr. 8, 1998 (video, AP).

261   "looked shocked": David Gardner, "Private Shame of the Public Star," *Daily Mail*, Apr. 9, 1998.

262   "I'm sorry": Nick Hopkins & David Gardner, "Michael's Photo Trap," *Daily Mail*, Apr. 10, 1998.

262   **"I've got"**: John South & Darryl Wrobel, "How AIDS Tragedy Drove George Michael to Public Shame," *National Enquirer*, Apr. 28, 1998.

262   **"I guess"**: Michael Pagnotta to JG, July 10, 2017.

262   **"ZIP ME"**: *Sun*, Apr. 9, 1998.

262   **"Gay George?"**: Caroline Graham, "The Cop George Fancied," *Sun*, Apr. 14, 1998.

262   **"Heavy smoker"** . . . **"happened"**: Dominic Mohan, "He's Trying to Give Up Fags," *Sun*, Apr. 11, 1998.

262   **"Some might"**: Boy George, "We Are Sisters Under the Skin," *Daily Express*, Apr. 9, 1998.

263   **"rocked"**: Billy Masters to JG, June 13, 2018.

263   **"I said to"**: David Geffen to JG, Sept. 5, 2017.

263   **"Live and"**: Thomas Whittaker, "Boy George: He's Done No Wrong," *Sun*, Apr. 9, 1998.

263   **"Americans"**: "Celebrity Scandals in the 1990s—from Donald Trump to Bill Clinton," *Newsweek*, Sept. 7, 2017.

264   **"My parents"**: Emily Yoshida, "Hugh Grant's Very English Comeback," *Vanity Fair*, Aug. 13, 2019.

264   **"I made"**: Andros Georgiou, *Rock: The Luckiest Man in Pop*, 455.

265   **"preying"**: Lynda Lee-Potter, "It's Just Obscene to Glorify George," *Daily Mail*, Apr. 15, 1998.

265   **"What he"**: Richard Littlejohn, "Imagine George Michael Doing That in the Ladies," *Sun*, Apr. 14, 1998.

265   **"crashed"**: "Babylon and On!," *New York Post*, Apr. 9, 1998.

265   **"in a *toilet?*"**: *VH1 News*, Apr. 1998.

265   **"Gay people"**: Simon Napier-Bell to JG, Sept. 7, 2018.

265   **"has lost"**: Martin Samuel, "Why George's Arrest Is a Crying Shame," *Daily Express*, Apr. 10, 1998.

266   **"What flaming"**: Matthew Parris, "What's George Done That Is So Dreadful?," *Sun*, Apr. 11, 1998.

266   **"we pride"**: Lesley White, "Tragedy of a Private Public Man," *Sunday Times*, Apr. 12, 1998.

266   **"I *never*"**: Judy Wieder, "George Michael' All the Way Out," *Advocate*, Jan. 19, 1999.

266   "carefully": Nicola Pittam, "Dressed to Grill," *Daily Mail*, Nov. 25, 1998.

267   "It's good": John Hiscock, "George Michael Faces the World," *Daily Telegraph*, Apr. 11, 1998.

267   "Guys" . . . "recently": Nick Hopkins, "I've Nothing to Be Ashamed of Says Michael," *Daily Mail*, Apr. 11, 1998.

267–68 "implying" . . . "take on it:" Peter Sheridan, "I Won't Have Sex in Public Again, Pledges George," *Express*, Dec. 4, 1998.

268   "He was stammering": Jim Moret to JG, Nov. 26, 2017.

269   "He looked": Moret.

269   "He's a very": "Singer's Gift," *Times*, Apr. 13, 1998.

270   "He was treated": Chris Heath to JG, July 10, 2017.

270   "Everyone has" . . . "us girls": Ben Proctor, "We Guessed He Was Gay but We Love Him Anyway," *Sun*, Apr. 9, 1998.

270   "nice" . . . "trousers down": Peter Sheridan, "I Won't Have Sex in Public Again, Pledges George."

270–71 "Gay men" . . . "were doing": John Duran to JG, Aug. 20, 2018.

271   "sat in": "George Finds Time to Reflect," *Daily Express*, Apr. 20, 1998.

271   "I always": GM, *Desert Island Discs*, BBC Radio 4, Sept. 30, 2007.

CHAPTER TWENTY

272   "victim's" . . . "for sure": John Hiscock, "George Michael Given £500 Fine and Counseling," *Daily Telegraph*, May 15, 1998.

272   "I got": Peter Sheridan, "I Won't Have Sex in Public Again, Pledges George," *Express*, Dec. 4, 1998.

272   "If Mr.": Jasper Gerard, "Older and Out," *Times*, Nov. 7, 1998.

272   "Officials": John Glionna, "Beverly Hills Gets Vigilant in Curbing Sex Cruisers," *Los Angeles Times*, May 3, 1998.

272   "Singer": "Laugh Lines," *Los Angeles Times*, Apr. 26, 1998.

275   "heavy in": *Billboard*, Nov. 7, 1998.

275   "laughable": Richard Wallace, "Who the Hell Does George Thing He Is?," *Daily Mirror*, Nov. 25, 1998.

276   **"Come on"**: Tony Parsons, "Toilet Humor Out of Place, George," *Daily Mirror*, Oct. 12, 1998.

276   **"I was the"**: Sean Hoare & James Scott, "Cousin Walks Out on Cocky George," *Sun*, Nov. 1998.

277   **"They said"**: Derbeh Vance to JG, July 20, 2018.

277   **"I am fully"**: Nicola Pittam, "Dressed to Grill," *Daily Mail*, Nov. 25, 1998.

278   **"She probably"**: *Parkinson*, Dec. 5, 1998.

278   **"a watershed"**: "22 George Michael," *Independent*, June 26, 2005.

278   **"Whether he"**: Michael Cashman, "TV Star Michael Cashman's Verdict," *Daily Mirror*, Apr. 10, 1998.

279   **"He was like"**: Michael Odell, "New Direction," *South Bend Tribune*, Aug. 8, 1999.

279   **"wimpy"**: "George Michael TV," MTV, Nov. 4, 1998.

279   **"wall-to-wall"** . . . **"industry"**: *Parkinson*, Dec. 5, 1998.

279   **"I don't"**: Jim Moret to JG, Nov. 26, 2017.

279   **"I was so"**: "Coming Out" radio interview, c.1999.

280   **"emotional"** . . . **"evidence"**: Marcelo Rodriguez, Plaintiff-appellant, v. Georgios Kyriacos Panayiotou, Defendant-appellee, U.S. Court of Appeals, Dec. 3, 2002.

280   **"It spread"**: John Duran to JG.

280   **"They would"**: "George Michael TV," *MTV*, Nov. 4, 1998.

CHAPTER TWENTY-ONE

281   **"former pinup"**: Nicole Martin, "Bad Vibes Between the Bachelor Boys," *Daily Telegraph*, Dec. 11, 1999.

281   **"GEORGE!"**: Niall Flynn to JG, Apr. 19, 2020.

281   **"First I'd"**: Matthew Wright, "George Arrives Flushed," *Daily Mirror*, Apr. 1, 1999.

281   **"I don't"**: *Jo Whiley Show*, BBC Radio 1, Mar. 18, 2002.

282   **"pop in"**: Phil Palmer to JG.

283   **"George's phrasing"**: David Finck to JG, Apr. 15, 2018.

283   **"You would"**: Jill Dell'Abate to JG, Apr. 15, 2018.

283   **"In case"**: David Finck to JG, Apr. 15, 2018

283   "He told": Jill Dell'Abate to JG.

284   "I saw": Helen Merrill to JG, Dec. 19, 2017.

284   "He was a": Phil Palmer to JG.

284   "although": Jill Dell'Abate to JG.

284   "We only": Q, Mar. 2000.

284   "The last": Capital FM Radio, Dec. 10, 1999.

285   "tone": Neil McCormick, "Pop CDs," Daily Telegraph, Dec. 4, 1999.

285   "It's such": Chris Heath to JG, July 10, 2017.

285   "He evidently": Tom Moon, "The Music Report," Philadelphia Inquirer, Jan. 2, 2000.

286   "everything from" . . . "humor": "You've Got a Heart of Pure Gold, George," Daily Mirror, Sept. 18, 1999.

286   "I'm not": Danny Cummings to JG, May 26, 2018.

287   "He wanted": Johnny Douglas to JG, July 10, 2019.

287   "This is": "A Boy's Own Story," Guardian, Dec. 4, 1999.

287   "totally": "Coming Out" radio interview, c.1999.

288   "Fourteen million": Staying Alive, MTV, Dec. 1, 1998.

288   "I don't": GM, internet talkback, georgemichael.com, July 21, 1998.

288   "a dubious": Ray Mark Rinaldi, "Heroes Are Hard to Find When They're Hiding," St. Louis Post-Dispatch, Apr. 23, 2000.

288   "and we": Judy Wieder to JG, March 23, 2018.

289   "No one": Elizabeth Birch to JG, July 8, 2020.

289   "He would": Judy Wieder to JG.

290   "I told him": Elizabeth Birch to JG.

290   "Garth will": Chris Willman, "Behind the Scenes at Equality Rocks," Entertainment Weekly, Apr. 14, 2000.

290   "We got": Danny Cummings to JG.

290   "A handful": " 'Equality Rocks' Brings Singers, Actors to Stage," Pacific Daily News (Guam), May 2, 2000.

291   "Hey": Gina Vivinetto, "Equal Parts Human Rights and Huge Talent," Tampa Bay Times, May 5, 2000.

291   "I'm not": " 'Equality Rocks' Brings Singers, Actors to Stage."

291   "We'd given": Elizabeth Birch to JG.

291   "declined": Marc Sandalow, "Gay Rally in Washington Bares Deep Divisions," San Francisco Chronicle, Apr. 29, 2000.

291 **"tried to"**: "Tracks," *Courier-Journal* (Louisville, KY), May 6, 2000.

291 **"People were"**: Judy Wieder to JG.

292 **"as though"**: Elizabeth Birch to JG.

293 **"He bellyached"**: Gina Vivinetto, "Equal Parts Human Rights and Huge Talent."

293 **"He knew"**: Danny Cummings to JG.

293 **"crushed"**: Judy Wieder to JG.

293 **"Michael never"**: "Garth and George Just Say No," *Us*, Oct. 30, 2000.

CHAPTER TWENTY-TWO

294 **"You don't" . . . "on TV"**: Johnny Douglas to JG, July 10, 2019.

294 **"a whole"**: Adam Mattera, "George Michael: Days of the Open Hand," *Attitude*, May 2004.

295 **"Kenny was"**: Niall Flynn to JG, Apr. 7, 2020.

295 **"so George"**: Andrea Duncan Mao, "Whitney, George Michael Team for Duet," *MTV News*, Mar. 1, 2000.

295 **"absolutely"**: Margaret Lyons, "What We Learned from Cissy Houston on *Oprah*," *Vulture*, Jan. 29, 2013.

295 **"I know"**: "Whitney: Barry Walters Pops the Question," *Out*, May 2000.

296 **"very cool"**: Marilyn Beck & Stacy Jenel Smith, "Whitney Still a Hit with Producer," New York *Daily News*, Apr. 4, 2000.

296 **"It sounded"**: Niall Flynn to JG, Apr. 7, 2020.

296 **"George didn't"**: Johnny Douglas to JG.

296 **"faking"**: J. D. Considine, "Houston Takes Ill-Advised Liberties with Her Greatest Hits," *Baltimore Sun*, May 25, 2000.

297 **"the most"**: Anne Spackman, "Most Expensive House in Britain Just Got Dearer," *Times*, Sept. 13, 2002.

297 **"The swimming"**: Anthony Mitchell, "George's 'Tacky Eyesore' Rocks Village Neighbors," *Sunday Express*, Apr. 29, 2001.

298 **"I wanted"**: George Michael, "I Bought Lennon's Piano from a Better Age of Pop," *Sunday Times*, Oct. 22, 2000.

298 **"People are"**: "Pop Bites Back at Bono," *New Music Express*, Oct. 24, 2000.

298   **"has become"**: Neil McCormick, "The Death of Pop," *Daily Tele-graph*, Nov. 4, 2000.

298   **"He was constantly"**: Johnny Douglas to JG.

299   **"If I was"**: Mark Allen, "George Michael Unzipped," *Marie Claire*, Oct. 2004.

300   **"so desperate"**: "Colin Paterson Gets George Michael's Freeek! On," *Observer*, Mar. 9, 2002.

300   **"Look, I'm"**: Johnny Douglas to JG.

300   **"There was tension"**: Mike Southon to JG, May 7, 2020.

301   **"one of"**: Sarah Baxter, "Landslides of Lovely People," *Sunday Times*, May 4, 1997.

301   **"*Turn on*"**: Johnny Douglas to JG.

301   **"He didn't"**: Niall Flynn to JG, Apr. 7, 2020.

302   **"that Elton"** . . . **"a woman"**: Tim Searle to JG, July 11, 2020.

302   **"I remember"**: Niall Flynn to JG, Apr. 7, 2020.

303   **"He was bang-up"**: Giles Pilbrow to JG, Jan. 2, 2020.

303   **"a hero"**: Piers Morgan, "I Read Pilger in the Mirror . . . and I Got Angry at the World," *Daily Mirror*, July 1, 2002.

304   **"washed-up"**: Bill Hoffmann, "Pop Perv's 9/11 Slur," *New York Post*, July 2, 2002.

304   **"I am definitely"**: Matthew Tempest, "George Michael Lampoons 'Poodle' Blair," *Guardian*, July 1, 2002.

304   **"COWARD"** . . . **"cop-out"**: "George Michael Defends 'Shoot the Dog,'" CNN.com, July 5, 2002.

304   **"After watching"**: "Oh No, the Righteous Rockers Are Staging a Comeback," *Sunday Times*, July 7, 2002.

304   **"brave"**: "Now Woody Takes on the Warmongers," *Daily Mirror*, Aug. 9, 2002.

304   **"fucking"**: Shuan Ponsonby, "Cosmic Slop #95: A New Hope," *Getintothis.co.uk*, Jan. 12, 2017.

305   **"I was accused"**: Tim Searle to JG.

305   **"I would never"**: "George Michael Defends 'Shoot the Dog,'" CNN.com, July 5, 2002.

305   **"fascist"**: *HARDtalk*, BBC News Channel, Feb. 25, 2003.

305   **"was all"**: Tim Searle to JG.

305   **"You know"**: Mark Allen, "George Michael Unzipped."

305   **"due to"**: "Madonna pulls Anti-War Video," *Billboard*, Apr. 1, 2003.

305   **"worse than"**: Mark Allen, "George Michael Unzipped."

305   **"He wasted"**: Niall Flynn to JG, Apr. 7, 2020.

306   **"I have absolutely"**: *HARDtalk*, BBC News Channel, Feb. 25, 2003.

307   **"Which one?"**: *The Graham Norton Show*, Channel 4 (UK), Feb. 28, 2003.

307   **"We should"**: Martin Evans & David Smith, "George Is Back After 17 Years," *Daily Express*, Mar. 7, 2003.

307   **"I am proud"**: Don McLean Official Website, Apr. 11, 2003.

308   **"It went around"**: Niall Flynn to JG, Apr. 7, 2020.

308   **"Everyone could"**: Thomas Andrei, "Le quartier de George Michael ne se remet toujours pas de son 'départ,'" *Greenroom*, Dec. 22, 2017.

308   **"She leapt"** . . . **"messages"**: Gary Jones, "George Break-In Trauma," *Daily Mirror*, Nov. 25, 2004.

309   **"The sofa"**: Niall Flynn to JG, Aug. 20, 2020.

309   **"I thought"**: Johnny Douglas to JG.

309   **"I sensed"**: Phil Palmer to JG.

309   **"I never"**: Billy Masters to JG, June 13, 2018.

309   **"No jealousy"**: Piers Morgan, "My Relationship with Kenny Is Open, Not in an Emotional Sense . . . Purely Physical," *Daily Mirror*, July 2, 2002.

310   **"sitting"**: John O'Brien, "'I Go with Gay Strangers. We Have Our Own Code,'" *Independent*, July 30, 2006.

310   **"were either"**: Adam Mattera, "George Michael: Days of the Open Hand."

310–11   **"I've already"** . . . **"breath, George"**: "Quote of the Day," *Gazette* (Montreal), Apr. 13, 2004.

311   **"gave me"**: Mark Allen, "George Michael Unzipped."

311   **"I really"**: Piers Morgan, "My Relationship with Kenny Is Open."

311   **"first proper"** . . . **"this one"**: "Michael's Latest 'For the Boys,'" *Calgary Herald*, Apr. 17, 2004.

311   **"It's supposed"**: Adam Mattera, "George Michael: Days of the Open Hand."

311   **"That's why"**: Johnny Douglas to JG.

CHAPTER TWENTY-THREE

312 **"suggests"**: Peter Paphides, "Losing Patience," *Times*, Mar. 20, 2004.

312 **"often angry"**: Paul Connolly, "You've Gotta Have Faith," *Times*, Feb. 28, 2004.

312 **"For years"**: David Thomas, "Taking the Michael!," *Daily Mail*, Mar. 12, 2004.

312 **"It gives"**: Alexis Petridis, *Guardian*, Mar. 11, 2004.

312 **"The bits"**: Andy Gill, "New Releases," *Independent*, Mar. 12, 2004.

312 **"I can't"**: "George Michael Rules British Radio," *South Florida Sun-Sentinel*, Apr. 29, 2004.

313 **"This isn't"**: "George Michael Requires 'Patience,'" AP (Akron Beacon Journal) June 6, 2004.

313 **"George Michael"**: Mary Lamey, *The Gazette* (Montreal), May 27, 2004.

313 **"George Michael's"** . . . **"from fame"**: *Tampa Tribune*, May 26, 2004.

314 **"George Michael"**: Doug Camilli, "George Michael Retires, Sort of," *Gazette*, Mar. 13, 2004.

315 **"terrified"**: Johann Hari, "Talk Without Prejudice," *Independent*, Dec. 9, 2005.

315 **"Those of"**: "George Michael Dumps Chat Room," *Argus Leader*, July 9, 2004.

315 **"surrounded"**: Janet Street-Porter, "Back in the Closet, George. We Only Want Your Songs," *Independent*, Dec. 11, 2005.

315 **"I know"**: Allyson Lieberman, "Pal to Spill George Michael Dirt," *New York Post*, May 16, 1999.

316 **"He betrayed"**: Danny Cummings to JG, May 26, 2018.

316 **"I am sorry"**: *Rock: The Luckiest Man in Pop* (2012), 308.

316 **"We have never"** . . . **"fans do"**: "By George," *Chicago Tribune*, Dec. 17, 2004.

316 **"If I"**: Laura Benjamin, "George Gives 'Gossip' Elton a Handbagging," *Daily Mail*, Dec. 15, 2004.

317 **"chills"**: Nicola Methven, "George on Drugs," *Daily Mirror*, Oct. 20, 2006.

318 **"These days"**: Cheryl Stonehouse, "The Man George Michael Always Wanted to Be," *Daily Mirror*, Apr. 19, 2006.

318   **"spends"**: Simon Hattenstone, "George Michael: 'I'm Surprised I've Survived My Own Dysfunction'," *Guardian*, Dec. 4, 2009.

318   **"No one"**: Cheryl Stonehouse, "The Man George Michael Always Wanted to Be"

318   **"hasn't experienced"**: Simon Hattenstone, "There Was So Much Death," *Guardian*, Dec. 8, 2005.

319   **"twenty-two"** . . . **"any joy"**: *George Michael: A Different Story*, (documentary), 2005.

319   **"I just"**: James Christopher, "On the Couch, the Male Kylie Laments His Idol Years in Pop," *Times*, Feb. 18, 2005.

319   **"I have got"**: James Sturke, "George Michael Says Pop Is 'Dead' as He Plans Exit," *Independent*, Feb. 17, 2005.

319   **"He's had"**: Janet Street-Porter, "Back in the Closet, George. We Only Want Your Songs."

319   **"I absolutely"**: Adam Mattera, "George Michael: Days of the Open Hand," *Attitude*, May 2004.

319   **"I could get . . . nothing"**: "Making It Legal," *Courier Journal* (Louisville, KY), Dec. 1, 2005.

319   **"I think"**: "No Dress Rehearsal," *Statesman Journal* (Salem, OR), May 8, 2006.

320   **"I'm a dirty"**: Simon Hattenstone, "There Was So Much Death."

320   **"huge amount"**: Johann Hari, "Talk Without Prejudice."

320   **"champagne"**: Stephen Moyes, "George's Secret Addiction," *Sun*, Jan. 21, 2017.

322   **"sex toys"**: Fiona Cummins & Caroline Hedley, "George's Gimp," *Daily Mirror*, Feb. 28, 2006.

322   **"vanilla"**: Robert Börjesson, "Jag är inget sexmonster," *Expressen* (Sweden), Apr. 5, 2007.

322   **"I don't know"**: Ciar Byrne, "George Michael: 'My Career's on Track and I'm Planning a Tour,'" *Independent*, Apr. 21, 2006.

322   **"Is this"**: Sarah White & Mark Jagasia, "George: Drugs Arrest Was My Own Fault as Usual," *Daily Express*, Feb. 28, 2006.

322   **"It's my own . . . nodded off"**: Adam Sherwin, "George Michael Blames It on Elton," *Times*, London, *Calgary Herald*, Apr. 21, 2006.

322   **"I promise"**: Ben Hoyle, "It Is My Own Stupid Fault—As Usual,"
Times, Feb. 28, 2006.

323   **"He didn't look" . . . "repairs"**: Laurie Hanna, "Wham! Scram!,"
Daily Express, Apr. 17, 2006.

323   **"a lot of"**: Lee Musiker to JG, Sept. 2, 2020.

323   **"It was nothing"**: "George Michael Plans to Tour the World," *Central
New Jersey Home News*, Apr. 22, 2006.

324   **"The subtext"**: Ciar Byrne, "George Michael: 'My Career's on Track.'"

324   **"Did I"**: Eva Simpson, "Elton's Fury at George's 'Blame,'" *Daily
Mirror*, Apr. 22, 2006.

324   **"This is not"**: Craig McLean, "What's Up with George Michael?,"
Daily Telegraph, Oct. 9, 2006.

324   **"Just What"**: "George: I've Got No Drug Problem," *Daily Mirror*,
Oct. 3, 2006.

324   **"Get Help"**: Fiona Cummins, "Get Help, George," *Daily Mirror*,
Mar. 1, 2006.

324   **"Believe me"**: *The Last Days of George Michael*, Channel 5 (UK),
Mar. 23, 2017.

324   **"I think he"**: Richard Alleyne, "Troubled Pop Star Allegedly Ran
into 3 Cars," Daily Telegraph, Apr. 19, 2006.

324   **"a sad"**: Brian Reade, "Don't Make a Drama Out of Mid-Life Crisis,"
Daily Mirror, Apr. 20, 2006.

324   **"the fear"**: Cheryl Stonehouse, "The Superstar Running Away from
Himself," *Daily Express*, Feb. 28, 2006.

324   **"surrounded"**: Phil Palmer to JG.

325   **"Suggesting"**: Niall Flynn to JG, Apr. 19, 2020.

325   **"I was star-struck"**: "Mutya Buena Teams Up with George Michael,"
popdirt.com, Sept. 12, 2006.

325   **"The sappy"**: Heath McCoy, "Season's Greatest Hits," *Calgary Herald*,
Dec. 23, 2006.

325   **"I want to"**: *George Michael: The Road to Wembley*, (documentary),
2007.

326   **"a pot-bellied"**: Neville Thurlbeck, "George's Sex Shame," *News of
the World*, July 23, 2006.

326   **"George is not"**: Nicole Lambert, "Erratic George Michael's New Shame," *Daily Mail*, July 24, 2006.

327   **"I mean"**: Sarah Tetteh, "George: I'm Like a Gay Rooney," *Daily Mirror*, July 26, 2006.

327   **"He now"**: Neil McCormick, "George Michael's Image Will Outlast the Scandal," *Daily Telegraph*, Sept. 15, 2010.

327   **"I'm not doing"**: Neville Thurlbeck, "George's Sex Shame."

327   **"I don't have"**: *Parkinson*, ITV (U.K.), Apr. 21, 2006.

CHAPTER TWENTY-FOUR

328   **"They will"**: Claudia Goulder & Catherine Boyle, "George Has No Time for Scandal on US Return," *Daily Express*, Mar. 26, 2008.

328   **"he was uncompromising"**: Phil Palmer to JG.

329   **"George just"**: Danny Cummings to JG, May 26, 2018.

329   **"I truly"**: Craig McLean, "What's Up with George Michael?," *Daily Telegraph*, Oct. 9, 2006.

329   **"fervent fans"**: *La Vanguardia*, "George Michael reúne a 18.000 seguidores en el inicio de su gira europea," Sept. 23, 2006.

329   **"If you're"**: Recording, Madison Square Garden, July 21, 2008.

330   **"for my"**: Madison Square Garden.

330   **"Yeah, right!"**: Madison Square Garden.

330   **"The fact"**: Simon Napier-Bell to JG, Sept. 7 2018.

330   **"K, I"**: Napier-Bell.

330   **"There has"**: Tim Teeman, "Shallow Portrait of a Careless Whinger," *Times*, Nov. 1, 2016.

330   **"much more"**: Eva Simpson & Caroline Hedley, "George of the Rovers," *Daily Mirror*, Nov. 20, 2006.

330   **"George was"**: Phil Palmer to JG.

330   **"Thank you"**: Gavin Martin, "Bye George," *Daily Mirror*, Aug. 26, 2008.

330   **"a George"**: "George Michael brilla en Madrid," *El País*, Sept. 27, 2006.

331   **"I had no"**: Emily Miller, "George: I've Got No Drug Problem," *Daily Mirror*, Oct. 3, 2006.

331   "They cocoon": Fiona Phillips, "We're Losing Faith, George," *Daily Mirror*, Oct. 7, 2006.

331   "I felt": Niall Flynn to JG, Apr. 19, 2020.

332   "He was charming": Craig McLean, "What's Up with George Michael?"

332   "George Michael wishes": *George Michael—I'm Your Man: A South Bank Special*, Nov. 7, 2006.

333   "ridiculously": Tim Teeman, "Shallow Portrait of a Careless Whinger," *Times*, Nov. 1, 2006.

333   "GEORGE": *Daily Mirror*, Oct. 20, 2006.

333   "I did *not*": Chris Goodman, "George Gets the Party Started," *Daily Express*, Nov. 9, 2006.

333   "Every time": Johnny Douglas to JG, July 10, 2019.

333   "Trim": Chris Mugan, "Pop: George Michael," *Independent*, Nov. 21, 2006.

333   "He wears": Chris Goodman, "George Gets the Party Started," *Daily Express*, Nov. 19, 2006.

334   "because ultimately": Johann Hari, "Talk Without Prejudice," *Independent*, Dec. 9, 2005.

334   "Did they": Victoria Ward & Gary Anderson, "'I Did Take Drugs and Drive . . . I'm So Stupid,'" *Daily Mirror*, May 9, 2007.

334   "Not guilty": Will Pavia, "George Michael Admits Drug Charge," *Times*, May 9, 2007.

335   "I did something": Victoria Ward & Gary Anderson, "I Did Take Drugs and Drive . . . I'm So Stupid," *Daily Mirror*, May 9, 2007.

335   "I do not": "George Michael Ordered to Appear in Court," AP (*Daily Oklahoman*), Apr. 27, 2007.

335   "I'm glad": John Chapman, "'Unfit' George Is on the Road to Wembley After Escaping Prison," *Daily Express*, June 9, 2007.

336   "I think": GM, *Desert Island Discs*, BBC Radio 4, Sept. 30, 2007.

336   "He spoke": Paul Keilthy, *Camden New Journal*, "Court Sends George Michael to Sing Sing," Aug. 23, 2007.

336   "kind of": Will Harrison, "The Capsizing of Damien Hirst," *Baffler*, April 3, 2017.

337   "Most people": Jamie Stengle, "Pop Star's Foundation Brings Art to Texas," *Statesman Journal* (Salem, OR), Apr. 8, 2008.

338–39   "How about" . . . "bangs": Stephen Fry to JG, July 30, 2020.

340   "On reflection": Adam Sherwin, "George Michael HIV Interview Is Cut for Being 'Too Personal,'" *Times*, Sept. 21, 2007.

340   "I couldn't": Stephen Fry to JG.

340   "part of": "Still Making Waves," *Financial Times*, Jan. 28–29, 2012.

340–41   "I'd been" . . . "think so": GM, *Desert Island Discs*.

CHAPTER TWENTY-FIVE

342   "I was a": *Star Stories*, Channel 4 (U.K.), Sept. 22, 2006.

343   "I was really": *Freedom* (documentary), 2017.

343   "I was prepared": *The Red Line*, Pt. 2, BBC Radio 2.

343   "a hairy": *British Comedy Awards,* ITV, Dec. 6, 2008.

343   "Shut": *The Catherine Tate Show*, BBC2, Dec. 25, 2007.

343   "I grew" . . . "very shy": Greg Berlanti to JG, Sept. 26, 2020.

344   "It's a very": Adam Markovitz, *Entertainment Weekly*, Mar. 24, 2008.

344–45   "It seemed" . . . "bear it": Mark Kavanagh, "George Michael Live at the RDS, Dublin," *Hot Press*, June 14, 2007.

345   "Would you": *Eli Stone*, Episode 9, ABC-TV, Mar. 27, 2008.

345   "George . . .": *Eli Stone*, Episode 13, Apr. 17, 2008.

346   "When he": Greg Berlanti to JG.

346   "Yes, that": Chuck Barney, "Odd 'Eli Stone' Gets Off to a Solid Start," *Contra Costa Times*, Jan. 30, 2008.

346   "ex-Wham!": Kevin D. Thompson, "Smart Lawyer with Visions: It's So 1990s," *Palm Beach Post*, Jan. 31, 2008.

346   "One imagines": Randy Cordova, "Controversial '80s Icon Is Making a Comeback," *Gannett News Service*, July 29, 2008.

346   "He was": Phil Palmer to JG.

346   "Lord knows": Recording, GM, HP Pavilion, San Jose, CA, June 19, 2008.

347   "performed": A. D. Amorosi, "George Michael Tries to Atone for Lost Time," *Philadelphia Enquirer*, July 28, 2008.

347   **"had little"**: Jim Farber, "No Wham-Bam Show," New York *Daily News*, July 22, 2008.

347   **"He used"**: Phil Palmer to JG.

347   **"She had"** . . . **"my heart"**: Bret Witke to JG, May 1, 2020.

347   **"Sick"**: Leslie Gray Streeter, "Michael Gives It One More Try," *Palm Beach Post*, Aug. 8, 2008.

348   **"I do"**: Andrew Jameson, "George Michael Shock Funeral Tribute," *Daily Star*, Jan. 24, 2017.

348   **"COCAINE"**: *Daily Mirror*, Sept. 15, 2005.

349   **"the gay"** . . . **Do It"**: Nathan, Sara & Mike Sullivan, Lynsey Haywood, "Careless Weeper: Crying Star George 'Sorry' Over Crack," *Sun*, Sept. 22, 2008.

349   **"Oh no!"**: Tony Parsons, "Don't Go Down the Pan, George," *Daily Mirror*, Sept. 27, 2008.

350   **"I think there"**: Johnny Douglas to JG, July 10, 2019.

350   **"It pissed"**: Niall Flynn to JG, Apr. 7, 2020.

350   **"He just"**: Niall Flynn to JG, Apr. 19, 2020.

351   **"Hi Thierry"**: Philip Utz, "The Confessions of Manfred Thierry Mugler."

351   **"I said"**: Judy Wieder to JG, March 23, 2018.

352   **"Nobody knew"**: Niall Flynn to JG, Apr. 7, 2020.

352   **"George has"**: "George Michael Snags Big Book Deal," AP (*Reno Gazette*), Jan. 18, 2008.

352   **"the devil"**: *George Michael—I'm Your Man: A South Bank Special.* Nov. 7, 2006.

352   **"George didn't"**: Chris Cameron to JG, June 2, 2018.

353   **"Neither"**: "Wham! Star 'Stone-Cold Sober,' " *Independent*, Aug. 16, 2009.

353   **"The fact"**: Simon Price, "We Love You, George, but You Don't Make It Easy for Us," *Independent*, Aug. 16, 2009.

353   **"George Michael Shunts"**: Price.

353   **"Why should"**: Simon Hattenstone, "There Was So Much Death," *Guardian*, Dec. 8, 2005.

353   **"the überconfident"**: Joanna Weiss, " 'Out' from the Start, 'Idol' Rocker Seeks Own Way to Stardom," *Boston Globe*, June 14, 2009.

353 **"God-gifted"**: "Adam Lambert: 'George Michael Had a God-Gifted Voice from the Heavens,'" *Pressparty*, Aug. 21, 2017.

354 **"a genius"**: Stephen Moyes, "George's Secret Addiction," *Sun*, Jan. 21, 2017.

354 **"I can't"**: Joe McElderry, *The X Factor UK*, ITV, Dec. 12, 2009.

354 **"I really"**: Niall Flynn to JG, Aug. 20, 2020.

354 **"One can"**: "George Michael: December Song (I Dream of Christmas)," *Financial Times*, Dec. 20, 2008.

355 **"He said"** . . . **"George's video"**: Yibi Hu to JG, Sept. 24, 2020.

356 **"My ego"**: Simon Hattenstone, "George Michael: 'I'm Surprised I've Survived My Own Dysfunction,'" *Guardian*, Dec. 4, 2009.

CHAPTER TWENTY-SIX

357 **"George Michael"**: Adam Sherwin, "George Michael Puts Record Straight on Gay Lifestyle," *Independent*, May 12, 2011.

358 **"No, I"**: Mark Hughes, "Keep the Faith, George," *Independent*, Sept. 15, 2010.

358 **"a small"**: Laura Pitel & Steve Bird, "George Michael Jailed After Driving His Car into Shopfront While High on Drugs," *Times*, Sept. 15, 2010.

358 **"profound"**: "George Michael Pleads Guilty to Drug Offenses," AP (*The Oklahoman*), Aug. 27, 2010.

358 **"It does not"**: Mark Hughes, "Keep the Faith, George," *Independent*, Sept. 15, 2010.

359 **"There were"**: Sky News (AU), Sept. 15, 2010.

359 **"I thought"**: "George Michael Says He 'Deserved' to Go to Jail," *BBC News*, Mar. 6, 2011.

359 **"cockroaches"**: The Independent Monitoring Board, HMP Pentonville: Annual Report to the Secretary of State, Apr. 1, 2012–Mar. 31, 2013, p.16.

359 **"for sex"**: Emma Rowley, "Inmates Cheer George Michael as He Starts Jail Term," *Evening Standard*, Sept. 15, 2020.

359 **"Where's George"** . . . **"no freedom!"**: "Kenny Goss Manages a Smile," *Daily Mail*, Sept. 17, 2010.

360   "great" . . . "member": Agence France-Presse, "Jail Term for Driving on Drugs Was Karma, Michael Says," *Edmonton Journal*, Mar, 8, 2011.

360   "I'm going": Wesley Johnson, "George Michael Gains His Freedom," *Independent*, Oct. 12, 2010.

360   "Karmically": Agence France-Presse, "Jail Term for Driving on Drugs Was Karma, Michael Says."

360   "House music": Will Hodgkinson, "George Michael Issues Apology to Gays . . . with Strings Attached," *Times*, May 12, 2011.

360   "I'm going": Halina Watts, "George Michael Dance Record Ready for Release," *Daily Mirror*, Oct. 5, 2018.

361   "gay enough": Will Hodgkinson, "George Michael Issues Apology to Gays . . . with Strings Attached."

361   "because he": Yibi Hu to JG, Sept. 24, 2020.

361   "on the": *Up Close with George Michael, Pt. 2*, BBC Radio 2, Mar. 25, 2014.

362   "When it came": *The Red Line*, Pt. 2, BBC Radio 2.

362   "spendin' ": *Red Nose Day*, BBC 1/2, Mar. 18, 2011.

362   "my lovelies": GM, Twitter, July 11, 2011.

362   "OOOh": GM, Apr. 2, 2012.

362   "In the corner": Mark Sweney & Dugald Baird, "Jeremy Clarkson: A History of BBC Top Gear Controversies," *Guardian*, Mar. 10, 2015.

363   "pig-ugly": GM, Twitter, July 19, 2011.

363   "Just saw": GM, Feb. 5, 2012.

363   "Every radio": GM, July 5, 2012.

363   "Quite a": GM, Sept. 18, 2011.

363   "Murdoch's: GM, July 11, 2011.

363   "sat two": GM, July 7, 2011.

363   "Would you": Hayley Minn, "George Michael Turned Down Prince William," *Daily Mirror*, Dec. 27, 2016.

363   "surrounded": *Showbiz Tonight*, CNN, Apr. 25, 2011.

363   "At four": Chris Cameron to JG, June 2, 2018.

364   "to make": *Up Close with George Michael, Pt. 1*, BBC Radio 2, Mar. 18, 2014.

364   "He even": Ben Butler to JG, Feb. 5, 2018.

365   **"I think George"**: Phil Palmer to JG.

365   **"which is"**: GM, Twitter, Aug. 21, 2011.

365   **"I'm not"**: GM, Symphonica press conference, Royal Opera House, London, May 11, 2011.

365   **"I'm in need"**: Stephen Moyes, "George's Secret Addiction," *Sun*, Jan. 21, 2017.

365   **"We stripped"**: Henry Hey to JG, Feb. 5, 2018.

365   **"He was the"**: Ben Butler to JG.

366   **"Early on"**: Paul Spong to JG, Apr. 14, 2020.

366   **"My lovely"**: Recorded interview with Phil Marriott, July 2012.

366   **"was like"**: Caesar Gergess to JG, May 28, 2018.

366   **"fine art"**: "Fadi Fawaz 'Plans Art Exhibition,'" AP, Apr. 24, 2017.

367   **"Sun, sand"**: GM, Twitter, Feb. 3, 2012.

367   **"George was"**: Niall Flynn to JG, Aug. 20, 2020.

367   **"I'm looking"** . . . **"of it"**: *Go'morgen* (Danish TV), July 2011.

367   **"I've got to"**: Ben Walsh, "First Night," *Independent*, Aug. 23, 2011.

367   **"I could"**: David Finck to JG, Apr. 15, 2018.

368   **"He was not"**: Finck.

368   **"I'm gonna"**: Recording, GM, Sportpaleis, Antwerp, Belgium, Oct. 7, 2011.

368   **"This song"**: GM, Sportpaleis.

369   **"the nature"**: David Sinclair, "Simple and Stylish Cherry-Picking Through a Perfectly Polished Songbook," *Times*, Oct. 26, 2011.

369   **"This man"**: Noah Michelson, "First Listen: George Michael's 'Where I Hope You Are,'" *Out*, Aug. 23, 2011.

369   **"Come on"**: Ben Walsh, "First Night," *Independent*, Aug. 23, 2011.

370   **"It murmured"**: Ludovic Hunter-Tilney, *Financial Times*, Oct. 29, 2011.

370   **"swagger"**: Gregory Katz, "George Michael in Fine Voice on Live Album," AP, *News Messenger* (Fremont, OH), Mar. 20, 2014.

370   **"I have"**: GM, Twitter, Aug. 28, 2011.

370   **"he was smelling"**: Mike Southon to JG, May 7, 2020.

370   **"My voice"**: GM, Twitter, Oct. 12, 2011.

370   **"It was beautiful"**: Paul Spong to JG.

370   **"He never"**: David Finck to JG.

371   "one of the great" . . . "amazing": *Up Close with George Michael,* BBC Radio 2, Mar. 18 & 25, 2014.

371   "George's food": David Finck to JG.

371   "a bizarre" . . . "sense now": Mark McLean to JG, Nov. 12, 2019.

372   "Went for": GM, Twitter, Nov. 3, 2011.

372   "He was on": Mark McLean to JG.

372   "New George": *Vogue Italia,* Nov. 16, 2011.

372   "He seemed": Phil Palmer to JG.

372   "It's such a": GM, Twitter, Oct. 27, 2011.

372   "That fucking": David Finck to JG, July 8, 2019.

372   "you could": Phil Palmer to JG.

373   "The details" Ben Butler to JG.

373   "That's when": Butler.

CHAPTER TWENTY-SEVEN

374   "severe": Simon Boyle, "Ill George Tour Axed," *Daily Mirror,* Nov. 26, 2011.

374   "germs are": *Up Close with George Michael,* Pt. 2, BBC Radio 2.

374   "George Michael": Deborah Sherwood, "George Michael Beating Pneumonia Hell, Says Lover," *Daily Star,* Nov. 27, 2011.

374   "Apparently": *The Last Days of George Michael,* Channel 5 (U.K.), Mar. 23, 2017.

375   "vaguely Bristolian": "George Michael's Accent Switch During Pneumonia Battle," *Daily Express,* July 18, 2012.

375   "feeble" . . . "walk again": GM to Chris Evans, BBC Radio 2, July 17, 2012.

375   "I'm very" . . . "everyone": "George Michael's Health," *Sky News,* Dec. 23, 2011.

375   "Hey everyone": GM, Twitter, Dec. 23, 2011.

376   "best Christmas" . . . "lucky man": GM, Twitter, Dec. 26, 2011.

376   "I cannot": "George Michael 'Released from the Hospital,'" Music-News.com, Dec. 22, 2011.

376   "Pray for": "George Michael Blasts Christian Group That Prayed for His Death," *Tampa Bay Times,* Jan. 10, 2012.

376   **"totally"**: GM, Twitter, Jan. 3, 2012.

376   **"First real"**: GM, Twitter, Jan. 28, 2012.

377   **"*Change*** . . . **"thrilled with it"**: GM to Chris Evans, BBC Radio 2, July 17, 2012.

377   **"We would"**: Niall Flynn to JG, Apr. 7, 2020.

378   **"like, a"**: Niall Flynn to JG, Aug. 20, 2020.

378   **"David had"**: Henry Hey to JG, Feb. 5, 2018.

378   **"It became"**: Jill Dell'Abate to JG, Apr. 15, 2018.

378   **"was sending"**: Niall Flynn to JG, Aug. 20, 2020.

378   **"I love that"**: GM to Chris Evans, BBC Radio 2, July 17, 2012.

379   **"They were"**: Niall Flynn to JG, Jan. 21, 2021.

380   **"Everywhere"**: Johnny Douglas to JG, July 10, 2019.

380   **"quite pissed"**: Douglas.

380   **"We stood"**: Danny Cummings to JG, May 26, 2018.

380   **"Normally"**: Johnny Douglas to JG.

380   **"not the time"**: "George Michael Defends Olympics Closing Ceremony Song," *BBC News*, Aug. 14, 2012.

380   **"could do"**: Seth Abramovitch, *New Music Express, Aug. 14, 2012.*

380   **"Please join"**: GM, Twitter, Aug. 14, 2012.

380   **"It's not"**: Niall Flynn to JG, Apr. 19, 2020.

381   **"Doesn't it"**: Adrian Thrills, "A Professional Triumph . . . and a Deeply Personal One," *Daily Mail*, Sept. 6, 2012.

381   **"reinvented"**: David Sinclair, "Slick and Sharp—but Go Easy on the Cover Versions, George," *Times*, Sept. 18, 2012.

381   **"the major"**: "George Michael Cancels Australia Tour, Cites Anxiety," *Reuters*, Oct. 1, 2012.

381   **"That feeling"**: GM to Chris Evans, BBC Radio 2, July 17, 2012.

381   **"I have a"**: Henry Hey to JG.

381   **"which breaks"**: "George Michael Cancels Australia Tour, Cites Anxiety," *Reuters*, Oct. 1, 2012.

382   **"gave everybody"**: David Finck to JG, Apr. 15, 2018.

382   **"said were"**: Chris Heath to JG, July 10, 2017.

382   **"George wasn't"**: Johnny Douglas to JG.

382   **"I've reconciled"** . . . **"popstar"**: PopJustice.com, Oct.-Nov. 2011.

383   "We were in": Niall Flynn to JG, Aug. 20, 2020.

383   "I think": Judy Wieder to JG, March 23, 2018.

383   "champagne" . . . "champers": Stephen Moyes, "George's Secret Addiction," *Sun*, Jan. 21, 2017.

383   "passed out": Emmeline Saunders, "Suicidal George Michael Tried to Kill Himself FOUR Times, Claims Lover as He Recalls Finding Singer Dead in Bed," *Daily Mirror*, Sept. 24, 2018.

383   "He bounced": Paul Scott, "Did George Michael Hurl HIMSELF from His Range Rover at 70mph on the M1?," *Daily Mail*, May 24, 2013.

384   "I saw": Nigel Atkins, "George Fell into Fast Lane of M1," *Daily Mirror*, May 21, 2013.

384   "Even if " . . . "look good": Matt Wilkinson & Tom Morgan, "Scrape Me Up Before You Go Slow," *Sun*, May 20, 2013.

384   "There is": Tom Bryant, "George Didn't Try to Commit Suicide," *Daily Mirror*, May 24, 2013.

384   "He's perfectly" . . . "comment": Anthony France & Matt Wilkinson, "George Michael Airlifted to Hospital After Rush-Hour Crash," *Sun*, May 17, 2013.

384   "public interest": "Police Close Investigation into George Michael M1 Accident," *Independent*, June 5, 2013.

384   "Aren't you . . . would say": Alisha Rouse, "George Michael Tried to Stab Himself 25 Times in Rehab, Claims Ex-Lover," *Daily Mail*, Sept. 25, 2018.

385   "It was almost": Chris Cameron to JG, June 2, 2018.

385   "I'd love": GM to Chris Evans, BBC Radio 2, July 17, 2012.

CHAPTER TWENTY-EIGHT

386   "We found" . . . "for itself ": Vaughan Arnell to JG, Jan. 12, 2018.

387   "It's a very": Yibi Hu to JG, Sept. 24, 2020.

387   "the former": "George Michael 'Resting' After Hospital Stay," AP (*Times*), May 30, 2014.

388   "I'd go": Niall Flynn to JG, Jan. 29, 2021.

388   "He would": Barry Reynolds to JG, Sept. 26, 2019.

388   **"unique"**: "George Michael's Visit to Secretive Clinic," *Daily Mirror*, Mar. 16, 2017.

388   **"biochemical"**: kusnachtpractice.com.

388   **"What we"** . . . **"and loved"**: Paul Flynn & Matthew Todd, "Pride and Prejudice for Gay Men," *Guardian*, Feb. 19, 2011.

389   **"George Is"**: Pete Samson, "George Is a Crack Addict," *Sun*, July 12, 2015.

389   **"To my"**: GM, Twitter, July 12, 2015.

389   **"It's not"**: Niall Flynn to JG, Jan. 29, 2021.

390   **"Much stronger"**: Danny Cummings to JG, May 26, 2018.

390   **"it was impossible"**: Johnny Douglas to JG, July 10, 2019.

390   **"When someone's"**: Barry Reynolds to JG.

390   **"I remember"**: Tom Bryant, "I Found My Tragic George Dead in Bed," *Daily Mirror*, Dec. 27, 2016.

390   **"George didn't really"**: Niall Flynn to JG, Apr. 7, 2020.

391   **"He still"**: Niall Flynn to JG, Apr. 19, 2020.

391   **"He said"**: Niall Flynn to JG, Apr. 7, 2020.

391–92   **"I've got"** . . . **"garden"**: Kirsty Young to JG, Nov. 24, 2020.

392   **"My God"** . . . **"destiny"**: *The Red Line*, Pt. 1, BBC Radio 2.

392   **"I'm rich"**: Chris Gray & Saeed Shah, "Robbie Swings Historic Record Deal with EMI," *Independent*, Dec. 30, 2013.

393   **"People who"** . . . **"extreme"**: *The Red Line*, Pt. 1, BBC Radio 2.

393   **"We minimize"**: Kirsty Young to JG.

393   **"Even when"**: *The Red Line*, Pt. 2, BBC Radio 2.

393   **"We had"**: Kirsty Young to JG.

393   **"I just had"**: Johnny Douglas to JG.

394   **"George had"**: Niall Flynn to JG, Apr. 7, 2020.

395   **"upset"**: Howell Davies, "How I Found George Dead," *Sun*, Sept. 25, 2018.

395   **"I know"**: "Fadi Fawaz," *Data Lounge*, Jan. 2, 2018.

395   **"I have no"** . . . **"999"**: Howell Davies, "How I Found George Dead," *Sun*, Sept. 25, 2018.

396   **"Is the patient"** . . . **"hang up?"**: Recording, 999 call, Fadi Fawaz, Dec. 25, 2016.

396   **"It is with"**: Elysa Gardner & Andrea Mandell, "Singer George Michael, Dominant in 1980s, Dies," *USA Today*, Dec. 26, 2016.

397   **"the entire"**: Thomas Andrei, "Le quartier de George Michael ne se remet toujours pas de son 'départ,'" *Greenroom*, Dec. 22, 2017.

397   **"That's what"**: Kirsty Young to JG

397   **"I was in"**: Danny Cummings to JG.

397   **"I thought"**: Dee C. Lee to JG, Feb. 10, 2021.

397   **"George used"**: Rob Kahane to JG, 28, 2018.

397   **"I wanted"**: Christopher Bucktin, "Elton John Claims George Michael Died Because He Couldn't Deal with His Sexuality," *Daily Mirror*, Oct. 24, 2019.

397   **"I always"**: Michael Pagnotta to JG, July 10, 2017.

CHAPTER TWENTY-NINE

398   **"4ever"**: Char Adams, "Wham! Member Andrew Ridgeley and Singing Duo Pepsi and Shirlie Remember George Michael," *People*, Dec. 26, 2016.

398   **"a kind"**: *Daily Mirror*, Dec. 27, 2016.

398   **"My pleasure"**: David Baddiel, Twitter, Dec. 26, 2016.

398   **"I've lost"**: Benjamin Njoku, "Ex-Wham Singer George Michael Dies at 53," *Vanguard*, Dec. 27, 2016.

399   **"non-suspicious"**: John Herring, "George Michael Death Not Being Investigated by Major Crimes Unit, Say Police," *Newburytoday*, Jan. 6, 2017.

399   **"Where someone"**: Simon Boyle, "'He Never Stood His Ground,'" *Sun*, Jan. 10, 2017.

399   **"FUCK YOU"**: Fadi Fawaz, Twitter, Mar. 7, 2017.

399   **"I went to"**: Tom Bryant, "I Found My Tragic George Dead in Bed," *Daily Mirror*, Dec. 27, 2016.

399   **"The only"**: Marisa Laudadio, "George Michael's Boyfriend Tweets That Music Star Wanted to Kill Himself," *Wonderwall*, Jan. 1, 2017.

399–400 **"devastated"** . . . **"as he was"**: Laura Armstrong, "Dad's Probe Pain," *Sun*, Jan. 8, 2017.

400   **"Did I"**: Mark Jefferies & Nicola Bartlett, "George Hadn't Taken Heroin Before He Died," *Daily Mirror*, Dec. 28, 2016.

400   **"I just think"**: Stephen Moyes, "George's Secret Addiction," *Sun*, Jan. 21, 2017.

400   **"Any pretense"**: Moyes.

400   **"I think his"**: Zoie O'Brien, "George Michael's Ex-Lover Fadi Fawaz Is Seen Looking 'Sad and Lost,'" *Daily Mail*, Dec. 26, 2018.

400   **"natural causes"**: "George Michael Died of Natural Causes," *BBC News*, Mar. 7, 2017.

401   **"I am very"**: "The Truth Is Out . . . Really?," *Sun*, Mar. 8, 2017.

401   **"George died"**: Halina Watts, "George Michael's Family Hit Back," *Daily Mirror*, July 21, 2018.

401   **"family source"**: "George Michael 'Was Discovered Passed Out in Bath Full of Water After Overdosing on GHB,' Claims Pal," *Daily Mirror*, July 21, 2018.

401   **"I'm not"**: Johnny Douglas to JG, July 10, 2019.

401   **"We may"**: Ellie Harrison, "Andrew Ridgeley Still Has 'a Number of Questions' About George Michael's Death," *Independent*, Oct. 5, 2019.

402   **"Then the door"**: Niall Flynn to JG, Apr. 19, 2020.

402   **"donation"**: Mike Hamilton & Jane Atkinson, "Inside Star's Send-Off," *Sun*, May 6, 2017.

403   **"my place"**: Fadi Fawaz, Twitter, June 9, 2018.

403   **"An eye"**: Fawaz, Apr. 4, 2018.

403   **"George I am"** . . . **"burger"**: Zoe Shenton, "George Michael's Lover Fadi Fawaz Claims He's So Broke He 'Struggles to Buy Milk and Water,'" *Daily Mirror*, July 11, 2017.

403   **"Goerge Micheal [*sic*]"**: Fadi Fawaz, Twitter, Apr. 16, 2018.

403   **"It's a way"**: "Fadi Fawaz Selling George Michael's Possessions," AP, Apr. 17, 2018.

403   **"I feel"**: Fadi Fawaz, Twitter, Feb. 5, 2018.

404   **"savages"** . . . **"death"**: James Draper, "Fadi Fawaz Relives the Horror of Discovering George Michael's Body in Shocking Detail," *Daily Mirror*, Apr. 6, 2018.

404   **"To every"**: Fadi Fawaz, Twitter, Feb. 21, 2018.

404 **"All of"**: Amanda Platell, "Platell's People: Why George Michael Made Me Change My Own Will," *Daily Mail*, June 7, 2019.

404 **"George I hate"**: Fadi Fawaz, Twitter, Aug. 4, 2018.

405 **"renovating"**: Rebecca Lewis, "George Michael's Ex Fadi Fawaz Goes 'Absolutely Berserk' as He 'Destroys Pop Star's Home'," *Metro*, July 14, 2019.

405 **"absolutely"** . . . **"flying everywhere"**: Rebecca Lewis, "George Michael's Ex . . ."

405 **"Every fixture"**: Eve Wagstaff, "Fix Me Up Before You Go Go," *Sun*, August 17, 2019.

405 **"sleeping in"**: Amanda Devlin, "Troubled Times," *Sun*, Feb, 6, 2020.

405 **"George Michael was"**: Joel Adams, "George Michael's Former Boyfriend Fadi Fawaz Disgusts Singer's Fans," *Daily Mail*, Oct. 30, 2019.

405 **"He never"**: Ishani Ghose, "George Michael Was HIV Positive, Lousy in Bed and 'Never Wrote His Own Music,' Says Ex Fadi Fawaz, *Meaww*, Oct. 31, 2019.

406 **"said that"**: Emma James, "George Michael's Ex Fadi Fawaz Arrested After 'Attacking Parked Cars with Hammer," *New York Post*, Aug. 18, 2020.

406 **"I will revenge"**: Fadi Fawaz, Twitter, Apr. 15, 2018.

406 **"And no"**: Fawaz, Apr. 16, 2018.

406 **"exactly as"**: "George Michael: New Song by Late Star to Get First Play," *BBC News*, Sept. 6, 2017.

406 **"David trying"**: *Rock: The Luckiest Man in Pop* (2012), 325.

406 **"George was"**: Niall Flynn to JG, Jan. 21, 2021.

406 **"I've got"**: Johnny Douglas to JG.

407 **"choir"**: David Grant, "Boy George Has Some Harsh Words About That Posthumous George Michael Single," *Queerty*, Sept. 7, 2017.

407 **"It's absolute"**: Deon Estus to JG, May 2, 2019.

407 **"essentially"**: Mikael Wood, "Little More Than a Careless Whisper," *Los Angeles Times*, Oct. 21, 2017.

408 **"incredibly"**: David Fear, " 'Last Christmas' Review," *Rolling Stone*, Nov. 6, 2019.

408 **"fifteen of"**: Niall Flynn to JG, Aug. 20, 2020.

409   **"under"**: Thea Jacobs, "Bid Me Up," *Sun*, March 15, 2019.

409   **"in his"**: Raven Saunt & Harry Howard, "George Michael's 'Devastated' Family Vow His Ex-Lover Kenny Goss Will Get Nothing After He Sued the Late Singer's Estate Demanding £15,000 A MONTH," *Daily Mail*, Oct. 11, 2020.

409   **"We will be"**: Alahna Kindred & Alex Matthews, "Swerve the Bad," *Sun*, Dec. 27, 2019.

410   **"I think"** . . . **"out why"**: *The Red Line*, Pt. 1, BBC Radio 2.

EPILOGUE

411   **"GEORGE"**. . . **"you want"**: "The Sex Life Celebration of George Michael," *HuffPost* video, Apr. 8, 2017.

411   **"We wanted"**: Dan Glass to JG, June 19, 2017.

412   **"So many"** . . . **"vulnerability"**: "The Sex Life Celebration of George Michael," *HuffPost* video, Apr. 8, 2017.

412   **"I think he"**: *The Red Line*, Pt. 2, BBC Radio 2.

412   **"For all"**: "Stubble and Strife," *Observer*, May 12, 1996.

413   **"Pop singers"**: Ellyn Solis to JG, May 23, 2017.

413   **"I find"**: Johnny Douglas to JG, July 10, 2019.

413   **"Somewhere along"**: Steve Pond, "George Michael, Seriously," *Rolling Stone*, Jan. 28, 1988.

413   **"When I"**: Billy Masters to JG, June 13, 2018.

413   **"culture of"**: Julianne Escobedo Shepherd, "George Michael, a Worthy Conduit for All Our Desires," *Jezebel*, Dec. 28, 2016.

413   **"British"**: A. D. Amorosi, "Sam Smith Shows Why He's a Brit Soul Master," *Philadelphia Inquirer*, Jan. 14, 2015.

414   **"He sent"**: Mesfin Fekadu, "Outtakes: Sam Smith on George Michael, Rihanna and Drinking," AP, Nov. 15, 2017.

414   **"We can"**: Stephen Fry to JG, July 30, 2020.

415   **"the emotional"**: Will Automagic to JG, July 19, 2019.

415   **"Pop music"**: Danny Cummings to JG, May 26, 2018.

415   **"Maybe"**: Barb Jungr to JG, June 7, 2018.

COMMERCIAL ALBUM DISCOGRAPHY

With Wham!

Fantastic (1983)
Make It Big (1984)
The Final (1986)
Music from the Edge of Heaven (1986)
Twelve Inch Mixes (1988)
The Best Remixes (1989)
The Best of Wham!: If You Were There (1997)
Japanese Singles Collection: Greatest Hits (2020)

Solo

Faith (1987)
Listen Without Prejudice Vol. 1 (1990)
Older (1996)
Ladies & Gentlemen: The Best of George Michael (1999)
Songs from the Last Century (1999)
Twenty Five (2006)
Patience (2004)
Faith (Deluxe Collector Edition) (2010)
Symphonica (2014)
Listen Without Prejudice / MTV Unplugged (Deluxe Edition) (2017)
Last Christmas (soundtrack) (2019)

ACKNOWLEDGMENTS

To everyone who spoke with me for this book, my heartfelt thanks for sharing your memories and insights. All of you made it possible for me to tell this story.

I am immensely indebted to my first champion in this project, bassist David Finck, whose keen insights into George and his music set me on the right track. Søren Madsen gave me abundant and invaluable access to his vast collection of materials and his equally impressive store of knowledge. Recording engineer Niall Flynn spent many hours telling me about the man he worked with and observed at close range for twenty-one years; Niall made a crucial difference in my understanding of George Michael. Danny Cummings, George's longtime percussionist, welcomed me into his home in France and offered a compassionate view of the George he loved. Chris Cameron, George's keyboard player and musical director for most of his solo career, answered my questions speedily and incisively for three years.

Eric Brogger, Reed McGowan, Kenny Mellman, and James Spencer all shared their wisdom with me about George's music and the times through which he passed. Lawyer and former Sony executive Sylvia Coleman supplied me with essential documents and went out of her way to open doors. Journalist Thomas Andrei took me on an insider's walking tour of Highgate, one of George's London neighborhoods. Pierre Meirelles of Rio de Janeiro helped me unlock the story of the Brazilian love of George's life, Anselmo Feleppa; Gustavo Pace took the time to translate the more difficult Portuguese in my interviews with Anselmo's friends. Marco Antonio Valgiusti and Ben Glenn III gave me their valuable impressions of George's art collection. A great artist himself, photographer Bobby Miller took an author's photo that I treasure.

Others who connected me with interview sources or provided important information, materials, and advice include Penny Arcade, Jeffrey Burbank,

Jodi Burnett, Luiz Felipe Carneiro, Michael Cavadias, Steven Charlton, Nick De Biase, Alan Eichler, Jim Farber, Barbara Fasano, Jeff Fleming, David Freeland, Caesar Gergess, Caroline Graham, Maggie Carnes Hafner, Corky Hale, Glenn Hanna, Lauren Hanna, Keith Hartel, David Hurst, Elio Iannacci, Bradley Jones, Kieron Kawall, Lucy King, Matthias Künnecke, Marcelo Lago, Mark Lambert, Joe Levy, Holt McCallany, Jeff Macauley, Bob Merlis, Allen Mezquida, Helen Merrill, Steve Nathan, Vicky F. O'Neill, Lori Opendon, Phil Palmer, Craig Peikin, Alex Perry, Gill Pringle, Darren Ramirez, Steven Reigns, Mark Robertson, Graham Russell, Bill Sensenbrenner, Peter Sheridan, Steve Sidwell, Ken Siman, Xavier Smith, Jill Stean, James Sullivan, Sylvynho, Andrew Tobias, Roger Walker-Dack, Ron Weisner, and Paul Wexler. Abundant thanks to Paul Gomersall for generously allowing me to use his photos, and to Philip Thomas for providing images owned by his parents, Peter and Cordy Thomas. Mary Ellen Jensen of Alamy made my photo acquisition a breeze.

I could not have written this book without the resources of the British Library, whose superbly professional and cordial staff made my days there a joy. GMForever.com is the definitive database of substantial articles about George Michael; I turned to it again and again. Yogworld, another site devoted to George, is a bonanza of news, tidbits, and links that shine a light on the fine points of his career.

To the friends who hosted me in my research travels—Simon Wallace and Sarah Moule (London), Caesar Gergess (Paris), Delphine de Rohan-Chabot (La Baule, France), Mark Christian Miller (West Hollywood), and Joel Thurm (Laurel Canyon, Los Angeles), thank you for the privilege of using your guest bedrooms or sofas and for the joy of your company. Joel, Lisa Bond, Michael Childers, Tammy Faye, David Hurst, Barb Jungr, Richard Lamparski, Darren Ramirez, Ken Siman, and Sheila Weller all counseled and consoled me when I needed it.

My godsend of an agent, David Forrer, found this book a home and changed my life, as he has before. David Cashion, my original editor at Abrams, fought to give it that home; this book would not exist without him. His successor Chelsea Cutchens expertly and insightfully brought it into the light and paid careful attention to everything. So did Laura Cooke, who surpassed every other copy editor with whom I have ever worked, and proofreader Christopher Cerasi. Great thanks to attorney Julie Ford for giving the manuscript a scrupulous and expert legal read. I'm grateful to the rest of the Abrams team—managing editors Annalea Manalili and Kayla White, creative director and book designer Deb Wood, design manager Danny Maloney, senior designer Devin Grosz, production manager Sarah Masterson Hally, and digital and social media senior manager Mamie VanLangen—for their hard work and talent. Publicist Andrew Gibeley did a tirelessly resourceful and caring job of spreading the word about this book; he is the best at what he does. Most of all, thanks to my constant companion throughout this process, George Michael, whose talent and heart made me very glad I took this chance.

INDEX

Abdul, Paula, 131
activism, 301–7, 338–40, 361–64
Adele, 362, 412–13
Ægean Records, 241–42, 244–47, 316
Agressot, Patricia, 200
Ahmad, Shamsi, 23, 27, 31, 51
AIDS
    activism for, 338–40
    benefit album for, 180–81
    charity for, 239
    in culture, 186–89
    homophobia and, 84–85
    for MTV, 287–89
    sexual orientation and, 20, 65, 84–85,
        109–10, 112–13, 115, 139, 184–85,
        200–201
    World AIDS Day concert, 212–13
Ai Li, 76
"Ain't No Stoppin' Us Now," 241
Albarn, Damon, 224, 235
Allan, Robert, 24
Almond, Marc, 43–44
"Alone," 377
Altman, John, 8
"Amazing," 309, 330–31
"American Angel," 309
American Bandstand (TV show), 33–34
"American Life," 305
American Music Awards, 90–91
Anderson, J. T., 256–58
Anderson, Lindsay, 76, 79
Andrei, Thomas, 308, 397
Andrews, Brittany, 274
Animal Nightlife, 41
Appleyard, Bryan, 160
Aquilante, Dan, viii–ix
Arbagey, Joey, 279
Arias, Joey, 190–93
Arnell, Vaughan, 274, 386–87
arrests, 259–66, 270–73, 277–80, 334–35,
    348–49, 357–60
art collection, 336–38
"As," 279
Attitude (magazine), 7

Austin, David (née Mortimer), 407–8
    early career with, 15–17, 23, 38, 63, 101–2,
        104, 107–8
    support from, 374, 378, 389, 394, 406

Babylon Zoo, 235
"Back for Good," 225
Bad, 125–26, 129, 166
Badalamenti, Angelo, 231
"Bad Boys," 37
Baddiel, David, 398
Balance-Drew, Benjamin Paul "Plan B,"
    370–71
Bamigboye, Baz, 104
Bananarama, 64
Bangalter, Thomas, 317
"Banks of the Ohio," 4
Barber, Nicholas, 236
Bare, 156–57
Barlow, Gary, 225
Barrowclough, Anne, 94–95
Barry, Len, 109
Bartolomi, David, ix
Batties, Rebecca, 70
the Beat, 14
Beck, Jeff, 34–35
Beckenham, Kay, 122
Beckinsale, Kate, 245
Beckwith, Tamara, 271
Bee Gees, 10–11, 126, 259
Bell, Andy, 122
Bell, Max, 49
"Ben," 5
Bennett, Tony, 323, 364
"Bennie and the Jets," 119
Benton, Anthea, 220, 232–33, 274
Berk, Jane, 119
Berkmann, Marcus, 124, 140, 162
Berlanti, Greg, 343–46
Berry, Ken, 223
Berry, Nancy, 223
Beverly Hills Cop II (film), 110–12
Beyoncé, 351–52
Bicknell, Ed, 203

"Biko," 140
bin Laden, Osama, 304
Birch, Elizabeth, 289
Bitelli, Dave, 124–25
Bjork, 283
Blair, Iain, 84
Blair, Jerry, 159, 166
Blair, Tony, 301–7
Blake, John, 97
"Blame It on the Sun," 246
Blauel, Renate, 44
Blige, Mary J., 279
Blondie, 21, 31
"Body and Soul," 364
The Bodyguard (film), 200
Bolan, Marc, 34–35
Born in the U.S.A., 166
Bourke, Toby, 244–47, 250
Bowe, Lawrie, 352–53
Bowermaster, Jon, 133
Bowie, David, 9, 22
Bowling, Dan, 42
Boy George
    for Culture Club, 19, 29, 44, 64–65
    rivalry with, 80, 86, 105, 109–10, 136, 211,
        253, 258–59, 262–63, 287
Boyzone, 315
Bragg, Melvyn, 156, 333
Branson, Brad, 87–88, 174–75
Brazil, 171–75
Bricusse, Leslie, 345
Bright, Spencer, 169–70, 203
Brooks, Garth, 289–91, 293
"Brother, Can You Spare a Dime," 369
Brown, Divine, 262
Brown, Mick, 42, 68, 70, 140–41
Brown, Steve, 31, 33
Browne, David, 147
Brummel, Beau, 9
Buckley, Tim, 371
Buena, Mutya, 325
Burchill, Julie, 99
"Burn Rubber on Me (Why You Wanna Hurt
    Me)," 41
Burns, Hugh, 107
Bush, George W., 301–7, 330
Butler, Ben, viii, 373

Cameron, Chris
    collaboration with, x, 103–9, 131, 133,
        148–49, 152–53
    support from, 173, 199–200, 226, 229, 290,
        352, 363–64, 385

Camilli, Doug, 314
Campbell, Naomi, 228
"Candle in the Wind," 99, 249–50
"Can't Get Used to Losing You," 14
"Can't Smile Without You," 69
Careless Whisper, 337
"Careless Whisper"
    initial success of, 48, 56–57, 60–62, 71, 73,
        77, 90–91, 99
    legacy of, 119–20, 132–33, 173
Carey, Mariah, 207
Carlin, John, 180, 189, 194
Carmen, Jeanne, 274
Carneiro, Luiz Felipe, 172–74
"Cars and Trains," 294–95
Carson, Johnny, 87
Carter, Bob, 26
Carvey, Dana, 146–47
Cashman, Michael, 278
Cassidy, David, 5–6
censorship, 103–4, 112–14, 291
"Chameleon (Shed Your Skin)," 247
Chapman, Dinos, 337
Chapman, Jake, 337
Charles, Ray, 246
Charlton, Janet, 258
Chawla, Mukul, 358
Cheng Fangyuan, 78
Chidekel, David, 23–24, 51
"Chirpy Chirpy Cheep Cheep," 5
Christgau, Robert, 11
Clapton, Eric, 34–35
Clark, Dick, 34, 53
Clarke, Emilia, 408
Clarkson, Jeremy, 362–63
Climie, Simon, 95
Clinton, Bill, 263
"Club Tropicana," 23, 40–42, 46, 152
Coca-Cola, 144–47
Cocker, Jarvis, 224, 235
Coleman, Sylvia, 158, 167, 184, 206, 210,
    215, 218
Coleridge, Tania, 121
Collard, James, 250–51
"Come On!," 49
Come on Over, 285
coming out, 44–45, 201–2, 234, 254–59,
    274–77, 292–93
Common Hours, 21
Coney Island at Noon Saturday, July 5, 1942,
    156
Connolly, Paul, 312
Considine, J. D., 113, 296

"Constant Craving," 291
Cope, Nigel, 204
Corden, James, 361–62
Cornelius, Don, 146
Cosby, Bill, 80
"Cowboys and Angels," 151, 368
Cowell, Simon, 304, 354
Cowley, Patrick, 20
Craig-Martin, Michael, 337
Cran, Mark, 205–8, 214–16, 219
Crawford, Cindy, 163–65
Crawford, Robyn, 296
"Crazyman Dance," 179–80
"Credit Card Baby," 58
Cromelin, Richard, 181
Crowley, Gary, 49
Cui Jian, 78
Culture Club, 19, 29, 44, 64–65, 110
Cummings, Danny, 316, 397, 415
    after Wham!, 104–5, 107–8, 124, 144,
        148–49, 152, 169, 173–74, 213, 286, 290,
        293, 328–29
    for Wham!, vii–viii, 6–7, 38, 47–48, 53, 61,
        75, 77, 89, 94, 98
Curtis, Tony, 267
Cushnan, Ruadhri, 299, 325
Cyrus, Miley, 398

Daft Punk, 317
Daggett, Chris, 107, 116–17
D'Angelo, Andrew, 60
Dann, Trevor, 112
D'Arby, Terence Trent, 232–33, 386
Davis, Clive, 95, 376
Davis, Jeff, 115
Davis, Shan, 260
Day, Doris, 55, 282–83
Day, Spencer, 163
Dean, Mark, 23–25, 27, 32, 34–35, 45–46,
    50–51
death, 393–403
De Atley, Richard, 147
"December Song (I Dreamed of Christmas),"
    354–55
Deevoy, Adrian, 29, 125, 131, 135, 138, 143,
    157, 202
DeGeneres, Ellen, 251–52, 288
"Delilah," 4
Dell'Abate, Jill, 283–84, 364, 378
DeMacque, Helen "Pepsi," 45, 67, 70, 76,
    89–90, 98, 157, 317, 401–2
DeMann, Freddy, 34
Derek, Bo, 347

"Desafinado," 214
Desert Island Discs (radio show), 340–41
Diana (Princess), 82, 211–13, 248–50, 363,
    415
Diaz, John, 111
Dickins, Rob, 223
"A Different Corner," 87–88, 98, 133, 330
A Different Story (documentary), 316–19
Dire Straits, 203
Dirty Dancing (soundtrack), 125–26, 145
Donovan, Jason, 171
"Don't Let the Sun Go Down on Me," 82, 354
"Do They Know It's Christmas?," 67, 69, 81
Douglas, Johnny
    collaboration with, 230–32, 236–38, 242,
        273, 294, 296, 298, 333, 350, 377, 380
    support from, ix, 300, 380, 390, 393–94,
        401, 406, 413
Downs, Alan, 388–89
"Do You Really Want to Hurt Me," 19
"Do You Really Want to Know," 189
Dranoff, Béco, 214
drug use, 320–27, 331–33, 386–93
Dunk, Marcus, 161
Duran, John, 256–57, 270–71, 280
Dylan, Bob, 160

The Eagles, 222
The Eagles, 222
"The Edge of Heaven," 94
"Edith and the Kingpin," 282
Eggar, Robin, 68
Eli Stone (TV show), 343–46
Elizabeth II (queen), 79–80
Ellen (TV show), 251–52
Emin, Tracey, 336–37
Epic Records, 29, 50, 56, 61–62
Equality Rocks concert, 288–93
Erasure, 122
Erotica, 166
Estus, Deon
    after Wham!, 130, 132–33, 148, 170, 202
    for Wham!, 39, 45, 58, 60, 75–76, 100,
        103–4
Etheridge, Melissa, 254, 288, 291
Eurythmics, 42–43
Evangelista, Linda, 163–65, 189, 192–93
Evans, Chris, 51, 100, 252, 377–78, 385
"Every Other Lover," 382
"Everything She Wants," 59, 73, 110, 119,
    133, 330
the Executive, 14–15, 17
Expensive Habits (Garfield), 51

Extended Plaything, 184, 209
Extras (TV show), 342–43
Eyre, Tommy, 39, 49–50, 60

Faith, 109, 118, 120, 124–29, 144–48, 166, 215
"Faith," 108–9, 120–21, 125–26, 147
Faith tour, viii
Falwell, Jerry, 252
fame, 38–43, 71–74, 314–19
Fantastic, 39, 46
"Fantasy," 394, 407
Farber, Jim, 186–87, 347
"Fastlove," 230–34, 236–37, 292
"Father Figure," 106–7, 121, 126, 147, 168–69, 172, 213, 313, 369
Fawaz, Fadi, viii, 366–67, 369, 372, 374–77, 383–85, 393–97, 399–406
Fayed, Emad "Dodi," 249
Fear, David, 408
"Feeling Good," 345–46, 369
Feleppa, Alexandre, 201
Feleppa, Alice, 201
Feleppa, Amodeo, 176, 201
Feleppa, Anselmo
    memories of, 226, 234, 237, 254, 292, 385, 391–92
    relationship with, vii, 174–79, 181, 184–86, 196–202
Fernandes, Pat, 29, 54, 86, 123
Fernandes, Rosa, 174, 177, 200
Fernley, Robert, 93
Filippello, Connie, 56, 63, 75, 138, 237, 261, 276, 374, 384, 396, 404
The Final, 94–95
Fincher, David, 164–65
Finck, David, 283, 364–65, 367–68, 369, 381–82
Finnigan, Judy, 326–27
Fiorentino, Donya, 92, 99
Five Live, 188–89
"Flawless (Go to the City)," 311, 330
Flax, Bob, 127
Flynn, Niall, 350–51, 406, 408
    collaboration with, 301–3, 305–6, 354, 377–78
    support from, 229, 246–47, 281, 295, 296, 309, 325, 331–32, 367, 380, 383, 387–89, 391
Foreign Skies (documentary), 79, 98
"Forget Me Nots," 231
"For the Love of You," 282
Fowler, Jon, 174–75
Fox, Katherine, 384

Fox, Neil, 284–85
Frankie Goes to Hollywood, 43–44, 103, 199
Franklin, Aretha, 95–97, 101, 141
Franklin, Cecil, 96–97
Franklin, C. L., 97
Frears, Stephen, 144
"Free," 232
Freedom (autobiography/documentary), 391–92, 407–8
"Freedom," 58, 73, 90–91, 99, 110, 415
"Freedom! '90," 160, 163–70, 173, 181, 227–28, 292, 379, 414
Freedomfest, 140
"Freeek!," 299–300, 308
"Freeway of Love," 95
Frost, David, 218–19
Fry, Stephen, 338–40, 414
Fulfillingness' First Finale, 151
funeral, 401–2
Furnish, David, 319
Fürstenberg, Egon von, 177

Gabriel, Peter, 140
Gabrin, Chris, 30
Gallagher, Liam, 380
Gallagher, Noel, 235, 304
Gannon, Louise, 163
Gantner, Carrillo, 78
Gap Band, 41
Garcia, Tony, 101–3, 151
Garfield, Simon, 51, 224
Garfunkel, Art, 30
Garratt, Sheryl, 45, 228–29
Gately, Stephen, 287
Gavin & Stacey (TV show), 361–62
Gaye, Marvin, 140, 142, 299, 370
gay marriage, 319–20
Geary, Charlie, 256
Geffen, David, ix, 25, 59, 221–23, 225, 232, 238, 263
Geffen Records, 219
Geldof, Bob, 66–69, 81, 91
"George Is a Crack Addict" (Georgiou, J.), 389
George Michael: A Different Story (documentary), 184–85, 317–19
Georgiou, Alex, 383
Georgiou, Andros, 316
    business with, 241–47, 272–73, 276
    friendship with, 2, 6, 9–11, 14, 67–69, 78, 96, 123, 147, 185, 199, 201, 226, 232, 264
Georgiou, Dimitrios, 1
Georgiou, Jackie, 389

Gervais, Ricky, 342–43, 412
Getz, Stan, 215
Gibbins, Duncan, 42, 53, 56–57, 61
Gilberto, Astrud, 214–15
Gilberto, João, 148, 214–15
Gill, Ian, 46
Gilmour, Andrew, 336
"The Girl from Ipanema," 214
Glass, Dan, 411–12
Gleadall, Pete, 290
Glitter, Gary, 98
"Going to a Town," 365, 368
Golding, Henry, 408
Goldsmith, Harvey, 47, 81, 91–92, 286
Goldstein, Patrick, 137
Goldstone, Don, 198, 255
Gomersall, Paul, 39, 53, 58, 67, 103, 106,
    214–15, 229
Goodbye Yellow Brick Road, 9
Goodman, Chris, 333
Gore, Al, 103–4
Gore, Tipper, 103–4, 114, 291
"Go See the Doctor," 113
Goss, Earl, 262
Goss, Kenny, 358–59, 399–400
    art collection with, 336–38, 402, 409
    privacy with, 241–42, 248, 255, 258–62,
        277, 283
    relationship with, 309–10, 313, 319–20,
        329–30, 348–50, 356, 369
Goss, Ozell, 262
Graff, Gary, 160
Graham, Bill, 81
Graham, Caroline, 64, 261–62
Grant, David, 407
Grant, Hugh, 264
"The Grave," 307
Gray, Charles, 219
Gregory, Steve, 60–61
Grein, Paul, 124
Grubman, Allen, 117–18, 127, 208
Guanabara, Lucia, 174–77, 185, 200–201
"Guilty Feet," 19, 23, 31, 34, 48
Gundersen, Edna, 236
Guns N' Roses, 187

Hall, Fawn, 122
Halliwell, Geri, 247–48, 302–3, 356
Hamnett, Katherine E., 54
"Hand to Mouth," 107
"Happy," 180, 189
"Hard Day," 107, 125–26
Hari, Johann, 188, 315, 320

Haring, Bruce, 183
Harrelson, Woody, 304
Harrison, Colin, 12–13
Harrison, George James, 12
Harrison, Lesley Angold
    childhood with, 1–3, 9, 12–14, 27
    support from, 100, 132, 202, 242–44,
        249–50, 333–34
Harry, Debbie, 21
Hattenstone, Simon, 13, 318, 352–53, 355–56
Hayes, Lynda, viii, 31–33
health concerns, 376–79
"Heal the Pain," 151, 325
Heath, Chris, 38, 43, 113, 135, 155–56, 162,
    168, 190–91, 270, 285, 382
"Heat Wave," 53
Heche, Anne, 252, 288
Henley, Don, 219
"Heroes Are Hard to Find When They're
    Hiding" (Rinaldi), 288
Hey, Henry, 39, 364–65, 368, 378, 381
Heyward, Nick, 98
Hiding Out (documentary), 291–93
Hilburn, Robert, 125, 147, 160
Hill, Dave, 125
Hirst, Damien, 336–37, 408
HIV. See AIDS
Hodgkinson, Will, 360
Hoffmann, Bill, 304
Holden, Stephen, 105, 124, 148, 234
Holiday, Billie, 108, 282
Holliman, Shirlie, 98, 247
    before Wham!, 10, 18–19, 21–22, 26–28
    with Wham!, 30, 32–33, 41–42, 44–45, 92
Homem-Christo, Guy-Manuel de, 317
homophobia, 6, 12–13, 16–17, 43–45, 65
    AIDS and, 84–85
    in Brazil, 171–72
    censorship and, 291
    coming out and, 274–77, 292–93
    in culture, 181, 187, 251–53, 279–80
    at MTV, 193
Hooke, Peter Van, 7–8
Hope, Ryan, 378–79
Hopkinson, Frank, 38
Hotel California, 222
Houston, Cissy, 295
Houston, Whitney, 95, 200, 295–97, 376–77,
    379
Howarth, Gerald, 307
Hu, Yibi, 354–55, 361, 387
Hucknall, Mick, 212–13
Huey Lewis and the News, 90–91

Human Touch, 166
Hunt, Dennis, 63, 126–27, 142
Hunter, James, 162
Hunter-Tilney, Ludovic, 369–70
Hussein, Saddam, 301–3

Iberman, Mel, 222
"I Can't Make You Love Me," 240
Ice on Fire, 81
"Idol," 371
Ienner, Don, 158, 183, 196, 206–7
"If I Told You That," 296–97
"I Knew You Were Waiting (for Me)," 95–97,
    101, 133, 141
illness, 372–76
I'm Coming to Take You to Lunch (Napier-
    Bell), 75
"I'm Your Man," 89–90, 99, 173, 230
influences, 5–8
Innervision, 23–25, 27, 30–32, 35–37, 46,
    50–51
In the Lonely Hour, 414
"I Remember You," 283, 287, 292, 369
Isley Brothers, 282
"It Doesn't Really Matter," 229
Iversen, Peter, 103
I Want My MTV (Marks and Tannenbaum),
    111
"I Want Your Sex," 101–5, 108, 110–16, 118,
    132–36, 140, 193, 208, 231, 291

Jackman, James, 377
Jackson, Freddie, 126–27
Jackson, Janet, 113
Jackson, Kevin, 156
Jackson, Michael, 5, 44, 64, 117–18, 125–26,
    129, 141, 166, 264, 268, 295
Jacobs, Danny, 170
Jagger, Mick, 62
Janes, Hannah, 386
Jankel, Chaz, 8
Jardine, Cassandra, 212
Jasmin, Paul, 87
Jenkins, Garry, 122
Jerkins, Rodney, 295–96
"Jesus to a Child," 228–30, 232, 234–35
Jeung, Kathy, 86–87, 110–11, 116–17, 123,
    127, 142, 347
Jobim, Antônio Carlos, 178, 214, 234
Joel, Billy, 118
John, Elton, 181–82, 208, 287, 371
    friendship with, 97–99, 139, 243, 248–50,
    302, 316–17, 323–24, 356, 381–82, 397

    as idol, 9, 11, 13, 30, 44, 58–59, 73
    privacy for, 81–82, 109, 122, 187, 265,
        275–76, 319
"John and Elvis Are Dead," 300, 368
Johnson, Don, 92
Johnson, Holly, 109, 199
Jones, Bradley, 255
Jones, Grace, 87
Jones, Lesley-Ann, 86, 241
Jones, Tom, 4
Joseph, Joe, 217
*Joseph and the Amazing Technicolor
    Dreamcoat* (Webber), 8
Jungr, Barb, 42, 415

Kahane, Rob, 154, 397
    business with, 100–101, 106, 110, 113,
        116–18, 122, 137, 143–44, 147, 148,
        152–53, 157–59, 161, 164, 167, 170,
        172–73, 194, 202
    as confidante, 182–84, 198–201, 204, 206,
        209, 215–18, 239
    early career for, 25–26, 83, 90, 92, 96
Kahn, Joseph, 299
Katz, Gregory, 370
Katzenburg, Jeffrey, 222
Kavanagh, Mark, 344–45
Keating, Ronan, 315
Keeps, David, 187
Keilthy, Paul, 336
Kemp, Martin, 247
Kemp, Shirlie, 404
Kerzner, Sol, 91
"Killer," 213, 235
King, Jonathan, 179, 218, 220, 221
"Kiss," 104–5, 110–11
"Kissing a Fool," 8, 108, 370
Knight, Gladys, 146
Kool Moe Dee, 113
Kreins, Edward T., 256, 261
Kunick Leisure, 91–92

Ladies and Gentlemen, 273–74, 276, 278–79,
    338
Lady Gaga, 398
"Lady Marmalade," 133
Lago, Marcelo, 176
Lambert, Adam, 353
Lambie, Jim, 337
Lamey, Mary, 313
Landers, Jay, 160, 167, 259
Landmen, Beth, 117–18
Lane, Nathan, 288, 291

lang, k.d., 212–13, 254, 288, 290–91
Last Christmas (film), 407–8
"Last Christmas" , 408, 52, 67–69, 98, 334, 413
The Last Resort with Jonathan Ross (TV
   show), 114–15
Lawson, Gail, 122
lawsuit, 203–11, 214–19
Leahy, Dick, 25–26, 46, 83, 118, 195–96, 199,
   204, 223–24
"Learn to Say No," 101
Leaver, Andrew, 14, 16–17, 20
Leaver, Scott, 15
Le Beat Route, 19, 21
Le Bon, Simon, 99
Lee, Dee C., 27–31, 36, 41–42, 44–45, 397. *See
   also* Wham!
Lee, Peggy, 413
Lee, Sammy, 260
Lee-Potter, Lynda, 265
LeFevre, Benji, 134
legacy, 406–15
Lemire, Christy, 313
Lemon, Brendan, 254
Lennon, John, 150–51, 236, 297
Leno, Jay, 272
Leonard, Tom, 251
Leopold, Bill, 289
Lepage, Mark, 203
"Let Her Down Easy," 386–87
"Let's Wait Awhile," 113
Letterman, David, 276–77
Lewinsky, Monica, 264
Like a Prayer, 166
Lindbergh, Peter, 163
Lippert, Barbara, 145
Lippman, Michael, 101, 114, 167, 398
Listen Without Prejudice Vol. 1, 155–63,
   165–68, 179, 181, 207–9, 215–16, 224
Listen Without Prejudice Vol. 2, 177–81, 184,
   189, 194
Littlejohn, Richard, 265
"Little Willy," 5
Live Aid concert, 81–82
Live in London, 354
"Living for the City," 245
"Livin' La Vida Loca," 283
"Loaded," 149–50, 415
Lobel, Phil, 116
"Look at Your Hands," 107–8
Lord, Rebecca, 274
Lorde, 415
Louganis, Greg, 287
"Love Action (I Believe in Love)," 301

"Love is a Losing Game," 341, 368
"Love Machine," 40, 77
"Love's in Need of Love Today," 80–81,
   109–10, 133, 213
Lucas, Sarah, 337
Lucky Town, 166
Lynskey, Dorian, 199

MacPherson, Andrew, 284
Madeley, Richard, 326–27
Madonna, 30, 53, 141, 152, 164, 189, 305,
   310, 398
Make It Big, 57–61, 73
Mandela, Nelson, 140
"Mandy," 251
Manilow, Barry, 69, 251
Marks, Craig, 111
Marshall, Joe, 354–55, 361
Marshall, Katherine, 334–35
Martha and the Vandellas, 53
Martin, George, 63
Martin, Ricky, 283
Marx, John, 83
Masters, Billy, 49, 72–73, 157, 263, 309, 413
Match of the Day (TV show), 52
Mathes, Rob, 284, 369
Mattera, Adam, 7, 86, 116, 165
Mavros, Michael, 6
May, Brian, 188–89
McCartney, Paul, 150–51, 236, 325
McCole, Tara, 270
McCormick, Neil, 298, 324, 327
McCoy, Heath, 325
McDowell, Carrie, 113
McElderry, Joe, 353–54
McGowan, Reed, 166, 237–38
McLean, Craig, 324, 332
McLean, Don, 307
McLean, Mark, 365, 368, 371–72
McMullen, Jeff, 135–37
McNichol, Steve, 227
McRae, Carmen, 143
Medina, Roberto, 172–73
Mellman, Kenny, 55
Mendonça, Newton, 214
Mercury, Freddie, 11–13, 61, 82, 101, 186–89,
   407
Mercury Fading, 243
Merrill, Helen, 283–84
Metal Fucking Rats (Webster and Noble), 337
Mezquida, Allen, 60–61
Michael, Deno, 15
Michael, George. *See specific topics*

Middle of the Road, 5
Middleton, Kate, 363
Miller, Dennis, 146–47
Miller, Harland, 337
Minogue, Kylie, 171, 380
"Miss Sarajevo," 282
Mitchell, Joni, 282
Mohan, Dominic, 262
"Monkey," 105, 107, 131, 347
Montanna, June, 122
Montgomery, Carolyn, 85
Moon, Tom, 124, 162, 285
Moorish, Lisa, 230
Morahan, Andy, 79, 94, 96, 110–11, 300, 370
Moret, Jim, 268–69, 279–80
Morgado, Robert, 223
Morgan, Dennis, 95
Morgan, Piers, 137, 200, 303, 311
Morris, Southan, 317
Morrison, Bryan, 25, 35
Morrison, Mark, 243
Morse, Steve, 72
Mortimer, David. *See* Austin, David
Moss, Kate, 348–49, 378–80
"Mother's Pride," 151–52, 181, 208
Motown Returns to Apollo (TV special), 80
Mottola, Tommy, 158–60, 183, 207, 209
Moulder, Dave, 78
Mournian, Tomas, 289
Moyet, Alison, 108
MTV, 29–30, 89–90, 113–14, 152, 193, 287–89
MTV Unplugged, 240
Mugler, Thierry, 189–93, 351–52
Munk, David, 162
Murdoch, Rupert, 64, 137, 332, 352, 363
Murphy, Eddie, 264
Murrell, Trevor, 39
Music and Lyrics (film), 317
Music from the Edge of Heaven, 94
"My Baby Just Cares for Me," 287, 369
"My Cherie Amour," 3
My Life, 279
My Love Is Your Love, 295–96
"My Mother Had a Brother," 294

Napier-Bell, Simon
    support from, 93, 101–2, 224, 330
    for Wham!, 2, 34–37, 47, 50–51, 54, 56,
        61–62, 68, 73–76, 79, 87, 90–92
Napster, 240
NetAid concert, 286
Newlands, Willy, 74
Newley, Anthony, 345

Newmar, Julie, 190–91
New Order, 282, 357
New Religion (Lucas), 337
Newton-John, Olivia, 4
"New York City Boys," 291
"Nikita," 81
Noble, Tim, 337
Nobleman, Marc Tyler, 121
Nomis Management, 91–92
Norris, John, 280
Norton, Graham, 352–53
"Nothing Looks the Same in the Light," 40
"Nothing to My Name," 78
Novarro, Ramon, 11
Novik, Dave, 119, 158, 183

O'Brien, John, 310
O'Connor, John, 349
O'Connor, Sinéad, 282–83
O'Donnell, Rosie, 287
O'Dowd, George, 19
Off the Charts (Haring), 183
Ohga, Norio, 158, 195–96
Older, ix, 226, 229–38, 240, 243, 292
"Older," 240
"1-2-3," 109
"One in a Million," 187
"One More Try," 126, 133
"One Year of Love," 61
Ono, Yoko, 298
"Outside," 273–75, 330
overdose, 387–88

Pafford, Steve, 114
Page, Jimmy, 34–35
Pagnotta, Michael, 30, 122, 168–70, 204,
    217–20, 262, 397
Palmer, Phil
    after Wham!, 148–49, 166, 242, 247, 282,
        284, 309, 324–25, 330, 346, 365, 372
    with Wham!, 47–48
Panayiotou, Georgios Kyriacos, 1–3
Panayiotou, Kyriacos, 1
Panayiotou, Melanie, 1–2, 17, 49, 57, 153, 397,
    402, 409–10
Panayiotou, Yioda, 1–2, 402, 404
Panos, Jack, 1–3, 6, 9, 14, 21, 25, 27, 99–100,
    132, 202, 334, 401–2
"Papa Was a Rolling Stone," 169
Paphides, Peter, 312
Parker, Jonathan, 204, 209, 211, 214–17
Parkinson, Michael, 278, 327
Parnell, Ric, 8

Parris, Matthew, 170–71, 266
Parsons, Tony, 156–57, 198, 211, 254, 258–59, 262, 276, 349
The Partridge Family, 5–6
Passengers, 282
Paterson, Colin, 300
Patience, 311–14
"Patience," 311
Paul, Henri, 249
Pavarotti, Luciano, 208
Payne, Steve, 257–58, 266, 279
Peel, John, 98–99
Peele, Beverly, 190, 192
Peikin, Craig, 77, 84–85
Pepsi, 144
Perkins, John, 358–59
Petridis, Alexis, 312
Pet Shop Boys, 288, 291, 379
Philips, Chuck, 158
Phillips, Fiona, 331
Pike, Tony, 41–42, 44
Pilbrow, Giles, 302
Pilger, John, 301
Plan B, 370–71
Platell, Amanda, 404
pneumonia, 372–76
Police, 285
Pollock, Gordon, 204–11
Pope, Tim, 36
Porter, Chris, 26, 48, 53, 58, 60, 103, 105–6, 149–50, 178, 202, 226–27, 229
Pourikou, Kyriakos, 400
"The Power of Love," 90–91
"Praying for Time," 150–51, 160, 163, 240, 346, 353–54, 368
"Precious Box," 300
Previn, André, 365
Price, Simon, 43, 59, 353
Prince, 90–91, 103–5, 110–11, 168, 220, 240–41
Pringle, Gill, 139, 211–12
prison, 358–60
Pritchett, Georgia, 302
Project Angel Food, 277–78
Purple Rain, 168

Queen, 11–12
Queen Latifah, 288–89

Radel, Cliff, 112
Radley, Norman, 297
Raitt, Bonnie, 240
Ramone, Phil, 282–83, 323, 364, 377–78

Rampton, James, 170
Random Events Tend to Cluster (Wieder), 254
Rantzen, Esther, 239
"Rapper's Delight," 21
"Rapture," 21, 31
"A Ray of Sunshine," 40, 47
"The Recluse," 370–71
"Red Dress," 154
Red Hot + Blue (benefit album), 180–81
Red Hot + Dance (TV special), 189, 194, 208, 215
Red Hot + Rio (benefit album), 214–15
Red Nose Day telethon, 357, 361–62
Rees, Jasper, 169
Rees-Jones, Trevor, 249
rehab, 386–89
Reid, Mike, 240
Reiner, Ira, 272
relationships, 86–88, 99–100, 348–50
"Relax," 43–44, 103
Resen, Morten, 367
Reynolds, Barry, 388, 390
Richard, Cliff, 113
Richards, Andy, 59
Richie, Lionel, 267
Ridgeley, Albert, 9
Ridgeley, Andrew, 97–99, 154–55, 261, 318, 398. *See also* Wham!
  as colleague, 38–39, 44–45, 51–53, 62–63, 92–95, 110, 141, 147, 173–75
  early career of, 8–10, 13–15, 17–24, 26–29, 32, 37, 75, 78
Rihanna, 368
Rimalower, Ben, 130
Rinaldi, Ray Mark, 288
"Rio," 41
Robinson, Smokey, 80
Rock in Rio (Carneiro), 172
Rock Me Tonight, 126–27
Rodgers, Nile, 394, 407
Rodriguez, Marcelo, 260, 280
Rodwell, Paul, 24
Rogers, Patrick, 165
Rogers, Shorty, 53
Rolling Stones, 415
Rose, Axl, 187
Rosen, Hilary, 289
Rosenthal, Robert, 126
Ross, Jonathan, 114–15
"Round Here," 300
"Roxanne," 285
Rubin, Charles, 272, 277–78

Rushen, Patrice, 231
Russell, Paul, 24, 46, 51, 127, 158–59, 167,
    184, 194–96, 210, 215–16
Russell, Tony, 46, 50, 101, 117–18, 127,
    157–59, 183–84, 194–96, 208, 210,
    223–24, 263
"Russian Roulette," 368
Rutter, Simon, 407

Saint Sebastian, Exquisite Pain (Hirst),
    337
Samuel, Martin, 265
Samuelson, Debbie, 29–30, 62
Sandall, Robert, 161
Sanderson, Lisa, 290
Sandow, Greg, 155
Saturday Night Fever (soundtrack), 10–11
Saturday Superstore (TV show), 32–33
Scargill, Arthur, 68–69
Schulhof, Mickey, 128, 167, 195–96, 222
Schwarzenegger, Arnold, 263
Scott, Norman, 27–28
Sealey, Diane Catherine. See Lee
Searle, Tim, 302, 305
Sebastian, Tim, 306
"Secret Love," 282–83
Sepúlveda, Robert, Jr., 395
"Seventeen," 22
Sex Pistols, 22
"Sexual Healing," 140
sexual orientation, 11–13, 16
    AIDS and, 20, 65, 84–85, 109–10, 112–13,
        115, 139, 184–85, 200–201
    in solo career, 100, 116–17, 121–22,
        134–36, 170–75, 186–89
    during Wham!, 19–20, 36, 43–45, 81–82,
        85–88, 176–79
"Shake," 154
Shamblin, Allen, 240
Shaw, Phil, 90
Shepard, Dennis, 291
Shepherd, Julianne Escobedo, 413
Sherwin, Adam, 340, 357
Shields, Brooke, 87
"Shoot the Dog," 301–8, 312, 330, 347
Shriver, Maria, 263, 268
Sidwell, Steve, 103, 226
"Sign O' the Times," 160
Simone, Nina, 345, 370
Simply Red, 212, 243
Simpson, O. J., 268
Sinatra, Frank, 160–61
Sinclair, David, 235, 381

Sitrick, Michael, 267
Skapinker, Michael, 209
Skipwith, Michael, 248
Smallwood, David, 388
Smith, Andrew, 237
Smith, Giles, 216
Smith, Richard, ix, 114, 144, 234, 250
Smith, Sam, 414
Snyder, Michael, 173
Soft Cell, 43–44
"Solar Power," 415
Solid Gold (TV show), 33–34
Solis, Ellyn, 61, 251, 412–13
solo career
    activism in, 361–64
    in California, 198–200
    contracts for, 117–18, 158–63, 194–97,
        221–24
    criticism of, 163–67, 236–38, 312–14
    failure in, 379–80, 382–83
    Faith for, 124–29
    friendships in, 247–50
    image in, 111–15, 120–23, 134–41, 179–80,
        189–93, 202–10, 211–13, 219–20,
        250–53, 266–71, 281–85, 308–11,
        351–55
    lawsuit during, 203–11, 214–19
    management in, 182–84, 232–36
    personal life in, 239–43
    publicity for, 118–20, 244–47, 273–77,
        285–90, 297–300, 340–41, 355–56
    of Ridgeley, Andrew, 154–55
    self-recreation in, 155–58
    sexual orientation in, 100, 116–17, 121–22,
        134–36, 170–75, 186–89
    songwriting in, 148–53, 224–32, 294–97,
        382–83
    start of, 101–9
    success in, 110–11, 143–48
    touring for, 109–10, 130–34, 141–42,
        168–70, 181–82, 290–93, 325–26,
        328–31, 333–36, 342–48, 364–73,
        381–82
    World AIDS Day concert for, 212–13
"Someone Saved My Life Tonight," 282
A Song for You, 296
Songs from the Last Century, 285, 364–65
"Song to the Siren," 371
Son of Albert, 155
Southon, Mike, 90, 96, 110, 164, 190–91, 300,
    370
"Spaceman," 235
Spears, Britney, 310

Spencer, James, 21, 28, 40, 84
Spice Girls, 247–48
Spielberg, Steven, 222
"Spinning the Wheel," 231–34, 237, 330
Spirits Have Flown, 126
Spiro, Brian, 334–35
Spong, Paul
    support from, 103, 108, 366, 370
    with Wham!, 52–53, 58, 61, 63, 70,
        75–78, 90
Springfield, Dusty, 35, 291, 371
Springsteen, Bruce, 117–18, 129, 166
Stag, Paul, 365, 367, 383, 400
Stansfield, Lisa, 187
"Star People," 227
Stephen Fry, 338–40
Stephens, Andy, x, 159, 180, 184, 232, 261,
    263, 276, 303, 351–52
Sting, 243
Stonehouse, Cheryl, 318
Stone Roses, 199
"The Strangest Thing," 227
Streeter, Leslie Gray, 348
Street-Porter, Janet, 213, 315–17, 319
Streisand, Barbra, 259, 271
Strummer, Joe, 94
"Suffragette City," 22
Sugababes, 325
Sugarhill Gang, 21
suicide attempt, 383–85
Sullivan, James, 15–16, 19–20
Summers, Gordon "Jazz," 34–36, 38, 46–47,
    52, 54, 61–62, 79, 82–83, 91–92
Summerskill, Ben, 171
Sweet, 5, 22
"Sweet Dreams (Are Made of This)," 42–43
Sweeting, Adam, 134, 151, 169
Sylvynho, 176–77, 200
"Sympathy for the Devil," 415
Symphonica, 365, 386–87
Symphonica show, 364–73

tabloids, 404–6
    arrests in, 260–66, 270–73, 277–80,
        334–35, 348–49, 357–60
    privacy and, 64–67, 136–38, 211, 322–24,
        326, 398–99
"Tainted Love," 43–44
Take That, 224–25
Tannenbaum, Rob, ix, 57, 80, 96, 111
Tatchell, Peter, 171, 253
Taupin, Bernie, 11, 282, 371
Tay, Richard, 28

Taylor, Elizabeth, 186–87
Tebbit, Norman, 92
Teeman, Tim, 330, 333
Teller, Al, 61, 118
Ten Good Reasons, 171
Tennant, Helen, 122
Tennant, Neil, 254, 288
Thatcher, Margaret, 68, 94
"That Old Devil Called Love," 108
"They Won't Go When I Go," 151
"This Is How (We Want You to Get High),"
    377, 408
"This Kind of Love," 382
Thompson, Emma, 407–8
Thompson, Howard, 62, 121
Thorncroft, Antony, 98
Thriller, 126, 166
"Through," 367
Timberlake, Justin, 310–11
Tisch, Laurence, 128
"To Be Forgiven," 229
Todd, Matthew, 357
"Too Funky," 189, 194
Top of the Pops (TV show), 5, 32–33, 46, 55,
    120
Torrington, Andrew, 335
Townshend, Pete, 57
Trigger, 247
Trojan Souls, 382
The Trojan Souls, 199
"True Faith," 282, 357, 361–64, 369
Tunnel of Love, 129
Turlington, Christy, 163–65
"Turn to Gold," 101
Twain, Shania, 285
Twenty Five, 325–26, 333
25 Live Tour, 342–48
2DTV, 302–5
Tyrrell, Thomas, 127

Üffenvanken, Marchelo, 274
"Uh Uh, No No Casual Sex," 113
United Kingdom (U.K.), vii
Untitled (God) (Craig-Martin), 337
Up Close with George Michael (documentary),
    371
Ure, James "Midge," 67–68

Vance, Derbeh, 277
Vandross, Luther, 180
Vaughan, Arnell, 232–33
The Velvet Rage (Downs), 388–89
Versace, Gianni, 138

the Vibrators, 17
"Village Ghetto Land," 140
Vivinetto, Gina, 293
Wainwright, Rufus, 238, 365
"Waiting (Reprise)," 329
"Waiting for That Day," 150, 163, 181
"Wake Me Up Before You Go-Go," 52–55, 62, 73, 77
Walden, Narada Michael, 95–96
Wallace, Richard, 275–76
Wallinger, Karl, 218
Walsh, Ben, 369
Walters, Barry, 295–96
"Waltz Away Dreaming," 244–45
Warleigh, Ray, 60
Warwick, Dionne, 146
Washbourn, Amanda, 26–27
Waterman, Pete, 218
Watley, Jody, 101
Watson, Sam, 270
"We Are the Champions," 82
Webber, Andrew Lloyd, 8
Webster, Sue, 337
Weegee, 156
Weisner, Ron, 33, 246
Weiss, Joanna, 353
Weller, Paul, 68–69
"We Shall Be Free," 289, 291
Wexler, Jerry, 48
Wham!. See also specific topics
    image for, 29–33, 37, 43–45, 67–69, 79–82, 84–86, 89–91
    leadership for, 33–36, 45–51, 57–61, 91–95
    publicity for, 22–29, 38–43, 51–55, 56–57, 61–63, 64–67, 71–74, 95–99
    on tour, 69–71, 75–79, 82–84
Wham! George Michael & Me, 44
"Wham Rap! (Enjoy What You Do?)," 22, 27, 37, 98, 378
What's the 411?, 279
"Where I Hope You Are," 369
Whiley, Jo, 281, 314
White, Barry, 112
White, Jim, ix, 99, 123, 236
White, Lesley, 266
White, Ryan, 135
"White Light," 378–81
Who's Zoomin' Who?, 95–97
Wickham, Vicki, 35, 371
Wieder, Judy, 100, 121, 254, 288–89, 291, 293, 351–52, 383
"Wig-Wam Bam," 22
Wilker, Deborah, 162

Will Automagic (deejay), 415
Will & Grace (TV show), 252
William (prince), 363
Williams, Alex, 117–18
Williams, Andy, 14, 143
Williams, Robbie, 225, 392–93
Willis, Peter, 137
Willman, Chris, 114
Wilson, Pete, 181
Winehouse, Amy, 341, 364, 368, 407
Winfrey, Oprah, 251, 313–14
Witke, Bret, 52, 86, 107, 116–17, 133, 347
Wittstock, Melinda, 203
Wonder, Stevie, 3, 80–81, 152–53, 245–46
Wood, Mikael, 407
Woodward, Karen, 174, 318
World Party, 218
"Wrap Her Up," 81
Wright, Yvonne Lowrene, 151

Yates, Paula, 66
Yetnikoff, Walter, 61, 117–18, 128–29, 158
Yibi Hu, 77
Yoshida, Emily, 264
"You and I," 363–64
"You Have Been Loved," 240, 250, 368
Young, Kristy, 134, 152–53, 178, 271, 340–41, 391–93, 410
"Young Guns (Go for It!)," 31–34, 36, 98
"You've Changed," 282, 368

Zadrick, Shana, 190
Zielinski, Christoph, 374
Zito, Torrie, 283–84